which is organized into eight major sec
tions: Introduction and Summary; Educa
tional Disadvantage and Child Develop
ment; Inequality in Education; Schoo
Integration; Education of Language Mi
norities; Making Education More Respon
sive; Education Finance; and Rural Educa
tion.

# TOWARD EQUAL EDUCATIONAL OPPORTUNITY

# TOWARD EQUAL EDUCATIONAL OPPORTUNITY

## THE REPORT
## of the
## SELECT COMMITTEE ON
## EQUAL EDUCATIONAL OPPORTUNITY
## UNITED STATES SENATE

Edited,
with a new Introduction,
by
Francesco Cordasco
Montclair State College

AMS Press, Inc.
New York

 Published in the United States of America by AMS Press, Inc., 56 East 13th Street, New York, New York 10003.

**Library of Congress Cataloging in Publication Data**

United States. Congress. Senate. Select Committee on Equal Educational Opportunity.
Toward equal educational opportunity.

Reprint of the 1972 ed. published by the U.S. Govt. Print. Off., Washington, which was issued as Report no. 92-000 of the United States Senate, 92nd Congress, 2nd Session.
Bibliography: p. 441
1. Educational equalization—United States.
I. Cordasco, Francesco, 1920- ed. II. Title. III. Series: United States. 92nd Congress, 2nd Session, 1972. Senate. Report no. 92-000.
LA210.U56 1974 370.19 74-8765

ISBN: 0-404-11622-1

Manufactured in the United States of America

## TABLE OF CONTENTS

# INTRODUCTION

## I.

The Select Committee on Equal Educational Opportunity of the United States Senate was established on February 19, 1970 "to study the effectiveness of existing laws and policies in assuring equality of educational opportunity, including policies of the United States with regard to segregation on the ground of race, color, or national origin, whatever the form of such segregation and whatever the origin or cause of such segregation, and to examine the extent to which policies are applied uniformly in all regions of the United States."(1) Chaired by Senator Walter F. Mondale of Minnesota,(2) the Select Committee's deliberations continued for almost three years; the Committee "heard teachers, students, parents, academic experts, school administrators and government officials. . . . [The Committee] printed a record which, in over 13,000 pages, provides a complex picture—a human picture, of courageous efforts by dedicated men and women who work daily to overcome obstacles which appear insurmountable, alongside scenes of cruelty and disregard for the needs of children."

The final *Report* of the Committee was submitted on December 31, 1972. In the foreword to the final report, Chairman Mondale observed:

> It is the promise of fairness, of equal opportunity, which is at stake in the findings of our Select Committee. As we point out, there is much that is impressive and even remarkable about the American system of public education and what it has done, and it is doing, to provide better opportunities for millions of Americans. But the plain fact is that full educational opportunities—so fundamental to success in American life—are denied to millions of American children who are born poor or nonwhite.

It is this final *Report*(3) which is being re-published, since the report is, in essence, a guide to and a summary of the 13,000 pages of testimony and exhibits which constitute a vast repository of information on educational practice and opportunity in the United States in the early 1970's. In a very real sense, the Senate Select Committee on Equal Educational Opportunity undertook an investigation for which no private group had the resources in time, money, and staff; and since the Select Committee made very clear recommendations, its findings not only provide an historical corpus on educational conditions and practice in the United States in the 1970's, but also a national recognition of educational needs with a commitment (however incompletely implemented) to meeting these needs. As a national document, the importance of the *Report* cannot be overemphasized. It may well be that the Select Committee's deliberations, findings, and recommendations will rank in significance with those of the famous Plowden *Report* published in England in 1967.(4)

In its deliberations, the Select Committee chose to view its assignment in a very broad scope. Its major point of departure was a study of the causes and effects of racial and socioeconomic isolation, the status of school desegregation and integration, but it did not limit itself to civil rights issues, and examined "that area of public and social policy where quality education and civil rights law meet."

> In response to our charge we have therefore viewed public education from many perspectives. We have conducted intensive hearings on education finance and the distribution of educational resources. We have studied the special education problems of children whose first language is other than English, including American Indians, Mexican Americans, Puerto Ricans and Oriental Americans. We have heard testimony about residential segregation and Federal housing policies and programs, and we have looked at the administration of Federal aid to educational programs, preschool and child development, the special education problems of both urban and rural school districts, research and information in education, and a variety of other aspects of public elementary and secondary education.
>
> We have heard testimony from more than 300 witnesses including elementary, junior, and senior high school students and their parents, teachers, school principals and superintendents, school board members, educational economists, lawyers, psychologists, sociologists, State, local and Federal public officials, representatives of civil rights and other nonprofit organizations, and other experts and laymen. Members and staff have reviewed hundreds of reports and other materials, commissioned our own research studies and visited schools and classrooms in Alabama, California, Florida, Louisiana, Massachusetts, Michigan, Mississippi, New York, Pennsylvania, South Carolina, Texas, West Virginia and the District of Columbia. Our hearings record covers more than 11,000 pages of printed testimony and supporting materials.(5)

## II.

At the outset the Committee attempted to define the term "equal educational opportunity." The term is in many ways elusive, but the Committee's definition is both precise and direct: "As we will use the term, equal educational opportunity refers both to the results of education and the way those results are produced."(6) In further elaboration of its cogently laconic definition, the Committee observed:

> It is a fundamental goal of our democratic system that life's opportunities be distributed on the basis of each individual's capacity and choice and that no individual be denied the chance to succeed because of his membership in a racial, religious, social, economic, or other group in society. The extent to which this goal is met is the test of both equal opportunity in our society and equal educational opportunity. Thus, in terms of the outcomes of formal

> schooling, equal educational opportunity is achieved when representative individuals with similar abilities and making similar choices within each group in society have the same chance to participate and succeed in life's activities.
>
> But equal educational opportunity must also be defined in terms of the absence of inequality in the process of schooling and its components. Much of this report concerns the elements of inequality in the educational process: For example, the separation of students by race and social and economic class, the inequitable distribution of educational resources and the ways minority-group children are treated in school.
>
> Children from different backgrounds begin school at different starting lines. They therefore have different educational needs. As used in this Report, equal educational opportunity, then, also refers to the absence of those educational practices that help produce the unequal results of education. Stated positively it is the availability on the basis of need of all those material and human, tangible and intangible things that society puts into its schools, and that collectively affect the process of formal schooling.
>
> It is with these concepts in mind that we have examined public elementary and secondary education.(7)

The Committee accepted, in a very real sense, the broad implications of its definition of equal educational opportunity. In essence, the majority opinion in the Committee proposed that schools do make a difference, and the Committee directly confronted the issues raised by the Coleman *Report*:

> Throughout our history, society has recognized the crucial role of formal education in the life of every citizen. It has been assumed that a child's cognitive skills—particularly his ability to communicate, together with his opportunities as a young adult for further education, a decent job and income and his ability to provide his children with these opportunities—are all, in large measure, for better or worse, determined by his experience in school. Thus, it has been assumed that the quantity and quality of an individual's schooling both relate to his success in later life. Quality is usually measured by student performance on standardized achievement tests. Quantity is usually measured by the years of schooling completed.
>
> Yet, in recent years, since the publication of the Coleman Report, *Equality of Educational Opportunity*, in 1966, there has been widespread debate among experts about the relative influence on a child's performance in school, of his family background and socioeconomic status on one hand, and his experience in school on the other. There is no argument about the fact that advantaged children and children from deprived home environments enter school at different starting lines. There is no doubt that a child's communicative skills, knowledge, perceptions and attitudes—all his experiences during his preschool years—fundamentally determine where he begins the first grade. But there is no agreement about what happens after

that.

Dr. Coleman and others who have analyzed the Coleman Report data have concluded that schools have little effect independent of the child's background. Thus, at least in terms of academic achievement, they say that schools generally fail to narrow the gaps between advantaged and disadvantaged students and that disadvantaged students are likely to leave school in a worse position, academically, relative to their peers, than when they entered.

On the other side are experts who conclude that there is a clear and independent relationship between what schools do and the results they produce. Critical of the procedures and statistical methodology of the Coleman Report, they cite research studies showing that children from deprived homes generally attend schools which have fewer and lower quality educational services and less experienced staff. They conclude that the facilities and quality of education in a school have a direct bearing on how well children preform.

Taking this debate one step further, some observers—citing the contradictory nature of evidence that compensatory education and other aid to education programs have generally succeeded in raising levels of academic achievement—seriously doubt that more such efforts or more money can provide equal education opportunity in our public school systems. Yet, on the other side, there is also evidence that in many communities, compensatory education, integration and other efforts, all of which cost money, have produced measurable increases in the academic achievement of disadvantaged children.

We are persuaded that there is merit to both sides of these arguments. A child's socioeconomic status, his parents' educational level and occupational status, the extent to which he and his family are the victims of racial discrimination and all the other elements of his home environment determine in large measure his performance in school and his success or failure in life.

But we are convinced that schools also make a difference. We believe that money wisely spent on education, the existence or absence of modern up-to-date facilities and instructional materials, the presence or absence of well-trained, qualified, sensitive teachers and staff, the socioeconomic mix of the students in classrooms, and all the other attributes of a school and the activities that take place within it also account for the success or failure of individual students and of groups of students in the schools and classrooms of this Nation.(8)

The national debate on the equality of educational opportunity ("Do the Schools Make a Difference?") has largely been argued along the lines which the Committee correctly perceived: if its historical antecedents extend back to the days of John Dewey and Horace Mann, its major protagonists on the contemporary scene have been Daniel Patrick Moynihan, Christopher Jencks, James Coleman, Thomas Pettigrew, and, tangentially (with considerable controversy), the psychologists, Arthur Jensen, Richard Herrnstein, and others who resurrected the old argument of the black-white IQ controversy.

III.

The famous Coleman *Report*(9) is a massive exposition of 737 pages followed by 548 pages of statistical explanation. Its genesis lay in Section 402 of the Civil Rights Act which ordered the Commissioner of Education to conduct a survey "concerning the lack of availability of equal educational opportunities for individuals by reason of race, color, religion or national origin." Coleman and his associates collected data in 4000 schools from about 600,000 children and 60,000 teachers. Although it may well be, as has been suggested, that Congress "was setting out to document the obvious in order to arm the Administration with a public relations bludgeon to overcome opposition"(10), Coleman's findings were not what was expected (Coleman, himself, has observed halfway through the study that "the study will show the difference in the quality of schools that the average Negro child and the average white child are exposed to. You know yourself that the difference is going to be striking.") The major surprising message of Coleman's report appeared to be that the effect of schools on the equality of opportunity had been exaggerated. Coleman put it in these words:

> One implication stands out above all: That schools bring little influence to bear on a child's achievement that is independent of his background and general social context; and that this very lack of independent effect means that the inequalities imposed on children by their home, neighborhood, and peer environment are carried along to become the inequalities with which they confront adult life at the end of school. For equality of educational opportunity through the schools must imply a strong effect of schools that is independent of the child's immediate social environment, and that strong independent effect is not present in American schools.(11)

Although the findings of the Coleman *Report* have been disputed, reanalysis of the data indicates that the initial findings are largely correct. Daniel Patrick Moynihan and Thomas Pettigrew organized at the Harvard School of Education a Seminar on the Equality of Educational Opportunity Report (SEEOR). Its meetings were initiated in the fall of 1966 after the Coleman *Report* had been officially released in July. The seminar's findings were published in 1972(12) with Frederick Mosteller, Professor of Mathematical Statistics at Harvard University, and Moynihan as co-editors. With many of the participants in the seminar contributing chapters, the Mosteller/Moynihan volume substantiated by reanalysis the significant findings of Coleman, *i.e.*:

- The vast majority of black and white children attend schools that are segregated by color.

- Contrary to the general assumption, though schools for black and white children were "separate," they were nearly "equal" in physical facilities, formal curricula, and teacher characteristics, given controls for regional differences; black-white school differences were simply not there.

- Even where there were measured differences between the facilities, curricula, and teacher characteristics, they had very little effect on the performance of either white or black students as measured by standardized tests.

- The two most significant variables which displayed a consistent relation with test performance were those of social class of the parents and social class of fellow students.

Later in 1972, Christopher Jencks, who had participated in the Pettigrew-Moynihan seminar, published, along with seven colleagues, still another work which reanalyzed the Coleman findings.(13) Although there are some distinctively original assessments in the Jencks volume, its conclusion largely substantiate the Coleman findings, *e.g.*:

- Access to the resources of schools is distributed quite unequally, being directly related both to social class position and length of time spent in school

- No evidence was found that differences between schools contribute significantly to cognitive inequality

- The family background of an individual is more influential in determining how much schooling he receives than either intelligence (measured by IQ) or quality of schooling

- The occupation one eventually attains is directly affected by educational background, and educational background is influenced by family background: thus family background becomes the more important of several factors ultimately influencing occupational status

- Education influences the options one has for first entering a particular occupation, but it does not have much effect on earnings or competence within that occupation

In a sense, Jencks goes beyond Coleman in suggesting that reform within the schools can ultimately have only marginal effect on the inequality which exists outside the schools. Jencks summarizes his position thusly:

> There seem to be three reasons why school reform cannot make adults more equal. First, children seem to be far more influenced by what happens at home than by what happens in school. They may also be more influenced by what happens on the streets and by what they see on television. Second, reformers have very little control over those aspects of school life that affect children. Reallocating resources, reassigning pupils, and rewriting the curriculum seldom change the way teachers and students actually treat

> each other minute by minute. Third, even when a school exerts an unusual influence on children, the resulting changes are not very likely to persist into adulthood.(14)

Further exacerbating the national disputations on the equality of educational opportunity were the incursions into the debate of the educational psychologists. Arthur Jensen of the University of California at Berkeley created a furor with an article published in late 1969 in which he argued two basic propositions: that research findings suggested that heredity explains more of the differences in IQ between individuals than does environment, and that heredity accounts for the differences between the average IQ's of groups as well as between those of individuals.(15) Jensen had opened up the old argument of the black-white IQ controversy, and the statistical refinements from which a theory of innate biological inferiority has been argued. Used by conservatives, the propositions espoused by Jensen argued against continued heavy expenditures for education, and against desegregation. For the liberal community, the lower average performance of blacks was due either to cultural bias in the tests used or to unfavorable environmental factors which necessitated greater efforts on the part of social policy makers.(16)

## IV.

Against this background of debate, the Senate Select Committee had to develop a defensible posture, for the question of equal educational opportunity intractably impinged on the greater question of the pervasive inequality in American society. If one wished to reduce the inequality in American society, it seemed more advantageous to attack it directly than to attempt to ameliorate it through reforming the institution of the school, which is only tangentially related to the creation of that inequality. In other words, if people are to be made more equal in income, opportunities for mobility, and job security, then it is necessary to deal with the consequences of differential family backgrounds in terms of socioeconomic variables rather than school curricula, teachers' credentials, school facilities (or their absence), and the like.

The Committee did not skirt the issues; it could not have, had it chosen to do so. Its answers were, again, forthright:

> All too often we tend to deal with problems in our society as though the institutions which affect our lives and opportunities are unrelated to each other. For example, national policies and programs are developed to create full employment, decent housing, reform welfare, eliminate hunger, provide child care or health care or overcome educational disadvantage. Yet, we often act as though each were a separate solution to an isolated condition. Each in turn has its day in court as "the Nation's number one priority." Each has its own experts and advocates who tend to view their solution to a particular problem as the one which will take care of many or most of the other problems in society as well.
>
> This is certainly true of education. After 2 years of hearings and other studies, it is tempting to conclude

that—if schools could provide all the skills children need for adulthood, if schools could succeed in motivating children where their home life has failed, if schools were free of discrimination and had the resources to meet the needs of every child—the cycle of poverty and disadvantage would be broken. While we believe great progress would result, such a conclusion is both unrealistic and unwarranted. For no one institution in society can, or should, be expected to overcome the failure of all others.

No discussion of educational opportunity can fail to recognize the relationship of educational inequality to other inequalities in society. No design for the reform of public education, no program which promises full opportunity for disadvantaged children in school, will fully succeed unless it is accompanied by efforts to overcome the consequences of inadequate health care and nutrition, unemployment, substandard housing, and other conditions which combine to deny equality of opportunity to millions of children and adults. No policy designed to eliminate racial and ethnic discrimination in education can fully succeed without similar efforts to eliminate discrimination in a broad range of other areas such as housing, employment, voting rights and access to public accommodations.

It is not within the mandate of this committee to examine in depth or recommend policies and programs to alleviate these other inequalities in our society. But it is appropriate not only to make note of them, but to put them in perspective as we discuss inequality in educational opportunity. For the child from a disadvantaged family, poverty, unemployment, welfare dependency, hunger, poor health and substandard and overcrowded housing are the conditions of a depressing and damaging environment into which he is born and raised and which dominate his life while he is in school and after his schooling—unless something intervenes to break the cycle of poverty. All these conditions converge on the educational process. Often for the child—whose parents never completed high school, or whose father is unemployed or whose family is on welfare—life at home, in his years both before and during school, is a fight for survival. Often there are no children's books or magazines, few toys and none of the educational stimuli that most children take for granted. Except for school, television my be his only sustained contact with the world outside his urban ghetto or rural slum neighborhood. The child who lacks proper food at home is often dull and listless, often sick. If he is one of the 7.5 million poor children who receive a free or reduced-price meal, lunch at school may be his only nutritious meal. The child who arrives at school without breakfast simply cannot learn on an empty stomach.(17)

A wide range of individual and minority views challenged the Committee's majority view.(18) Reflecting the black-white IQ controversy, Senator McClellan of Arkansas lamented, "the tendency in many areas is to tell individuals and groups that lower achievement levels is [*sic*] due to discrimination rather than unequal ability. This is often misleading and obviously promotes racial disharmony." However, Senator Spong of Virginia cautioned the Committee:

> To me, the evidence is far from clear that busing and racial balance bring the desired educational response, that they are a panacea for the educational ills of our Nation. We engage in what I have often referred to as the "politics of over-promise" if we present busing or racial balance as such to any group.
>
> With the Coleman Report, the reanalysis of the Coleman Report, the other data which has been collected and the work of this committee ending in inconclusive findings about the value and results of various desegregation attempts and education programs, it would be an easy thing to call for an additional study. In a way, that seems to be what is required. Yet, that could lead to no more resolute conclusion and in the meanwhile the situation demands attention. A more positive approach, perhaps, is to admit that our knowledge is incomplete, the available research inconclusive, and to move within limited bounds.
>
> Aside from the legal and constitutional questions which must be decided, there are substantive questions regarding education and our Nation's priorities which must also be considered. There is significant disaffection with U.S. education today. Questions range from the relevance of the curricula to the lifestyles of students to the failure of the system to meet the needs of many students.(19)

Senator Ervin of North Carolina saw the Committee's positions in direct conflict with the Congress's intent:

> Whatever one may think of the numerous assertions concerning the value of integrated education set forth in the majority report—assertions which are very much still a matter of dispute among professional educators—no American citizen who believes in constitutional government and in the sanctity of local control over education can be comforted by this committee's Report respecting school integration. At least in this part of its Report, the committee appears to be more committed to equal mixing of bodies in the schools than to the subject with which it was charged—equal educational opportunity. I am compelled to reach such a conclusion because the committee has clearly accepted, even advocated, the dangerous pattern of judicial and bureaucratic tyranny over local school boards which has emerged over the past few years.
>
> I submit that the positions set forth in this part of the committee's Report not only directly conflict with Congress' expressed opposition to forced intergration—especially when involving massive busing of schoolchildren—but also run counter to fundamental constitutional and legal principles long cherished in our Republic.(20)

In a strongly worded dissent, Senators Hruska of Nebraska,

Dominick of Colorado, and Cook of Kentucky leveled a series of criticisms against the *Report*, although they did not dispute the broad thrust of it:

> Despite the fact that the Report has summarized numerous suggestions of educators on how to improve school practices, and made a number of specific recommendations about steps to be taken by Congress and the Executive Branch to administer existing programs more uniformly; it is felt that in certain areas the Report falls short of being an adequate guide for Federal efforts to advance equality of educational opportunity. The following criticisms should be made:
>
> - Despite its great length, the Report fails to deal with a number of widely discussed innovative or cost-cutting techniques, which bear on equal educational opportunity, such as educational vouchers, performance contracting, or year-round schools.
> - The Report slights the complex relationships in school governance, and says little, if anything, about the roles of Chief State School Officers, school boards, central staffs and school superintendents. These relationships bear directly on efforts to assure quality education. Nor does the Report deal adequately with the role of professional associations or unions in the field of education.
> - The Report is much stronger in documenting what is wrong with the schools than in mapping positive approaches. It does not suggest approaches which could be used to provide quality education for *all* children. Nor does it endorse fresh innovative strategies for Federal involvement in the education of children. It quite properly bemoans past failures, and then recommends that additional money be spent to fix wrongs which were not put right by largely unsuccessful programs in the past.
> - The financial recommendations of the Report do not take into consideration the changing trends in national enrollment and, even more regrettably, fail to map out an adequate Federal policy for equalizing or providing adequate resources for quality education in the wake of *Serrano* and related decisions.
>
> In the light of these shortcomings, we feel that dissenting views to the conclusions of the Report are in order.(21)

The minority dissent is a combination of sectional politics, the disenchantment with Federal educational interventions the success of which was doubted, and, in a small measure, the recognition of the uncertainties which flowed from the Coleman study and its reanalysis.

## V.

As I noted at the beginning of this introduction, the Senate Select Committee *Report* provides a vast repository of information on educational practice and opportunity in the United States in the early 1970's: putting aside all other considerations, the document has a single, commanding importance. It is a register of contemporary education practice the data of which clearly delineate an absence of the equality of educational opportunity for millions of American children. It is a *national* document which articulates a national consciousness, and its recommendations, if only partially implemented, provide the agenda out of which educational opportunity for disenfranchised children will emerge.

How comprehensive the Committee *Report* is as a register of contemporary educational practice is apparent in a skeletal overview of its concerns. The framework of the *Report* incorporates dimensional discussions of the nature of educational inequality, the intricacies which surround school integration, the education of language minorities (non-English speaking children), the school and its community, educational finance, and rural education. The completeness of treatment for each of these areas is best indicated by examining the *Report's* schema for Part IV (Chapters 14-19). It is a miniature text on "school integration."(22)

This imposing agendum for the discussion of the most important educational issue facing the United States in the 1970's is a *complete* discussion. It is cogent, thorough, dispassionately objective in its review of the extant data and there can be little objection to its carefully considered set of recommendations. The Committee was precisely correct in noting that "the focus of national debate on the misleading issues of 'massive busing' and 'racial balance' has contributed to deteriorating public confidence in the justice of constitutional requirements and in the essential fairness of our judicial system. Our national commitment to equality of educational opportunity is in jeopardy.(23)

## VI.

One question remains: why has so little attention been paid to the *Report* of the Senate Select Committee? The answer is not simple. The disbanding of the Committee sponsoring the *Report* certainly deflected interest from it. From its publication, the *Report* was in short supply, and no Congressional enthusiasm was evident for acknowledging or encouraging distribution of it. In addition, the *Report* was published just before Watergate inquiries began, and it may have just disappeared into the mass of *dejecta membra* which lay strewn over the Congressional landscape in 1973. In a way the fate of the *Report* was not unlike that of the Riles *Report* on urban education which, in a period of presidential and Congressional stability, had been largely unacknowledged and left unimplemented, even if its importance continues undiminished.(24) It may be that the neglect of the Committee's *Report* is due to the post-Coleman disillusionment which has dampened the ardor of Congressional support for educational spending. Probably, this post-Coleman disenchantment, further exacerbated by the attacks on integration, is the main reason for the *Report's* neglect.

> The post-Coleman challenge to the case for spending money on education is beginning to echo through the halls of Congress, ominously for the supporters of federal aid to education, who include both Representative John Brademas, Democrat of Indiana, the chairman of the House Select Subcommittee on Education, and one of his Republican colleagues, Representative Albert Quie of Minnesota. In a recent speech Quie has made it plain that he remains to be convinced that compensatory education makes no difference. John Brademas is afraid that the social science findings, misunderstood or deliberately misrepresented, will be used to justify savage cuts in federal aid to elementary and secondary education and to make opposition to such programs respectable. He is deeply skeptical of the case against the efficacy of education spending, pointing out not only that federal aid still amounts to only 7 percent of the cost of elementary and secondary schooling but also that in many cases funds intended under Title I for compensatory education for underprivileged children have been indiscriminately spent for political reasons on middle-class children, so that few valid conclusions can be drawn from the experience of Title I. He feels adrift without adequate information, while the opponents of educational spending are able to use the social scientists' evidence, often disingenuously. In his own reelection campaign in Indiana last fall he was amused, but not happy, to find his Republican opponent quoting what he called the "Colombo report" (meaning the Coleman report) to him.
>
> Education lobbyists claim that the "Jencks report" has been freely cited by the Nixon Administration's Office of Management and Budget on Capitol Hill in justification of the cuts in the fiscal 1974 budget. And even in some of the more conservative governors' offices, one lobbyist for elementary and secondary education told me there is a widespread feeling that "Coleman and Jencks" have the effect of giving education a low priority.(25)

Perhaps the liberal education policies which animate the spirit of the Committee's *Report*, "and the intellectual assumptions on which they were built, are in bad trouble."(26) I would, however, reject Christopher Jencks' ingenuous postulate that "We must reject the conservative notion that income inequality is largely due to the fact that men are born with unequal abilities and raised in unequal home environments."(27) There may be more sophistry than social science in Jencks' animadversions.

In a symposium convened by the editors of the *Harvard Educational Review* on Jencks' *Inequality*,(28) a group of black social scentists and educators were invited to participate. In their contribution the black academicians observed:

> Neither Christopher Jencks nor his ideological forbears will dissuade black advocates from their commitment to educational equity. We never defined educational success as a synonym for social or economic success and therefore

> have no illusions about the limited role of public instruction in the redress of black grievance. Even so, it is well to point out to polemicists like Jencks that we reserve for ourselves the right to decide the criteria for determining when, and whether, public instruction is fulfilling its obligation to poor and black children.(29)

It is in the perspectives of these sentiments that the *Report* of the Senate Select Committee on Equal Educational Opportunity is to be understood.(30)

Francesco Cordasco, *Professor of Education*
*Montclair State College*

NOTES

(1) Pursuant to Senate Resolution 359, February 19, 1970 (91st Congress, 2nd Session).

(2) Other members included Senators John L. McClellan (Arkansas); Warren G. Magnuson (Washington); Jennings Randolph (West Virginia); Daniel K. Inouye (Hawaii); Birch Bayh (Indiana); William B. Spong, Jr. (Virginia); Sam J. Ervin, Jr. (North Carolina); Adlai E. Stevenson III (Illinois); Roman L. Hruska (Nebraska); Jacob K. Javits (New York); Peter H. Dominick (Colorado); Edward W. Brooke (Massachusetts); Mark O. Hatfield (Oregon); Marlow W. Cook (Kentucky).

(3) *Toward Equal Educational Opportunity*. The Report of the Select Committee on Equal Educational Opportunity. United States Senate . . . Together with Additional, Individual, and Minority Views (Washington: United States Government Printing Office, 1972). The text of *Committee Hearings* was separately issued (paginated consecutively, pp. 1-11, 155) between April 20, 1970 and December 3, 1971 (see *Report*, pp. 423-424); *Committee Prints* appeared between September 1970 and December 1972 (see *Report*, p. 425). The *Report* was issued as a *Committee Print*.

(4) Central Advisory Council for Education. *Children and their Primary Schools* (London: Her Majesty's Stationery Office, 1967). "The Report of the Central Advisory Council on Education in England, *Children and their Primary Schools*, familiarly known as the Plowden Report in honor of its chairman, was the most important government-sponsored document about primary education published in thirty years. The Council carefully gathered evidence from a wide spectrum of sources over an extended period of time. In 1970, three years after its publication, most people acknowledged that the Report represented a fair summary of enlightened professional opinion. Few felt that it was very far in advance of common practice; rather it gave semi-official endorsement to changes already underway and made modest recommendations for more widespread implementation during the 1970's. There is some indication that *Children and their Primary Schools* represents a combination of positions of the enlightened, middle-of-the-road members of the educational establishment." Robert J. Fisher, *Learning How to Learn: The English Primary School and American Education* (New York: Harcourt Brace Jovanovich, 1972), p. 29.

(5) *Report of the Select Committee on Equal Educational Opportunity*, pp. 1-2. The Committee's enquiries were not comprehensive: there are significant exclusions. "This committee has not had sufficient time to examine many important aspects of public education which we would like to have studied. We have not, for example, examined the potential contribution of private schools for providing equal educational opportunity. We have not studied equal opportunity in higher education or the impressive potential role of vocational and career education. There are other matters that relate to equality in educational opportunity which we have touched upon generally, but not examined in sufficient depth to make detailed recommendations: For example, classroom teaching techniques and instructional methods, the role of schools of

education in the training of teachers, the influence of teacher and other educational organizations on educational policy and practices, and the administration of schools and school districts. We especially regret that time and the nature of the committee's mandate did not permit us to study the special problems of rural education in greater depth. We recommend that other appropriate committees undertake intensive studies of these aspects of education." (p. 4)

(6) *Report*, p. 3.

(7) *Ibid.*

(8) *Report*, pp. 4-5.

(9) James S. Coleman, *et al.*, *Equality of Educational Opportunity* (Washington: United States Government Printing Office, 1966). The summary of the Coleman *Report* is reprinted in Francesco Cordasco, *et. al.*, eds. *The School in the Social Order: A Sociological Introduction to Educational Understanding* (Scranton: International, 1970), pp. 107-149.

(10) Godfrey Hodgson, "Do Schools Make a Difference?" *Atlantic* (March 1973), p. 37.

(11) Coleman, p. 325.

(12) Frederick Mosteller and Daniel P. Moynihan, eds., *On Equality of Educational Opportunity: Papers Deriving from the Harvard University Faculty Seminar on the Coleman Report* (New York: Random House, 1972). In the Preface, Mosteller and Moynihan observed: "The report on Equality of Educational Opportunity appeared in the summer of 1966. From the first it was clear that this was a study of the greatest consequence, but also that the educational community and the public at large would have great difficulty assessing its implications. The methodological sophistication of the analysis, and the inherent difficulty of the material itself, made much of the report all but inaccessible to non-specialists. Moreover, the analysis of the data had been carried out in a matter of months, there being a legislative deadline for the report. While this was a feat of seldom equaled physical and intellectual exertion, it nonetheless suggested that further work could and should be done. As a most original step, the Office of Education initiated this idea by suggesting in the Report that scholars carry our further analyses. Finally, the Federal government, or at least the higher reaches of the Department of Health, Education, and Welfare, had shown serious concern over what seemed to the 'anti-education' findings of the study." (p. ix). For an earlier set of analyses of the Coleman *Report*, see a special issue of the *Harvard Educational Review* on "Equal Educational Opportunity," vol. 38 (Winter 1968).

(13) Christopher Jencks, *et. al*, *Inequality: A Reassessment of the Effects of Family and Schooling in America* (New York: Basic Books, 1972). Jencks' volume is not limited to a reanalysis of Coleman data; it examines, as well, a wide range of other studies (*e.g.*, the Project Talent survey), and Census Bureau studies of social mobility and income distribution. Reference should be made to Jencks' essay, "The Coleman Report and the Conventional Wisdom," in the Mosteller/Moynihan volume.

(14) Jencks, *Inequality: A Reassessment*, pp. 255-256. Donald M. Levine, in his examination of the Jencks volume, commends its "laying to rest much mistaken conventional wisdom" about schooling in America, but he cautiously notes that "its conclusions for educational policy and policy analysis are extreme and, ultimately, do little service in the cause of a more rational allocation of educational resources." Donald M. Levine, "Educational Policy after Inequality," *Teachers College Record*, vol. 75 (December 1973), pp. 149-179. See also a special issue of the *Harvard Educational Review*, "Perspectives on Inequality" (vol. 43, February 1973), which includes Christopher Jencks' "Inequality in Retrospect," in which he notes: "In any event, the purpose of *Inequality*, was not to argue the case for socialism, which is complex and problematic. Neither, as the book makes clear, was its purpose to argue against school reform. Rather, the aim of the book was to show that one specific, widely-held theory about the relationship between school reform and social reform was wrong. According to that theory, the degree of inequality in incomes

is determined by the degree of inequality in skills. These, in turn, depend on family background, genes, and schooling. The evidence presented in *Inequality* seems to me to show that variations in family background, IQ genotype, exposure to schooling, and quality of schooling cannot account for most of the variation in individual or family incomes. This means we must reject the conservative notion that income inequality is largely due to the fact that men are born with unequal abilities and raised in unequal home environments. We must also reject the liberal notion that equalizing educational opportunity will equalize people's incomes. The evidence in *Inequality* cannot carry us much further, even though its rhetoric sometimes tries." (p. 128).

(15) Arthur Jensen, "How Much Can We Boost IQ and Scholastic Achievement?" *Harvard Educational Review*, vol. 39 (1969), pp. 1-123. Jensen proposes that individuals with low IQ's are different in genetic makeup from those who possess high IQ's, although he admits that environmental factors can influence IQ differences. From studies conducted in the United States and England, Jensen concludes that 80 per cent of one's intelligence as measured by IQ tests is due to heredity and 20 per cent to environment. Further, Jensen maintains that the overwhelming influence of genetic factors (.80 versus .20) explains not only IQ differences among individuals *within* the same group, but also *between* groups as aggregates. In Jensen's view, blacks as a group do less well in areas such as abstract reasoning and problem solving than whites and Orientals: he imputes these differences to factors of inheritance and matters of genetic structure and brain formation. Compensatory education programs (essentially, federal interventions) have failed, Jensen reasons, because they have ignored heredity and its impact on performance.

(16) For reactions to Jensen's article (and the involvements in the controversy of Richard Herrnstein and David K. Cohen) see Godfrey Hodgson, *loc. cit.*, pp. 39-40. For violent disagreements with Jensen, see Charles Silberman, *Crisis in the Classroom* (New York: Random House, 1970) who accuses him of raising "an ugly question"; and F.L. Morris, *The Jensen Hypothesis: Social Science Research or Social Science Racism* (Los Angeles: University of California, Center for Afro-American Studies, 1971). For an overview of the controversy, see Alan Gartner, *et. al.*, eds., *The New Assault on Equality: IQ and Social Stratification* (New York: Harper & Row, 1973). Reference should also be made to the *Harvard Educational Review* Reprint series which include *Environment, Heredity, and Intelligence* (No. 2), and *Science, Heritability, and IQ* (No. 4) which include the text of the Jensen article, responses to the article, and a reply by Dr. Jensen (No. 2); and a collection of papers largely stimulated by the Jensen article (No. 4).

(17) *Report*, pp. 7-8.

(18) *Report*, pp. 367.

(19) *Report*, p. 393.

(20) *Report*, p. 408.

(21) *Report*, p. 410.

(22) *Report*, pp. XVI-XVII.

(23) *Report*, p. 263. The Committee further observed: "At the same time, public discussion has largely ignored both the benefits of integrated education, and the legitimate concerns of parents—concern of minority group parents that their children not be subjected to unfair and discriminatory treatment within desegregated schools, concerns of all parents that desegregation improve and not impair their children's educational opportunities.

"The immediate losers have been the Nation's children. And the greatest losers are the 11 million children already attending 1,500 desegregating school districts. Negative leadership discourages the local support necessary for successful school integration, and compounds the already difficult jobs of teachers and local school officials." (*loc. cit.*)

(24) The Urban Education Task Force was one of a number of task forces convened by Robert H. Finch, then Secretary of Health, Education, and Welfare. The Urban Education Task Force was headed by Wilson C. Riles and was assigned by Dr. James E. Allen, Jr. (then Assistant Secretary/Commissioner

of Education-designate) a high priority in seeking solutions for the deepening urban educational crisis. The Task Force completed its *Report* in November/December 1969, and submitted it to Dr. Allen in January 1970. For whatever reasons, the *Report* was not made public, and its publication in the *Congressional Record* (January 19-20, 1970) by Representative Jeffery Cohelan (*D., California*) brought it to attention. The complete text of the *Report* is available in *The Urban Education Task Force Report. Final Report of the Task Force on Urban Education to the Department of Health, Education, and Welfare.* Wilson C. Riles, Chairman (New York: Praeger, 1970). The summary of the *Final Report* is reprinted in Francesco Cordasco, *The Equality of Educational Opportunity: A Bibliography of Selected References* (New York: Rowman and Littlefield, 1973), pp. 59-79.

(25) Godfrey Hodgson, *loc. cit.*, p. 45.

(26) "What can be said, at the end of the first stage of the Coleman doctrine, is that whether you believe with Daniel Patrick Moynihan that liberal education policies of the last few generations have succeeded so well that they have run into diminishing returns, or with Christopher Jencks that they have proved disappointing—those policies, and the intellectual assumptions on which they were built, are in bad trouble. They have lost support in the ranks of the social scientists who provided America, from Roosevelt to Johnson, with a major part of its operating ideology." Godfrey Hodgson, *loc. cit.*, p. 46.

(27) Christopher Jencks, "Inequality in Retrospect," *loc. cit.*

(28) See footnote 14, *infra*. The symposium was also issued separately by the *Harvard Educational Review* in its Reprint Series (No. 8, 1973).

(29) *Perspectives on Inequality*, p. 55. "Although the work of Gunnar Myrdal and psychologists such as Kenneth Clark gave intellectual support to the reforms of the early 1960's, reaction since then has gained momentum, and it would appear today that the liberal scholars have been swept from the field by the Shockleys, Jensens, Banfields, Moynihans—and now by Jencks. Such research from eminent social scientists, who are based at the nation's most prominent centers of higher learning, though they differ in approach, all seem to point to the conclusion that blacks and lower class people are about where they ought to be in the society—at the bottom—and that all efforts to move them, or let them move themselves, are futile." (*loc. cit.*, p. 43).

(30) "If we accept the correctness of these three propositions—that compulsory public schooling will be with us for the foreseeable future; that the organizational arrangements inside schools legitimate current patterns of inequality, but do not create them; and that reforming schools does not necessarily imply dealing with the inequalities of the larger society—then we might consider the following implications. First, we can liberate ourselves from the shackling myths of what schools are supposed to be doing, both for the benefit of the students and for the larger society. We can put down the notions that schools are the 'great equalizer' that provides everyone equal access to the mobility escalators. Rather, we can recognize the realities of how schools reinforce social class differences and act to preserve the current arrangements. There is little possibility of transforming the schools to the point where they do not serve this legitimatizing function if it is not first acknowledged that in fact they do." Ray C. Rist, *The Urban School: A Factory for Failure. A Study of Education in American Society* (Cambridge: MIT Press, 1973), p. 253.

[COMMITTEE PRINT]

92D CONGRESS } SENATE { REPORT
2d Session } { No. 92–000

# TOWARD EQUAL EDUCATIONAL OPPORTUNITY

## THE REPORT

OF THE

## SELECT COMMITTEE ON EQUAL EDUCATIONAL OPPORTUNITY UNITED STATES SENATE

PURSUANT TO

S. RES. 359, FEBRUARY 19, 1970

A Resolution Authorizing a Study of the Effectiveness of Existing Laws in Assuring Equality of Educational Opportunity

AND SUBSEQUENT

Resolutions Authorizing Expenditures of the Select Committee on Equal Educational Opportunity

TOGETHER WITH

ADDITIONAL, INDIVIDUAL, AND MINORITY VIEWS

DECEMBER 31, 1972

U.S. GOVERNMENT PRINTING OFFICE
WASHINGTON : 1972

## UNITED STATES SENATE

### SELECT COMMITTEE ON EQUAL EDUCATIONAL OPPORTUNITY

(Created pursuant to S. Res. 359, 91st Congress)

WALTER F. MONDALE, Minnesota, *Chairman*

JOHN L. McCLELLAN, Arkansas
WARREN G. MAGNUSON, Washington
JENNINGS RANDOLPH, West Virginia
DANIEL K. INOUYE, Hawaii
BIRCH BAYH, Indiana
WILLIAM B. SPONG, Jr., Virginia
SAM J. ERVIN, Jr., North Carolina
ADLAI E. STEVENSON III, Illinois

ROMAN L. HRUSKA, Nebraska
JACOB K. JAVITS, New York
PETER H. DOMINICK, Colorado
EDWARD W. BROOKE, Massachusetts
MARK O. HATFIELD, Oregon
MARLOW W. COOK, Kentucky

WILLIAM C. SMITH, *Staff Director and General Counsel*

MEMBERS OF THE COMMITTEE ON THE JUDICIARY

JOHN L. McCLELLAN, Arkansas
THOMAS J. DODD, Connecticut [1]
BIRCH BAYH, Indiana
SAM J. ERVIN, Jr., North Carolina

ROMAN L. HRUSKA, Nebraska
MARLOW W. COOK, Kentucky

MEMBERS OF THE COMMITTEE ON LABOR AND PUBLIC WELFARE

JENNINGS RANDOLPH, West Virginia
WALTER F. MONDALE, Minnesota
HAROLD E. HUGHES, Iowa [2]
ADLAI E. STEVENSON III, Illinois

JACOB K. JAVITS, New York
PETER H. DOMINICK, Colorado

MEMBERS AT LARGE

WARREN G. MAGNUSON, Washington
DANIEL K. INOUYE, Hawaii
WILLIAM B. SPONG, Jr., Virginia

EDWARD W. BROOKE, Massachusetts
MARK O. HATFIELD, Oregon

[1] Not reelected to 92d Congress, replaced by Senator Ervin.
[2] Resigned from committee at start of 92d Congress, assigned to Senator Stevenson.

# LETTERS OF TRANSMITTAL

December 31, 1972.

Hon. James O. Eastland,
*Chairman, Committee on the Judiciary,*
*U.S. Senate, Washington, D.C.*

Dear Mr. Chairman: Under the authority of Senate Resolution 359, 91st Congress, 2d Session, as amended by subsequent resolutions, I am submitting on behalf of all the members of the Select Committee on Equal Educational Opportunity the committee's final report.

As you know, the Select Committee on Equal Educational Opportunity was established on February 19, 1970, "to study the effectiveness of existing laws and policies in assuring equality of educational opportunity, including policies of the United States with regard to segregation on the ground of race, color, or national origin, whatever the form of such segregation and whatever the origin or cause of such segregation, and to examine the extent to which policies are applied uniformly in all regions of the United States."

I am forwarding additional copies of the Select Committee's final report under separate cover—should you wish to make them available to the members of your committee.

With warmest regards.

Sincerely,

Walter F. Mondale, *Chairman.*

DECEMBER 31, 1972.

Hon. HARRISON A. WILLIAMS,
*Chairman, Committee on Labor and Public Welfare,*
*U.S. Senate, Washington, D.C.*

DEAR MR. CHAIRMAN: Under the authority of Senate Resolution 359, 91st Congress, 2d Session, as amended by subsequent resolutions, I am submitting on behalf of all the members of the Select Committee on Equal Educational Opportunity the committee's final report.

As you know, the Select Committee on Equal Educational Opportunity was established on February 19, 1970, "to study the effectiveness of existing laws and policies in assuring equality of educational opportunity, including policies of the United States with regard to segregation on the ground of race, color, or national origin, whatever the form of such segregation and whatever the origin or cause of such segregation, and to examine the extent to which policies are applied uniformly in all regions of the United States."

I am forwarding additional copies of the Select Committee's final report under separate cover—should you wish to make them available to the members of your committee.

With warmest regards.

Sincerely,

WALTER F. MONDALE, *Chairman.*

# FOREWORD

For nearly 3 years the U.S. Senate Select Committee on Equal Educational Opportunity has tried to examine the way in which American public education serves those whose voices are heard least—children and families from racial and ethnic minority groups, or who are simply poor.

We have heard teachers, students, parents, academic experts, school administrators and government officials. We have commissioned staff studies and academic research. And we have printed a record which, in over 13,000 pages,* provides a complex picture—a human picture, of courageous efforts by dedicated men and women who work daily to overcome obstacles which appear insurmountable, alongside scenes of cruelty and disregard for the needs of children.

It is the promise of fairness, of equal opportunity, which is at stake in the findings of our Select Committee. As we point out, there is much that is impressive and even remarkable about the American system of public education and what it has done, and it doing, to provide better opportunities for millions of Americans. But the plain fact is that full educational opportunities—so fundamental to success in American life—are denied to millions of American children who are born poor or nonwhite.

As Chairman of this Select Committee, and of the Subcommittee on Children and Youth, and as a member of other committees which deal with human problems—the Select Committee on Nutrition and Human Needs, the Subcommittees on Manpower and Poverty, Education, Health, Housing and Migratory Labor, and the Special Subcommittee on Indian Education—it has been my opportunity and challenge to witness firsthand the children and families who suffer the adversity and hopelessness which this Report describes.

I have seen the lives of disadvantaged children all over this country—on reservations, in ghettos, in migrant camps and pockets of rural poverty. Statistics can never tell the full story:

- Of a disconsolate and disoriented migrant mother standing blank-faced with her rickets-ridden infant, unable to answer any question about herself or her child.
- Of the hurt and anger in the eyes of black parents and children in a Southern livingroom describing a segregated swimming pool built with Federal funds and hand-me-down school books.
- Of a class of dispirited Eskimo children who speak only Eskimo, taught by a white teacher who speaks only English from a "Dick and Jane" textbook—with illustrations which show nothing of them or what they could know.

*See Select Committee References, pp. 423–440.

- Of the cold, military-like environment of a Federal boarding school for Navajo elementary children—children who must spend months away from their families, often beginning at age 5.

The literature is full of such examples—of children and families living in despair in our country. Some, such as Dr. Robert Coles, have spent their lives chronicling the devastation.

The causes are not hard to find. There is a long and continuing record of racial, ethnic, and economic discrimination. Minority group and disadvantaged children—despite their greater needs—usually have not been given access to equal educational resources. It is especially true that they have been denied the special help they need to overcome the educational handicaps of poverty, discrimination and cultural isolation. And mindlessness, bureaucratic unresponsiveness, and sometimes arrogance and intolerance, take their toll.

To learn well, a child must be genuinely respected and valued for who he is—himself, his culture and language, his family. He must believe in himself. Yet our educational system frequently has great difficulty accepting and building upon differences. Too often I have seen dedicated people trying to "save" children from their families' history and culture. I don't believe it works. We must learn to respect children for themselves, and permit them to build on their own backgrounds.

Our Select Committee has recommended several steps that we believe would substantially help to improve the educational opportunities of these children. Undoubtedly many will argue with the specifics of these recommendations.

But, what is important—and, in my opinion, what is missing—is a deep and strong national commitment to justice for disadvantaged children. Erik Erickson once said, "the most deadly of all possible sins is the mutilation of a child's spirit . . ." We *are* mutilating the spirits of millions of American children every day, and it is surely a sin.

Failure to obtain an adequate education is a personal tragedy for these cheated children and their families. But the Nation's loss is still greater. We are wasting the lives of children who could become happier, more employable, more contributing citizens, and better able to help their own families. Those of us who are more fortunate know of this waste, and must suffer great guilt.

We have just completed a remarkable and breathtaking effort at manned exploration of the moon. It was an impressive human accomplishment. But, I have never seen anything as thrilling, impressive, or beautiful as the face of a happy, healthy, confident child. Nothing should haunt us more than the face of a child who knows he has failed. I have seen hundreds of them—I know there are countless more.

We can and must commence a massive and full-hearted effort to stop this devastation—and to match the priceless potential of these magnificent children with the resources and affection which they need and deserve.

WALTER F. MONDALE, *Chairman*,
*Select Committee on Equal Educational Opportunity.*

# SUMMARY OF CONTENTS

# CONTENTS

# Part I
# Introduction and Summary

## Chapter 1—Overview

### A. Introduction

> In these days it is doubtful that any child can reasonably be expected to succeed in life if he is denied the opportunity of an education. Such an opportunity, where the State has undertaken to provide it, is a right which must be made available to all on equal terms . . . We conclude that in the field of public education the doctrine of "separate but equal" has no place. Separate educational facilities are inherently unequal.
>
> *Brown v. Board of Education, 1954*

On February 19, 1970, this committee was created "to study the effectiveness of existing laws and policies in assuring equality of educational opportunity, including policies of the United States with regard to segregation on the ground of race, color, or national origin, whatever the form of such segregation, and to examine the extent to which policies are applied uniformly in all regions of the United States."

It was the Senate's concern that such laws and policies have not been applied uniformly that gave rise to the establishment of the Select Committee. We have examined this question. We have studied the causes and effects of racial and socioeconomic isolation and we have reviewed the status of school desegregation and integration efforts North, South, East and West, whether undertaken in compliance with Federal or State law or voluntarily. But we have not limited our studies to civil rights issues, for we have also tried to look at that area of public and social policy where quality education and civil rights law meet.

In response to our charge we have therefore viewed public education from many perspectives. We have conducted intensive hearings on education finance and the distribution of educational resources. We have studied the special education problems of children whose first language is other than English, including American Indians, Mexican Americans, Puerto Ricans and Oriental Americans. We have heard testimony about residential segregation and Federal housing policies and programs, and we have looked at the administration of Federal aid to education programs, preschool and child development, the special education problems of both urban and rural school districts, research and information in education, and a variety of other aspects of public elementary and secondary education.

We have heard testimony from more than 300 witnesses including elementary, junior, and senior high school students and their parents, teachers, school principals and superintendents, school board members, educational economists, lawyers, psychologists, sociologists, State, local and Federal public officials, representatives of civil rights and other nonprofit organizations, and other experts and laymen. Members and staff have reviewed hundreds of reports and other materials, commissioned our own research studies and visited schools and classrooms in Alabama, California, Florida, Louisiana, Massachusetts, Michigan, Mississippi, New York, Pennsylvania, South Carolina, Texas, West Virginia and the District of Columbia. Our hearings record covers more than 11,000 pages of printed testimony and supporting materials.

We have found neither uniformity in the enforcement of our Nation's civil rights laws as they affect education nor equality of educational opportunity in many of our Nation's schools. For most American children, our public education system is eminently successful. We have found great progress. But we have also found that public education is failing millions of American children who are from racial and language minority groups, or who are simply poor.

It is failing because most children who are from minority groups or speak a different language at home or are poor, whatever their race or heritage, are often in schools and classrooms with fewer educational resources. It is failing because these children are treated, usually unwittingly, but sometimes as a result of discrimination and racial prejudice, in ways which are insensitive and unresponsive to their backgrounds and cultures. It is failing because poor and minority group children are often isolated in schools and classrooms where they fail to receive the kind of stimulating experiences which most American middle-class children can take for granted. Education is failing these children because the quality of most American education is largely determined by the wealth of students' families and their communities. And it is failing because many of those school systems which are attended by disadvantaged children are somehow institutionally unresponsive to their needs.

This failure is costly to both the individual and the Nation. It is at least partly responsible for the cost to the Nation in combating crime and supporting welfare, and it results in a substantial loss to our national economy in terms of personal income and tax revenues.

The task ahead is to develop education systems in every community in this Nation which are sensitive and responsive to the needs and backgrounds of all children, and particularly minority-group children and children from educationally and economically disadvantaged homes. We must begin to build an educational system in which cultural diversity and pluralism are both accepted and supported.

We must find ways to make schools—particularly those in large school districts—more a part of their community, and involve communities in their schools. We must make it possible for the clients of education to participate more meaningfully in the decisions made about their education.

We must change the systems by which the financial and human resources for education are now distributed so that those resources are raised and distributed equitably, with the objective that every school in this Nation have the resources to provide the best possible education. We must rescue, with Federal funds, those school systems presently facing a fiscal crisis which threatens to erode the quality of education they are now providing. As we allocate the resources for education we must also assure that those good schools, which are now providing excellent opportunities for their students, are not required to reduce their resources or diminish the quality of education they are now providing.

We must do this and more if equal educational opportunity is to become a reality rather than just a long-sought goal.

But we will fail in these tasks unless we proceed with the job of eliminating racial discrimination, and unless we pursue efforts to encourage quality integrated education. It is among our principal conclusions—as a result of more than 2 years of intensive study—that quality integrated education is one of the most promising educational policies that this Nation and its school systems can pursue if we are to fulfill our commitment to equality of opportunity for our children. Indeed, it is essential, if we are to become a united society which is free of racial prejudice and discrimination.

### B. Equal Educational Opportunity: A Definition

Before summarizing the committee's central conclusions and recommendations, it is important to define the term "equal educational opportunity."

As we will use the term, equal educational opportunity refers both to the results of education and the way those results are produced.

It is a fundamental goal of our democratic system that life's opportunities be distributed on the basis of each individual's capacity and choice and that no individual be denied the chance to succeed because of his membership in a racial, religious, social, economic, or other group in society. The extent to which this goal is met is the test of both equal opportunity in our society and equal educational opportunity. Thus, in terms of the outcomes of formal schooling, equal educational opportunity is achieved when representative individuals with similar abilities and making similar choices within each group in society have the same chance to participate and succeed in life's activities.

But equal educational opportunity must also be defined in terms of the absence of inequality in the process of schooling and its components. Much of this report concerns the elements of inequality in the educational process: For example, the separation of students by race and social and economic class, the inequitable distribution of educational resources and the ways minority-group children are treated in school.

Children from different backgrounds begin school at different starting lines. They therefore have different educational needs. As used in this Report, equal educational opportunity, then, also refers to the absence of those educational practices that help produce the unequal results of education. Stated positively it is the availability on the basis of need of all those material and human, tangible and intangible things that society puts into its schools, and that collectively affect the process of formal schooling.

It is with these concepts in mind that we have examined public elementary and secondary education.

## C. Our Unfinished Business

This committee has not had sufficient time to examine many important aspects of public education which we would like to have studied. We have not, for example, examined the potential contribution of private schools for providing equal educational opportunity. We have not studied equal opportunity in higher education or the impressive potential role of vocational and career education. There are other matters that relate to equality in educational opportunity which we have touched upon generally, but not examined in sufficient depth to make detailed recommendations: For example, classroom teaching techniques and instructional methods, the role of schools of education in the training of teachers, the influence of teacher and other educational organizations on educational policy and practices, and the administration of schools and school districts. We especially regret that time and the nature of the committee's mandate did not permit us to study the special problems of rural education in greater depth. We recommend that other appropriate committees undertake intensive studies of these aspects of education.

In addition there are other forms of inequality in our society which relate to education that we have not had a chance to study: Discrimination based upon sex, religion or age, for example, or the inequalities to which the mentally retarded and physically handicapped, or those with special learning disabilities, are subjected.

We have concentrated particularly upon the education of children from racial and language minority groups and children who are from educationally and economically deprived homes. We have not, however, examined in detail the special education problems of American Indians or the children of migrant farm workers. The education of these children has been thoroughly studied by two subcommittees of the Committee on Labor and Public Welfare—the Subcommittee on Migratory Labor and the Special Subcommittee on Indian Education. We have drawn from the work of these two subcommittees in this report. In 1969, the Indian Education Subcommittee issued its report, *Indian Education: A National Tragedy—A National Challenge*, after 2½ years of intensive hearings and travel. That report has led to the enactment of specific legislation designed to deal with the specific educational problems of American Indians. On June 8, 1972, for example, the Congress enacted the Indian Education Act as part of the Education Amendments of 1972.

## D. Schools Can Make a Difference

Throughout our history, society has recognized the crucial role of formal education in the life of every citizen. It has been assumed that a child's cognitive skills—particularly his ability to communicate, together with his opportunities as a young adult for further education, a decent job and income and his ability to provide his children with these opportunities—are all, in large measure, for better or worse, determined by his experience in school. Thus, it has been assumed that the quantity and quality of an individual's schooling both relate to his success in later life. Quality is usually measured by student performance on standardized achievement tests. Quantity is usually measured by the years of schooling completed.

Yet, in recent years, since the publication of the Coleman Report, *Equality of Educational Opportunity*, in 1966, there has been widespread debate among experts about the relative influence on a child's performance in school, of his family background and socioeconomic status on one hand, and his experience in school on the other. There is no argument about the fact that advantaged children and children from deprived home environments enter school at different starting lines. There is no doubt that a child's communicative skills, knowledge, perceptions and attitudes—all his experiences during his preschool years—fundamentally determine where he begins the first grade. But there is no agreement about what happens after that.

Dr. Coleman and others who have analyzed the Coleman Report data have concluded that schools have little effect independent of the child's background. Thus, at least in terms of academic achievement, they say that schools generally fail to narrow the gaps between advantaged and disadvantaged students and that disadvantaged students are likely to leave school in a worse position, academically, relative to their peers, than when they entered.

On the other side are experts who conclude that there is a clear and independent relationship between what schools do and the results they produce. Critical of the procedures and statistical methodology of the Coleman Report, they cite research studies showing that children from deprived homes generally attend schools which have fewer and lower quality educational services and less experienced staff. They conclude that the facilities and quality of education in a school have a direct bearing on how well children perform.

Taking this debate one step further, some observers—citing the contradictory nature of evidence that compensatory education and other aid to education programs have generally succeeded in raising levels of academic achievement—seriously doubt that more such efforts or more money can provide equal educational opportunity in our public school systems. Yet, on the other side, there is also evidence that in many communities, compensatory education, integration and other efforts, all of which cost money, have produced measurable increases in the academic achievement of disadvantaged children.

We are persuaded that there is merit to both sides of these arguments. A child's socioeconomic status, his parents' educational level and occupational status, the extent to which he and his family are the victims of racial discrimination and all the other elements of his home environment determine in large measure his performance in school and his success or failure in life.

But we are convinced that schools also make a difference. We believe that money wisely spent on education, the existence or absence of modern up-to-date facilities and instructional materials, the presence or absence of well-trained, qualified, sensitive teachers and staff, the socioeconomic mix of the students in classrooms, and all the other attributes of a school and the activities that take place within it also account for the success or failure of individual students and of groups of students in the schools and classrooms of this Nation.

Yet to say all these things are important does not resolve the debate about what attributes of education make the most difference or what policies or programs are most likely to provide equal educational opportunity. In attempting to find answers to these questions we have sought the advice and opinions of leading experts and practitioners. We have reviewed the literature on equal educational opportunity.

We have found the experts' analyses of the problems most helpful. But we have found an appalling lack of concrete solutions. And, we are distressed that so few of the experts are able to provide answers. Perhaps this is because education is one of the most complex and least understood of all human endeavors. In any event, there is a serious knowledge gap about the education of disadvantaged children in this country.

Thus, it has been less difficult for us to assess the extent and causes of inequality in education than it has been to devise ways of making education more responsive and sensitive to the needs of minority group and disadvantaged children. We do not purport to have all the answers. We have no single solution to propose that we know will lead to equality in educational opportunity; nor do we believe there is a single policy or program that can alone assure educational success. Many hopeful proposals that we might be implementing have not been tried. Others have been undertaken with so little effort that they have been inadequate to meet the goals for which they were designed. We think there must be a combination of policies and programs to make our schools succeed for those whom they now fail. We must provide the resources necessary to overcome the disadvantages that children from poor families and deprived home environments bring to school. But those resources must be combined with an attitude of sensitivity and respect for children of all backgrounds. At the same time, we must enhance our present efforts and undertake new ones to upgrade the quality of education for all children. We must develop new approaches, try new programs, and greatly expand efforts to learn what will work for minority and disadvantaged children.

In the 1960s, the Federal Government for the first time in our history became directly involved in a major effort to support public education. We launched a major program to compensate for the educational disadvantage of children from poor families. At the same time, we undertook to abolish dual, separate systems of education for black- and white children. Now, in the early 1970s, largely through court challenges, we would appear to be launching a third major effort to eliminate the inequities in the ways in which we pay for education and distribute resources to our schools.*

Each of these efforts, to compensate for educational disadvantage, to integrate our schools, and to reform school finance, is essential. But they tend to be looked upon as alternatives. When we think we have discovered that one strategy has not met our expectations, we proceed to the next and when that appears difficult we launch another, never having adequately tried or funded the last.

Compensatory education, school integration and reform in school finance, together with the other policies and programs recommended in these pages, should not be looked upon as alternative strategies. They should proceed together, with adequate support to make them successful.

Thus, we are persuaded that there must be a combination of strategies and programs which will permit schools as institutions and

---

*An issue now before the U.S. Supreme Court in *San Antonio* v. *Rodriguez*.

those in them to re-examine themselves. While we cannot write a prescription which assures educational success, we believe we can prescribe a number of hopeful processes which will more likely lead to equality of educational opportunity, and which will make our public schools more responsive to the needs and desires of poor and minority group children.

## E. Education in Perspective

All too often we tend to deal with problems in our society as though the institutions which affect our lives and opportunities are unrelated to each other. For example, national policies and programs are developed to create full employment, decent housing, reform welfare, eliminate hunger, provide child care or health care or overcome educational disadvantage. Yet, we often act as though each were a separate solution to an isolated condition. Each in turn has its day in court as "the Nation's number one priority." Each has its own experts and advocates who tend to view their solution to a particular problem as the one which will take care of many or most of the other problems in society as well.

This is certainly true of education. After 2 years of hearings and other studies, it is tempting to conclude that—if schools could provide all the skills children need for adulthood, if schools could succeed in motivating children where their home life has failed, if schools were free of discrimination and had the resources to meet the needs of every child—the cycle of poverty and disadvantage would be broken. While we believe great progress would result, such a conclusion is both unrealistic and unwarranted. For no one institution in society can, or should, be expected to overcome the failure of all others.

No discussion of educational opportunity can fail to recognize the relationship of educational inequality to other inequalities in society. No design for the reform of public education, no program which promises full opportunity for disadvantaged children in school, will fully succeed unless it is accompanied by efforts to overcome the consequences of inadequate health care and nutrition, unemployment, substandard housing, and other conditions which combine to deny equality of opportunity to millions of children and adults. No policy designed to eliminate racial and ethnic discrimination in education can fully succeed without similar efforts to eliminate discrimination in a broad range of other areas such as housing, employment, voting rights and access to public accommodations.

It is not within the mandate of this committee to examine in depth or recommend policies and programs to alleviate these other inequalities in our society. But it is appropriate not only to make note of them, but to put them in perspective as we discuss inequality in educational opportunity. For the child from a disadvantaged family, poverty, unemployment, welfare dependency, hunger, poor health and substandard and overcrowded housing are the conditions of a depressing and damaging environment into which he is born and raised and which dominate his life while he is in school and after his schooling—unless something intervenes to break the cycle of poverty. All these conditions converge on the educational process. Often for the child—whose parents never completed high school, or whose father is unemployed or whose family is on welfare—life at home, in his years both before and during school, is a fight for survival. Often there are no childrens' books or magazines, few toys and none of the educational stimuli that most children take for granted. Except for school, television may be his only sustained contact with the world outside his urban ghetto or rural slum neighborhood. The child who lacks proper food at home is often dull and listless, often sick. If he is one of the 7.5 million poor children who receive a free or reduced-price meal, lunch at school may be his only nutritious meal. The child who arrives at school without breakfast simply cannot learn on an empty stomach.

One of education's most basic tasks is to equip children for a vocationally productive adult life. Schools generally succeed in equipping most of their graduates with the basic skills and motivations to function in society and hold a decent job. But that is little consolation for 4.7 million unemployed citizens or to 2 million underemployed who can find only part-time work. It is little satisfaction to 13.7 million wage earners—whose pay is less than a poverty income—or to the minority American who is jobless or unable to advance his career because of employment discrimination. As long as the promise of a full employment economy remains unfulfilled, the most equal and best educational system we can devise will be useless to those of its beneficiaries who are the victims of an economic system in which unemployment is a fact of life. Moreover, uncertainty about the prospects for future employment—in an economy where so many teenagers and young adults cannot find jobs—often impedes the child's incentive to learn in school.

But inadequate education also results in unemployment. Our public schools today are failing millions of children who simply do not acquire the basic skills and knowledge—whose aspirations and perceptions of themselves and trust in the institutions that affect their lives are so low that they simply cannot function in society.

An August 1970 survey conducted by Louis Harris and Associates for the National Reading Council showed that 18.5 million Americans—13 percent of our citizens 16 years and older—are so deficient in basic ability to read and write they are unable to meet the normal demands placed upon them in society. Among these 18.5 million are 6.3 million Americans who have no more than a fifth grade education. But the rest have gone beyond the fifth grade and perhaps completed elementary school or even a year or two of high school. Their level of comprehension of routine written material is so low that they have difficulty in filling out simple application forms or understanding written instructions. They have difficulty preparing tax returns, applying for public assistance or medical benefits, passing written examinations for driver's licenses, and performing other communicative tasks.

For these people unemployment and menial, low-paying jobs are the inevitable consequence of low educational attainment and school failure.

# Chapter 2—Summary of the Report

## A. Inequality in Education

### 1. THE EDUCATION OF MINORITY-GROUP AND DISADVANTAGED CHILDREN

In our more than 2 years of hearings and studies we have concentrated primarily upon the education of those who are denied equal opportunity in our society—children from poor families, whatever their race or heritage, and children who are members of racial and language minority groups.

We have tried to look at education from a perspective from which institutions in our society rarely view themselves—from the standpoint of those whom the system has failed. We have found failure and we have much to criticize. But if we are critical of an institution which is failing millions of school-age youngsters, we are also mindful that the vast majority are being well prepared and will leave school with the skills, knowledge and motivations they need to succeed in life.

In the course of our studies we have learned much that is good about public education in America. There is no doubt that our schools have provided each successive generation of American children with the knowledge and skills they need to lead productive and satisfying lives in a growing, increasingly complex society.

Each year more children are attending schools for longer periods and learning more. Between 1950 and the present, the proportion of elementary school students completing high school has increased from 50 to more than 75 percent. During the same period the college entrance rate has doubled. To rate our public educational system an overall success would be an understatement. From the standpoint of most Americans, it has served our Nation superbly.

But that cannot be said with respect to the education of most children in poverty—living in the rural slums or urban ghettos or isolated suburban pockets of America. And cannot be said for most poor children—black children, or Mexican American, or Puerto Rican, or Portuguese, or Oriental, or American Indian, or other children who are from racial minorities whose first language is not English.

About one-fifth, or 9.3 million of our Nation's 46.3 million students in public preschools and elementary and secondary schools, are members of minority groups. At the same time another 20 percent are from families with incomes under $5,000 a year, and about 4 million are from families with annual incomes less than $3,000 per year. Also, 12.2 million students are in families where the head of the household has no more than 8 years of school, and 10.5 million are children with unemployed or underemployed parents. These and other statistics—the 8.7 million children who arrive at school each day without a nutritious breakfast, the fact that at least 5 million children live in substandard housing units, and the high incidence of inadequate health care for perhaps as many as 21 million children of all ages—indicate the magnitude of disadvantaged among our Nation's school- and preschool-age population. We estimate that at least 12 million and perhaps as many as 20 million of the Nation's school-age population of 59 million, between 3 and 17, are from either economically or educationally disadvantaged homes.

For most of these children formal education is a yearly repetition of accelerating failure. Our public education system has failed and continues to fail successive generations of children from disadvantaged and minority group backgrounds—millions of children who leave school years behind in achievement and without the skills, knowledge or motivation they need to succeed in life. The result is that our public schools not only perpetuate but often exacerbate rather than help overcome the economic, social and racial inequalities in our society.

The typical child who is black, Mexican American, Puerto Rican, American Indian, a member of another racial- or language-minority group, or poor white and living in a rural community, is likely to achieve in school at two-thirds the rate of the average child. On entering the third grade he is often already a year behind. By the 12th grade he is likely to be 4½ years behind.

But the real story of educational failure was related to the committee in the testimony of witnesses, many of them professional educators, from communities across the country. It is a tale of devastating personal tragedy of enormous consequences to individual children. Here is a sampling of some of the things we heard about the performance of disadvantaged children.

- In the ghetto schools of Hartford, Conn., the average IQ scores of black elementary schoolchildren show a steady decline between the 4th and the 8th grade from 94 to 86. This 8th grade score is only 6 points above the IQ level at which the laws of Connecticut permit institutionalization in special schools for the mentally retarded.
- Similarly, at the preschool level, in the Edgewood school district of San Antonio, Tex., Chicano children at the age of 3 score an average of 104 in IQ tests. At age 4 their average is 90. By the time they are 5, and ready to enter the first grade, it is 70.
- In the typical Philadephia inner city elementary school, 65 percent of the students score in the 16th percentile in the Iowa Test of Basic Skills—so low they are simply not functioning as students.
- Of the Mexican-American students in Texas, 56.8 percent leave school before completing the 8th grade; 78.9 percent drop out before high school graduation. One expert estimated 20 percent of migrant children never attend school at all.
- There are 7,800 Puerto Rican students in the public schools of Newark, N.J. Only 96 are in the 12th grade; in Boston between 1965 and 1969, only 4 out of 7,000 Puerto Rican schoolchildren graduated from high school; and in Chicago, the Puerto Rican dropout rate before high school graduation is 60 percent.

- Two-thirds of all American Indian adults have never gone beyond elementary school; 10 percent of those over 14 never went to school at all; and probably as many as half the American Indian children enrolled in school today will not finish high school.

These are but a few examples of the tragic educational failure of minority group and disadvantaged children.

### 2. THE ELEMENTS OF INEQUALITY IN EDUCATION

Today and throughout our history, where a person is born, his race, his native language, his cultural background and his parents' income and occupation are the principal factors that determine where he lives and the quality of his education. The child from a disadvantaged home usually enters school already behind in his ability to communicate and relate to the new world around him. He goes to school with others from similar backgrounds and often to a school with inadequate facilities. He is often taught by less-qualified teachers who are insensitive to his culture and background, and who label him as different, slow in learning and likely to fail. He is often tested and tracked in a class for slow learners. He is more likely than the child from an advantaged home to drop out before graduation. If he does graduate he is usually years behind in achievement; he seldom continues his education and is likely to return to all the handicaps of the environment into which he was born. This is the unequal life of the disadvantaged schoolchild.

There are three principal, interrelated ways in which the process of education in this Nation is unequal.

*First*, children from minority and economically disadvantaged families live their lives isolated from the rest of society. The fact is that education in this country is still—for the most part—segregated by race, economic and social class. By any reasonable measure, except in the 11 Southern States, we have hardly begun the task of eliminating the segregation of minority group and disadvantaged students in our Nation. Nationally, 5.9 million out of 9.3 million minority-group students, or more than 60 percent, still attend predominantly minority-group schools. At the same time 72 percent of the Nation's nonminority-group students attend schools which are at least 90 percent nonminority. Four million minority-group students attend schools which are 80 percent or more minority, and 2 million are in classes which are 99–100 percent minority.

By every standard of measurement there has been pronounced reduction in the isolation of black students in the 11 Southern States during the past 4 years. However, during the same period, the change in other regions of the country has been infinitesimal. In 1968, 78.8 percent of the South's black students were in 80–100 percent minority schools. By 1971, that figure was reduced to 32.2 percent. This reduction almost entirely accounted for a 22.1 percent nationwide reduction in the proportion of black students in 80–100 percent minority schools during the same period.

But even more dramatic has been the near elimination of all-black schools in the South. In 1968, 68 percent of the South's black students were in all-black schools. By September 1971, that figure was reduced to 9.2 percent.

Minority-group children are more isolated in large school districts than in small ones. About one-half of the Nation's black students are in our 100 largest school districts. These school districts, which include all the Nation's large cities, are the most segregated in the Nation. Nearly 75 percent of the black students in these districts were in 80–100 percent minority schools, and 60 percent were in 95–100 percent minority schools in the Fall of 1971.

*Second*, minority and disadvantaged children are often treated in unequal ways by schools themselves.

Their performance, their aspirations and motivations are often adversely affected by the attitudes and expectations of their teachers—who often label them as inferior, and destined to fail. The disadvantaged child is often tracked in a class or other group of "slow learners" or "underachievers." In short, these children are subjected to a labeling process according to their background rather than their ability or potential—a process which deeply affects a child's attitudes about himself, his family, his culture and virtually assures school failure and a life of unequal opportunity after school.

One of our witnesses described these unequal practices as they affect Spanish-speaking children:

> The injuries of the Latin American child have been inflicted by those who have claimed to teach and motivate him, and who have, in reality, alienated him, and destroyed his identity through the subtle rejection of his language [which nobody speaks], his culture [which nobody understands], and ultimately him [whom nobody values].*

*Third*, the financial resources for public elementary and secondary education are both raised and distributed inequitably so that the quality of a child's education is largely dependent upon the taxable wealth of each school district and its citizens. As a result, most children from low-income families and those who live in communities with low tax bases or high public service costs attend schools with fewer and lower quality educational services.

The disparities in school expenditures across the Nation can only be described as spectacular. They exist among States, among school districts within States and among schools within school districts. Among the 50 States the range of per-pupil expenditures is from $1,429 in Alaska to $489 in Alabama. Within almost every State the highest spending school district spends at least twice as much as the lowest spending school district and variations of 3-, 4-, and 5-to-1 are not uncommon.

In short, poor children usually attend poor schools. They are the victims of the fact that most of the resources for education in this Nation are allocated in a manner which assures that the best education that money can buy is available to children in wealthy communities, and the lowest quality education goes to those in the poorest communities.

These three factors—segregation of minority-group and disadvantaged children in fact, if not in law; the unequal practices and treatment to which they are subjected, and the inequality in educa-

---

*Hearings of the U.S. Senate Select Committee on Equal Educational Opportunity, Part 4. *Mexican-American Education*, Aug. 18, 1970, p. 2392.

tional resources—combine to produce inequality in American public elementary and secondary education. Together they produce educational failure in the form of low aspirations and motivations, high dropout rates, and low achievement.

### 3. THE PRIMARY CAUSES OF EDUCATIONAL INEQUALITY

What these elements of educational inequality—segregation, economic discrimination, malnutrition and the unequal treatment of, and unequal resources for, minority-group and poor children—add up to is a system which is failing millions of children. The reasons for that failure are complex. But they add up to a central finding of our work:

It is not that children fail. It is our Nation that has failed them.

They are the victims—the victims of racial discrimination and class prejudice, poor schools, unfit housing, inadequate health care, malnutrition, unemployment and poverty. They are the victims of virtually every institution in our society—of which our public education system is among the most important—institutions that are insensitive and unresponsive to the needs of racial minorities and disadvantaged groups. The fact is that many of the school systems in this Nation that are confronted with children from families whose racial or cultural heritage or spoken language are different from those of most white middle-class American children are somehow institutionally unable to respond to their needs.

The reasons for this insensitivity are many and complex. In part, they have to do with questions which are beyond the scope of our committee's work: The theory and practice of teaching, how children from different backgrounds learn most effectively, what should be in their curriculum, whether they should be instructed in an atmosphere which is open and informal or structured and formal. These are questions to which educators seem to not have found answers.

From this committee's perspective this lack of response is, in part, a matter of attitude; and, in part, a matter of the way schools and educators relate to their clients. Minority and disadvantaged groups in this Nation often see themselves as the powerless victims of an educational system—run by a professional and political establishment which systematically excludes them from the process by which schools are governed, and from the decisions made about the education of their children.

They see their children's future in the hands of people who often fail to understand their needs and aspirations, and who are insensitive to their heritage and culture and the values they consider important—a condition that Charles Silberman has called "mindlessness." They are powerless to affect the policies of school boards, school administrators and others who distribute the resources, assign the principals and teachers, set the curriculum, and make the other decisions that affect their children's education.

To minority groups, education often remains a closed institution controlled by the majority. They have waited nearly 20 years since the *Brown* decision held out the prospect of integrated education. They have watched, and they have sometimes been the victims rather than the beneficiaries, of a slow, painful process of change, more often than not accompanied by white resistance—usually overt and sometimes violent. They know that, nationwide, most schools which were separate and unequal in 1954 remain that way today; and they know that, even where desegregation has been accomplished, control over the educational process often remains exclusively in the hands of those who fought to retain separate and unequal schools.

Many feel they have waited long enough. They feel as Kenneth Haskins expressed it to the committee:

> All of the work done by black people and some white people to alter the situation so that equality could be achieved has not changed the basic fabric of this country. We still have a society that can tolerate or encourage a school system that fails poor black children, but would immediately mobilize itself if it was not educating middle-class white children. . . .
>
> It is upon this base that the present educational system is built. . . . In any case, black people feel they can no longer accept their definitions from white America. Growing numbers of others—Indians, Puerto Ricans, Mexican Americans, and some poor whites—are reaching similar conclusions.*

It is this unresponsiveness to the needs and desires of minority groups that has led many to seek not just proportional representation—on school boards, in administrative positions and on faculties—but control of their own schools and school systems. Some seek "community control" as an alternative to school integration. Not so much, perhaps, because they reject integration as a promising path to educational equality, but because they simply no longer believe that our governmental and educational institutions are going to let it happen in a way that gives them an equal chance—the right to decide for themselves, make choices about their own and their children's futures.

It is important to understand not just that our institutions have failed to respond but the reasons why. The reasons are rooted in our history—that part of our history of which we are reminded almost daily as minority groups struggle for equal rights in this country.

In 1968, the National Advisory Commission on Civil Disorders warned that "Our Nation is moving toward two societies, one black, one white—separate and unequal." The Commission called for "a commitment to national action—compassionate, massive and sustained—backed by the resources of the most powerful and richest nation on this earth. From every American it will require new attitudes, new understanding, and, above all, new will."

The warning has gone largely unheeded. The commitment has not been made. Perhaps the reason is that neither our people nor their institutions have been able to shed the basic attitudes about race and status that are rooted in our past.

Not long ago in our history, virtually every nonwhite group was prevented by law or custom from an adequate education, gainful employment, political participation and, in most instances, ownership of land and other property. The doors to collective advancement were simply kept closed to blacks, browns, reds and other racial minorities.

But the removal of legal impediments to equality has not enabled nonwhite Americans to gain the social status, economic and political power necessary to gain parity in society or control their own destinies.

---

******Ibid.***, Part 13, *Quality and Control of Urban Schools*, July 27, 1971.**

Attitudes and customs are not easily changed—they will only change with time. But the more often we are reminded, as a people, that we are a society that too often defines people by color and class rather than by their abilities and accomplishments, the more likely we are to eliminate the vestiges of racial and ethnic intolerance that prevent us from becoming one society in which equality of opportunity is a reality.

#### 4. THE COSTS OF INADEQUATE EDUCATION

The real costs of inadequate education and the lack of equal educational opportunity in this country are, for the most part, immeasurable.

For the individual, educational failure means a lifetime of lost opportunities. But the effects are visited on the Nation as well, for society as a whole also pays for the undereducation of a significant segment of its population.

Unemployment and underemployment due to low levels of educational attainment and underachievement reduce many citizens' earning power. Reduced earnings translate into fewer total goods and services, less tax support for government, and require the use of public budgets to pay for services that would otherwise be provided through personal resources.

Families whose incomes are below the poverty line must be supported with tax dollars to pay for food, housing, health services, job training, remedial education, income maintenance and other services.

Low educational attainment is also an important contributor to crime. The tie between education and juvenile delinquency has been well documented. The costs of crime prevention and control, also our judicial and penal systems, are higher to the extent that higher educational attainment and achievement would result in reduced juvenile delinquency and adult crime.

Nor are these costs limited to the present generation, for the children of those who are denied a decent education are themselves more likely to suffer the same educational and social consequences as their parents.

A study estimating the magnitude of these costs was undertaken for this Select Committee by Professor Henry M. Levin of the Stanford University School of Education, Entitled "The Costs to the Nation of Inadequate Education," the study concludes that the failure of 3.18 million American men—between the ages of 25 and 34—to graduate from high school will cost $237 billion in lost personal income over the lifetimes of this group of young adults.

The study further demonstrates that of this amount, Federal, State, and local governments will lose $71 billion in tax revenues of which $47 billion would have been added to the Federal treasury, and $24 billion would have been paid to State and local governments.

The study estimates that the cost of providing high school completion among the same population group would have been approximately $40 billion. As a result, the government revenues generated by this investment would have exceeded government expenditures by more than $30 billion. Each dollar invested in high school completion for these young men would have generated approximately $6 of national income over their lifetimes.

Dr. Levin's study estimates that $3 million of the Nation's annual welfare expenditures are attributable to inadequate education; and, that of the annual cost of crime, inadequate education is responsible for another $3 billion each year.

Dr. Levin's study is the first attempt to place dollar estimates on the loss to our society of educational neglect. It is particularly important in view of the present national concern about financial inequality in education and the need to overcome the fiscal crisis faced by many of our school systems.

As Dr. Levin concludes, for each dollar we invest in public education, there is likely to be a six-fold return on our national investment—just in terms of the production of income alone. And every $4 invested to provide a minimum of high school completion will generate $7 in additional tax revenues to Federal, State, and local governments.

## B. The Preschool Years

### 1. CHILD DEVELOPMENT

*Findings*—Nothing is more central to the problem of equal educational opportunity than the experiences children have—or do not have—during the early childhood years.

The opportunities and the environments that America's 21 million children under 6 are now experiencing—and that the children who follow them will experience—are among the major determinants of their future success or failure.

The beginning years of life are critical for a child's intellectual growth, and for his social, emotional, physical, and motivational development. These early years are the formative years. They are the years in which permanent foundations are laid for a child's feelings of self-worth, his sense of self-respect, his motivation, his initiative, and his ability to learn and achieve.

Fortunately for most children, the preschool years are usually spent in a secure and stimulating environment where they receive the physical and mental nourishment necessary for development. The child from an affluent family who enters school at the age of 6 often has behind him a full and complex learning history. The variety of skills this well-endowed 6-year-old brings to school with him are impressive. Yet he was born with none of these specific abilities. He has learned them all from interactions with his environment. In short, his "cognitive development" is already well advanced. He also, as a rule, has had his medical and dental needs attended to; and he has never been truly hungry or undernourished.

But this is seldom the case for 3.2 million preschool children living in poverty. For them the early years can be a depressing, deadening, tragic experience.

Regardless of the love and attention these children receive from their families—and however strong their family ties—many are growing up without adequate nutrition and health care; and without the active mental and intellectual stimulation that is necessary during their early years.

Many of these children are depressed, withdrawn, and listless. Parents and child development specialists report that, in the beginning, it is difficult to get some of them to smile or show interest in anything around them. Young children in some deprived homes are considered well behaved if they sit quietly in a corner during the day—instead of talking, playing, and exploring. The frequent moving and use of many different babysitters make some of them confused, insecure and, in extreme cases, emotionally disturbed and hyperactive. Sometimes there are no books or magazines in their homes, no clocks, or radios, and what few toys there are usually have no educational value for the child.

In addition, many poor children—Mexican Americans, Indians, Eskimos, Puerto Ricans, Portuguese, Asians, and members of the other minority groups—grow up learning English as a second language, or not at all. Besides being burdened with possible nutritional and intellectual deprivation in their early years, many are confronted with an alien language and an alien culture when they begin school.

These are the more than 3 million preschool children of poverty. There are over 5 million preschool children whose mothers are working. Some of these children are receiving healthful and stimulating care while their parents work. But many are not. Many are left in purely custodial and unlicensed day-care centers, and others—the so-called latchkey children—are left alone to look after themselves. And their numbers are growing.

- In 1971, 43 percent of the Nation's mothers worked outside the home—compared to only 18 percent in 1948.
- One out of every three mothers with preschool children is working today—compared to one out of eight in 1948.
- In 1971, 1.3 million mothers, of children under 6, were bringing up children without a husband, and 50 percent of these mothers worked.

Yet, there are fewer than 700,000 spaces in licensed day-care centers to serve the over 5 million preschool children whose mothers work.

Many of these early inequities can be prevented. That is the lesson of our best preschool education programs, including Head Start and their necessary counterparts like Follow Through. Promising results have been produced in a wide variety of quality preschool education efforts ranging from programs involving regularly scheduled home visits by tutors who work with both the child and his parents to the more familiar part- or full-day education programs such as Head Start or Nursery School. These quality early childhood programs have shown that good preschool programs can significantly enhance the development of a child in later years. But they do not show—and this fact cannot be overemphasized—that quality preschool programs alone will guarantee that children reach their full potential.

Early childhood services are not an inoculation that lasts for life. There are no magic periods in childhood. Child development is continuous and enrichment in the preschool years must be followed by stimulating education during the school years, or else much of the gains will be lost.

The implications of both past experience and research are quite clear:

- A child's chance for an equal educational opportunity begins long before he enters school.
- The home environment, or the day-care environment, in which a preschool child spends his time can have a major impact on his future educational career.

- Quality preschool programs for children and parents can help eliminate much of the deficit normally produced by poverty or custodial day care.
- Deep and meaningful parent involvement is essential for the success of early childhood efforts.
- We must have a continuity between the early childhood programs and subsequent educational endeavors in the elementary schools to sustain the gains they make.

*Recommendations*—The committee recommends, therefore, legislation to create voluntary comprehensive well-financed, child development programs for families and children that:

- Strengthen family life and family capabilities.
- Assure adequate health, nutritional and educational opportunities in the early childhood years.
- Provide home-based programs drawing on the talents and resources of parents as the primary educational influence on their children.
- Upgrade day-care programs into truly developmental and educationally stimulating experiences rather than purely custodial and sometimes damaging parking lots for children.
- Involve parents and other family members in all aspects of these programs including staffing, decisionmaking and training.
- Provide expanded opportunities for staff training and research.
- Offer maximum flexibility, within the national standards of excellence, for local groups to adopt programs consistent with their needs.
- Promote social and economic diversity—rather than a track system—for the preschool years.
- Provides family services in the home.
- Involve Follow Through Programs and other improvements in the elementary schools to provide the essential continuity between early enrichment and later educational programs.

It should be noted that the 92d Congress has already considered legislation* along these lines. The committee hopes that full consideration leading to enactment of our recommendations will be undertaken early in the 93d Congress.

### 2. CHILDREN'S TELEVISION

*Findings*—Television is a major influence on the development of children. Ninety-seven percent of American families own television sets. The average American school-age child watches between 22 and 25 hours of television each week. By the time he is 16, he is likely to have

*S. 3617, "The Comprehensive Head Start, Child Development, and Family Services Act of 1972," which passed the Senate during the 2d Sess., 92d Cong.

watched between 15,000 and 20,000 hours of television, while at the same age he has spent only 10,000 hours in school.

The wide availability and pervasiveness of television have stimulated concern about its effects on children. Among the specific subjects of concern are the high incidence of violence and the distorted portrayal of minority groups on the screen. At the same time there is no doubt that television can be a positive force in the life of a child—that all the hours spent in front of the TV set can help him to learn to read and count, and expose him to ideas and people that he does not encounter in his normal home and school life.

"Sesame Street," created by the Children's Television Workshop, is a children's program designed to offer educational content to preschool youngsters, particularly those from disadvantaged families. The evaluation of the first year of "Sesame Street" suggests that such programs offer great potential as a tool for providing equal educational opportunity to all American children. The single most important conclusion of the study was that regardless of race, ethnic background, or economic status the more a child watched "Sesame Street" the more he learned. "Sesame Street" and its companion for elementary school children, "The Electric Company," are the only shared educational experiences of many white, black, and other minority-group young children in America. These programs are outstanding examples of how television can further educational opportunity.

We believe integrated children's educational television performances have the potential to further equal educational opportunity—both in the home and in the classroom. We endorse the recently enacted authorization of $60 million over the next 2 fiscal years to provide grants to public and private nonprofit agencies for the production and development of integrated children's educational television programs.

*Recommendations*—We Recommend:

- That the Congress appropriate the full $60 million authorized for fiscal years 1973 and 1974 for integrated children's educational television programs under the Emergency School Aid Act.
- That during this 2-year period, Congress and the Department of Health, Education, and Welfare carefully review both the cognitive and affective results of children's educational television programs—results which will be available through implementation of the requirement in the Emergency School Aid Act that funded programs be subjected to comprehensive evaluation.
- That an appropriate number of new children's educational television programs should be designed and directed to meet the needs of minority group children in particular geographical areas of the United States.
- That in 1974, Congress consider a permanent authorization for the development and implementation of integrated children's educational television programs.
- That greater efforts be made to encourage the development of educational television programs for children under commercial sponsorship.

In the final analysis it is the television industry itself which will determine whether children's programing will play a constructive role in enhancing equal educational opportunity.

## C. The School Years

### 1. SCHOOL INTEGRATION

*Findings*—For more than a century, the goal of this Nation has been a just and open society—in which citizens associate freely as they wish, in which race and religion are no handicap—and, above all, a society in which each child is born with a real and equal chance for a productive and useful life. Achievement of that goal cannot be grounded upon a system of public education which perpetuates for all time the results of past racial discrimination. The Supreme Court's comment in *Brown* v. *Board of Education* is even truer today:

> In these days, it is doubtful that any child may reasonably be expected to succeed in life if he is denied the opportunity of an education. Such an opportunity, where the State has undertaken to provide it, is a right which must be made available to all on equal terms.

And yet racial discrimination, including the deliberate segregation of children by race or national origin, is widespread in public school systems throughout this country. In the 17 Southern and Border States, strictly segregated dual school systems were required by State statute from the earliest days of public education. And a growing number of Federal courts have found segregation in public education caused by subtler means in the North and West as well. In South Holland, Ill., a U.S. District Court found schools located in the center rather than at the boundaries of segregated residential areas in order to achieve school segregation, school assignment policies under which black children living nearer to white schools attended black schools while white children living nearer to black schools attended white schools, schoolbuses used to transport students out of their neighborhoods to achieve segregation. Federal courts have found discrimination in Pontiac and Detroit, Mich., in Pasadena and San Francisco, Calif., in Denver, Colo., in Indianapolis, Ind., in Minneapolis, Minn., and elsewhere.

The 18 years since the Supreme Court's landmark decision in *Brown* v. *Board of Education*—and, in particular, the 8 years since adoption of the Civil Rights Act of 1964—have presented a clear test of our commitment to equal opportunity for all American children. The Nation continues to wrestle with its conscience, and the outcome remains in doubt. It is clear as this report is published that our national commitment to nondiscrimination in public education is in serious jeopardy.

Proposals were introduced in the 92d Congress for constitutional amendments, and for legislation which—if held constitutional—would severely limit or eliminate the power of Federal courts and agencies to remedy the establishment or maintenance of racially discriminatory school systems. These proposals are likely to be advanced again in the new 93d Congress. Public opinion polls over the last 2 years show a marked decrease in support, not for desegregation itself, but for means of remedying segregation without which discriminatory dual school systems must be allowed to continue.

Perhaps the saddest aspect of the current debate over school desegregation has been its focus on the misleading issues of "busing" and "racial balance" and its consequent disregard for the real issues affecting the well-being of the millions of children, minority group and nonminority group, whose futures are now at stake in desegregated schools.

It should be clearly understood that Federal law requires only an end to officially sponsored segregation in public education, which violate the 14th Amendment to the U.S. Constitution, and the Civil Rights Act of 1964. Federal law does not require a "racial balance". Nor can Federal law require school systems to adopt the creative educational approaches which can build upon desegregation to create quality, integrated education; this is a local responsibility, although we believe the Federal Government can and should provide help to school districts to make desegregation educationally successful.

There are only two forms of school desegregation in this country—desegregation undertaken as a matter of voluntary local (or, in some instances, State) decision, and desegregation undertaken to remedy officially sponsored segregation which violates the Equal Protection Clause of the 14th Amendment.

Federal courts, and Federal agencies under the Civil Rights Act of 1964, act only to remedy segregation imposed by the discriminatory acts of public authorities, and even then they do not require any "racial balance" in the schools. Chief Justice Berger's opinion for a unanimous Supreme Court in *Swann* v. *Charlotte-Mecklenburg*, decided in April of 1971, should have put this issue to rest:

> The constitutional command to desegregate schools does not mean that every school in every community must always reflect the composition of the school system as a whole.

"Racial balance" is not required. What is required is "a plan that promises realistically to work . . . until it is clear that State-imposed segregation has been completely removed."

The issue of "busing"—although it has been at the center of debate since adoption of the Civil Rights Act of 1964—is just as misleading—as the issue of "racial balance". The facts speak for themselves:

- According to HEW's 1970 school survey, 42 percent of all American public school students are transported to their schools by schoolbus.
- HEW estimates that only 3 percent of all public school busing is for the purpose of desegregation.
- The Department of Transportation attributes less than 1 percent of the annual increase in student transportation to school desegregation.

Transportation of students is so common in school districts throughout the Nation that there can be no legitimate reason to forbid its use as one tool in remedying discrimination.

In most cases, if not all, transportation has been held within reasonable limits. In the 23 largest school districts undergoing desegregation in the Fall of 1971, the Department of HEW estimates that the proportion of students transported rose by only 7.5 percent.

And where courts and Federal agencies have required use of transportation, often it has been to assure that the results of desegregation will be more stable, and that desegregation will not be limited to the minority-group and nonminority-group working class populations who typically live in adjoining neighborhoods.

Like any other tool, transportaton can be abused. But the Supreme Court has established a standard of reasonableness—that transportation should not be required where "time or distance of travel is so great as to risk either the health of the children or significantly impinge on the educational process." The Supreme Court has noted that "the time of travel will vary with many factors, but none more than the age of the students." Thus the Congress in the Education Amendments Act of 1972 has reaffirmed that standard, and expressly applied it to proceedings under Title VI of the Civil Rights Act of 1964. Under both Supreme Court rule and legislative provision, transportation that exceeds reasonable limits can be judicially challenged and judicially remedied.

Transportation under court order has caused serious hardship in a number of communities, not because of the time or distance of travel, but because an insufficient supply of schoolbuses has required schools to be placed on double or even overlapping triple sessions in order to permit existing buses to make several runs.

In Nashville, Tenn., for example, no funds were available for more buses to support a 20-percent increase in the proportion of students transported. Schools were put on triple sessions so that existing buses could make additional runs; the result was severe hardship to many families, which has seriously undermined support for the school program. Numbers of other communities suffered similar hardships.

And educational services in many of these communities have been reduced in order to meet unavoidable additional costs. Increased transportation expenses, while often large in dollar terms, are generally small in terms of total school operating budgets. An increase of 20 percent in the proportion of students transported in Tampa, Fla., for example, increased operating expenses by $767,000—less than 0.4 percent of the total school budget. But already overstrained education budgets cannot absorb these increased costs without sacrificing existing education programs.

As Nashville, Tenn., Superintendent Elbert Brooks testified:

> . . . neither those who support integration, nor those who tolerate integration, will accept for long their children's continued exposure to hardship and danger brought about by inadequate transportation services.

The hardships brought about by inadequate transportation services could have been avoided if the Department of Health, Education, and Welfare had not restricted use of funds under the $75 million Emergency School Assistance Program, earmarked to meet special needs of desegregating school districts, by prohibiting support for transportation of students. Fortunately, efforts to impose similar restrictions on the recently-adopted Emergency School Aid Act—establishing a comprehensive program to support both legally required and voluntary integration efforts—were defeated. The committee hopes that Federal funds will be available to support the added costs of desegregation-related transportation next Fall.

School desegregation does present critical problems—the problem of guaranteeing minority-group parents that their children will not be victims of discrimination within desegregated schools, and the problem of guaranteeing all parents that their children's education will be improved by integration. Continued preoccupation with the false issue of whether a single child should be transported to achieve desegregation will not help address these real problems.

We would do well to learn from the children themselves. A survey, conducted by the Resource Management Corporation for the Office of Education, of students attending 252 desegregating school districts which received Emergency School Assistance Program funding during the 1970–71 school year, found:

> About 70 percent of blacks and about 60 percent of whites agreed that both races were becoming more openminded as a result of interracial busing.

*Integration and Educational Opportunity*—*Equality of Educational Opportunity*, commonly known as the "Coleman Report," was commissioned under the authority of Section 402 of the Civil Rights Act of 1964, and contains the findings of a study conducted for the Office of Education by a research team under Dr. James S. Coleman of Johns Hopkins University. The study is based on surveys of 570,000 students and 60,000 teachers attending 4,000 schools during the 1965–66 school year.

The report found achievement highly related to family background, and found that differences in traditional measures of school quality—per-pupil expenditures on staff, library volumes per student, science lab facilities, presence of guidance counselors, etc.—had little apparent effect on achievement.

But the report also found that socioeconomic status of fellow students did have a strong relationship to academic achievement of minority-group children.

In Dr. Coleman's words:

> . . . if schools are racially homogeneous or economically homogeneous, the disadvantages a working-class or Negro child, or a Puerto Rican child, or a Mexican-American child experiences in his home environment are multiplied by the disadvantages he experiences in his school environment.

At the same time, when children from educationally disadvantaged homes attend schools with predominantly middle-class, educationally advantaged student bodies, educational disadvantage resulting from home environment is reduced, although not eliminated.

Important support for the Coleman findings concerning the importance of socioeconomic integration is found among the studies contained in *On Equality of Educational Opportunity*, a collection of reanalyses of the Coleman data by members of the Harvard University faculty. (See Chapter 12.)

In his controversial book *Inequality*, which is in large part based on analyses of the 1965 Coleman data, Christopher Jencks estimates that racial-socioeconomic integration alone will reduce the gap in achievement test scores between black- and white children and between rich and poor children by 10 to 20 percent.*

We agree with Jencks' observation that the available data are murky. We agree with his finding that racial-socioeconomic integration is more likely to produce achievement gains than simply equalizing school resources. And, while reducing aggregate inequality by 20 percent would be a substantial achievement, we find real promise that where carefully designed educational programs provide for focused remedial services within a racially and economically integrated setting, substantially more dramatic gains can be achieved.

There are weaknesses in the Coleman data. For example, only 65 percent of school districts asked to participate responded; and technical questions have been raised regarding the report's analysis. More importantly, the study is simply a "snapshot" of conditions in American public schools during the 1965–66 school year. While it describes the condition of children in integrated and segregated schools during that year, it cannot follow their progress through school to show, for example, the effect of integration on a group of students over time, as so-called "longitudinal" studies are designed to do.

These shortcomings have provoked an academic debate which continues to the present day. But despite its imperfections, the Coleman Report is the most impressive research ever conducted in the field of education. And the report does provide substantial evidence, which withstands reanalysis, that socioeconomic integration may well be the most hopeful strategy for improving the educational opportunities of educationally disadvantaged children. It is not that minority-group children can only learn alongside nonminority children; it is that disadvantaged children tend to benefit from a stable, advantaged classroom environment.

Well-controlled "longitudinal" studies of the impact of the school integration on children's academic achievement over time are disappointingly few and far between.

However, we do find a broad range of evidence, from the results of achievement testing programs to the testimony of teachers and school administrators serving throughout the Nation, that school integration can be an academic as well as a social success, and that compensatory education programs are most likely to produce significant and lasting gains when special educational efforts are combined with socioeconomic integration.

For example, Project Concern is a voluntary program which presently transports 1,500 innercity Hartford, Conn., schoolchildren to classes in 14 suburban communities.

A survey conducted in the program's third year (1968–69) discloses that children who had spent their careers in Project Concern (first, second and third graders) were substantially outperforming their innercity peers.

This evidence is supported by a careful longitudinal study of 25 Project Concern children attending schools in Cheshire, Conn., in the 1968–69 and 1969–70 school year. The students attended grades 1–4 in 1968–69, their first year in the program. The study indicates that, be-

*Inequality: Reassessment of the Effect of Family and Schooling in America*, Christopher Jencks, et al., Basic Books, New York, 1972.

tween November 1968 and November 1969, students experienced an average 4-month gain in reading and verbal skills. By November of 1969 these students' average and median achievement in reading, language and arithmetic was at or above the national average.

Increased academic achievement is not the only benefit of Project Concern. Testimony from innercity and suburban students demonstrates growth in ability to deal comfortably with interracial social contact. And children have not been the only beneficiaries. A number of innercity parents of participating children have moved to the suburban communities where their children attend school. Participation by innercity parents in school activities is high; during the 2-year experimental period, 90 percent of the innercity parents attended all major activities.

The Berkeley, Calif., Unified School District serves approximately 15,000 students in kindergarten through 12th grade. The student body is 45 percent black, 3 percent Chicano, 9 percent Asian and other minorities, and 43 percent white.

Berkeley is the largest school district in the Nation to integrate all of its schools voluntarily, and the most widely acclaimed "success story"—not because every problem has been solved, but because the Berkeley community, diverse as it is, is working together toward better education for all its children. This unity of commitment was not obtained easily. There were 12 years of open—and often angry—public debate from the first public demand for school integration in 1957 to the implementation of the final plan in the Fall of 1969.

Before the plan was implemented, school officials engaged in an intensive effort to involve all elements of the Berkeley community in planning for desegregation. Two major committees composed of school officials, parents, and other community members were established—one to review logistics and the other to review instructional programs. In addition, small meetings were held in homes throughout Berkeley to inform parents and other interested persons about the plan and to gather their reactions. This process of both informing the community at large about the integration plan and involving interested persons in its design is viewed by parents and school officials as central to the development of public support for the plan implemented in the Fall of 1969.

The process of integration has enabled the Berkeley school system to confront the need to improve its academic program for all students. And it has helped the Berkeley community to confront its racial division.

Mrs. Louise Stoll, a white parent, testified:

> It is my belief that the people for whom I can speak, young white- and black-liberal families living in Berkeley, I think we have been given a rare privilege in Berkeley to find out what real problems are now in racial relations, because we have gotten over the mechanical aspect of moving children around the community. It is an exciting thing to be a part of working out these problems. They have to be worked out or there is no future for us, and we are all committed to that.

Berkeley completed only its third year of integration in June of 1972. At this early time, integration does appear to have increased the academic achievement of disadvantaged minority-group children in the early grades; on completing second grade, the first "school generation" to attend only integrated schools (children who began integrated kindergarten in 1968) is as much as 3 months ahead of preintegration performance levels in reading.

The Coleman Report's findings and the preliminary results of the Berkeley and Hartford programs receive further confirmation from a 2-year longitudinal study of kindergarten and first-grade students in New Haven, Conn., conducted by Dr. Willa A. Abelson of Yale University, under the direction of Dr. Edward Zigler—until recently Director of the HEW Office of Child Development. Dr. Abelson's report concludes:

> . . . the longitudinal data which we have tracing academic growth during the first 2 years of school supports the findings of Coleman and others indicating that children living in poverty areas of the city achieve more optimally in classes with mixed enrollments. These results suggest that the difference in attainments appears gradually, and is quite evident in the reading area by the end of first grade.

None of these longitudinal studies is conclusive. Integration plans have not been in operation long enough for conclusive results. But the results do support the Coleman findings.

We are also aware of several studies showing little academic benefit from integration. Some of these studies appear to have concentrated on the impact of integration on academic achievement at the high school level, while immediate achievement gains appear most likely when integration begins in the elementary years. Other studies appear not to distinguish between purely racial desegregation and integration which is economic as well as racial. In most, no effort is made to determine whether schools provide friendly and hospitable environments based on mutual respect, or to measure the impact of remedial programs.

The committee is not in a position to reconcile each conflicting research study. But we do find that the evidence, taken as a whole, strongly supports the value of integrated education, sensitively conducted, in improving academic achievement of disadvantaged children, and in increasing mutual understanding among students from all backgrounds.

This conclusion is supported by the experience of growing numbers of educators from throughout the Nation.

Hoke County is a small rural community of 18,000 in eastern North Carolina. Its schools serve 4,850 children: 50 percent black, 35 percent white, and 15 percent Lumbee Indian. Hoke County had a triple school system—separate schools and classes for each group—and a triple transportation system.

In 1968 and 1969, the county eliminated its triple system and established a unitary system under which each school reflected the countywide population distribution.

Donald Abernethy, Hoke County's school superintendent, described the results:

> You would see them standing around in clusters on the campus. This was at first. Now you see very little of this. The children have learned to get along with each other. They respect one another. They vote for each other in elections . . .

The Harrisburg, Pa., school system, serving over 12,000 students, nearly 58 percent of whom are from minority groups, was completely desegregated in the Fall of 1971 under the requirement of State law. Superintendent David H. Porter testified:

> You had to witness firsthand the fact that 2 years ago students and teachers were merely accepting a certain methodical dullness about education. Students went to school not really to learn and teachers not really to teach. It was merely a place you were supposed to be for 5 days a week . . .
>
> We probably would not have admitted to any failure because we probably would not have recognized it.
>
> It's strange the way a school system can die before your very eyes as you mistake the death rattle for the sound of children learning. The cycle had to be broken . . .
>
> The mandate from the State Human Relations Commission to eliminate de facto segregation, though castigated by many, may well have been precisely the right thing at the right time. Not only did it wake us up to our responsibilities in race relations but it made us aware of the educational and administrative flaws that were permeating our entire system.
>
> The change has been dramatic. Walk into an early childhood center or an elementary school and look at the faces, hear the sounds, watch the kids at work and play. You can't show it on paper yet, but down inside you know it's working.

Dr. E. Ray Berry, superintendent of the desegregated Riverside, Calif., system testified:

> I see desegregation as an important element. I think it is quite possible to adequately educate minority children in a segregated situation academically; there are fine ways to turn them on, take the lid off, create the attitude about education; but I really believe it is far easier in an integrated situation, and ultimately I think it is the only answer in terms of if we really believe in an integrated society. I don't see any other way to do it.

He presented the results of a survey of parents:

> Over 80 percent of the parents believed that the quality of education was as good or better in integrated schools than before integration.
>
> Approximately 90 percent of the parents said that their children liked school and seldom or never wished to go to another school.
>
> After 3 years of integration, over 90 percent of the parents were opposed to the idea of separate schools. The responses were not significantly different when the three ethnic groups were compared with each other.

Dr. Elbert Brooks, superintendent in Nashville, Tenn., where there is organized opposition to court-ordered desegregation testified:

> I cannot accept the argument which many give that we are ruining our school system by integration. I think that there are many factors in favor from an educational standpoint and from a social standpoint of integrating schools.

And a recent study conducted by the U.S. Commission on Civil Rights gives every cause for optimism. The Commission staff conducted intensive on-site visits to five school districts recently desegregated in order to comply with constitutional requirements for elimination of discrimination—Tampa, Fla.; Pasadena, Calif.; Pontiac, Mich.; Winston-Salem and Charlotte, N.C. As the former Commission Chairman, Dr. Theodore Hesburgh, testified before the House Judiciary Committee:

> What the staff members found stands in stark contrast to the newspaper headlines and the television newscasts. Despite some opposition to desegregation, they did not find parents blocking the school entrances, teachers resigning in droves, or pupils engaged in continuous disorders. On the contrary, the staff found schools being conducted in an atmosphere of relative peace, harmony and efficiency, in an atmosphere consistent with the Nation's ideals.

And a recent survey conducted by the Resource Management Corporation for the Office of Education confirms these expectations. The study, of 879 schools in desegregating districts which received assistance under the Emergency School Assistance Program for the 1970–71 school year, found:

- Forty-one percent of students attending desegregated schools for the first time reported changes for the better on "going to school with students of another race," while only 5 percent reported changes for the worse.
- Eighty percent of students interviewed agreed that "students are cooperating more and more as the year goes on."
- While 33 percent of black students and 23 percent of white students said they would rather go to another school if they could, only 6 percent reported they did "not like it here" and 80 percent reported learning more in school than the previous year.
- A substantial majority of teachers and principals reported improvement in interracial relationships among students, and only 2 percent reported worsening relationships.

The report concludes:

> There is strong evidence that the racial climate improved during the 1970–71 school year in many respects and rarely worsened.

Clearly, there are many educationally disadvantaged children in our great urban ghettos who cannot be given the opportunity to attend economically and racially integrated schools, despite our best efforts.

We must increase our efforts to provide effective compensatory education services for all educationally disadvantaged students. However, the evidence appears to be that a dollar spent on compensatory education is far more likely to produce results in a quality integrated setting. A case in point is provided by the California study, conducted by Dr. Herbert Kiesling for the Rand Corporation and cited as evidence for the success of compensatory efforts in the Presidential message of March 17, 1972, submitting the Student Transportation Moratorium Act and Equal Educational Opportunities Act to Congress. While the study did show dramatic improvement from specialized reading programs in projects costing in excess of $250 per pupil, the successful schools did not have majority-disadvantaged student bodies.

We find that if racial-socioeconomic integration is combined with major efforts to strengthen curricula, improve teaching methods, substantially reduce class size and encourage the meaningful involvement of parents and community members, school integration can be the basis for impressive improvement in the educational achievement of minority-group and low-income students, and can immeasurably enrich the capacity of all students for life in a complex and multiracial society.

We are joined in our conclusions by the American Federation of Teachers, the Council of Chief State School Officers, the National Education Association, the 1972 Report of the President's Commission on School Finance, the White House Conference on Children, and by the National Advisory Committee on the Education of Disadvantaged Children, which found in its latest report that: "Desegregation is the best form of compensatory education." Our conclusion is also bolstered by a memorandum submitted by HEW Secretary Elliot Richardson in support of the proposed "Equal Educational Opportunities Act." The memorandum states:

> We know that children learn less effectively when there is a great degree of economic or racial isolation.

We find that integrated schools can provide better educational opportunities for all children. But desegregating a school—simply "mixing bodies"—does not insure the benefits of integrated education. "Desegregated" schools in which minority-group students are treated as "second-class citizens," or in which a few students from relatively advantaged backgrounds are overwhelmed by a majority of students from the poorest and most deprived backgrounds, can become a nightmare.

Dr. Thomas Pettigrew, a social psychologist specializing in the subject of school desegregation, succinctly stated the distinction between a "desegregated" and an "integrated" school when he testified:

> . . . an *integrated* school refers to an interracial facility which boasts a climate of interracial acceptance.

Our 2½ years of study have convinced us that there are six basic elements in successful school integration, whether integration takes place under court order or voluntarily, whether districtwide or in a single school—and that these elements must be supported by human and financial resources.

*Community Participation*—The first and essential element is community participation. School officials must make every effort to involve a broad cross section of the community in planning for integration—not just those who agree that integration is desirable, but those who are "neutral" and those who disagree as well.

Involving the total community in planning for integration is not an easy task for school officials, and it may appear to be an inefficient approach to decisionmaking. But the effort is worthwhile. By assuring that all segments of the community are fully involved in the development of the plan, resistance can be minimized and public support, which is essential to the success of any integration program, can be significantly increased. And the plan itself may be made more responsive to the community's needs.

*Socioeconomic Diversity*—It seems clear from the available research that increased academic performance for disadvantaged children cannot be expected to flow from racial or ethnic desegregation alone. The key element in increasing academic performance of low-income children, whether or not they are from minority groups, appears to be socioeconomic integration. In addition, parents of more advantaged children are justifiably concerned over possible assignment of their children to schools with majority-disadvantaged student bodies.

We believe that, wherever possible, students should be assigned, for purposes of desegregation, to stable schools containing a majority of educationally advantaged children, in order to achieve the most hopeful kind of integration.

It is one of the great tragedies of the last 8 years that the importance of assuring that school integration takes place along economic, as well as racial and ethnic lines, has received little attention from local school officials implementing integration plans and the Office of Education in rendering technical assistance. We are not suggesting "one-way" integration. We are suggesting that newly integrated schools should not ordinarily contain a majority of disadvantaged students. Where both racial and socioeconomic integration are achieved, integrated schools have the best chance to succeed, educationally and socially, for all their students.

*Importance of Early Integration*—Available research indicates that immediate benefits in terms of academic achievement are far more likely when integration takes place during the early years; the earlier integration takes place, the greater the gain that can be expected. And the potential for racial strain in high school is greatest when children have been segregated in earlier years.

We note that the "Equal Educational Opportunities Act" proposed by the Administration last July, and now before committees of the House and Senate, would effectively eliminate elementary schools from many desegregation plans by prohibiting the requirement of transportation below the elementary school level. This provision appears to run contrary to much that is known about constructive approaches to school integration.

*Integrated Classrooms*—The benefits of integrated education will be lost if classroom segregation takes place within supposedly integrated schools. No absolute rule is possible. Some courses, even in elementary grades, may require part-time grouping for effective instruction. But so-called "tracking," or grouping children on the basis of achievement test scores, must be held to a minimum; and individualized instruction should be used wherever possible to permit the education of children from various achievement levels within a single classroom.

*The Language Minorities*—Students of Mexican American, Indian, Puerto Rican, Portuguese and Oriental backgrounds and other children from families with strong commitment to ethnic heritage and language, require unique attention during the desegregation process.

But integrated education can be of special importance to language-minority children. As HEW Secretary Elliot Richardson told the committee:

> . . . the maintenance of ethnic isolation creates for the Spanish-speaking or Indian language-speaking child the additional disadvantage of depriving him of the most important resource of English language skill development—regular interaction and communication with English-speaking children.

While school integration is as socially and educationally advantageous for language-minority children as it is for other children, great care must be taken to assure that integration does not deprive these children of access to bilingual and bicultural programs designed to make them fluent in both English and the language spoken at home, and fully aware of their own cultural heritage. And every effort should be made to use these children as resources for the development of language skills and cultural knowledge in nonlanguage minority children.

*Mutual Understanding and Respect*—The most important aspect of a successfully integrated school is a warm and supportive environment for children from all racial and economic backgrounds, based upon mutual respect and acceptance among students and faculty.

These human qualities cannot be produced by a formula. But their development can be strongly assisted. In-service faculty training designed to encourage sensitivity to the needs of children from varying backgrounds should be provided on a continuing basis. Where possible, student-teacher ratios should be reduced, by employing additional professional staff, and by use of paraprofessional and volunteer aides. And curriculum and course content should be reviewed and revised to assure accurate treatment of racial and national origin minorities, and that materials and course content are relevant and not offensive to all children who study them.

### 2. LEGITIMATE CONCERNS

The intense debate over the issues of "busing" and "racial balance" has tragically blinded many to the legitimate concerns of parents from all racial and economic backgrounds.

Often parents are understandably concerned that desegregation may result in transfer of their children from schools with middle-class student bodies and highly motivated teachers to schools with educationally disadvantaged student bodies, where teacher motivation and academic opportunities may be decidedly inferior. At the same time, the evidence strongly indicates that integration is most likely to produce achievement gains for educationally disadvantaged students when schools contain a majority of more advantaged students.

Integrated schools with stable, majority-advantaged student bodies promise the greatest benefit to disadvantaged children; and they respond to the most pressing concerns of many parents of more advantaged children. Integration plans should reflect this principle to the fullest possible extent; and yet, the vital importance of socioeconomic considerations to successful school integration has largely escaped attention.

Minority-group teachers and community leaders often fear that desegregation may lead to further discrimination even more damaging than that involved in segregation itself. In too many instances these fears have been borne out. An on-site survey of 295 districts conducted by six civil rights groups in the Fall of 1970 with the help of roughly 100 volunteer lawyers found widespread cases of discriminatory policies and practices. HEW reports demotion or dismissal of over 4,000 black teachers and administrators in only five States during the 1971–72 school year. And yet, prompt and effective law enforcement can deter much of this "second generation" discrimination and avoid the need for a decade of private litigation and local struggle, which will take its toll on the educations of countless children. Also largely overlooked by public discussion has been the need for early integration.

Finally, the public debate has too often ignored the evidence that integrated education, sensitively conducted, is valuable for all children concerned. And yet, the great majority of educators and agencies concerned with educational policymaking agree that quality integrated education—in schools which are economically, as well as racially integrated, where resources are available for compensatory education and for special services, such as individualized instruction, to meet the educational needs of all students and, most important, where there is a warm attitude of human acceptance on the part of parents and school personnel—is among the most hopeful strategies for the education of disadvantaged children, and that its benefits extend to children of the more affluent as well.

Perhaps President Nixon said it most clearly:

> We all know that desegregation is vital to quality education—not only from the standpoint of raising the achievement levels of the disadvantaged, but also from the standpoint of helping all children achieve a broad-based human understanding that is increasingly essential in today's world.

### 3. METROPOLITAN APPROACHES

Residential segregation is a fact of American life. And as a result of residential patterns existing with remarkable similarity throughout the United States, segregated schools are also a fact of life in this country. Over 80 percent of all black metropolitan residents live in central cities, while more than 60 percent of white metropolitan residents live in suburbs.

Of minority-group students, 62.4 percent outside the South attend centercity school districts in which a majority of students are from minority groups.*

And, many low-income white families—like minority-group families—are condemned to certain sections of a metropolitan area, where their children often attend economically segregated schools.

As Dr. Thomas Pettigrew testified before the Senate Education Subcommittee:

> Even if we did not have school segregation within districts, we would still face a national problem of segregation across districts.

Low-income Americans—both minority group and nonminority group—who find themselves restricted to the innercity, have seen jobs disappear. Nationally over the last two decades, 80 percent of the

*Department of HEW, Office for Civil Rights.

new jobs created in large metropolitan areas have been located in the suburbs.

But the heaviest toll of this closed society falls on children. Underfunded and inadequate schools attended by low-income children are too often educational graveyards. Many of their students are damaged by poor housing, malnutrition, inadequate intellectual stimulation in preschool years, by lack of preventive and diagnostic medical care. Their lives must be lived in an environment of social failure. And schools do little to overcome the handicaps with which these students enter.

Public schools alone may be unable to reverse the effect of educational deprivation in preschool years and the ongoing effects of confinement to a culture of poverty. Clearly child development services must be made available in preschool years to enable low-income families to place their children on a more competitive footing with the children of the more affluent. Clearly more effective forms of compensatory education must be found to help ghetto schools do a better job of preparing their students for successful lives. Programs of integration within centercity school systems and voluntary cooperation between urban and suburban school districts can make the educational benefits of integrated education immediately available to many ghetto children.

But none of these approaches is a panacea. The roots of the social and economic tensions which threaten to divide the Nation—and of much educational deprivation—lie in the extreme racial and economic segregation of our urban areas. Only by making real choice available—choice for low-income families to live near suburban employment and integrated suburban schools, choice for middle-income families to live near centercity jobs and send their children to integrated schools as good as those in the suburbs—can we defeat the destructive economic and educational impact of the ghetto.

The rigid economic and racial stratification of our urban areas did not take place by chance. Too often it has been encouraged by governmental action on the State, local and Federal levels.

In his testimony before the committee, HUD Secretary Romney explained that the cause lies in "our country's tormented history of race relations."

> Throughout most of that history the dominant majority supported or condoned social and institutional separation of the races. This attitude became fixed in public law and public policy at every level of government and every branch of government, and thus it was adopted as a matter of course by the Federal Government when it entered the housing field in the 1930s. It continued after World War II.

There can be no sweeping generalizations about the legal impact of the wide variety of governmental policies inhibiting the elimination of residential segregation. Individual actions by local authorities have been found violative of 14th Amendment protections against racial and ethnic discrimination.

On the other hand, the Supreme Court recently implied that at least some limitations may be constitutionally imposed to exclude families on the basis of low income, where racial motivation cannot be proved, which would be prohibited if the motivation were shown to be racial rather than economic. *James* v. *Valtierra*, 402 U.S. 137 (1971).

The law in this area is still in a state of flux; and it may be several years before a clear-cut legal pattern emerges.

The extent to which Federal courts may be prepared to require metropolitan cooperation for school desegregation, based on evidence of discriminatory actions by State and local authorities to encourage both residential and school segregation within metropolitan areas, is also unclear. There are two cases which currently raise this issue: *Bradley* v. *Richmond*, involving school districts in the Richmond, Va., metropolitan area; and, *Bradley* v. *Milliken*, involving the Detroit, Mich., metropolitan area. Neither of these cases has yet been finally decided.

The future of these housing and school desegregation decisions and the legal theories on which they rest cannot be predicted with confidence. What can be predicted is that courts are not the branch of government best equipped to deal with the extremely complex issues involved in breaking down racial and economic barriers within metropolitan areas, in ways that do justice to the legitimate concerns of all involved. A court cannot offer subsidies to compensate suburban communities for increased costs—including educational costs—of serving low-income families, or provide assistance to replace revenues lost through location of tax-free public housing units. A court is ill equipped to require that low-income housing be "scatter-site," rather than in huge apartment projects, or to implement the metropolitan planning needed to prevent some suburban communities from being swamped by low-income housing while others are untouched. But, if public officials at the local, Federal and State levels refuse to act, the courts will be left to their own, and very limited, devices.

### 4. ENCOURAGING INTEGRATION OF METROPOLITAN SCHOOLS

In many metropolitan areas, where centercity school districts contain concentrations of minority group and educationally disadvantaged children, the most promising approach to successful school integration would appear to be through cooperative, voluntary arrangements between city and suburban school systems.

Successful interdistrict integration programs involving attendance of centercity children in suburban schools have been implemented through cooperation of 30 school systems in the Boston, Mass., area (METCO), 5 school systems in Rochester, N.Y., and 14 Connecticut school districts (Project Concern)—including all the major cities in the State. However, these programs are limited in scope—involving fewer than 4,000 minority-group children—due in large part to an absence of adequate financing.

Other interdistrict approaches have been based on the concept of the "magnet school"—a ghetto school designed to attract advantaged students through an innovative educational program. Although a number of efforts to establish "magnet schools" have failed, the Trotter School in Boston and the World of Inquiry School in Rochester both have waiting lists of children from throughout their metropolitan areas.

With recent adoption of the Emergency School Aid Act, adequate financing will be available, for the first time, to support existing programs—including cost of services to improve educational quality for all children within integrated classrooms—and to support voluntary adoption of similar programs by other communities. The committee hopes that the availability of Federal financial assistance will encourage more voluntary cooperative efforts.

In addition, we believe that appropriate committees of the Senate and the House should consider special incentives and priority in the allocation of Federal assistance for education to support school districts in metropolitan areas which voluntarily achieve broad-based involvement in planning and implementation of cooperative school integration efforts.

### 5. PROVIDING CHOICE IN HOUSING

There can be no doubt that, in most areas of the country, there is substantial local resistance to low- and moderate-income housing and to the elimination of residential segregation.

And there are often sound and legitimate reasons for suburban opposition to certain forms of low- and moderate-income housing—concerns which can be met.

Some communities which have responsibly opened their doors to federally subsidized housing have found that—precisely because there are so few communities willing to do so—they are soon overburdened.

The construction of federally subsidized public housing takes land off the tax rolls, imposing a double burden on residential communities. Not only are children added to their school populations with special educational needs, but the tax base which must support those needs is depleted at the same time. Also low- and moderate-income housing may create increased demands for public health, transportation, welfare, law enforcement and other municipal services in addition to education.

HUD has taken an important step in the right direction through its new emphasis on scatter-site housing and small cluster developments in its regulations on "Projects Selection Criteria," which became effective on February 7, 1972.

Under the new regulation, Federal support will be denied to proposals for subsidized housing which threaten to "tip" already integrated residential areas. In addition, subsidized housing located in existing areas of minority concentration will be supported only under a State or local development plan which provides comparable opportunities to minority families in integrated areas, or where housing needs cannot otherwise be met.

However, the new regulations cannot be completely effective while their scope is limited to concern for the impact of Federal housing programs on segregation by race and national origin. The regulations should be broadened to reach the real problem, which is to provide wider choice in housing for all low-income families, while guaranteeing communities which accept federally assisted housing that they will not be overburdened.

And the Federal Government must seek to eliminate the financial burden on communities caused by low and moderate income housing.

Chapter 2 Section 6(d) (1) of the Housing and Urban Development Act of 1972, passed by the Senate on March 2, 1972, would eventually require all public housing projects to pay full real estate taxes. This provision would meet part of the local objections to public housing, by ending depletion of available local tax revenues; and the committee urges its adoption by the Congress.

But we must also deal with the increased burdens placed on municipal services by both low- and moderate-income housing.

Education is, by far, the local service most directly affected by the addition of low- and moderate-income housing. And the Congress has already acted to provide such a program of educational subsidies. The Elementary and Secondary Education Amendments of 1969, signed into law in April 1970, added a new "Clause (c)" to the existing program of School Assistance in Federally Affected Areas (the so-called "Impact Aid" Program) authorizing a Federal payment to compensate local school districts for serving students from tax-free federally assisted public housing—in much the same way that school districts are compensated for serving children who live on military bases, Indian reservations, and other tax-exempt federally owned property. Unfortunately, this provision has not been funded. Full funding of the "Clause (c)" program is an absolutely essential first step toward a rational housing policy; past failures to make funds available are inexcusable. We must begin by fully funding this program, and then expand the concept to other types of federally subsidized housing, and other municipal services in addition to education.

President Nixon's Task Force on Urban Renewal approved this type of incentive to local communities, urging:

> . . . that additional legislation be requested to provide special Federal aid to help suburban communities meet the increased costs of education, public health, transportation, and other municipal services that result directly from expanding the supply of low- and moderate-income housing in the community.

Far more attention must be paid to the design of low- and moderate-income housing, to assure that it is consistent and compatible with surrounding residential areas and to avoid large low-income housing units which become "mini-ghettos".

As Anthony Downs observed, Federal policy should encourage the "location of many new low and moderate income housing units in suburban areas both in relatively small clusters and in individual scatteration in middle-income neighborhoods."

HUD's recently adopted "Project Selection Criteria" require all proposals for subsidized housing to meet the objective of providing "an attractive and well-planned physical environment." If properly implemented these regulations could ensure that there will be no more large, institutionalized public housing projects which simply export a slice of urban poverty to the suburbs.

Present law permits Federal support for scatter-site housing and small multifamily units. But there is now only limited authority for a third approach: Making individual housing allowances to enable recipients to obtain existing rental housing.

The Housing and Urban Development Act of 1970 authorized the Secretary of HUD to conduct research programs to demonstrate the feasibility of providing low-income families with housing allowances to assist them in obtaining existing standard rental housing of their choice.

This program should be continued—with the aim of adopting new legislation extending rent subsidies and public housing rent allowances to individual households.

The immediate costs for scatter-site housing, small multifamily units and housing allowances may be higher than for the construction of conventional public housing units. But the social benefits, in terms of school integration, reduced crime, increased access to jobs and more hopeful environment can more than compensate for these increased costs.

The legitimate concerns of suburban and other middle-income communities—to avoid a deluge of low- and moderate-income housing, to avoid severe financial hardship, to preserve the character and appearance of their communities—must be met. But at the same time, more affluent communities should be encouraged to accept some Federally assisted housing, to permit a degree of choice, and access to suburban jobs, to families now confined to the city, and to halt the increasing metropolitan segregation by race and income which threatens to divide the Nation into hostile camps.

The Civil Rights Commission points out that HUD can, and should, take a more active role in encouraging rational site selection for federally assisted housing. We join the commission in suggesting that HUD:

> . . . affirmatively seek out applications from builders and sponsors for housing located so as to contribute to the healthy growth of the entire metropolitan area [and] provide assistance to them to assure that they are able to build on desirable sites.

Where zoning laws or other local ordinances discriminate against racial or national origin minorities, the committee believes that HUD is legally obligated to take enforcement action under Title VI of the Civil Rights Act of 1964 and the Fair Housing Act of 1968.

A recent statement on equal housing opportunity by the Leadership Conference on Civil Rights and nine other national public interest organizations aptly describes the need for adequate law enforcement in this field:

> The continuation of . . . Federal assistance unaccompanied by civil rights standards subverts our major national housing goal—to provide a decent home in a suitable living environment for all American citizens.

And the Federal Government is directly responsible for its own facilities location policies.

The U.S. Government employs over 6 million men and women; and increasingly Federal facilities—like many businesses—are moving from the central cities. In the Washington, D.C., area alone, for example, many Government agencies—including the Geological Survey, the National Bureau of Standards, the U.S. Public Health Service, and the Atomic Energy Commission—have recently moved or plan to move to the suburbs. Although it has great potential leverage on local communities because of the economic benefits flowing from location of Federal facilities, the Federal Government in relocating its facilities has made little or no effort on their part to insure that its low- and moderate-income employees can find accessible housing nearby. In fact, Federal moves into the suburbs often result in the loss of jobs to low- and moderate-income employees who can no longer reach their place of employment.

On June 14, 1971, the Department of Housing and Urban Development and the General Services Administration joined in a memorandum of understanding to help insure adequate housing near new Federal installations. Under this agreement HUD will advise GSA as to the availability of low- and moderate-income housing near a projected Government facility. If GSA must locate in an area where no such housing is available, HUD and GSA will join in a plan to provide such housing within 6 months after the facility is to be occupied. This new policy is an important step forward.

However, as Senator Ribicoff noted:

> It is still possible under the agreement to locate a facility well away from any housing. If a community has zoned out the possibility of low- and moderate-income housing, there is little HUD and GSA can do to provide it.

It is clear that the Federal Government has complete discretion in deciding where to locate its facilities. We believe that assurance of decent housing for low- and moderate-income employees should be obtained before final decision to locate a facility is reached.

#### 6. TOWARD A MORE COMPREHENSIVE APPROACH

As suggested earlier, HUD regulations under existing authority can go far toward meeting the concerns of many communities that lowering barriers to low- and moderate-income housing may result in an avalanche. And HUD can do more under existing authority to encourage and support sensible site selection. But unless suburban communities agree to remove barriers to subsidized housing, the major burden will continue to fall on central cities, and racial and economic division will continue to grow.

A most promising approach has been adopted by the Miami Valley Regional Planning Association. The association, which represents the communities of the Dayton, Ohio, metropolitan area is implementing a unique plan designed to disperse the anticipated need for low- and moderate-income housing throughout the five-county Dayton metropolitan area.

The basic premise of this plan, adopted unanimously by the member governments of the Planning Association in September 1970, is that every community in a metropolitan area will accept its "fair share" of the low- and moderate-income housing, required to meet the needs of the area's residents.

Although the "fair share" is a goal, it is also a *ceiling*—no community will receive low- or moderate-income housing in excess of its "fair share." As Mr. Dale Bertsch of the association testified:

> One of the major complaints which is heard by elected officials across our region, when they begin to advocate low and moderate income housing within their communities, is that certain communities within the suburbs are going to become the pressure relief valve for the central city. Therefore,

> it is anticipated, and we have used—the commission has used—the goal also as a shutoff valve for low and moderate income housing construction in the suburbs.

We do not pretend to have a detailed or final answer to the increasing educational, social and economic segregation of our metropolitan areas. But we do find that intense metropolitan segregation increasingly threatens the American commitment to equal opportunity based on individual merit. We believe that relevant committees of the House and Senate should consider legislation to support voluntary adoption of the "fair share" approach to allocation of federally subsidized housing in other metropolitan areas, and we believe that metropolitan plans should be encouraged to address the need to provide increased housing opportunities for middle-income families within central cities, as well as the need to provide housing opportunities for low-income families outside the central city.

## D. Recommendations

### 1. FEDERAL LEADERSHIP

The committee's fundamental and most basic recommendation is that the Congress and the Executive Branch unite in a national policy which supports the Constitution, recognizes the potential benefits of quality integrated education, and is committed to helping local communities assure that desegregation—whether voluntary or under legal requirement—is responsive to the legitimate concerns of parents and students from all backgrounds.

The focus of national debate on the misleading issues of "massive busing" and "racial balance" has contributed to deteriorating public confidence in the justice of constitutional requirements, and in the essential fairness of our judicial system. Our national commitment to equality of educational opportunity is in jeopardy.

At the same time, public discussion has largely ignored both the benefits of integrated education, and the legitimate concerns of parents—concern of minority-group parents that their children not be subjected to unfair and discriminatory treatment within desegregated schools, concerns of all parents that desegregation improve and not impair their children's educational opportunities.

The immediate losers have been the Nation's children. And the greatest losers are the 11 million children already attending 1,500 desegregating school districts. Negative leadership discourages the local support necessary for successful school integration, and compounds the already difficult jobs of teachers and local school officials.

We must unite in an effort to make school desegregation work, or fail a fundamental test of our national character. As President Nixon said in his March 1970 message on school desegregation:

> Few issues facing us as a Nation are of such transcendent importance: important because of the vital role that our public schools play in the Nation's life and in its future; because the welfare of our children is at stake; and because it presents us a test of our capacity to live together in one Nation, in brotherhood and understanding.

### 2. Rejection of Constitutional Amendments

We recommend rejection of any proposal to amend the U.S. Constitution which would limit the existing authority of Federal courts to remedy racially discriminatory school segregation.

### 3. Rejection of "Student Transportation Moratorium Act" and "Equal Educational Opportunities Act"

We recommend against adoption of the "Student Transportation Moratorium Act," and the "Equal Educational Opportunities Act" proposed by the administration last Spring.

The "Equal Educational Opportunities Act" attempts to place severe limits on the power of the courts to remedy officially imposed school segregation—by prohibiting requirement of any additional transportation at the elementary school level and by making transportation a remedy of "last resort" at the secondary level.

The proposed Student Transportation Moratorium Act would prohibit implementation of desegregation plans requiring *any* change in existing transportation patterns during a period designed for congressional action on the "Equal Educational Opportunities Act." The "Moratorium" would go so far as to prohibit adoption of plans transporting children shorter distances to achieve desegregation, and in many cases, would effectively require preservation of dual school systems intact during its life.

We find that guidelines for student transportation developed by the Supreme Court in *Swann* v. *Charlotte-Mecklenburg*, and applied to administrative proceedings under the Civil Rights Act by the Education Amendments of 1972, establish a sensible, enforceable and uniform standard for the use of transportation in eliminating the effects of racially discriminatory student assignment policies. Transportation will not be required over times and distances which risk children's health or impinge on their educations. If individual desegregation plans require unreasonable transportation, there are judicial remedies.

We find both of these legislative proposals to be of highly doubtful constitutionality. But beyond their probable unconstitutionality, the "Equal Educational Opportunities Act" and the "Student Transportation Moratorium Act" would severely restrict remedies for unconstitutional school segregation while compounding the legitimate concerns which lie behind much opposition to school desegregation.

Without transportation, much unlawfully established segregation must be allowed to persist. The desegregation which does take place will often disproportionately involve nonminority-group students from less affluent, blue-collar families whose homes are adjacent to minority-group residential areas. Student bodies of desegregated schools will more often be predominantly minority group and predominantly educationally disadvantaged—encouraging "white flight," jeopardizing the academic benefits of integration, provoking legitimate concern of parents of more advantaged students assigned to these schools, and rendering the tasks of teachers and school officials far more difficult. Desegregation of elementary schools, where educational benefits are greatest, will be highly restricted, while desegregation of junior and senior high schools can be expected to be far less successful if based upon extensive segregation in elementary schools.

### 4. ENCOURAGING VOLUNTARY INTEGRATION

The committee strongly recommends Federal incentives to encourage voluntary school integration. We agree with the National Advisory Committee on the Education of Disadvantaged Children that "desegregation is the best form of compensatory education." And properly conducted, it can better prepare all children for life in a multiracial society.

The recently adopted $1 billion-a-year Emergency School Aid Act provides the necessary support for voluntary integration; it is essential that the bill be fully funded.

### 5. A UNIFORM NATIONAL POLICY OF LAW ENFORCEMENT

In exercising their responsibilities under the Civil Rights Act of 1964, the Departments of Justice and HEW must enforce constitutional 14th Amendment and Civil Rights Act guarantees against discrimination in public education on a uniform, national basis. If additional funds are required, they should be requested.

We note that the recently adopted Education Amendments of 1972 authorize Federal district courts in their discretion to award the payment of reasonable attorneys' fees and costs to successful plaintiffs in suits to enforce the 14th Amendment and the Civil Rights Act in the area of public education. We strongly believe that continued private litigation is an essential component of a successful national strategy. And we recommend that Federal assistance be made available, so that payment of attorneys' fees does not deplete education budgets.

### 6. FULL FUNDING OF EMERGENCY SCHOOL AID ACT

On June 23, 1972, the President signed into law the Emergency School Aid Act, as part of the comprehensive Education Amendments of 1972. The Act, which replaces the temporary $75 million Emergency School Assistance Program established by special appropriation in the Fall of 1970, authorizes an annual expenditure of $1 billion to support a broad range of programs and projects related to the achievement of equal educational opportunities.

Because this bipartisan legislation implements many of this committee's basic recommendations, we are most disappointed that funding was not requested in time for the beginning of the present school year. We are also gravely concerned by reports that—although $230 million were appropriated by the Congress in October for the remainder of this school year—administrative delays may prevent even continued funding of programs which received assistance for the first semester under the earlier Emergency School Assistance Program.

We recommend:

- Continued funding of programs and projects, for both school districts and nonprofit organizations, which received assistance for the first semester of this year through immediate additional appropriations for the original ESAP program.

- Full funding of the new Emergency School Aid Act for the 1973–1974 school year. If the request is contained in the President's January budget message, school districts will have ample time to prepare for the implementation of programs next Fall. We note that the $1 billion authorized by the Act for the 1973–74 school year is identical with the President's original request for the current 1972–73 school year.

### 7. FUNDING FOR TRANSPORTATION

We urge the Department of HEW to respect the clear mandate of the Congress, which defeated proposals to prohibit expenditure of Federal funds for desegregation-related transportation, by making funds under the new ESAA available, upon request of local officials, to support reasonable transportation.

### 8. ACTION AGAINST DISCRIMINATORY TREATMENT OF TEACHERS AND ADMINISTRATORS

We recommend prompt and decisive action by the Departments of Justice and Health, Education, and Welfare against discriminatory treatment of minority group teachers in recently desegregated school systems.

### 9. ACTION AGAINST "SECOND-GENERATION" DISCRIMINATION

Similarly, prompt and effective action must be taken to remedy discrimination against minority group children within "desegregated" schools.

We recommend prompt publication of a memorandum, promised to the committee in June of 1970, establishing Federal policy under Title VI of the Civil Rights Act of 1964 with respect to "second-generation" discrimination. And we recommend that the Departments of HEW and Justice enter into cooperative arrangements which will assure compliance of school districts desegregating under court order as well as under Title VI plan—a policy which was promised to the committee in the Spring of 1970 and never implemented.

### 10. DENIAL OF TAX-EXEMPT STATUS TO "SEGREGATION ACADEMIES"

The courts have held that so-called "segregation academies"—schools established for the purpose of circumventing public school desegregation—are legally prohibited from receiving tax-favored status as charitable organizations: *Green* v. *Connally*, aff'd 404 U.S. 997 (1971). We urge that firm steps, including site visits, be taken to enforce this legal mandate.

### 11. ECONOMIC INTEGRATION

We recommend that desegregation plans avoid wherever possible the establishment of schools with majority-disadvantaged student bodies.

### 12. PARENT, STUDENT AND COMMUNITY INVOLVEMENT

We recommend that school offiicals make every effort to involve a broad cross section of the community in planning for integration, including students, teachers, parents, representatives of business and labor groups, and other interested community members.

By assuring that all segments of the community are fully involved in the development of plans, resistance can be minimized, the public support which is essential to the success of any desegregation program can be substantially increased, and desegregation plans themselves can be made more responsive to community needs.

### 13. INTEGRATED CLASSROOMS

The committee recommends that school districts avoid classroom segregation along racial, ethnic or socioeconomic lines within desegregated schools wherever possible. Federal enforcement officials should take prompt action against unconstitutional discriminatory practices within "desegregated" schools. And, in administering the Emergency School Aid Act, the Office of Education should encourage applications which support classroom integration.

### 14. MUTUAL UNDERSTANDING AND RESPECT

To encourage the development of supportive classroom environment, we recommend that implementation of plans for school integration be accompanied by:

- Integration of faculty and staff.
- In-service faculty training on a continuing basis, to encourage sensitivity to the needs of children from varying backgrounds.
- Reduction of student/adult ratios through employing additional professional and paraprofessional staff, and through use of volunteer aides, to permit more individual attention to each child.
- Review of course content and materials to assure accuracy, sensitivity, and relevance for all students.

The committee notes that Federal financial assistance to support these activities will be available under the recently adopted Emergency School Aid Act.

### 15. FAIR TREATMENT FOR LANGUAGE-MINORITY CHILDREN

Desegregation plans should include provisions for services to meet the needs of Mexican Americans, Puerto Rican, Oriental, Portuguese, Indian and other children with special language-related educational needs.

### 16. EARLY INTEGRATION

We recommend that local school officials, and the Office of Education in providing technical assistance and administering the Emergency School Aid Act, bear in mind the crucial importance of integration during the elementary grades.

### 17. MULTIDISTRICT SCHOOL INTEGRATION

We recommend Federal financial support for voluntary multidistrict cooperative integration efforts.

We also recommend that appropriate committees of the Congress consider special incentives and priority allocation under general education programs to encourage voluntary metropolitan planning for school integration.

### 18. THE EDUCATION PARK

We recomend Federal support for the construction of some model education parks, serving perhaps 12,000 to 20,000 students from kindergarten through high school, on a campus where space can be made available for location of junior college and postsecondary vocational facilities. To avoid the creation of an unwieldly and remote bureaucracy, we recommend that parks be divided into "mini-schools" of fewer than 600 students.

### 19. INTEGRATION OF NONPUBLIC SCHOOLS

We note that Federal assistance is authorized under the Emergency School Aid Act for the purpose of encouraging and supporting school integration efforts by nonpublic schools, and urge that the Department of HEW make use of this authority.

### 20. HOUSING OPPORTUNITIES

The committee recommends an active role by the Department of Housing and Urban Development in encouraging rational site selection for federally assisted housing—both to encourage development of low- and moderate-income housing opportunities outside areas of present concentration, and to assure that communities which accept low- and moderate-income housing are not overburdened

We recommend that the Departments of Justice and Housing and Urban Development exercise their responsibilities under Title VI of the Civil Rights Act of 1964 and the Fair Housing Act of 1968 to take action against laws, other ordinances and practices which discriminatorily restrict housing opportunities on the basis of race or national origin.

We recommend adoption, by Executive order, of Federal policy under which Federal agencies will obtain assurance of adequate housing opportunities for low- and moderate-income employees as a prerequisite to location or relocation of facilities.

In the absence of adoption of such a policy, the committee recommends adoption of legislation similar to S. 1283, the Government Facilities Location Act, to accomplish these purposes.

We recommend that relevant committees of the Senate and House consider legislation to establish incentives for voluntary adoption of metropolitan plans based on the "fair share" approach to allocation of federally subsidized housing; such plans should be encouraged to address the needs for increased middle-income housing opportunities within central cities, as well as to provide housing opportunities for low-income families outside the central city.

Action to increase the opportunities of low-income families must be accompanied by action to protect the legitimate interests of suburban and other middle-income communities.

We recommend vigorous application of the "Project Selection Criteria" which became effective February 1, 1972, to prevent funding of subsidized housing which threatens to "tip" already integrated residential areas. We recommend immediate expansion of the scope of these regulations beyond their present concern with preventing resegregation by race and national origin to a broader concern with preventing concentration of low- and moderate-income housing, regardless of the race or national origin of its occupants.

We recommend immediate funding of "Clause (c)" of the "Impact Aid" program under P.L. 81–874—which has gone without funds since its enactment in 1970—to compensate public schools for the extra costs of serving children from public housing, and for the concurrent loss of public housing property from the tax rolls.

We recommend enactment of legislation to provide similar support for welfare, law enforcement, health and other additional costs, as recommended by the President's Task Force on Urban Renewal.

We recommend payment of real estate taxes by federally subsidized public housing projects, as provided in Chapter 2 Section 6(d)(1) of the proposed Housing and Urban Development Act of 1972, which has passed the Senate and was pending in House Committee at the close of the 92d Congress.

And, we recommend exploration of federally guaranteed insurance to protect home values in communities accepting federally subsidized low- and moderate-income housing.

The committee recommends that HUD require adequate attention to the design of low- and moderate-income housing, to assure that housing is compatible with surrounding residential areas. To avoid large low-income housing units which become "mini-ghettos," we recommend location of federally subsidized housing in small clusters and on a scatter-site basis in middle-income neighborhoods, and we recommend continued experimentation with housing allowances, which enable recipients to obtain existing rental housing on the open market.

## E. The Education of Language Minorities

### 1. Findings

The American child whose first language is other than English suffers a double disadvantage. Like the black child and poor white child he is probably isolated in a rural slum or urban ghetto community where he was born and lives and goes to school. If he is poor, he probably attends a school with other poor children of the same racial or ethnic background. And often it is an older school with less qualified teachers and fewer resources.

But when he arrives at school he faces a special disadvantage, for his language and culture are different and they are often neither valued nor understood by those who teach him and run his school. Often his language is considered alien, his culture unimportant, and his manner unusual. He is probably told he must learn in English, a language which may be alien to him or at least is seldom spoken at home. He enters a new world where the values his parents taught him are now often rejected, tacitly if not explicitly. He may be asked to change into something different. He is sometimes even forbidden to speak his native language in school.

Unable to conform to his new world, the language-minority child is often labeled and stamped as inferior. He is tested. But the test he takes was probably designed for middle-class English-speaking "Anglo" children. If he fails or does poorly, he is then often tracked into a class with slow learners. He may then see himself as inferior. He soon learns that his heritage is not regarded by others as important, for there is little in his curriculum or his textbooks about his heroes or the history of his people. His world at home is simply excluded from this world at school.

This is the plight of hundreds of thousands of language-minority children—children whose heritage in Spanish, Mexican, Puerto Rican, Portuguese, Chinese, Japanese, Filipino, Korean, American Indian or whose forebears may be from any of a large number of other foreign lands.

Unfortunately, all too often fluency in a foreign language is looked upon by public school systems as a handicap for the child who is deficient in his ability to communicate in English. While detailed surveys have not been undertaken for language-minority groups, the U.S. Census Bureau estimates that of the 9.2 million Spanish-surnamed Americans in the United States, only half usually speak English at home. In a survey conducted by the U.S. Civil Rights Commission in 1969 it was estimated that nearly half the Mexican-American first graders in Arizona, California, Colorado, New Mexico and Texas are deficient in English when they arrive at school.

Even greater proportions of American Indian children are deficient in English. In its report, "Indian Education: A National Tragedy—A National Challenge," the Special Subcommittee on Indian Education concluded that more than half our Indian youths between the ages of 6 and 18 use their native language at home and that two-thirds of Indian children entering BIA schools have little or no skill in English.

The language-minority child not only arrives at school with this handicap, he is immediately subjected to practices and policies and sometimes even legal prohibitions which attempt to keep him from communicating in his native language. In fact, until recently, many States had legal prohibitions forbidding teaching in public schools in any language other than English.

But even in the absence of official State laws prohibiting foreign languages in schools there are still school districts which prohibit or discourage the speaking of foreign languages.

These rules are enforced, often rigidly, through various forms of punishment: Detention after school hours, the payment of a few pennies in fines for each word of Spanish spoken, suspension from school, and even, sometimes, corporal punishment.

The rejection of the minority child's language is also accompanied by the exclusion of his culture from the school curriculum. Most schools offer neither Spanish-surnamed, Indian, Oriental or other foreign language children an opportunity to learn about their heritage or folklore. Their textbooks either ignore the history of their people or present a distorted picture based on false stereotypes.

Witnesses before this and other committees described history texts with degrading characterizations of Hispanic, Oriental and American Indian peoples. They also described school censorship practices which deprive language-minority children of the opportunity for exposure to the conditions of their people in America today.

These are among the unequal practices to which the language-minority child is subjected in school. But they are perhaps only the symptoms of a more fundamental cause of educational inequality for the language-minority child—exclusion from the process by which decisions are made about the education of minority-group and disadvantaged children. For the language minorities and for other disadvantaged groups most public school systems are a closed society. All too often educational decisions are made about disadvantaged children without consultation with or explanation to those who are affected and in some school districts school officials are openly hostile to language-minority groups.

It is clear from all the testimony we have heard—from the educators, students and other observers from both minority and non-minority groups that unless ways can be found to involve minority groups in their own education and in their own schools, for them public education will remain unequal and their lives will remain a series of lost opportunities.

### 2. RECOMMENDATIONS

*Community Participation in Education*—The effective participation of language-minority groups, including parents, students and other community representatives is the cornerstone of any effort to deal with the problems of language-minority children. We recommend that school systems take steps to directly involve language-minority parents, students and other community residents in both the development and implementation of bilingual education programs and teaching materials. More than that, language minorities must become involved in the educational process. Without their direct and active participation we do not believe it likely that their language and culture will become an accepted, successful part of education. To assure the full participation of language minorities in bilingual education programs we recommend that Title VII of the Elementary and Secondary Education Act be amended to require the same conditions for eligibility for funds as are now provided in the bilingual provisions of the Emergency School Aid Act of 1972. Thus, Title VII should be amended to require that before a school district is eligible to receive a grant it must establish a community committee which will fully participate in both the development and implementation of the program to be funded. Further, Title VII should be amended to assure that private, nonprofit organizations in cooperation with local school districts, as well as districts themselves, may receive grants to develop bilingual and bicultural education curricula designed to develop reading, writing and speaking skills in both English and the family language of language-minority children, and to develop understanding of the history and cultural backgrounds of language-minority groups on the part of both language-minority and English-speaking children.

To be eligible, the private nonprofit agency must establish a policy board which is representative of the community.

Under these provisions both the policy board of the private curriculum development agency and school district community committee must be representative of parents, school officials, teachers and other citizens. At least half the members must be parents and at least half members of language-minority groups.

We believe these provisions for private nonprofit organization curriculum development and for the establishment of community committees are among the most constructive and promising provisions that the Congress has adopted in Federal education legislation.

*Bilingual Education Programs*—Neither the levels of participation nor the resources available for Title VII are adequate to meet the needs of this Nation's language-minority students.

In terms of the needs of language-minority children, Title VII has been starved for funds. In the first year of the program's operation, fiscal year 1969, Congress appropriated only $7.5 million despite an authorization of $30 million. During the past year, 1972, $35 million was appropriated out of an authorized $100 million, enough to serve only 109,000 children and, of these, an estimated 30 percent were not language-minority children. For the present year, congressional efforts to increase Title VII funding to $60 million died with the veto of the Labor-HEW Appropriations Bill.

This compared with an HEW estimate that 5 million school-age children in the United States have at least some need for special language training.

Moreover, the funds that have been spent have not been distributed equitably. Illinois, which has 75,000 Spanish-speaking schoolchildren (3.6 percent of the country's total) received only $220,000 of Title VII funds during fiscal year 1971 (1 percent of the funds). This amounted to $2.90 for each Spanish-speaking student. New York, with 315,000 students, received $8,720,000 or $7.70 per Spanish-speaking student. The top 10 States, with nearly 700,000 Spanish-speaking students received between $10.17 and $41.55 per student.

We recommend that future funds for new bilingual education projects including those made available by the Emergency School Aid Act be allocated to help equalize the previous inequitable distribution of funds.

Together, Title VII of ESEA and the bilingual education programs of the Emergency School Aid Act are potentially the most promising programs designed to meet the needs of language-minority students. We recommend the full funding to the maximum authorized limit of both these programs. The Emergency School Aid Act bilingual education programs have not yet become operational. When they do, we recommend that Bilingual Education Act programs be administered in coordination with the new ESAA Program.

At the end of 2 years, when the Emergency School Aid Act is scheduled to expire, these programs should be merged under Title VII. During the 2-year period we believe it is essential that HEW undertake a comprehensive evaluation of bilingual education programs. The Office of Education has recently funded an evaluation study designed to determine which bilingual programs are most effective. We hope that as a result of this study the Office of Education will be able to provide a set of models which have proved successful and which can be replicated by school districts wishing to undertake bilingual education.

At the end of this 2-year period and with the help of a comprehensive evaluation, the Congress ought then be in a position to transform Title VII into a nationwide bilingual education program which can help financially hard-pressed school districts throughout the United States meet the needs of those children from families and communities where the dominant language is other than English.

*Bilingual Educational Personnel*—The effectiveness of any bilingual education effort depends largely on the availability of teachers, principals, counselors and other educational personnel who are capable of meeting the needs of language-minority children. Only if educators are sensitive to the needs of these children, understand and respect the language they speak and the culture and heritage of which they are proud will education be a successful experience for minority-group children whose first language is not English.

There is presently a totally inadequate supply of trained teachers and other school personnel who are either themselves members of language-minority groups or who are adequately trained to meet the need for bilingual education.

There are a number of reasons for this lack of adequate personnel for bilingual education.

*First*, the recruitment and training of bilingual teachers and administrative personnel has been largely neglected by our public school systems and by teacher education institutions.

*Second*, there has been neither an adequate commitment nor sufficient resources for the recruiting and training of bilingual teacher aides and paraprofessionals from minority groups.

*Third*, State legal requirements which are designed to set minimum standards for the employment of educational personnel often operate to discriminate against language-minority educators.

We recommend that teacher training institutions in this country, particularly those in regions of the Nation containing substantial numbers of language-minority citizens, include in their curricula programs designed to acquaint prospective teachers with the culture and heritage of language-minority children. We recommend that teachers be encouraged to concentrate in this vital field and that a major effort be undertaken by teacher training institutions to recruit members of language-minority groups.

We recommend that intensive and well-planned in-service training programs be developed for teachers and school administrators who are employed by school systems with large numbers of language-minority children. These programs should be designed to make teachers and administrators aware of the cultural heritage and history of language-minority children. Teachers should be encouraged to attend in-service Summer institutes such as those that were previously funded under the National Defense Education Act. These institutes can provide an effective and invaluable experience and improve teaching effectiveness for those teachers who have language-minority students in their classes.

Paraprofessionals are an invaluable aid to teachers, administrators and counselors in working with all children. But this is particularly true with language minorities.

We believe that every school system should endeavor to recruit community people as teacher aides to help meet the pressing needs for bilingual educational personnel.

Children learn effectively from other children. In California, several school districts have undertaken programs in which volunteer high school and college students tutor and counsel young children on a one-to-one basis. Where these student-teachers are themselves bilingual they have served an especially crucial role supplementing the formal education of language-minority children. These California projects have been funded by the Bilinqual Education Act. We recommend that similar projects be funded in other school districts.

Finally, ways must be found to ease the present restrictions in many States which operate to impede the recruitment of educators who are from language-minority groups.

Certification requirements have recently become the subject of successful court challenges. Objective standards for qualification are important to school systems in maintaining professional capability, but they can and have operated to exclude the very people that our public schools so vitally need. The committee endorses the principle of certification, but believes it must be implemented with much greater flexibility and sensitivity than has been heretofore practiced.

## F. Education Finance

### 1. FINDINGS

*The Present System*—Our Nation's present arrangements for raising and distributing money for public education are both complex and fundamentally unfair; and while the details differ, the pattern is similar in nearly every State.

The basic source of education finance is the local real estate property tax, which provides more than one-half of all school revenues. Heavy reliance on the local property tax enables rich school districts with large tax bases to spend large amounts for their children's education with low tax rates, while poor school districts which tax themselves more heavily still spend less.

The inequity of this tax system is not corrected by the bewildering variety of aid formulas through which the States finance most of the remaining costs of public education. In general, these formulas fail to equalize the revenue-raising abilities of rich and poor school districts; and, at worst, they aggravate the inequities resulting from reliance on local property tax.

The California Supreme Court has found that our typical State system of education finance conditions the fundamental right to education "on wealth, classifies its recipients on the basis of their collective affluence and makes the quality of a child's education depend upon the resources of his school district and ultimately upon the pocketbook of his parents." *Serrano* v. *Priest*, 487 P. 2d 241 (1971). And differences in wealth create disparities in the ability of States to finance education nearly as great as the disparities among local governments.

In short, the way we finance our schools embodies the very definition of inequality in educational opportunity.

The existence of such inequitable school finance systems alone would be enough to warrant fundamental reform. But these inequities are aggravated by the most serious fiscal crisis in education since the Depression. In nearly every area of the Nation, education costs have risen dramatically; and they continue to rise at a rate which threatens to outstrip the capacities of State and local governments to raise the revenues needed to meet present educational needs.

We face a financial crisis of emergency proportions which strikes not only large city school systems—with overwhelming educational problems, rising cost levels for education and other municipal services, and declining tax bases—but many rural and suburban school districts as well. As a result, teachers have been laid off, schools are closing early and basic educational programs are being curtailed.

Thus, we have an outmoded, unfair system of financing public education in this country and a state of near bankruptcy in many school systems.

Once again, in the face of decades of inaction by State and Federal authorities, the courts are taking the lead. On August 30, 1971, the California Supreme Court ruled in *Serrano* v. *Priest* that State-local systems of school finance which link access to education funds with local wealth in real property valuation violate the Equal Protection Clause of the 14th Amendment to the U.S. Constitution. Similar rulings have been handed down in cases affecting Texas and New Jersey. The *Serrano* principle is presently before the U.S. Supreme Court in *Rodriquez* v. *San Antonio Independent School District.* If *Rodriquez* is upheld, substantial changes will be required in the school finance systems of most, if not all, States.

But regardless of the Supreme Court's ultimate legal decision, the States and the Federal Government have both an opportunity and a responsibility to correct the inequities which the courts have brought to public attention. The challenge presented by *Serrano* and its progeny is to devise a system of education finance which allocates assistance fairly, on the basis of need, rather than arbitrarily, on the basis of local wealth.

While education is primarily a State function, the opportunity of every schoolchild for an equal education is a fundamental right in which the Nation as a whole, and every one of its citizens, has a stake. The Federal Government can and should assist hard pressed State and local governments in providing excellent educational opportunities for all children.

Our fairness in dealing with reform of education finance over the next decade will provide yet another test of our commitment to equal educational opportunity.

*The Federal Role in Education Finance*—Present Federal aid for public elementary and secondary education is totally inadequate to deal with the growing fiscal crisis in education finance—it does not begin to provide the resources necessary to cope with the educational problems of disadvantaged children; and, it has a negligible impact on the problem of financial inequity. In the last decade, Federal funds for public elementary and secondary schools have increased from $650 million to about $3.1 billion. Over the past 4 years the increase in Federal funds has been negligible; and, in fact, the Federal Government now provides less than 8 percent of the revenues for public education—and this share has steadily decreased since 1968.

In the face of a fiscal crisis in many school systems and totally inadequate funding of compensatory education programs, the Federal budget for fiscal year 1973 provides no increase in appropriations for compensatory education under Title I of the Elementary and Secondary Education Act—the largest single source of Federal funds for elementary and secondary schools. While Federal aid to education is leveling off and the Federal share declining, the costs of education are rising.

Compounding the inadequacy of Federal aid is the fact that no school district can count on the same amount, much less an increase, from one year to the next. New York City, for example, received from major Federal educational programs $31.48 for each pupil in 1966, $79.22 in 1967, and $39.89 in 1968.

Not only is Federal support for education declining and fluctuating, it fails to direct resources where the needs are greatest—toward offsetting the inequalities in State and local finance systems. In the aggregate, Federal aid does have a mildly equalizing affect because of the impact of compensatory education for educationally disadvantaged low-income children under Title I of the Elementary and Secondary Education Act, which provides nearly 40 percent of the Federal funds for elementary and secondary education. Within metropolitan areas, however, Federal funds are completely insufficient to overcome the advantages of those school districts with high tax bases.

### 2. RECOMMENDATIONS

*First*, we recommend immediate expansion of Title I of the Elementary and Secondary Education Act through Congressional adoption of an additional new program, modeled on the President's compensatory education proposals of March 17, 1972, with an initial authorization of $1.5 billion annually.

These funds would be expended in direct project grants from the Office of Education to school systems agreeing to use the new funds, together with funds received under the preexisting Title I program, for highly concentrated well-evaluated, compensatory services in reading and math.

If vigorously administered by the Office of Education, such a new program can bring about the concentration of funds and focus on specific program goals which have been lacking in so many projects funded under Title I. As the President said:

> While there is a great deal yet to be learned about the design of successful compensatory programs, the experience so far does point in one crucial direction: To the importance of providing sufficiently concentrated funding to establish the educational equivalent of a "critical mass," or threshold level. Where funds have been spread too thinly, they have been wasted or dissipated with little to show for their expenditure. Where they have been concentrated, the results have been frequently encouraging and sometimes dramatic.

The new programs, combined with a continuation of Title I could provide compensatory services averaging $300 a year to 10 million of the estimated 17 million Title I-eligible students beginning in the

Fall of 1973. Effective administration on the local and Federal levels and full evaluation can build the record for increased funding to extend full compensatory help to all disadvantaged children by the Fall of 1975.

*Second*, we recommend that beginning next fiscal year and for at least the 3 succeeding fiscal years, $5 billion in additional Federal funds be authorized and appropriated for a new program to encourage and support reform of elementary and secondary education financing, along the following lines:

(a) Allocation of funds according to a formula which takes account of the varying ability, and effort, of States to adequately finance public education.

(b) Grant of financial assistance for implementation of State plan to provide fairer treatment for the many rural and suburban, as well as centercity, school districts which have inadequate revenue-raising ability under existing school finance systems.

(c) Provision that local education agencies be required to adopt effective procedures, including objective measurements of educational achievement, for the annual evaluation of the effectiveness of education programs. In addition, States should be encouraged to undertake comprehensive statewide educational assessment programs.

We believe our recommendations for these substantial increases in Title I funds and new funds for elementary and secondary education will relieve the immediate financial crisis in public education, fulfill the promise and potential of compensatory education that was made when the Elementary and Secondary Education Act was passed in 1965, and encourage the States to shift from regressive inequitable education finance structures to progressive and equitable finance plans.

*Third*, we recommend more adequate funding of existing Federal elementary and secondary education programs, including support for vocational education and the education of handicapped children. And we note our recommendations contained elsewhere in this Report, for full funding of the Indian Education Act, the Bilingual Education Act (Title VII of the Elementary and Secondary Education Act of 1965), and the Emergency School Aid Act.

## G. Making Education More Responsive

### 1. SCHOOLS AND THEIR COMMUNITIES

Money is not the only resource necessary to make education in the 1970s and 1980s more effective. There are resources within business, universities, cultural institutions, service and other community organizations that are equally important, readily available and now largely unused in public education. Schools can and should make use of these resources. Much, if not most learning, occurs outside the classroom. Schools should find ways to make the community part of the school learning experience.

Libraries, museums and zoos have long been used as resources outside the school. But they are almost always underused.

Perhaps the most successful and best publicized effort to integrate community resources into the formal learning process was the Parkway Program—the "School Without Walls"—developed several years ago in Philadelphia. This program made extensive use of the museums, theatres, libraries, businesses and government offices in downtown Philadelphia as learning, research and work experience sites for high school students.

In testimony before this committee, witnesses urged that schools be more open, less rigid and more in tune to the "real world" outside the classroom and that students be given an opportunity to understand how what they learn in school applies to their interests, concerns and needs.

Using community institutions would not only benefit students, it would help involve the community in the education of its children. Businessmen, lawyers, accountants, public officials, people in hospitals and industry and others could design educational programs to inform and educate young people about what they do and how they do it.

Beyond expanding the physical learning site, there are other ways that the educational process can be restructured to take advantage of extra-school resources. It has long been established for example that children learn effectively from other children. Where schools have had older children tutor younger children the experience has been found to benefit both.

The testimony of several witnesses before the committee demonstrated that schools can develop new and imaginative and often unused ways to make use of community resources and people and make them a part of the learning process. Such approaches will help make education a more practical and real experience and at the same time tap new, available and inexpensive resources that ought to be a part of formal education.

A number of educators have proposed that schools be open longer hours and more days and that they provide both educational and non-educational services for adults as well as children.

A school might be open, for example, on a 12- to 14- hour basis 6 or 7 days a week. New school activities and educational programs might be planned, implemented and evaluated with the participation of parents, students and others in the community. Aside from the formal curriculum, later afternoon activities could be provided not just for children in the school, but for other children in the community as well. Education courses could be available for adults in the evening and the school would be open whenever possible for other kinds of community activities and meetings. The school could also be used to provide services such as health, legal aid and employment counseling. Paraprofessionals could be used both as teacher aides and in noneducational activities. The school itself would thus function as a community center for the educational and other community needs of all people in the neighborhood.

### 2. CHANGING ROLES FOR EDUCATORS AND THEIR CLIENTS

The growing demands for accountability in public education are in part a reflection of the fact that many schools are failing minority group and disadvantaged children and are often unable to recognize their needs. But they are also rooted in feeling among many parents and students from all backgrounds that public education is too often a closed society, overly defensive to criticism, and often resistant to change.

Often parents and students see themselves excluded from direct participation in educational matters. Increasingly, they are questioning the validity of the decisions professionals are making for them. Increasingly they question the right of professionals to make such decisions *for* them and whether these decisions are made with their best interests in mind.

Moreover, in many communities the present educational structure does not provide its clients adequate information about student and school performance, or the data with which the public can judge the quality of education in the school district or a particular school by comparing it with that in other communities or schools.

There are a number of actions which we believe should be taken to assure that parents, students and community residents have the information necessary to evaluate the performance of their schools, enable clients to participate in decisions about education policy and programs, and afford choices among alternative methods of instruction, curricula and types of schools.

We believe that any system designed to make schools more responsive must have four key elements:

*First*, parents and students should become directly involved in school affairs.

*Second*, the fullest possible, accurate information must be publicly available on school performance and other essential aspects of school life.

*Third*, school principals should be relieved of many of their present administrative burdens so they can be more active participants in the educational process and made more responsible for the outcomes of their schools.

*Fourth*, all teachers must become sensitive to diversity and to the backgrounds of different children and be free to innovate, experiment and develop new instructional techniques.

*Community Participation*—One of the keys to successful school integration is the full and complete participation of students, parents, teachers and other community residents in the design of plans, educational programs and extracurricular activities. Successful community participation in education is a two-way street. School administrators and professional educators must view community residents as an essential resource in educational decisionmaking. At the same time, parents and students must participate constructively and cooperatively. We believe the establishment of community committees should be encouraged in all school districts.

Parent-citizen committees adequately representative of minority groups should be established for both individual schools and school districts with representatives of parents, students—at least at the high school level—and teachers. These committees, working with school superintendents, school principals, and other school officials should help design and recommend specific, objective goals for education, explore new educational programs, innovations, suggest changes in educational programs, and help develop appropriate ways to measure student performance and evaluate school performance. The committees might also explore new classroom techniques, find ways to involve the community in school activities, develop plans to make use of community resources, and help make the school become a more community-oriented institution, responsive to its clients.

These parent-citizen committees should receive financial support and have sufficient resources to tap the expertise of disinterested technicians and others who could be helpful in providing advice, counsel, technical assistance and in developing ways to ask the right questions.

*The Role of the School Principal*—In many ways the school principal is the most important and influential individual in any school. He is the person responsible for all the activities that occur in and around the school building. It is his leadership that sets the tone of the school, the climate for learning, the level of professionalism and morale of teachers and the degree of concern for what students may or may not become. He is the main link between the school and the community and the way he performs in that capacity largely determines the attitudes of students and parents about the school. If a school is a vibrant, innovative, child-centered place, if it has a reputation for excellence in teaching, if students are performing to the best of their ability, one can almost always point to the principal's leadership as the key to success.

We believe there is a need to revitalize the leadership role of school principals, reduce their administrative burdens and permit them to exercise the kind of responsibility necessary to make education work. At the same time, we believe if schools are to be more accountable to their clients, as the person most responsible for education where it happens, the principal should also be the person who is held accountable for the performance of the school, its teachers and students.

Accordingly, we urge that school districts take the following steps toward these goals:

*First*, the school principal should be unburdened from as many of his present administrative burdens as possible and given greater autonomy and responsibility for the improvement of instruction and other activities involving students within the school. The principal and teachers should be free to experiment with new teaching methods and select appropriate instructional materials to meet the needs of individual students and students from diverse backgrounds. To the extent possible the States should relax their present restrictions on curriculum requirements and other matters to accomplish these aims.

*Second*, in exercising these responsibilities, principals should consult fully and directly with parent-citizen school committees described in the previous section. Changes in present educational practices, the development of new techniques and the design of new programs should be a cooperative effort among the principal, teachers, parents and students involved in the school.

*Third*, in order to relieve the school principal from his present administrative burdens, he should have the resources to select a school administrator or manager to fill a position with the rank of assistant principal. The administrator should be responsible for noneducational, administrative and managerial functions at the school.

*Fourth*, States and local communities should review the processes by which principals are selected including the possibility of consultation with the clients of education as part of the selection process. Academic credentials, seniority, and administrative ability are important qualifications for any school principal. But we believe more attention should also be paid to those essential traits which define a prospective principal's capacity for educational leadership so that the selection process will be conducted in a manner to assure the appointment of qualified educators who are both leaders of teachers and responsive to the needs and desires of parents and students.

*Fifth*, consideration should also be given by States and school districts to the publication of an annual evaluation of school performance which would include the results of standardized achievement tests in schools and school districts. These results should be presented in such fashion that educators and their clients will be able to assess how well schools are doing.

*Teachers and Their Education*—It is the interaction between teacher and child that lies at the heart of the educational process. Effective teaching is the essential condition for education and insensitive or inadequate teaching will at least result in a lost opportunity, if not damage to the child.

No significant or lasting changes in education can take place in our schools without both the participation and leadership of teachers, their organizations and the people and institutions involved in teacher education and development.

*Incentives for Education Quality*—Many critics have suggested that the incentive structure of schools does not place enough emphasis on the provision of quality education to the schools' primary clients—its students.

The committee received testimony from representatives of the State of Michigan school system concerning an innovative program it has instituted to provide incentives for quality education. Michigan awards State aid to school districts partially on the basis of the educational progress of a school district's educationally disadvantaged students.

We believe schools should be provided encouragement for performing their basic functions well. We recommend that Title I be amended to give States the option of participating in a new, federally funded. education achievement bonus program. Under this program, school districts would be provided a bonus for each Title I student who made adequate educational progress as measured by annual tests in reading and math. The bonus could be used by the school district as general assistance and would be in addition to regularly received Title I funds. The program would provide a strong incentive for school districts to find organizational structures and teaching techniques capable of teaching their Title I pupils effectively.

We believe more teacher education should take place in public schools. Teachers should spend more time away from the physical setting and atmosphere of a college or university and work in classrooms with experienced teachers at various times throughout their period of training.

All too often today teacher education is largely removed from the practical day-to-day elementary and secondary school experience. In most schools of education, except for a short student-teaching experience, preparation is conducted within the college or university and the aspiring teacher must demonstrate his or her skills in the traditional way by taking tests and writing papers.

One way of assuring that new teachers have the kind of practical training they need is to provide that a greater share of the responsibility for training teachers be undertaken by experienced classroom teachers not only with the student teacher in the public school classroom but also by bringing experienced teachers into teacher colleges and schools of education.

*Teacher Centers*—Teacher education does not stop with the issuance of a certificate or graduate degree. It is a continuous process of development. We believe teachers must have the time, free from their classroom duties, to acquire new knowledge about subjects taught, about new classroom instructional methods and learn about new developments in education. They should have the opportunity to share experiences with each other so that new information will be disseminated into a variety of classrooms and schools.

One of the most hopeful, innovative models for the in-service development of teachers that the committee has found is the teacher centers, a concept that has become both popular and useful to teachers in England.

The teacher center concept is based upon the proposition, with which this committee is in complete accord, that fundamental educational change can best come through those charged with the responsibility for delivering educational services, that is, teachers. If education is to become more responsive, teachers must be able to define their own problems and work out ways to meet their needs in the classroom.

Initiated, organized and run by teachers, the primary function of the teacher center, as described by Professor Stephen K. Bailey of Syracuse University, is to "make possible a review of existing curricula and other educational practices by groups of teachers and to encourage teacher attempts to bring about changes."

More than 500 such centers now exist in England.

While some centers meet after school, others meet in evenings, on weekends, holidays and more extensive sessions during the summer break.

> The teachers' center also promotes and provides exhibits of new textbooks, programmed instruction, audio-visual aids, homecrafts and handicrafts and student art. Promotional and information activities (bulletins, newsletters, posters, etc.) are disseminated to keep all teachers and other interested people in the area informed about programs and exhibits. After school experimental classes on family life, adolescent identity crises, and community problems are undertaken with selected students.*

Professor Bailey stated further that "the key to the success and enthusiasm associated with the teacher center notion is control by local teachers". While some centers may be organized around subject areas such as mathematics, English, or reading, others may be organized by grade or region or focus on broader concepts such as child behavior or group dynamics. The alternatives are broad enough to include those seeking both general and specific knowledge.

The committee believes that the teacher center concept can have important implications for improved teacher and student performance in public schools in this country. With the cooperation of teacher

---

*Teachers Centers: A British First *Phi Delta Kappan*, November 1971.

organizations we believe teachers should endeavor to better mobilize their forces for educational progress than they have heretofore. Certainly, an American version of teacher centers could begin a process of relevant self-appraisal and development.

We believe a substantial effort should be undertaken with Federal funds to establish teacher centers in several communities throughout the United States. There is ample authority under existing programs for the funding of such centers and we recommend that Congress appropriate funds sufficient to establish teacher centers in a variety of school districts next year. Once experience demonstrates their effectiveness such a program can be expanded in future years.

## H. Rural Education

### 1. FINDINGS

More than 53 million Americans—about 26 percent of our population—live outside the Nation's metropolitan areas.

Among the Nation's nearly 70 million children under 18, 24.4 million live in communities of less than 10,000. Of these, 4.7 million live in towns with a population of between 2,500 and 10,000; 2.2 million are in communities with 1,000 to 2,500 residents; and 17.5 million live in what the census classifies as "other rural areas"—including 3.1 million who live on the Nation's farms. About 5 million of these rural children are from families with incomes below the poverty level.

Smallness can be both an advantage and a disadvantage. The small school district seldom has overcrowded classrooms and teachers are more likely to be acquainted with their student's parents. The small school is more likely to be closely tied to the community. Often it is the social center for the community. It is this sense of community, the feeling on the part of parents and students that they are participants in education, that is so seldom present in large school systems, especially in urban areas and particularly for minority groups.

But more often smallness means isolation; and it means inadequate facilities, low per-pupil expenditures, limited educational curricula and inadequately trained, low-paid teachers.

Teachers' salaries, for example, are often as much as $2,000 or $3,000 less in rural than in other areas. This makes it extremely difficult for rural areas to attract well-trained teachers, especially those with advanced degrees.

Rural school districts also suffer from inadequate educational resources. Many rural school districts simply lack the tax base necessary to raise sufficient funds for public education. This often makes it impossible to support modern facilities, pay teachers decent salaries, purchase modern instructional equipment which can facilitate modern learning techniques or offer advanced courses in sciences and other subjects. The small school district faces an additional financial disadvantage, for research studies show that the per-pupil cost of educational services increases as the number of students in the school decreases. Many rural schools are for this reason economically inefficient.

Equally, if not more important, is the lack of adequate vocational training in rural school districts. Most rural youth today neither live on farms nor plan careers in agriculture upon graduation. Yet, much of the vocational training in rural school districts is agriculturally oriented. More than 300,000 American youth migrate from rural to urban areas each year. They move from the small towns, particularly in the rural South, to the major cities of the North and to other metropolitan areas in their own and nearby States. More often than not these youthful Americans are ill-prepared for urban living; untrained for available jobs; and, all too often, are consigned to a life of poverty in the innercity more devastating than that from which they have escaped.

All these disadvantages of rural education result in lower achievement, low aspirations and motivations and low educational attainment among many rural schoolchildren.

### 2. RECOMMENDATIONS

- We recommend that the States, with Federal help, undertake to develop area vocational schools to serve several school districts at one time. The area schools established by South Carolina—which are attended part time by children and adults and provide basic literary, job-oriented vocational and technical training—should be examined as a possible model.
- We recommend that the States consider the full assumption of student transportation costs in rural areas, as one way of relieving rural school districts of a major financial burden.
- We recommend the establishment of additional federally financed Regional Education Service Agencies modeled after those established by the Appalachian Regional Commission. These agencies provide a variety of educational services to combinations of two or more school districts that wish to join together in efforts that the school districts could not afford to undertake alone—services such as guidance counseling, job placement for high school seniors, bilingual education teachers, and administrative services. RESAs not only provide much needed educational services; also, they make it possible for school districts to preserve the advantages of smallness and, at the same time, provide those services which only larger school districts can afford.
- We recommend the establishment of a rural school division in the U.S. Office of Education so that rural education will have a Federal spokesman whose sole task is to represent the interests of more than 24 million children in small towns and other rural areas in our Nation. This rural school division should act as the principal Federal agency for the development of rural education programs and also be the advocate for rural school districts within the Federal bureaucracy—so that these districts can compete for Federal funds on equal terms.
- Finally, Federal aid to education programs must be both designed and administered with a recognition of the special needs of rural areas. Those rural school districts, which are isolated and have low tax bases, should receive increased financial assistance.

# Part II

# Educational Disadvantage and Child Development

## Chapter 3—The Nation's Disadvantaged Children

This report is about elementary and secondary education—how it fails millions of children from deprived backgrounds, how the resources for it are inequitably distributed, how black and other minority children are separated and discriminated against in school and how our educational system often fails to respond to the needs and desires of those they serve.

But above all, this is a report about children. And it is important at the outset to define whom we are talking about. While available data do not provide the exact number of disadvantaged children in the United States, there are a number of useful indicators which can serve to adequately define the dimensions of the problem.*

Nearly 70 million of our 203 million citizens are under 18 years old. About 59 million are between the ages of 3 and 17, who, for the purpose of the 1970 Census, are considered to be the Nation's preschool and school-age population.

Of these 59 million, just over 52 million are enrolled in some type of schooling. About 46 million are in public preschools and elementary and secondary schools; nearly 6 million are in private and special schools. Another 7 million children, ages 3–17, are not enrolled in any type of school or educational program and there are just over 17 million preschool age, from under 1 year of age to under 5 years of age.

### A. The Nation's Minority and Nonminority Group Children

Approximately 20.9 percent of the Nation's children are members of minority groups.** This same ratio carries over into our public schools, where there are 37.9 million nonminority and 9.3 million minority group children.

---

*Except where otherwise noted, the statistics used in this chapter are derived from U.S. Census Bureau Reports resulting from the 1970 Decennial Census.

**For purposes of this chapter, minority group children include those who are black, Spanish-surnamed, Portuguese-speaking, American Indian, Asian-Americans, Eskimos, Hawaiians, and other members of identifiable minority groups.

**Table 3–1.**—*Minority and nonminority students in public preschools and elementary and secondary schools* [1]

| | Numbers | Percent |
|---|---|---|
| All students | 44, 900, 000 | 100. 0 |
| Nonminority | 37, 900, 000 | 79. 1 |
| Minority | 9, 300, 000 | 20. 9 |
| Black | 6, 700, 000 | 14. 9 |
| Spanish-surnamed | 2, 200, 000 | 5. 1 |
| American Indian | 197, 000 | . 4 |
| Oriental | 209, 000 | . 5 |

[1] Source: HEW, *Directory of Public Elementary and Secondary Schools in Selected Districts*, Fall, 1970.

## B. Children From Low-Income Families

Approximately 20 percent of all children live in families with incomes under $5,000 per year. About 5 million children are in families with annual incomes of less than $3,000 a year. Among public school and preschool children, more than 8.7 million, or 19 percent, are in families with incomes of less than $5,000 a year. Add to this, 1.8 million children who are not in school, and another 400,000 in private schools, and a total of 10.9 million children are in such families.

By race, 13.8 percent white public-school-age children are in families with incomes of less than $5,000, while 46.8 percent of blacks are from such families.

Of the Nation's 59 million school-age children, 4 million are in families with incomes under $3,000. Nearly 3.2 million public school and preschool children and 757,000 who are not in school are in such families. In public schools and preschools, 4.4 percent of the white children, 20.7 percent of the black children and 28 percent of the Spanish-surnamed school children are in families with less than $3,000.

At this writing, detailed indices are not available for Spanish-surnamed, American Indian and Oriental school children. We do know, however, that 28 percent of Mexican-American school-age children are from families with incomes of less than $3,000; and that half of all American Indian families have incomes of less than $2,000 with 75 percent less than $3,000. Thus, one can safely assume that close to three of every four of the Nation's American Indian school children are living in poverty-stricken families.

With the widespread recognition that socioeconomic status of the home environment strongly relates to the educational achievement of the school child, these then are the figures setting forth the initial educational and economic disadvantage—with minority group children having poverty indices four to seven times that of white children.

The following tables show the 1970 Census distribution of the Nation's school and nonschool children economically and by race.

TABLE 3-2.—*Economic status of family members, ages 3-17, by family income and race* [1]

[Numbers in thousands and percentages]

| | Total | Under $3,000 | $3,000 to $4,999 | Under $5,000 | $5,000 to $7,499 | $7,500 to $9,999 | $10,000 to $14,999 | $15,000 to plus | Not reported |
|---|---|---|---|---|---|---|---|---|---|
| All children | 59, 081 | 4, 012 | 6, 894 | 10, 906 | 9, 815 | 10, 740 | 14, 379 | 9, 103 | 4, 139 |
| Percent | | 6. 7 | 11. 6 | 18. 4 | 16. 6 | 18. 1 | 24. 3 | 15. 4 | 7. 0 |
| Total enrolled, all schools | 51, 874 | 3, 254 | 5, 819 | 9, 073 | 8, 342 | 9, 298 | 12, 969 | 8, 574 | 3, 589 |
| Percent | | 6. 2 | 11. 2 | 17. 5 | 16. 1 | 18. 0 | 25. 0 | 16. 5 | 7. 0 |
| Total enrolled in public preschools and schools | 45, 770 | 3, 144 | 5, 556 | 8, 700 | 7, 687 | 8, 202 | 11, 084 | 6, 985 | 3, 114 |
| Percent | | 6. 8 | 12. 1 | 19. 0 | 16. 7 | 17. 9 | 24. 2 | 15. 2 | 6. 8 |
| Total not enrolled in schools | 7, 235 | 757 | 1, 076 | 1, 833 | 1, 473 | 1, 442 | 1, 410 | 529 | 505 |
| Percent | | 10. 4 | 14. 8 | 25. 3 | 20. 3 | 19. 9 | 19. 4 | 7. 2 | 7. 6 |
| Total enrolled in private schools | 6, 077 | 110 | 263 | 373 | 655 | 1, 096 | 1, 885 | 1, 589 | 475 |
| Percent | | 1. 8 | 4. 3 | 6. 1 | 10. 7 | 18. 0 | 31. 0 | 26. 1 | 7. 8 |
| All white children | 49, 946 | 2, 230 | 4, 651 | 6, 881 | 7, 903 | 9, 617 | 13, 509 | 8, 568 | 3, 467 |
| Percent | | 4. 5 | 9. 3 | 13. 8 | 15. 9 | 19. 2 | 27. 0 | 17. 1 | 6. 9 |
| All nonwhite children | 9, 135 | 1, 782 | 2, 243 | 4, 025 | 1, 912 | 1, 123 | 870 | 535 | 672 |
| Percent | | 2. 0 | 24. 0 | 44. 1 | 21. 0 | 12. 2 | 9. 5 | 5. 8 | 7. 3 |
| All black children | 8, 334 | 1, 747 | 2, 153 | 3, 900 | 1, 754 | 1, 008 | 738 | 363 | 572 |
| Percent | | 21. 0 | 25. 8 | 46. 8 | 21. 0 | 12. 1 | 8. 8 | 4. 3 | 6. 8 |

[1] Numbers and percentages in this and other tables in this chapter may not total due to standard statistical error, rounding, etc. They are, however, accurate estimates derived from separate 1970 Census Reports.

TABLE 3-3.—*Total school-age population, ages 3–17 by family income distribution*

[By number of students in thousands and percentages]

| | Total | Annual income | | | | | | |
|---|---|---|---|---|---|---|---|---|
| | | Under $3,000 | $3,000 to $4,999 | $5,000 to $7,499 | $7,500 to $9,999 | $10,000 to $14,999 | $15,000 plus | Not reported |
| All races | 59, 082 | 4, 011 | 6, 895 | 9, 816 | 10, 740 | 14, 378 | 9, 102 | 4, 104 |
| Percent | | 6. 7 | 11. 6 | 16. 6 | 18. 1 | 24. 3 | 15. 4 | 7. 0 |

TABLE 3-4.—*Total public and preschool enrollment, ages 3–17, by race and family income*

[By number of students in thousands and percentages]

| | Total | Annual income | | | | | | |
|---|---|---|---|---|---|---|---|---|
| | | Under $3,000 | $3,000 to $4,999 | $5,000 to $7,499 | $7,500 to $9,999 | $10,000 to $14,999 | $15,000 plus | Not reported |
| All races | 45, 700 | 3, 144 | 5, 556 | 7, 687 | 8, 202 | 11, 084 | 6, 985 | 3, 114 |
| Percent | | 6. 8 | 12. 1 | 16. 7 | 17. 9 | 24. 2 | 15. 2 | 6. 8 |
| White | 38, 271 | 1, 681 | 3, 962 | 6, 083 | 7, 270 | 10, 377 | 6, 581 | 2, 586 |
| Percent | | 4. 4 | 9. 6 | 15. 9 | 19. 0 | 27. 1 | 17. 2 | 6. 7 |
| Black | 6, 890 | 1, 433 | 1, 787 | 1, 481 | 843 | 613 | 276 | 456 |
| Percent | | 20. 7 | 25. 9 | 21. 4 | 12. 2 | 8. 8 | 4. 0 | 6. 6 |

TABLE 3–5.—*Children not enrolled in school, ages 3–17, by race and family income*

[By number of students in thousands and percentages]

| | Total | Annual income | | | | | |
|---|---|---|---|---|---|---|---|
| | | Under $3,000 | $3,000 to $4,999 | $5,000 to $7,499 | $7,500 to $9,999 | $10,000 to $14,999 | $15,000 plus | Not reported |
| All races | 7, 235 | 757 | 1, 076 | 1, 474 | 1, 442 | 1, 409 | 528 | 551 |
| Percent | | 10. 4 | 14. 8 | 20. 3 | 19. 9 | 19. 4 | 7. 2 | 7. 6 |
| White | 5, 997 | 458 | 751 | 1, 240 | 1, 317 | 1, 318 | 488 | 426 |
| Percent | | 7. 6 | 12. 5 | 20. 6 | 21. 9 | 21. 9 | 8. 1 | 7. 1 |
| Black | 1, 131 | 292 | 315 | 210 | 110 | 81 | 24 | 99 |
| Percent | | 25. 8 | 27. 8 | 18. 5 | 9. 7 | 7. 1 | 2. 1 | 8. 7 |

TABLE 3–6.—*Total public nursery and kindergarten school enrollment by race and family income*

[By number of students in thousands and percentages]

| | Total | Annual income | | | | | |
|---|---|---|---|---|---|---|---|
| | | Under $3,000 | $3,000 to $4,999 | $5,000 to $7,499 | $7,500 to $9,999 | $10,000 to $14,999 | $15,000 plus | Not reported |
| All races | 3, 021 | 270 | 380 | 507 | 599 | 728 | 363 | 175 |
| Percent | | 8. 9 | 12. 5 | 16. 7 | 19. 8 | 24. 0 | 12. 0 | 5. 7 |
| White | 2, 444 | 132 | 244 | 398 | 512 | 685 | 328 | 145 |
| Percent | | 5. 4 | 10. 0 | 16. 3 | 20. 9 | 28. 0 | 13. 4 | 5. 9 |
| Black | 515 | 134 | 121 | 105 | 76 | 31 | 25 | 22 |
| Percent | | 26. 0 | 23. 5 | 20. 4 | 14. 7 | 6. 0 | 4. 8 | 4. 3 |

TABLE 3–7.—*Public elementary school enrollment, grades 1–8, by race and family income*

[By number of students in thousands and percentages]

| | Total | Annual income | | | | | | |
|---|---|---|---|---|---|---|---|---|
| | | Under $3,000 | $3,000 to $4,999 | $5,000 to $7,499 | $7,500 to $9,999 | $10,000 to $14,999 | $15,000 plus | Not reported |
| All races | 29, 908 | 2, 150 | 3, 910 | 5, 169 | 5, 449 | 6, 993 | 4, 122 | 2, 116 |
| Percent | | 7. 2 | 13. 1 | 17. 3 | 18. 2 | 23. 3 | 13. 8 | 7. 1 |
| White | 24, 805 | 1, 155 | 2, 628 | 4, 093 | 4, 832 | 6, 527 | 3, 838 | 1, 732 |
| Percent | | 4. 6 | 10. 5 | 16. 5 | 19. 4 | 26. 3 | 15. 4 | 6. 9 |
| Black | 4, 706 | 980 | 1, 239 | 999 | 561 | 412 | 185 | 329 |
| Percent | | 20. 8 | 26. 3 | 21. 2 | 11. 9 | 8. 7 | 3. 9 | 7. 0 |

TABLE 3–8.—*Total public high school enrollment, grades 9–12, by race and family income*

[By number of students in thousands and percentages]

| | Total | Annual income | | | | | | |
|---|---|---|---|---|---|---|---|---|
| | | Under $3,000 | $3,000 to $4,999 | $5,000 to $7,499 | $7,500 to $9,999 | $10,000 to $14,999 | $15,000 plus | Not reported |
| All races | 12, 841 | 724 | 1, 266 | 2, 011 | 2, 154 | 3, 363 | 2, 500 | 823 |
| Percent | | 5. 6 | 9. 8 | 15. 6 | 16. 7 | 26. 1 | 19. 4 | 6. 4 |
| White | 11, 022 | 394 | 820 | 1, 592 | 1, 926 | 3, 165 | 2, 415 | 709 |
| Percent | | 3. 6 | 7. 4 | 14. 4 | 17. 4 | 28. 7 | 21. 9 | 6. 4 |
| Black | 1, 669 | 319 | 427 | 377 | 206 | 170 | 66 | 105 |
| Percent | | 19. 1 | 25. 5 | 22. 5 | 12. 3 | 10. 1 | 3. 9 | 6. 2 |

## C. Children and Their Parents' Educational Attainment

The educational attainment of a child's parents provides one index of his educational advantage and disadvantage. Thus, for example, educational psychologists have widely held that the more advanced a parent's educational attainment, the more likely that he will expose his children to books and other learning stimuli. The census has provided figures on the numbers of school-age children by various categories and the years of school completed by their family head.

As is shown in Table 3–9, in 1970 more than 6.5 million, or 11 percent of all school-age children, live in families where the head of the household has less than an 8th grade education. 12.2 million, or 20.5 percent, have parents who never attended high school; and 23.2 million, or 39 percent of all school-age children have parents who failed to complete high school.

Table 3–9.—*School-age children, 3–17, by educational attainment of family head, 1970*

[Numbers in thousands]

| | Family head school years completed | | | |
|---|---|---|---|---|
| | Less than 8 years | 8 years | Less than 12 years | No college |
| Total children, 59,570 | 6, 542 | 12, 215 | 23, 240 | 44, 237 |
| Percent | 11 | 20. 5 | 39 | 74. 2 |

Table 3–10 breaks these figures down by race.

Table 3–10.—*School-age children, 3–17, by race and educational attainment of family head*

[Numbers in thousands]

| | Family head school years completed | | | |
|---|---|---|---|---|
| | Less than 8 years | 8 years | Less than 12 years | No college |
| Total children: | | | | |
| White, 44,576 | 4, 116 | 8, 447 | 16, 280 | 21, 041 |
| Percent | 9. 2 | 18. 5 | 36. 5 | 47. 4 |
| Black, 8,221 | 2, 067 | 3, 025 | 5, 364 | 7, 274 |
| Percent | 25. 1 | 36. 7 | 65. 2 | 88. 2 |

Reports on other minority-group children and their parents' educational attainment levels are not available from any Government agency at this time. It is known, however, that among adult American Indians, two-thirds have never gone beyond the elementary school level, one-quarter have less than 5 years of education and 10 percent of all American Indians over 14 years of age have never attended any school. For those who have attended federally supervised schools, the average educational level is 5 years.*

**Indian Education: A National Tragedy—A National Challenge,* U.S. Senate Special Subcommittee on Indian Education, 91st Cong., 1st Session, 1969.

Committee witnesses testified that 79 percent of all Mexican Americans between the ages of 20 and 49 have not completed high school. And, it has been estimated that 15–20 percent of the total Mexican-American population in the United States has never seen the inside of a school building.*

The picture of educational achievement for Puerto Ricans is equally discouraging. In 1969, it was found that the average education for Puerto Ricans 25-and-over is 8.3 years. Fifteen percent of those Puerto Ricans 25-and-over have high school diplomas. In 1970, only 1.5 percent of this group had college degrees.

Presented below are tables showing the distribution of public school children according to the educational attainment of their family heads:

---

*Hearings of the U.S. Senate Select Committee on Equal Educational Opportunity, Part 4—*Mexican Education*, Aug. 18, 19, 20, 21, 1970, p. 2573.

**TABLE 3-11.**—*Total public school enrollment and educational attainment level of family head*

[Number of students in thousands, completed grade level of family head, and percentage distribution]

| All races | Total | Years of school completed— 0 to 4 | 5 to 7 | 8 | 1 to 3, high school | High school graduate | 1 to 3, college | College, 4 or more |
|---|---|---|---|---|---|---|---|---|
| Nursery and kindergarten | 3, 006 | 59 | 164 | 224 | 555 | 1, 183 | 348 | 472 |
| Percent | | 1. 9 | 4. 4 | 7. 4 | 18. 4 | 39. 3 | 11. 2 | 15. 6 |
| Elementary, grades 1 to 8 | 29, 779 | 916 | 2, 573 | 2, 720 | 5, 652 | 10, 674 | 2, 980 | 4, 265 |
| Percent | | 3. 0 | 8. 6 | 9. 1 | 18. 9 | 35. 8 | 10. 0 | 14. 3 |
| High school, grades 9 to 12 | 13, 508 | 389 | 1, 109 | 1, 511 | 2, 632 | 4, 437 | 1, 406 | 2, 023 |
| Percent | | 2. 8 | 8. 2 | 11. 1 | 19. 4 | 32. 8 | 10. 4 | 14. 9 |
| Total | 46, 293 | 1, 364 | 3, 846 | 4, 455 | 8, 839 | 16, 294 | 4, 734 | 6, 760 |
| Percent | | 2. 1 | 8. 3 | 9. 6 | 19. 0 | 35. 2 | 10. 2 | 14. 6 |
| Cumulative | | | 5, 210 | 9, 665 | 18, 504 | 34, 798 | | |
| Percent | | | 11. 2 | 20. 8 | 39. 9 | 75. 1 | | |

TABLE 3–12.—*White public school enrollment and educational attainment level of family head*

[Number of students in thousands, completed grade level of family head, and percentage distribution]

| White children | Total | Years of school completed— | | | | | | |
|---|---|---|---|---|---|---|---|---|
| | | 0 to 4 | 5 to 7 | 8 | 1 to 3, high school | High school graduate | 1 to 3, college | College 4 or more |
| Nursery and kindergarten | 2, 432 | 40 | 78 | 168 | 404 | 998 | 299 | 444 |
| Percent | | 1. 6 | 3. 2 | 6. 9 | 16. 6 | 41. 0 | 12. 2 | 18. 2 |
| Elementary, grades 1 to 8 | 24, 678 | 614 | 1, 711 | 2, 149 | 4, 229 | 9, 387 | 2, 677 | 3, 911 |
| Percent | | 2. 4 | 6. 9 | 8. 7 | 17. 1 | 38. 0 | 10. 8 | 15. 8 |
| High school, grades 9 to 12 | 11, 469 | 229 | 705 | 1, 257 | 2, 051 | 4, 071 | 1, 258 | 1, 897 |
| Percent | | 1. 9 | 6. 1 | 10. 9 | 18. 8 | 35. 5 | 10. 9 | 16. 5 |
| Total | 38, 579 | 883 | 2, 494 | 3, 574 | 6, 684 | 11, 456 | 4, 234 | 6, 252 |
| Percent | | 2. 3 | 6. 5 | 9. 3 | 17. 3 | 30. 0 | 11. 0 | 16. 2 |
| Cumulative | | | 3, 377 | 6, 951 | 13, 635 | 25, 091 | | |
| Percent | | | 8. 7 | 18. 0 | 35. 3 | 65. 0 | | |

**TABLE 3–13.—*Black public school enrollment and educational attainment level of family head***

[Number of students in thousands, completed grade level of family head, and percentage distribution]

| Black children | Total | Years of school completed— 0 to 4 | 5 to 7 | 8 | 1 to 3, high school | High school graduate | 1 to 3, college | College, 4 or more |
|---|---|---|---|---|---|---|---|---|
| Nursery and kindergarten | 512 | 19 | 76 | 53 | 140 | 158 | 41 | 24 |
| Percent | | 3.7 | 14.8 | 10.3 | 27.3 | 30.8 | 8.0 | 4.6 |
| Elementary, grades 1 to 8 | 4,705 | 291 | 801 | 525 | 1,364 | 1,174 | 255 | 295 |
| Percent | | 6.1 | 17.2 | 11.1 | 28.9 | 24.9 | 5.3 | 6.2 |
| High school, grades 9 to 12 | 1,873 | 148 | 384 | 226 | 549 | 336 | 126 | 105 |
| Percent | | 7.6 | 20.5 | 12.0 | 29.3 | 17.9 | 6.7 | 5.6 |
| Total | 7,090 | 458 | 1,261 | 804 | 2,053 | 1,668 | 422 | 424 |
| Percent | | 6.4 | 17.7 | 11.3 | 28.9 | 23.5 | 5.9 | 6.0 |
| Cumulative | | | 1,719 | 2,523 | 4,576 | 6,244 | | |
| Percent | | | 24.2 | 35.6 | 64.5 | 88.0 | | |

**TABLE 3–14.—*Total public, private, special and nonschool enrollment, ages 3–34, by family head***

[Number of students in thousands, completed grade level of family head, and percentage distribution]

| | Total | Years of school completed— 0 to 4 | 5 to 7 | 8 | 1 to 3, high school | High school graduate | 1 to 3, college | College, 4 or more |
|---|---|---|---|---|---|---|---|---|
| All races: | | | | | | | | |
| Number | 59,570 | 738 | 4,804 | 5,673 | 11,025 | 20,997 | 6,221 | 9,112 |
| Percent | | 1.2 | 8.1 | 9.5 | 18.5 | 35.2 | 10.4 | 15.3 |

TABLE 3-15.—*Total children not enrolled in school, ages 3–17, by race and family head*

[Number of students in thousands, completed grade level of family head, and percentage distribution]

| | Total | Years of school completed— | | | | | | |
|---|---|---|---|---|---|---|---|---|
| | | 0 to 4 | 5 to 7 | 8 | 1 to 3, high school | High school graduate | 1 to 3, college | College, 4 or more |
| All races: | | | | | | | | |
| Number | 7, 200 | 339 | 776 | 925 | 1, 447 | 2, 420 | 580 | 697 |
| Percent | | 4. 7 | 10. 8 | 12. 8 | 20. 0 | 33. 6 | 8. 0 | 9. 7 |
| White: | | | | | | | | |
| Number | 5, 997 | 209 | 530 | 757 | 1, 149 | 2, 152 | 527 | 614 |
| Percent | | 3. 5 | 8. 8 | 12. 6 | 19. 1 | 35. 9 | 8. 8 | 10. 2 |
| Black: | | | | | | | | |
| Number | 1, 131 | 118 | 230 | 154 | 286 | 242 | 45 | 74 |
| Percent | | 10. 4 | 20. 3 | 13. 6 | 25. 3 | 21. 4 | 4. 0 | 6. 5 |
| Nonwhite: | | | | | | | | |
| Number | 1, 249 | 130 | 246 | 168 | 298 | 268 | 53 | 83 |
| Percent | | 10. 4 | 19. 7 | 13. 4 | 24. 0 | 21. 4 | 4. 2 | 6. 6 |

### D. Children of the Unemployed

About 4.4 million children (6.2 percent of all children under 18) lived in families where the head of the household did not work at all during 1970. Another 12.1 million were in homes where the breadwinner worked only part of the year. Thus, a total of 16.5 million children (23.2 percent) were in families whose head was either unemployed or underemployed. It is reasonable to assume that about the same proportion, or 10.5 million, of the Nation's public school and preschool children are children of the unemployed and underemployed.

### E. Hungry Children

According to the Senate Select Committee on Nutrition and Human Needs, there are approximately 25.5 million Americans living in families whose incomes are insufficient to purchase a nutritionally adequate diet. About 10.5 million are children under 18. Federal family food assistance programs, the Food Stamp and Commodity Distribution Programs, reach only about 44 percent of the estimated 14 million persons who must have aid to escape malnutrition. The U.S. Senate Select Committee on Nutrition and Human Needs estimates that of those who do not receive food assistance and need it, 3.8 million are children.

The U.S. Department of Agriculture estimates that 9.3 million schoolchildren are eligible for free and reduced-price school meals. Of those eligible, 7.5 million now receive school lunch and 520,000 receive school breakfast each day. Thus, our school breakfast programs fail to reach 8.7 million eligible low-income schoolchildren and 1.8 million receive neither breakfast nor lunch at school.*

### F. Children Living in Substandard Housing

According to the 1970 Census, 4.7 million housing units in this country are substandard in that they lack adequate plumbing facilities. An even larger number of housing units, 5.2 million, are overcrowded. It has been estimated that at least 5 million children live in these substandard housing units.

### G. Children With Inadequate Health Care

There is no available comprehensive index of the inadequacy of child health care in the United States. However, there are a number of fairly reliable indicators. It has been estimated, for example, by the American Academy of Pediatrics that 18 million children under age 17 may have never seen a physician and that 21 million see a doctor less often than once a year.

There are other, more specific indications of the magnitude of the child health crisis in this country:

- The report of the 1971 White House Conference on Children and Youth notes that about 12 million children need special care for eye conditions; more than 3 million are afflicted with speech im-

---

*U.S. Senate Select Committee on Nutrition and Human Needs, committee print, *Hunger in the Classroom: Then and Now*, January 1972.

pediments; over 2 million have untreated orthopedic handicaps; and 75 percent of all children in families with annual incomes of less than $2,000 and 66 percent in families earning less than $4,000 have never seen a dentist.

- The U.S. Department of Health, Education, and Welfare in a survey in the 1960s reported that among young children, age 6–11, one out of 12 had a speech defect, one out of nine had faulty vision, and that among children, age 5–14, one in four had never seen a dentist, with poor children having an average of 3.5 decayed, untreated teeth.
- In 1968, it was estimated that 10 percent of the children enrolled in the Nation's public schools had moderate to severe emotional problems, and only 5 percent of the children needing psychiatric care received it. One of every three poor children has serious emotional problems that require treatment. As of 1970, over 2.5 million young people under the age of 20 were mentally retarded—with between 100,000–200,000 babies born mentally retarded each year.

As a report of the 1971 White House Conference on Children and Youth stated:

> These and other health needs are not being met because of inadequate preventive diagnostic and treatment services in low-income areas particularly in major cities. Children from these areas often enter school without previous medical or dental care. At this time in many outpatient departments, children are waiting 5 to 7 hours to be seen hurriedly by a physician. When health problems are discovered through school examinations community agencies often lack the resources to provide treatment and follow-up care.

### H. Migrant Children

Nearly 350,000 children, the vast majority from minority groups, belong to migrant families who depend for their living on an agricultural economy that requires them to be almost constantly mobile. Fully one-fourth of the Nation's migratory labor force in 1967 were youths between the ages of 14 and 17. The average annual farm wage of a migrant worker is $987.

Hunger and malnutrition are common among these families. Their average life span is 49 years. The death rate from pneumonia and flu for migrants is twice the national rate; the infant mortality rate is 125 percent of the national rate; and the accident rate is three times the national rate.

These children have a median educational level of 6.2 years. Seventeen percent of migrants are illiterate; 25 percent have never attended school or not gone beyond the fourth grade.

### I. Indian Children

Roughly 250,000 Indian children attend elementary and secondary schools. Over two-thirds attend local public elementary schools, with the remainder attending schools operated by the Bureau of Indian Affairs or private organizations.

The public school education received by Indian students has been subsidized to some extent by the Federal Government since the 1890s. The purpose of the legislation appeared to be twofold. First, it gave legislative authority to the policy of integrating Indians into the white culture, thus establishing the goal of assimilation with the public schools as the vehicle for attaining that goal. Second, it established the precedent of providing subsidies to public schools in order to encourage them to assume the responsibility for Indian education.

This approach, initially established by authorizing the Office of Indian Affairs to reimburse public schools for the extra expense incurred by instructing Indian children, was formalized by the enactment of the Johnson-O'Malley Act of 1934, which permitted the Bureau of Indian Affairs to contract with States to provide for the education of Indian students. Indian education was further subsidized in 1951 with the enactment of the federally impacted area legislation—Public Laws 815 and 874 of the 81st Congress. Indian children have, since 1966, also benefited from specific participation in various programs under the Elementary and Secondary Education Act.

In spite of these Federal efforts, the Indian Education Subcommittee in 1969 found Indian education to be a national tragedy. Some of its general findings include the following:

- Dropout rates are twice the national average in both public and Federal schools. Some school districts have dropout rates aproaching 100 percent.
- Achievement levels of Indian children are 2 to 3 years below those of white students.
- One-fourth of elementary and secondary school teachers—by their own admission—would prefer not to teach Indian children.
- Indian children, more than any other minority group, believe themselves to be "below average" in intelligence, even though evidence is contrary to this belief.

## J. The Nation's Disadvantaged Schoolchildren

These statistics indicate the magnitude of the health, food, family education, employment, housing and income problems of our Nation's children.

Fifty-nine million children are between the ages of 3 and 17. They are the Nation's preschool and school-age population. It is difficult to pinpoint the exact number of these children who should be classified as economically or educationally disadvantaged.

The U.S. Office of Education classifies almost 17 million children in this manner using family income, children receiving AFDC, children in institutions for the neglected or delinquent, children in foster homes, migrant children and handicapped children as the criteria.

However, for the purposes of this Report, it would appear more appropriate to use a number of different indices from recent census and other data presented above to determine the approximate number who are economically and educationally disadvantaged among the Nation's school population. Even so, it is not possible to define a clear line between "advantaged" and "disadvantaged." It might be said, for example, that 8.6 million children from families with less than $5,000 in income are "disadvantaged", while 16.5 million with family incomes of more than $10,000 are "advantaged." But income alone is not a sufficient criteria and such a demarcation would fail to account for family size.

Nor is the educational level of the child's parents alone a sufficient criterion. Certainly the majority of the 6.5 million children whose family head has less than an 8th grade education are educationally disadvantaged. So are a large proportion of another 16.7 million children whose parents attended but did not complete high school. But it is impossible to say all such children are.

Nevertheless, taking together a number of the separate indices presented in the sections of this chapter will provide an appropriate range of numbers of disadvantaged school and preschool children.

- *Minority Group Students:* 9.3 million of all children enrolled in public school are from minority groups.
- *Low Income Students:* 10.9 million school and preschool children are in families whose annual incomes are less than $5,000.
- *Parent Education Level:* 23.2 million students have parents who failed to complete high school, and 12.2 million are in families where the head has no more than 8 years of schooling.
- *Employment:* 10.5 million are school children of the unemployed and underemployed.
- *Hunger:* 8.5 million school children from low income families probably arrive at school without a nutritious breakfast; 3.8 million do not receive family food assistance they need and 1.8 million receive neither breakfast nor lunch at school.
- *Health:* Between 18 and 21 million children have seldom or never seen a doctor.
- *Housing:* About 5 million children live in substandard housing.

From these and other data we believe it is reasonable to estimate that at least 12 and perhaps as many as 20 million of the Nation's 59 million school and preschool-age children are economically or educationally disadvantaged.

# Chapter 4—The Preschool Years

Nothing is more central to the problem of unequal educational opportunity than the experiences children have—or do not have—during their early childhood years.

The opportunities and the environments that America's 21 million children under age 6 are now experiencing—and that the children who follow them will experience—are among the major determinants of their future success or failure.

## A. Studies and Reports

The influence of the early childhood environment is one of the principal messages of the massive 1966 study conducted for the Office of Education entitled *Equality of Educational Opportunity*. That study, the so-called Coleman Report, found that the home environment—including factors such as parents' education, reading material in the home, and the educational desires parents hold for their children—was the most important element in determining how well a child does in school.

That, also, is the finding of numerous studies and reports reviewed by our committee, and the conclusion shared by most witnesses who testified before us.

The recent report of the President's Commission on School Finance put it this way:

> We cannot ignore many research findings which lead us to believe that much of the lack of success of past efforts has been because we started too late in a child's life. . . .
>
> We believe that the Federal Government should encourage the development of early childhood education programs for all children and that financial assistance should be provided for children from low-income families.

The 1971 report of the Education Commission of the States called for developmental programs for children younger than age 6. It urged that they be designed for:

> Improving the inadequate day care situations to which many children in this country are now exposed . . . detecting and preventing future problems for the 10 to 15 percent of children who might be physically or mentally handicapped or have learning disabilities . . . providing help to any parent wanting to become a more effective parent.

The National Advisory Commission on Civil Disorders concluded that "the time has come to build on the proven success of Head Start and other preschool programs. . . ."

The Committee for Economic Development in March 1971, stated that "the most effective point at which to influence the cumulative process of education is in the early preschool years . . ." and "there is evidence that effective preschooling gives the best return on the educational investment." That CED report concluded: "Preschooling is desirable for all children, but it is a necessity for the disadvantaged. Without it there is little possibility of achieving equality in education."

Perhaps the most persuasive and compelling points were made by the 1970 White House Conference on Children.

In a unique weighted vote the delegates to that conference—representing parents, pediatricians, health and welfare experts, university researchers, authorities in practically every area of children's needs, and children themselves—voted as their first priority the provision of "comprehensive family-oriented child development programs including health services, day care and early childhood education."

The message of these findings holds true for all American children. It is particularly true for the 3.2 million preschool children living in poverty and many of the 5.8 million preschool children whose mothers are working.

## B. The Beginning Years of Life

The beginning years of life are critical for a child's intellectual growth, and for his social, emotional, physical and motivational development. These early years are the formative years. They are the years in which permanent foundations are laid for a child's feelings of self-worth, his sense of self-respect, his motivation, his initiative and his ability to learn and achieve.

A child's intelligence is not fixed, once and for all, at birth. We have learned that his intelligence is shaped by his experiences, and that his mental development is significantly influenced by the conditions and the environment he encounters in the first few years of life.

And children are most eager and often most able to learn during their early childhood years. As Dr. Benjamin Bloom concluded in "Stability and Change in Human Characteristics":

> As time goes on . . . more and more powerful changes are required to produce a given amount of change in a child's intelligence . . . and the emotional cost it exacts is increasingly severe . . . . To a very great extent a child's experiences at the beginning are critical determinants of his entire future life.

### 1. THE NEEDS OF POOR CHILDREN

All too often, the early experiences of America's poor children are depressing and deadening. Regardless of the love and attention these children receive from their families, many of them are growing up without adequate nutrition and health care, and without the educational activities and opportunities during their early years that are conducive to later success in school.

Recent findings by the Mississippi Medicaid Commission indicate the magnitude of unmet health needs alone. The extent of undetected and untreated health problems among the poor children examined by the commission—and their implications for child development—are staggering. The commission found 1,301 medical abnormalities in the 1,178 children it examined, including: 305 cases of multiple cavities; 97 cases of faulty vision; 217 cases of enlarged tonsils; 57 cases of hernia; 48

cases of intestinal parasites—mostly hookworm; 53 cases of poor hearing; and 32 other medical conditions requiring immediate treatment.

As a result of deficiencies such as these, many of these children are depressed, withdrawn and listless. Parents and child development specialists report that in the beginning it is difficult to get some of them to smile or show interest in anything around them. Young children in some of these homes are considered well behaved if they sit quietly in a corner during the day, instead of talking, playing and exploring. Frequent moving and the use of many different babysitters make some of the children confused, insecure and, in extreme cases, result in emotional disturbances and hyperactivity. Sometimes there are few books or magazines in these homes, no clocks or radios, and what few toys there are may have little educational value for the child.

In addition to the possible nutritional and intellectual deprivation in their early years, many poor children—Mexican Americans, Puerto Ricans, Indians, Eskimos, Portuguese, Asians and other language minorities—all too often are confronted with an alien culture and language when they enter school.

As Dr. Norman Drachler, former Superintendent of the Detroit Public Schools, testified about the experiences some of these children have: "a child who comes from a disadvantaged home brings with him to school not merely his pencils and his books, but also the burden of his environment."

### 2. ENVIRONMENTAL HANDICAP

One excellent explanation of the way this so-called "environmental handicap" can develop and influence a child's educational career was provided in testimony before the committee. Harold Howe, vice president of the Ford Foundation and former U.S. Commissioner of Education, described it this way:

> Perhaps the best way to illustrate the idea of an environmental handicap is to describe an actual situation in which working mothers typically return to work some two months after giving birth to a child. During the time that they are working, the child will be placed with another mother whose business is taking in children of working mothers, each of whom might pay a dollar a day or so to have her children cared for during working hours. In such a center will be children from several months of age up to 4 or 5 years, and an individual caretaker might look after up to 10 or 12 such children in her home.
>
> For the caretaker who had neither training nor equipment and facilities to provide a stimulating environment the entire emphasis is frequently on the passivity of children. The child who doesn't cry, who doesn't need attention, who doesn't ask questions after he has learned to speak, who doesn't move about—in other words the child who does not seek, demand, and get stimulation and is least troublesome to the person in charge—is the child who gets rewarded. Such an environment discourages the early and very significant development of every aspect of human sensitivity and potential. The qualities fortified in children so treated are the qualities which lead to failure in school. The lack of positive

stimulation from human contact, from active exploration of objects, from verbal interchange, and from the kind of play through which a child learns shapes and sizes and colors depresses and inhibits the development of capabilities which are extremely important not only for success in school but for success in life. The development of language as a most important component of any individual's growth often suffers in this sort of environmental handicapping system.

Contrast this situation with many well-financed day care or preschool arrangements staffed by trained personnel in which stimulation of all kinds is provided. Children get all sorts of attention and praise for their achievements on a regular basis from interested adults, they are encouraged to talk over their ideas and feelings, to handle objects, explore the differences of sound, shape, color, texture in all kinds of materials, to solve problems—and therewith their early intellectual development is much advanced. Further, a child is offered choices to set his own pace, and develop goals of his own—thereby giving him a sense of power over his environment.

Add to this the situation in the home for many of the kinds of families which would make use of the type of day care activity described two paragraphs above, homes in which economic handicaps deny proper nutrition and certain aspects of stimulation, even though just as much love and care may be present as in the middle class home, and you get a picture of environmental denial which pyramids in its effect on children as they mature. Indeed, the handicaps from the home are probably much more important than those growing from ill designed day care.

Children who have these environmental "handicaps" typically enter a school system which has set its task and its expectations in terms of more fortunate children. Early in such a schooling arrangement the child who comes with a handicap finds the school saying to him in no uncertain terms that he is not a success, that he doesn't measure up, that there is something wrong with him. Whether the individual teacher ever utters such words or not, the operation of the entire system effectively carries the message . . .*

President Nixon, shortly after he took office, recognized the severity of this need. In his 1969 Economic Opportunity Message to Congress, he stated:

So crucial is the matter of early growth that we must make a national commitment to providing all American children an opportunity for healthful and stimulating development during the first 5 years of life.

Later that same year, when he created the Office of Child Development in HEW to serve as the focal point for this effort, the President summarized the need many poor children have for child development and preschool education opportunities. He said:

---

*Hearings of the U.S. Senate Select Committee on Equal Educational Opportunity, Part 12—*Compensatory Education and Other Alternatives in Urban Schools*, Aug. 3, 1971.

We have learned, first of all, that the process of learning how to learn begins very, very early in the life of the infant child. . . . Children begin this process in the very earliest months of life, long before they are anywhere near a first grade class, or even kindergarten, or play school group. We have also learned that for the children of the poor, this ability to learn can begin to deteriorate very early in life, so that the youth begins school well behind his contemporaries and seemingly rarely catches up. He is handicapped as surely as a child crippled by polio is handicapped; and he bears the burden of that handicap through all his life. It is elemental that, even as in the case of polio, the effects of prevention are far better than the effects of cure.

Increasingly we know something about how this can be done. With each passing year—almost with each passing month, such is the pace of new developments in this field of knowledge—research workers in the United States and elsewhere in the world are learning more about the way in which an impoverished environment can develop a "learned helplessness" in children. When there is little stimulus for the mind, and especially when there is little interaction between parents and child, the child suffers lasting disabilities, particularly with respect to the development of a sense of control of his environment. None of this follows from the simple fact of being poor, but it is now fully established that an environment that does not stimulate learning is closely associated in the real world with poverty in its traditional forms. As much as any one thing it is this factor that leads to the transmission of poverty from one generation to the next. It is no longer possible to deny that the process is all too evidently at work in the slums of America's cities, and that is a most ominous aspect of the urban crisis.

It is just as certain that we shall have to invent new social institutions to respond to this new knowledge.

This learned helplessness doesn't have to exist. Fortunately for most children, it doesn't. Most children's early years are spent in a more secure and stimulating environment where they receive the physical and mental nourishment necessary for development. Some have the additional advantage of a private preschool experience.

### 3. EDUCATIONAL ADVANTAGES OF A PRIVILEGED ENVIRONMENT

The child from a privileged family who enters school at the age of 6 often has behind him a full and complex learning history.

The variety of skills this well-endowed 6-year-old brings to school with him are impressive. Yet the child was born with none of these specific abilities. He has learned them all from interactions with his environment. In short, his "cognitive development" is already well advanced. He also, as a rule, has had his medical and dental needs attended to. And, he has never truly been hungry or undernourished.

Some economists have tried to explain and measure the educational value of a privileged environment. They have tried to measure the degree to which a child's home provides him with experiences and skills which help him at school. This measure—which yields a rough estimate of what might be called "the value of the middle class environment"—is not perfect. It makes a number of assumptions which do not always hold true.

For example, indifferent parents can damage a child no matter how wealthy or well educated they may be. Conversely, some of the most poverty stricken or undereducated parents are able to provide their children with the emotional security and support necessary to succeed in school and in life.

In general, however, all other things being equal, these economists concluded that wealthier and better educated parents have privileges and advantages that often permit them to better prepare their children for school than do impoverished and deprived parents. Dennis Dugan, a Notre Dame economist, has made some tentative analyses in this area. He has measured the amount of time a mother spends with her child in activities which have educational benefit; and, he has assigned a value to the time she spends with her child which reflects the money she could have earned if she had spent that time in regular employment.

Dr. Dugan assumed that a better educated mother can generally command a higher salary than an undereducated mother. He further assumed that the more educated mother is presumably better equipped to impart school-related experiences and skills to her child. He therefore placed a higher value on her time.

His estimates suggest that by the first grade level:

- A child whose mother had had less than an 8th grade education has only about $2,700 "embodied" in him.
- In contrast, a child whose mother had 5 or more years of college has $9,300 "embodied" in him.

And this discrepancy grows as the child progresses through school, since Dugan further finds that the more educated woman is able to continue devoting more time to her children, and her time continues to be valued more highly.

In addition, this analysis does not even reflect the fact that wealthier parents actually spend more for their children's education and educational-related activities than poor parents, and, that their children normally attend schools benefiting from higher per-pupil expenditures than do the children of the poor.

These calculations suggest that the added educational value brought to the preschool years by a middle-class environment as opposed to an impoverished environment could be as high as $6,000 to $7,000. Clearly, they are not complete enough to say that with any certainty. But, they do reflect—at least in a rough financial sense—some of the educational advantages available to children who grow up in a privileged environment. And—if they are multiplied by the 3.2 million preschool children living in poverty—they suggest that poor children, as a group, enter school with approximately $20 billion less invested, or embodied, in their educational development than they might have had if they had been born to a middle-class environment.

And these dollar differences which Dr. Dugan found are accurate and useful predictors of skills students eventually achieve.

But most poor children—and many children of working parents who have spent their preschool years in custodial day-care conditions—arrive at school without these general advantages and assets.

Many have not received sufficient nutrition, health care and intellectual stimulation. Many have not received the educational benefits of a "middle-class environment," whatever that is worth. As Dr. Julius Richmond observed, "approximately one-third of our children are being raised in environments that virtually insure failure in society's major institutions for all children—schools."

Our committee's findings sadly support that conclusion.

According to studies presented by Dr. Alexander Plante and Mrs. Gertrude Johnson of the Connecticut State Department of Education, a review of the Hartford, Conn. public education system reveals the inability of many ghetto schools to prevent this cumulative deficit from growing. Their testimony shows that the average IQ of fourth graders in the Hartford ghetto schools was 94 in 1965. Two years later—when that class was in the sixth grade—its average IQ had dropped to 88. In another 2 years, in the eighth grade, it was 86—only 6 points above the IQ level at which children become candidates for institutionalization in Connecticut facilities for the retarded.

Similarly third graders in Washington, D.C., test 4 months behind students in 11 other big cities. By the ninth grade they are 1.6 years behind other big city students; and, even further behind—some 2.2 years behind—the national average.

In short, damage is done in the crucial early years, and often our educational institutions are unable to repair it in later life. The cycle of need rolls on.

### C. Day Care Needs

In addition to the children of the poor, there are over 5 million preschool children whose mothers are working. Some of these children are receiving healthful and stimulating care while their parents work. But many are not. Many are left in purely custodial and unlicensed day-care centers, and others—the so-called "latchkey" children—are left alone to look after themselves. And their numbers are growing dramatically:

- In 1971, 43 percent of the Nation's mothers worked outside the home, compared to only 18 percent in 1948.
- One out of every three mothers with preschool children is working today, compared to one out of eight in 1948.
- In 1971, 1.3 million mothers of children under 6 were bringing up children without a husband, and half of these mothers worked.
- Yet, there are fewer than 700,000 spaces in licensed day-care centers to serve the over 5 million preschool children whose mothers work.

And although some existing Federal programs, such as Title IV of the Social Security Act, help provide day care for these children, much of it is inadequate. Dr. Edward Zigler, former Director of HEW's Office of Child Development, has estimated that only about 20 percent of these day-care programs are developmental, or comprehensive, and stated that in "many instances we are paying for service that is harmful to children."

Dr. Zigler's assessment is supported by a recent Office of Economic Opportunity report, "Day Care: Resources for Decisions," which concluded:

> Over 90 percent of all full-day centers in the United States are privately operated for profit . . . Most are custodial programs because that's all most working mothers can afford . . . Day care in America is a scattered phenomena; largely private, cursorily supervised, growing and shrinking in response to national adult crises, largely unrelated to children's needs . . .

### D. Successful Preschool Education Programs

Many of these early inequities can be prevented. That is the lesson of our best preschool education programs, including Head Start and their necessary counterparts like Follow Through.

Promising results have been produced in a wide variety of quality preschool education efforts ranging from programs involving regularly scheduled home visits by trained persons who work with both the child and his parents to the more familiar part-day or full-day programs located in centers. For example:

- The Infant Research Project in Washington, D.C., directed by Dr. Earl Schaefer, sent tutors into the home 1 hour each weekday to work with mothers and their young children during the period from ages 16 months to 3 years. During the 1½ years this program provided services, the children being tutored maintained an average IQ of 105, while a control group of comparable ghetto youngsters in that neighborhood who did not receive tutoring experienced an average IQ decline of 19 points. After services were terminated at age 3, the gap between those who had received tutoring and those who had not, decreased over time. But a full 3 years after all services had ended, those who had received help at those early ages still registered an average advantage of 7 IQ points compared to those who had received no early assistance.
- A program directed by Merle Karnes at the University of Illinois provided a weekly course in child development to disadvantaged mothers over a 15-month period which began when their children were between the ages of 1 and 2 years old. In these classes the mothers were provided with educational toys designed to create opportunities for verbal interaction between themselves and their infants, and trained in teaching techniques. At the end of the program the children whose mothers participated had an average IQ of 106, 16 points higher than the average of a comparable group of youngsters whose mothers had not participated in this program.
- The Verbal Interpretation Project in Nassau County, N.Y., directed by Phyllis Levenstein, sent trained workers on semiweekly half-hour visits to the homes of disadvantaged youngsters with kits of toys and books designed to stimulate interaction between mother and child. The children participating registered initial average gains of 15 to 20 IQ points; and, 3 years after the program had ended still maintained this 15–20 point advantage over comparable children who had not participated in this program.

- The preschool program conducted in the Englewood School District in San Antonio, Texas, described by Dr. Cardenas in his testimony before our Committee, serving predominately Spanish-speaking preschool children, underscored the importance of providing preschool education to children at early ages. Three-year-olds participating for the first time in a preschool program made greater gains than 4- or 5-year-olds participating for the first time in the same program.
- And the Syracuse Day Care Project directed by Dr. Julius Richmond and Dr. Bettye Caldwell produced average IQ gains of 17 points among impoverished 1- to 4-year olds who had been in the program for 2 years.

### E. Continuity and Parental Involvement Essential

These early childhood programs and others like them hold tremendous promise for reducing some of the barriers that now exist to equal educational opportunity.

They have revealed the exciting IQ gains that disadvantaged youngsters can score, and the IQ losses they can avoid, if support and assistance is provided to them and their parents during the early years of life. They have reported very encouraging improvements in equally important but harder to measure areas such as the confidence, motivation, cooperation and self-respect of the youngsters served. And, in many cases, they have provided essential medical and nutritional services which have detected and treated literally thousands of physical defects and handicaps.

These encouraging findings are one of the central messages in the seven longitudinal studies of preschool education recently released by the Office of Child Development. In every case, these seven preschool programs had an immediate and positive impact on the child's performance, as measured by IQ gains, cognitive and language tests and teacher's observations regarding motivation and social competence. And in some cases, these longitudinal studies revealed how the effects of quality preschool programs on the intellectual performance of disadvantaged children can last into primary school age, even when no further enrichment is provided in school.

These studies support the conclusion that many Americans have been operating on for years. As Dr. James W. Guthrie stated in his testimony before the committee:

> For the person who has any doubt about the advantages of early childhood education, I think he only has to observe the behavior of middle- and upper-class parents who can afford this kind of schooling for their children. They seek it wherever possible . . .

Perhaps most importantly, these longitudinal studies reveal that early childhood services are not an innoculation that lasts for life. There are no magic periods in childhood. And programs that operate on any other assumption are running a high risk of producing encouraging gains that will be largely washed out after the program ends. Child development is continuous, and enrichment in the preschool years must be followed by stimulating education during the school years or else much of the earlier improvements will be lost.

An equally important finding from this longitudinal research concerns the importance of deep and meaningful parent involvement in preschool efforts. Of all the programs reviewed, the most promising were those that used the parent as the primary teacher or tutor. These home-based programs were extremely successful not only in producing IQ gains, but also in maintaining them over a period of time. While there are clearly situations in which these programs are not possible—such as cases in which both parents have to work—the findings underscore the importance of assuring that early childhood programs are designed to supplement and support the strengths of the family, not replace or weaken them.

In short, these longitudinal studies reveal that we now have even more reason to believe that good, early childhood programs can significantly enhance the development of a child in later years. They underscore the fact that neglect, hunger, inadequate health care and lack of educational opportunities during the first 5 years of life can cripple a child's development for life or at least make it exceedingly difficult and expensive to restore and recover what has been lost. Also, they show how quality preschool efforts, providing maximum support for and responsibilities to parents, can prevent much of this destruction from occurring. But they do not reveal—and this fact cannot be overemphasized—that quality preschool programs alone will guarantee that children will reach their full potential.

The implications of all this research are quite clear:

- A child's chance for an equal educational opportunity begins long before he enters school.
- The home environment—or the day-care environment—in which a preschool child spends his time can have a major impact on his future educational career.
- Quality preschool programs for children and parents can help eliminate or reduce the deficit normally produced by poverty or custodial day care.
- Deep and meaningful parent involvement is essential for the success of early childhood efforts.
- And, there must be a continuity between the early childhood programs and subsequent educational endeavors in the elementary schools to sustain the gains they make.

## F. Recommendations

The committee recommends, therefore, the creation of voluntary comprehensive, well-financed child development programs for families and children that:

- Strengthen family life and family capabilities.
- Assure adequate health, nutritional and educational opportunities in the early childhood years.
- Provide home-based programs drawing on the talents and resources of parents as the primary educational influence on their children.

- Upgrade day-care programs into truly developmental and educationally stimulating experiences rather than purely custodial and sometimes damaging parking lots for children.
- Involve parents and other family members in all aspects of those programs including staffing, decision making, and training.
- Provide expanded opportunities for staff training and research.
- Offer maximum flexibility, within the national standards of excellence, for local groups to adopt programs consistent with their needs.
- Promote social and economic diversity—rather than a track system—for the preschool years.
- Involve follow-through programs and other improvements in the elementary schools to provide the essential continuity between early enrichment and later educational programs.

It should be noted that the 92d Congress has already considered legislation* along these lines. The committee hopes that full consideration leading to enactment of our recommendations will be undertaken early in the 93d Congress.

These recommendations will require a substantial investment of funds. They will require commitment and effort. But they are necessary.

The Coleman Report, as well as any other, reminds us of the consequences of ignoring the home environment and the preschool years. It concluded:

> Taking all these results together, one implication stands out above all: That schools bring little influence to bear on a child's achievement that is independent of his background and general social context; and that this very lack of an independent effect means that the inequalities imposed on children by their home, neighborhood and peer environment are carried along to become the inequalities with which they confront adult life at the end of school.

If our country is really serious about making equal educational opportunity a reality, the committee finds it is essential to make available, to families that request them, preschool services of the highest quality. We recommend that we begin immediately to make these opportunities and services available and give substance to what President Nixon so correctly identified as "a national commitment to providing all American children an opportunity for healthful and stimulating development during the first 5 years of life."

---

*S. 3617, "The Comprehensive Head Start, Child Development, and Family Services Act of 1972," which passed the Senate during the 2d Sess., 92d Cong.

# Chapter 5—Children's Television

## A. The Effects of Television on Young Children

Television is a major influence on the development of children. The average American school-age child watches between 22 and 25 hours of television each week. By the time he is 16, he is likely to have watched between 15,000 and 20,000 hours of television, while at the same age he has spent only 10,000 hours in school.

Television ownership is nearly universal. Ninety-seven percent of American families own television sets. Studies have shown that 90 percent of families with yearly incomes of less than $5,000 have television sets. The Surgeon General's Scientific Advisory Committee on Television and Social Behavior found that "virtually all children in the United States have television sets in their homes."

In recent years, concern over the nature of the influence of television on children has intensified. First came a concern with the amount of violence on the screen, a concern that the pervasiveness of shows exhibiting violence would produce a generation more likely to turn to it as a way of solving their problems.

This concern about program content also led to a realization that television might become a positive force in the life of a child. Perhaps many of those hours spent in front of the TV set might help him to learn to read or count and expose him to new ideas and people.

Representatives of minority groups have pointed out that the America reflected in television shows excluded large segments of our society. Until very recently, blacks, Puerto Ricans, Spanish-surnamed, orientals, and American Indians rarely appeared on television except as caricatures or objects of ridicule—the forever-losing Indians on cowboy shows, or the prattling, sombrero-topped Mexican peddling corn chips or sleeping under a big tree.

Minority groups began to charge that television had become another instrument for oppressing minorities. As Dr. Chester Pierce, a professor of psychiatry at Harvard, told the committee, "Racism is both contagious and lethal. Thus, even in its entertainment posture, television must be careful not to aggravate a lethal, contagious public health illness."*

There is no doubt that children absorb what they see on the television screen. Tiny youngsters are adept at repeating advertising jingles and mimicking the antics of their favorite character actors and cartoon personalities. What they see and learn may create lasting impressions. The minority-group child, for example, seeing things and experiencing events that have no place in his reality, begins to

---

*Hearings of the U.S. Senate Select Committee on Equal Educational Opportunity, Part 2—*Equality of Educational Opportunity—an Introduction*, July 30, 1970.

look at television as that "other world"—a world in which he may never participate.

Television should become a strong force for promoting racial understanding and cultural diversity in the United States. Many American children between 3 and 5 years of age watch as much as 40 hours of television weekly since they are not yet regularly attending school. School psychologists have shown that the development of racial prejudice takes place in the absence of factual knowledge about other races. Television can be the means for providing such knowledge at these critical preschool ages.

Out of these concerns—the revulsion against violence and against the unfair portrayal of minority groups—and the belief that television can be both entertaining and a constructive force for learning—came "Sesame Street," an educational program aired at 3- to 5-year olds.

## B. Sesame Street

The creator of "Sesame Street," the Children's Television Workshop (CTW), decided to concentrate its efforts on a program that would attract children too young to be in school during the day—particularly disadvantaged children whom it hoped would benefit later in school from the headstart they might receive from a television program with educational content.

Preschoolers, CTW had found, make almost a full-time job of television viewing, watching an average of 8 hours a day. To compete with commercial television, CTW decided "Sesame Street" would have to make use of some of the animated cartoon and filmmaking techniques children were accustomed to seeing on other shows.

The curriculum of "Sesame Street" was structured to teach the naming of letters, recitation of numbers, the names of parts of the body, animals and machines; and other basic knowledge and skills.

But another major consideration in developing the program was the presentation of a television world that was both appealing and meaningful to minority and disadvantaged youngsters. As Joan Ganz Cooney, president of CTW, testified:

> Most black and other minority group children today are growing up seeing too few of their own people too seldom on television. It is bound to have an effect on them, on their perception of themselves and of the world around them; and this effect is not good for these children or for the society they will soon enter.*

After its first year CTW decided that to test the success of "Sesame Street" in teaching both academic skills and social attitudes to preschoolers, a systematic comprehensive evaluation would be required. As Mrs. Cooney stated:

> The major strategy was not merely to discover whether viewers learned more than nonviewers . . . The evaluation was also directed toward discovering which groups of children seem to benefit from viewing the show, what characterizes those who learn a great deal, how children react to

---

**Ibid.*

various techniques used in the show, and whether the children's reactions seem to be related to their learning.*

The completed evaluation conducted by the Educational Testing Service includes data on the impact of "Sesame Street" on 943 children, from both disadvantaged and advantaged backgrounds and from rural and inner city neighborhoods. The great majority of these children, 731, were considered to be "disadvantaged."

The single most important conclusion of the study was that the more a child watched "Sesame Street," the more he learned. This applied to all children studied—black, white, Spanish-speaking, rich and poor. Moreover, of those children who watched the show most often (an average of more than five times per week), disadvantaged children made larger achievement gains than advantaged children. Thus, there is some evidence that the program can help to close the gaps between advantaged and disadvantaged children.

The results of "Sesame Street" clearly offer hope for disadvantaged and minority children who might otherwise fall behind early in school.

In our judgment the "Sesame Street" experience is a hopeful example of how television can further educational opportunity. But "Sesame Street" not only teaches letters and numbers—it is the only shared educational experience of many white, black, and other minority group preschool children in America.

The effect of "Sesame Street" on the social attitudes of its viewers was not as systematically or conclusively studied as academic achievement. Mrs. Cooney told the committee that the "Sesame Street" researchers suspect that positive changes in social attitudes are occurring. Moreover, many comments received by CTW from viewers confirmed this. The changes in social attitudes resulting from viewing the program are currently being studied in the analysis of the second year of "Sesame Street."

We must acknowledge a body of opinion among educators holding that the methods of knowledge and skills transmission employed by "Sesame Street" do not necessarily best serve the intellectual development of its viewers. While we reached no judgment in relation to the validity of this body of opinion, we believe that "Sesame Street" has provided a dramatic breakthrough for the acceptance of "entertainment television" as a significant educational medium; it represents an important starting point rather than an unqualified successful conclusion in attempts by educators to harness the great educational potential of television.

## C. Continuing Problems

The findings of the "Sesame Street" study suggest that television has great potential as a tool for providing equal educational opportunity to all American children.

Television is pervasive, particularly in the homes of disadvantaged and minority families. In the Bedford-Stuyvesant area of New York City, for example, 90 percent of the families with less than $5,000 income have television sets and close to two-thirds have two sets. Ninety percent of the children between the ages of 3 and 5 in this area watched "Sesame Street," 60 percent four or more times a week.

*Ibid.

Clearly, television's potential for education in the home and in the school is virtually limitless. But the "Sesame Street" experience also points up the many problems to be solved before television can live up to its potential for promoting equal educational opportunity.

There is no evidence to show whether the early gains of disadvantaged youngsters who watch "Sesame Street" can be maintained, particularly if the children attend inferior inner city schools lacking in adequate facilities and staff.

"Sesame Street" is intended to reach only 3- to 5-year olds and there is no comparable study of the potential of television for older children.

The Children's Television Workshop program for older children, "The Electric Company"—which emphasizes the teaching of reading—has gone on the air this year. But during the 1971–72 television season—according to a study for the National Citizens Committee for Broadcasting—there was not a single weekday afternoon network children's program on commercial television.

The heavy emphasis on violence on children's television must also be noted. The Surgeon General's Scientific Advisory Committee on Television and Social Behavior* reported that children are exposed to a constant stream of violence throughout the day. Other surveys show the number of deaths that occur on the screen. For example, a *Christian Science Monitor* survey last year reported 125 killings in 74 hours of prime-time programs. An article, "TV and the Child: What Can Be Done" reported that "by the age of 14 the average child has seen 18,000 murders" on television.

Clearly, there is a need for a change in the way our Nation uses television. We must increase the number of positive programs like "Sesame Street," not only on public television, but on commercial television as well.

### D. Minority Employment

A small percentage of jobs in the television industry is held by members of minority groups. Mrs. Cooney described "Sesame Street" as having "probably the most thoroughly integrated behind-the-cameras team in the industry." But she added that the program "has problems recruiting adequately trained and experienced men and women from minority groups because of their systematic exclusion from so much of the American mainstream for so long."**

Until more members of minority groups are recruited, trained and hired by the industry, it is not to be expected that programing will be, as Mrs. Cooney put it, "useful or relevant" to all Americans. Even though public television has had a better minority employment record than commercial television, according to the Minority Affairs Office of the National Association of Educational Broadcasters, only 8 percent of the employees of public television stations were black, Spanish-surnamed, Oriental Americans or American Indian.

---

**Television and Growing Up: The Impact of Televised Violence*, report to the Surgeon General, U.S. Public Health Service, December 1971.

**Hearings of the U.S. Senate Select Committee on Equal Educational Opportunity, Part 2—*Equality of Educational Opportunity—An Introduction*, July 30, 1970.

## E. Recommendations

The committee received testimony from a number of experts and concerned citizens advocating a concerted effort to develop the potential of television.

Dr. James A. Perkins of the International Council for Educational Development stated that television could help "provide quality integrated education. . . . It can help to reinforce the child's positive experience with integration. . . . It can make children feel that an environment in which people of all races interact in positive ways is natural and pleasant." Dr. Perkins also suggested that television can provide learning experiences that avoid the underachiever's feelings of inferiority that can occur in other types of compensatory learning programs.

As Thomas P. F. Hoving, chairman of the National Citizens Committee for Broadcasting, stated to the Senate Education Subcommittee:

> If integration is ever to work, our children, during their crucial preschool years, must be exposed in a positive manner to the lifestyles and backgrounds of the various racial and ethnic groups that form American society. For most American families no such exposure is possible without the help of television.

The committee agrees with the observations of the Educational Testing Service in its evaluation of "Sesame Street":

> In general, Sesame Street achieved its goals. They were important goals. Since this experimental television program for preschoolers was so successful, it would be a travesty of responsible educational policymaking were not more, similarly conceived television programs funded, developed, researched, and presented.

We note with approval the fact that the Congress has recently authorized an appropriation of $60 million in fiscal years 1973 and 1974 to support the production and development of integrated children's educational television programs. This sum was included in the Emergency School Aid Act enacted by Congress on June 8, 1972. Under the provisions of that Act, the Commissioner of Education is authorized to fund up to 10 public or private nonprofit organizations which have the capability of providing expertise in the development of television programing and to pay the cost of development and production of integrated educational programs for children which are of both cognitive and effective educational value. Programs funded are expected to teach concrete academic skills, encourage interracial understanding and promote cultural diversity.

Recipients must also employ minority group persons in responsible positions and establish effective means for evaluating gains in cognitive and affective skills achieved by the children viewing the programs.

The Act also requires that programs developed be made available for transmission without charge to any commercial or public television station, school or other organization wishing to transmit the program.

Organizations receiving such funds are expected to develop additional programs for preschool and older children.

In this connection, we believe it would be wise to direct a number of these new programs to specific geographical areas such as the Southwestern and Northeastern portions of the United States with their large concentrations of Spanish-speaking American children.

We endorse this provision of the Emergency School Aid Act. The authorization for this program will terminate in June 1974. By that time, there should be ample opportunity to review the results of these new educational programs for children. If "Sesame Street" is any indication, and if these programs are developed and implemented as intended by the Congress—with sensitivity to the needs and desires of minority groups—we believe they will be successful.

We hope that at the end of 2 years the Congress will then be in a position to establish a further authorization for the continuing development of quality, integrated children's educational television programs.

Finally, we believe greater efforts should be made to encourage the development of educational programs for children under commercial sponsorship. Commercial as well as public television can become an effective means for providing equal educational opportunity for all children.

# Part III

# Inequality in Education

## Chapter 6—The Education of Minority Group and Disadvantaged Children

**The community has not wanted for all its children what the best parent wants for his own child. As a result, the public schools are failing dismally in what has always been regarded as one of their primary tasks—in Horace Mann's phrase, to be "the great equalizer of the conditions of men," facilitating the movement of the poor and disadvantaged into the mainstream of American economic and social life. Far from being "the great equalizer," the schools help perpetuate the differences in conditions, or at the very least, do little to reduce them. If the United States is to become a truly just and humane society, the schools will have to do an incomparably better job than they are now doing of educating youngsters from minority-group and lower-class homes.**

***—Charles E. Silberman***

Education is this Nation's largest enterprise. It involves, full time, nearly a third of our citizens and annual public expenditures exceeded only by those for national defense.

In 1970 more than 59 million persons were enrolled full or part time in public and private preschools, elementary and secondary schools, colleges and universities in the Nation. Seven and one-half percent of our work force, more than 6 million people, were employed in education.

Below college level in the school year 1970–71, 51.8 million students in public preschools and public and private elementary and secondary schools were taught by 2.3 million classroom teachers at an annual expenditure of about $50 billion. Those who taught and learned in public school attended 90,821 schools located in 17,995 separate school districts.

As a society, we are more deeply committed to the task of educating our children than to any other. Formal education is one of the most important determinants of the lifetime opportunities of each of our citizens. For most Americans and through most of our history, education has been a remarkable success.

At the beginning of our history, schooling was a commodity available only to the privileged and wealthy. In the early 19th century, we embarked upon what was then termed a "Great Experiment" in mass education—universal, free, public schooling for every child. It is not an exaggeration to state that the success of our educational system has been largely responsible for our development into the most economically productive society in the world. By historical and traditional standards, our illiteracy rate is almost infinitesimal. As a people, we read more than most others. We have produced our share of the world's artists, musicians, scientists, philosophers and statesmen.

Just in terms of growth our public school system has made phenomenal strides. In 1920, only 20 percent of the Nation's 17-year-olds attended public schools. Today nearly 80 percent of 17-year-olds are in school. In most modern European countries, between 25 and 35 percent in this age bracket attend school. In France, only one in 10, for example, is able to advance beyond the equivalent of a grade school education. In September 1971, the Office of Education calculated that 1971–72 enrollment in public and private institutions would increase for the 27th consecutive year to a record 60.2 million—nearly a third of the entire population.

The rate of educational attainment of our people has kept pace with the requirements of a growing, increasingly sophisticated and complex society. 2.7 million students will graduate from high school this year—a million more than in 1961. More significantly, while the secondary school enrollment increased 43 percent in 1961–71, the number of high school graduates increased 62 percent. For example, nationwide, students who entered the 5th grade in 1942–43, only half completed high school in 1950 and one-fifth went on to college. But 75.2 percent of entering 5th graders in 1962 completed high school in 1970 and 46 percent went on to college. In the past decade, the proportion of young adults, age 20–29, who completed at least a high school education increased from 65 to 82 percent for whites and from 40 to 62 percent for blacks and other minorities.

School retention rates have increased dramatically in the last decade as Figure 6–1 demonstrates.

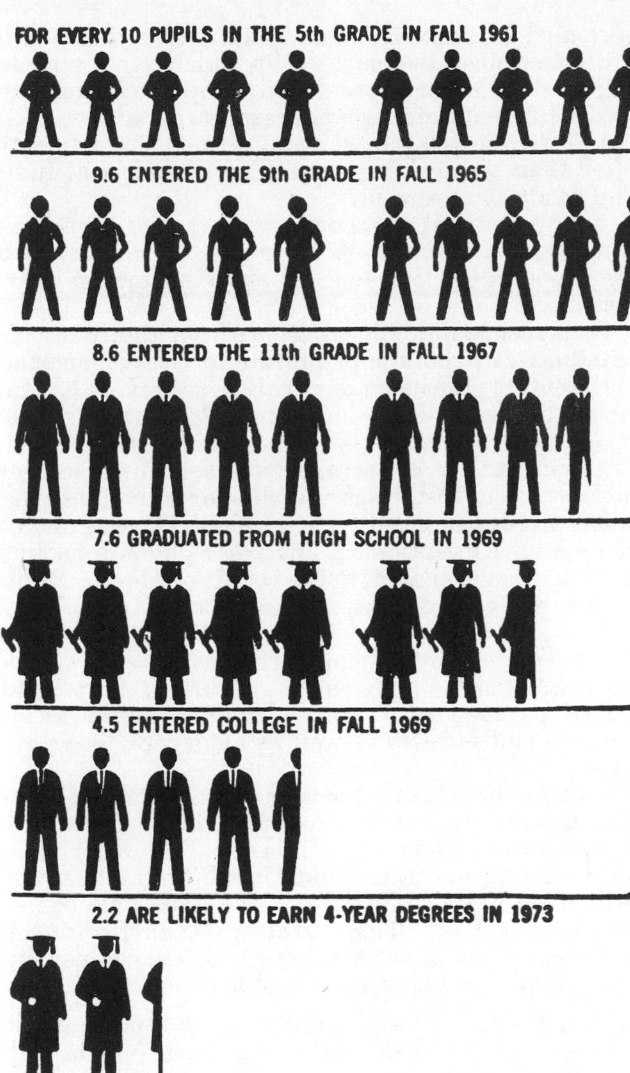
FOR EVERY 10 PUPILS IN THE 5th GRADE IN FALL 1961
9.6 ENTERED THE 9th GRADE IN FALL 1965
8.6 ENTERED THE 11th GRADE IN FALL 1967
7.6 GRADUATED FROM HIGH SCHOOL IN 1969
4.5 ENTERED COLLEGE IN FALL 1969
2.2 ARE LIKELY TO EARN 4-YEAR DEGREES IN 1973
SOURCE: U.S. Department of Health, Education, and Welfare, Office of Education, *Digest of Educational Statistics*, table 10.

FIGURE 6–1. Estimated retention rates, fifth grade through college graduation: United States, 1961 to 1973

Not only are a greater proportion of our youth completing more years of school and college; but, also, they are acquiring more knowledge about more things. A 1969 report by the Department of Health, Education, and Welfare, for example, found that schoolchildren in the lower grades learned more in the 1960s than their older brothers and sisters learned in the 1950s.

The report used findings of an Educational Testing Service study which recently assembled 186 instances in which comparable tests were given to large and roughly representative samples of elementary school students at two different times over the last two decades.

In all but 10 of the 186 paired comparisons, the later group performed better than the earlier group. The comparisons indicated an improvement of about 20 percent.

In short, what is learned in school has kept pace with the needs of an expanding society. Our schools have met the challenges of an industrial revolution in the 19th century and a technological revolution in the 20th century.

In these terms then, public education has been highly successful. But schooling in America, from the beginning of the "common school" in the early 19th century, has had a dual role in society. It has functioned as the principal means by which individuals learn the traditional communicative and other cognitive skills, acquire knowledge and develop and mature intellectually. At the same time, schooling has been viewed throughout most of our history as a device for providing equal opportunities among groups of children from diverse backgrounds. In the 19th century—at the inception of universal public schooling in this country—education was viewed, in the words of Horace Mann, as "the great equalizer of the conditions of men—the balance wheel of social machinery."

This did not mean equality among individuals. For it was recognized that among individuals, differences in abilities, efforts, and choices would produce a variety of outcomes in an industrial society which requires laborers and farmers as well as managers, lawyers, teachers, and scientists.

Thus, it has been the role of schools as "equalizers" to assure not that ours is a classless society, but as Professor Henry Levin of Stanford stated in a report to this committee, it has been education's role to:

> . . . assure that representative individuals born into any social class would have opportunity to achieve status as persons born into other social classes. That is, the opportunities for achieving life success for a son would not be determined by his father's achievements, but only by his own.*

It is in this sense that schools relate to equal opportunity in society. It is in this role that public education has often failed. And it is the failure to meet this test of equal educational opportunity that underlies much of the growing dissatisfaction with public education today. As we have pointed out earlier in this report, the responsibility for this failure does not fall on the shoulders of our public school systems alone. Yet schools play a major role in the development of every generation of Americans.

The fact is that—today, and throughout our history—where a person is born, the color of his skin, his language, national origin, cultural background, and his parents' social and economic status are the principal determinants of where he lives and of the quality of his education. The fact is that our public school system is too often failing the child

---

******The Costs to the Nation of Inadequate Education*, **Henry M. Levin, U.S. Senate Select Committee on Equal Educational Opportunity, committee print, February 1972.**

who is not born white, or who is born to a family whose first language is not English, or who is simply poor.

The child from an affluent family begins life with many advantages. His home environment, health care, nutrition, material possessions, and the educational and social status of his parents give him a head start in life and in school. He usually goes to school with children from similar backgrounds, with the same headstart, from the same community. His school is often modern, it has the most up-to-date facilities, instructional materials and techniques. He is usually taught by well-trained, well-motivated teachers who believe he can learn. He usually performs well in school and probably will go to college and often attends graduate school.

The typical child from a deprived home usually travels an entirely different road. His parents are poor. His father may be unemployed or underemployed. There are often few educational toys, books or other materials in his home. His only contact with a doctor may be in the emergency room of a general hospital. He usually enters school behind in ability to communicate and is often unable to relate to a world outside his home environment. Typically he fails to respond adequately in school. Most of his classmates are from similarly disadvantaged homes. And if he is black and poor, most of his classmates are black and poor. If he is of Spanish or Portuguese or Oriental or American Indian heritage he may speak only his native tongue at home. Yet he is usually expected to be proficient in English at school. His school is often old, drab, rundown, without proper facilities or equipment. He is often taught by less qualified or less experienced teachers who sometimes view him and his classmates as failures. Even if he is lucky enough to go to a better school with advantaged youngsters, he may be placed or "tracked" in a class for slow learners. He may well drop out of school before the 12th grade. But even if he graduates, he is often years behind his more affluent peers in academic achievement and is far less likely to continue his education. Because he is ill-equipped educationally and emotionally to compete in the American economy, he may live a life of deprivation and failure, in a cycle of poverty which is perpetuated from one generation to the next.

Simply stated, it is this contrast—between the advantaged child who receives the best education our public schools can offer, and the disadvantaged child who is often relegated to a second-class education—that best describes educational inequality in our public schools.

Just as inequality in education and other inequalities in our society are related, there are three interrelated ways in which schools produce unequal results:

*First*, minority group and disadvantaged children and their families are predominantly isolated from the rest of society both by where they live and the schools they attend. Education in this country is still, far too often, separated by race, ethnic origin, and social class.

*Second*, educational and other practices within schools often initiate or increase inequalities among groups of students. These practices include the ways in which the child and his teacher relate to each other; the assignment, or tracking of students; the curriculum to which the child is exposed; and, finally the ways in which his performance is evaluated.

*Third*, the schools attended by minority group and poor children are often those with the least in resources. The facilities and services in our public schools are often distributed in inverse relation to need. The ways in which most of the tax dollars for education are raised and spent tend to provide that the best education resources are available in the wealthiest communities and the worst in the poorest communities.

These three factors, isolation in school and in impoverished homes and neighborhoods, unequal school practices, and inequality in educational resources, combine to produce inequality in American public education. They are closely related. Together they produce poor school performance, high dropout rates and low educational attainment.

# Chapter 7—Isolation in the United States

## A. The Extent of Student Isolation

Counting the number of minority and nonminority-group children in our Nation's schools has become the principal measure of progress in school desegregation in recent years. The Department of Health, Education, and Welfare now conducts a yearly survey of elementary and secondary school districts in all States except Hawaii. The survey provides seven different measures of minority and nonminority-group school isolation and includes all but the smallest school districts. The numbers of black, Spanish-surnamed, Oriental Americans, American Indian and nonminority students are provided for each school and school district. The results are published showing the number and percentage of each group of students in schools in which minority groups comprise 0–49.9, 50–100, 80–100, 90–100, 95–100, 99–100 percentage of the student body respectively.

These statistics provide useful measurements of year-to-year progress in reducing minority group isolation in States and regions, and by size or other characteristic of a given school district. But such measurements imply that some fixed proportion of minority to nonminority-group students defines the schools in a geographic area as "segregated" or "desegregated." Clearly, a 100 percent black school in a majority white school district is segregated in fact, if not in law. Or conversely, a 100 percent white school in a majority black district is a segregated school. Certainly also, a school that is "racially balanced" so that the percentage of each group of students is precisely the same as the percentage of each group in a given school district is "desegregated." Even if "racial balance" was the legal test of a desegregrated school or adopted as a matter of public policy—which it is not—it would be impossible to devise a universally applicable measurement of desegregation because the proportion of minority and nonminority-group students in the schools of each district would necessarily depend upon the proportion in the district as a whole.

In any case, the law neither imposes racial balance as the criterion for the dismantling of a dual school system nor defines a segregated school as one which is in some fixed disproportion to such balance. It requires simply that schools not be identifiable racially as a result of official action as schools for a particular group of children. That is a test which is simply not mathematical; and, the results of this have produced different proportions of minority to nonminority-group children in different schools within a district, as well as among school districts within a State or region.

Under these circumstances, the Elementary and Secondary School Survey is, at best, an inadequate measure of school segregation and desegregation and, at worst, a misleading indicator of legal compliance. When used to measure legal compliance it fosters the public misconception that the law requires racial balance. It should not be used—as it is at present—as a measure of desegregation enforcement results.

The survey nevertheless does provide useful information on the extent to which minority and nonminority-group children attend the same or separate schools. It does measure school isolation which may be the result, alone or in combination, of official governmental actions, private decisions; or, in some school districts, compliance with court-ordered or Title VI desegregation plans. For this purpose the survey does provide valid indices of one facet of educational inequality—in the vast majority of minority-group dominated schools, racial and ethnic isolation is usually synonymous with socioeconomic isolation, and often second-class educational services. The result is low educational attainment and achievement and a perpetuation of the preschool and postschool cycle of poverty and disadvantage.

### 1. MINORITY-GROUP ISOLATION NATIONALLY AND BY STATE AND REGION

Significant progress has been made in reducing minority-group isolation in school districts in the 11 Southern States in the past several years. Nationally, however, in 1970—of a total of 9.3 million minority-group students—5.9 million, or more than 60 percent, attended predominantly minority-group schools. At the same time, 72 percent of the Nation's nonminority-group students attended more than 90 percent nonminority schools.

Four million minority-group students are in schools which are 80 percent or more minority and 2 million are in schools which are 99–100 percent minority. The following table indicates the percentages of each minority group in the Nation's schools at increasing levels of isolation.

TABLE 7–1.—*Percent of minority-group students attending public school at increasing levels of isolation in the continental United States (Fall 1970)*[1]

| Percent minority schools | All minorities | Black | Spanish-surnamed | Oriental | American Indian |
|---|---|---|---|---|---|
| 50 to 100 | 62. 6 | [1] 66. 9 | 55. 8 | 29. 4 | 33. 5 |
| 80 to 100 | 44. 0 | [1] 49. 4 | 33. 1 | 13. 1 | 21. 4 |
| 90 to 100 | 37. 0 | 43. 3 | 22. 9 | 7. 7 | 13. 9 |
| 95 to 100 | 31. 5 | 38. 2 | 16. 3 | 4. 0 | 6. 8 |
| 99 to 100 | 21. 4 | 28. 0 | 5. 8 | . 7 | 1. 9 |
| 100 | 10. 5 | [1] 14. 0 | 1. 8 | . 1 | 1. 8 |

[1] Figures are for Fall 1970. Fall 1971 estimates are available for black students in 50 to 100 percent, 80 to 100 percent, and 100 percent minority group schools. They are 64.4 percent, 45.9 percent, and 11.6 percent respectively.

Among 49 States (excluding Hawaii which was not surveyed) and District of Columbia, 8.6 million of 9.4 million or 91.5 percent of the

Nation's minority-group students are in 24 States and the District of Columbia.

Among these jurisdictions, the District of Columbia has the highest percentage of minority-group students (95.5) and the highest percentage of minority-group children in isolated schools. The incidence of racial isolation within a State is usually a reflection of urban patterns. Among the States, Illinois has the highest incidence of school isolation. The following table shows the percentage of minority-group students attending schools at various levels of isolation in these 24 States and the District of Columbia.

TABLE 7–2.—*Percent of minority-group students attending school at increasing levels of isolation in 24 States and the District of Columbia (Fall 1970)*

| State | Percent minority schools | | | | |
|---|---|---|---|---|---|
| | 50 to 100 | 80 to 100 | 90 to 100 | 95 to 100 | 100 |
| Continental United States | 62. 6 | 44. 0 | 37. 0 | 31. 5 | 10. 5 |
| 24 States and District of Columbia | 64. 7 | 45. 6 | 38. 4 | 32. 8 | 11. 1 |
| Alabama | 63. 4 | 48. 1 | 44. 0 | 38. 8 | 20. 0 |
| Arizona | 55. 2 | 35. 4 | 19. 0 | 9. 6 | . 7 |
| Arkansas | 56. 6 | 21. 6 | 18. 3 | 15. 3 | 8. 5 |
| California | 50. 7 | 30. 5 | 24. 4 | 20. 8 | 1. 8 |
| Colorado | 40. 0 | 17. 2 | 9. 4 | 7. 2 | 0 |
| District of Columbia | 98. 5 | 96. 4 | 94. 4 | 92. 3 | 33. 3 |
| Florida | 51. 5 | 32. 3 | 24. 2 | 19. 0 | 8. 2 |
| Georgia | 63. 7 | 39. 1 | 34. 3 | 30. 6 | 16. 7 |
| Illinois | 79. 3 | 68. 4 | 63. 9 | 59. 6 | 30. 0 |
| Indiana | 66. 2 | 51. 9 | 43. 3 | 36. 7 | 12. 1 |
| Louisiana | 68. 3 | 46. 8 | 40. 5 | 36. 6 | 23. 7 |
| Maryland | 65. 1 | 51. 8 | 48. 5 | 44. 4 | 25. 0 |
| Michigan | 73. 0 | 58. 5 | 51. 6 | 44. 4 | 9. 0 |
| Mississippi | 73. 5 | 48. 3 | 35. 4 | 29. 8 | 10. 8 |
| Missouri | 77. 3 | 66. 4 | 61. 2 | 57. 1 | 29. 2 |
| New Jersey | 66. 6 | 45. 3 | 37. 4 | 30. 8 | 5. 2 |
| New Mexico | 71. 9 | 37. 2 | 18. 9 | 9. 4 | 1. 3 |
| New York | 74. 7 | 57. 7 | 49. 2 | 38. 2 | 7. 8 |
| North Carolina | 47. 0 | 18. 4 | 14. 5 | 12. 8 | 6. 6 |
| Ohio | 68. 7 | 53. 0 | 46. 3 | 39. 9 | 13. 1 |
| Pennsylvania | 72. 0 | 56. 3 | 48. 8 | 42. 3 | 4. 4 |
| South Carolina | 55. 0 | 29. 0 | 22. 0 | 17. 1 | 7. 0 |
| Tennessee | 67. 2 | 59. 5 | 55. 1 | 49. 7 | 25. 7 |
| Texas | 69. 4 | 49. 9 | 39. 4 | 32. 5 | 7. 6 |
| Virginia | 57. 2 | 30. 0 | 24. 1 | 20. 4 | 10. 0 |

These 24 States include all 11 Southern States, two of the six border States and 11 of the 32 Northern and Western States as divided regionally by the HEW survey. As the following table shows, the two Border States, Maryland and Missouri, show the highest levels of school isolation in each minority isolation category, and while the South has a somewhat higher percentage of minority-group students in 100 percent minority schools than the North, it has fewer such children in schools which are less than 100 percent minority than the rest of the country.

TABLE 7–3.—*Percent of minority-group students attending school at increasing levels of isolation in 24 States* [1] *by geographic region (Fall 1970)*

| Area | Percent minority schools | | | | |
|---|---|---|---|---|---|
| | 50 to 100 | 80 to 100 | 90 to 100 | 95 to 100 | 100 |
| Continental United States | 62. 6 | 44. 0 | 37. 0 | 31. 5 | 10. 5 |
| 24 States and District of Columbia | 64. 4 | 45. 6 | 38. 4 | 32. 8 | 11. 1 |
| 11 Northern and Western States | 65. 3 | 47. 5 | 40. 0 | 33. 6 | 8. 3 |
| 2 Border States | 69. 9 | 57. 6 | 53. 5 | 49. 4 | 26. 6 |
| 11 Southern States | 62. 2 | 40. 3 | 33. 0 | 28. 1 | 12. 0 |

1 Containing 91.5 percent of the Nation's minority group students.

Among the remaining 25 States which have 8.5 percent of the Nation's minority-group school population, the indices of school isolation are dramatically lower than in the 24 States and in the Nation as a whole.

TABLE 7–4.—*Percent of minority-group students attending school at increasing levels of isolation in 25 States* [1] *by geographic region (Fall 1970)*

| Area | Percent minority schools | | | | |
|---|---|---|---|---|---|
| | 50 to 100 | 80 to 100 | 90 to 100 | 95 to 100 | 100 |
| Continental United States | 62. 6 | 44. 0 | 37. 0 | 31. 5 | 10. 5 |
| 24 States and District of Columbia [2] | 64. 7 | 45. 6 | 38. 4 | 32. 8 | 11. 1 |
| 25 States [1] | 36. 0 | 24. 2 | 18. 9 | 14. 7 | 2. 4 |
| 21 Northern and Western States | 36. 1 | 23. 1 | 16. 9 | 12. 3 | 1. 8 |
| 4 Border States | 35. 6 | 26. 8 | 23. 7 | 20. 5 | 3. 9 |

1 Containing 8.5 percent of the Nation's minority-group students.
2 Containing 91.5 percent of the Nation's minority-group students.

### 2. BLACK STUDENT ISOLATION, BY STATE AND REGION

Of the Nation's 6.7 million black students, 6.2 million or 93 percent are concentrated in 21 States and the District of Columbia. The District of Columbia, Illinois and Michigan, in that order, contain the highest indices of black student isolation.

TABLE 7–5.—*Percent of Negro students attending school at increasing levels of isolation in 21 States and District of Columbia (Fall 1970)*

| State | Percent minority schools | | | | |
|---|---|---|---|---|---|
| | 50 to 100 | 80 to 100 | 90 to 100 | 95 to 100 | 100 |
| Continental United States | 66. 9 | 49. 4 | 43. 3 | 38. 2 | 14. 0 |
| 21 States and District of Columbia | 68. 3 | 50. 5 | 44. 5 | 41. 8 | 14. 8 |
| Alabama | 63. 5 | 48. 2 | 44. 1 | 38. 9 | 20. 0 |
| Arkansas | 57. 0 | 21. 8 | 18. 5 | 15. 5 | 8. 6 |
| California | 74. 2 | 57. 8 | 51. 5 | 46. 7 | 5. 0 |
| District of Columbia | 98. 8 | 97. 0 | 95. 0 | 92. 9 | 33. 5 |
| Florida | 51. 6 | 33. 0 | 26. 3 | 21. 9 | 9. 8 |
| Georgia | 64. 1 | 39. 4 | 34. 5 | 30. 8 | 16. 8 |
| Illinois | 85. 7 | 77. 6 | 75. 0 | 71. 2 | 36. 2 |
| Indiana | 69. 7 | 54. 9 | 48. 1 | 41. 3 | 13. 9 |
| Louisiana | 68. 7 | 47. 3 | 41. 0 | 37. 1 | 24. 0 |
| Maryland | 67. 0 | 53. 4 | 49. 9 | 45. 7 | 25. 7 |
| Michigan | 80. 8 | 65. 3 | 57. 8 | 49. 8 | 10. 1 |
| Mississippi | 73. 6 | 48. 4 | 35. 5 | 29. 9 | 10. 8 |
| New Jersey | 68. 0 | 50. 3 | 42. 4 | 3C. 3 | 6. 6 |
| New York | 71. 2 | 55. 1 | 48. 1 | 38. 9 | 9. 0 |
| Missouri | 79. 9 | 68. 7 | 63. 4 | 59. 1 | 30. 2 |
| North Carolina | 45. 9 | 17. 2 | 13. 7 | 12. 2 | 6. 8 |
| Ohio | 72. 8 | 56. 5 | 49. 4 | 42. 8 | 14. 0 |
| Pennsylvania | 73. 7 | 58. 0 | 50. 5 | 44. 3 | 4. 7 |
| South Carolina | 55. 2 | 29. 1 | 22. 1 | 17. 2 | 7. 0 |
| Tennessee | 67. 7 | 60. 0 | 55. 5 | 50. 1 | 25. 9 |
| Texas | 65. 1 | 52. 6 | 46. 7 | 41. 9 | 14. 0 |
| Virginia | 58. 6 | 30. 8 | 24. 7 | 20. 9 | 10. 3 |

These 21 jurisdictions include the 11 Southern States, two of six Border States and eight from the North and West. The 11 Southern States are generally 15 to 20 percentage points below the eight Northern and Western States.

TABLE 7–6.—*Percent of Negro students attending school at increasing levels of isolation in 21 States[1] by geographical region (Fall 1970)*

| Area | Percent minority schools | | | | |
|---|---|---|---|---|---|
| | 50 to 100 | 80 to 100 | 90 to 100 | 95 to 100 | 100 |
| Continental United States | 66. 9 | 49. 4 | 43. 3 | 38. 2 | 14. 0 |
| 21 States and District of Columbia | 68. 3 | 50. 5 | 44. 5 | 41. 8 | 14. 8 |
| 8 Northern and Western States | 75. 2 | 60. 4 | 54. 0 | 47. 5 | 13. 0 |
| 2 Border States | 72. 1 | 58. 0 | 55. 2 | 51. 0 | 27. 5 |
| 11 Southern States | 60. 9 | 39. 3 | 33. 3 | 29. 2 | 14. 1 |

[1] Containing 94 percent of the Nation's black students.

### 3. SPANISH-SURNAMED STUDENT ISOLATION BY STATE AND REGION

The HEW survey counted 2.3 million students of Spanish heritage in the United States, the Nation's second largest minority group. All but 191,000 live in 10 States, with the largest number in California (706,000), Texas (566,000), New York (316,600) and New Mexico (109,300). They are the largest student minority group in Arizona (19.7%), California (15.5%), Colorado (14.6%), New Mexico (38.9%) and Texas (21.5%). In New Mexico and New York they are more isolated in school than black students; and, in California and Illinois they are substantially less isolated than black students. As the following table shows, Spanish-surnamed students are substantially more segregated in New York and Texas than in the other eight States.

TABLE 7–7.—*Percent of Spanish-surnamed American students attending school at increasing levels of isolation in 10 States (Fall 1970)*

| States | Percent minority schools | | | | |
|---|---|---|---|---|---|
| | 50 to 100 | 80 to 100 | 90 to 100 | 95 to 100 | 100 |
| Continental United States | 55. 8 | 33. 1 | 22. 9 | 16. 3 | 1. 8 |
| 10 States | 59. 2 | 35. 3 | 24. 5 | 17. 5 | 1. 9 |
| Arizona | 51. 6 | 30. 5 | 14. 5 | 8. 1 | . 5 |
| California | 39. 2 | 17. 2 | 11. 4 | 8. 2 | . 1 |
| Colorado | 39. 2 | 13. 1 | 4. 7 | 2. 4 | 0 |
| Connecticut | 54. 0 | 26. 9 | 18. 3 | 14. 6 | 0 |
| Florida | 53. 0 | 30. 1 | 14. 8 | 5. 0 | . 3 |
| Illinois | 53. 1 | 26. 4 | 11. 0 | 4. 0 | . 2 |
| New Jersey | 67. 2 | 30. 8 | 23. 0 | 13. 1 | . 5 |
| New Mexico | 71. 5 | 33. 2 | 14. 2 | 7. 7 | . 8 |
| New York | 83. 4 | 64. 5 | 53. 4 | 39. 7 | 6. 3 |
| Texas | 73. 1 | 48. 4 | 34. 5 | 26. 1 | 2. 9 |

Regionally, Spanish-surnamed students are more isolated in school in the four Northeastern States than in the five Southwestern States.

TABLE 7–8.—*Percent of Spanish-surnamed American students attending school at increasing levels of isolation in 10 States by geographic region (Fall 1970)*

| Area | Percent minority schools | | | | |
|---|---|---|---|---|---|
| | 50 to 100 | 80 to 100 | 90 to 100 | 95 to 100 | 100 |
| Continental United States | 55. 8 | 33. 1 | 22. 9 | 5. 8 | 1. 8 |
| 5—Arizona, California, Colorado, New Mexico, Texas | 54. 6 | 30. 3 | 19. 9 | 14. 4 | 1. 2 |
| 4—Connecticut, Illinois, New Jersey, New York | 75. 1 | 52. 4 | 41. 1 | 29. 5 | 4. 3 |

The U.S. Civil Rights Commission undertook a detailed study of ethnic isolation of Mexican Americans in the five Southeastern States. Based upon school year 1968–1969 data, the study was first published in August 1970, as the first of two reports on Mexican-American Education.

In summary the Commission found:

> There are about 2 million Spanish-surnamed students, including Mexican Americans, Puerto Ricans, Cubans, and other Latin Americans, in the public schools of the continental United States. The second largest minority group in the public schools, they constitute about 5 percent of the total U.S. school population.
>
> Approximately 1.4 million, or 70 percent of the Spanish-surnamed pupils, attend school in the five Southwestern States of Arizona, California, Colorado, New Mexico, and

Texas. Almost all of these pupils are Mexican Americans. The largest minority group in the schools of the region, they comprise 17 percent of the total enrollment. More than 80 percent are in two States, California and Texas, with nearly 50 percent in California alone. However, Mexican Americans constitute more of the enrollment (38 percent) in New Mexico than in any other State.

The Mexican-American population is primarily urban. The majority of Mexican-American pupils attend school in large urban districts that have enrollments of 10,000 or more. In each State, one or more of the large urban districts contain a significant proportion of the Mexican-American enrollment: Los Angeles, Calif.; San Antonio, El Paso, and Houston, Tex.; Denver, Colo.; Albuquerque, N. Mex.; and Tucson, Ariz.

Within each of the States the Mexican-American school population is concentrated in specific regions or geographic areas. In Texas nearly two-thirds of all Mexican-American pupils attend school in the counties located along or near the Mexican border. In this area, about three of every five students are Mexican Americans. To a lesser extent Mexican Americans also are concentrated in the counties of north-central New Mexico, southern Colorado, southern Arizona, and in the agricultural valleys and southern coastal areas of California.

While Mexican-American pupils are unevenly distributed among the States and concentrated in specific geographic areas within each State, they are also concentrated, or isolated, in districts and schools of the Southwest. About 404,000 Mexican-American pupils, or 30 per cent of this ethnic group's enrollment in the Southwest, attend schools in approximately 200 predominantly (50 percent or more) Mexican-American districts in the region.

The largest number of predominantly Mexican-American districts is in Texas. Ninety-four predominantly Mexican-American districts, almost all of which are located in the southern part of the State, contain nearly 60 percent of the State's total Mexican-American enrollment. About 20 percent of Texas' Mexican-American students attend school in districts which are nearly all—80 percent or more—Mexican Americans.

Most of the other predominantly Mexican-American districts are in California and New Mexico. Together, these States contain as many predominantly Mexican-American districts as Texas—about 90; however, the total Mexican-American school population of these districts is much smaller. They include only about 94,000 Mexican-American pupils—55,000 in California and 39,000 in New Mexico.

The isolation of Mexican-American pupils in predominantly Mexican-American districts results in part from their concentration in specific geographic areas of each State. However, many of these students are isolated in districts which are contiguous to predominantly Anglo districts. In San Antonio, five districts located in the heart of the city are predominantly Mexican-American and contain 90 percent of all Mexican Americans in the area. Well over 50 percent of the Anglo public school enrollment is in eight predominantly Anglo districts which surround the core city. Each of the five predominantly Mexican-American districts borders on one or more of the Anglo districts.

A large proportion of the Mexican-American enrollment in the Southwest also tends to be concentrated in a comparatively small number of schools. Approximately 1,500 schools—12 percent—are predominantly Mexican-American. They house about 635,000 pupils, or 45 percent of the total Mexican-American enrollment in the Southwest. Nearly 300,000 pupils, or more than 20 percent, are in schools which have between 80–100 percent Mexican-American student body. These pupils are most severely isolated in schools in Texas and New Mexico. In these two States, two-thirds of all Mexican-American students attend predominantly Mexican-American schools. In Texas about 40 percent are in schools nearly all Mexican American. Students of this minority group are least isolated in California, where less than 30 percent are found in predominantly Mexican-American schools.

At the elementary school level, Mexican Americans experience the greatest degree of ethnic isolation. One-half of the Mexican-American elementary students attend predominantly Mexican-American schools, while about 35 percent of their secondary school enrollment is in predominantly Mexican-American schools.*

The Civil Rights Commission is also presently engaged in an extensive study of public education for Puerto Rican children in New York City. All the statistical dimensions have not yet been determined; however, certain preliminary findings indicate that the isolation of Puerto Rican students is of great magnitude:

- In 1970, New York City comprised 68.2 percent of the New York SMSA population. While 59.4 percent of the whites in the SMSA live in New York City, 97.4 percent of the Puerto Ricans in the SMSA live in the city, mostly in three innercity boroughs.
- In these three innercity districts—Manhattan, Bronx, and Brooklyn—the white population has dropped 26.2 percent, from 77.3 to 51.1 percent, over the last 10 years. During the same period, the nonwhite and Puerto Rican population increased from 22.7 to 49.9 percent.

### 4. ORIENTAL AMERICANS

Approximately 209,000 Oriental Americans** were in elementary and secondary public schools in September 1970. Nearly half, 104,800,

---

**Ethnic Isolation of Mexican Americans in the Public Schools of the Southwest*, U.S. Commission on Civil Rights, August 1970.

**This figure excludes the State of Hawaii, where the native population is largely of oriental heritage, and where, because institutions reflect that heritage, school attendance figures cannot reasonably be said to identify "isolation" with all the connotations that word carries in this Report.

were in California. The next largest numbers were in the States of New York (21,770) and Washington (10,439). Nationally, 29.4 percent of Oriental Americans are in predominantly minority schools and 13.1 percent are in schools which are 80–100 percent minority—substantially lower incidences of isolation than for black or Spanish-surnamed students.

In California 39.5 percent of oriental students are in predominantly minority schools and 16.2 percent are in 80–100 percent minority schools. In New York, 48 percent are in predominantly minority schools and 32.2 percent are in 80–100 percent minority schools. The figures for the State of Washington are 22 percent and 2.7 percent respectively.

The following table shows the percentage of oriental students attending minority-group schools in those States in which there are more than 2,000 oriental students.

TABLE 7–9.—*Percent of Oriental students attending schools at increasing levels of isolation in 15 States (Fall 1970)*

| State | Oriental students | Percent minority schools | | |
|---|---|---|---|---|
| | | 50 to 100 | 80 to 100 | 90 to 100 |
| Continental United States | 209, 092 | 29. 4 | 13. 1 | 7. 7 |
| Arizona | 2, 045 | 14. 1 | 5. 3 | . 9 |
| California | 104, 821 | 39. 5 | 16. 2 | 8. 2 |
| Colorado | 3, 095 | 8. 6 | 4. 5 | 1. 1 |
| Illinois | 7, 511 | 15. 4 | 8. 3 | 7. 1 |
| Maryland | 2, 655 | 1. 0 | . 2 | 0 |
| Massachusetts | 4, 348 | 22. 7 | 15. 8 | 5. 8 |
| Michigan | 4, 165 | 9. 7 | 4. 3 | 3. 2 |
| New Jersey | 6, 993 | 20. 1 | 6. 8 | 3. 9 |
| New York | 21, 770 | 48. 0 | 32. 2 | 26. 3 |
| Ohio | 3, 380 | 5. 8 | 2. 2 | 1. 5 |
| Oregon | 3, 314 | . 6 | . 1 | . 1 |
| Pennsylvania | 2, 408 | 2. 6 | . 7 | . 7 |
| Texas | 4, 217 | 17. 8 | 6. 4 | 2. 8 |
| Virginia | 2, 969 | 4. 3 | 1. 0 | . 2 |
| Washington | 10, 439 | 22. 0 | 2. 7 | . 1 |

## 5. AMERICAN INDIANS

There are 197,100 American Indian students in the Nation's non-Federal public schools. Oklahoma, Arizona, New Mexico, California, North Carolina, Washington, and Alaska, in that order, have the largest numbers of American Indian students. Nationally, these students are much less isolated in school than either black or Spanish-surnamed students and somewhat more isolated than Oriental students. Yet, in Arizona and New Mexico, 54.1 percent and 63.1 percent, respectively, attend 80–100 percent minority-group schools.

The following table shows the percentage of American Indian students attending increasing levels of minority-group schools in those States in which there are more than 2,000 American Indian students.

TABLE 7-10.—*Percent of American Indian students attending schools at increasing levels of isolation in 20 States (Fall 1970)*

| State | American Indian students | Percent minority schools | | |
|---|---|---|---|---|
| | | 50 to 100 | 80 to 100 | 90 to 100 |
| Continental United States | 197, 109 | 33. 5 | 21. 4 | 13. 9 |
| Alaska | 10, 070 | 38. 4 | 29. 8 | 14. 1 |
| Arizona | 19, 575 | 64. 4 | 54. 1 | 31. 7 |
| California | 16, 842 | 17. 1 | 3. 8 | 2. 0 |
| Idaho | 2, 192 | 5. 8 | 0 | 0 |
| Illinois | 2, 526 | 15. 0 | 6. 0 | 4. 0 |
| Michigan | 4, 375 | 4. 0 | 1. 8 | . 8 |
| Minnesota | 7, 172 | 5. 2 | . 5 | . 5 |
| Montana | 8, 434 | 48. 3 | 27. 5 | 18. 0 |
| Nebraska | 2, 134 | 53. 8 | 3. 1 | 2. 7 |
| Nevada | 2, 839 | 25. 3 | 17. 7 | 9. 0 |
| New Mexico | 19, 216 | 83. 4 | 63. 1 | 45. 1 |
| New York | 5, 669 | 25. 0 | 20. 2 | 9. 3 |
| North Carolina | 14, 168 | 78. 0 | 48. 8 | 36. 1 |
| Oklahoma | 28, 647 | 6. 9 | . 1 | . 1 |
| Oregon | 3, 721 | 11. 7 | 11. 6 | 11. 6 |
| South Dakota | 7, 536 | 30. 2 | 17. 6 | 9. 0 |
| Texas | 3, 588 | 38. 5 | 33. 1 | 31. 6 |
| Utah | 4, 733 | 14. 2 | 11. 4 | 3. 2 |
| Washington | 10, 611 | 15. 8 | . 7 | . 2 |
| Wisconsin | 7, 069 | 23. 6 | 7. 5 | 6. 9 |

## B. School Isolation Trends

### 1. BY REGION: 1968–71

By any standard of measurement there has been a pronounced reduction in black student isolation in the 11 Southern States during the past 4 school years. During the same period, the change in the remaining States has been negligible.

In 1968, 78.8 percent of the South's black students were in 80–100 percent minority schools. By 1971 that figure was reduced to 32.2 percent. This reduction almost entirely accounted for a 22.1 percent nationwide reduction in the proportion of black students in 80–100 percent minority schools during the same period.

But even more dramatic has been the near elimination of all-black schools in the South. In 1968, 68 percent of the South's black students were in all-black schools. By September 1971, that figure was reduced to 9.2 percent.

TABLE 7-11.—*Black student isolation by geographic area, Fall 1968–Fall 1971*

[Figures are percentages]

| Geographic area | Percent minority schools | | |
|---|---|---|---|
| | 50 to 100 | 80 to 100 | 100 |
| Continental United States: | | | |
| 1968 | 76.6 | 68.0 | 39.7 |
| 1971 | 64.4 | 45.9 | 11.6 |
| Difference | −12.2 | −22.1 | −28.1 |
| 32 Northern and Western States: | | | |
| 1968 | 72.4 | 57.4 | 12.3 |
| 1971 | 72.2 | 57.1 | 11.2 |
| Difference | −.2 | −.3 | −1.1 |
| 11 Southern States: | | | |
| 1968 | 81.6 | 78.8 | 68.0 |
| 1971 | 56.1 | 32.2 | 9.2 |
| Difference | −25.5 | −46.6 | −58.8 |
| 6 Border States and District of Columbia: | | | |
| 1968 | 71.6 | 63.8 | 25.2 |
| 1971 | 69.5 | 60.9 | 24.2 |
| Difference | −2.1 | −2.9 | −1.0 |

## 2. BY STATE: 1968–70

Among the 21 States, which, together with the District of Columbia, contain 94 percent of the Nation's black students, only those in the South had any significant reduction in school isolation. Thus, for example, while Florida, Georgia, Louisiana and Mississippi each reduced the proportion of black students in 80-100 percent minority schools by more than 40 percent, the isolation of black students in such schools in New York, New Jersey, Michigan and Ohio increased between 1 and 5 percentage points.

TABLE 7–12.—*Black student isolation in 21 States,*[1] *from Fall 1968 to Fall 1970*[2]

[Figures are percentages]

| State | Percent minority schools | | | | | |
|---|---|---|---|---|---|---|
| | 50 to 100 | | 80 to 100 | | 100 | |
| | 1968 | 1970 | 1968 | 1970 | 1968 | 1970 |
| 11 Southern States: | | | | | | |
| Alabama | 91. 7 | 63. 5 | 91. 5 | 48. 2 | 85. 6 | 20. 0 |
| Arkansas | 77. 4 | 57. 0 | 74. 9 | 21. 8 | 71. 7 | 8. 6 |
| Florida | 76. 8 | 51. 6 | 73. 8 | 33. 0 | 59. 1 | 9. 8 |
| Georgia | 86. 0 | 64. 1 | 84. 5 | 39. 4 | 76. 4 | 16. 8 |
| Louisiana | 91. 1 | 68. 8 | 89. 1 | 47. 3 | 81. 9 | 24. 0 |
| Mississippi | 93. 3 | 73. 6 | 92. 7 | 48. 4 | 88. 2 | 10. 8 |
| North Carolina | 71. 7 | 45. 9 | 67. 2 | 17. 2 | 59. 0 | 6. 8 |
| South Carolina | 85. 8 | 55. 2 | 84. 7 | 29. 1 | 79. 3 | 7. 0 |
| Tennessee | 78. 8 | 67. 7 | 75. 5 | 60. 0 | 58. 7 | 25. 9 |
| Texas | 74. 7 | 65. 1 | 67. 3 | 52. 6 | 43. 5 | 14. 0 |
| Virginia | 73. 1 | 58. 6 | 70. 2 | 30. 8 | 58. 0 | 10. 3 |
| 8 Northern and Western States: | | | | | | |
| California | 77. 5 | 74. 2 | 62. 0 | 57. 8 | 7. 2 | 5. 0 |
| Illinois | 86. 4 | 85. 7 | 76. 9 | 77. 6 | 38. 6 | 36. 2 |
| Indiana | 70. 0 | 69. 7 | 55. 5 | 54. 9 | 12. 8 | 13. 9 |
| Michigan | 79. 4 | 80. 8 | 64. 3 | 65. 3 | 9. 0 | 10. 1 |
| New Jersey | 66. 1 | 68. 0 | 48. 2 | 50. 3 | 7. 3 | 6. 6 |
| New York | 67. 7 | 71. 2 | 50. 0 | 55. 1 | 7. 5 | 9. 0 |
| Ohio | 72. 3 | 72. 8 | 57. 0 | 56. 5 | 13. 2 | 14. 0 |
| Pennsylvania | 72. 5 | 73. 7 | 58. 2 | 58. 0 | 4. 4 | 4. 7 |
| 2 Border States: | | | | | | |
| Maryland | 68. 9 | 67. 0 | 58. 5 | 53. 4 | 31. 2 | 25. 7 |
| Missouri | 75. 4 | 79. 9 | 70. 2 | 68. 7 | 33. 4 | 30. 2 |

[1] Containing 94 percent of the Nation's black students.
[2] 1971 figures are not available.

### 3. LARGE CITY SCHOOL DISTRICTS: 1968–71

Among the Nation's 100 largest school districts which were surveyed both in 1968 and 1971, 28 significantly reduced black-student isolation during that period. All but two—Wichita, Kans., and Las Vegas, Nev.—were in the South. Ten were in Florida. Little if any reduction in school isolation occurred during this period in the remaining large districts and many became more school-isolated.

TABLE 7–13.—*Decrease in black student isolation in 28 large school districts from Fall 1968 to Fall 1971*

[Figures in percentages]

| School district | Percent minority schools | | | | | |
|---|---|---|---|---|---|---|
| | 50 to 100 | | 80 to 100 | | 100 | |
| | 1968 | 1971 | 1968 | 1971 | 1968 | 1971 |
| Brevard County, Fla. (Titusville) | 30. 2 | 10. 5 | 30. 2 | 10. 5 | 30. 2 | 0 |
| Broward County, Fla. (Fort Lauderdale) | 85. 5 | 21. 3 | 79. 7 | 8. 0 | 68. 9 | 2. 3 |
| Charleston County, S.C | 87. 2 | 71. 3 | 84. 2 | 62. 4 | 84. 2 | 24. 9 |
| Charlotte-Mecklenburg County, N.C | 72. 3 | 2. 1 | 68. 1 | 1. 5 | 39. 0 | 0 |
| Chatham County, Ga. (Savannah) | 90. 7 | 40. 6 | 86. 5 | 7. 6 | 77. 1 | 0 |
| Clark County, Nev. (Las Vegas) | 51. 9 | 32. 4 | 51. 9 | 18. 7 | 0 | 3. 7 |
| Dade County, Fla. (Miami) | 87. 6 | 77. 0 | 82. 0 | 53. 2 | 48. 6 | 12. 9 |
| DeKalb County, Ga. (Decatur) | 55. 4 | 29. 7 | 47. 0 | 22. 2 | 10. 2 | 0 |
| Duval County, Fla. (Jacksonville) | 87. 4 | 64. 0 | 87. 4 | 38. 2 | 76. 7 | 23. 3 |
| East Baton Rouge Parish, La | 94. 4 | 77. 1 | 94. 2 | 72. 0 | 80. 0 | 21. 0 |
| Escambia County, Fla. (Pensacola) | 77. 5 | 57. 6 | 71. 3 | 15. 2 | 70. 0 | 0 |
| Fort Worth, Tex | 90. 3 | 78. 6 | 85. 4 | 67. 0 | 60. 7 | 20. 4 |
| Greenville County, S.C | 85. 2 | . 9 | 83. 3 | 0 | 74. 3 | 0 |
| Hillsborough County, Fla. (Tampa) | 81. 7 | 2. 2 | 77. 4 | . 5 | 64. 3 | 0 |
| Jefferson County, Ala. (Birmingham) | 97. 0 | 60. 6 | 96. 7 | 56. 7 | 96. 7 | 30. 0 |
| Jefferson Parish, La. (Gretna) | 79. 5 | 6. 1 | 79. 5 | . 6 | 79. 5 | 0 |
| Mobile County, Ala | 89. 1 | 64. 2 | 87. 5 | 44. 2 | 59. 9 | 15. 3 |
| Muscogee County, Ga. (Columbus) | 92. 9 | 4. 0 | 87. 5 | 1. 6 | 70. 0 | 1. 6 |
| Nashville-Davidson County, Tenn | 83. 2 | 17. 3 | 69. 4 | 0 | 51. 8 | 0 |
| Norfolk, Va | 88. 5 | 49. 6 | 82. 3 | 1. 2 | 49. 6 | 0 |
| Orange County, Fla. (Orlando) | 79. 9 | 47. 7 | 77. 1 | 28. 3 | 77. 1 | 4. 9 |
| Palm Beach County, Fla | 81. 4 | 37. 1 | 79. 5 | 10. 8 | 72. 3 | 0 |
| Pinellas County, Fla. (Clearwater) | 78. 3 | 5. 2 | 73. 2 | 0 | 25. 9 | 0 |
| Polk County, Fla. (Bartow) | 67. 3 | 20. 1 | 66. 7 | 11. 7 | 66. 7 | 0 |
| Richmond, Va | 93. 6 | 93. 9 | 88. 6 | 36. 5 | 78. 0 | . 1 |
| Virginia Beach, Va | 37. 8 | 0 | 37. 8 | 0 | 29. 2 | 0 |
| Wichita, Kans | 54. 5 | . 3 | 53. 4 | 0 | 0 | 0 |
| Winston-Salem-Forsyth County, N.C | 84. 7 | 4. 3 | 84. 7 | 2. 7 | 70. 9 | 0 |

It should be noted that despite the substantial progress in reducing black-student isolation in the Southern States and in these cities:

- In the 28 districts named in Table 7–13, 44,956 black students remain in 100 percent minority schools.
- In the 11 Southern States in which 27.2 percent of the student population is black; more than half (1,761,589 out of 3,139,436) of the black students attend predominantly minority schools; nearly a third, 1,010,558 attend 80–100 percent minority schools, and 290,390 students remain in 100 percent minority-group schools.
- In the 25 largest Southern school districts covered by the 1971 survey, black students make up 32.4 percent of the school enrollment and more than half, 58.4 percent, attend 80–100 percent minority schools.

- As indicated in the following table, in most of the largest school districts in Texas and Louisiana black students remain highly isolated.

TABLE 7–14.—*School isolation in Texas and Louisiana cities (Fall 1971)*

[In percentage]

| School district | Black students | Percent minority schools | | |
|---|---|---|---|---|
| | | 50 to 100 | 80 to 100 | 100 |
| Austin, Tex | 14. 7 | 63. 9 | 58. 1 | 8. 6 |
| Caddo Parish (Shreveport), La | 49. 6 | 74. 5 | 66. 6 | 30. 3 |
| Corpus Christi, Tex | 5. 7 | 94. 5 | 80. 0 | . 6 |
| Dallas, Tex | 36. 3 | 85. 0 | 83. 4 | 10. 5 |
| East Baton Rouge, La | 39. 0 | 77. 1 | 72. 0 | 21. 0 |
| Fort Worth, Tex | 28. 3 | 78. 6 | 67. 0 | 20. 4 |
| Houston, Tex | 37. 8 | 91. 3 | 86. 0 | 8. 7 |
| Orleans Parish (New Orleans), La | 71. 4 | 93. 4 | 80. 8 | 47. 2 |
| San Antonio, Tex | 15. 5 | 91. 7 | 71. 2 | 12. 6 |

#### 4. SPANISH-SURNAMED STUDENT ISOLATION TRENDS

While there has been some nationwide progress in reducing the school isolation for black students, nearly all of which is attributable to Federal court orders and Title VI desegregation plans in Southern States, there has been no appreciable decrease in school isolation of Spanish-surnamed students. Of the 10 States in which more than 90 percent of the Nation's Spanish-surnamed students reside, in none has there been any appreciable reduction in school isolation over the past 4 years. In most of these States and in most large cities with significant Spanish-surnamed populations there have been slight increases.

### C. Isolation in Large City School Districts

About half the Nation's black students, 3.4 million, are in our 100 largest school districts. These districts are, by far, the most segregated in the Nation. They include all the Nation's large cities. Collectively their school population in the Fall of 1971 was 34 percent black; and, in 1970 18.2 percent Spanish-surnamed. At that time—and there has been little appreciable overall change since—73.4 percent of these district's black students were in 80–100 percent minority schools and 59 percent were in 95–100 percent minority schools. Spanish-surnamed students were similarly isolated with 52 percent in 80–100 percent minority schools. Even more significant, schools in large districts are well above the rest of the Nation in incidence of minority-group isolation.

The following table compares isolation levels of black and Spanish-surnamed students in large school districts with isolation levels in the Nation and in those States which contain most of the Nation's minority-group students.

TABLE 7-15.—*Black and Spanish-surnamed student isolation in large school districts (1970)*

[Figures are percentages]

| Area | Percent | Percent minority schools: 50 to 100 | 80 to 100 | 90 to 100 | 95 to 100 | 100 |
|---|---|---|---|---|---|---|
| Black student isolation: | | | | | | |
| 100 largest school districts | 32.3 | 83.9 | 71.8 | 65.7 | 59.0 | 21.0 |
| Continental United States | 14.9 | 66.9 | 49.4 | 43.3 | 38.2 | 14.0 |
| 21 States and District of Columbia[1] | 18.5 | 68.3 | 50.5 | 44.5 | 41.8 | 14.8 |
| Spanish-surnamed student isolation: | | | | | | |
| 31 largest school districts | 18.2 | 74.7 | 52.0 | 39.2 | 28.7 | 2.8 |
| Continental United States | 5.1 | 55.8 | 33.1 | 22.9 | 16.3 | 1.8 |
| 10 States[2] | 11.7 | 59.2 | 35.3 | 24.5 | 17.5 | 1.9 |

[1] Containing 94 percent of the Nation's black students.
[2] Containing 88 percent of the Nation's Spanish-surnamed students.

Large city school district black student populations range from 95.2 percent in Washington, D.C. and 72.1 percent in Atlanta, Ga., to 2.6 percent in Albuquerque, N. Mex. The schools of the District of Columbia are, by definition, minority-group isolated schools. No significant decrease in school isolation is possible within such a district. On the other hand, in a city such as Fresno, Calif.—where 9.3 percent of the students are black and 51 percent of such students are in 90–100 percent minority schools—it is obvious that racial isolation exists in a school district where it is certainly mathematically feasible to eliminate.

No assessment of racial or ethnic isolation in schools or school districts can fail to take account of the relationship between the percentage of minority-group students in the district as a whole and the percentage attending schools at any particular level of isolation. In Table 7–16, large school districts are set forth in order of decreasing percentages of black students in the district.

Surveys of large school districts were conducted in 1965, 1968, 1970 and 1971. However, not all such districts were surveyed in each of those years. Moreover, statistics were gathered for different levels of school isolation in different years. Hence, the following table contains only such figures as are available for the year indicated.

TABLE 7–16.—*Black-student isolation in large city school districts, ranked by percentage of black students in the district*

| School district | Percent black | 50 to 100 percent | | | | 80 to 100 percent | | | 90 to 100 percent | | | 100 percent | | |
|---|---|---|---|---|---|---|---|---|---|---|---|---|---|---|
| | | 1965 | 1968 | 1970 | 1971 | 1968 | 1970 | 1971 | 1965 | 1968 | 1970 | 1968 | 1970 | 1971 |
| Washington, D.C., 1971 | 95.2 | 99.3 | 99.1 | 98.8 | 99.7 | 96.5 | 97.0 | 97.6 | 90.4 | 94.2 | 95.0 | 27.8 | 33.5 | 35.2 |
| Compton, Calif., 1971 | 85.0 | | | 100.0 | 100.0 | | 92.7 | 97.8 | | | 90.5 | | 15.8 | 7.4 |
| Atlanta, Ga., 1971 | 72.1 | 98.8 | 94.6 | 93.4 | 92.0 | 91.8 | 87.0 | 85.9 | 97.4 | 90.0 | 77.9 | 78.1 | 33.6 | 21.6 |
| Newark, N.J., 1971 | 72.0 | 90.3 | 97.9 | 97.1 | 97.4 | 88.4 | 91.2 | 91.3 | 51.3 | 85.6 | 86.4 | 19.3 | 19.8 | 22.5 |
| Orleans Parish, La., 1971 | 71.4 | | 91.2 | 92.2 | 93.4 | 83.3 | 81.9 | 80.8 | | 81.2 | 78.6 | 62.3 | 48.5 | 47.2 |
| Richmond, Va., 1971 | 69.1 | 98.5 | 93.6 | 88.3 | 93.9 | 88.6 | 56.8 | 36.5 | 98.5 | 84.6 | 44.7 | 78.0 | 9.6 | .1 |
| Baltimore City, Md., 1971 | 68.2 | 92.3 | 92.3 | 90.6 | 90.8 | 83.8 | 81.0 | 84.1 | 84.2 | 78.6 | 79.2 | 43.5 | 42.9 | 42.6 |
| St. Louis, Mo., 1971 | 67.7 | 93.7 | 92.9 | 97.5 | 97.9 | 89.0 | 87.9 | 89.8 | 90.9 | 87.6 | 82.7 | 49.9 | 49.8 | 47.5 |
| Gary, Ind., 1971 | 67.5 | 94.8 | 96.9 | 96.5 | 96.2 | 90.7 | 91.7 | 95.7 | 89.9 | 85.0 | 85.7 | 32.4 | 39.1 | 17.4 |
| Detroit, Mich., 1971 | 65.0 | 91.5 | 91.0 | 94.2 | 93.7 | 79.1 | 79.3 | 78.6 | 72.3 | 69.0 | 73.9 | 10.6 | 13.7 | 12.1 |
| Philadelphia, Pa., 1970 | 60.5 | 90.2 | 90.4 | 92.6 | | 76.9 | 80.2 | | 72.0 | 67.1 | 70.0 | 4.3 | 5.1 | |
| Oakland, Calif., 1971 | 58.1 | 83.2 | 94.5 | 93.5 | 93.7 | 77.1 | 75.2 | 73.1 | 48.7 | 63.4 | 58.6 | 4.7 | 2.6 | 1.6 |
| Cleveland, Ohio, 1971 | 57.3 | 94.6 | 95.2 | 95.8 | 95.4 | 90.8 | 90.9 | 91.3 | 82.3 | 86.0 | 89.2 | 24.7 | 34.8 | 35.4 |
| Birmingham, Ala., 1971 | 56.4 | | 92.8 | 84.2 | 86.1 | 92.7 | 73.5 | 74.7 | | 91.6 | 69.7 | 84.6 | 33.5 | 34.6 |
| Chicago, Ill., 1971 | 55.8 | 96.9 | 96.8 | 97.0 | 97.8 | 90.3 | 91.8 | 91.6 | 89.2 | 86.6 | 89.7 | 47.4 | 45.4 | 46.1 |
| Memphis, Tenn., 1971 | 53.7 | 98.8 | 97.4 | 93.5 | 92.9 | 95.4 | 90.1 | 89.2 | 95.1 | 92.7 | 89.5 | 73.3 | 49.8 | 41.5 |
| Kansas City, Mo., 1971 | 52.2 | 85.5 | 86.0 | 90.7 | 90.3 | 78.1 | 83.4 | 86.4 | 69.1 | 69.8 | 74.8 | 14.6 | 14.9 | 24.9 |
| Caddo Parish, La., 1971 | 49.6 | | 97.5 | 74.3 | 74.5 | 97.4 | 68.0 | 66.6 | | 97.4 | 65.1 | 94.0 | 44.5 | 30.3 |
| Louisville, Ky., 1971 | 48.8 | 84.5 | 86.5 | 88.3 | 87.3 | 64.9 | 77.4 | 82.3 | 69.5 | 52.7 | 68.4 | 7.8 | 4.3 | 15.6 |
| Chatham County, Ga., 1971 | 48.2 | | 90.7 | 80.5 | 40.6 | 86.5 | 67.1 | 7.6 | | 86.5 | 48.5 | 77.1 | 15.6 | 0 |
| Charleston County, S.C., 1971 | 48.0 | | 87.2 | 69.2 | 71.3 | 84.2 | 59.9 | 62.4 | | 84.2 | 53.7 | 84.2 | 13.6 | 24.9 |
| Norfolk, Va., 1971 | 47.9 | | 88.5 | 67.1 | 49.6 | 82.3 | 55.9 | 1.2 | | 79.6 | 46.3 | 49.6 | 26.1 | 0 |
| Cincinnati, Ohio, 1971 | 46.1 | 88.0 | 78.1 | 83.1 | 86.3 | 50.9 | 54.0 | 54.9 | 49.4 | 43.9 | 39.5 | 16.9 | 15.7 | 10.6 |
| Mobile County, Ala., 1971 | 45.9 | 99.9 | 89.1 | 81.8 | 64.2 | 87.5 | 54.4 | 44.2 | 99.9 | 87.5 | 47.1 | 59.9 | 10.1 | 15.3 |
| Dayton, Ohio, 1971 | 42.7 | | 89.1 | 87.0 | 84.4 | 82.7 | 77.8 | 78.1 | | 82.7 | 73.4 | 22.2 | 9.5 | 14.6 |
| Pittsburgh, Pa., 1971 | 41.1 | 82.8 | 78.7 | 76.7 | 76.6 | 60.0 | 57.5 | 61.6 | 49.5 | 52.5 | 56.5 | 9.8 | 13.2 | 9.5 |
| Flint, Mich., 1971 | 40.9 | 85.9 | 75.8 | 81.0 | 79.6 | 42.4 | 38.2 | 46.6 | 67.9 | 37.3 | 30.4 | 0 | 2.1 | 1.9 |
| Buffalo, N.Y., 1971 | 39.5 | 88.7 | 73.0 | 73.2 | 72.6 | 65.1 | 59.7 | 59.0 | 77.0 | 62.6 | 56.1 | 5.6 | 6.6 | 14.0 |
| Baton Rouge Parish, La., 1971 | 39.0 | | 94.4 | 78.0 | 77.1 | 94.2 | 71.9 | 72.0 | | 91.0 | 68.7 | 80.0 | 29.1 | 21.0 |
| Houston, Tex., 1971 | 37.8 | 97.6 | 94.7 | 91.6 | 91.3 | 90.9 | 85.4 | 86.0 | 93.0 | 88.0 | 73.7 | 64.5 | 8.8 | 8.7 |

| | | | | | | | | | | | | | | |
|---|---|---|---|---|---|---|---|---|---|---|---|---|---|---|
| Indianapolis, Ind., 1971 | 37. 7 | 84. 2 | 77. 6 | 79. 5 | 76. 5 | 62. 5 | 60. 3 | 60. 1 | 70. 5 | 57. 6 | 55. 6 | 10. 8 | 8. 7 | 12. 7 |
| Dallas, Tex., 1971 | 36. 3 | 90. 3 | 97. 9 | 97. 3 | 85. 0 | 93. 0 | 94. 1 | 83. 4 | 82. 6 | 87. 6 | 91. 4 | 32. 1 | 23. 2 | 10. 5 |
| Rochester, N.Y., 1971 | 35. 7 | ------ | 54. 4 | 59. 1 | 51. 0 | 34. 4 | 44. 2 | 33. 7 | ------ | 12. 1 | 24. 2 | 0 | 0 | 0 |
| New York, N.Y., 1971 | 34. 3 | 55. 5 | 80. 3 | 83. 7 | 83. 9 | 60. 5 | 65. 7 | 69. 2 | 20. 7 | 52. 2 | 57. 9 | 10. 2 | 11. 9 | 6. 0 |
| Muscogee County, Ga., 1971 | 32. 5 | ------ | 92. 9 | 88. 0 | 4. 0 | 87. 5 | 85. 8 | 1. 6 | ------ | 87. 5 | 80. 9 | 70. 0 | 61. 9 | 1. 6 |
| Charlotte-Mecklenburg County, N.C., 1971 | 31. 8 | ------ | 72. 3 | 9. 3 | 2. 1 | 68. 1 | 4. 1 | 1. 5 | ------ | 58. 9 | 1. 8 | 39. 0 | 0 | 0 |
| Boston, Mass., 1971 | 31. 7 | 79. 5 | 76. 7 | 82. 0 | 85. 1 | 54. 5 | 65. 1 | 63. 2 | 35. 4 | 43. 1 | 52. 0 | . 3 | 11. 0 | 1. 3 |
| Duval County, Fla., 1971 | 31. 3 | ------ | 87. 4 | 74. 4 | 64. 0 | 87. 4 | 57. 5 | 38. 2 | ------ | 87. 4 | 54. 9 | 76. 7 | 37. 0 | 23. 0 |
| San Francisco, Calif., 1971 | 30. 4 | 72. 3 | 84. 5 | 85. 8 | 90. 6 | 46. 6 | 55. 5 | 22. 3 | 21. 1 | 34. 3 | 31. 7 | . 4 | 1. 1 | 1. 3 |
| Winston-Salem-Forsyth County, N.C., 1971 | 29. 4 | ------ | 84. 7 | 63. 0 | 4. 3 | 84. 7 | 57. 4 | 2. 7 | ------ | 84. 4 | 57. 0 | 70. 9 | 43. 8 | 0 |
| Palm Beach County, Fla., 1971 | 28. 6 | ------ | 81. 4 | 74. 9 | 37. 1 | 79. 5 | 40. 6 | 10. 8 | ------ | 76. 2 | 29. 4 | 72. 3 | 0 | 0 |
| Escambia County, Fla., 1971 | 28. 4 | ------ | 77. 5 | 58. 7 | 57. 6 | 71. 3 | 16. 6 | 15. 2 | ------ | 70. 0 | 3. 8 | 70. 0 | 0 | 0 |
| Forth Worth, Tex., 1971 | 28. 3 | ------ | 90. 3 | 90. 2 | 78. 6 | 85. 4 | 80. 0 | 67. 0 | ------ | 85. 4 | 75. 3 | 60. 7 | 48. 4 | 20. 4 |
| Richmond, Calif., 1971 | 28. 3 | 82. 9 | 61. 6 | 49. 7 | 51. 2 | 43. 4 | 33. 2 | 30. 8 | 39. 2 | 34. 8 | 29. 9 | 5. 1 | 3. 0 | 2. 9 |
| Columbus, Ohio, 1971 | 28. 2 | 80. 8 | 71. 2 | 74. 1 | 71. 9 | 56. 9 | 53. 0 | 53. 9 | 34. 3 | 40. 7 | 45. 2 | 3. 1 | 2. 2 | 1. 7 |
| Milwaukee, Wis., 1971 | 28. 0 | 86. 8 | 87. 6 | 87. 8 | 85. 2 | 75. 9 | 76. 2 | 78. 8 | 72. 4 | 63. 2 | 60. 4 | 15. 5 | 0 | 5. 6 |
| Akron, Ohio, 1971 | 27. 8 | ------ | 62. 3 | 63. 5 | 66. 3 | 39. 4 | 49. 3 | 40. 2 | ------ | 23. 7 | 23. 8 | 3. 9 | 0 | 2. 9 |
| Nashville-Davidson County, Ky., 1971 | 27. 2 | ------ | 83. 2 | 75. 0 | 17. 3 | 69. 4 | 67. 0 | 0 | ------ | 61. 3 | 62. 4 | 51. 8 | 21. 1 | 0 |
| Toledo, Ohio, 1971 | 27. 2 | ------ | 77. 4 | 75. 9 | 77. 5 | 64. 1 | 59. 3 | 59. 4 | ------ | 52. 4 | 48. 5 | 9. 8 | 3. 5 | 2. 6 |
| Jefferson County, Ala., 1971 | 26. 7 | ------ | 97. 0 | 80. 7 | 60. 6 | 96. 7 | 78. 4 | 56. 7 | ------ | 96. 7 | 77. 6 | 96. 7 | 47. 8 | 30. 0 |
| Dade County, Fla., 1971 | 25. 7 | ------ | 87. 6 | 78. 3 | 77. 0 | 82. 0 | 53. 1 | 53. 2 | ------ | 80. 7 | 41. 9 | 48. 6 | 12. 3 | 12. 9 |
| Los Angeles, Calif., 1971 | 24. 9 | 87. 5 | 95. 3 | 94. 1 | 93. 2 | 88. 2 | 87. 1 | 86. 6 | 39. 5 | 83. 0 | 83. 3 | 12. 3 | 8. 7 | 7. 6 |
| Oklahoma City, 1971 | 23. 6 | 96. 8 | 87. 5 | 78. 6 | 78. 1 | 83. 3 | 75. 1 | 68. 3 | 90. 5 | 83. 3 | 75. 1 | 5. 7 | 22. 8 | 32. 1 |
| Broward County, Fla., 1971 | 23. 3 | ------ | 85. 5 | 47. 9 | 21. 3 | 79. 7 | 41. 1 | 8. 0 | ------ | 79. 7 | 39. 2 | 68. 9 | 15. 8 | 2. 3 |
| Prince Georges County, Md., 1971 | 22. 4 | ------ | 43. 9 | 59. 2 | 61. 3 | 25. 6 | 35. 0 | 39. 8 | ------ | 20. 7 | 20. 2 | 13. 9 | 2. 3 | 1. 5 |
| Greenville, County, S.C., 1971 | 22. 2 | ------ | 85. 2 | 1. 5 | . 9 | 83. 3 | . 6 | 0 | ------ | 83. 3 | 0 | 74. 3 | 0 | 0 |
| Polk County, Fla., 1971 | 22. 1 | ------ | 67. 3 | 27. 5 | 20. 1 | 66. 7 | 12. 1 | 11. 7 | ------ | 66. 7 | 11. 4 | 66. 7 | 0 | 0 |
| Jefferson Parish, La., 1971 | 20. 7 | ------ | 79. 5 | 51. 3 | 6. 1 | 79. 5 | 36. 3 | . 6 | ------ | 79. 5 | 31. 7 | 79. 5 | 19. 5 | 0 |
| Hillsborough County, Fla., 1971 | 19. 5 | ------ | 81. 7 | 76. 6 | 2. 2 | 77. 4 | 62. 8 | . 6 | ------ | 73. 3 | 49. 4 | 64. 3 | 11. 3 | 0 |
| Orange County, Fla., 1971 | 18. 4 | ------ | 79. 9 | 59. 3 | 47. 7 | 77. 1 | 52. 0 | 28. 3 | ------ | 77. 1 | 33. 3 | 77. 1 | 16. 6 | 4. 9 |
| Omaha, Nebr., 1971 | 18. 0 | 81. 1 | 79. 5 | 73. 3 | 70. 7 | 55. 0 | 64. 3 | 61. 6 | 47. 7 | 39. 1 | 48. 0 | 0 | 0 | 0 |
| Sacramento, Calif., 1971 | 16. 3 | ------ | 29. 7 | 34. 2 | 36. 0 | 5. 3 | 3. 8 | 6. 7 | ------ | 3. 5 | 3. 3 | 0 | 0 | 0 |
| Pinellas County, Fla., 1971 | 16. 3 | ------ | 78. 3 | 54. 5 | 5. 2 | 73. 2 | 20. 9 | 0 | ------ | 72. 1 | 20. 0 | 25. 9 | 4. 8 | 0 |
| Denver County, Colo., 1971 | 15. 7 | 75. 2 | 80. 0 | 55. 4 | 54. 7 | 65. 9 | 44. 5 | 36. 5 | 29. 4 | 56. 1 | 37. 5 | 0 | 0 | 0 |

TABLE 7-16.—*Black-student isolation in large city school districts, ranked by percentage of black students in the district.*—Continued

| School district | Percent black | 50 to 100 percent | | | | 80 to 100 percent | | | 90 to 100 percent | | | 100 percent | | |
|---|---|---|---|---|---|---|---|---|---|---|---|---|---|---|
| | | 1965 | 1968 | 1970 | 1971 | 1968 | 1970 | 1971 | 1965 | 1968 | 1970 | 1968 | 1970 | 1971 |
| Fort Wayne, Ind., 1971 | 15.6 | 82.9 | 73.1 | 70.4 | 48.8 | 57.1 | 49.2 | 36.1 | 60.8 | 32.2 | 40.6 | 0 | 0 | 0 |
| San Antonio, Tex., 1971 | 15.5 | 77.2 | 89.4 | 90.7 | 91.7 | 85.6 | 67.1 | 71.2 | 65.9 | 85.3 | 60.1 | 52.7 | 11.1 | 12.6 |
| Wichita, Kans., 1971 | 15.5 | 89.1 | 54.5 | 35.6 | .3 | 53.4 | 31.5 | 0 | 63.5 | 47.4 | 31.5 | 0 | 4.0 | 0 |
| Austin, Tex., 1971 | 14.7 | 86.1 | 86.9 | 84.0 | 63.9 | 86.0 | 78.5 | 58.1 | 86.1 | 84.6 | 78.5 | 22.2 | 14.7 | 8.6 |
| Tulsa, Okla., 1971 | 14.1 | 98.7 | 84.4 | 72.5 | 59.7 | 77.0 | 68.7 | 51.2 | 90.7 | 77.0 | 68.7 | 45.7 | 17.7 | 10.1 |
| Anne Arundel County, Md., 1971 | 12.9 | ------ | 19.7 | 21.3 | 21.1 | 2.5 | 3.5 | 3.1 | ------ | 0 | 2.4 | 0 | 0 | 0 |
| Clark County, Nev., 1971 | 12.9 | ------ | 51.9 | 37.7 | 32.4 | 51.9 | 30.0 | 18.7 | ------ | 51.9 | 30.0 | 0 | 5.4 | 3.7 |
| Seattle, Wash., 1970 | 12.8 | 60.4 | 55.2 | 59.4 | ------ | 24.4 | 25.1 | ------ | 9.9 | 8.1 | 3.1 | 0 | 0 | ------ |
| Rockford, Ill., 1971 | 12.8 | ------ | 41.5 | 44.1 | 44.3 | 10.6 | 7.8 | 8.3 | ------ | 0 | 7.8 | 0 | 0 | 0 |
| San Diego, Calif., 1971 | 12.8 | 73.3 | 74.9 | 67.9 | 64.8 | 64.3 | 56.3 | 55.6 | 13.9 | 54.7 | 46.4 | 0 | 0 | 0 |
| Brevard County, Fla., 1971 | 11.1 | ------ | 30.2 | 11.2 | 10.5 | 30.2 | 11.2 | 10.5 | ------ | 30.2 | 11.2 | 30.2 | 0 | 0 |
| Virginia Beach, Va., 1971 | 10.2 | ------ | 37.8 | 12.6 | 0 | 37.8 | 12.6 | 0 | ------ | 37.8 | 12.6 | 29.2 | 0 | 0 |
| Long Beach, Calif., 1971 | 10.1 | ------ | 63.4 | 65.0 | 65.5 | 12.4 | 0 | 0 | ------ | 0 | 0 | 0 | 0 | 0 |
| Portland, Oreg., 1971 | 9.8 | 59.2 | 42.6 | 37.9 | 47.6 | 24.9 | 21.3 | 21.2 | 46.5 | 20.5 | 17.4 | 0 | 0 | 0 |
| Minneapolis, Minn., 1971 | 9.7 | 39.2 | 29.2 | 42.4 | 35.2 | 0 | 0 | 6.7 | 0 | 0 | 0 | 0 | 0 | 0 |
| Fresno, Calif., 1971 | 9.3 | ------ | 84.2 | 75.6 | 71.0 | 76.6 | 67.0 | 64.0 | ------ | 76.6 | 51.2 | 11.3 | .3 | .3 |
| Des Moines, Iowa, 1971 | 8.4 | ------ | 43.0 | 41.5 | 42.8 | 11.3 | .6 | 8.0 | ------ | 0 | 0 | 0 | 0 | 0 |
| De Kalb County, Ga., 1971 | 7.2 | ------ | 55.4 | 29.5 | 29.7 | 47.0 | 14.7 | 22.2 | ------ | 47.0 | 14.7 | 10.2 | .9 | 0 |
| St. Paul, Minn., 1971 | 7.0 | ------ | 12.4 | 35.4 | 31.6 | 12.4 | 10.7 | 9.6 | ------ | 12.4 | 10.7 | 0 | 0 | 0 |
| Kanawha County, W. Va., 1971 | 6.6 | ------ | 18.1 | 13.8 | 12.6 | 0 | 0 | 0 | ------ | 0 | 0 | 0 | 0 | 0 |
| Corpus Christi, Tex., 1971 | 5.7 | ------ | 98.3 | 97.3 | 94.5 | 78.5 | 84.0 | 80.0 | ------ | 77.6 | 54.0 | 25.6 | .5 | .6 |
| Tucson, Ariz., 1971 | 5.3 | ------ | 81.1 | 73.0 | 69.7 | 34.5 | 34.6 | 35.4 | ------ | 23.7 | 18.5 | 0 | 0 | 0 |
| Jefferson County, Ky., 1971 | 3.8 | ------ | 26.4 | 19.0 | 14.2 | 26.4 | 19.0 | 14.2 | ------ | 26.4 | 19.0 | 0 | 0 | 0 |
| El Paso, Tex., 1971 | 3.0 | ------ | 38.2 | 42.2 | 29.1 | 28.3 | 20.3 | 18.5 | ------ | 25.9 | 18.5 | 4.3 | 3.2 | 0 |
| Cobb County, Ga., 1971 | 2.9 | ------ | 6.7 | 0 | 0 | 6.7 | 0 | 0 | ------ | 6.7 | 0 | 6.7 | 0 | 0 |
| Albuquerque, N. Mex., 1971 | 2.6 | ------ | 72.4 | 63.8 | 65.6 | 51.2 | 38.0 | 46.9 | ------ | 31.4 | 27.1 | 0 | 0 | 0 |

## Chapter 8—The Causes of Racial Isolation and Segregation in Public Schools

School segregation is but one of the ways racial and socioeconomic groups are separated in our society. Its causes are varied and complex. In many States it started with the passage of constitutional and statutory provisions requiring racially separate dual schools systems. But today, particularly in metropolitan areas, it is mainly the result of two factors which often interact to determine the racial and socioeconomic compositions of public schools. The first is the existence of segregated residential patterns, often created, sanctioned and perpetuated by the policies and practices of governmental agencies, public officials and private organizations. The second factor is the actions of school authorities which often assure that schools are racially and socioeconomically homogeneous institutions.

### A. Segregated Housing

Residential segregation is a fact of American life. Segregated residential patterns exist with remarkable similarity throughout the United States; and segregated schools follow those patterns.

As Robert Carter, President of the National Committee Against Discrimination in Housing, told the committee:

> Because housing segregation has spread so far and has become so entrenched throughout the United States, and because of the use of the neighborhood school, school segregation has become more widespread. The trend seems to be one way—toward increased school separation. . . . We have tied a policy of school organization (which we label *de facto* school segregation) to a policy of housing segregation.*

The extent of racial segregation by residence has been well documented. Demographer Karl E. Taeuber, who developed a "segregation index" for 207 American cities—all the cities for which census data are available by block and which had at least 1,000 nonwhite households in 1960—reached this depressing conclusion:

> No elaborate analysis is necessary to conclude from these figures that a high degree of residential segregation based on race is a universal characteristic of American cities. This segregation is found in the cities of the North and West as well as of the South; in large cities as small; in nonindustrial cities as well as industrial; in cities with hundreds of thousands of Negro residents as well as those with only a few

*Hearings of the U.S. Senate Select Committee on Equal Educational Opportunity, Part 5—*De Facto Segregation and Housing Discrimination*, Aug. 25, 1970; p. 2645.

thousand, and in cities that are progressive in their employment practices and civil rights policies as well as those that are not.*

This conclusion was based on 1960 Census data. But the picture was no better during the decade of the 1960s. Dr. Taeuber examined special census data for 13 cities to assess trends in population, migration, and residential segregation from 1960 to mid-decade. He concluded that:

. . . In these cities the demographic trends of the 1950s are continuing. There is a net out-migration of white population, and in several cities a decline in total population. Negro population is growing rapidly, but natural increase rather than net in-migration increasingly is the principal source. The concentration of whites in the suburbs and Negroes in the central cities is continuing. Within the cities, indices of racial residential segregation generally increased. The combination of small increases in residential segregation and large increases in the Negro percentage has greatly intensified the magnitude of the problems of segregation and desegregation of neighborhoods, local institutions, and schools.**

There is no dispute about the "universality" of residential segregation in this country—and its impact on education. Speaking for the present Administration, George Romney, Secretary of Housing and Urban Development, told the committee that

. . . metropolitan areas today consist of miles of slums, miles of gray areas, and miles of sprawling suburbs, some modest and some affluent. These are the miles which separate the black and the poor from good schools, and from new promising job opportunities. And with this physical separation has come a decreasing ability of people of differing backgrounds to communicate with each other about the problems which clearly affect everyone.***

The 1970 Census figures show no relief from the Nation's increasing residential segregation. In 66 Standard Metropolitan Statistical Areas in which more than half of all our citizens live, the white population of the central cities declined between 1960 and 1970 by 2 million, or 5 percent, while the black population increased by nearly 3 million or 35 percent.

Conversely, in these cities' suburbs, the white population increased by 12.5 million and the black population by less than 1 million. As a result, the black percentage in the suburbs increased from 4.2 percent in 1960 to only 4.5 percent in 1970.

While Dr. Taeuber's studies have shown that residential segregation based on race is greater than residential segregation based on economic class, it is clear that Americans are not separated by race alone. In many suburban areas of the country, there are no housing opportunities for low- and moderate-income white Americans; and efforts to provide such housing are often met with strong local opposition.

---

**Ibid.*, p. 2736.
***Ibid.*, p. 2746.
****Ibid.*, August 26, 1970, p. 2756.

Thus, many low-income white families—like minority-group families—are consigned to their own neighborhoods in metropolitan areas. Also, their children often attend schools dominated by other children from nonaffluent families.

So in housing as well as in schools, Americans are walled off by both race *and* economic class.

Those low-income Americans who cannot live where they choose—whether white or nonwhite—are losing the basic chance to help themselves. For with the exodus to the suburbs have gone the economic heart beat of the cities—jobs:

- Nationally over the last two decades, 80 percent of the new jobs created in large metropolitan areas have been located in the suburbs.
- Of the 990,000 new jobs created between 1959 and 1967 in the New York metropolitan region, 75 percent were located outside the city. And most of the new jobs in the city were for more affluent white collar workers.
- The Census Bureau estimates that the number of men employed in the central cities decreased by 2 percent from 1960 to 1970. During this same period, male employment outside the central cities increased by 35.4 percent.

In his 1971 housing message, President Nixon assessed the impact of this job trend on minority Americans. He observed that the:

> Price of racial segregation is being paid each day in dollars: In wages lost because minority Americans are unable to find housing near the suburban jobs for which they could qualify. Industry and jobs are leaving central cities for the surrounding areas. Unless minority workers can move along with the jobs, the jobs that go to the suburbs will be denied to the minorities—and more persons who want to work will be added to the cities' unemployment and welfare rolls.

The President also pointed out that involuntary racial separation inevitably leads to "the waste of human resources through the denial of human opportunity."

> No Nation is rich enough and strong enough to afford the price which dehumanizing living environments extract in the form of wasted human potential and stunted human lives—and many of those living environments in which black and other minority Americans are trapped are dehumanizing.

### B. The Causes of Residential Segregation

As in the case of school segregation, housing segregation is seldom a matter of individual choice. It is clear that Federal, State and local governmental practices, at every level, have contributed to the housing segregation which exists today. These actions combine with those of private organizations such as lending institutions, real estate brokerage firms, land developers and others to establish and maintain residential segregation.

In his testimony before the committee, Secretary Romney placed this in historical perspective. The answer, he said, lies in "our country's tormented history of race relations."

> . . . Throughout most of that history, the dominant majority supported or condoned social and institutional separation of the races. This attitude became fixed in public law and public policy at every level of government and every branch of government, and thus it was adopted as a matter of course by the Federal Government when it entered the housing field in the 1930s. It continued after World War II.*

As Secretary Romney indicated, the Federal Government played a major role in building ghettos and creating residential segregation through:

- The massive public housing projects which often deliberately reinforced segregated living patterns.
- The Federal highway programs which often helped destroy viable urban communities and often divided inner cities from their suburbs.
- Urban renewal programs which promised better neighborhoods, but often produced other, more crowded slums.
- Permitting local governments to pass on the location of Federal low-income housing.
- The location of Federal offices in suburbs which barred low and moderate income housing.

Since World War II, the FHA and Veterans' Administration have financed more than $120 billion worth of new housing. Less than 2 percent of this has been available to nonwhite families, and much of that on a strictly segregated basis.

The Federal Government's involvement in residential segregation was not a matter of inadvertence or neglect. It was conscious, stated policy. For example, the official FHA *Underwriting Manual* for 1938 contained the following warning: "If a neighborhood is to retain stability, it is necessary that properties shall continue to be occupied by the same social and racial group." The Manual, in effect until the Supreme Court ruled in 1948 that racial covenants were not enforceable in the courts, recommended use of restrictive covenants to keep out "inharmonious racial groups." Indeed, it provided a model restrictive covenant for those needing assistance in pursuing this policy.

Secretary Romney acknowledged that a variety of Federal programs are, in part, responsible for today's segregated living patterns and cited the FHA's role in creating and maintaining segregated housing:

> Unfortunately, the sound policy objectives of FHA were accompanied by both official and informal Federal encouragement of racial segregation. FHA refused to provide insurance in integrated neighborhoods on the grounds that the financial risk to the Government was too great. As a matter of fact, Congress declared as a matter of policy that the FHA had to limit insurance to those instances where they could prove the economic feasibility of the insurance, and with the attitudes that existed, this tended to be a restrictive policy.

* * * * * * *

---

**Ibid.*, p. 2775.

In addition to preventing minorities from gaining access to new housing, FHA policies also generally withheld insurance from existing housing in central city areas. This practice, called "redlining," involved an unwritten but well-understood agreement between financial institutions and FHA that many central city neighborhoods occupied largely by minority groups had an unfavorable economic future.*

In addition to the Federal Government, other levels of government have also pursued policies designed to perpetuate residential segregation. In some cases, local efforts to exclude low- and moderate-income housing have been quite blatant. For example, many communities have rezoned parcels of land to block federally subsidized housing.

Richard Bellman, a staff attorney for the National Committee Against Discrimination in Housing described such local barriers in testimony before the committee:

In my opinion, one of the most serious impediments to the creation of integrated communities is the imposition by local communities of restrictive and exclusionary building code and land use requirements which effectively foreclose construction of new housing for low- and moderate-income citizens. . . . Many suburban cities and towns have simply zoned all residential areas exclusively for single family uses eliminating the possibility of construction of townhouses and apartment units for the poor. Some communities impose large lot or minimum floor space requirements which have the same result. Other communities raise arbitrary building code requirements, or encourage construction only of luxury type apartments while refusing to approve multiple dwellings with units to accommodate larger families.**

Mr. Bellman cited a number of examples of action by local public officials to block housing projects sponsored by minority citizen groups:

. . . In Lackawanna, N.Y., city officials denied a nonprofit sponsor a building permit for construction of a Department of Housing and Urban Development Section 236 project in an exclusively white ward; in Lawton, Okla., the City Council refused to rezone a parcel of land in a white section to a multi-family residential classification to enable construction of a Section 236 project; in Lansing, Mich., a voter referendum action challenging a rezoning blocked construction of a turkey housing project in a white area; in Union City, Calif., another citizen referendum challenge wiped out a rezoning which would have enabled a Mexican-American housing sponsor to build a 280 unit Section 236 project near to a new white single-family residential tract.

In each one of these cases minority group housing sponsors sought to build projects in areas which would provide decent housing in an integrated environment. In each case vehement opposition was raised by white citizens and in each case public action was taken which was clearly arbitrary and racially discriminatory. The Lackawanna and Lawton cases resulted

*_Ibid._, p. 2755.
**_Ibid._, p. 2910.

in findings by Federal courts that invidious racial discrimination in fact had motivated public officials.*

Another major barrier to the creation of integrated housing opportunities is the practice by many city housing authorities of confining public housing developments to ghetto areas within the city. Such practices, of course, reinforce and expand the ghetto—thereby hastening white flight from the city and making it more difficult to attract white families back to the city.

Increasingly, many of these practices are being challenged in State and Federal courts. Many courts have found such practices violate the "equal protection" clause of the 14th Amendment and other constitutional guarantees. On the other hand, the Supreme Court, in *James* v. *Valtierra*, 402 U.S. 137 (1971), held that absent any evidence of racially discriminatory intent, a State law requiring prior approval of federally subsidized housing projects by local referendum does not, on its face, violate the Constitution.

Thus, there can be no sweeping generalizations about the legal impact of the wide variety of local policies inhibiting the elimination of residential segregation. The law in this area is still in a state of flux, and it may be several years before a clear-cut legal pattern emerges.

But there can be no doubt that in most areas of the country, there is substantial local resistance to low- and moderate-income housing and to the elimination of residential segregation. In 1968, the National Advisory Commission on Civil Disorders found:

> Housing programs serving low-income groups have been concentrated in the ghettos. Nonghetto areas, particularly suburbs, for the most part have steadfastly opposed low income, rent supplement, or below-market interest rate housing, and have successfully restricted use of these programs outside the ghetto.

The result of these governmental policies and actions has been a pervasive segregation that flows from residence: Isolation in schools, jobs, public services, consumer markets—in nearly every area of human endeavor and opportunity.

The pattern of combined governmental official action which produces residential and school isolation in most of our large cities was best described by the Federal District Court in Michigan in *Bradley* v. *Milliken*, Civ. Act. 35257 (E.D. Mich. 1971), the Detroit school desegregation case decided in September 1971:

> The city . . . is a community generally divided by racial lines. Residential segregation within the city and throughout the larger metropolitan area is substantial, pervasive and of long standing. Black citizens are located in separate and distinct areas within the city and are not generally to be found in the suburbs. While the racially unrestricted choice of black persons and economic factors may have played some part in the development of this pattern of residential segregation, it is, in the main, the result of past and present practices and customs of racial discrimination, both public and private, which have and do restrict the housing opportunities of black people . . .

---

* *Ibid*, p. 2910.

Government actions and inaction at all levels, Federal, State and local, have combined, with those of private organizations, such as loaning institutions and real estate associations and brokerage firms, to establish and to maintain the pattern of residential segregation throughout the . . . metropolitan area. It is no answer to say that restricted practices grew gradually . . . or that since 1948 racial restrictions on the ownership of real property have been removed. The policies pursued by both government and private persons and agencies have a continuing and present effect upon the complexion of the community—as we know, the choice of a residence is a relatively infrequent affair. For many years FHA and VA openly advised and advocated the maintenance of "harmonious" neighborhoods, that is, racially and economically harmonious. The conditions created continue. . . . The actions or the failure to act by the responsible school authorities, both city and State, were linked to that of these other governmental units.

When we speak of governmental action we should not view the different agencies as a collection of unrelated units. Perhaps the most that can be said is that all of them, including the school authorities, are, in part, responsible for the segregated condition which exists. And we note that just as there is an interaction between residential patterns and the racial composition of the schools, so there is a corresponding effect on the residential pattern by the racial composition of the schools.

### C. Local School Policies and Practices

As the court said in *Bradley* v. *Milliken*, there is an interaction between residential patterns and the racial composition of schools. Each affects the other. Thus, the official policies and practices of some school boards in school districts throughout the country along with residential segregation, have sanctioned and perpetuated racial isolation in public schools. These policies and practices include the gerrymandering of attendance zones and school boundary lines; the changing of grade structures; changes in feeder patterns from elementary and junior and senior high schools; the use of buses to transport children to racially segregated schools out of their neighborhoods; the assignment of teachers on the basis of race; the construction of new schools and additions to old schools, and the assignment of children on the basis of race to special education classes and other actions.

Many of these practices, while seemingly innocent on their face and ostensibly undertaken for educational or economic reasons, are intentionally designed to result in the maintenance of segregated education.

A typical example of such practices was found by the U.S. District Court in Indiana to have existed since well before the *Brown* decision in the city of Indianapolis. In that case the court found that despite the repeal of State school segregation laws in 1949 the Indianapolis school board perpetuated a dual school system both before and after the *Brown* decision.

Between 1949 and 1954 the court found that:

In some instances where desegregation would have resulted if children had been assigned to the closest school, they were assigned to segregated schools farther from their homes . . .

Boundary lines were drawn with knowledge of racial residential patterns and the housing discrimination underlying it. Not only did the board not attempt to promote desegregation, but the boundary lines tended to cement in the segregated character of the elementary schools. In some instances, segregation was promoted by drawing boundary lines which did not follow natural boundaries or were not equidistant between schools . . .

Since 1954, the Court said,

. . . the most notable nonracial characteristic of the school system has been growth . . . This growth caused overcrowding problems in many schools at one time or another, and the board had available, and employed, various techniques to deal with this overcrowding.

Among these techniques were attendance zone boundary changes, the construction of additions, the construction of new schools, the provision of transportation or the adjustment of existing transportation, alteration in grade structure, and the location or relocation of special education classes in elementary schools . . .

The defendant board has constructed numerous additions to schools since 1954; more often than not the capacity thus created has been used to promote segregation. It has built additions at Negro schools and then zoned Negro students into them from predominantly white schools; it has built additions at white schools for white children attending Negro schools; it has generally failed to reduce overcrowding at schools of one race by assigning students to use newly built capacity at schools of the opposite race . . .

During the post-1954 period, the board perpetuated segregation through the use of optional attendance zones. Specifically, in areas of racially mixed residential patterns students were given options between predominantly Negro and predominantly white elementary schools, and where entire elementary districts covered both Negro and white neighborhoods, graduates were given options between predominantly Negro and predominantly white high schools. White students in optional zones almost always attended white schools . . .

The board has perpetuated segregation through the construction of new schools. Specifically, new elementary schools to be attended by students of predominantly one race have been constructed adjacent to schools attended primarily by students of the opposite race . . .

The board has perpetuated segregation by transporting students from overcrowded schools of one race to schools of the same race rather than to available nearby schools of the opposite race. In contrast to the current local and national hullabaloo about busing, the board's minutes record no citizen protests to the busing of white students to white schools.

The board has also perpetuated segregation in the assignment of special education classes. Specifically, it has maintained predominantly Negro and predominantly white special education departments at contiguous Negro and white schools and has shifted special education classes between schools with a resultant increase in segregation . . .

Some of the board's 1954–68 segregation practices are evident in simple boundary changes . . . According to the evidence, there have been approximately 350 boundary changes in the system since 1954. More than 90 percent of these promoted segregation.

In a number of cases involving school districts throughout the country the courts have found some or all these practices to exist. Whether or not intentionally designed to perpetuate racial isolation in public schools, they are typical of the actions which have been undertaken in hundreds of school districts not yet taken to court.

## D. State Dual School Systems

Finally, the most obvious cause of school segregation stems from the existence of State laws designed either to sanction dual school systems or avoid the establishment of unitary school systems. Before the Supreme Court's 1954 decision in *Brown* v. *Board of Education*, in many States, segregated schools were initially established and maintained under the mandate of State constitutional and statutory law. Schools were segregated as a matter of accepted public policy.

This was true in Northern as well as most Southern and Border States. It was the official legal policy of the State of Indiana, for example, to separate black and white students before 1949. The same was true for Arizona and Wisconsin until 1951, as well as the States of the Deep South until the *Brown* decision in 1954. In fact, before the *Brown* decision, all but six States—Hawaii, Maine, Nevada, New Hampshire, Vermont and Washington—at one time or another legally sanctioned some form of racial separation by State constitution, statute or judicial decision.

These laws were held to violate the Federal Constitution in 1954. However, in many Southern States, legislatures enacted statutes designed to perpetuate the operation of segregated school systems by sanctioning such devices as divesting local school boards of the authority to assign children to particular schools, "tuition grants," "freedom of choice" and by other means in an effort to frustrate execution of the Supreme Court's decisions. These efforts to resist school desegregation culminated with the enactment of antibusing statutes by State legislatures, North and South, designed to prohibit the assignment of students on account of race for purposes of desegregation.

These and other similar legal devices designed to avoid school desegregation have now all been declared unconstitutional. Further, through enforcement of Title VI of the Civil Rights Act of 1964 and with Supreme Court decisions such as *Green* v. *New Kent County*, 391 U.S. 430 (1968), most of the dual school systems in the South that originated and were perpetuated through the sanction of unconstitutional State laws have now been declared unconstitutional.

But, as the previous discussion demonstrates, much of the remaining school isolation in the South and nearly all of it in other areas of the country is the result of a combination of factors which converge to produce both residential and school segregation.

# Chapter 9—Unequal and Discriminatory Educational Practices

The assignment of disadvantaged and minority group children to separate schools is only one of the ways in which schools create and maintain inequality. The educational process itself favors middle and upper class, nonminority children and often suppresses the aspirations of children from disadvantaged groups.

A child's success in school is affected for better or worse by the attitudes and expectations of his classroom teachers and school staff, by his placement in a particular class or learning group, by the process of testing and evaluation to which he is continually subjected and in other ways that schools as institutions treat children.

Usually these practices are undertaken with the best of intentions for seemingly valid educational reasons. But all too often they constitute acts of unconscious and sometimes deliberate discrimination against minority group children. Either way, they tend to label children according to their background rather than their ability or potential. They play a major role in determining a child's life chances, for they deeply affect a child's attitudes about himself and his culture, his opportunity to achieve to the best of his ability in school, the possibility of further education after high school and his place in society at the end of his educational career.

As Dr. Mark R. Lohman, Professor of Education, University of California at Riverside, told the Select Committee, there are "hundreds of subtle ways in which schooling is rigged so that the middle class is continuously the winner . . ."*

From the time he enters kindergarten or first grade, the minority group or disadvantaged child is the loser. Dr. David Sanchez, a member of the San Francisco school board described how schools injure the Spanish-speaking child:

> The injuries of the Latin American child have been inflicted by those who have claimed to teach and motivate him, and who have, in reality, alienated him, and destroyed his identity through the subtle rejection of his language (which nobody speaks), his culture (which nobody understands), and ultimately, him (whom nobody values).**

Dr. Sanchez' description applies equally to the black, Oriental American, American Indian, Spanish-speaking, or other minority or poor white child in many schools.

---

*** Hearings of the U.S. Senate Select Committee on Equal Educational Opportunity, Part 20—*Unequal School Practices*, Nov. 8, 1971.**

**** *Ibid.*, Part 4—*Mexican American Education*, Aug. 18, 1970, p. 2392.**

## A. Teacher Attitudes and Expectations

In many ways the school teacher is the most influential person in a child's life outside his home. Studies show that in most classes children spend 80 percent of their time listening to their teachers. A schoolchild spends about a third of his waking hours 5 days a week, 9 months at year in school. The interaction between teacher and child lies at the heart of the educational process. Perhaps more than any other factors, the ability of the teacher and how the teacher and child relate to each other determine success in school. A child's teacher plays a crucial, sensitive and personal role in his development, next only to that of the child's parents, his siblings and perhaps his peers.

The disadvantaged child's failure in school is often rooted in his deprived home life before he arrives in the classroom. But his first contact with his teacher begins a process that may well perpetuate inequality. He learns quickly what his teacher expects of him. And the teacher's expectation affects his performance, a phenomenon called by sociologists the "self-fulfilling prophecy." Simply defined, it means that people tend to do what others expect and these expectations evoke behavior that makes the expectations come true. Thus, a teacher who believes for whatever reason that a child is likely to fail will often place that child either in the teacher's own mind or physically, with a group of other children about whom he or she has similar attitudes. Or, as Charles Silberman has described the "self-fulfilling prophecy" in *Crisis in the Classroom:*

> The teacher who assumes that her students cannot learn is likely to discover that she has a class of children who are indeed unable to learn; yet another teacher, working with the same class but without the same expectation, may discover that she has a class of interested learners. The same obtains with respect to behavior: The teacher who assumes that her students will be disruptive is likely to have a disruptive class on her hands.

Many teachers understandably prefer to teach well motivated, high achieving students. Formal teacher training tends to be oriented toward the training of white, middle-class students. Many find it difficult to understand and teach children from races or cultures different from their own.

What is communicated to the disadvantaged child is an attitude toward his cultural, ethnic and racial upbringing and his role in life. He may be seen as unruly and apathetic and told to be obedient, respectful and quiet rather than seen as being able, responsible, active and curious.

As Professor Kevin Ryan of the University of Chicago stated in a report to the Select Committee:

> Even those [teachers] who are free of conscious and subconscious racism are usually ill at ease with the children of blacks, Mexican Americans, Indians, and even poor whites. Their training gives them little understanding of, and therefore little respect for, the culture, mores, and life styles of these groups.

The result is a paradox. The students whom teachers enjoy teaching the most may need these teachers less than those students in poor schools in disadvantaged neighborhoods that teachers understandably want to avoid. It is the student who is rejected as unworthy who needs closer, more sensitive contacts with teachers and more intensive formal instruction.

Dr. Uvalde Palomares, one of the leading experts in the Nation on the education of language minority children, was the Select Committee's first witness in April 1970. Though he described his own personal experiences as a Chicano child from the fields of California when he entered school and came in contact for the first time with his new teacher in an alien environment, he stated his experiences were typical of thousands of Chicano children today in the schools of the Southwest.

> Imagine a 3-year-old boy . . . he is picking prunes and putting them in the box . . . his parents are very proud, he is busy . . . he is proud of the fact that he is moving fast and not sitting still because that is not valued in the field . . . he is aggressive . . . proud to a certain degree of his aggressiveness . . . particularly physical aggressiveness . . .
>
> He is going to interact with the teacher the same way that he was interacting with his parents . . . he is going to interact physically; he is moving fast . . .
>
> Now, the minute the teacher starts to interact with the child she is going to have certain expectancies from him. One of them is that the child can sit still; the child can pay attention . . . The child enters ready to do the things he is complimented for and lives for. Immediately the teacher tries to deal with it. How is she going to deal with the whole business of his moving about fast and pushing kids out of the way and trying to get his own and never wanting to sit still, of not asking permission to go to the bathroom . . .
>
> Neither party is guilty certainly of doing anything on purpose . . . both the child and the teacher are struggling to communicate and understand each other. Here is essentially what happens. The teacher looks at the behavior of the child and labels it . . . as flighty, hyperactive, overly aggressive . . . disrespectful. Yet all the child is doing is what he was brought up to do by parents and farmers in the community who thought he would make an excellent worker in the field.
>
> He enters the first grade. The effort by the teacher then becomes to slow him down, to get him to sit still, to get him to pay attention. The first and most significant problem that happens is that she tries to get him to stop speaking Spanish . . .
>
> The teacher starts speaking only English to him; the child begins to turn himself off; something begins to happen to that child that the teacher doesn't like. He begins to develop a bad concept. He begins to see himself as a bad kid. Nobody can really understand why . . . when he walked in that room he might have been hyperactive, flighty, overly aggressive. But he was also brighteyed. He was interested; he was trying, he was involved . . .
>
> As the teacher begins to quiet him down and show him in her own way that he must slow down he begins to slow down . . . At the same time something begins to happen to

those eyes . . . His eyes begin to dull . . . Where the teacher used to worry about his acting out in early age now he doesn't act out . . . He will notice that the teachers aren't really concerned and that they are beginning to use other words; he is kind of dull, uninterested . . .

In this child's third year, in the second grade he is being called dumb; he forgets easily; he is taught one thing today, cannot remember others. By now he is almost 2 years behind . . . Suddenly they become very worried and they begin to give him tests . . . Findings show that the child has really fallen behind now and he is something of a problem child and he must be dealt with remedially . . .

If you walk into the classroom, you find that the teacher unwittingly is forcing him into a position where he is developing bad feelings about himself, beginning to see himself as inferior, beginning not to like school and he is already starting the process of dropping out.*

Dr. Palomares did not blame the teachers. As he stated, the teachers he was describing really care for their children. They are eager to start communicating with them. The teacher's way of dealing with the child whom she labels as a problem and who comes from a different cultural background is identical, Dr. Palomares pointed out, to the way she would relate to the child from her own middle class background where it is important to sit still and pay attention. As Dr. Palomares said:

The teacher is treating the middle class and the Chicano farm child both equally, but by treating them both equally she is rendering unequal opportunity to the Chicano child because his problem is not that he is sick or bad, but that he is ignorant.

The treatment of schoolchildren who speak their native language at home and have little knowledge of English when they arrive at public school can only be described as having a devastating effect on the child. One committee witness, José V. Uriegas, a member of the Texas State Advisory Committee on Civil Rights, estimated that 95 percent of the Chicano children in Uvalde, Tex., speak Spanish almost exclusively before they enter school. He described what happens to the Chicano child in the Uvalde school system:

I don't think it takes a professional psychologist to see the psychological damage that is done to a child who has for 7 years been speaking Spanish at home which in many instances is the only way he can communicate with his parents and his relatives. Up to the age of 7 he has never been told this is bad, that this is inadequate, or that he is inferior because of this, and then on the first day of school he is confronted by a gringo teacher and is forced to change his entire person.

Take Juan Lopez on his first day of school. Because the teacher is incapable of saying Juan Lopez she changes his name to Johnny Lopey or something like that. Already the acculturation begins. The psychological damage is enormous. I

---

* *Ibid.*, Part 1A, *Equality of Educational Opportunity, An Introduction*, Apr. 20, 1970, p. 22.

don't think I have to go into much detail. When he is told he is going to be punished for speaking Spanish, it is something he never thought was wrong.

When the insinuation is made or he is directly told that his language is inferior, that his language is no good, that he has to learn how to speak English or else he will never succeed and he is confronted with this the damage is irreparable.

They are not asking him to change within the next few years, they are asking him to change that same day and he is put aside in the room as someone who is different and inferior. You have to put yourself in the shoes of that 7-year-old kid to appreciate what this educational system is doing to him.*

The 30,000 Puerto Ricans in Boston have a 62 percent illiteracy rate not only in English but in Spanish. When the Puerto Rican child enters school he is faced with an alien language. He must adjust to a new culture.

He has learned his values and his self-worth from his parents. When he enters the first grade in a public school where the teachers speak only English and teach a different culture, he is immediately and totally frustrated.

He goes home seeking help from his parents. They cannot help him. He not only loses respect for himself, but he quickly loses respect for his parents and the value system and the language that they taught him.

These and numerous other descriptions of the problems of Spanish-speaking children were heard by the committee.

While this kind of insensitive treatment is generally a result of mindlessness on the part of teachers, school administrators and others, it is sometimes combined with racial and ethnic prejudice. For example, according to the Coleman Report, one-fourth of the elementary and secondary school teachers in schools with Indian children—by their own admission—preferred not to teach the Indian child. Teachers and school administrators are probably no more free of racial attitudes than others, and in many schools, minority-group children are exposed to insulting remarks and humiliating actions which reinforce their already developed sense of inferiority and breed hostility and anger.

Charles Silberman refers to a number of personally observed examples in his book: The teacher who chastizes the black child for calling out an answer but compliments the white child for the same behavior; the black youngster who is told to "put your dirty hand down"; the school in southern Texas where Chicano children are "forced to kneel in the playground and beg forgiveness if they are caught talking to each other in Spanish"; the elementary class in Tucson, Ariz., where poor children must drop a penny in a bowl for every word of Spanish they utter.

Others have noted the adjectives sometimes used in schools to describe black students—lazy, high-strung, rebellious, inferior, superstitious, unstable, dull, stupid and ignorant—and contrasted them with descriptions of white children by the same people: happy, cooperative, energetic, curious, attentive, bright and ambitious.

These words and day-to-day actions, sometimes deliberate, but usual-

---

* *Ibid.*, Part 4, *Mexican-American Education*, Aug. 19, 1970, p. 2515.

ly mindless and unwitting, stamp the child from a minority group with an indelible label of inferiority—a label which in itself has devastating effects on the child in class but which also becomes part and parcel of his formal education. What begins as an informal labeling process becomes the justification for grouping and evaluation practices that further serve to foster inequality.

## B. Tracking

Tracking, or ability grouping, along with testing is probably one of the most controversial subjects among educators today. Tracking may be defined as the separation of children by their aptitudes or abilities in separate classes or separate groups within classes either part time or full time. During the decade of the 1950s it became the common practice in most schools. A 1962 survey, for example, showed that 77 percent of the elementary schools and 90 percent of the secondary schools in the country were using some form of tracking. Proponents of tracking viewed it as a sensible and rational way of organizing students by allowing them to compete against classmates at their own ability level and as a device for permitting students to progress at different rates through the school curriculum. It was viewed as the closest approximation that schools could come in meeting the individual curricular needs of each student. Further, it made the instructional process easier and less complicated for the teacher.

Thus, tracking arose not as a device for the separation of children by race or social class but as an impartial device which was thought to yield better educational results.

More recently, however, its educational value has been questioned by professional educators. Many studies have found, for example, that bright students as measured by IQ scores do not learn any more efficiently or achieve at a higher rate when placed in homogeneous as opposed to heterogeneous classes. In other words, they do not gain by being placed in special tracks.

But it is the student who is placed in the lower track who is seriously hurt by this system. In the overwhelming majority of cases, lower socioeconomic class and minority group students consistently fill the bottom rungs of the tracking system. Thus, whether there is an apparent educational justification for it or not, tracking in fact often separates students by race and socioeconomic status within schools. This separation produces no less adverse effects upon disadvantaged children than the segregation of children in separate schools.

The decision to place a child in a particular class or group usually involves several factors. Formally, it is supposed to be made on the basis of cognitive skills, usually achievement in verbal ability and mathematics. In fact, however, placement decisions are often made on the basis of a teacher's recommendations which reflect the child's attitudes, whether he is a disciplinary problem, whether he cooperates in class and whether he responds as the teacher expects. Often social status and race enter into the decision.

Teachers and counselors often expect lower-class and minority-group children to be slower, less responsive and have lower aspirations. They are referred to as "underachievers" or "late bloomers" when in fact they may be as bright and have as high a learning potential as the middle class children who, it is assumed, will achieve at a faster rate.

By the end of the child's first year, his rating in class becomes converted into a recommendation to his next teacher. Children are thus divided by groups receiving and using different instructional materials, treated differently and achieving, as they are expected to, at different levels. By the time he enters high school the student may already, in effect, be tracked for life; for his counselor, because of his prior record or because he is from a minority group, or both, advises against college preparation or other post-high school education.

Regardless of the reasons for placing the child from a lower socioeconomic status family in a lower track, it is the effect on that child that renders tracking a major device for perpetuating educational inequality. As Dr. Lohman told the committee, "Grouping has the dangerous potential of forming an iron cast around a child's potential to grow." Students know what their position in a track means. They know that it is their schools' way of telling them whether they are bright, average or stupid. A student labels himself and his peers and he develops negative attitudes about himself associated with that label. Many educators believe that is one of the major reasons compensatory education has often had such a small impact on achievement scores. There is abundant and increasing evidence that students in lower tracks are severely hurt, not only in terms of achievement, but in terms of their future aspirations, in self-esteem, motivation and their attitudes about themselves. Tracking thus serves to reinforce inequality between socioeconomic classes of students. It tends to separate them on the basis of their race and background. It tends to keep them separated on that basis throughout their educational careers and in later life.

## C. Testing and Evaluation

The testing of schoolchildren is one of the most hotly debated aspects of education. Some educators would abandon testing altogether, but most, while recognizing that tests are fraught with cultural biases and often used for the wrong purposes, recognize that there must be some way of measuring educational progress. In fact, if schools are to be held accountable for the effectiveness of their efforts, many argue that the public has a right to demand some type of testing as a way of evaluating school performance.

In any case, for present purposes, it is important to point out the ways in which testing may be misused as a device to perpetuate school inequality.

An estimated $300 million is invested each year in this Nation in the "testing" of public school children. It has been estimated that our nearly 46 million public school children take an average of three standardized tests every year. These tests usually fall into three categories: IQ tests, school subject achievement tests and aptitude tests.

Studies show that most teachers believe that IQ tests are among the most important factors in determining a child's ability and his potential to succeed in school. However, many studies have also shown that IQ tests are culturally biased. When their use to stratify children on the basis of their ability is combined with their cultural bias, IQ tests can become a device for perpetuating inequality based on cultural differences.

In 1969, the Association of Black Psychologists called for a moratorium on all IQ testing charging that these tests label black children as uneducable, place black children in special classes, assign black children to lower educational tracks, perpetuate inferior education, deny black children higher educational opportunities, and destroy the growth and development of blacks.

When he first enters school, the child is confronted with an IQ test which will open his cumulative record and thereafter may determine the course of his education. If he scores 100 or more, he is probably accepted as a "normal" child deserving of the regular educational treatment and environment. But should he score less than 100, he may find himself labeled "retarded" and quickly tracked into special classes.

When children learn the results of IQ tests, they gain impressions about their own potential and what they can aspire to be. Dr. Lohman stated this problem in his report to the committee:

> A long literature has accumulated demonstrating that IQ tests are culture bound and to some degree reflect a particular social class bias. In the United States an IQ test has some measure of usefulness with middle- and upper-middle class children who are white. For other ethnic groups and social classes the IQ measure loses its validity and for children from a minority culture it should not be used at all because it discriminates unfairly on the basis of social and cultural experiences.
>
> Particularly at an early age a child from a poor, nonwhite background is unlikely to have experienced a similar environment, verbally or physically, to a white middle-class child. The items on the most frequently used IQ tests are drawn from and the norms are established for children from white and middle-class backgrounds. It should not surprise anyone that a child whose cultural and environmental experiences differ substantially from society's majority will test differently.

Dr. Lohman further pointed out that when children from low income families enter school with skill deficits as compared with more affluent children, the effect of standardized achievement testing is to lock them into their low status position and to establish a learning hierarchy.

Most achievement tests are of the type classed as "norm reference tests." They are designed to report the child's position relative to his peers. The "norm" or the average of all those tested, is the reference point to which an individual child's score can be compared.

The tests then compare a child's actual grade level with the grade level at which he tests. Thus, a child in the eighth month of the third grade is at the 3.8 grade level. His test may show him as having a grade level equivalent in a particular subject below or above that number.

As Dr. Lohman points out, the concept of the norm, while highly useful in understanding student performance, should not be used to compare the student with his classmates, for by definition it separates the winners from the losers. No child below the norm is successful: those at it are mediocre, and those above, superior. While the norm itself doesn't say this, teachers, school administrators and parents interpret the results in this way, and society distributes its rewards for successful educational achievement and its choices for higher education in a similar pattern.

## D. Curriculum

Educators who design curricula, especially in such subjects as English and the social sciences, must make choices about what literature should be read or what events or leaders in history are important to include in school textbooks. Often these choices are based upon the dominant cultural values of the society.

In many schools, literature courses seldom include black, American Indian, Portuguese, Spanish or Oriental heritage authors. The same is often true of other ethnic cultures. History and other texts seldom mention or fairly portray the contributions of important minority group figures.

Such narrowly based curricula carry a message to the children of nonwhite and ethnic backgrounds. It tells them their past, their culture, their heros are unimportant. It tells them they must learn only about a culture which may seem alien to them.

The phenomenon of "cultural ethnocentrism" often dominates our public school curriculum. Its damage is directed at the minority-group child's self-esteem and motivation to perform, both of which affect his achievement in school. Unfortunately, it is the exceptional teacher who is bold or creative enough to design her own curriculum units to bridge the cultural gap in the classroom. School systems tend to press teachers to stick to the text and curriculum imposed from outside the classroom rather than encourage innovation.

There is another important way in which school curriculum creates and perpetuates inequality. As Dr. Mark Lohman has pointed out in his study, most curricula, particularly in elementary school, are based on a "building block concept of development." Curriculum planners and textbook writers develop their materials in logical and more increasingly difficult steps. The child who fails in one of these steps may nevertheless be promoted to the next. He fails the next steps. Or he may be placed behind in a remedial class using a textbook used by his peers a year or more ago, reinforcing his feeling of failure.

Present school curricula are not designed deliberately to discriminate against the poor or minority-group student. Until recently, however, there were a good many instances in which school textbooks portrayed minority-group figures in a misleading, condescending or even racist manner. A passage from a textbook on the history of Alabama which was required reading in Alabama schools as late as the Spring of 1970 is illustrative. In a chapter entitled "Reconstruction in Alabama", there appears the following description of the Ku Klux Klan:

> The loyal white men of Alabama saw they could not depend on the laws or the State government to protect their families. They knew they had to do something to bring back law and order, to get the government back in the hands of honest men who knew how to run it.
>
> It happened that at this time a band of white-robed figures appeared on the streets of Pulaski, Tenn. No one knew who they were. They rode through the town like ghosts and then disappeared. Soon other robed bands were seen all over the

> South, including Alabama. This organization became known as the Ku Klux Klan. General Nathan B. Forrest was one of the leaders of the Klan.
>
> The Klan did not ride often, only when it had to. But whenever some bad thing was done by a person who thought the "carpetbag law would protect him, the white-robed Klan would appear on the streets. They would go to the person who had done the wrong and leave a warning. Sometimes this warning was enough, but if the person kept on doing the bad, lawless things the Klan came back again.
>
> They held their courts in the dark forests at night; they passed sentence on the criminals and they carried out the sentence. Sometimes the sentence would be to leave the State.*

In 1969, before the Indian Education Subcommittee, Will Antell of the Minnesota Department of Education described a standard textbook used until recently in public schools attended by American Indian children:

> One of the standard textbooks in Minnesota has been Marion Antoinette Ford's book "Star of the North."
>
> As we have observed and looked at this book we find it historically inaccurate and we find it very distasteful and offensive to the American Indian, Minnesota Indian, particularly.
>
> It cites them constantly as lazy, as doing a lot of drinking, of massacring white people, on the warpath, and in one particular section as I recall it, they referred to the American Indian male, saying the only work that he ever did was to stamp on wild rice during the wild rice season.
>
> There are implications like this throughout the textbooks. Lately, Indian communities have been protesting this. The school systems are beginning to respond to this and are taking them out of use.

While these may be extreme examples of distorted or racist texts, there is no doubt that school curriculum remains today a major contributing cause of educational inequality.

### E. School Isolation and School "Charters"

There is another factor which contributes to the separation of school children on the basis of race and social and economic class. It involves the notion of a school's "charter" or reputation. Within a large metropolitan area some communities' school systems have reputations for excellence while others are labeled as inferior. Some suburban schools, for example, are generally thought to be superior to those in cities or contiguous rural areas. But even within the same community, schools have what Dr. Mark Lohman of the University of California at Riverside describes as "positive or negative charters"; some schools are labeled as good, others as bad, and a few superior. They are so labeled even though within a community the facilities and the quality of teaching are similar in each school.

The school with a reputation for excellence attracts high achieving youngsters from higher socioeconomic status families. When new

---

* *Know Alabama, An Elementary History*, Ocosley, Stewart, and Chappell, Colonial Press, 1957, p. 145.

families move into the community they usually inquire where "the best schools" are located. If it is within their financial means they will seek to live in these schools' attendance zones, areas which are also by reputation "the best" neighborhoods. Evidence of this is found, for example, in the way suburban homes are advertised in the classified pages as being located near a particular school regarded as superior to other schools in the community.

The schools in these neighborhoods may indeed be better and it is only natural that parents seek to live near the best schools. But as Dr. Lohman observed in testimony before the Select Committee, "It is the social and economic prestige of the parents who send their children to school rather than some special characteristic of the school itself that determines its reputation for excellence."

Schools within communities and school districts within larger areas are thus tagged as either having high achieving, highly motivated students expected to attend college or as having low achieving students with low aspirations who are less likely to continue their education and are likely to enter low status occupations.

The reputation, good or bad, feeds itself. Each type of school tends to attract more of the same kinds of students. Those with good reputations are almost always attended by white students of affluent families. Those with negative charters and poorer reputations have higher proportions of nonwhite and middle- or low-income students. No matter what their aptitudes or intelligence might be, these children are not expected to achieve, and their school is not expected to have much influence on their future.

A school's charter is thus one more factor which tends to perpetuate the educational inequality among children from different socioeconomic backgrounds.

### F. Desegregation Without Integration

Teacher attitudes, insensitivities, and expectations, tracking and testing, the use of ethnocentric and culturally biased instructional materials and the notion of a school's charter are among the everyday practices that perpetuate inequality in education. Whether they result from what many education critics term "mindlessness" or from deliberate discrimination against minority-group children, they operate to place the minority group child in an inferior status throughout his school career.

The elimination of such practices ought to be one of the principal aims of the school desegregation effort. Yet these and other practices operate to deny equality and perpetuate isolation and segregation even within schools in school districts that are formally desegregated.

Physical desegregation—that is, the elimination of separate or dual schools to which children are assigned by race or social class—does not by itself necessarily produce educational equality or even reduce inequality. A later chapter will discuss the positive steps which should be taken to make desegregation successful in both human and educational terms. But in defining the ways in which schools perpetuate inequality, mention must be made of the kinds of discriminatory practices and the treatment of black and other minority-group children in many desegregated schools and school systems—practices that can lead to the failure of school desegregation as a device for ending educational inequality.

In the Summer of 1970, the committee held extensive hearings on the status of legal desegregation. Many of the witnesses were concerned not just with formal legal compliance, but with what has been described as a "second generation" of segregation problems.

As Mrs. Ruby Martin, former director of the Office of Civil Rights, stated:

> We are getting away from counting heads—how many bodies are together—and we are now thinking about individuals and what happens to individuals.*

At the time of these hearings, it was clear that many communities had failed to take the actions necessary to turn their desegregated schools into sensitive, humane, integrated community institutions. Students, parents, teachers and others related the following practices:

- The discriminatory firing and demotion of black teachers, principals and other administrators.
- The refusal to treat black students arriving at formerly all-white schools as equals. Black students in many such schools were excluded from extra-curricular activities such as student councils, elections for class officers, cheerleading, athletics and other activities. The symbols of success and school spirit—the trophies and school colors and emblems that meant so much to the students in their former black school—were "lost" or "not displayed."
- The suspension or expulsion and the imposition of punishment for disciplinary infractions on black students without similar treatment of white students.

This kind of treatment was often described as systematic, deliberate and calculated.

These and other similar practices were characterized by the students themselves in these words:

> What is happening by desegregating the schools in this way . . . is that you are creating a hostile environment in which black students cannot even get the little bit of training that they got in the black schools much less talk about education.**

This statement is a tragic testament to the problems involved in many schools and school districts which have failed to realize that desegregated education is not synonymous with integrated education.

---

* Hearings of the U.S. Senate Select Committee on Equal Educational Opportunity, Part 3B—*Desegregation Under Law*, June 18, 1970, p. 1311.

** *Ibid.*, p. 1318.

# Chapter 10—Poor Children in Poor Schools

The isolation and separation of disadvantaged and minority group children by school and by residence and the practices which relegate them to a status of inferiority combine with a third way in which schools provide the disadvantaged child with second-class educational opportunities. The schools which our Nation's low-income children attend are often those with fewer and lower quality educational services. They are the schools where educational dollars are either fewer or purchase less.

Our Nation's system of school finance is in a state of fiscal crisis both because the resources devoted to education are inadequate and because money for education is raised and distributed inequitably. The children who need the most often have the least. Part VII presents a complete review of the problems of educational finance. This chapter reviews the inequalities in school expenditures and services and the relationships between money, educational quality and student socioeconomic status.

### A. Student Socioeconomic Status and the Quality of School Services

Experts differ on the extent to which poor or minority group children attend schools or live in school districts where they receive fewer or lower quality school services. (The relationship between educational resources and achievement is discussed in the following chapter.) The committee and its staff have reviewed a number of studies which attempt to answer this question. The two most notable and comprehensive are the Coleman Report *Equality of Educational Opportunity*, and a survey of schools and school districts in Michigan sponsored by the Urban Coalition and reported in *Schools and Inequality* by Guthrie, Kleindorfer, Levin and Stout. The first three authors testified at the committee's hearings.

The Coleman Report has been the subject of much controversy and challenge. A reanalysis of that report which is reprinted in the recently published book, *On Equality of Educational Opportunity*, edited by Frederick Mosteller and Daniel Moynihan, concludes that there is little racial or social class bias in the allocation of resources among northern urban elementary schools. Another analysis of the Coleman data concluded that schools which were almost all black had similar resources as schools which were nearly all white within regions of the country, but that there were substantial variations among regions, particularly in the South as opposed to other areas.

The report *Schools and Inequality* is both the most comprehensive review of the research on this issue and the most concentrated study to date of the relationships between pupil socioeconomic status, the qual ity of available school services, pupil achievement, and student post-school performance. It surveyed a large variety of school districts in a typical industrial State containing large cities and suburbs as well as rural areas with low population densities. It measured a much larger number and variety of educational services than the Coleman Report. While this study's conclusions with respect to resources and pupil achievement and post-school performance are discussed in Chapter 12, for present purposes, as the authors state, the study demonstrates rather conclusively that:

> To be a lower socioeconomic status elementary school child is to experience an extraordinary probability of being discriminated against. High quality school services are provided to children of wealthy homes. Poor quality school services are provided to children from poor homes.

The authors found that among school districts in Michigan those with higher percentages of students from affluent families had more and better administrative services, equipment and facilities, curricular offerings, instructional innovations, and special education services for the handicapped. They found these school districts had more teachers enrolled in graduate courses and other in-service training activities, superintendents with more years of formal schooling, and more staff personnel with specialized functions. On another level, among schools within districts, it was found that low socioeconomic status schools tended to be housed in older buildings on smaller building sites and were more crowded, less well equipped and had fewer library books per thousand students. Low socioeconomic status schools were also less likely to have a school nurse or infirmary room. They were less likely to have remedial education services, services for speech correction or special classes for students deficient in English, for students with physical handicaps, or for students with behavior and adjustment problems. Teachers in these schools had lower scores in verbal ability, low estimates of the academic abilities of their students and low perceptions of the general reputations of their schools.

In summary, the authors found for the typical industrial State that they were studying that the quality of school services is "tied tightly to the child's social and economic circumstances" . . . and that "socioeconomic status is an excellent predictor of available school services." They found that the relationship between socioeconomic status and the quality of school services held true among school districts, among individual schools within districts and between low- and high-income student groups.

That there are wide disparities in school quality between schools with predominantly low-income students and those with mostly affluent students was also related by other committee witnesses. The Edgewood School District in San Antonio is the poorest in the San Antonio area. It is also 93 percent Chicano and 3.5 percent black. It has a dropout rate of more than 50 percent. Over 52 percent of its teachers in the school year 1969–70 were uncertified.

As anyone who has visited the schools in Harlem or other Northern city ghettos will confirm, urban black children are often in schools that are older, larger, more crowded, on smaller sites, with fewer library books, often no auditorium or gymnasium and fewer science laboratory facilities. The teachers in these schools have, on the average, a lower level of verbal skill than those in more affluent neighborhoods.

Dr. Mark R. Shedd, then Superintendent of Schools in Philadelphia described these conditions in compelling terms:

> Let me just describe, briefly, what a ghetto school is really like, using one of ours in Philadelphia as an example.
>
> Unless you have visited such a school and seen firsthand the conditions with which students and teachers have to contend, you can't know their frustration and depression.
>
> Here are some facts about one such school in North Philadelphia. The school was constructed before 1905 and is non-fire resistant. It's old and dilapidated. It's a firetrap.
>
> The school has none of the modern facilities built into the newer schools. There's no cafeteria, which means no School Lunch Program. There's no auditorium which means no assembly programs.
>
> There's no gymnasium and, therefore, no organized physical education program. The best the kids can hope for is a little exercise in the basement near the boiler and the furnace, or perhaps in the yard when the weather's nice.
>
> The heating system is deficient. Some of the classrooms are consistently around 50 degrees, all winter long. Children dress in coats to keep warm.
>
> When you add to that the many broken windows, damaged sashes and frames—which create drafts and noises throughout the building—learning becomes secondary to just keeping warm.
>
> Perhaps you are beginning to see that it is not a very pretty picture that I am painting. But I am not finished yet.
>
> The roof leaks and water has caused damage to the building. Paint and plaster are cracked, peeling, and falling throughout the building.
>
> The school has one set of toilets for the children, which is located in the basement.
>
> The teachers have no lounge, dining area nor office space. All special services are crowded in to one converted classroom. The only men's room is on the third floor.
>
> The morale of both pupils and teachers is understandably low. It's not easy to come to a building, day after day, which is literally falling apart.
>
> When you add the problems of the community—such as a lack of community facilities, the high percentage of children from low-income families who come to school hungry each day, the large numbers of youngsters with low-achievement scores in basic skills—teaching also can become a very frustrating experience.
>
> As an example, of the 540 pupils in the school, 65 percent scored below the 16th percentile on the Iowa test of basic skills—which is considered to be the minimum functioning level for pupils.
>
> And this problem is compounded when you realize that the faculty is comprised of 45 percent of inexperienced teachers,

teachers with 2 years' experience or less. It is also apparent how woefully inadequate are the number of positions allotted for necessary services.

In this school there are only 12 positions for art, music, remedial education, counseling, and special programs for educationally, physically, and emotionally handicapped.

This falls far short of providing the help that is needed for pupils who begin their education with social, cultural, and economic handicaps. Yet these conditions are prevalent in some 30 other school buildings in Philadelphia.

And I say, 30 school buildings that are firetraps. But large numbers of additional buildings—while facilities might be of more recent construction—would still reflect the same test score failure.

We simply can't go on like this any more.*

Research, personal observations and the statements of witnesses before the committee clearly demonstrate the relationship between the resources and services which our schools provide and the socioeconomic status of schoolchildren in this country. In short, poor children usually attend poor schools, and those who need the most generally get the least in resources and services.

## B. Disparities in School Spending

The disparities in school expenditures across the Nation can only be described as extreme. They exist among States, among districts within States and among schools within school districts. They are further compounded by the fact that the cost of providing educational and other services is often higher in many districts as for example in large cities where a large proportion of the Nation's disadvantaged children live and attend schools which are more isolated by race and family-income status than in other areas.

### 1. PER-PUPIL EXPENDITURES FROM STATE TO STATE

The average per pupil expenditure in the United States for the school year 1970–71 was $858. However, as Table 10–1 indicates, the range among the States was almost three to one. At one extreme was Alaska** with $1,429 per pupil and New York with $1,370 per pupil. These States spent 166.5 percent and 159.6 percent of the national average, respectively. At the opposite pole were Mississippi which spent $521 per pupil and Alabama with an expenditure of $489—60.7 percent and 56.9 percent of the national average, respectively.

---

*Hearings of the U.S. Senate Select Committee on Equal Educational Opportunity Part 16A, *Inequality in School Finance*. Sept. 21, 1971.

** The figure for Alaska reflects about a 33 percent greater cost-of-living compared with other areas of the United States.

TABLE 10-1.—*Estimated expenditure per pupil in ADA, public elementary and secondary schools, by State, 1970–71* [1]

| State | Expenditure per pupil | | | |
|---|---|---|---|---|
| | Total [2] | Current | Capital outlay | Interest on school debt |
| 1 | 2 | 3 | 4 | 5 |
| United States | $1,008 | $858 | $119 | $31 |
| Alabama | 572 | 489 | 68 | 15 |
| Alaska | 1,897 | 1,429 | 418 | 50 |
| Arizona | 985 | 808 | 161 | 16 |
| Arkansas | 665 | 578 | 65 | 22 |
| California | 1,060 | 879 | 148 | 33 |
| Colorado | 902 | 780 | 98 | 24 |
| Connecticut | 1,082 | 997 | 53 | 32 |
| Delaware | 1,298 | 954 | 285 | 59 |
| District of Columbia | 1,250 | 1,046 | 204 | ---------- |
| Florida | 954 | 776 | 159 | 19 |
| Georgia | 729 | 634 | 68 | 27 |
| Hawaii | 1,144 | 951 | 184 | 9 |
| Idaho | 761 | 629 | 89 | 43 |
| Illinois | 1,112 | 937 | 139 | 36 |
| Indiana | 1,025 | 770 | 215 | 40 |
| Iowa | 1,104 | 944 | 139 | 21 |
| Kansas | 860 | 771 | 77 | 12 |
| Kentucky | 709 | 621 | 65 | 23 |
| Louisiana | 904 | 806 | 71 | 27 |
| Maine | 885 | 763 | 100 | 22 |
| Maryland | 1,240 | 968 | 228 | 44 |
| Massachusetts | 980 | 856 | 78 | 46 |
| Michigan | 1,126 | 937 | 147 | 42 |
| Minnesota | 1,241 | 1,021 | 172 | 48 |
| Mississippi | 553 | 521 | 24 | 8 |
| Missouri | 843 | 747 | 73 | 23 |
| Montana | 1,000 | 866 | 113 | 21 |
| Nebraska | 837 | 683 | 128 | 26 |
| Nevada | 911 | 808 | 60 | 43 |
| New Hampshire | 918 | 729 | 158 | 31 |
| New Jersey | 1,207 | 1,088 | 78 | 41 |
| New Mexico | 912 | 776 | 126 | 10 |
| New York | 1,561 | 1,370 | 143 | 48 |
| North Carolina | 714 | 642 | 60 | 12 |
| North Dakota | 761 | 689 | 49 | 23 |
| Ohio | 891 | 778 | 89 | 24 |
| Oklahoma | 746 | 676 | 61 | 9 |
| Oregon | 1,079 | 935 | 121 | 23 |
| Pennsylvania | 1,191 | 948 | 188 | 55 |
| Rhode Island | 1,147 | 983 | 127 | 37 |
| South Carolina | 753 | 656 | 84 | 13 |
| South Dakota | 826 | 713 | 101 | 12 |
| Tennessee | 670 | 601 | 47 | 22 |
| Texas | 775 | 636 | 111 | 28 |
| Utah | 739 | 643 | 82 | 14 |
| Vermont | 1,162 | 1,061 | 75 | 26 |
| Virginia | 923 | 800 | 99 | 24 |
| Washington | 1,018 | 873 | 112 | 33 |
| West Virginia | 704 | 624 | 71 | 9 |
| Wisconsin | 1,078 | 977 | 67 | 34 |
| Wyoming | 1,012 | 927 | 67 | 18 |
| Outlying areas: | | | | |
| American Samoa [3] | 634 | 634 | ---------- | ---------- |
| Canal Zone | 1,139 | 1,104 | 35 | ---------- |
| Guam | 854 | 804 | 50 | ---------- |
| Puerto Rico | 416 | 383 | 33 | ---------- |

[1] Digest of Educational Statistics, 1971, National Center for Educational Statistics, U.S. Department of Health, Education, and Welfare.
[2] Includes current expenditures, capital outlay, and interest on school debt.
[3] Data for 1969–70.

Source: U.S. Department of Health, Education, and Welfare, Office of Education, *Fall 1970 Statistics of Public Schools;* and unpublished data.

### 2. UNEQUAL PER-PUPIL EXPENDITURES WITHIN STATES

There is a wide variety in the ways in which the 50 States finance education. In some States, for example, school health and other non-educational services are financed through agencies other than the school system and may not show up in school expenditure statistics. Thus State expenditure comparisons do not present an accurate picture of school finance disparities. But more important, interstate differences, which average out high and low school district costs, mask a much wider range of differences in per-pupil expenditures among school districts within States. Table 10–2 shows per-pupil expenditure ranges within each of the 50 States. In nearly every State the highest spending school district spends at least twice as much as the lowest spending school district. Variations of 3-, 4-, and 5-to-1 are not uncommon, and at the extreme—in Wyoming and Texas—the highest spending school district spends more than 20 times as much as the lowest.*

TABLE 10–2.—*Intrastate disparities in per-pupil expenditures, 1969–70* [1]

| | High | Low | High/low index |
|---|---|---|---|
| Alabama | $581 | $344 | 1.7 |
| Alaska | 1,810 | 480 | 3.8 |
| Arizona | 2,223 | 436 | 5.1 |
| Arkansas | 664 | 343 | 2.0 |
| California | 2,414 | 569 | 4.2 |
| Colorado | 2,801 | 444 | 6.3 |
| Connecticut | 1,311 | 499 | 2.6 |
| Delaware | 1,081 | 633 | 1.7 |
| District of Columbia | | | |
| Florida | 1,036 | 593 | 1.7 |
| Georgia | 736 | 365 | 2.0 |
| Hawaii | | | |
| Idaho | 1,763 | 474 | 3.7 |
| Illinois | 2,295 | 391 | 5.9 |
| Indiana | 965 | 447 | 2.2 |
| Iowa | 1,167 | 592 | 2.0 |
| Kansas | 1,831 | 454 | 4.0 |
| Kentucky | 885 | 358 | 2.5 |
| Louisiana | 892 | 499 | 1.8 |
| Maine | 1,555 | 229 | 6.8 |
| Maryland | 1,037 | 635 | 1.6 |
| Massachusetts | 1,281 | 515 | 2.5 |
| Michigan | 1,364 | 491 | 2.8 |
| Minnesota [2] | 903 | 370 | 2.4 |
| Mississippi | 825 | 283 | 3.0 |
| Missouri | 1,699 | 213 | 4.0 |
| Montana average of groups | 1,716 | 539 | 3.2 |
| Nebraska average of groups | 1,175 | 623 | 1.9 |
| Nevada | 1,679 | 746 | 2.3 |
| New Hampshire | 1,191 | 311 | 3.8 |
| New Jersey, 1968–69 | 1,485 | 400 | 3.7 |
| New Mexico | 1,183 | 477 | 2.5 |
| New York | 1,889 | 669 | 2.8 |
| North Carolina | 733 | 467 | 1.4 |
| North Dakota county averages | 1,623 | 686 | 2.3 |
| Ohio | 1,685 | 413 | 4.0 |
| Oklahoma | 2,566 | 342 | 7.5 |

[1] Hearings of the U.S. Senate Select Committee on Equal Educational Opportunity, Part 16A—*Inequality in School Finance,* Sept. 22, 1971.
[2] Does not reflect subsequent reforms.

*These extreme disparities probably reflect the existence of rich, very small school districts.

TABLE 10-2.—*Intrastate disparities in per-pupil expenditures, 1969–70*—Continued

| | High | Low | High/low index |
|---|---|---|---|
| Oregon | 1,432 | 399 | 3.5 |
| Pennsylvania | 1,401 | 484 | 2.9 |
| Rhode Island | 1,206 | 531 | 2.3 |
| South Carolina | 1,741 | 350 | 5.0 |
| South Dakota | 610 | 397 | 1.5 |
| Tennessee | 700 | 315 | 2.4 |
| Texas | 5,334 | 264 | 20.2 |
| Utah | 1,515 | 533 | 2.3 |
| Vermont | 1,517 | 357 | 4.2 |
| Virginia | 1,126 | 441 | 2.6 |
| Washington | 3,406 | 434 | 7.8 |
| West Virginia | 722 | 502 | 1.4 |
| Wisconsin | 1,432 | 344 | 4.2 |
| Wyoming | 14,554 | 618 | 23.6 |

NOTES

For New Jersey data are for fiscal year 1969 since fiscal year 1970 data were not yet available.
For Alaska data represent revenue per pupil.
For Montana and Nebraska data are high and low of average for districts grouped by size.
For North Dakota data are averages of expenditures of all districts within a county.
Data are not fully comparable between States since they are based entirely on what data the individual State included in their expenditures-per-pupil analysis.

Source: State reports and verbal contacts with State officials.

### 3. UNEQUAL EXPENDITURES AMONG SCHOOLS WITHIN DISTRICTS

The most immediate impact of school expenditures occurs in individual schools. There have been few efforts to examine disparities in the amounts spent per pupil within individual school districts. Few districts break down their expenditures on a school-by-school basis. However, patterns of discrimination in which school districts have assigned fewer resources to schools attended by minority group and low socioeconomic status students have been found in a number of cities. A Syracuse University study of three New York school districts in 1971 found that schools with high concentrations of low-achieving students received fewer funds from State and local sources than did schools with high proportions of high achieving students. The most widely reported instance of differences in intradistrict expenditures involved the District of Columbia case of *Hobson* v. *Hansen* 269 S. Supp. 401, Aff'd 408 52d 175 in 1967. In that case it was demonstrated that substantially more money was spent on pupils in white-dominated schools that in black-dominated schools in the Nation's capital. The average per-pupil expenditure in elementary schools was found to range from $216 per child in the black ghetto schools to a high of $627 in the affluent white schools, a difference of $411. According to Julius Hobson's testimony before the committee,* by 1968 this difference had increased to $506 and "data for 1970 showed that the differential had reached an unbelievable amount of $1,719 between the lowest elementary school expenditure per pupil and the highest elementary school expenditure per pupil."

In the Education Amendments of 1970, Congress attempted to exert its influence on intradistrict spending disparities by requiring

*Hearings of the U.S. Senate Select Committee on Equal Educational Opportunity, Part 16A, *Inequality in School Finance*, Sept. 23, 1971.

that all school districts which receive funds under Title I of the Elementary and Secondary Education Act of 1965 (targeted to children from low-income families) use State and local funds "to provide services in project areas which, taken as a whole are at least comparable to services being provided in areas in such districts which are not receiving funds under this title (Sec. 141(a)3)." This provision did not take effect until the 1972–73 school year; thus it is difficult to assess its impact. The committee is hopeful that the Office of Education will enforce its requirements vigorously, thus assuring that Federal compensatory education funds will be spent for the supplemental purposes for which they were intended.

### 4. CITIES AND THEIR SUBURBS

Disparities in per-pupil expenditures can be found among all types of school districts—urban, suburban and rural.

Many large cities, for example, spend at or above their State's average in per-pupil expenditure. However, others often spend substantially less than some of their richer suburbs. Furthermore, at least in terms of pupil-teacher ratio, many cities get less for their money. Table 10–3 shows the 1967 difference between central city and high spending suburban school districts in eight major metropolitan areas. It also shows the pupil-teacher ratios in each area. In every case, city students had both less money spent on their education and higher pupil-teacher ratios. Los Angeles, for example, spent $601 per pupil with 27 pupils in each classroom, while Beverly Hills spent $1,192 per pupil with a pupil-teacher ratio of 17-to-1. New York City spent $854 per pupil, while Great Neck, Long Island, spent $1,391 with four fewer students in each class.

TABLE 10–3.—*Comparison of pupil/teacher ratio in selected central cities and suburbs, 1967* [1]

| City and suburb | Pupil/teacher ratio | Per pupil expenditures |
|---|---|---|
| Los Angeles | 27 | $601 |
| Beverly Hills | 17 | 1, 192 |
| San Francisco | 26 | 693 |
| Palo Alto | 21 | 984 |
| Chicago | 28 | 571 |
| Evanston | 18 | 757 |
| Detroit | 31 | 530 |
| Grosse Pointe | 22 | 713 |
| St. Louis | 30 | 525 |
| University City | 22 | 747 |
| New York City | 20 | 854 |
| Great Neck | 16 | 1, 391 |
| Cleveland | 28 | 559 |
| Cleveland Heights | 22 | 703 |
| Philadelphia | 27 | 617 |
| Lower Merion | 20 | 733 |

[1] Hearings of the U.S. Senate Select Committee on Equal Educational Opportunity, Part 16A, *Inequality in School Finance,* Sept. 22, 1972.

## C. DO DISADVANTAGED CHILDREN ATTEND LOW QUALITY, POOR SCHOOLS?

The disparities in school expenditures among States, school districts and schools do not alone demonstrate that there is a relationship between student socioeconomic status and educational resources. Do poor children go to poor schools?

While there have been no nationwide studies which establish that in every State poor children attend poor schools, available evidence does demonstrate that both the quality and quantity of the educational services available to low-income children tend to be inversely related to the proportions of such children in school districts and in schools within districts.

### 1. EDUCATIONAL EXPENDITURES AND PERSONAL INCOME

Variations in per-pupil expenditures from State to State do not necessarily correlate with incidence of disadvantage among students in each State. However, many States which spend less on education per pupil also generally have lower per capita and family incomes. Conversely, many States with high educational expenditures show higher measures of personal income. Table 10-4 compares per pupil expenditures in the 50 States with their per capita incomes.

TABLE 10-4.—*State expenditures per-pupil and per-capita income*

| State | Estimated Expenditure per pupil in ADA, 1970-71 (1) | Percent o f U.S. average | Per-capita personal income, 1969 (2) | Per-capita personal income as percent of national average, 1969 (3) |
|---|---|---|---|---|
| Alaska | $1,429 | 166.5 | [1] $4,460 | 121.0 |
| New York | 1,370 | 159.6 | 4,442 | 120.5 |
| New Jersey | 1,088 | 126.8 | 4,241 | 115.0 |
| Vermont | 1,061 | 123.6 | 3,247 | 88.1 |
| Minnesota | 1,021 | 118.9 | 3,635 | 98.6 |
| Connecticut | 997 | 116.2 | 4,595 | 124.6 |
| Rhode Island | 983 | 114.5 | 3,858 | 104.6 |
| Wisconsin | 977 | 113.8 | 3,632 | 98.5 |
| Maryland | 968 | 112.8 | 4,073 | 110.5 |
| Delaware | 954 | 111.1 | 4,107 | 111.4 |
| Hawaii | 951 | 110.8 | 3,928 | 106.5 |
| Pennsylvania | 948 | 110.4 | 3,659 | 99.2 |
| Iowa | 944 | 115.8 | 3,549 | 96.3 |
| Illinois | 937 | 109.2 | 4,285 | 116.2 |
| Michigan | 937 | 109.2 | 3,994 | 108.3 |
| Oregon | 935 | 108.9 | 3,573 | 96.9 |
| Wyoming | 927 | 108.0 | 3,353 | 90.4 |
| California | 879 | 102.4 | 4,290 | 116.4 |
| Washington | 873 | 101.7 | 3,848 | 104.4 |
| Montana | 866 | 100.9 | 3,130 | 84.9 |
| Massachusetts | 856 | 99.7 | 4,156 | 112.7 |
| Arizona | 808 | 94.1 | 3,372 | 91.5 |
| Nevada | 808 | 94.1 | 4,458 | 120.9 |
| Louisiana | 806 | 93.9 | 2,781 | 75.4 |
| Virginia | 800 | 93.2 | 3,307 | 89.7 |
| Colorado | 780 | 90.9 | 3,604 | 97.7 |
| Ohio | 778 | 90.6 | 3,738 | 101.4 |
| Florida | 776 | 90.4 | 3,525 | 95.6 |
| New Mexico | 776 | 90.4 | 2,897 | 78.6 |
| Kansas | 771 | 89.8 | 3,488 | 94.6 |
| Indiana | 770 | 89.7 | 3,687 | 100.0 |
| Maine | 763 | 88.9 | 3,054 | 82.8 |
| Missouri | 747 | 87.0 | 3,458 | 93.8 |
| New Hampshire | 729 | 84.9 | 3,471 | 94.1 |
| South Dakota | 713 | 83.1 | 3,027 | 82.1 |
| North Dakota | 689 | 80.3 | 3,012 | 81.7 |

[1] The figure for Alaska should be reduced by 30 percent to make the purchasing power generally comparable to figures for other areas of the United States.

TABLE 10-4.—*State expenditures per pupil and per capita income*—Continued

| State | Estimated Expenditure per pupil in ADA, 1970-71 (1) | Percent of U.S. average | Per-capita personal income, 1969 (2) | Per-capita personal income as percent of national average, 1969 (3) |
|---|---|---|---|---|
| Nebraska | 683 | 79. 6 | 3, 609 | 97. 9 |
| Oklahoma | 676 | 78. 7 | 3, 047 | 82. 6 |
| South Carolina | 656 | 76. 4 | 2, 607 | 70. 7 |
| Utah | 643 | 74. 9 | 2, 997 | 81. 3 |
| North Carolina | 642 | 74. 8 | 2, 888 | 78. 3 |
| Texas | 636 | 74. 1 | 3, 259 | 88. 4 |
| Georgia | 634 | 73. 8 | 3, 071 | 83. 3 |
| Idaho | 629 | 73. 3 | 2, 953 | 80. 1 |
| West Virginia | 624 | 72. 7 | 2, 603 | 70. 6 |
| Kentucky | 621 | 72. 3 | 2, 847 | 77. 2 |
| Tennessee | 601 | 70. 0 | 2, 808 | 76. 2 |
| Arkansas | 578 | 67. 3 | 2, 488 | 67. 5 |
| Mississippi | 521 | 60. 7 | 2, 218 | 60. 2 |
| Alabama | 489 | 56. 9 | 2, 582 | 70. 0 |
| United States | 858 | 100. 0 | 3, 687 | 100. 0 |

Source: U.S. Department of Commerce, Regional Econom'cs Division: *State and Regional Personal Income in 1969*. Survey of Current Business 59: 33-44; August 1970, p. 35.

There is a direct correlation between family income and school revenue. Even within suburban areas of metropolitan areas there is a disparity between high- and low-family incomes and the corresponding per pupil revenues. Table 10-5 ranks suburban school districts in five metropolitan areas by median family income. It reveals a general pattern of higher school revenues in higher income communities.

TABLE 10–5.—*Suburban income and school revenues in five metropolitan areas, 1967*

| Income category | Boston suburbs | | | Los Angeles suburbs | | | New York suburbs | | |
|---|---|---|---|---|---|---|---|---|---|
| | Number[1] | Income range | Per pupil revenue | Number | Income range | Per pupil revenue | Number | Income range | Per pupil revenue |
| High | 3 | $9, 000–9, 363 | $860 | 2 | $8, 600–11, 977 | $1, 071 | 5 | $10, 500–14, 459 | $1, 455 |
| Moderately high | 8 | 7, 300–8, 900 | 784 | 17 | 7, 400–8, 600 | 682 | 13 | 8, 000–10, 000 | 1, 172 |
| Moderately low | 11 | 6, 300–7, 300 | 720 | 19 | 6, 400–7, 400 | 656 | 18 | 6, 500–8, 000 | 1, 068 |
| Low | 6 | 5, 900–6, 300 | 683 | 4 | 6, 100–6, 400 | 685 | 7 | 5, 500–6, 500 | 1, 026 |
| | | | | Houston suburbs | | | Detroit suburbs | | |
| High | | | | 1 | $7, 200–8, 929 | $477 | 3 | $8, 700–14, 717 | $877 |
| Moderately high | | | | 5 | 6, 300–7, 200 | 615 | 12 | 7, 400–8, 700 | 693 |
| Moderately low | | | | 4 | 5, 000–6, 300 | 528 | 11 | 6, 600–7, 400 | 631 |
| Low | | | | 2 | 3, 700–5, 000 | 472 | 5 | 5, 600–6, 600 | 738 |

[1] Number of school systems.

Source: The Policy Institute of the Syracuse University Research Corp.

## 2. MONEY AND EDUCATIONAL SERVICES

There is also evidence that school districts which spend more per pupil generally pay higher teacher salaries, have more and better trained teachers, more counselors and other services proportionate to the number of students. It is self-evident that if the cost of services is held constant the more a school district has to spend the more educational services it can provide. Thus a high spending school is more likely, for example, to have more books in school libraries, use more instructional aids to supplement basic texts, offer a more varied curriculum, and provide a greater variety of extra-curricular activities for its students.

One example of the relationship between per pupil expenditures and educational services is provided in the Table 10–6. It shows the variations in teachers salaries, teacher qualifications, numbers of counselors and other professionals in six school districts in the San Antonio area of Texas. As this table demonstrates, the higher the per-pupil expenditure, the higher the teacher salaries, the more teachers there are with advanced training, the more teachers there are with masters degrees, the lower the student-counselor ratio and the more professional personnel of all kinds there are in the district relative to the number of students.

TABLE 10–6.—*The relationship between district wealth and educational quality, Texas school districts categorized by equalized property valuation and selected indicators of educational quality*

| Selected districts from high to low by market value per pupil [1] | Total revenues per pupil [2] | Professional salaries per pupil [2] | Percent, teachers with masters degrees [3] | Percent of total staff with emergency permits [2] | Counselor-student ratios [2] | Professional personnel per 100 pupils |
|---|---|---|---|---|---|---|
| Alamo Heights | $595 | $372 | 40 | 11 | 645 | 4. 80 |
| North East | 468 | 288 | 24 | 7 | 1, 516 | 4. 50 |
| San Antonio | 422 | 251 | 29 | 17 | 2, 320 | 4. 00 |
| North Side | 443 | 258 | 20 | 17 | 1, 493 | 4. 30 |
| Harlandale | 394 | 243 | 21 | 22 | 1, 800 | 4. 00 |
| Edgewood | 356 | 209 | 15 | 47 | 3, 098 | 4. 06 |

[1] Policy Institute, Syracuse University Research Corp., Syracuse, N.Y.
[2] *Ibid.*
[3] U.S. District Court, Western District of Texas, San Antonio Division, *Answers to Interrogatories*, civil action No. 68-175-SA.

NOTE.—Table from evidentiary affidavit of Joel S. Berke in *Rodriguez* v. *San Antonio School Districts*.

### 3. SCHOOL EXPENDITURES AND EDUCATIONAL AND INCOME DISADVANTAGE

In many school districts, educational dollars must serve a large proportion of needy students. This is true particularly in large cities, poorer suburbs, and rural areas. At the same time, such districts seldom spend more, and often they provide fewer dollars and receive less State aid than communities with fewer disadvantaged children. This is illustrated by a representative sample of New York State school districts. Table 10–7 groups 119 city and noncity school districts by property wealth categories. City and noncity school districts are contrasted with respect to their education tax rates, their tax rates for all municipal functions, the amount of State aid available, total per pupil expenditures; and finally, by two measures of educational need—the percentage of school district pupils scoring two or more grade levels below the norm, and the percentage of students from families receiving welfare payments.

As this survey shows, while the city school districts have somewhat lower education tax rates, they consistently have higher tax rates for all functions than noncity communities. Moreover, they receive somewhat less State aid and their per-pupil expenditures are lower than those in the noncity school districts. But more important, these lower expenditures must serve a student population which is much more educationally disadvantaged and income disadvantaged than the school population outside the city.

TABLE 10-7.—*Selected data for 119 New York State school districts, city and noncity, within wealth groups*

| Full taxable property value per pupil[1] (city-noncity) | School tax rate | | Total tax rate | | Total State aid | | Total expenditures per pupil | | Percent of pupils 2 or more grade levels below the norm | | Percent of pupils from families receiving AFDC | |
|---|---|---|---|---|---|---|---|---|---|---|---|---|
| | Noncity | City | Noncity | City | Noncity | City | Noncity | City | Noncity | City | Noncity | City |
| $48,000 and above: | | | | | | | | | | | | |
| Noncity (N=8) | $16.78 | $11.84 | $34.18 | $37.15 | $351.25 | $351.0 | $1,320 | $1,187 | 17.7 | 34.0 | 5.6 | 15.0 |
| City (N=1) | | | | | | | | | | | | |
| $45,938–$3,634: | | | | | | | | | | | | |
| Noncity (N=8) | 19.53 | 16.23 | 34.73 | 45.57 | 383.37 | 356.25 | 1,203 | 1,146 | 15.0 | 31.5 | 4.5 | 17.3 |
| City (N=4) | | | | | | | | | | | | |
| $35,396–$24,150: | | | | | | | | | | | | |
| Noncity (N=29) | 19.42 | 16.43 | 33.81 | 37.80 | 475.72 | 463.44 | 1,088 | 1,011 | 14.7 | 27.8 | 2.3 | 12.7 |
| City (N=9) | | | | | | | | | | | | |
| $23,610–$12,190: | | | | | | | | | | | | |
| Noncity (N=49) | 18.57 | 15.91 | 35.92 | 41.41 | 629.24 | 566.85 | 998 | 972 | 17.5 | 22.3 | 3.8 | 8.6 |
| City (N=7) | | | | | | | | | | | | |
| $11,741 and below: | | | | | | | | | | | | |
| Noncity (N=5) | 14.96 | | 43.21 | | 619.0 | | 1,014 | | 18.4 | | 3.0 | |
| City (N=0) | | | | | | | | | | | | |

[1] In weighted average daily attendance.

Source: Joel S. Berke, Robert J. Goettel, Ralph W. Andrew. "Equity in Financing New York City's Schools: The Impact of Local, State, and Federal Policy." Education and Urban Affairs, vol. IV, No. 2, February 1972 (forthcoming).

# Chapter 11—Unequal Educational Performance and the Consequences of Educational Inequality

The elements of educational inequality—the isolation of minority-group and disadvantaged children, the unequal treatment of such children, and the inequities in school resources—all influence the unequal performance of children during and after their formal education. This performance can be measured in terms of two major outcomes of schooling. The first are the results of standardized achievement tests which measure the child's cognitive skills—his ability to read, write and demonstrate mathematical skills and otherwise communicate and display a knowledge about a particular subject. The second is educational attainment or the number of years of school completed. These two, educational achievement and attainment, are the traditional measurements of school performance.

But schools also deal with values and emotions as well as with intellectual development. They are a part of life's experiences that teach people how to feel and act as well as to think. One way or another children develop or fail to develop attitudes and character traits such as creativity, curiosity, self-respect, self-assurance and self-confidence, perseverance, the capacity for self-criticism and self-evaluation and all the other terms which define the aspirations, motivations and perceptions of individuals.

Charles Silberman has stated as well as anyone how schools relate to these so-called "affective" skills.

> Children are taught a host of lessons about values, ethics, morality, character and conduct every day of the week, less by the content of the curriculum than by the way schools are organized, the ways teachers and parents behave, the way they talk to children and to each other, the kinds of behavior they approve or reward and the kinds they disapprove or punish.*

We know of no nationwide studies which measure these "affective" outcomes of formal education in terms of race or social class. In any event, these are not outcomes that can be very effectively measured.

However, a reanalysis of the Coleman Report data, "A Study of Our Nation's Schools" sponsored by the Department of Health, Education, and Welfare, showed that achievement on standardized tests correlates closely with the attitudinal and motivational outcomes in school.

---

*Hearings of the U.S. Senate Select Committee on Equal Educational Opportunity, Part 1A, *Equality of Educational Opportunity, An Introduction*, Apr. 29, 1970, p. 205.

## A. The Limitations of Achievement Tests

The misuses of testing and how it leads to tracking and other devices that perpetuate inequalities in school were discussed in Chapter 9. Achievement testing is one of the most hotly debated educational subjects today. We do not intend to enter into that debate, but before presenting the available evidence on school achievement it is appropriate to mention some of the criticisms. They were well articulated by Dr. Lawrence F. Read, school superintendent from Jackson, Mich. Dr. Read's testimony before the committee challenges this process of evaluation on the following grounds, among others:

- Uniform systems of testing artifically determine educational objectives and tend to freeze the curriculum so that the entire educational process is devoted solely to the acquisition of certain cognitive skills.
- Testing regiments and mechanizes the entire education process, emphasizes memoraization as the major factor in the learning process and de-emphasizes those components of the learning process that are either not measurable or that we do not know how to measure--motivation, self-concepts, and the rapport that, exists between the teacher and the student.
- Testing reduces the teacher to the status of a tutor for examinations, forces the teacher unwittingly to devote most if not all his efforts to "teaching to the test" instead of trying to individualize the learning process and create the kind of learning environment with which every child is comfortable.
- Testing stimplates standardization, uniformity and creates serious barriers to growth, evolution and improvement and innovation in education.

Whatever the merits of these criticisms the fact is that achievement tests are the only presently available measurements for determining the results of education. They cannot measure attitudes or character but, as the Coleman Report states, they do measure skills that are

> . . . among the most important in our society for getting a good job and moving up to a better one, and for full participation in an increasingly technical world. Consequently, a pupil's test results at the end of public school provide a good measure of the range of opportunities open to him as he finishes school—a wide range of choice of jobs or colleges if these skills are very high; a very narrow range that includes only the most menial jobs if these skills are very low.

Achievement tests can also be useful in identifying needs and priorities and for planning and directing the improvement of education. Perhaps more important, they are essential to any system of accountability in education today. Schools must be held accountable for teaching basic skills. The school that fails in this task can do so with impunity unless some objective measurement of achievement is available to its clients.

In assessing school performance, standardized achievement tests have several other drawbacks. First, there is no standardized achievement test given nationwide. On the contrary, there are more than half a dozen well-recognized and widely used tests. Unfortunately, however, these tests do not have common norms; they are given at different times, for different purposes and under conditions over which the designers of the test have no control. Further, it is often difficult to equate the results of one test with those of others. Moreover, even where the same test is given within a school, school district or State, it is often given in different grades at different times during the school year.

These problems are further compounded by the fact that the results of achievement tests are easily subject to misinterpretation, misrepresentation and oversimplification; and they may be reported to the public in a form which makes the data misleading or largely unusable.

It is with a recognition of all these criticisms and limitations that measurements of school achievement are used in this report to illustrate the wide disparities between the performance of minority and nonminority group and disadvantaged and advantaged children.

## B. Inequality in Student Achievement

While there is no standardized national achievement test, some 42 States conduct statewide testing programs and standard testing is conducted in nearly every school district in the Nation. The vast majority measure the following cognitive skills: Word knowledge and discrimination, reading and spelling ability and arithmetic in two parts—concepts and problem-solving and arithmetic computation.

Most achievement tests are classed as "norm reference tests", that is they show the relative position of the child in relation to his peers who took the same test. The "norm", or average of all those students tested for purposes of standardization, is the reference point used to determine the child's position. In terms of grade level, achievement tests compare the child's actual grade level with his achieved grade level. Thus, for example, a child achieving at the norm when he begins the third grade when he has been tested will have both an actual grade level and an achieved grade level, or as it is usually expressed, a "grade level equivalent" of 3. If he progresses in school according to the norm he will achieve at the rate of 1 year or 1 month for each year or month spent in school.

The 1970 Census provides numbers and percentages of school-age students, 3 to 17 years old at or below grade level. Table 11–1 shows the percentages and numbers of students by race who were two or more years below grade, a year below grade, on grade and one or more years above grade. As these figures indicate, among all races, 9.4 million students (18 percent) in this country are a year or more below where they should be in school, while 5.4 million (10.3 percent) are a year or more above and 37.2 million (71.3 percent) are achieving on grade. At the same time, 1.5 million students (3 percent) are two or more years below grade. There are nearly three times the proportion of blacks in this category as whites.* The white students, 1 million or 2.4 percent are two or more years below grade while 442,000 (6.2 percent) black students are in this category.

---

*"White" students for purposes of this census report includes minorities other than blacks.

TABLE 11–1.—*Grade level equivalents by race, 1970*

[Numbers and percentages of students]

| | Number enrolled (thousands) | 2 or more years below | 1 or more years below | 1 year below | In modal | 1 or more years above |
|---|---|---|---|---|---|---|
| All races: | | | | | | |
| Number | 52, 201 | 1, 542 | 9, 442 | 7, 900 | 37, 247 | 5, 401 |
| Percent | | 3. 0 | 18. 1 | 15. 1 | 71. 3 | 10. 3 |
| Whites: | | | | | | |
| Number | 44, 412 | 1, 078 | 7, 430 | 6, 352 | 32, 422 | 4, 582 |
| Percent | | 2. 4 | 16. 7 | 14. 3 | 73. 0 | 10. 3 |
| Blacks: | | | | | | |
| Number | 7, 108 | 442 | 1, 909 | 1, 467 | 4, 289 | 835 |
| Percent | | 6. 2 | 26. 8 | 20. 6 | 60. 3 | 11. 7 |

Many years of research on test score results, measuring in terms of grade level equivalents the relative scores of racial and ethnic groups, provide a general indication of the relative performance ratings of our public school population. They show that on the average there is a gap between the performance of minority and nonminority and between advantaged and disadvantaged public school children—a gap which is not only usually maintained throughout 12 years of schooling but which steadily increases between the sixth and 12th grades.

At the sixth grade level in reading, verbal ability and mathematics, for example, research shows that nationwide black students trail white students by 3, 2 and 2.5 years, respectively. Upon high school completion this gap increases to 3.4, 3.8 and 5.5 years respectively. So that, as a general proposition, it can be stated that black students graduate 4.3 years behind white students in their overall performance on achievement tests. The results are similar, and in some instances the gap is wider, when Spanish-surnamed, American Indian and other language-minority students are compared with the majority group or "Anglo" students.

When the white school population enters the sixth grade, on the average it is achieving at about the 6.7 level in reading, verbal ability and mathematics. Yet, the average minority-group student doesn't reach the sixth grade level until he is in the eighth grade and in the 12th grade his reading performance is at the ninth grade level.

The most comprehensive assessment of school achievement ever undertaken in this country is contained in the Coleman Report. That survey encompassed approximately 600,000 students in 4,000 elementary and secondary schools across the United States. It provided the educational community and the Nation with their first full-scale look at the educational disparities above the fifth grade among various ethnic and racial groups and among students from different socioeconomic backgrounds. However, the tests were taken in 1965 and the results are now more than 7 years old. Thus while they do provide a general picture of the gaps between minority-group and disadvantaged students on the one hand and advantaged students on the other, they do not necessarily reflect the present relative standings of the various groups. Moreover, they do not reflect variations in dropout rates among groups which tends to distort the true picture of achievement levels. With these limitations in mind, the results of the Coleman survey are shown in Table 11–2 which shows each group's scores in verbal ability.

TABLE 11–2.—*Grade level equivalents for various groups in verbal ability*

| | Grade 6 | Grade 9 | Grade 12 |
|---|---|---|---|
| Negro | 4. 4 | 7. 0 | 8. 8 |
| White | 6. 5 | 9. 8 | 12. 9 |
| Puerto Rican | 3. 4 | 7. 0 | 9. 3 |
| Mexican | 4. 5 | 7. 5 | 9. 4 |
| Indian | 4. 8 | 7. 7 | 10. 5 |
| Oriental | 5. 9 | 9. 0 | 11. 8 |

Source: Tetsuo Okada, Wallace M. Cohen, and George W. Mayeske, "Growth in Achievement for Different Racial, Regional, and Socioeconomic Groupings of Students," U.S. Office of Education, May 16, 1969.

As Table 11–2 shows, within each group, the grade level of academic achievement increases as each progress through school. However, there is a wide variation in the level of achievement between the groups in each grade. And the gaps between whites and most other groups generally increase between grade six and grade 12. And at 12th grade most minority groups are from 2½ to 4 years behind.

When these verbal achievement test data are broken down by the socioeconomic status of students within each group, as Table 11–3 shows, it is clear that the socioeconomic status of the student determines educational achievement in a major way. Thus, for example in the 12th grade the High SES white students achieve above a grade equivalent of more than 14 while the low SES white is at 10.6. Similarly there is more than a 2½ year gap between the high and low SES black or Mexican American.

TABLE 11–3.—*Grade level equivalents for social class groups*

| Grades: | 6 | | | 9 | | | 12 | | |
|---|---|---|---|---|---|---|---|---|---|
| Ethnic Group — SES: | Low | Medium | High | Low | Medium | High | Low | Medium | High |
| Negro | 4. 1 | 4. 7 | 5. 3 | 6. 5 | 7. 3 | 8. 4 | 8. 1 | 9. 3 | 10. 7 |
| White | 5. 6 | 6. 5 | 7. 3 | 8. 1 | 9. 5 | 11. 4 | 10. 6 | 12. 6 | (1) |
| Puerto Rican | 3. 1 | 3. 6 | 4. 6 | 6. 6 | 7. 2 | 8. 4 | 8. 8 | 9. 8 | 10. 6 |
| Mexican | 4. 1 | 4. 8 | 5. 7 | 6. 9 | 7. 8 | 9. 0 | 8. 9 | 9. 8 | 11. 6 |
| Indian | 4. 4 | 5. 1 | 6. 0 | 7. 1 | 8. 2 | 9. 7 | 9. 0 | 11. 2 | 13. 7 |
| Oriental | 4. 7 | 6. 1 | 7. 0 | 8. 0 | 9. 3 | 10. 3 | 10. 7 | 11. 8 | (1) |

1 Denotes GLE equal to or greater than 14.

Source: Tetsuo Okada, Wallace M. Cohen, and George W. Mayeske, "Growth in Achievement for Different Racial, Regional, and Socioeconomic Groupings of Students," U.S. Office of Education, May 16, 1969.

These tables demonstrate that except for Oriental students who are about a year behind white students in verbal ability and reading and just below whites in mathematics, the minority-group students studied—American Indians, Spanish-surnamed Americans and blacks—are grouped together behind their white peers. At the same time within each group there is a clear correlation between socio-economic class and grade level achievement.

What we see then is a dismal picture of the academic achievement of minority and disadvantaged groups in this Nation. But it is probably more instructive to ask what it will take to close the gaps. This is perhaps best illustrated by what a number of research studies have referred to as the "disadvantaged norm of academic achievement." The disadvantaged norm, as opposed to the "national norm," is a composite performance line of the following student groups; blacks, Mexican Americans, Puerto Ricans, American Indians, and Southern rural and Appalachian whites—a total of some 12.5 million public school children. As a general proposition they are the under-achievers in our school population. As a group they achieve in school at a rate approximately two-thirds that of the average nonminority, nondisadvantaged child—a rate which produces the ever-widening gap as these children progress through their educational careers.

Stated another way, minority and disadvantaged students perform at a grade level equivalent rate of .67 years for each school year, or a monthly rate of 2 months for every 3. The disadvantaged-norm children, instead of achieving 9 months' growth during the 9-month school year, achieve only 6 months' growth.

On entering the third grade the disadvantaged-norm child has an achievement level equal to that of the average second grade student. Thus, he already has a year to make up. But what is distressing to note in the disadvantaged-norm child, achieving at two-thirds the rate of the average child cannot hope to close the gap unless he achieves at a rate well above the average student, that is, much faster than the national norm rate of 1 month or 1 year for every month or year of instruction. Therefore, if an educational program produces learning at the rate of 2 months for every 3 months in school, the average disadvantaged child will continue along the disadvantaged-norm line. If his achievement rate is moved up to 4 months for every 5 months in school he progresses only slightly above the disadvantaged-norm line and doesn't begin to close the gap. If the school program moves his learning rate to a 1-to-1 basis equal to the national norm learning rate, the average disadvantaged child's regression has been arrested; but he will continue to achieve at a constant rate one or two grades below his peers throughout his entire school career. In order to close the gap between the average nonminority, nondisadvantaged child and the average disadvantaged child, schools must produce a learning rate of 4 months for every 3 months in school, a rate exactly twice the rate which this child is now achieving. The later this acceleration begins, the higher the rate must be if the disadvantaged child is to achieve at the national norm when he graduates from high school. Beginning in the third grade, for example, the rate would have to be just twice the 2-to-3 disadvantaged-norm rate. Thus, in the 9-month school year he would have to achieve at the rate of 12 months instead of his current rate of six. Chart 11–4 illustrates this analysis graphically using the commonly accepted national norm growth rate of 10 months for every school year—with the disadvantaged growth rate at 7 months.

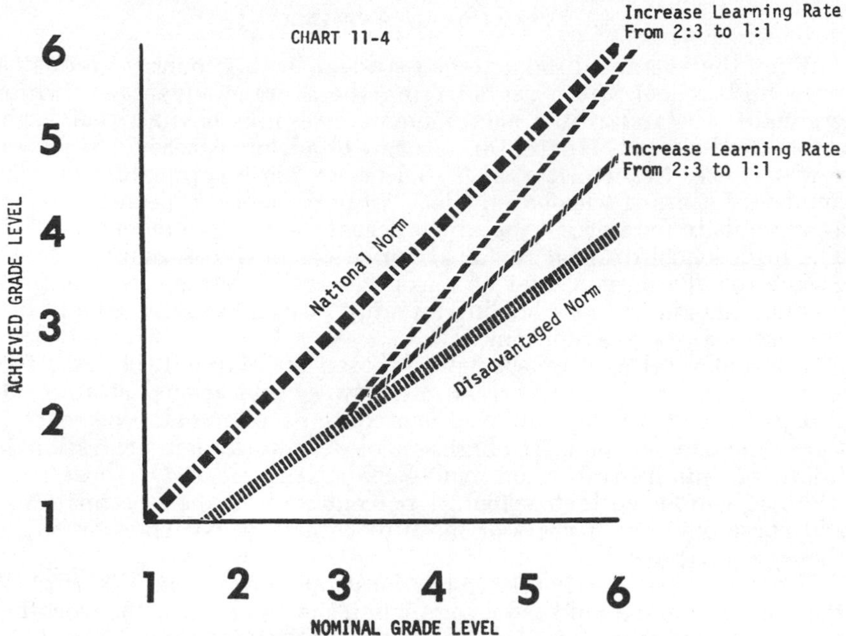


This illustrates not only the magnitude of the problem but the difficulty of overcoming it. It is tempting when we look at the achievement tests results of compensatory education programs or school integration to bemoan the fact that little seems to have been accomplished. But when one realizes that starting as early as the third grade, the average disadvantaged child will have to learn at twice the rate of the average child in order to catch up, it is perhaps understandable that programs designed to upgrade the education of minority groups and poor children produce results which are at best disappointing and certainly wide of their goals.

The committee has received a great many reports on achievement testing of minority and disadvantaged children and has heard school administrators and others relate the test scores of children in their communities. It heard, for example, that in many of the ghetto elementary schools in Philadelphia 65 percent of the pupils score below the 16th percentile in the Iowa Test of Basic Skills—the minimum level, below which a student simply learns nothing. The committee heard testimony that in Boston 62 percent of the Puerto Rican adults are illiterate in both English and Spanish. In 87 New York City schools with Puerto Rican majorities, 85 percent are below grade level in reading and a third are 2 years below grade level. In Chicago, Puerto Rican public school children are an average of 4 years behind in reading. Spanish-surnamed students in California leave the 12th grade 3½ years behind and in Illinois 5 years behind. Texas describes 40 percent of its Spanish-speaking citizens as functional illiterates.

The testimony and achievement studies reviewed confirm the view that it will take a monumental effort to reverse this pattern of inequality in achievement.

## C. Educational Attainment

When the average disadvantaged student in this country graduates from high school 3 to 5 years behind the average advantaged white graduate on standardized achievement tests, it is obvious that high school graduation is far from an accurate or adequate measure of school performance. Nevertheless, as a society we place a premium on the number of years of school completed. A high school certificate is almost a prerequisite for a decent job, and a decent job means a decent income. The high school dropout is, for all practical purposes, unemployable except for the most menial of tasks. There is a strong relationship between the amount of schooling an adult citizen has received and his occupational status and income.

A recently released census survey based on March 1972 data, for example, shows a direct correlation between educational attainment and job level.* Among employed men 25 to 64 years old, 9 percent of those who had not completed high school were working in professional, technical, administrative or managerial occupations. Of those men who had completed high school 21 percent were in these occupations, and those who had 4 years or more of college 80 percent worked in these occupations.

Income is also directly related to educational attainment. The higher the number of years of school completed, the more likely the working man in this country is to have an income of $10,000 or more. In 1971, among employed men who had not completed high school, 33 percent had incomes below $6,000; while only 13 percent of high school graduates had incomes below this level. Forty-three percent of those who had 4 or more years of college had incomes of $15,000 and over in 1971 compared with only 6 percent of those who were not high school graduates. As Table 11–5 shows, the higher the educational attainment, the higher the income.

Table 11–5.—*Level of school completed by employed males, 25 to 64 years old, by income in 1971*

[Numbers in thousands. Noninstitutional population,

| Income | Total | Not high school graduate | High school graduate: No years of college | High school graduate: 1 to 3 years of college | High school graduate: 4 years of college or more |
|---|---|---|---|---|---|
| Total, 25 to 64 years | 38, 448 | 13, 192 | 13, 554 | 4, 945 | 6, 756 |
| Under $3,000 | 2, 263 | 1, 314 | 501 | 208 | 240 |
| $3,000 to $5,999 | 5, 489 | 3, 032 | 1, 635 | 427 | 395 |
| $6,000 to $9,999 | 13, 064 | 5, 253 | 5, 132 | 1, 444 | 1, 235 |
| $10,000 to $14,999 | 11, 216 | 2, 853 | 4, 598 | 1, 807 | 1, 958 |
| $15,000 and over | 6, 416 | 741 | 1, 688 | 1, 060 | 2, 927 |
| **Percent** | | | | | |
| Total, 25 to 64 years | 100. 0 | 100. 0 | 100. 0 | 100. 0 | 100. 0 |
| Under $3,000 | 5. 9 | 10. 0 | 3. 7 | 4. 2 | 3. 6 |
| $3,000 to $5,999 | 14. 3 | 23. 0 | 12. 1 | 8. 6 | 5. 8 |
| $6,000 to $9,999 | 34. 0 | 39. 8 | 37. 9 | 29. 2 | 18. 3 |
| $10,000 to $14,999 | 29. 2 | 21. 6 | 33. 9 | 36. 5 | 29. 0 |
| $15,000 and over | 16. 7 | 5. 6 | 12. 5 | 21. 4 | 43. 3 |

*U.S. Bureau of the Census, Current Population Reports, Series p. 20, No. 243.

According to the 1970 Census, the Nation as a whole is moving toward higher levels of educational attainment. Of our population over 35, for example, only about 19 percent have completed some college while for those in the 25- to 34-year age group about 30 percent have a college degree. In the last 10 years the incidence of high school completion among young adults, age 25 to 29, has risen from 60.7 percent to 74.7 percent. This improvement has been demonstrated among both blacks and whites. In 1970, 55.8 percent of all black adults between the ages of 25 and 30 have completed high school as compared with 38.6 percent in 1960. For white adults in this age bracket, the percentages are 77 and 63.7 percent, respectively.

In all, 56.1 percent of all American men over 25 years of age have completed high school. This compares with 41.1 percent in 1960, 34.3 percent in 1950 and 24.5 percent in 1940.

While the number of years of education completed by our population as a whole and by minority as well as nonminority groups has risen substantially over time, there are still wide gaps in school years completed between minority and nonminority adults. Below the high school level for example, 14.6 percent of black adults over 25 have less than 5 years of education as compared with 4.5 percent of white adults. Of black adults, 43.8 percent have less than 9 years schooling compared with 26.6 percent for whites. This gap at the elementary school level is even more pronounced for Spanish-speaking citizens. Of Spanish-speaking adults, 46.3 percent have less than 9 years of education. At the high school level, 54.5 percent of whites have completed high school as have 31.4 percent of blacks and 36 percent of Spanish-speaking Americans.

In terms of median years of school completed, the white population over 25 has completed 12.1 years; blacks 9.8 years and Spanish-speaking Americans 9.6 years.

There is no question that, by these measures, Spanish-speaking Americans are one of our Nation's most disadvantaged minorities. Abundant evidence of this was presented at the committee's Mexican-American and Puerto Rican education hearings:

- Although Spanish-surnamed students make up more than 14 percent of the public school population of California less than 0.5 of 1 percent of the college students enrolled in the seven campuses of the University of California are of this group.
- Ninety-two Mexican-American students are enrolled in the Nation's medical schools, 0.25 of 1 percent of 37,756 medical students.
- In 1969, there were only 300 Mexican-American students at the University of Texas out of a total enrollment of 35,000. Mexican Americans make up 18 percent of the Texas population.
- In Chicago, 60 percent of all Puerto Rican students dropout before they finish high school. Only 18,000 Puerto Ricans are enrolled in the public school system. Just 4,000 are in high schools.
- In Newark, N.J., out of 7,800 Puerto Rican students, 96 are in the 12th grade.
- Philadelphia's Puerto Rican dropout rate is 70 percent.
- There are more than 100,000 Puerto Ricans in Massachusetts. Two hold masters degrees.

# Chapter 12—Schools or Family Background and Educational Performance: What Makes the Difference?*

The preceding chapters of this report have reviewed the elements of educational inequality: The separation of minority-group students by school and residence, the school practices which often place minority group and disadvantaged students in an inferior status and the inequalities in school resources and services which distinguish schools for the rich from those for the poor.

Chapter 11 presents the evidence of inequality in student performance in terms of educational attainment, academic achievement and the other results of formal education. But is there a cause and effect relationship between what schools do and how students perform? Do schools make a difference? Or are children destined to perform according to their socioeconomic status?

Much has been written about the relationship between a child's family background, socioeconomic status and home environment on the one hand, and his performance in school on the other. There is no doubt that the advantaged child and the child from the deprived-home environment begin at different starting lines in their school careers. There is no doubt that a child's verbal skills, his knowledge of other basic skills, his motivation, his perception of himself and his attitudes toward others and toward his surroundings—all his experiences during the first 4 or 5 years of life—determine where he is when he starts school.

But there is no agreement about what happens after that—about what makes the difference once a child enters school and proceeds with 12 years of formal education.

What is it that produces unequal educational outcomes between minority and nonminority and between advantaged and disadvantaged children? Is success in school determined by the things schools make available to their students or by the things students bring with them to school, or some combination of each? Most importantly, can school programs be modified and strengthened to make greater opportunities available to disadvantaged children?

We searched in vain for clear answers to these questions. Unfortunately, we found that the experts are uncertain and that there is great disagreement among them.

Some educators say that schools have little or no effect independent of the child's background. Other educators believe that a clear and independent relationship exists between what schools do and the results they produce. They note, as discussed in the previous chapter, that children from deprived homes generally attend those schools which

---

*See also Chapter 16—*Integration andn Educational Opportunity*, p. 217.

have fewer and lower quality educational services. They conclude further that educational services have a direct bearing on how well children perform.

The debate became public with the release of *Equality of Educational Opportunity*, Coleman's Report, in 1966. Since that time, educators, sociologists, statisticians and others have analysed, reanalysed, challenged and counterchallenged the report's methods and conclusions.

We cannot, in this Report, review the history of these responses or, more than by way of a summary, review the results of this massive, landmark study and the other studies which reach different results with respect to these questions.

## A. The Coleman Report

The conclusions drawn from the Coleman data by the Coleman Report have been reaffirmed by exhaustive reanalyses, the results of which are published in the recent volume, *On Equality of Educational Opportunity*, a compilation of papers deriving from the Harvard University seminar on the Coleman Report, edited by Frederick Mosteller and Daniel Moynihan.

The major conclusion of the Coleman study as stated in the report itself is that:

> Schools bring little influence to bear on a child's achievement that is independent of his background and general social context; and . . . this very lack of an independent effect means that the inequalities imposed on children by their home, neighborhood, and peer environment are carried along to become the inequalities with which they confront adult life at the end of school.

In other words, the principal sources of inequality of educational opportunity stem from student home environment and family background. Schools receive students who already differ in their skills, knowledge and attitudes and therefore begin their education on different starting lines. Formal education seldom closes the gaps between such students.

This conclusion is based upon the following general findings of Dr. Coleman's Report and the reanalyses of it:

- Variations in academic achievement in school are determined primarily by family background, home environment and the social class of students. The differences in schools' physical facilities, formal curricula and school staff characteristics account for relatively little of the differences in achievement among students. This is true for both black and white students.*

- Most of the variation in student achievement occurs within the same school while very little occurs between schools. The school-to-school achievement variation is almost entirely due to the educational backgrounds and aspirations of students. Thus, the attributes of a given school as a whole, as opposed to the attributes of the teachers and students in it, account for very little of the variation in individual achievement between schools.

---

**Ibid.*

- The strong relation of family economic and educational backgrounds of students to their achievement does not diminish as the student progresses in school; rather, it increases, at least during elementary school years.
- As currently organized, schools are predominantly culturally homogeneous and racially segregated. This cultural and racial homogeneity maintains and reinforces the differences that are imposed by family backgrounds and social origins.
- What differences there are in school factors such as facilities, curriculum, teachers, etc., have a stronger effect—up or down—on the recorded achievement of minority pupils than on nonminority students.
- Of all the possible in-school variations, the strongest factor is the quality of the teacher, particularly the teacher's verbal ability.
- One pupil attitude factor, the extent to which the student feels he can control his own destiny—or so-called "fate control"—is more strongly related to achievement than other in-school factors. Minority pupils—except for Orientals—show far less belief than nonminorities that they can control their own futures and environments; but, when they do have that conviction, their achievement levels tend to be higher than nonminorities who do not hold that conviction.

Dr. Coleman restated these findings himself by testifying:

> The sources of inequality of educational opportunity appear to lie first in the home itself and the cultural differences immediately surrounding the home; then they lie in the school's ineffectiveness to free achievement from the impact of the home and in the school's cultural homogeneity which perpetuates the social influences of the home and its environs.

### B. Contrary Evidence

The findings and conclusions of the Coleman Report, particularly the conclusion that there is little relationship between school factors and achievement levels, are by no means accepted by all educators or other observers who have studied the issue.

In a major critique of the Coleman Report, Professors Samuel Bowles of Harvard University and Henry M. Levin of Stanford University concluded that a number of the Coleman Report's findings, including those relating to the ineffectiveness of school resources, were not substantiated by evidence collected in the survey.*

And the basic Coleman data have been subject to criticism owing to a large number of schools which failed to respond to the survey, various errors in the ways in which information was collected and in the biases or inaccuracies of the response which form the basis of the Coleman Report's statistics.

In addition, there is a large body of research which appears to demonstrate that school factors including school facilities, instructional

---

**Ibid.*

materials, and the attributes of teachers and staff and other educational services do bear a direct relationship to the performance of students in school.

In the 1969 Urban Coalition Study, *Schools and Inequality*, Professors Guthrie, Kleindorfer, Levin and Stout review the results of 17 studies dealing with the relationship between school services and student achievement. In addition, they present their own findings in the State of Michigan. On the basis of these studies they conclude:

> . . . It is evident there is a substantial degree of consistency in the studies' findings. The strongest findings by far are those which relate to the number and quality of professional staff, particularly teachers. . . . Teacher characteristics, such as verbal ability, amount of experience, salary level, amount and type of academic preparation, degree level, and employment status (tenured or non-tenured) [are] significantly associated with one or more measures of pupil performance.

In addition they found that student performance was related to the frequency of contact and proximity of students to professional staff in terms of student-staff ratios, classroom size, school size, and the length of the school year.

They state that a number of studies, including their own, suggest that the age of school buildings and the adequacy and amount of physical facilities are also "significantly linked to increments in scales of pupil performance." Finally, because all of these school factors cost money, the authors found that expenditures per pupil and teacher salary levels "are correlated significantly with pupil achievement levels."

The Urban Coalition's study concludes:

> A relationship exists between the quality of school services provided to a pupil and his academic achievement, and that relationship is such that higher quality school services are associated with higher levels of achievement.
>
> There can be little doubt that schools have an effect that is independent of the child's social environment. In other words, schools do make a difference.

### C. Who Is Right?

This committee, of course, does not have the scientific expertise to determine who is right—Dr. Coleman and those who support his conclusions, or the authors of the Urban Coalition study. We can only conclude from our review of the available evidence that there is merit to both sides of the argument. Our record supports the Coleman Report's conclusion that family background is presently the single most important factor in determining academic performance. But we also suspect that the later, more specifically focused Urban Coalition study was far more precise in identifying the existence of resource disparities which the earlier study missed, and that the Urban Coalition study therefore does accurately find independent links between achievement and the existing patterns of resource allocation. Our best judgment is that both school quality and family background relate significantly to school performance.

Regardless of the outcome of the debate over the general impact of existing resource disparities on the achievement of disadvantaged children, our study of school integration and compensatory education programs (Chapters 16 and 25) does provide convincing evidence that resources can be employed in particular ways which will substantially improve opportunities for disadvantaged children. This finding is not inconsistent with the Coleman Report, which argues only that differences in school resources and expenditures as employed in 1965 in general had little effect on academic achievement. The Report does not deal with the effectiveness of focused compensatory efforts, and the Report provides strong supportive evidence of the benefits of socio-economic integration.

Several recent publications, however, most notably Christopher Jencks' controversial book *Inequality*,* have gone far beyond the Coleman Report's findings to argue not only that schools generally do not presently entirely overcome the effects of educational disadvantage—a finding with which we agree—but that schools cannot substantially improve the academic performance of disadvantaged children—and that efforts to improve schools should focus only on making them pleasant places to be.** Further, Jencks suggests that family background has little impact on economic success in life. We simply do not believe the evidence supports these drastic conclusions.

---

**Inequality: A Reassessment of Family and Schooling in America*, Christopher Jencks, and Marshall Smith, Henry Acland, Mary Jo Bane, David Cohen, Herbert Gintis, Barbara Heyns and Stephen Michelson.

**Jencks also suggests that education has little independent effect on lifetime earnings, and that there is more economic mobility in our society than is commonly supposed. These arguments are effectively rebutted in Levin, "The Social Science Objectivity Gap", *Saturday Review*, December 1972.

# Chapter 13—The Costs of Inadequate Education

The costs of inadequate education are, for the most part, immeasurable. For the individual, educational failure means a lifetime of lost opportunities. But the effects are visited on the Nation as well, for society as a whole also pays for the undereducation of a significant segment of its population.

Unemployment and underemployment due to low levels of educational attainment and underachievement reduce many citizens' earning power. Reduced earnings translate into fewer total goods and services, less tax support for Government, and require the use of public budgets to pay for services that would otherwise be provided through personal resources. Families whose incomes are below the poverty line must be supported with tax dollars to pay for food, housing, health services, job training, remedial education, income maintenance and other services. Low educational attainment is an important contributor to crime; the costs of crime prevention and control and our judicial and penal systems are higher to the extent that higher educational attainment and achievement would result in reduced juvenile delinquency and adult crime.

The Nation also pays for inadequate education in the reduced political participation of persons with low educational attainment. Studies show that persons with less formal schooling are less likely to register or vote and less informed about political issues. To the degree that other groups in society thereby become a more powerful political constituency for public officeholders, those who fail to participate are underrepresented in and powerless to effect the actions of the legislative and executive branches of State, local and National Government.

Finally, the costs of poor education are not just limited to the present generation. The children of persons with inadequate education are themselves more likely to suffer the same educational and social consequences as their parents.

A study estimating the magnitude of some of these costs was undertaken for the committee by Dr. Henry M. Levin, Associate Professor at the Stanford University School of Education. Dr. Levin's study is the first attempt to place dollar estimates on the loss to our society of educational neglect. His report, which has been published separately by the committee, is a landmark in educational economic research. It is particularly important in the context of the current national concern about inequality in educational finance and the prospect that the Federal Government and the States will undertake large increases in their respective shares of the costs of public education.

## A. Summary of Dr. Levin's Findings on the Costs of Inadequate Education

The purpose of the Levin study was to estimate costs to the Nation of educational neglect where an inadequate education is defined as attainment of less than high school education. In summary, the study found:

1. The failure to attain a minimum of high school completion among the population of males 25–34 years of age in 1969 was estimated to cost the Nation:

- $237 billion in income over the lifetime of these men.
- $71 billion in foregone government revenues of which about $47 billion would have been added to the Federal Treasury and $24 billion to the coffers of State and local governments.

2. In contrast, the probable costs of having provided a minimum of high school completion for this group of men was estimated to be about $40 billion.

- Thus, the sacrifice in national income from inadequate education among 25- to 34-year-old males was about $200 billion greater than the investment required to alleviate this condition.
- Each dollar of social investment for this purpose would have generated about $6 of national income over the lifetime of this group of men.
- The government revenues generated by this investment would have exceeded government expenditures by over $30 billion.

3. Welfare expenditures attributable to inadequate education are estimated to be about $3 billion *each year* and are probably increasing over time.

4. The costs to the Nation of crime that is related to inadequate education appears to be about $3 billion *a year* and rising.

5. Inadequate education also inflicts burdens on the Nation in the form of reduced political participation and intergenerational mobility, as well as higher incidence of disease. It is difficult to attempt any monetary estimate of these costs.

## B. An Investment in High School Completion

### 1. Defining Educational Inadequacy

There are at least two ways of defining educational inadequacy. The first concentrates on the overall concept of education in society. Educational failure is viewed in terms of inequality in the distribution of the rewards of schooling and, particularly recently, as the result of institutional inflexibility, wastefulness and an inability or unwillingness to adapt to change.

The second and more traditional way of defining inadequate education is to view educational success and failure in terms of quantity and quality of school experience. Rightly or wrongly our society rewards individuals largely according to their educational attainment. This definition is accepted here because of our inability to assess the effects and consequences of the more significant aspects of inadequate education suggested in the first definition.

Any demarcation between adequate and inadequate education is an arbitrary one, but it is clear that an adequately educated person should be able to cope with such routine tasks as preparing work papers, tax forms, passing written examinations for a drivers license, and applying for insurance benefits. Given this, and the relative importance of a high school education for job opportunities, for purposes of assessing its costs it is reasonable to define inadequate education as any level of education below high school graduation.

### 2. THE INCIDENCE OF LOW EDUCATIONAL ATTAINMENT

According to Census data, in March 1969* nearly half of all citizens 25 years of age and over—and two-thirds of our black population—lack a high school diploma.

But this certainly overstates educational inadequacy, since many older persons entered the labor force at a time when the need for a high school diploma was not clearly established as a prerequisite for social mobility, job level and other benefits. In contrast, youngsters who do not complete high school today enter the work force with an educational liability which will most likely plague them increasingly through their careers. In addition, the general upward trend toward more schooling has meant that among younger adults the proportion who have not completed high school is much lower than among the population as a whole.

Among young adults, age 25–29 for example, about 25 percent failed to complete high school; although about 40 percent of black men and nearly 50 percent of all black women in this age group did not attain this level. Thus the incidence of high school completion is much greater among young adult whites than blacks.

For purpose of analyzing the Nation's investment in high school completion, the category of young men age 25–34 was chosen since they represent a group with the most recent educational experience—they have completed their education and they are at the beginning of their work careers. In 1969, there were 11.8 million men in this category of whom approximately 12 percent were nonwhite. Table 13–1 shows the educational attainment of white and nonwhite men in this age group. Young men, 2.6 million white and 583,000 nonwhite, failed to complete high school. This represents 44 percent of all nonwhite men age 25–34 and 25 percent of all white men in this age group.

---

*Dr. Levin's Report uses 1969 Census estimates. The 1970 Census was not available when Dr. Levin's research was undertaken, but the 1970 data would not appreciably change the conclusions of his study.

TABLE 13-1.—*Educational attainment for males 25 to 34 years of age, March 1969, by race*

[Numbers in thousands]

| | Elementary | | High school | | College | | | | | |
|---|---|---|---|---|---|---|---|---|---|---|
| | Less than 8 years | 8 years | 1 to 3 years | 4 years | 1 year | 2 years | 3 years | 4 years | 5 or more years | Total |
| White males | 537 | 561 | 1, 499 | 4, 161 | 630 | 686 | 286 | 1, 191 | 960 | 10, 467 |
| Percentage | 5. 1 | 5. 3 | 14. 3 | 39. 8 | 6. 0 | 6. 5 | 2. 7 | 11. 3 | 9. 2 | 100 |
| Nonwhite males | 145 | 85 | 353 | 491 | 48 | 58 | 10 | 71 | 61 | 1, 319 |
| Percentage | 10. 9 | 6. 4 | 26. 7 | 37. 2 | 3. 8 | 4. 4 | 0. 8 | 5. 3 | 4. 6 | 100 |

Source: U.S. Department of Commerce, Bureau of the Census, "Educational Attainment: March 1969," "Population Characteristics," current Population Reports, series P-20, No. 194 (Feb. 19, 1970), table 1.

## 3. LOSS IN NATIONAL INCOME FROM EDUCATIONAL INEQUALITY

The following table shows the numbers of men age 25–34 who would have increased their educational attainments through high school and beyond if all such men had completed a minimum of high school attainment.

TABLE 13–2.—*Estimates of number of males 25 to 34 years of age who would have increased their educational attainments under a national policy providing a minimum of high school completion*

[In thousands]

| | Number of additional persons completing level | | |
|---|---|---|---|
| | White | Nonwhite | Total |
| From— | | | |
| Less than 8 years | 537 | 145 | 682 |
| 8 years | 561 | 85 | 646 |
| 1 to 3 years high school | 1, 499 | 353 | 1, 852 |
| To high school completion. | | | |
| From high school completion to— | | | |
| 1 to 3 years college | 418 | 94 | 512 |
| 4 years college | 223 | 50 | 273 |
| 5 or more years college | 195 | 44 | 239 |

Census data permit the estimation of lifetime incomes according to educational attainment level. Table 13–3 shows estimated lifetime incomes from age 18 for men by race and educational attainment.

TABLE 13–3.—*Estimated lifetime incomes from age 18 for males by race and educational attainment*

| Level of schooling completed | Lifetime income | | |
|---|---|---|---|
| | All males | White | Nonwhite |
| Elementary: | | | |
| Less than 8 years | $206, 000 | $219, 500 | $155, 900 |
| 8 years | 263, 000 | 276, 100 | 176, 700 |
| High school: | | | |
| 1 to 3 years | 282, 000 | 300, 400 | 204, 200 |
| 4 years | 336, 000 | 347, 000 | 242, 900 |
| College: | | | |
| 1 to 3 years | 378, 000 | 384, 600 | 292, 300 |
| 4 years | 489, 000 | 497, 500 | 348, 200 |
| 5+ years | 544, 000 | 554, 000 | 387, 800 |

But to apply these estimates to an analysis of increased high school completion and associated college participation would be to ignore the effects of such increases on the labor market; of possible differences in ability between present dropouts and those who graduate from high school; and of other factors. Accordingly, these figures must be adjusted for other influences that affect earnings before a conversion of the foregone income due to inadequate schooling can be computed. After considering these factors it seemed appropriate to reduce the lifetime income gains represented by Table 13–3 by a factor of 25 percent.

As this table shows, the difference in expected lifetime incomes between men with 8 years of schooling and those with high school completion is about $73,000 for the overall population; and differences in lifetime income between high school dropouts and graduates are in the $40,000–$50,000 range. At the college level, a graduate receives about $150,000 more than a high school graduate.

Since Table 13–3 reflects the additional lifetime income generated by greater schooling attainments and Table 13–2 represents those additional educational attainments, the total income lost by not having invested in a minimum of high school completion for this group of men can also be calculated.

TABLE 13–4.—*Estimate of incomes forgone by failure to invest in a minimum of high school completion for all males 25 to 34 years old*

| | Gross income forgone (billions) | After 25 percent ability adjustment |
|---|---|---|
| White: | | |
| High school completion | $178 | $133.5 |
| College | 90 | 67.5 |
| Total whites | 268 | 201.0 |
| Nonwhite: | | |
| High school completion | 32 | 24.0 |
| College | 16 | 12.0 |
| Total nonwhites | 48 | 36.0 |
| Total all males 25 to 34 years old | 316 | 237.0 |

Table 13–4 presents incomes foregone by our society as a result of its failure to invest in a minimum of 4 years of high school for all males 25–34 years of age. The gross income loss calculated is $316 billion over the lifetime of this group. This in turn is reduced by 25 percent as the estimated portion of the difference between the incomes of persons of varying levels of educational attainment that is attributable to the fact that persons of higher abilities complete more schooling.

When adjusted by this factor, the net amount of national income loss is $237 billion. This amount is composed of about $157.5 billion that emanates directly from the additional high school completions and another $79.5 billion for the men who would have continued their education beyond this level had they received high school diplomas.

*Thus, the failure to have invested in an adequate education among men 25–34 years is likely to cost society about $237 billion in lost income over the lifetime of these men.*

#### 4. LOST TAX REVENUES

Any substantial loss of national income is also tantamount to a large loss of tax revenues at all levels of government. In 1969, government tax receipts represented about 31 percent of personal income, rising from 23.5 percent in 1949. About two-thirds of these public revenues went to the Federal Government and about one-third was collected by State and local governments. Thus, almost a third of any reduction in national income would represent a diminution in revenues for the support of public goods and services.

On the basis that about 30 percent of the national income lost by not investing in adequate education will represent a reduction in tax collections, the sacrifice for the public sector from having failed to make this investment for the 25- to 34-year-old group of males is about $71 billion. Of that amount, about $24 billion would have represented the additional contribution to State and local governments, and about $47 billion would have been added to the Federal Treasury. Given the fact that an increasing proportion of national income is being channeled to the Government sector over time, the $71 billion estimate is likely to be a conservative one.

### 5. THE RELATIONSHIP BETWEEN HIGH SCHOOL COMPLETION, PRODUCTIVITY AND INCOME

Before calculating the cost of providing high school completion, it is appropriate to ask how higher levels of education can lead to higher levels of productivity and income.

As compared with those who have obtained their high school diplomas and perhaps attended college, persons with less than high school completion are likely to be found in the lower paying occupations, to be receiving lower earnings even within an occupation, and to be more susceptible to unemployment and underemployment. These differences in experiences reflect themselves in differences in economic productivity and earnings.

There are at least three reasons that workers with more education are likely to be more productive and derive higher earnings than those with lower educational attainments. First, additional schooling provides one with a greater set of skills such as language and numerical proficiency, conceptual skills, and vocational abilities, both specific and general, which improve productivity.

Second, additional schooling tends to inculcate persons with specific attitudes and behaviors that help them to function in the large enterprises that characterize much of both the government and the private sector.

Third, it has been suggested that in a society characterized by rapid technological change, education makes a contribution to productivity by creating a greater ability to adapt to such change. Studies of agriculture, for example, have found that the more highly educated farmers tend to adopt productive innovations earlier than those with lesser education.

Finally, as an adjunct of this, it is possible that the technology of production in a society reflects the educational mode of the labor force. That is, as average skill levels rise, capital that is introduced into the production process makes use of the greater abundance of such labor force capabilities. The result is that low skill opportunities decline as the educational attainment of the work force rises. Unfortunately, this means that the portion of the population with considerably less than average attainment finds that the relative demand for its services is declining.

### 6. THE COST OF PROVIDING ADEQUATE EDUCATION THROUGH HIGH SCHOOL COMPLETION

What would have been the additional national investment required to raise the level of educational attainment as reflected in Table 13–4? To calculate this investment it is necessary to determine the cost of both high school completion and the additional cost for those who would also complete one or more years of higher education.

Using U.S. Office of Education 1970 estimates of $1.214 per year of additional secondary schooling and $2,545 per year of college attendance, the cost of providing a minimum of high school completion for all males who would otherwise not graduate is estimated at about $13.4 billion; and the cost of providing additional education to those persons among this group who would continue their education beyond high school is about $9 billion, or a total of $22.5 billion. This figure represents a lower limit on the public's investment for eliminating inadequate education, for it does not take into consideration the massive increases in expenditures on potential dropouts which would be required to fulfill the minimum goal of high school completion.

To derive the upper limit of added investment necessary to attain high school completion for the same group, it is assumed that additional expenditures must take place at both the elementary and secondary levels for each potential dropout. This additional expenditure is calculated to raise spending to about $1,450 per year for each eligible person at the elementary grades and over $2,400 a year at the secondary level, an increase by several factors over present compensatory efforts for disadvantaged children.

Such a substantial infusion would represent an investment of about $34 billion more than the lower limit of $23 billion. Thus, $57 billion is the approximate upper estimate on spending required to alleviate undereducation among the 25- to 34-year-old group of men.

Selecting the midpoint of the range between $23 billion and $57 billion as the most reasonable estimate of costs, the investment figure required to alleviate the costs of poor education among the 25- to 34-year-old male group is approximately $40 billion. Clearly, the more effectively the Nation can focus its schools on the needs of potential dropouts, the lower the additional investment required to attain a minimum of high school completion.

### 7. HIGH SCHOOL COMPLETION AS A NATIONAL INVESTMENT

It is clear that the national cost of educational neglect far exceeds the national investment required to alleviate this problem. Among 25- to 34-year-old men alone, the expected increase in lifetime income would have been about $237 billion had all members of the group completed a minimum of high school. In contrast, the national investment required to fulfill such an objective would have cost only about $40 billion. Thus, on the basis of this analysis the costs to society of inadequate education are nearly $200 billion in excess of the costs of maintaining a program of high school completion for the group of men studied. Each dollar of investment in their education would generate an additional $6 of national income over the lifetime of the 25- to 34-year-old men. The additional $237 billion in lifetime income that is presently foregone by insufficient education would have provided about

$71 billion in additional revenues to Federal, State and local governments. Finally, government treasuries would have received an excess of more than $30 billion over the costs of the program.

## C. Inadequate Education and Welfare Expenditures

In fiscal year 1970, welfare assistance programs cost the Nation about $12.8 billion. The Federal Government was responsible for slightly over half of these welfare costs, the States for about 38 percent and the local governments for just under 11 percent.

In addition, unemployment compensation paid $4.3 billion in benefits to the jobless.

Not all welfare costs are education-related. However, there are several categories that probably have a direct relationship to inadequate education: Aid for Dependent Children (AFDC), Medical Assistance Payments related to AFDC, and Unemployment Compensation. Eligibility for each of these benefits is contingent on income or employment, which in turn are at least partly a function of education.

### 1. AFDC

By far the largest proportion of AFDC families are those in which the mother is the only parent at home. A study conducted in 1967 found that among all women, about 55 percent had completed a minimum of high school, among female heads of families the figure was 42 percent; but among AFDC mothers, only 20 percent had reached this level of attainment.

The increased employability of AFDC recipients when they have higher educational attainment is reflected in Table 13–5 which shows the number of months of employment in the 37 months prior to receipt of AFDC payments in 1967.

Table 13–5.—*Number of months of employment during 37-month period prior to receipt of AFDC payments, 1967*

| Education level | Number of months employment | | | | |
|---|---|---|---|---|---|
| | Unemployed | Up to 12 | Up to 24 | Up to 36 | 37 |
| None | 73. 4 | 10. 1 | 5. 0 | 2. 9 | 7. 9 |
| 8 | 48. 7 | 20. 6 | 11. 7 | 8. 8 | 8. 8 |
| 9 to 11 | 37. 5 | 25. 0 | 15. 2 | 12. 1 | 8. 7 |
| 12 | 28. 5 | 24. 9 | 20. 4 | 14. 6 | 9. 8 |

Source: U.S. Department of Health, Education, and Welfare. Social and Rehabilitation Service, "Welfare Policy and Its Consequences for the Recipient Population: A Study of the AFDC Program" (Washington, 1969), table 5.8.

The probability and duration of employment is thus a direct function of education level. Moreover, even when women with low educational attainment were employable, the earnings were frequently too low to make them financially independent.

In the cases where fathers are present there is a similar pattern of educational disability as shown in Table 13–6. While about 58 percent of the male adult population in 1967 had completed at least 12 years of schooling only 9 percent of AFDC incapacitated males and 16 percent of AFDC unemployed males had attained this level.

TABLE 13–6.—*Educational attainment for males, March 1967*

[In percent]

| Educational attainment | All males 18 to 64 | AFDC incapacitated | AFDC unemployed |
|---|---|---|---|
| 0 to 4 years | 3. 9 | 40. 2 | 16. 8 |
| 5 to 8 years | 18. 8 | 36. 8 | 34. 4 |
| 9 to 11 years | 19. 0 | 14. 2 | 32. 8 |
| 12 years | 32. 7 | 6. 7 | 12. 8 |
| More than 12 years | 25. 3 | 2. 2 | 3. 2 |

Source: For all males, U.S. Department of Commerce, Bureau of the Census, Current Population Reports, series P–20, No. 169, "Educational Attainment: March 1967," table 1. For AFDC males, U.S. Department of Health, Education, and Welfare, Social and Rehabilitation Service. Findings of the AFDC Study, Pt. I (Washington, July 1970) tables 29 and 33.

### 2. GENERAL ASSISTANCE

General Assistance is a residual program designed to provide aid for single persons, childless couples under 65, families with children and employed male heads, and others who are not eligible for other programs. State and local practices differ, and it is therefore difficult to generalize about specific provisions of General Assistance programs. The basic nature of the programs in providing support to low-income households, however, suggests the same type of ties to insufficient education that are evident for the AFDC programs.

### 3. UNEMPLOYMENT INSURANCE

The objective of unemployment insurance is to provide cash benefits to regularly employed workers during limited periods of involuntary unemployment. Many educationally disadvantaged persons are not covered by the program, since those who have never held jobs or who have worked only for short intervals are ineligible for benefits. Moreover, the fact that benefits are related to previous earnings means that persons with lower educational attainment and earnings will receive lower benefits.

Obviously, not all people receiving unemployment insurance benefits are educationally disadvantaged in the conventional sense. But it is the so-called marginal worker—the worker who is the least able to adapt to changing technology because of limited skills—who is the most susceptible to unemployment in industries characterized by technological change. Accordingly, it is reasonable to conclude that inadequate education is a partial cause of unemployment insurance expenditures.

### 4. THE COST OF WELFARE ATTRIBUTABLE TO INADEQUATE EDUCATION

Given the relative uncertainty of how much of the welfare burden should be allocated to inadequate education, it seems reasonable to estimate such costs on the basis of two presumptions: (1) Only the education-related categories of welfare should be considered in the analysis; and, (2) both an intuitive upper limit on the proportion of these expenditures attributable to poor education and a lower limit should be investigated. It would seem that the midpoint of the range established by these boundaries would be the best assessment of the welfare costs associated with undereducation. It is probable that between one-half and one-quarter of the costs of AFDC, medical assistance and general assistance costs, and that between 15 and 25 percent of employment compensation costs are attributable to low educational attainment.

The following table shows the estimated costs of welfare attributable to not providing a minimum of high school completion for all citizens. The upper limit of such costs is estimated to be about $4 billion a year. The lower limit is set at about $2.1 billion a year. The midpoint of this range is about $3 billion a year, a figure which is considered as being the most reasonable overall estimate of costs of welfare incurred because of insufficient education.

TABLE 13-7.—*Estimated cost of welfare expenditures from inadequate education in 1970*

| | *Millions* |
|---|---|
| Aid to families with dependent children | $4,082 |
| Medical assistance | 1,199 |
| General assistance | 640 |
| Public assistance total | 5,921 |
| Unemployment compensation | 4,322 |
| Upper estimate: | |
| Public assistance total X50 percent | 2,961 |
| Unemployment compensation X25 percent | 1,081 |
| Upper estimate total | 4,042 |
| Lower estimate: | |
| Public assistance total X25 percent | 1,480 |
| Unemployment compensation X15 percent | 648 |
| Lower estimate total | 2,128 |

Source: AFDC. General Assistance and Medical Assistance Expenditures—Sources of Funds Expended for Public Assistance Payments, table 1, 25 percent of medical assistance payments were approximated as AFDC share. The 1968 share was 27.9 percent. See U.S. Department of Health. Education, and Welfare. Social and Rehabilitation Service. Medicaid, Selected Statistics 1951–69. Unemployment compensation payments are taken from U.S. Department of Health, Education, and Welfare, Social Security Bulletin (April 1971), table M1.

Alleviating inadequate education, then, would reduce the Nation's welfare costs by about $3 billion, or 15–20 percent of the present welfare burden carried by the taxpayer. To the degree that the Nation shifts to an income maintenance program it is likely that the impact of inadequate education on these costs will be even greater.

## D. Inadequate Education and the Costs of Crime

For the year 1965, the President's Commission on Law Enforcement and Administration estimated that the economic impact of crime and related expenditures was $21 billion. Research on juvenile and adult crime indicates that low educational attainment is clearly a contributing factor to the high crime rate.

Inmates of correctional institutions have completed far less schooling than the population as a whole. For example, in a test administered to newly admitted felons in California in 1968, it was shown that 56 percent scored at eighth grade level or below in standardized achievement tests, compared with the median level of more than 12 years for the general adult population in the State. Parallel studies for

Texas and New Jersey have shown similar inmate educational retardation.

The tie between low educational attainment and juvenile delinquency has been well documented. Even when factors such as race, family size and income, IQ scores, and presence of both parents in home were taken into account, one study found that high school dropouts were three to five times more likely than high school graduates to be arrested for committing a juvenile crime. Similar studies in other areas of the Nation have found the same negative association between education and delinquency.

### 1. THE RELATIONSHIP BETWEEN CRIME AND INSUFFICIENT EDUCATION

Several theories have been suggested for the higher delinquency rate of high school dropouts. Some researchers assert that poor quality of education (that is, irrelevant content, and the treatment of students in low-status fashion and preparing them for low-paying jobs) is a major school-linked cause of rebellion and delinquency.

There is also evidence relating income and employment to criminal behavior. One study, for example, found that a 10 percent rise in family income can be expected to reduce delinquency by 15–20 percent. Further, in an analysis of three U.S. cities, there appeared to be an increase of about 2.5 percent in the delinquency rate associated with each 10 percent increase in the rate of unemployment (from 5 to 5.5 percent, for example).

### 2. THE COSTS OF EDUCATION-RELATED CRIME

Table 13–8 shows estimates of the economic impact of crime for 1965, as compiled by the President's Commission on Law Enforcement and Administration of Justice.

TABLE 13–8.—*Economic impact of crimes and related expenditures, 1965*

| | *Millions* |
|---|---|
| Crimes against persons: | |
| Homicide | $750 |
| Assault | 65 |
| Total | 815 |
| Crimes against property: | |
| Property destroyed: Arson and vandalism | 300 |
| Involuntary transfer: | |
| Unreported commercial theft | 1,400 |
| Robbery | |
| Burglary | 600 |
| Larceny | |
| Auto theft | |
| Embezzlement | 200 |
| Fraud | 1,350 |
| Forgery and other | 82 |
| Total | 3,932 |

TABLE 13–8.—*Economic impact of crimes and related expenditures, 1965*—Continued

| | *Millions* |
|---|---|
| Other crimes: | |
| Driving under influence | 1,816 |
| Tax fraud | 100 |
| Abortion | 120 |
| Total | 2,036 |
| Illegal goods and services: | |
| Narcotics | 350 |
| Loan-sharking | 350 |
| Prostitution | 225 |
| Alcohol (tax loss) | 150 |
| Gambling | 7,000 |
| Total | 8,075 |
| Public law enforcement and criminal justice: | |
| Police | 2,792 |
| Corrections | 1,034 |
| Prosecution and defense | 125 |
| Courts | 261 |
| Total | 4,212 |
| Private costs related to crime: | |
| Prevention services | 1,350 |
| Prevention equipment | 200 |
| Insurance (overhead costs) | 300 |
| Private counsel, bail, witness expenses | 60 |
| Total | 1,910 |
| Total | 20,980 |

Though the total economic impact of crime was estimated at about $21 billion for 1965, not all of these amounts are social costs in the sense that society has made sacrifices of these magnitudes. Further, not all of the social costs are derived from education-related crimes.

To be considered education related, a crime should satisfy two criteria. First it should reflect crimes that are likely to decline if there were a reduction in the incidence of inadequate education. Second, it should measure a "real" sacrifice in the Nation's resources rather than just a transfer of them from one group in society to another.

The following categories seem to reflect a social burden and appear to be related to poor education: crimes against persons, property destroyed by arson and vandalism, public law enforcement and criminal justice expenditures and private costs related to crime. Crimes against persons accounted for about $815 million in 1965 in foregone income and medical expenses; property destroyed by arson and vandalism amounted to about $300 million. Much of the public law enforcement and criminal justice expenditures of over $4 billion and the private costs related to crime of almost $2 billion should be applied to the estimate of the education-related costs of crime.

Not reflected in Table 13–8 is the loss of income and national output reflected by the large source of manpower that is imprisoned. The income that is foregone by inmates in correctional institutions has been calculated to be about $1 billion.

Table 13–9 shows the estimated costs of crime attributable to inadequate education. These are based upon 1965 estimates.

TABLE 13–9.—*Estimated costs of crime attributable to inadequate education*

| | *Millions* |
|---|---|
| Costs of crimes against persons and property: | |
| Homicide | $750 |
| Assault | 65 |
| Arson and vandalism | 300 |
| Total | 1,115 |
| Law enforcement and judicial | 4,212 |
| Private costs | 1,910 |
| Foregone income of inmates | 1,000 |
| Total | 8,237 |

As Table 13–9 shows, the annual cost of crime which is likely to decline with an increase in educational attainment is approximately $8.2 billion. It is not possible to determine the exact proportion of this amount that is attributable to insufficient education. However, it is reasonable to assume that between a quarter and a half the total cost, that is, between $2 billion and $4.1 billion, represents the cost of crime attributable to inadequate education. Both rising costs and increased crime rates would indicate these costs are considerably higher at the present time.

## E. Other Social Costs of Inadequate Education

Society bears other costs attributable to inadequate education. While monetary estimates cannot be calculated for them, our Nation unquestionably pays substantially for the fact that lower levels of political participation, lack of intergenerational mobility and poor health are all associated with low educational attainment.

### 1. INADEQUATE EDUCATION AND POLITICAL PARTICIPATION

The poorly educated tend to participate less in the political process. As a result, government is biased in favor of the more educated and wealthy and public policies and programs often work against the poorly educated.

Born into poor families, the undereducated feel that their plight is hopeless, that participation in politics will not significantly change their lives. Feeling powerless, citizens may vent their frustration in the form of riots, demonstrations and other such disruptions, as we have witnessed frequently in recent years.

The impact of schooling can be substantial in overcoming the lack of political participation. In a study of some 10,000 elementary schoolchildren, the school was found to be the "central, salient, and dominant force" in the political socialization of the young child. Schooling imparts a theoretical knowledge of political institutions and information on the practical aspects of the system. The importance of voter registration and exercising one's franchise are emphasized. Moreover, education provides access to information on political and social issues which tends to create a greater personal predisposition toward concern over political matters.

A recent survey by the Bureau of the Census on the 1968 presidential election and earlier surveys carried out by other groups have confirmed that the likelihood of voting is directly related to the educational attainment of the population. The following table shows this pattern for the 1968 presidential election.

TABLE 13–10.—*Reported voter participation in 1968 presidential election*

| Years of schooling | Proportion voting | | | |
|---|---|---|---|---|
| | Whites | | Blacks | |
| | Males | Females | Males | Females |
| 0 to 4 | 45. 4 | 32. 0 | 43. 2 | 34. 7 |
| 5 to 7 | 60. 5 | 46. 1 | 54. 9 | 53. 5 |
| 8 | 68. 4 | 59. 8 | 59. 7 | 53. 3 |
| 9 to 11 | 67. 5 | 62. 7 | 61. 7 | 59. 4 |
| 12 | 76. 3 | 75. 6 | 74. 8 | 69. 5 |
| 13 to 15 | 80. 7 | 82. 5 | 79. 7 | 79. 4 |
| 16 | 85. 2 | 84. 2 | 85. 8 | 83. 7 |
| 17 or more | 86. 4 | 88. 3 | 88. 4 | ---------- |

Source: U.S. Department of Commerce, Bureau of the Census, "Years of School Completed—Reported Voter Participation in 1968 and 1964 for Persons 25 Years Old and Over, by Race and Sex, in the United States: November 1968." Current Population Reports, series P 20, No. 192, table 11.

### 2. INADEQUATE EDUCATION AND INTERGENERATIONAL MOBILITY

The children of parents with inadequate education are themselves likely to suffer from poor education. Research has shown that the higher the educational attainment of a child's parents the child is not only likely to attain more schooling but he is also likely to show higher scores on achievement tests at every level of schooling. Thus, the alleviation of inadequate education in this generation will likely have a salient effect on reducing it in the next generation as well. Conversely, the present burden of undereducation will likely translate into future costs for the society our children inherit.

### 3. INADEQUATE EDUCATION AND POOR HEALTH

Inadequate education can affect health levels in a variety of ways.

*First*, less educated persons are not as likely to be aware of the symptoms of certain serious illnesses whose early detection is crucial for cure or control.

*Second*, knowledge of nutritional requirements, prenatal care, and preventative health precautions are less widespread among persons who lack adequate schooling.

The specific role of education in exacerbating health problems has been addressed in several studies. Usually though, the educational factors are subsumed under other related socioeconomic factors such as occupation, which are in themselves heavily influenced by educational attainment. The lower the occupational level of fathers, for example, the higher the rate of infant mortality both during the fetal stage and during early childhood. A similar pattern is reflected in death rates of adults and the incidence of disease according to occupational category. A study of severe psychological disorders found that the lower socioeconomic groups were much more likely to fall prey to schizophrenia and paranoia than the higher groups. Here again the role of inadequate education was strongly implied.

## F. Significance of the Levin Findings

The Levin study assesses only part of the costs to our society of inadequate education. It focuses only on high school graduation as one index of educational inadequacy. In assessing the loss to our national income it focuses only upon 3.2 million men between the ages of 25 and 34. It does not, for example, attempt to document the additional costs which we pay for the fact that millions of American youth who, now and in the past, have graduated from high school but failed to receive the equivalent of a 12th grade education. It is, however, a significant and landmark contribution to our knowledge, as it demonstrates that the failure of our educational system is tremendously costly to our society. It does demonstrate that for each dollar we invest in public education there will be a five- or six-fold return on our investment—just in terms of the production of national income alone. And, every $4 invested to provide a minimum of high school completion will generate $7 in additional tax revenues to Federal, State and local governments.

The Levin study emphasizes the costs to the Nation of inadequate education and the benefits that would flow to our entire society under a policy of minimum high school completion. If, as Dr. Levin demonstrates, the benefits of a major effort to improve education accrue nationally, the Nation as a whole should certainly pay a substantial portion of the cost. Of $71 billion in additional tax revenues which would be produced if the 25- to 34-year-old group were all to have completed high school, $47 billion would be collected by the Federal Treasury while $24 billion would be collected by State and local governments. Two-thirds of these additional revenues would, therefore, be collected by the Federal Government. Yet, at the present time, the Federal Government supports only about 7 percent of the total costs of public education with the States supplying 41 percent and local governments 52 percent of these expenses.

If, as Dr. Levin estimates, $40 billion is required to generate this $71 billion in additional Government tax revenues, under our present system of education finance less than $3 billion of that $40 billion would be provided by the Federal Government with a return to the Federal Treasury of $47 billion. At the same time, $37 billion would have to be invested by State and local governments with a return to them of only $24 billion.

What these figures indicate is that State and local governments now bear the major share of educational expenses. At the same time, the Federal Government does not support education at a level commensurate with the return on its investment. On this basis there is ample justification for increased Federal support of education.

We believe it appropriate, here, to set forth a detailed description of the Levin Report and its findings.

# Part IV
# School Integration

## Chapter 14—A Basic Commitment

> **All persons born or naturalized in the United States and subject to the jurisdiction thereof are citizens of the United States, and of the State wherein they reside. . . . No State shall . . . deny to any person within its jurisdiction the equal protection of the laws.**
> ***14th Amendment to the U.S. Constitution***

For more than a century, the goal of this Nation has been a just and open society—in which citizens associate freely as they wish, in which race and religion are no handicap, above all, a society in which each child is born with a real and equal chance for a productive and useful life. Achievement of that goal cannot be grounded upon a system of public education which perpetuates, for all time, the results of past racial discrimination. The Supreme Court's comment in *Brown* v. *Board of Education*, 347 U.S. 483 (1954), is even truer today:

> In these days, it is doubtful that any child may reasonably be expected to succeed in life if he is denied the opportunity of an education. Such an opportunity, where the State has undertaken to provide it, is a right which must be made available to all on equal terms.

Yet racial discrimination, including the deliberate segregation of children by race or national origin, is widespread in public school systems throughout this country. In the 17 Southern and Border States, strictly segregated dual-school systems were required by State statute from the earliest days of public education. And a growing number of Federal courts have found segregation in public education caused by subtler means in the North and West as well. In South Holland, Ill., a U.S. District Court found schools located in the center rather than at the boundaries of segregated residential areas in order to achieve school segregation, school assignment policies under which black children living nearer to white schools attended black schools while white children living nearer to black schools attended white schools, schoolbuses used to transport students out of their neighborhoods to achieve segregation, Federal courts have found discrimination in Pontiac and Detroit, Mich., in Pasadena and San Francisco, Calif.; in Denver, Colo.; in Indianapolis, Ind.; in Minneapolis, Minn., and elsewhere.

The 18 years since the Supreme Court's landmark decision in *Brown* v. *Board of Education*, and, in particular, the 8 years since adoption of the Civil Rights Act of 1964, have presented a clear test of our commitment to equal opportunity for all American children. The Nation continues to wrestle with its conscience. And the outcome remains in doubt. It is clear as this report is published that our national commitment to nondiscrimination in public education is in serious jeopardy.

Proposals were introduced in the 92d Congress for constitutional amendments and for legislation which—if held constitutional—would severely limit or eliminate the power of Federal courts and agencies to remedy the establishment or maintenance of racially discriminatory school systems. These or similar proposals are likely to be advanced again in the 93d Congress. Public opinion polls over the last 2 years show a marked decrease in support, not for desegregation itself, but for means of remedying segregation without which discriminatory dual school systems must be allowed to continue. Perhaps the saddest aspect of the current debate over school desegregation has been its focus on the misleading issues of "busing" and "racial balance" and its consequent disregard for the real issues affecting the well-being of the millions of children whose futures are now at stake in desegregated schools.

There are only two forms of school desegregation in this country: desegregation undertaken as a matter of voluntary local—or, in some instances, State—decision, and desegregation undertaken to remedy officially sponsored segregation which violates the Equal Protection Clause of the 14th Amendment to the U.S. Constitution.

Federal courts, and Federal agencies under the Civil Rights Act of 1964 act only to remedy segregation imposed by the discriminatory acts of public authorities. Even then, they do not require any "racial balance" in the schools. Chief Justice Burger's opinion for the unanimous Supreme Court in *Swann* v. *Charlotte-Mecklenburg*, decided in April of 1971, should have put this issue to rest:

> The constitutional command to desegregate schools does not mean that every school in every community must always reflect the composition of the school system as a whole.

"Racial balance" is not required. What is required is "a plan that promises realistically to work . . . until it is clear that State-imposed segregation has been completely removed."

The issue of "busing"—although it has been at the center of debate since adoption of the Civil Rights Act of 1964—is just as misleading. The facts speak for themselves:

- According to HEW's 1970 school survey, 42 percent of all American public school students are transported to their schools by buses; an additional 25 percent ride public transportation.
- HEW estimates that only 3 percent of all public school busing is for the purpose of desegregation.
- The Department of Transportation attributes less than 1 percent of the annual increase in student transportation to school desegregation.

Transportation of students is so common in school districts throughout the Nation that there can be no legitimate reason to forbid its use as one tool in remedying discrimination.

In most, if not all cases, transportation has been held within reasonable limits. In the 23 largest school districts undergoing desegregation in the Fall of 1971, the Department of HEW estimates that the proportion of students transported rose by only 7.5 percent.

Where courts and Federal agencies have required use of transportation, often it has been to assure that the results of desegregation will be more stable—that desegregation will not be limited to the minority- and nonminority-group working class populations who typically live in adjoining neighborhoods.

Transportation, like any other tool, can be abused. But the Supreme Court has established a standard of reasonableness—that transportation should not be required where "time or distance of travel is so great as to risk either the health of the children or significantly impinge on the educational process." The court has noted that "the time of travel will vary with many factors, but none more than the age of the students." The Congress in the Education Amendments of 1972 has reaffirmed that standard, and expressly applied it to proceedings under Title VI of the Civil Rights Act of 1964. Under both Supreme Court rule and legislative provision, transportation that exceeds reasonable limits can be judicially challenged and judicially remedied.

Tragically, intense debate over the false issues of "busing" and "racial balance" have blinded many to the legitimate concerns of parents from all racial and economic backgrounds.

Often parents are understandably concerned that desegregation may result in transfer of their children from schools with middle-class student bodies and highly motivated teachers to schools with educationally disadvantaged student bodies, where teacher motivation and academic opportunities may be decidedly inferior. At the same time, the evidence strongly indicates that integration is most likely to produce achievement gains for educationally disadvantaged students when schools contain a majority of more advantaged students. Integrated schools with majority-advantaged student bodies promise the greatest benefit to disadvantaged children; and they respond to the most pressing concerns of many parents of more advantaged children. Desegregation plans should reflect this principle to the fullest possible extent; and, yet, the vital importance of socioeconomic considerations to successful school desegregation has largely escaped attention.

Minority-group teachers and community leaders often fear that desegregation may lead to further discrimination even more damaging than that involved in segregation itself. In too many instances these fears have been borne out. An on-site survey conducted by six civil rights groups, in the Fall of 1970, with the help of about 100 volunteer lawyers found widespread discriminatory policies and practices within "desegrated" schools. The findings of the civil rights groups were, in large part, confirmed by subsequent studies performed by the Department of Health, Education, and Welfare.

HEW's study of only five States found demotion or dismissal of over 4,000 black teachers and administrators during the 1971–72 school year. And yet, prompt and effective law enforcement can deter much of this "second generation" discrimination, and avoid the need for a decade of private litigation and local struggle—which will take its toll on the education of countless children.

Also largely overlooked by public discussion has been the need for early integration. The evidence reviewed by the committee strongly indicates that substantial gains in achievement of disadvantaged children are most likely when children are first integrated during the elementary grades. And integrated experiences in later grades appear far more likely to be successful when children have attended integrated elementary schools. Legislative proposals submitted by the administration last Spring, would severely limit integration at the elementary school level by prohibiting any increase in transportation to achieve desegregation, precisely at the level where some transportation is most needed, because of the inability of children to walk longer distances. Yet the administration proposals would support extensive desegregation—including use of increased transportation, where necessary—at junior and senior high school levels. Our record strongly indicates that enactment of such an approach would represent a mistake in judgment, of the most serious order.

Finally, the public debate has too often ignored the evidence that integrated education, sensitively conducted, is valuable for all children concerned. Yet, the great majority of educators and agencies concerned with educational policymaking agree that quality integrated education—in schools which are economically, as well as racially integrated; in which resources are available for compensatory education and for special services, such as individualized instruction, to meet the educational needs of all students; in which there is a warm attitude of human acceptance on the part of parents and school personnel—is among the most hopeful strategies for the education of disadvantaged children, and, that its benefits extend to children of the more affluent as well.

Continued support for school desegregation was recommended by both the 1971 White House Conference on Children and the 1972 Report of the President's Commission on School Finance. The most recent report of the National Advisory Committee on the Education of Disadvantaged Children found that, "desegregation is the best form of compensatory education." The educational importance of school integration is affirmed by the National Education Association, the American Federation of Teachers, and the Council of Chief State School Officers. Even the memorandum submitted by HEW Secretary Richardson in support of the proposed "Equal Educational Opportunities Act", which would severely limit constitutional enforcement, states:

> We know that children learn less effectively when there is a great degree of economic or racial isolation.

And perhaps President Nixon said it most clearly in his congressional message of May 21, 1970:

> We all know that desegregation is vital to quality education—not only from the standpoint of raising the achievement levels of the disadvantaged, but also from the standpoint of helping all children achieve a broad-based human understanding that increasingly is essential in today's world.

# Chapter 15—School Desegregation and the Law

## A. A Brief Background

Since ratification of the 14th Amendment in 1868, racial equality under law has been a fundamental principle of the American legal system. That was not always the case. For over 300 years, virtually all black Americans had been denied the most basic rights of American citizenship. In 1865, nearly 90 percent of all Americans of African descent were slaves. These black people were not American citizens; at law they were considered the personal property of their owners. They were not entitled to the vote, nor to due process of law in the courts. They were not permitted to own possessions, or even to marry without proprietary consent. The average life expectancy of black Americans was two-thirds that of whites.

Perhaps the most graphic description of the total subordination of Negroes in America before the Civil War is provided by the Supreme Court's 1857 decision in *Dred Scott* v. *Sandford*, 60 U.S. 303. There the court invalidated the "Missouri Compromise," an Act of Congress excluding slavery from portions of the Northwest Territories—as an unconstitutional restriction of the property rights of slaveowners and potential slaveowners. Those property rights were guaranteed against Federal infringement under the due process clause of the 5th Amendment to the U.S. Constitution.

The court held that in the eyes of the Constitution black Americans were:

> . . . considered as a subordinate and inferior class of beings, who had been subjugated by the dominant race, and, whether emancipated or not, yet remained subject to their authority, and had no rights or privileges but such as those who held the power and the government might choose to grant them.

Following the Civil War, dramatic changes in the legal status of Negro Americans were attempted through constitutional amendment. In 1865, the 13th Amendment outlawed slavery and involuntary servitude—except as punishment for crime. Ratification of the 14th Amendment followed in 1868, conferring citizenship on *all* persons born within the United States and guaranteeing the rights of due process of law and equal protection of the laws to all persons. The trilogy of civil rights amendments was completed in 1869 with the 15th Amendment by prohibiting denial of the vote on the basis of race.

These changes in the legal status of racial minorities were not cheaply purchased. They came at the cost of 4 years of Civil War, 529,000 American lives, and sectional bitterness that continues to divide the Nation, although with decreasing force, to the present day.

However, the adoption of the civil rights amendments did not confer immediate equality of legal status upon American blacks. State laws required segregation in public places, restrictive covenants in land deeds prohibiting sale to members of racial minorities, literacy requirements for voting with "grandfather" clauses to protect illiterate whites registered prior to passage of the 15th Amendment, "white primaries", job discrimination, and other discriminatory practices were adopted in much of the Nation to confine blacks to second-class citizenship. And, notwithstanding the civil rights amendments, many of these practices received the express approval of the Federal judiciary. In *Plessy* v. *Ferguson*, 163 U.S. 537, decided in 1896, the Supreme Court led the way. Upholding a Louisiana law requiring separate railway cars for whites and Negroes, the court said:

> The object of the [14th] amendment was undoubtedly to enforce the absolute equality of the two races before the law, but in the nature of things, it could not have been intended to abolish distinctions based upon color . . . Laws permitting and even requiring separation, in places where they are liable to be brought into contact, do not necessarily imply the inferiority of either race to the other, and have been generally, if not universally recognized as within the competency of the State legislatures in the exercise of their police power. The most common instance of this is connected with the establishment of separate schools for white and colored children, which have been held to be a valid exercise of the legislative power even by courts of States where the political rights of the colored race have been longest and most earnestly enforced. [Citing *Roberts* v. *City of Boston*, 5 Cush. 198 (1894).]

The court continued:

> We consider the underlying fallacy of the plaintiff's argument to consist in the assumption that the enforced separation of the two races stamps the colored race with a badge of inferiority. If this be so, it is not by reason of anything found in the act, but solely because the colored race chooses to put that construction upon it . . . Legislation is powerless to eradicate racial instincts, or to abolish distinctions based upon physical differences, and the attempt to do so can only result in accentuating the difficulty of the present situation.

Meaningful enforcement of the civil rights amendments has taken place only in the last quarter century.

Perhaps the decisive moment was the Supreme Court's crucial decision in *Shelly* v. *Kramer*, 334 U.S. 1 (1948), that the equal protection clause prohibits enforcement by State courts of land deed restrictions prohibiting the transfer of land to members of racial minorities.

In the area of education, three cases* required the admission of Negro students to State-run white institutions of higher education—on the ground that educational opportunities of equivalent value were not made available in State-run schools for black students. Then the

---

**Sipes* v. *Board of Regents of University of Oklahoma*, 332 U.S. 631; *Sweatt* v. *Painter*, 339 U.S. 629; *McLaurin* v. *Oklahoma State Regents*, 339 U.S. 637.

dam broke in 1954, with *Brown* v. *Board of Education*. There the court ruled maintenance of officially segregated public schools unconstitutional—even where State and local authorities have attempted in good faith to provide equivalent facilities, equipment and personnel in both black and white schools.

*Brown* effectively removed the legal underpinnings of *Plessy* v. *Ferguson*, ended the doctrine of "separate but equal," and laid the groundwork for a new equal protection clause jurisprudence.

## B. School Desegregation Under Law—1954–72

### 1. 1954–64—"ALL DELIBERATE SPEED"

The first *Brown* decision in 1954 established the legal principle that assignment of children on the basis of race to segregated schools violates the equal protection clause.

> . . . segregation of children in public schools solely on the basis of race, even though the physical facilities and other tangible factors may be equal, [does] deprive the children of minority groups of equal educational opportunity.

Following that decision, the Court scheduled additional arguments to consider the issue of remedy, inviting the U.S. Attorney General and the Attorneys General of the States to participate.

These arguments led to the second *Brown* decision, in May of 1955, 349 U.S. 294, which held that, in view of the administrative difficulties involved, complete elimination of dual school systems was not immediately required. Instead, segregated school districts were permitted a "period of transition" of unspecified duration, during which elimination of officially sanctioned segregation was to go forward "with all deliberate speed."

The initial response of lower Federal courts to *Brown II* was to require the implementation of so-called "free choice" desegregation plans on a grade-a-year basis. In the first year of such a plan, a Negro first-grade student would be given the opportunity to attend either the "black" school he would have attended under legal segregation, or any school formerly restricted to whites serving his grade. White first-grade students would be given a similar choice. All older students would continue to be restricted to racially segregated schools. In the second year, the "choice" option would be extended to children in both the first and second grades, and so on.

The initial response to court orders requiring even this limited desegregation was the "massive resistance" movement. By the end of 1953, every State with schools segregated by law in 1954, except Tennessee, had adopted some form of statute authorizing school closing to avoid desegregation. Four States completely prohibited expenditure of State funds for desegregated education. Eight States supported substitution of racially exclusive (white) private schools for desegregated public schools, and five States authorized transfer of public school property to private schools. Ultimately, all 11 States with school systems segregated by law at the time of *Brown* repealed or modified compulsory attendance laws, and six States weakened or eliminated teacher tenure provisions.*

The Supreme Court, however, refused to back down, and President Eisenhower's intervention to protect black students enrolled in Little Rock's Central High School demonstrated that State governments would not be permitted to ignore court orders. It became clear that State officials could effectively defy Federal authority only by closing the schools. By the Winter of 1958, the issue had become the future of public education and the stability of the governmental process, rather than segregation versus desegregation; and the "massive resistance" movement had lost the initiative.

Despite the decline of "massive resistance", only token progress toward school desegregation was made between the second *Brown* decision in 1955 and passage of the Civil Rights Act of 1964, nearly 10 years later. As the first decade after *Brown* drew to a close in the Spring of 1964, only 2.25 percent of Negro children in the 11 Southern States** attended school with whites; and faculty desegregation was practically nonexistent.

### 2. 1964–68—THE ESTABLISHMENT OF A FEDERAL ROLE

Before enactment of the Civil Rights Act of 1964, the Federal Government's involvement in the process of school desegregation amounted to little more than its amicus brief in *Brown* v. *Board of Education* and President Eisenhower's intervention with Federal troops to protect black students who had enrolled in Little Rock, Ark., Central High School in 1957. The Civil Rights Act, proposed by President John F. Kennedy in 1963, and enacted in a bipartisan effort the year after his assassination, led to substantial involvement by the Federal Government for the first time.

Title IV of this Act authorizes the Attorney General to file suit to obtain school desegregation upon receiving a citizen complaint. In addition, Title IV authorizes the Office of Education to render technical assistance to school districts preparing for desegregation; to conduct special training for school personnel in special educational problems occasioned by desegregation; and, to provide financial assistance to school districts for employment of desegregation specialists and in-service training of personnel.

---

*The weight of governmental authority fell with particular force upon the National Association for the Advancement of Colored People, which had taken a leading role in the *Brown* case and subsequent efforts to enforce its mandate. In five States, legislative committees conducted widely publicized investigations of subversive and un-American influences in the NAACP specifically and the civil rights movement generally. Other committees probed the NAACP for evidence of criminal law violations and tax evasions. Statutes designed to prevent the organization from supporting desegregation suits poured out of State legislatures. Existing laws regulating out-of-State corporations and concerning taxes and tax exemptions were applied harshly in the case of the association. Governors were granted emergency powers to halt organizational activity. State officials demanded that NAACP membership lists be made available for public inspection. State employees were required to list membership in the NAACP—grounds for dismissal for State employment.

**Alabama, Arkansas, Florida, Georgia, Louisiana, Mississippi, North Carolina, South Carolina, Tennessee, Texas, and Virginia.

Title IX of the Act authorizes intervention by the Attorney General in equal protection clause suits "of general public importance" brought by private parties.

Most important, Title VI of the Act requires all Federal agencies to assure that programs receiving Federal financial assistance are operated on a racially nondiscriminatory basis. Title VI provides:

> Sec. 601. No person in the United States shall, on the ground of race, color, or national origin, be excluded from participation in, be denied the benefits of, or be subjected to discrimination under any program or activity receiving Federal financial assistance.
>
> Sec. 602. Each Federal department and agency which is empowered to extend Federal financial assistance to any program or activity, by way of grant, loan, or contract other than a contract of insurance or guaranty, is authorized and directed to effectuate the provisions of Section 601 with respect to such program or activity . . .

Although Title VI applies to all programs of Federal financial assistance, its most immediate and dramatic impact was in the area of public education where Title VI imposes an affirmative duty on the Department of HEW to assure that school districts receiving Federal assistance operate their schools in compliance with 14th Amendment standards.

As the Fourth Circuit Court of Appeals held in *Taylor* v. *Cohen:*

> In Section 601 Congress sought to ban wrongs that result from denial of equal protection of the laws. Nothing in the Civil Rights Act of 1964 or its legislative history shows that Congress intended to appropriate money for any program that violates the constitutional rights of a citizen of the United States. 405 F. 2d 277 (4th Cir. *en banc* 1968)

HEW moved promptly to comply with its responsibilities under the Act. A basic regulation was adopted in November 1964. Under procedures adopted then, as modified in November 1967, termination of Federal assistance takes place only after opportunity for a hearing and decision by an independent Federal hearing examiner that a school district is in violation of current equal protection clause standards. The examiner's decision is subject to a chain of appeals including the Civil Rights Reviewing Authority (an independent board of legal experts), the Secretary of HEW, the Court of Appeals for the District of Columbia or for the circuit in which the school district is located, and finally the Supreme Court.

As a first step in achieving compliance, school systems were required to submit assurances of intent to comply with the Act prior to the opening of school year 1965–66. In April 1965, the first "General Statement of Policies Under Title VI of the Civil Rights Act of 1964 Respecting Desegregation of Elementary and Secondary Schools" was published.

These first "guidelines" called for extension of "free choice" to all grades in legally segregated school systems by the beginning of school year 1967–68. To achieve this goal, school districts which had operated on a completely segregated basis during the 1964–65 school year were required to implement "freedom of choice" at the rate of four grades a year—beginning in the Fall of 1965 and ending in the Fall of 1967—while districts which had already begun to implement "grade-a-year" plans could continue at a slower pace. Requirements with respect to faculties were limited to desegregation of faculty meetings and in-service programs.

The role of the HEW "guidelines" is often misunderstood. Although they have binding legal authority only to the extent that they accurately reflect the existing state of the law, the courts have given HEW policies "great weight" in deference to HEW's educational expertise and in the interest of uniformity—particularly with respect to proper procedures for the implementation of "freedom of choice" and the rate of progress that might be expected.*

In March 1966, the Department issued a "Revised Statement of Policies for School Desegregation Plans Under Title VI of the Civil Rights Act of 1964". The "revised guidelines" set out detailed procedures for "free choice" plans designed to assure that all students and their families were made aware of the availability of choice and were not subject to coercion from school personnel. In addition, they established the general standard that, in school districts desegrating under "free choice" plans, from 12–16 percent (depending on the degree of desegregation attained the previous year) of Negro children should be attending predominantly white schools by Fall of 1966. School systems failing to meet the targets were subject to closer examination to determine whether they were implementing the requirements of *Brown* in good faith. Where "free choice" did not promise adequate progress, then other means of desegregation, such as geographic zoning, might be required.

The "revised guidelines" for the first time set forth requirements for faculty desegregation, stating that:

> Staff desegregation for the 1966–67 school year must include significant progress beyond what was accomplished for the 1965–66 school year . . .

Although throughout 1966 and 1967 the Federal courts and HEW clearly saw "freedom of choice" as the major means of achieving school desegregation, doubts grew regarding the prospects for achieving effective elimination of dual school systems through continued reliance on that method. The "revised guidelines" stated:

> A free choice plan tends to place the burden of desegregation on Negro or other minority-group students and their parents. Even when school authorities undertake good faith efforts to assure its fair operation, the very nature of a free choice plan and the effect of longstanding community attitudes often tend to preclude or inhibit the exercise of a truly free choice by or for minority-group students.
>
> *　　*　　*　　*　　*　　*　　*
>
> The single most substantial indication as to whether a free choice plan is actually working to eliminate the dual school structure is the extent to which Negro or other minority group students have in fact transferred from segregated schools.

Also, similar misgivings were voiced by the courts. See, for example, *U.S.* v. *Jefferson County*.

---

* See *U.S.* v. *Jefferson County* 372 F. 2d 836 (5th Cir. 1966), *aff'd banc* 380 F. 2d 385 (1967), *cert. den.* 389 U.S. 840 (1967).

> . . . where a free choice plan results in little or no actual desegregation, or where, having already produced some degree of desegregation, it does not result in substantial progress, there is reason to believe that the plan is not operating effectively and may not be an appropriate or acceptable method of meeting constitutional and statutory requirements.

Although enforcement efforts were far from perfect (as the Civil Rights Commission pointed out in its 1967 report), over the first 4 years of its operation the Title VI enforcement mechanism proved effective in obtaining broad implementation of "free choice" plans. The percentage of black children attending school with whites in Southern States rose well over fivefold from 2.25 percent in 1964–65, to 6 percent in 1965–66, to 12.5 percent in 1966–67, and 13.9 percent in 1967–68.*

### 3. 1968–72—A CRISIS BUILDS

The second of the Supreme Court's three unanimous, pivotal school desegregation decisions was rendered on May 27, 1968. *Green* v. *County School Board of New Kent County, Virginia*, 391 U.S. 430, clarified two fundamental principles.

*First*, the court held that adoption of a "free choice" plan would not, in itself, satisfy the legal obligation to desegregate. Instead, the test of any desegregation plan was to be the extent of the desegregation it achieved. School districts were required to take whatever steps necessary to end the "pattern of separate 'white' and 'Negro' schools . . . to which *Brown I* and *Brown II* were particularly directed."

*Second*, the court abandoned the "all deliberate speed" formula of *Brown II* to hold that:

> The burden on a school board today is to come forward with a plan which promises realistically to work and promises realistically to work *now*.

Again, as in the case of the "free choice" guidelines, HEW and the Federal courts followed parallel courses. While Justice Department attorneys argued in favor of the final result in *Green*, the Department of HEW issued a new set of desegregation guidelines—"Policies on Elementary and Secondary School Compliance with Title VI of the Civil Rights Act of 1964"—adopting an identical position. The new guidelines, published in March 1968, and commonly known as the "National School Policies," predate the Supreme Court decision by nearly 2 months.

*Green* and the new guidelines signaled the end of the era of "free choice." The first 14 years since *Brown* had brought desegregation to less than 20 percent of black children in dual school systems established by State law. Now, courts and HEW would require more effective means—zoning, "pairing," grade reorganization—to achieve desegregation where "free choice" had failed. There was a new urgency. The "National School Policies" set a general target for full desegregation.

> Generally, school systems should be able to complete the reorganization needed for compliance with the law by the opening of the 1968–69 or, at the latest, 1969–70 school year.

---

* NOTE: Figures for 1964–65, 1965–66 and 1966–67 are for black children in schools with 5 percent or more white students. The figure for 1967–68 is for black children in predominantly white schools; the differences, for these years, between the two measures should be marginal.

And the Federal courts, interpreting the Supreme Court's mandate that desegregation be completed "at the earliest practicable date," agreed.

*The "July 3 Statement"*—A shift of Federal policy, however, became apparent with a joint statement, issued by the Attorney General and Secretary of HEW on July 3, 1969, announcing that primary responsibility for ultimate enforcement of school desegregation would be shifted from the HEW compliance mechanism established under Title VI of the Civil Rights Act to court suit by the Department of Justice.

The statement announced intention to transfer the burden of enforcement from Federal hearing examiners to the already overburdened Federal courts. There the pressures of other judicial business and more stringent rules of evidence make detailed and sensitive inquiries into the nature of the best remedy particularly difficult and inconvenient—especially in the many cases involving smaller districts. Before the July 3 statement, the Justice Department had concerned itself primarily with precedent-setting cases, relying on the Title VI mechanism to perform the bulk of more routine compliance activity.*

Far more important for the future, the July 3 statement placed the full burden of political responsibility for school desegregation—which had been shared between the Executive and Judicial Branches—solely on the shoulders of the Federal courts. And the Federal Judiciary—which can act only on a case-by-case basis, which cannot hold press conferences or address public meetings to argue in favor of its decisions, or to clear up misconceptions regarding the effect of its rulings—is not well equipped for political leadership.

*The Mississippi Delays—Confrontation with the Courts*—On August 25, 1969, the Secretary of HEW wrote three Federal district judges to request a 1-year delay in implementation of desegregation plans which had been prepared by HEW for 33 Mississippi school districts.**

Within 60 days, the delay had been rejected by the Supreme Court. In a brief, unanimous opinion, the court directed immediate implementation of the HEW-prepared plans.***

---

*The major justification advanced in favor of the new policy—that fund termination hurts only the children, and primarily poor children receiving compensatory education services under Title I of ESEA—is belied by the demonstrated extraordinary effectiveness of Title VI as a tool for obtaining compliance. The overwhelming majority of school districts entered into negotiated desegregation plans without ever undergoing termination of Federal assistance. By July 1969, 89 percent of school districts under HEW jurisdiction were in compliance with current standards, while only 3 percent—generally districts receiving only token amounts of Federal assistance—had been declared ineligible for Federal aid.

** Although Office of Education experts had found September implementation feasible (in some companion districts plans suggested postponing aspects of desegregation for a year because of need to construct new facilities), the Secretary wrote that implementation of the HEW-prepared plans would "in my judgment produce chaos, confusion and a catastrophic educational setback . . ."

*** Continued operation of segregated schools under a standard of allowing "all deliberate speed" for desegregation is no longer constitutionally permissible. Under explicit holdings of this Court the obligation of every school district is to terminate dual school systems at once and to operate now and hereafter only unitary schools. *Alexander* v. *Holmes County Board of Education*, 396 U.S. 19 (1969).

As a result of the efforts to secure delay, plans which had been prepared for orderly implementation in September were hastily placed in operation at midterm.

Two months later, on December 13, the Justice Department was again before the Supreme Court arguing for delay of HEW-prepared desegregation plans for 18 Louisiana school districts. Again, the court required immediate implementation of the plans in *Carter* v. *West Feliciana Parish*, 396 U.S. 226 (1970).*

These events did have a harmful effect on desegregation in the Fall of 1969. Paul Rilling, then Southeastern Regional Director for the Office for Civil Rights, told the committee:

> The results of this retreat in school desegregation have been to delay the pace of change, to rekindle resistance among bitter segregationists, and to isolate those local men who tried to move ahead on the basis of prior Federal commitments.**

Of 145 school districts in the States of Alabama, Florida, Georgia, Mississippi, Tennessee and South Carolina which had submitted desegregation plans to HEW calling for substantial steps in the Fall of 1969, 47—33 percent—reneged on their commitments. Of some 300 such school districts for the 11 Southern States, 95 reneged.

*Reemergence of Executive Leadership*—Beginning in the Spring of 1970, and continuing through Federal enforcement efforts in the Fall, a second, and affirmative, change in tone took place. In his Education Statement of March 3, 1970, the President emphasized continued support for school integration:

> I am well aware that "quality education" is already being interpreted as "code words" for a delay of desegregation. We must never let that meaning take hold. Quality is what education is all about; desegregation is vital to that quality; as we improve the quality of education for all American children, we will help them improve the quality of their own lives in the next generation.

On March 24, the President made a major statement on elementary and secondary school desegregation. To repair the "prevailing confusion," the President restated the commitment of his administration to enforce the Equal Protection Clause of the 14th Amendment:

> . . . some have interpreted various administration statements and actions as a backing away from the principle of *Brown*—and have therefore feared that the painstaking work of a decade and a half might be undermined. We are not backing away. The constitutional mandate will be enforced.

---

*The Committee was told that during this period desegregation plans prepared by Office of Education specialists at court request were subjected to special review.

Leon E. Panetta, Director of HEW's Office for Civil Rights at the time, testified:

> I was a part of a so-called "ad hoc committee" the purpose of which was to clear plans prepared by HEW educators before they were submitted to the courts, cleared not to insure they were educationally sound, or that they achieved maximum desegregation, but that they were politically sound.

** Hearings of the U.S. Senate Select Committee on Equal Educational Opportunity, Part 3A, *Desegregation Under Law*, June 15, 1970.

And the message proposed the expenditure of $1.5 billion over 2 years to support both desegregation under law and voluntary efforts by local communities to integrate their schools. In a later message submitting that legislation to the Congress, the President said:

> This Act deals specifically with problems which arise from racial separation, whether deliberate or not, and whether past or present. It is clear that racial isolation ordinarily has an adverse effect on education . . .
>
> * * * * * * *
>
> . . . the specific needs the Act addresses are immediate and acute. It represents a shift of priorities. It places a greater share of our resources behind the goal of making the desegregation process work, and making it work *now*. It also represents a measured step toward the larger goal of extending the proven educational benefits of integrated education to all children, wherever they live.

The renewed commitment carried over to the enforcement process. The Justice Department filed statewide desegregation suits in Georgia and Texas, initiated individual suits against roughly 50 school districts, and requested updated orders in numerous cases that had already been filed. As a result of these efforts, and similar efforts of private plaintiffs represented by such groups of the NAACP Legal Defense Fund, the Lawyers Committee for Civil Rights Under Law, and the Lawyers Constitutional Defense Committee, the percentage of black children attending majority white schools rose from 18.4 percent in 1968 to 39.1 percent in September of 1970, while even greater gains in faculty desegregation were achieved. This was a remarkable achievement, and it brought most Southern rural and small-town school districts into compliance with the requirements of the law.

But achievements in the Fall of 1970 were soon overshadowed.

*The Emergency School Assistance Program*—A makeshift $75 million appropriation "The Emergency School Assistance Program" to assist school districts desegregating under court order or Title VI plan was adopted in August 1970 and reenacted annually. But the major legislation which the President proposed was not adopted in 1970 or in 1971—adoption was completed only in June of 1972, and funds were not made available even in time for the opening of the 1972–73 school year. The $75 million special appropriation was too little, and establishment of the program through the appropriations process precluded the development of a comprehensive, detailed and well-considered program.

In addition, the special $75 million program was poorly managed during its first year of operation. An audit by the General Accounting Office, at the request of the committee, revealed:

> . . . in many cases, school districts did not submit with their applications, nor did HEW regional officers obtain, sufficient information to enable a proper determination that the grants were made in accordance with program regulations or that the grants were in line with the purpose of the program.

Inadequate action was taken, either administratively under Title VI or through court suit under Title IV, to prevent discrimination against black students, teachers and principals within so-called "desegregated" school districts. A survey, conducted by six civil rights groups, of 295 school districts receiving ESAP funds found widespread instances of discriminatory policies or practices, including segregation in supposedly "integrated" classrooms and facilities, segregation and other discrimination in transportation, faculty segregation, demotion or dismissal of black teachers and principals, violations of student assignment plans approved by courts or HEW, and furnishing of property and services to segregated private schools established to circumvent public school desegregation.*

And although precise figures are not available for 1970–71, HEW reports demotion or dismissal of 4,207 black teachers and administrators during the 1971–72 school year in the States of North Carolina, South Carolina, Georgia, Alabama, Mississippi, and Louisiana alone.**

1970–71 was the first school year in which substantial numbers of school districts began operation on a fully desegregated basis; the price of inadequate Federal action to curb "second-generation" discrimination during this first crucial year was great.

As Winifred Green of the American Friends Service Committee testified:

> Black parents find that there are two sets of laws, or at least two standards for obeying the law. When whites protested desegregation by sitting in principals' offices and picketing, no arrests were made. When black students peacefully protested conditions in their schools they were suspended, intimidated, harassed, and jailed.***

And white children, as well as black children, were victims of this unchecked wave of discrimination. In many communities, the result may be yet another generation of racial bitterness. George Fischer, President of the National Education Association, told the committee:

> The black children, by seeing black teachers and administrators downgraded or fired, are impressed with the feeling that blackness is a mark of inferiority. Their reaction in many cases is one of self-hate, although in recent years this has been replaced by feelings of rebellion. The white children, on the other hand, are led to believe that their whiteness makes them superior persons.***

Failure to act promptly against so-called "second-generation" discrimination poisoned the school experiences of thousands of schoolchildren in the Fall of 1970, A clear policy, backed by even a few well-publicized enforcement actions, would have deterred countless law violations. But a Federal policy statement on "in-school" discrimination, promised to the committee in June of 1970, was never issued, and a statement on faculty discrimination was not issued until January of the following year.

---

*The existence of widespread "second generation" discrimination in school systems receiving ESAP aid was confirmed in a report submitted by the Department of HEW to the Senate Subcommittee on Education, February 17, 1971. Instances of discrimination in school systems which did not receive ESAP assistance may well have been even greater.

** Hearings of the U.S. Senate Select Committee on Equal Educational Opportunity, Part 3A, *Desegregation Under Law*, June 16, 1970.

*** *Ibid.*

We do find that administration of the Emergency School Assistance Program improved substantially in the following, 1971–72, school year. Greatly improved procedures were adopted to assure both compliance with civil rights requirements and constructive use of ESAP funds. However, inadequate action continued to be taken under Titles IV and VI of the Civil Rights Act to combat "second-generation" discrimination.

*Swann v. Charlotte-Mecklenburg—A Crisis of Confidence*—For the most part, gains in desegregation achieved in the Fall of 1970 touched small towns and rural areas.

But the following Spring the Supreme Court ended any doubt as to whether larger school districts also were required to eliminate discriminatory school assignments—holding that additional transportation is among the tools which must be used where needed. In *Swann* v. *Charlotte-Mecklenburg* 402 U.S. 1 (1971), the third and most recent of the great desegregation cases. Chief Justice Burger ruled for a unanimous court:

> . . . techniques requiring the use of reasonable transportation must be used where necessary to eliminate racially identifiable schools which remain as vestiges of de jure segregation."

The initial response from the Executive Branch was constructive. On the day following the decision, the White House announced:

> The Supreme Court has acted and the decision is now the law of the land and it is up to the people to obey it. It is up to local school districts and courts to carry out the court decision. The Departments of Justice and HEW will carry out their statutory responsibilities.

But on July 30, school districts were informed by HEW that funds under the Emergency School Assistance Program would not be granted to support the additional cost of student transportation required to achieve desegregation. In the words of the HEW memorandum, school districts were "expected to fund their transportation needs through State and local sources."

And on August 3—when the bill had passed the Senate but was still before the House of Representatives—the administration requested an amendment to the $1.5 billion Emergency School Aid Act to bar any use of funds under the Act to support transportation of students.*

Denial of ESAP funds for additional transportation required under court orders and Title VI plans worked serious harm in the Fall of 1971. In Tampa, Fla., a 21 percent increase in the proportion of students transported forced the district to cancel a planned kindergarten program and assume a $1 million debt. As Superintendent Raymond Shelton testified:

> When demands are placed upon school systems without accompanying means to satisfy those demands, something must give. In our case it has been our kindergarten program,

---

*The statement announcing the request also announced that the Departments of Justice and HEW would disavow a desegregation plan involving increased transportation submitted by HEW for the Austin, Tex. Independent School District after the *Swann* decision. The statement was followed by repudiation of HEW plans drawn for Nashville, Tenn. and Corpus Christi, Tex.

teacher salaries, capital construction and most other parts of our educational program.*

In Nashville, Tenn., no funds were available for more buses to support a 20-percent increase in the proportion of students transported. Schools were put on triple sessions so that existing buses could make additional runs; the result was severe hardship to many families, which has seriously undermined support for the school program. And numbers of other communities suffered similar hardships.

The expense of desegregation-related transportation often is not great in terms of a school district's total budget. Added operating expenses for Tampa, Fla., for example, amounting to $767,000 were less than 0.4 percent of the total school budget. But without Federal help these funds must come through an increase in locally raised revenues or a cutback in educational services. And either of these measures can destroy the local support so crucial to the success of a desegregation program. As Nashville Superintendent Elbert Brooks testified:

> . . . neither those who support integration, nor those who tolerate integration will accept for long their children's continued exposure to hardship and danger brought about by inadequate transportation services.**

Reaction was not confined to the Executive Branch. In November 1971, the House of Representatives adopted the Emergency School Aid Act—which had earlier passed the Senate in modified form—as part of a comprehensive education bill, the Education Amendments of 1971. But in a session which lasted until after midnight, the House added a number of amendments designed to hamper 14th Amendment enforcement.

These amendments included provisions prohibiting use of Emergency School Aid Act funds for transportation; prohibiting expenditure of any Federal education funds for desegregation-related transportation; prohibiting the Departments of HEW and Justice from in any way requiring, supporting or encouraging transportation to achieve desegregation (effectively preventing Civil Rights Act and 14th Amendment enforcement in many cases); and prohibiting Federal district courts from making any desegregation order involving either transportation or assignment beyond "free choice" effective before all appeals had been exhausted.

A second debate occurred in the Senate the following February. Before sending the comprehensive education bill to conference with the House, the Senate rejected the House amendments, along with even more stringent proposals to limit the jurisdiction of Federal courts. The Senate expressed its support for constitutional standards, as defined by the Supreme Court in *Swann* v. *Charlotte-Mecklenberg*, by adopting a bipartisan compromise, the so-called Scott-Mansfield amendment, which would:

- Permit use of Federal funds to support desegregation-related transportation upon request of local school districts, so long as the time or distance of travel is not so great as to risk the health

---

*Hearings of the U.S. Senate Select Committee on Equal Educational Opportunity, Part 18, *Pupil Transportation Costs,* Oct. 6, 1971.

** *Ibid.*

of the children or significantly impinge on the educational process (the standard established by the Supreme Court in the *Swann* decision).

- Permit the Departments of Justice and HEW to apply current legal standards under the Civil Rights Act, subject to the Supreme Court's limitation on excessive use of transportation stated above.
- Require exhaustion of appeals prior to implementation of court orders for desegregation involving more than one local school district, to assure full consideration of the complex new issues involved in multi-district school desegregation cases.

Two weeks after conclusion of the Senate debate, the administration made a major policy announcement regarding school desegregation. Strongly attacking court rulings, the announcement called for congressional enactment of new laws, the "National Student Transportation Moratorium Act" and the "Equal Educational Opportunities Act".*

The substance of these proposals threatens a constitutional crisis over the respective authority of the legislative and judicial branches of Government and, if held constitutional, to rollback much of the progress in school desegregation achieved over the years since *Brown* v. *Board of Education.*

The proposed Moratorium Act was designed to halt any new court-ordered transportation to achieve desegregation for a year or until passage of the proposed Equal Educational Opportunities Act if enacted sooner. During its life the Moratorium, if adopted and held constitutional, would have prohibited Federal courts from requiring any change at all in existing transportation patterns in order to correct discriminatory school assignments.

The Moratorium would not have affected court orders existing at the time of its adoption—and therefore would have had no affect on existing desegregation. But it would, if held constitutional, have had a truly irrational impact on future court orders. The Act would have barred transportation of any student not previously transported, as well as transportation of any student to a different school from the one to which he had been bused under the segregated system. As a consequence, courts could not have acted even where students had been unnecessarily transported past the schools nearest their homes in order to maintain segregation. And courts would have been powerless to enter desegregation plans which maintained existing levels of transportation, but which called for transportation of children other than those presently transported to maintain segregation. It is quite clear that in many communities no effective desegregation would have been possible while existing transportation patterns were written in stone under the Moratorium.

The second proposal, the Equal Educational Opportunities Act, combined revision of Federal compensatory education programs with an effort to restrict the power of Federal courts to make use of transportation to achieve school desgregation. The Act would have redirected the $1 billion budgeted for school integration assistance (in-

---

*A nationally televised Presidential address delivered on Mar. 16, 1972, rejected a constitutional amendment "as an answer to the immediate problem" because the amendment approach had "a fatal flaw—it takes too long."

cluding compensatory services for children in desegregated schools) under the Emergency School Aid Act for fiscal year 1973, by removing the ESAs focus on encouraging school integration. According to the message submitting the legislation to the Congress, the $1 billion would have been used for "project grants" to school districts already receiving the $1.5 billion budgeted for compensatory education under Title I of the Elementary and Secondary Education Act, to provide selected schools with a "critical mass" of $300 per educationally disadvantaged student. This aspect of the Equal Educational Opportunities Act will be discussed more fully in Chapter 25. We note at this point, however, that additional funds can and should be devoted to compensatory education without sacrificing support for integrated education to do so.

Far more significant than the bill's provisions regarding Federal compensatory education programs were its efforts to place severe and retroactive limitations on the power of Federal courts to require transportation. Briefly, the bill included provisions to:

- Bar any increase in transportation (in average time, distance, or number of children) to achieve desegregation at the elementary school level.
- Make transportation a "remedy of last resort" on the secondary level, after first considering such "alternatives" as neighborhood zoning, construction of new schools, and construction or establishment of magnet schools or educational parks (ironically and confusingly, several of these "alternatives" such as educational parks and magnet schools typically involve transportation of students)—and only in conjunction with a long-term plan for adoption of an "alternative" method.
- Stay all orders involving increased transportation until all appeals are denied.
- Require that all court orders for desegregation lapse after 10 years, and all orders involving transportation after 5 years.
- Permit reopening of all existing court orders to conform them to the terms of the EEO Act.

A version of the Equal Educational Opportunities Act, which was in at least one respect still more restrictive than the original proposal, passed the House of Representatives late in the last Congress.* Efforts to obtain Senate passage in the closing days of the session, and without committee consideration, were unsuccessful.

*Constitutionality of the Proposals*—It is clear that both the Moratorium Act and those provisions of the Equal Educational Opportunities Act attempting to limit the authority of Federal courts presented serious constitutional problems. Although the Equal Educational Opportunities Act would have severely limited judicial requirement of transportation, and prohibited requirement of plans involving additional transportation on the elementary level, the Supreme Court in

---

*The House-passed bill would limit desegregation-related transportation to the "next nearest" school, but would extend this limitation to desegregation of secondary as well as elementary grades. In other important respects the House-passed Equal Educational Opportunities Act closely resembled the original Administration proposal.

*Swann* v. *Charlotte-Mecklenburg* held, in a unanimous opinion by Chief Justice Burger, that reasonable busing may be required as one device for ending officially sponsored public school segregation. In the words of the court:

> We find no basis for holding that the local school authorities may not be required to employ bus transportation as one tool of school desegregation. Desegregation plans cannot be limited to the walk-in school.

The Chief Justice observed that:

> Bus transportation has been an integral part of the public education system for years, and was perhaps the single most important factor in the transition from the one-room schoolhouse to the consolidated school.

The *Swann* case involved additional transportation of over 6,000 elementary school students.

And the Moratorium appears equally to have flown in the face of established constitutional principles. The effect of the Moratorium in many cases would have been to render substantial desegregation extremely difficult, since it would have permitted no rearrangement at all of existing transportation patterns. In *Alexander* v. *Holmes County*, 396 U.S. 19 (1970), the Supreme Court held that, 18 years after *Brown*, the Constitution requires immediate desegregation.

> . . . continued operation of segregated schools under a standard of allowing "all deliberate speed" for desegregation is no longer constitutionally permissible. Under explicit holdings of this Court the obligation of every school district is to terminate dual school systems at once and to operate now and hereafter only unitary schools.

It is argued that although Congress cannot alter the substance of the 14th Amendment rights, it can properly establish guidelines with respect to remedy. This may well be so. But the administration proposals attempted to impose severe limitations on a remedy which the Supreme Court has found essential to the vindication of constitutional rights. In *North Carolina* v. *Swann*, a companion case to the *Charlotte-Mecklenberg* decision, the court struck down a North Carolina statute prohibiting use of transportation to achieve school desegregation stating that:

> Transportation has long been an integral part of public educational systems and it is unlikely that a truly effective remedy can be applied without continued reliance upon it.

We doubt that Congress has the power to remove essential remedies—since, with no remedy, the constitutional right is of little value.

The constitutional justification for the proposed legislation was weak. Whether the Moratorium and Equal Educational Opportunities Acts would have been ultimately upheld or rejected as unconstitutional they would, if enacted, have precipitated a confrontation between legislative and judicial branches of Government from which neither could have emerged unscathed.

And even though these proposals were not passed by the 92d Congress, they have done great damage. They have lent strong support to those who argue that Federal courts, and in particular the Supreme

Court, are acting irresponsibly. With their focus on the misleading issues of "busing" and their misguided implication that desegregation should be pursued more actively in later than in earlier grades, they have further distracted attention from the real and legitimate concerns of families and educators in 1,500 desegrating school districts.

We note that the Education Amendments of 1972, P.L. 92–318, contain essentially the Senate's provision requiring the Supreme Court's standard of reasonableness to be applied with respect both to funding for desegregation and related transportation and to continued Federal enforcement activity under the Civil Rights Act. In addition, the Education Amendments contain the Emergency School Aid Act, which will provide financial assistance to school districts desegregating voluntarily or under legal requirement. In our judgment, further congressional intervention in the law enforcement process is not warranted.

### 4. MISCONCEPTIONS

A dramatic erosion in public support for effective school desegregation has taken place in recent years.

As recently as March 1971, a Harris poll of 1,600 families found 47 percent of parents willing to have their children bused for desegregation under court order, and only 41 percent opposed. But by March 1972, only 25 percent were willing; and 69 percent were opposed. Ironically, however, 83 percent of parents whose children were bused for all reasons were "satisfied with busing," and 89 percent found busing "convenient." We are convinced that this change in public attitude is due in large part to a lack of constructive national leadership in both the legislative and executive branches of Government.

Transportation of students is essential to American public education, segregation or integration aside. Twenty million elementary and secondary schoolchildren, 42 percent of our public school enrollment, rode 256,000 school buses 2.2 billion miles last year. Since 1919, every State has supported pupil transportation with public funds. The cost of student transportation last year reached nearly $1.5 billion, roughly 5 percent of public education expenditures.

There can be no justification for flatly prohibiting the use of so common a tool to achieve elimination of racially discriminatory school assignments.

And in fact, the Supreme Court rulings do not require transportation—or any other method for achieving school desegregation—to achieve "racial balance." They require desegregation only upon proof that school districts, alone, or in combination with other government agencies, have purposefully caused segregation to exist.* And even then, no "balance" is required. In the words of Chief Justice Burger:

> The constitutional command to desegregate schools does not mean that every school in every community must always reflect the composition of the school system as a whole. *Swann* v. *Charlotte-Mecklenburg*, 402 U.S. 1 (1971).

What the court has required is "a plan that promises realistically to work . . . until it is clear that State-imposed segregation has been completely removed."

---

*See Section 5 of this chapter, pp. 213–15.

Where schools have been located on the basis of race, or where gerrymandering of school zones together with discrimination in the sale or rental of housing had lead to creation of racially segregated residential areas, reasonable transportation may be the only method available to remedy the effects of past discrimination.

The Federal courts are firmly committed to a rule of reasonableness in the use of transportation to achieve desegregation. In *Swann* v. *Charlotte-Mecklenburg*, Chief Justice Burger's unanimous opinion sets forth sensible guidelines to protect against abuse:

> An objection to transportation of students may have validity when the time or distance of travel is so great as to risk either the health of the children or significantly impinge on the educational process.

And the court recognized that the younger the children are, the more stringently the standards must be applied.

> It hardly needs stating that the limits on time of travel will vary with many factors, but probably with none more than the age of the students.

This same standard has been applied to administrative enforcement actions under Title VI of the Civil Rights Act by the so-called "Scott-Mansfield" amendment to P.L. 92–318, the Education Amendments of 1971, signed by the President, June 23, 1972.

The court and the Congress have adopted a sensible, rational and flexible approach. If individual lower court orders have unreasonably required excessive transportation of students, this error can be corrected through appeal to higher federal courts. But there is little evidence, as a general proposition, of the "excessive busing" which has been discussed in such emotional terms.*

This finding is supported by the so-called "Lambda Report," a study prepared for the Department of HEW by the Lambda Corp. The study of desegregation in 29 metropolitan areas concludes that desegregation placing all minority-group children in majority white schools can be accomplished by transporting only an additional 10 percent of the enrollment. The projections of the Lambda Report are borne out in practice. Increases of over 20 percent in the proportion of students transported are extremely rare; and the cost of transportation even after desegregation rarely exceeds 3 percent of school district operating budgets. (See figures 15–1 and 15–2.)

As the Report confirms, transportation of students is particularly important to desegregation of elementary schools, since high schools and junior high schools typically draw students from broader attendance areas.

In view of the facts, the approach taken by the proposed "Equal Educational Opportunities Act" is particularly unfortunate. The result of this legislation would be to restrict desegregation at all levels, but its effect would be particularly severe at the elementary school level where it would prohibit any increase in transportation. And yet, all the evidence which we have gathered in 2½ years points to the conclusion that desegregation is most likely to be academically beneficial and socially constructive if it begins in the early grades. The Equal Educational Opportunities Act would, if adopted and held constitu-

---

*See page 187, chapter 14.

tional by the courts, freeze the school desegregation process into the approach—moderate desegregation in junior high school and high school, but extensive segregation in grades one through six—least likely to produce educational benefits for the children involved, and least likely to promote constructive results as they grow older.

Transportation under court order has caused serious hardship in a number of communities, not because of the time or distance of travel, but because an insufficient supply of school buses has required schools to be placed on double or even overlapping triple sessions in order to permit existing buses to make several runs.

And even so, educational services in many of these communities have been reduced in order to meet unavoidable additional costs. Although increased transportation expenses are small in terms of total school operating budgets, typically no more than 1 or 2 percent, already overstrained education budgets cannot absorb these increased costs without sacrificing existing education programs.

Court-ordered desegregation is costing Pontiac, Mich. $700,000—the cost of new transportation each year. Pontiac has had to cut educational programs to meet these costs. Dr. Dana Whitmer, Superintendent of Pontiac Public Schools, said:

> The school district programs are impoverished this year as compared with last year . . . the quality of things available is less and I cannot argue that that doesn't affect the quality of education in the school district.*

G. Holmes Braddock, the chairman of the school board in Dade County, Florida testified before the House Education Committee last June:

> The financial impact of desegregation is placing severe demands and burdens on the affected school systems.

Dade County has a $250 million school budget. Additional transportation is costing $670,000 per year.

Pasadena, Calif., is using $300,000 in Federal Impact Aid, which would otherwise be used for instructional programs, to support court-ordered transportation.

Harrisburg, Pa., is desegregating under State administrative procedures. Additional transportation expenses are more than $500,000 a year. Harrisburg has had to cut additional programs to pay for busing. Superintendent David H. Porter testified:

> We need help. We need it badly. If we are going to see a rekindling of pride and enthusiasm for the American way of life, we have got to make education work . . . hopefully we are not too late.**

In Nashville, Tenn., because of an inadequate number of school buses, opening times for schools have been staggered so that some children start school as early as 7 a.m. and others arrive home after dark. The inconvenience this has caused seriously threatens public support for education in Nashville.

---

*Hearings of the U.S. Senate Select Committee on Equal Educational Opportunity, Part 19B, *Equal Educational Opportunity in Michigan*, Nov. 4, 1971.

***Ibid.*, Part 14, *State Role in School Desegregation, Pennsylvania*, August 4, 1971.

The hardships brought about by inadequate transportation services could have been avoided if the Department of Health, Education, and Welfare had not refused to permit use of funds under the $75 million Emergency School Assistance Program, earmarked to meet special needs of desegregating school districts, to support transportation of students. Fortunately, efforts to impose similar restrictions on the Emergency School Aid Act recently signed into law were defeated. The committee hopes that Federal funds will be available to support the added costs of desegregation-related transportation next Fall.

School desegregation presents critical problems among which are guaranteeing minority-group parents that their children will not be victims of descrimination within desegregated schools and guaranteeing all parents that their children's education will be improved by integration. Continued preoccupation with the false issue of whether a single child should be transported to achieve desegregation will not help address those real problems.

We would do well to learn from the children themselves. A survey conducted by the Resource Management Corporation for the Office of Education of students attending 252 desegregating school districts which received Emergency School Assistance Program funding during the 1970–71 school year found:

> About 70 percent of blacks and about 60 percent of whites agreed that both races were becoming more openminded as a result of interracial busing.

FIGURE 15–1.—*Increase in pupil transportation in school districts due to desegregation court orders**

| District | Total enrollment prior court order | Total bused in district prior court order | Percent of enrollment bused in district | Total enrollment after court order | Total bused after court order | Percent of enrollment bused after court order | Percent public enrollment transported Statewide |
|---|---|---|---|---|---|---|---|
| Arlington | [1] 24, 390 | 9, 532 | 39. 0 | [2] 23, 133 | 8, 588 | 37. 0 | 63. 0 |
| Asheville | [3] 8, 381 | None | None | [1] 8, 241 | 2, 170 | 26. 3 | 62. 2 |
| Charlotte | [3] 84, 518 | 29, 737 | 35. 1 | [1] 82, 507 | 39, 080 | 47. 3 | 62. 2 |
| Duval | [1] 122, 493 | 38, 750 | 31. 6 | [2] 118, 217 | 44, 706 | 37. 8 | NA |
| Greensboro | [1] 31, 901 | 10, 781 | 33. 8 | [2] 30, 105 | 16, 689 | 55. 4 | 65. 0 |
| Hillsborough | [1] 105, 347 | 32, 406 | 30. 8 | [2] 102, 728 | 52, 795 | 51. 4 | NA |
| Jackson | [1] 30, 937 | 2, 127 | 7. 0 | [2] 29, 031 | 7, 300 | 25. 0 | 58. 7 |
| Lynchburg | [1] 11, 590 | None | None | [2] 11, 700 | 4, 478 | 38. 0 | 63. 0 |
| Manatee | [3] 16, 923 | 6, 628 | 39. 2 | [1] 17, 386 | 8, 287 | 47. 7 | NA |
| Nashville | [1] 94, 170 | 34, 000 | 36. 0 | [2] 87, 000 | 49, 000 | 56. 0 | 49. 0 |
| Norfolk | [3] 59, 429 | 7, 500 | 12. 6 | [2] 50, 791 | 15, 000 | 29. 5 | 63. 0 |
| Orange | [1] 85, 270 | 32, 964 | 38. 7 | [2] 86, 705 | 35, 713 | 41. 2 | NA |
| Pinellas | [1] 85, 117 | 36, 588 | 43. 0 | [2] 86, 880 | 36, 888 | 42. 5 | NA |
| Raleigh | [1] 23, 469 | 1, 342 | 5. 7 | [2] 22, 236 | 10, 126 | 45. 5 | 65. 0 |
| Richmond | [1] 47, 988 | [4] 13, 916 | 29. 0 | [2] 44, 989 | 17, 563 | 39. 0 | 63. 0 |
| Roanoke | [1] 19, 284 | 2, 150 | 11. 1 | [2] 18, 294 | 4, 665 | 25. 5 | 63. 0 |
| Winston-Salem | [3] 50, 462 | 18, 444 | 36. 5 | [2] 50, 070 | 32, 220 | 64. 3 | 65. 0 |

[1] 1970–71 school year.
[2] 1971–72 school year.
[3] 1969–70 school year.
[4] Of the total of 13,916, 8,500 rode Virginia Transit Co. buses and 5,416 rode school district-owned buses.
*Prepared by NAACP Legal Defense and Information Fund, Inc.

FIGURE 15-2.—*Cost of student transportation in individual school districts where desegregation occurred**

| District | Average cost per pupil prior to desegregation | Total operating cost for transportation prior to desegregation | Percent transportation cost of total operating school budget prior to desegregation | Average cost per pupil after desegregation | Total operating costs for transportation after desegregation | Percent transportation cost of total operating school budget after desegregation |
|---|---|---|---|---|---|---|
| Operating expenses: [1] | | | | | | |
| Arlington | $61. 15 | $709, 300 | 2. 8 | NA | NA | NA |
| Greensboro | NA | NA | NA | [2] NA | [2] NA | NA |
| Jackson | 79. 50 | 169, 103 | . 6 | $56. 17 | $410, 110 | 1. 8 |
| Lynchburg | None | None | None | 32. 90 | 147, 350 | 1. 3 |
| Nashville | 39. 71 | 1, 574, 790 | 2. 3 | 49. 00 | 2, 704, 228 | 3. 8 |
| Norfolk | None | None | None | None | None | None |
| Orange | 30. 02 | 989, 614 | 1. 8 | 30. 58 | 1, 092, 175 | 1. 9 |
| Raleigh | 75. 01 | [3] 100, 669 | . 7 | 24. 69 | 250, 061 | 1. 7 |
| Richmond | 32. 31 | 175, 000 | . 4 | 28. 46 | 500, 000 | 1. 1 |
| Roanoke | 55. 58 | 137, 393 | . 8 | [4] 30. 65 | 207, 699 | 1. 1 |
| Winston-Salem | 20. 26 | 373, 838 | 1. 8 | 30. 67 | [5] 988, 454 | 4. 0 |
| Total cost of transportation: | | | | | | |
| Asheville [6] | None | None | None | 56. 95 | 123, 598 | NA |
| Charlotte | 15. 97 | 475, 000 | . 8 | 27. 32 | 1, 067, 691 | 1. 6 |
| Duval [6] | 31. 90 | 1, 236, 157 | 1. 3 | 48. 91 | 2, 186, 590 | 2. 2 |
| Hillsborough | 37. 23 | 1, 206, 708 | 1. 35 | 37. 38 | 1, 973, 728 | 1. 7 |
| Manatee | 51. 70 | 342, 696 | 2. 3 | 46. 39 | 384, 468 | 2. 5 |
| Pinellas | 29. 40 | 1, 075, 850 | 1. 4 | 55. 38 | 2, 042, 970 | 2. 4 |

[1] Some figures may include spare parts or minor capital outlays.
[2] No city school district money was spent. State expenditures are not availablé.
[3] This includes lunchroom and administrative salaries; thus transportation above is considerably less.
[4] For elementary students on school-owned buses. $35 per student per year is spent for 900 elementary students on public buses contracted for by the district. This cost is based upon the number of routes. $63 per student per year is spent for 1,000 secondary students who cannot afford the student fare.The cost is based upon 35 cents per day per student times 180 school days.
[5] About $269,300 is paid from local funds for supplements for bus drivers' salaries and for transporting elementary students who are not eligible for State reimbursement.
[6] Asheville and Duval Counties own no buses but contract with a private carrier for all transportation.
[7] Includes leasing of 18 private buses.
* Prepared by NAACP Legal Defense and Information Fund, Inc.

### 5. A UNIFORM NATIONAL POLICY?

In establishing this committee, the Senate charged it with responsibility to

> Study . . . policies of the United States with regard to segregation on the grounds of race, color, or national origin, whatever the form of such segregation and whatever the origin or cause of such segregation, and to examine the extent to which policies are applied uniformly in all regions of the United States.

Discrimination in public education is not confined to any area of this Nation. In the 17 Southern and Border States purposeful segregation was created by State law—and continued by a decade and a half of desegregation plans which accomplished desegregation for only 14 percent of black children before the Supreme Court acted in 1968 to provide a new and tougher set of rules. As Chief Justice Burger's opinion in the *Charlotte-Mecklenburg* case remarks:

> The failure of local authorities to meet their constitutional obligation aggravated the massive problem of converting from the State-enforced discrimination of racially separate school systems. This process has been rendered more difficult by changes since 1954, in the structure and patterns of communities, the growth of student population, movement of families, and other changes, some of which had marked impact on school planning, sometimes neutralizing or negating remedial action before it was fully implemented.

In many Northern communities, segregated schools have been established by more subtle means.

South Holland, Ill. provides an example. There, a U.S. District Court found:

- Schools were located in the center rather than at the boundaries of segregated residential areas in order to achieve school segregation.
- School assignment policies were adopted under which black children living nearer to white schools attended black schools, and white children living nearer to black schools attended white schools.
- School buses were used to transport students out of their "neighborhoods" in order to achieve segregation.
- Teachers were assigned on a racial basis.

In Pasadena, Calif., a Federal District Court found:

- School zone boundaries were "gerrymandered" to concentrate black students in particular schools and whites in others—and transportation was provided to permit white students to avoid integration.
- The size of schools was regulated to assure that integration would not take place—and portable classrooms were located at black elementary schools to prevent assignment of students to adjoining white schools.

- Transfers out of "neighborhood schools" were permitted where the purpose was clearly to foster segregation.
- The great majority of black teachers and administrators were assigned to black schools—and even substitute teachers were assigned on a racial basis.
- Less well-educated, less experienced and lower-paid teachers were concentrated in black schools.
- Qualified black teachers were denied advancement to administrative positions on the basis of race.

And residential segregation in Pasadena was no accident. The Court found that from 1948 to 1968 virtually every Pasadena realtor refused to sell homes in white residential areas to Negroes. In fact, Pasadena realtors interpreted their code of ethics to render such sales unethical.

The findings of the Federal courts regarding segregation in Pasadena and South Holland are by no means unique. Findings of discrimination provide the basis for a growing number of Federal desegregation orders—Detroit, Pontiac, Kalamazoo and Ferndale, Mich.; San Francisco, Oxnard and Pasadena, Calif.; South Holland, Ill.; Indianapolis, Ind.; Clark County, Nev.; Denver, Colo.; Minneapolis, Minn., and numerous other communities. Court records reveal gerrymandering of school zones, assignment of faculty on a racial basis, transportation of students to maintain segregation, location of new school sites, and discriminatory allocation of resources, often combined with officially sanctioned residential segregation, producing school segregation that is far from "adventitious" in many Northern and Western communities. The courts have held officially sanctioned segregation in public education illegal wherever found.

In the first years after the Civil Rights Act of 1964 which authorized Federal enforcement of nondiscrimination in public education, Federal enforcement activities understandably centered on those areas where rigid segregation required under State law had continued virtually unaffected by the Supreme Court's 1954 ruling in *Brown*. The lack of enforcement activity outside these States in later years is less easy to understand, particularly in view of two congressional expressions of concern—first in the HEW Civil Rights appropriation for fiscal year 1969, and second in the "Stennis Amendment" to the Elementary and Secondary Education Amendments adopted in the Spring of 1970—that the law be enforced uniformly throughout the Nation.

Where intent to discriminate must be proven through a detailed factual presentation, as in most "Northern" school desegregation cases, enforcement is far more time-consuming than where intent to discriminate appears from the face of a State statute, as in most "Southern" cases. Preparation and trial of the Pasadena desegregation case alone, for example, occupied approximately 2 man-years of Federal attorneys' time.

But this cannot explain the fact that although the Justice Department has served as plaintiff in school desegregation cases effecting 526 school districts since 1964, only seven of those school districts are located outside the 17 Southern and Border States; or that of 3,625 districts subject to compliance investigation by HEW as of October 1971, only 69 compliance actions were taken against districts outside those States. Nor does it explain the fact that, although there are at least 22 successful or pending school desegregation law suits outside the 17 Southern and Border States, the Federal Government serves as plaintiff in only five.

Congressional concern has been reemphasized in the recently adopted Education Amendments of 1972, which repeat the provision of the "Stennis Amendment" calling for a uniform policy of law enforcement and provide that rules of evidence must be applied uniformly throughout the Nation. It is incumbent on the Departments of Justice and HEW to correct any regional bias in their law enforcement programs. If additional funds are needed, they should be immediately requested.

We are particularly pleased that the Emergency School Aid Act, recently enacted as part of the comprehensive Education Amendments, grants authority to Federal courts to award reasonable attorneys' fees and costs to successful plaintiffs in suits to enforce the nondiscrimination guarantees of Title VI and the 14th Amendment in the area of public education. As the record demonstrates, private litigation may be the best immediate route to a uniform national policy of law enforcement; clearly it is needed to reach the many cases of "second-generation" discrimination which now go untouched. Even under the best of circumstances, private litigation would be needed to supplement an active Federal enforcement program.

We believe, however, that consideration should be given to payment of the fees from a Federal fund—as with indigents' attorneys' fees under the Criminal Justice Act—rather than from school district budgets.*

---

*The provision in the form reported from Committee in the Senate provided for Federal payment, and was subsequently modified by amendment on the Senate floor.

## Chapter 16—Integration and Educational Opportunity

The committee is deeply disturbed by the lack of well-organized, strategic research to more closely determine the educational effects of school integration, and to explore the best educational techniques for use within integrated schools. Eighteen years after *Brown* v. *Board of Education* the research on this topic is haphazard, often reaching irreconcilably conflicting conclusions. We note that the lack of adequate educational research is not limited to the area of school integration; it is characteristic of all education policy, including the broad question of the education of disadvantaged children, or "compensatory education," in which the largest share of Federal education funds is invested.

The National Institute of Education, newly established under the Education Amendments of 1972, is charged with the responsibility for assuring pragmatic, technically sound and relevant research into these questions. The committee believes that the work of the National Institute may be a determining factor in the success or failure of American public education in the remainder of this century.

Our survey of the evidence that is available demonstrates a definite, positive relationship between racial-socioeconomic integration and academic achievement of educationally disadvantaged children. This relationship is strongest when integration begins in the first years of schooling and is strengthened by special efforts to improve school curricula and teaching methods.

We find that if racial-socioeconomic integration is combined with major efforts to strengthen curricula, improve teaching methods, better train teachers, substantially reduce class size and encourage the meaningful involvement of parents and community members, school integration can be the basis for impressive improvement in the educational achievement of minority-group and low-income students, and can immeasurably enrich the capacity of all students for life in a complex and multiracial society.

We are joined in our conclusions by the American Federation of Teachers, the Council of Chief State School Officers, the National Education Association, the President's Commission on School Finance, the White House Conference on Children, and by the National Advisory Committee on the Education of Disadvantaged Children, which found in its 1971 Report that "desegregation is the best form of compensatory education." Our conclusion is also bolstered by a recent memorandum submitted by HEW Secretary Elliot Richardson in support of the proposed "Equal Educational Opportunities Act." The memorandum states:

> We know that children learn less effectively when there is a great degree of economic or racial isolation.

## A. The Coleman Report and Related Studies

A summary of the Coleman Report's major findings is contained in Chapter 12. As discussed in that chapter, the Report found achievement highly related to family background. It also found that differences in traditional measures of school quality—per-pupil expenditures on staff, library volumes per student, science lab facilities, presence of guidance counselors, etc.—had little apparent effect on achievement.

But the report also found that socioeconomic status of fellow students did have a strong relationship to academic achievement of minority group children. In the words of the report:

> Attributes of other students account for far more variation in the achievement of minority-group students than any attribute of school facilities and slightly more than do attributes of staff.

As Dr. Coleman testified before the committee, educational disadvantage which springs from a home environment in which parents themselves lack educational advantages is reinforced by schools with segregated, low-income student bodies with such strength that known teaching strategies often appear powerless to combat it.

In Dr. Coleman's words:

> . . . if schools are racially homogeneous or economically homogeneous, the disadvantages a working-class or Negro child, or a Puerto Rican child, or a Mexican-American child experiences in his home environment are multiplied by the disadvantages he experiences in his school environment.

At the same time, when children from educationally disadvantaged homes attend schools with predominantly middle class, educationally advantaged student bodies, educational disadvantage resulting from home environment is reduced, although not eliminated.

As Dr. Coleman testified:

> . . . what seems to occur is this: That a child's family background being essentially in closest proximity to him, has a powerful effect, and that effect both occurs before age 5, and beyond.
>
> . . . the second most proximate environment of the child is the school environment of other children, and as this environment comes to cumulate over a period of time, it does begin to counteract or support—depending upon whether it is like his own family background, or different from his own family background—the effects of his own family background. As a consequence, the cognitive effects of school integration increase fairly linearly over the period of time he is in school.

We wish to stress that the disadvantage of which we are speaking relates only to the preparation of children to do well academically in school. As Dr. Coleman testified:

> Children from middle class ordinarily have greater educational resources in their homes than children from working classes; and white children ordinarily have greater educational resources in their homes than do Negro children, or Puerto Rican children, or Mexican-American children.

This does not mean that economically disadvantaged families fail to provide warm and supportive homes for their children. The following exchange between Senator McClellan and Dr. Uvaldo Palomares is highly relevant.

> Senator McClellan. Do you believe the fact that the child was working with his parents in gathering prunes that his parent's supervision became a handicap to that child when he got to school, caused that child to react differently than he normally would have if he had not been engaged in that relationship in association with his parents?
>
> Dr. Palomares. I, personally, don't think it is a bad thing or a handicap. I think it is a good thing. I think in terms of the expectancies of the teacher of behavior in the classroom it was a handicap.*

Important support for the Coleman findings concerning the importance of socioeconomic integration is found among the studies contained in *On Equality of Educational Opportunity*, a collection of reanalyses of the Coleman data by members of the Harvard University faculty. (See Chapter 12.)

Chapter 2 of the Harvard report contains a reanalysis of the Coleman conclusions by Prof. Christopher S. Jencks. Dr. Jencks' study, limited to data concerning sixth grade students in Northern metropolitan school districts, concludes:

> Poor black sixth graders in overwhelmingly middle-class schools were about 20 months ahead of poor black sixth graders in overwhelmingly lower-class schools. Poor students in schools of intermediate socioeconomic composition fell neatly in between. The difference for poor white sixth graders were similar.

When Jencks further controlled the data to account for the possibility that "poor" children achieving well actually came from better-educated families than the average "poor" child, poor white sixth graders in middle-class schools scored 10 months ahead of poor white sixth graders in lower-class schools; and poor black students in middle-class schools continued to score almost 20 months ahead of similar children in disadvantaged schools.

In his controversial book *Inequality*,** which is in large part based on analyses of the 1965 Coleman data, Christopher Jencks estimates that racial-socioeconmoic integration alone will reduce the gap in achievement test scores between black? and white children, and between rich and poor children by 10 to 20 percent.

We agree with Jencks' observation that the available data are murky. We agree with his finding that racial-socioeconomic integration is more likely to produce achievement gains than simply equalizing school resources. And, while reducing aggregate inequality by 20 percent would be a substantial achievement, we find real promise that where carefully designed educational programs provide for focused

---

*Hearings of the U.S. Senate Select Committee on Equal Educational Opportunity, Part 1A, *Equality of Educational Opportunity: An Introduction*, Apr. 20, 1970.

***Inequality: A Reassessment of the Effect of Family and Schooling in America* Christopher Jencks, et al., Basic Books, New York, 1972.

remedial services within a racially and economically integrated setting, substantially more dramatic gains can be achieved.

There are weaknesses in the Coleman data. For example, only 65 percent of school districts asked to participate responded; and technical questions have been raised regarding the report's analysis.*

More importantly, the study is simply a "snapshot" of conditions in American public schools during the 1965–66 school year. While it describes the condition of children in integrated and segregated schools during that year, it cannot follow their progress through school to show, for example, the effect of integration over time, as so-called "longitudinal" studies are designed to do. And the fact that the survey was conducted in 1965 is, itself, a limiting factor. Practically all desegregation in that year resulted either from the exercise of "free choice" by black families in 17 Southern and Border States, or by "neighborhood" assignment in the North—and many of these "neighborhoods" were in the process of changing in racial and socioeconomic compositions, creating a unique set of conditions within schools.

The Report simply did not measure conditions in school districts which had completed desegregation under legal requirement. Nor did the report measure conditions to be found where local school authorities have made a conscious effort to provide racial and socioeconomic integration in one or more schools. And perhaps most important, in few, if any, of the schools represented in the Coleman data were there any efforts to train teachers, revise curriculum, provide for increased individualized instruction or other efforts to assure the success of school integration.

Most academic studies of school desegregation, including those which are most negative, rely heavily on the Coleman data, and its weaknesses contribute to the confusion. But despite its imperfections, the Coleman Report is the most impressive research ever conducted in the field of education. In the words of Professors Mosteller and Moynihan:

> The findings constitute the most powerful empirical critique of the myths (the unquestioned basic assumptions, the socially received beliefs) of American education ever produced. It is the most important source of data on the sociology of American education yet to appear. It was the most complex analysis ever made of educational data in such quantity. And, again, it is more than that. Flowing from the very provisions of the Civil Rights Act of 1964, it is a document of profound significance for the future of racial and ethnic relations in America.

And the report does provide substantial evidence, which withstands reanalysis, that socioeconomic integration may well be the most hopeful strategy for improving the educational opportunities of educationally disadvantaged children. It is not that minority-group children can only learn alongside nonminority children; it is that disadvantaged children tend to benefit from a stable, advantaged classroom environment.

---

*Marshall Smith, in Chapter 6 of the Harvard study, goes so far as to argue that defects in the survey and analysis invalidate the report's conclusions.

## B. Evaluation of Existing Integration Programs

As mentioned earlier, well-controlled studies of the impact of school integration on children's academic achievement are disappointingly few and far between.

However, we do find a broad range of evidence, from the results of achievement testing programs to the testimony of countless teachers and school administrators, that school integration can be an academic as well as a social success, and that compensatory education programs are most likely to produce significant and lasting gains when special educational efforts are combined with socioeconomic integration.

### 1. PROJECT CONCERN—HARTFORD, CONN.

For example, Project Concern is a voluntary program which presently transports 1,500 innercity Hartford, Conn., schoolchildren to classes in 14 suburban communities. Children given an opportunity to participate in the program are randomly selected from schools with high proportions of educationally disadvantaged children and in which over 85 percent of the children are black and Puerto Rican.

Not more than three and no less than two Project Concern children are placed in any suburban classroom. Both the centercity and suburban school districts participate on a voluntary basis, with the centercity district paying for tuition, transportation and additional support from a team consisting of a professional teacher and a mother from the target area, who serves as a nonprofessional aide. One "team" is assigned to each 25 innercity children.

A preliminary study was conducted during the 1966–67 school year, with an experimental group of 255 students, of whom 213 received supportive services.

After 1 year, children in kindergarten through third grade showed significant gains in achievement and mental ability. Children in grades four through six did not. Children who had received supportive services achieved at higher levels than children who had not. (In subsequent years all students participating in the program received supportive assistance, as did their suburban classmates.)

A survey conducted in the program's third year (1968–69) discloses that children who had spent their careers in Project Concern (first, second and third graders), were substantially outperforming their innercity peers—by as much as a full year at the end of the third grade. The data is unfortunately inconclusive, since no less than seven separate achievement tests were used by the participating school districts, and roughly half of the Project Concern children did not receive tests at all; however, what data there is supports the testimony of Project Concern administrators, parents and students that the project is an educational success.

This evidence is supported by a careful longitudinal study of 25 Project Concern children attending schools in Cheshire, Conn. in the 1968–69 and 1969–70 school year.* The students attended grades 1–4 in 1968–69, their first year in the program. The study indicates that between November 1968, and November 1969, students experienced an

---

*Hearings of the U.S. Senate Select Committee on Equal Educational Opportunity, Part 1B, *Equality of Educational Opportunity: An Introduction*, p. 590.

average 4-month gain in reading and verbal skills. By November of 1969, these students' average and median achievement in reading, language and arithmetic * was at or above the national average.

Increased academic achievement is not the only benefit of Project Concern. Testimony from innercity and suburban students demonstrates growth in ability to deal comfortably with interracial social contact. And children have not been the only beneficiaries. A number of innercity parents of participating children have moved to the suburban communities where their children attend school. Participation by innercity parents in school activities is high; during the 2-year experimental period, 90 percent of the innercity parents attended all major activities. Mrs. Richard Stockwell, a suburban parent, testified:

> The thing I have learned from Project Concern is that when all people are together that have the same income, the same interests, they do the same things; they get a very false sense of values and things become important such as how close your grass is cut or how many clubs you belong to and the kinds of things that are really so unimportant. When you widen the people who lived with you and whom you know, then you begin to talk about things that are more important, and you are more a part of America.**

### 2. BERKELEY, CALIF.

The Berkeley, Calif. Unified School District serves approximately 15,000 students in kindergarten through 12th grade. The student body is 45 percent black, 3 percent Chicano, 9 percent Asian and other minorities, and 43 percent white.

Berkeley is the largest school district in the Nation to integrate all of its schools voluntarily, and the most widely acclaimed "success story"—not because every problem has been solved, but because the Berkeley community, diverse as it is, is working together toward better education for all its children. This unity of commitment was not obtained easily. There were 12 years of open and often angry public debate from the first public demand for school integration in 1957 to the implementation of the final plan in the Fall of 1969.

Berkeley has had a single desegregated high school since the 1890s. There was, however, extensive racial and economic segregation in junior high school and elementary schools. With considerable public controversy, the city's junior high schools were integrated in the Fall of 1964 through grade reorganization, converting three junior high schools serving grades 7–9 to a single 9th grade center and two 7th–8th grade centers.

Because of strong community opposition, plans for integration of elementary schools were not implemented in 1964. In fact, adoption of the junior high school desegregation plan alone led to an unsuccessful election to recall school board members.

In 1967, the board did vote to desegregate elementary schools by "pairing" with two-way busing. Elementary schools which formerly

---

*Gain in arithmetic scores was relatively slight and may lack statistical significance.

**Hearings of the U.S. Senate Select Committee on Equal Educational Opportunity, Part 1A, *Equality of Educational Opportunity: An Introduction*, May 5, 1970.

served grades K–6 now serve K–3 or 4–6; 3,500 children travel an average 15–20 minutes each way, at a per-pupil cost of 45 cents a day.

Before the plan was implemented, however, school officials engaged in an intensive effort to involve all elements of the Berkeley community in planning for desegregation. Two major committees composed of school officials, parents, and other community members were established—one to review logistics and the other to review instructional programs. In addition, small meetings were held in homes throughout Berkeley to inform parents and other interested persons about the plan and to gather their reactions. This process of both informing the community at large about the integration plan and involving interested persons in its design is viewed by parents and school officials as central to the development of public support for the plan implemented in the Fall of 1968.

As Dr. Neil Sullivan, then Superintendent of the Berkeley school system, testified:

> The Berkeley plan was acceptable to all, not only because it was fair to all but because all segments of the community participated in its development. Our goal was not simply integrated education, but quality integrated education. To this end, all parties, students, teachers, administrators, and citizen groups ranging from the conservative elements, the John Birch Society, to the Black Panthers participated.*

Some of the basic pressure for school integration in Berkeley, as in Hartford and in most other American communities, came from black parents seeking better education for their children; but a consensus in the black community was not instantly achieved. As Dr. W. Hazaiah Williams, a black member of the Board of Education testified:

> You need to also understand that within the black community there was a wide range, and continues to be a wide range, of definition about what we ought to be doing; and so it took a whole lot of internal debate on the issue to get the black community to [decide on integration]."
>
> . . . We had in the black community the experience of hammering through and reaching consensus; and this, itself, is a story that is not in the record, because the way the black community moves, this is not in the documents; but it obviously happened and we were involved in that happening, and with a lot of us it was a lot of trauma.**

Once consensus was reached, however, the black community in Berkeley was a powerful force for an integration plan under which the burdens would be borne equally by majority- and minority-group students, for teacher curricula sensitive to minority students' educational needs, and for increased employment of minority-group teachers, administrators, counselors, and other staff. And in Berkeley the school system is moving to meet these goals.

The process of desegregation has enabled the Berkeley school system to confront the need to improve its academic program for all students.

---

**Ibid.*, Part 2. *Equality of Educational Opportunity: An Introduction, Continued*, May 21, 1971.

***Ibid.*, Part 9A, *San Francisco and Berkeley, California*.

And it has helped the Berkeley community to confront its racial division.

Mrs. Louise Stoll, a white parent, testified:

> It is my belief that the people for whom I can speak, young white and black liberal families living in Berkeley, I think we have been given a rare privilege in Berkeley to find out what real problems are now in racial relations, because we have gotten over the mechanical aspect of moving children around the community. It is an exciting thing to be a part of working out these problems. They have to be worked out or there is no future for us, and we are all committed to that.*

Mrs. Amanda Williams, a black parent, had much the same message. She told the committee:

> I believe you and I share a fearful concern that the growing sentiment in America will be separate but equal in its new dress. I believe we also share that parents know that separate is unequal. No amount of educational resources by information, nor effort, can dispel this knowledge. This knowledge is a poison in our country which has and will continue to subvert educational efforts aimed at the changing educational opportunities without integration.**

Berkeley completed only its third year of integration in June of 1972. At this early time, desegregation does appear to have increased the academic achievement of disadvantaged minority-group children in the early grades; on completing second grade, the first "school generation" to attend only integrated schools (children who began integrated kindergarten in 1968) was as much as 3 months ahead of preintegration performance levels in reading.

School integration does show important promise of increasing the academic performance of minority-group children in Berkeley; and academic performance of white children has clearly not suffered. Even so, integration has not proved an instant solution to every problem.

As in Project Concern, the major academic impact of desegregation has been limited to children first integrated in earlier grades. And social divisions based on race have continued to affect Berkeley High School; *** although it is hoped that this will change as children integrated at an early age move into the high school.

But integration has helped the Berkeley community toward a deep commitment to improved educational opportunities for all its children

Mrs. Velma Bradley, president of the Berkeley PTA, summed up the Berkeley experience:

---

**Ibid.*

***Ibid.*

***With financial assistance from HEW under Title II of ESEA, Berkeley has implemented two small scale, racially exclusive "Experimental Schools"—"Black House" and "Casa La Raza"—providing full- and part-time instruction to high school students through a curriculum heavily oriented toward "black" and "Chicano" studies. These schools, which serve 209 full-time and part-time students (who also attend Berkeley High), are designed to test the ability of schools oriented around "black studies" or "Chicano studies" to increase the academic motivation of students uninterested in standard offerings. These experiments should provide valuable insight. It would appear, however, that the objectives of the experimental schools could have been achieved without restricting participation to members of a single racial or ethnic group.

> I think in Berkeley we have an involvement across the board of many, many parents, black parents helping white parents and white parents helping black parents, and so on, and students trying to help each other, too.*

### 3. NEW HAVEN, CONN.

The Coleman Report's findings and the preliminary results of the Berkeley and Hartford results receive further confirmation from a 2-year longitudinal study of kindergarten and first grade students in New Haven, Conn. conducted by Dr. Willa A. Abelson of Yale University, under the direction of Dr. Edward Zigler (now director of the HEW Office of Child Development). Dr. Abelson's Report ** concludes:

> . . . the longitudinal data which we have tracing academic growth during the first 2 years of school supports the findings of Coleman and others indicating that children living in poverty areas of the city achieve more optimally in classes with mixed enrollments. These results suggest that the difference in attainments appears gradually, and is quite evident in the reading area by the end of first grade. On the other hand, both the achievement and other data on intellectual development which we have collected show no difference in the academic progress of middle class children who have gone to school for 2 years in classes where a majority of the pupils is lower class as compared to middle class children in segregated middle class schools.

None of these longitudinal studies is conclusive. Desegregation plans have not been in operation long enough for conclusive results. But the results do support the Coleman findings.

We are also aware of several studies showing little academic benefit from desegregation. Some of these studies appear to have concentrated on the impact of desegregation on academic achievement at the high school level, while immediate achievement gains appear most likely when integration begins in the elementary years. Other studies appear not to distinguish between purely racial desegregation and integration which is economic as well as racial. In most, no effort is made to determine whether schools provide friendly and hospitable environments based on mutual respect, or to measure the impact of remedial programs. And integration programs which fail to "narrow the gap" between students are not necessarily failures. As disadvantaged students tend to fall farther and farther behind as they grow older, simply holding the gap constant can be an impressive accomplishment.

The committee is not in a position to reconcile each conflicting research study. But we do find that the evidence taken as a whole strongly supports the value of integrated education, sensitively conducted, in improving academic achievement of disadvantaged children, and in increasing mutual understanding among students from all backgrounds.

---

*Hearings of the U.S. Senate Select Committee on Equal Educational Opportunity. Part 9A, *San Francisco and Berkeley, California*.

**_Ibid._, Part 1A, *Equality of Educational Opportunity: An Introduction*, p. 262.

Empirical studies of desegregation are regrettably few, and haphazard in nature. Well-controlled studies are needed to determine the precise impact of varying degrees of socioeconomic integration, the best kinds of teacher training and supportive services to provide, the impact of varying class size and of using innovative techniques such as individualized instruction or student-to-student-teaching. As we stated earlier, it is our urgent hope that the newly established National Institute of Education will undertake to fund this desperately needed research.

However, the empirical studies which do exist are supported by the experience of growing numbers of educators from throughout the Nation.

Hoke County is a small rural community of 18,000 in eastern North Carolina. Its schools serve 4,850 children: 50 percent black, 35 percent white, and 15 percent Lumbee Indian. Hoke County had a triple school system—separate schools and classes for each group—and a triple transportation system.

In 1968 and 1969, Hoke County eliminated its triple system and established a unitary system under which each school reflected the countywide population distribution. It didn't just mix the children together and forget them once they entered the schoolhouse door. It tested every child to determine his level of achievement and took account of the low-achieving students' special needs. It made sure that no teachers or principals were displaced or demoted—in fact, Indian and black personnel were promoted. County school officials talked with fearful parents and counseled apprehensive students; they integrated all extracurricular activities so that every school-sponsored organization had representatives of all races in both its membership and its leadership.

Donald Abernethy, Hoke County's school superintendent, described the results:

> When we first integrated you would see in the lunchroom for example, tables of black kids, tables of red kids, and tables of white kids. They were not mixed up.
>
> You would see them standing around in clusters on the campus. This was at first. Now you see very little of this. The children have learned to get along with each other. They respect one another. They vote for each other in elections . . .
>
> Students also had fears and concerns. An example of a fear is best expressed by the Indian student who, after attending the integrated high school several weeks, was talking with his former principal who asked how the student was liking the new school. "I like it," the Indian reported. "You know, Mr. Oxendine, some of those white boys are not as smart as I am." Of course, the remark revealed a feeling of inferiority that had been imposed upon the Indian by the segregated system. For the first time, he had realized that he could perform as well as some of his white counterparts.*

And there has been academic improvement as well. Before integration, white sixth graders were a year ahead of their Indian and black counterparts. By 12th grade the gap was 2 full years. At the end of the first year of integration, white students continued to progress

---

**Ibid.*, Part 3A, *Desegregation Under Law*, June 17, 1970.

as before. Black students' rate of achievement was more than 50 percent better as a result of integrated schooling.

Could this have happened without integration. The superintendent thought not:

> I don't think it would ever happen if we kept the schools segregated and kept pouring in money for compensatory education in segregated schools. But I believe in an integrated system; that we will eventually work it out.

The Harrisburg, Pa., school system, serving over 12,000 students, nearly 58 percent of whom are from minority groups, was completely desegregated in the fall of 1971 under the requirement of State law. Superintendent David H. Porter testified to the results:

> You had to witness firsthand the fact that 2 years ago students and teachers were merely accepting a certain methodical, dullness about education. Students went to school not really to learn and teachers not really to teach. It was merely a place you were supposed to be for 5 days a week . . .
>
> We probably would not have admitted to any failure because we probably would not have recognized it.
>
> It's strange the way a school system can die before your very eyes as you mistake the death rattle for the sound of children learning. The cycle had to be broken . . .
>
> The mandate from the State Human Relations Commission to eliminate de facto segregation, though castigated by many, may well have been precisely the right thing at the right time. Not only did it wake us up to our responsibilities in race relations but it made us aware of the educational and administrative flaws that were permeating our entire system.
>
> The change has been dramatic. Walk into an early childhood center or an elementary school and look at the faces, hear the sounds, watch the kids at work and play. You can't show it on paper yet, but down inside, you know it's working.*

Dr. E. Ray Berry, superintendent of the desegregated Riverside, Calif., system testified:

> I see desegregation as an important element. I think it is quite possible to adequately educate minority children in a segregated situation academically, there are fine ways to turn them on, take the lid off, create the attitude about education, but I really believe it is far easier in an integrated situation, and ultimately I think it is the only answer in terms of if we really believe in an integrated society. I don't see any other way to do it.**

Dr. Berry told how the parents feel about integrated education. He presented the results of a questionnaire:

> Over 80 percent of the parents believed that the quality of education was as good or better in integrated schools than before integration.
>
> Approximately 90 percent of the parents said that their children liked school and seldom or never wished to go to another school.

---

**Ibid.*, Part 14, *State Role in School Desegregation: Pennsylvania,* Aug. 4, 1971.
***Ibid.*, Part 9A, *San Francisco and Berkeley, California,* Mar. 6, 1971.

> After 3 years of integration, over 90 percent of the parents were opposed to the idea of separate schools. The responses were not significantly different when the three ethnic groups were compared with each other.

Dr. Elbert Brooks, superintendent in Nashville, Tenn., where there is organized opposition to court-ordered desegregation testified:

> I cannot accept the argument which many give that we are ruining our school system by integration. I think that there are many factors in favor from an educational standpoint and from a social standpoint of integrating schools.*

Dr. Wayne Teague, superintendent of schools in Auburn, Ala., testified before the Education Subcommittee:

> For the black students who have been to white schools for more than a year, there is just no comparison in the rates of achievement they are making now and what they did in the past.

Superintendent Teague also testified to improving interracial acceptance at the high school level:

> We saw cheerleaders elected from both races. We saw athletic teams elected from both races, and it seems that students are accepting each other very well this year.

And a recent study conducted by the U.S. Commission on Civil Rights gives every cause for optimism. The Commission staff conducted intensive on-site visits to five recently desegregated school districts—Tampa, Fla.; Pasadena, Calif.; Pontiac, Mich.; Winston-Salem and Charlotte, N.C. As the former Commission Chairman, Dr. Theodore Hesburg, testified before the House Judiciary Committee:

> . . . we were not concentrating on noncontroversial and "success-story" instances of desegregation. Rather we selected what we considered to be a representative sampling of cities in which busing has been used to a significant degree.
>
> Our staff talked with parents, students, teachers, principals, superintendents, school board members, community leaders, and people from all walks of life, races and ethnic groups. What the staff members found stands in stark contrast to the newspaper headlines and the television newscasts. Despite some opposition to desegregation, they did not find parents blocking the school entrances, teachers resigning in droves, or pupils engaged in continuous disorders. On the contrary, the staff found schools being conducted in an atmosphere of relative peace, harmony and efficiency, in an atmosphere consistent with the Nation's ideals.
>
> The protests have subsided and the television cameras have moved on to other subjects. Students, parents, teachers and administrators are calmly proving to the world that desegregation can work. In some cases, organizations have been formed to counter the more combustible rumors. Some stu-

---

**Ibid.*, Part 18, *Pupil Transportation Costs*, Oct. 6, 1971.

> dents who previously resisted desegregation—and they probably were simply echoing the prejudices of their parents—now prefer to stay just where they are, even if it means a daily bus ride of 15 to 30 minutes.

Experience confirms predictions that school integration does improve interracial acceptance. Harvard psychologist Dr. Thomas Pettigrew testified:

> In 1966, the U.S. Commission on Civil Rights, as part of its broader study of racial isolation of the public schools (1967), a study in which I participated, interviewed representative samples of white and black adults in northern and western cities.
>
> Black adults who themselves attended integrated schools as children have more positive racial attitudes and more often send their children to integrated schools than comparable black adults who attended only segregated schools as children.
>
> They are typically making more money and are more frequently in white collar occupations than previously segregated blacks of comparable origins.
>
> Similarly white adults who experienced as children integrated schooling differ from comparable whites in their greater willingness to reside in an interracial neighborhood, to have their children attend interracial schools and to have black friends.
>
> For both black and white adults, then, integrated education did in fact prepare its products for interracial living as adults.*

A recent survey conducted by the Resource Management Corporation for the Office of Education confirms these expectations. The study, of 879 schools in desegregating districts which received assistance under the Emergency School Assistance Program for the 1970–71 school year, found:

- 41 percent of students attending desegregated schools for the first time reported changes for the better on "going to school with students of another race", while only 5 percent reported changes for the worse.
- 80 percent of students interviewed agreed that "students are cooperating more and more as the year goes on".
- While 33 percent of black students and 23 percent of white students said they would rather go to another school if they could, only 6 percent reported they did "not like it here" and 80 percent reported learning more in school than the previous year.
- A substantial majority of teachers and principals reported improvements in interracial relationships among students, and only 2 percent reported worsening relationships.

---

**Ibid.*, Part 2, ***Equality of Educational Opportunity, An Introduction, Continued***, May 13, 1971.

The report concludes:

> There is strong evidence that the racial climate improved during the 1970–71 school year in many respects and rarely worsened.*

#### 4. CONCLUSION

Clearly, there are many educationally disadvantaged children in our great urban ghettos who cannot be given the opportunity to attend economically and racially integrated schools, despite our best efforts. Franklin White, general counsel to the New York City Council on Human Rights, told the committee:

> Our first concern must be that black children be provided a better educational opportunity. And for many, integration is simply possible.**

We must increase our efforts to provide effective compensatory education services for all educationally disadvantaged students. However, the evidence appears to be that a dollar spent on compensatory education is far more likely to produce results in a quality integrated setting. A case in point is provided by the California study, conducted by Dr. Herbert Kiesling for the Rand Corp. and cited as evidence for the success of compensatory efforts in the President's message of March 17, 1972 submitting the Moratorium and Equal Educational Opportunities Acts to Congress. While the study did show dramatic improvement from specialized reading programs in projects costing in excess of $250 per pupil, the successful schools did not have majority-disadvantaged student bodies.

Every Government commission or agency to study the question has reached the same conclusion—integrated education, sensitively conducted, can improve educational opportunities of disadvantaged children from all backgrounds. This conclusion is supported by major education organizations and by teachers and administrators throughout the Nation.

---

*We note that Harvard Prof. David J. Armor reports that voluntary integration of junior and senior high school students in the METCO program—a program of urban-suburban integration in the Boston, Mass. area—led to increased racial identity of black students, measured by responses to questions such as "If you could be in any school you wanted, how many students would be white", "most black people should live and work in black areas, and most whites should live and work in white areas", and "black and white persons should not intermarry."

Armor's students remained integrationists in sentiment and experienced relatively small changes in opinion. On a scale from 0 (antiseparatist) to 4 (separatist) bused students moved from a rating of 1.4 to a rating of 1.8 from 1968 to 1970, while control students moved from 1.4 to 1.5. Although the percentage reporting spending "most free time with other black students" rose from 40 percent to 59 percent over the same period, 63 percent continued to report "white students are friendly."

It is impossible to determine the extent to which Armor's findings are unique to the Boston program or to students just integrated at the junior or senior high school level.

And it is difficult to draw conclusions from Armor's findings beyond the self-evident conclusion that urban high school students are experiencing an increase in racial identity. The extent to which answers to Armor's questionnaire reflect deep-seated changes in opinion is impossible to determine. One measure, however, is provided by the fact that few students have left the program, which is based on voluntary choice.

**Hearings of the U.S. Senate Select Committee on Equal Educational Opportunity, Part 5, *De Facto Segregation and Housing Discrimination*, Aug. 27, 1970.

But the value of integrated education goes far beyond its potential impact on academic achievement alone. In a society increasingly divided along racial and social class lines, the social skills that can be learned in a sensitively conducted integrated school may be the most crucial lesson which can be imparted by public education.

# Chapter 17—Achieving Integrated Schools

## A. The Model—Stable, Quality Integrated Schools

Nearly 3 years of study have led the Select Committee to the conclusion that school integration along racial and socioeconomic lines, sensitively conducted, provides the best hope for improving the educational opportunities of educationally disadvantaged children.

We agree with the testimony of Dr. James S. Coleman, perhaps the most distinguished researcher in the field, that disadvantaged students attending segregated schools are:

> . . . deprived of the most effective educational resources contained in the schools: those brought by other children as the result of their home environments.*

We have no doubt that integrated schools can provide better educational opportunities for all children. But desegregating a school—simply "mixing bodies"—does not insure the benefits of integrated education. "Desegregated" schools in which minority group students are treated as second-class citizens, or in which a few students from relatively advantaged backgrounds are overwhelmed by a majority of students from the poorest and most deprived backgrounds, can become a nightmare.

Dr. Thomas Pettigrew, a social psychologist specializing in the subject of school desegregation, succinctly stated the distinction between a "desegregated" and an "integrated" school when he testified:

> An *integrated* school refers to an interracial facility which boasts a climate of interracial acceptance.

Our nearly 3 years of study have convinced us that there are six basic elements in successful school integration, whether integration takes place under court order or voluntarily, whether districtwide or in a single school.

### 1. COMMUNITY PARTICIPATION

The first essential element is community participation. School officials must make every effort to involve a broad cross-section of the community in planning for integration—not just those who agree that integration is desirable, but those who are "neutral" and those who disagree as well. Representative committees, including teacher and student representatives, as well as representatives of parents and the community at large, should be established to participate fully with school officials in development of the physical plan for desegregation and in planning changes in the instructional program—in curriculum, teacher training, instructional methods—to accompany desegregation.

---

*Hearings of the U.S. Senate Select Committee on Equal Educational Opportunity, Part 1A—*Equality of Educational Opportunity, An Introduction*, Apr. 21, 1970.

It is suggested that half the membership of these committees should be composed of members of minority groups, even where minority group persons do not compose half the membership of the community at large, to ensure a frank and equal consideration of the needs of all the children involved. The planning process should include a series of open hearings, conducted on an impartial basis to provide every parent, teacher and interested community member with a full opportunity to understand the nature of the plan and the additional changes that accompany it, and to offer comments at a time when those comments can be seriously considered in drawing up the final plan.

Involving the total community in planning for desegregation is not an easy task for school officials, and it may appear to be an inefficient approach to decisionmaking. But the effort is worthwhile. By assuring that all segments of the community are fully involved in the development of the plan, resistance can be minimized and public support, which is essential to the success of any desegregation program, can be significantly increased. And the plan itself may be made more responsive to the community's needs.

The importance of full community participation is borne out by the success of desegregation programs—such as those conducted under court order in Tampa, Fla. and voluntarily in Berkeley, Calif.—where the greatest efforts have been made to involve the public. Tampa School Superintendent Raymond Shelton cited a major reason for the "unusual" public support received by the Tampa desegregation plan:

> The method in which the desegregation plan was developed through the involvement of the community with committees composed of large numbers of people from all walks of life and all areas of the community, including the student bodies of the individual high schools.*

Mrs. Amanda Williams, a Berkeley mother, told the committee:

> In Berkeley we had house meetings with parents coming together, and counselors were hired in the school district at the elementary and intermediate schools, which proved helpful in all instant feedback to parents' problems and concerns. The superintendent and his team of school administrators went into homes to listen and offer solutions to problems. I feel leadership both of the school district and staff is the primary cause for success. You have to have an administration that will listen to all concerns and problems and deal with them so that confidence will be built where parents feel they are wanted and needed.
>
> I believe that has been one of the things that has made Berkeley's integration in school work.
>
> * * * * * * *
>
> There is something to be learned in Berkeley. The Berkeley experience is a multiple achievement, in which the parents whose children are bused have played a key role. We seek to express and expose the fantasies and to share the realities in our experience of integrating the school district. We want to tell the parents and each individual school its constituency met

---

**Ibid.*, Part 18—*Pupil Transportation Costs*, Oct. 6, 1971.

and dealt with the very real problems that an integration program presents. Most important we want to tell you that Berkeley is getting on with the educational issues that every urban school faces which Berkeley now confronts to make our schools responsive to community needs.*

The importance of public participation is recognized by the Fourth and Fifth Circuit Court of Appeals, which require the establishment of biracial committees as a standard practice in school desegregation cases, by the Department of Health, Education, and Welfare, which has administratively required formation of biracial committees by recipients of assistance under the $75 million Emergency School Assistance Program, and by the Congress, which has required recipients of funds under the $2 billion Emergency School Aid Act to adopt committee and open hearing procedures along the lines discussed here.

### 2. SOCIOECONOMIC DIVERSITY

As discussed at length in Chapter 16, it seems clear from the available research that increased academic performance for disadvantaged children cannot be expected to flow from racial or ethnic desegregation alone. The key element in increasing academic performance of low income children, whether or not they are from minority groups, appears to be socioeconomic integration.

HEW Secretary Richardson testified:

> Children learn more from each other than from any other resource of the education environment.

And parents of more advantaged children are justifiably concerned over possible assignment of their children to schools with majority-disadvantaged student bodies.

We believe that, wherever possible, students should be assigned for purposes of desegregation to schools containing a majority of educationally advantaged children in order to achieve the most hopeful kind of integration. It is one of the great tragedies of the last 8 years that the importance of assuring that school desegregation takes place along economic, as well as racial and ethnic lines, has received little attention from local school officials implementing desegregation plans and the Office of Education in rendering technical assistance. We are not suggesting "one-way" desegregation. We are suggesting that newly-desegregated schools should not ordinarily contain a majority of disadvantaged students. Where both racial and socioeconomic integration are achieved, integrated schools have the best chance to succeed, educationally and socially, for all their students.

### 3. IMPORTANCE OF EARLY INTEGRATION

We agree with the testimony of Dr. Neil Sullivan, Commissioner of Education for the State of Massachusetts:

> The payoff in school integration is in early childhood and primary schools . . . Where we need to start school inntegration is where it is easiest to accomplish educationally, where the payoff is, in the primary schools, in early childhood.*

---

**Ibid.*, Part 9A—*San Francisco and Berkeley, Calif.*

***Ibid.*, Part 2—*Equality of Educational Opportunity, An Introduction*, May 21, 1970.

As discussed at length in Chapter 16, immediate benefits in terms of academic achievement are far more likely when integration takes place during the early years; and the earlier integration takes place, the greater the gain that can be expected. As Dr. Sullivan and others also testified, the potential for racial strain in high school is greatest when children have been segregated in earlier years.

We note that the "Equal Educational Opportunities Act" proposed by the President would effectively eliminate elementary schools from many desegregation plans by prohibiting the requirement of transportation below the elementary school level. This provision appears to run contrary to much that is known about constructive approaches to school desegregation.

### 4. INTEGRATED CLASSROOMS

The benefits of integrated education will be lost if classroom segregation takes place within supposedly integrated schools. So-called "tracking", or grouping children on the basis of achievement test scores, must be held to a minimum; and individualized instruction should be used wherever possible to permit the education of children from various achievement levels within a single classroom.

No absolute rule is possible. Clearly students who have not studied algebra should not be enrolled in calculus courses. Some courses, even in elementary grades, may require part-time grouping for effective instruction. But school authorities should bear in mind that where classification of children on the basis of achievement test scores results in racial segregation, not only are the benefits of integrated education lost, but the potential for racial polarization is greatly increased.

### 5. THE LANGUAGE MINORITIES

Students of Mexican American, Indian, Puerto Rican, Portuguese and Oriental backgrounds and other children from families with strong commitment to ethnic heritage and language, require unique attention during the desegregation process. The general educational needs of these children are discussed in Part V.

But integrated education can be of special importance to language minority children. As HEW Secretary Elliot Richardson told the committee:

> . . . the maintenance of ethnic isolation creates for the Spanish-speaking or Indian language-speaking child the additional disadvantage of depriving him of the most important resource of English language skill development—regular interaction and communication with English-speaking children.*

While school integration is as socially and educationally advantageous for language minority children as it is for other children, great care must be taken to assure that integration does not deprive these children of access to bilingual and bicultural programs designed to make them fluent in both English and the language spoken at home, and fully aware of their own cultural heritage.

Wherever possible, all students in areas of the Nation containing

---

**Ibid.*, Part 3C—*Desegregation Under Law*, Aug. 6, 1970.

large proportions of language minority persons should be involved in bilingual and bicultural programs, so that students using each other as resources can become fluent in both English and another language.

In desegregating school districts where bilingual, bicultural opportunities cannot be made universally available, care should be taken to cluster language minority students in particular schools so that special services can be made available. In a school district with 5 percent Chicano enrollment, for example, Chicano students might be concentrated so that they comprise 20 percent of the student body in the schools to which they are assigned, in order to make provision of bilingual services practical.

In addition, school districts should consider providing educational and cultural experiences to members of ethnic minorities outside the regular school day, by sponsoring neighborhood-based cultural activities or by permitting students to take advantage of existing opportunities on a release-time basis.

### 6. MUTUAL UNDERSTANDING AND RESPECT

The most important aspect of a successfully integrated school is a warm and supportive environment for children from all racial and economic backgrounds based upon mutual respect and acceptance among students and faculty.

These human qualities cannot be produced by a formula. But their development can be strongly assisted. In-service faculty training designed to encourage sensitivity to the needs of children from varying backgrounds should be provided on a continuing basis. Where possible, student-teacher ratios should be reduced, by employing additional professional staff, and by use of paraprofessional and volunteer aides. And curriculum and course content should be reviewed and revised to assure accurate treatment of racial and national origin minorities, and that materials and course content are relevant and not offensive to all children who study them. (See Chapter 9.)

Ultimately, the responsibility for successful integration falls upon each school and its teaching staff. As Dr. Uvaldo Palomares testified:

> . . . you have to start processes where that teacher and those youngsters begin to sit and look at each other, talk to each other, and start a way of communication.

### 7. ADEQUATE HUMAN AND FINANCIAL RESOURCES

The components of stable, quality integrated education require the availability of adequate financial resources to provide additional teachers and paraprofessional staff for more individualized instruction, for curriculum revision, for remedial services, for teacher training and efforts to strengthen school-community relations. The Congress has authorized Federal assistance to help provide these resources under the Emergency School Aid Act, signed into law last June 23. The committee urges that the full $2 billion annual appropriation initially proposed by the President and authorized under the bill be made available for the school year beginning next fall.

## B. Techniques for Achieving School Desegregation

There are a limited number of techniques open to a school district for desegregating its schools, whether voluntarily or under legal mandate.

### 1. GEOGRAPHIC ZONING

It may be possible to achieve desegregation simply by redrawing school zone lines. Where zone lines have been distorted ("gerrymandered") to achieve segregation, restoring the lines to their normal condition may be sufficient. Or it may be necessary to "redesign" the zone lines in a manner designed to encourage, rather than prevent desegregation.

In addition, "noncontiguous" zoning may be used. In figure 1, an example of noncontiguous zoning, the area (b), normally within the zone of school A, has been assigned to school B, and area (a), normally within the zone of school B, has been assigned to school A.

Figure 1--Noncontiguous zoning

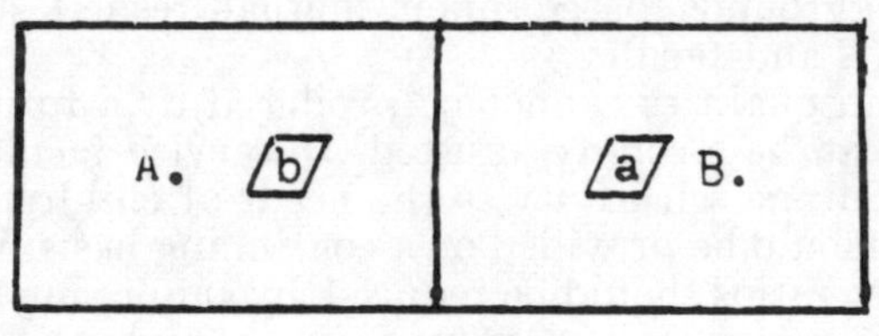


### 2. "PAIRING"

"Pairing" involves combining the student bodies with facilities of two or more schools serving the same grades. Both schools may continue to serve the same grades as before, simply exchanging a portion of their student bodies. Or "pairing" may be combined with "grade reorganization."

Figure 2--"Pairing" and grade reorganization

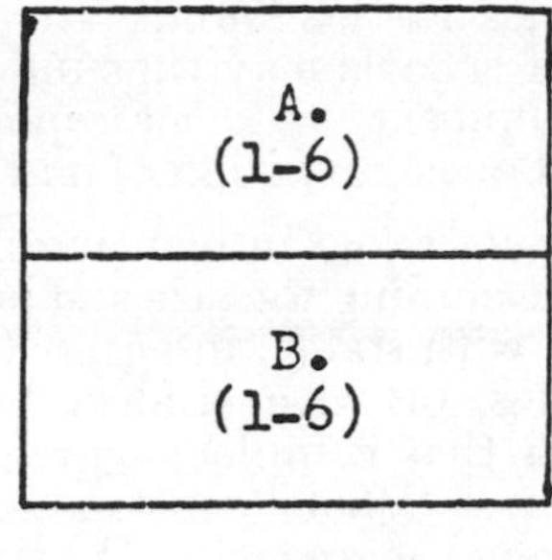


BEFORE

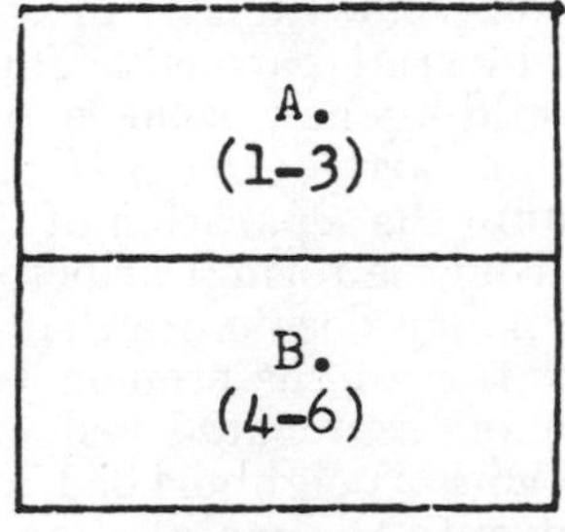


AFTER

**See Figure 2. Note that where "pairing" is combined with grade reorganization, students will often continue to attend the school nearest their homes serving the appropriate grade, and will continue to be assigned by geographic zone.**

3. SCHOOL CONSTRUCTION AND EDUCATION PARKS

Over the long term, school construction policies governing the size and location of new schools have a greater impact on racial segregation or integration of public schools than any other single school policy. As Chief Justice Burger commented in the *Charlottee-Mecklenburg* case:

> The construction of new schools and the closing of old ones is one of the most important functions of local school authorities and also one of the most complex. They must decide questions of location and capacity in light of population growth, finances, land values, site availability, through an almost endless list of factors to be considered. *The result of this will be a decision which, when combined with one technique or another of student assignment, will determine the racial composition of the student body in each school in the system. Over the long run, the consequences of the choices will be far reaching.* [Emphasis added] *

---

******Swann* v. *Charlotte-Mecklenburg*, 402 U.S. 1 (1971).**

Not only do school construction policies effect the immediate racial composition of newly constructed schools, but they also have a tremendous impact on the demographic composition of neighborhoods in later years. As the Chief Justice found:

> The location of schools may thus influence the patterns of residential development of a metropolitan area and have important impact on composition of inner city neighborhoods.

School districts cannot avoid influencing integration or segregation of their schools in determining the size and location of schools. Schools will either be located with stable, integrated student bodies, with segregated student bodies, or with student bodies so racially or economically imbalanced that complete segregation is bound to follow over a period of years. School construction can easily be used to further a policy of racial segregation. As the Chief Justice described the process:

> In addition to the classic pattern of building schools specifically intended for Negro or white students, school authorities have sometimes, since *Brown*, closed schools which appeared likely to become racially mixed through changes in neighborhood residential patterns. This was sometimes accompanied by building new schools in the areas of white suburban expansion farthest from Negro population centers in order to maintain the separation of the races with a minimum departure from the formal principles of "neighborhood zoning." Such a policy does more than simply influence the short-run composition of the student body of a new school. It may well promote segregated residential patterns which, when combined with "neighborhood zoning," further lock the school system into the mold of separation of the races.

But school construction policies can provide an equally powerful tool for achieving stable integration without inconvenience to the parents and children involved. If the best of all possible educational worlds is a stable, racially and economically integrated neighborhood school, school authorities can do much to achieve that goal through the intelligent planning of new construction.

A second method of achieving stable integration through school construction is the education park, envisioned as a device for achieving both improved and more economical educational offerings, and racial integration in large metropolitan areas. A metropolitan park would serve perhaps 12,000–20,000 students from kindergarten through high school—and should ideally include community college and post-secondary vocational facilities as well. To avoid creation of a massive and remote educational bureaucracy, each park might be divided into two or three high schools, eight to 10 junior high schools, 15 to 20 elementary schools, on a large campus.

Advocates of the educational park believe it has significant advantages as a method of achieving racially and socioeconomically integrated education in urban areas.

*First*, the park can be located on "neutral turf" between segregated residential areas, so that neither minority nor nonminority-group students are required to attend formerly "minority" or "nonminority" schools.

*Second*, improved specialized services can be made available— athletic facilities, individualized instruction, special services for handicapped and gifted children, wider course offerings in foreign languages, arts and sciences, more accessible vocational services—at reduced cost.

*Third*, location of junior college and post-secondary vocational facilities on the campus of an "education park" should facilitate cooperation between secondary and post-secondary education programs and significantly increase the accessibility of post-secondary education to students who might otherwise not take advantage of it.

Critics of the educational park concept have raised three major criticisms. First, the argument is made that gathering perhaps 15,000 children, of whom about 7,000 would be junior and senior high school students, in a single location would pose a potentially serious disciplinary problem. It would appear that the likelihood of disciplinary difficulties can be substantially reduced by subdividing the education parks into a number of small and responsive individual schools.

An initial capital cost which may exceed $50 million has provided a powerful disincentive to experimentation with the education park concept—in fact, although the concept of education parks has been fully developed since the mid-1960s, not even a single experimental park has been established. Finally, opponents of the park concept protest that a park serving a wider geographic area would render parent involvement in school activities far more difficult.

In fact, an education park might well encourage increased parent involvement through permitting establishment of *smaller* schools. While many elementary schools undergoing construction at the present time serve as many as 1,000 students for reasons of education economy, an education park would permit establishment of subschools serving as few as 400 or 500 students. The advantage of smaller and more personal schools, where teachers and administrators have far fewer parents with whom to deal, should outweigh any disadvantage inhering in the school location more distant from the family residence, Dr. Thomas F. Pettigrew told the committee:

> The criticism assumes that most urban public schools today are neighborhood-based, and that they generate considerable neighborhood involvement. Serious doubts can be raised about both assumptions; we may well be worrying about the loss of something already lost. In any event, there is no evidence to indicate that only a neighborhood-based school can generate parental concern, or that a metropolitan park could not duplicate this feat, or that there is a close and negative association between the size of the attendance area and involvement.*

We draw no final conclusions regarding the desirability of education parks. We do believe, however, that the opportunity to establish model parks should be opened to several communities through Federal financing of a substantial portion of the planning and construction costs. The version of the Emergency School Aid Act which passed the Senate would have directed experimentation with at least two parks. In the final version of the bill, however, the requirement

---

*Hearings of the U.S. Senate Select Committee on Equal Educational Opportunity, Part 2—*Equality of Equal Educational Opportunity, An Introduction*, May 13, 1970.

has been dropped; and although the Act continues to authorize support for experimentation with parks, the bill excludes elementary grades from the definition of "education park." We believe that integration programs which include the early years are far more promising than those which do not; we therefore would suggest that the Office of Education fund applications from communities which will themselves finance the elementary school aspects of a park, so that the concept can be tried once or twice in its entirety. And we urge modification of the statutory provision to permit this innovative strategy to be tried in practice.

#### 4. CHOICE, AND MAGNET SCHOOLS

As discussed in Chapter 15, courts have generally found so-called "freedom of choice" plans inadequate to meet constitutional requirements for rapid dismantling of racially discriminatory dual school systems. Choice remains available, however, as an approach to voluntary integration.

The simplest form of "choice" desegregation plan permits any parent to transfer his child to any school in the system, on a space-available basis. Where choices are not limited to those which favor desegregation, however, parents may misuse the plan to withdraw their children from newly-integrated schools, as happened under the Boston "Open Enrollment" plan, which actually worsened segregation of the Boston schools.

Choice plans limited to options which encourage desegregation can significantly increase desegregation where transfers are actively encouraged by school officials.

Although the typical choice plan permits nonminority-group students to transfer to predominantly minority-group schools, this option is seldom exercised. The concept of the "magnet school"—a ghetto school designed to attract advantaged students on a voluntary basis through provision of especially innovative school programs—is designed to encourage such transfer.

Attempts to establish magnet schools have met with only mixed success; at least two, however, the Trotter School in Boston, Mass. and the World of Inquiry School in Rochester, N.Y., have waiting lists of children from throughout their metropolitan areas.

Because of their high cost and uncertain success rate, magnet schools do not appear to be a broadly applicable approach to school integration. Much can be learned through establishment of these schools, however, and financial assistance under the Emergency School Aid Act should be made available to fund additional examples.

As discussed more fully in Chapter 18, "fair share-guaranteed access" plans, based on choice, remain perhaps the best hope for significant metropolitan desegregation across school district lines.

Under a "guaranteed access" plan, each participating suburban school system would voluntarily agree to accept up to a given number—a "fair share"—of centercity minority-group and educationally-disadvantaged children. A reasonable target might be agreement by suburban communities to accept up to one-half the proportion of minority-group and educationally-disadvantaged students found in the metropolitan area as a whole, as suggested by Senator Ribicoff's Urban Education Improvement Act. Care should be taken, however, to avoid scattering minority group children too thinly within suburban schools.* Centercity students would be selected according to parental choice.

This approach should go far toward meeting the legitimate concerns of suburban communities which fear that concentrations of educationally-disadvantaged students might make fundamental changes in the focus of their schools. School systems participating in a "guaranteed access" plan would be eligible for financial assistance under the Emergency School Aid Act to meet the added cost of additional services to both centercity and suburban children.

5. MODEL, STABLE, QUALITY INTEGRATED SCHOOLS

Where school districts are undertaking voluntary desegregation, the establishment of several model schools—alone or a first step or in combination with a broader "choice" plan—is helpful in demonstrating to the community that stable, quality integration can be educationally successful, and such efforts can teach us more about the elements of successful integration. Often, the establishment of truly integrated models, to which students are assigned on the basis of zoning, pairing, or other techniques, can build community support for integration more effectively than "choice" systems which typically result in only slight actual desegregation.

Model schools should contain a majority of more advantaged students, and a number of minority-group students which provides a fair test of broad integration of the district.

This approach to school integration, the establishment of "stable, quality integrated schools" has received the support of major education groups, including the National Education Association and the American Federation of Teachers. The version of the Emergency School Aid Act adopted by the Senate, with bipartisan support, required each applicant for assistance to establish at least one such model school. Although this requirement was deleted from the Act in Senate-House conference, the Office of Education and local communities undertaking desegregation programs should give this concept thorough consideration.

---

**Ibid.*

Dr. Pettigrew told the committeee:

> . . . there are data—I won't say they are as solid as I would like them to be—that suggest black children, when they are in small numbers, can be isolated . . . you get the idea that the isolated situation even more heightens the point I tried to make earlier on cross-racial acceptance . . . when you are the only black in the room and you have no support from other black children and little cross-racial acceptance you are in a bad way.

# Chapter 18—Metropolitan Approaches to Educational Equality

## A. Introduction

Residential segregation is a fact of American life. As a result of residential patterns existing with remarkable similarity throughout the United States, segregated schools are also a fact of life in this country. Over 80 percent of all black metropolitan residents live in central cities, while more than 60 percent of white metropolitan residents live in suburbs. And large percentages of nonminority group middle-class children who do reside in metropolitan cities attend nonpublic schools; according to testimony of Dr. Thomas Pettigrew, three-fifths of all nonminority-group students in Philadelphia and two-fifths of all such children in St. Louis and Boston do not attend public schools.

The result: 62.4 percent of minority-group students outside the South attend centercity school districts in which a majority of students are from minority groups.*

As Robert Carter, president of the National Committee Against Discrimination in Housing told the committee:

> Because housing segregation has spread so far and has become so entrenched throughout the United States, and because of the use of the neighborhood school, school segregation has become more widespread. The trend seems to be one way—toward increased school separation. Indeed, ours has already become two societies—one black and one white. . . . We have tied a policy of school organization (which we label *de facto* school segregation) to a policy of housing segregation.**

And as Dr. Thomas Pettigrew testified before the Senate Education Subcommittee:

> [E]ven if we did not have school segregation within districts, we would still face a national problem of segregation across districts.

The extent of America's residential segregation on the basis of race has been well documented. Demographer Karl E. Taeuber, who developed a "segregation index" for 207 American cities (all the cities for which block data are available and which had at least 1,000 nonwhite households in 1960), reached this depressing conclusion:

> No elaborate analysis is necessary to conclude from these figures that a high degree of residential segregation based on

---

*Department of Health, Education, and Welfare, Office for Civil Rights.

**Hearings of the U.S. Senate Select Committee on Equal Educational Opportunity, Part 5—*De Facto Segregation and Housing Discrimination*, Aug. 25, 1970.

race is a universal characteristic of American cities. This segregation is found in the cities of the North and West as well as of the South; in large cities as well as small; in nonindustrial cities as well as industrial; in cities with hundreds of thousands of Negro residents as well as those with only a few thousand, and in cities with only a few thousand, and in cities that are progressive in their employment practices and civil rights policies as well as those that are not.*

This finding was based on 1960 Census data. But in an article submitted to the committee by Dr. Taeuber and Reynolds Farley—entitled "Population Trends and Residential Segregation Since 1960"—the authors showed that the picture was no better during the decade of the 1960s. They examined special census data for 13 cities to assess trends in population, migration, and residential segregation from 1960 to mid-decade, and concluded that:

In these cities the demographic trends of the 1950s are continuing. There is a net out-migration of white population, and in several cities a decline in total population. Negro population is growing rapidly, but natural increase rather than net in-migration increasingly is the principal source. The concentration of whites in the suburbs and Negroes in the central cities is continuing. Within the cities, indices of racial residential segregation generally increased. The combination of small increases in residential segregation and large increases in the Negro percentage has greatly intensified the magnitude of the problems of segregation and desegregation of neighborhoods, local institutions, and schools.

Based on his studies Dr. Taeuber told the committee that "residential segregation is universal in American cities." Indeed, the committee found no dispute about the "universality" of residential segregation in this country—and its impact on education. Speaking for the present administration, George Romney, Secretary of Housing and Urban Development, told the committee that a "pattern of residential segregation . . . has come to characterize our great metropolitan areas." He testified that "deep divisions exist" and that our:

. . . metropolitan areas today consist of miles of slums, miles of gray areas, and miles of sprawling suburbs, some modest and some affluent. These are the miles which separate the black and the poor from good schools, and from new promising job opportunities. And with this physical separation has come a decreasing ability of people of differing backgrounds to communicate with each other about the problems which clearly affect everyone.**

The 1970 Census figures show no relief from our increasing residential segregation. As President Nixon observed in his June 11, 1971, Message on Equal Housing Opportunities:

In terms of racial concentration, the facts on housing occupancy revealed by the 1970 Census are compelling. In our 66 largest metropolitan areas, accounting for more than half the U.S. population—of which 49 are in the North and West—

---

**Ibid.*

***Ibid.*, Aug. 26, 1970.

the central city white population declined during the decade of the 1960s by about 2 million (5 percent)—while the black population increased almost 3 million (35 percent). This meant overall black population in central cities increased from 18 percent in 1960 to 24 percent in 1970.

In the suburban areas of these cities, however, the story was different. White population increased by 12.5 million (30 percent) and black population increased by less than 1 million (44 percent). The result was that the total black proportion of suburban population increased only from 4.2 percent in 1960 to 4.5 percent in 1970.

While Dr. Taeuber's studies have shown that residential segregation based on race is greater than residential segregation based on economic class, it is clear that Americans are not separated by race alone. In many suburban areas of the country, there are no housing opportunities for low and moderate income white Americans; and the efforts to provide such housing are often met with strong local opposition.

Thus, many low-income white families—like minority-group families—are condemned to certain sections of a metropolitan area, and their children often attend economically segregated schools.

So. in housing as well as in schools, there is growing isolation by both race and economic status in our metropolitan centers. And low-income Americans—both minority-group and nonminority-group—who find themselves restricted to the innercity have seen jobs disappear to the suburbs.

- Of the 990,000 new jobs created between 1959 and 1969 in the New York metropolitan region, 75 percent were located outside the city. The new jobs in the city were often for highly skilled or white-collar workers.
- Nationally over the last two decades, 80 percent of the new jobs created in large metropolitan areas have been located in the suburbs.
- The Census Bureau estimates that the number of males employed in American central cities decreased by 2 percent from 1960 to 1970. During this same period, male employment outside the central cities increased by 35.4 percent.

In his 1971 Housing Message, President Nixon assessed the impact of this job trend on minority Americans. He observed that the:

> . . . price of racial segregation is being paid each day in dollars: In wages lost because minority Americans are unable to find housing near the suburban jobs for which they could qualify. Industry and jobs are leaving central cities for the surrounding areas. Unless minority workers can move along with the jobs, the jobs that go to the suburbs will be denied to the minorities—and more persons who want to work will be added to the cities' unemployment and welfare rolls.

The President also pointed out the cost of this waste of human resources through the denial of human opportunity:

> No nation is rich enough and strong enough to afford the price which dehumanizing living environments extract in the

form of wasted human potential and stunted human lives—and many of those living environments in which black and other minority Americans are trapped are dehumanizing.

But the heaviest toll of this closed society falls on our children. Underfunded and inadequate schools attended by low-income children are too often educational graveyards. Many of their students are damaged by poor housing, malnutrition, inadequate intellectual stimulation in preschool years by lack of preventive and diagnostic medical care. Their lives must be lived in an environment of social failure, and schools do little to overcome the handicaps with which these students enter.

In Hartford, Conn., for example, the average IQ of fourth graders in ghetto schools was 94 in 1965. Two years later, when that class was in the sixth grade, its average IQ had dropped to 88. In another 2 years, in the eighth grade, it was 86—only six points above the IQ level at which children became candidates for institutionalization in Connecticut facilities for the retarded.

The failure of centercity school systems to meet the needs of their educationally disadvantaged students has many causes, each discussed at length elsewhere in this report.

- Often centercity school systems are underfinanced as compared with many of the wealthier suburban systems with which they must compete, and yet face the need to pay higher salaries and provide more expensive remedial and special services.* Many cities where per capita tax effort average 40 percent higher than in surrounding areas, cannot afford increased expenditures for education.

- Ghetto schools may well receive less adequate material support and attract less effective teaching staffs than schools with more advantaged student bodies elsewhere in the same school district.

- Remote, cumbersome bureaucracy and failure to invite parental involvement in school activities may render schools unnecessarily insensitive to the needs of their students.

- But the most important factor may be the ghetto itself. Children raised in the bleakest poverty, almost completely isolated from the mainstream of urban life over their entire upbringing, are simply at an educational disadvantage.

Public schools alone may be unable to reverse the effect of educational deprivation in preschool years and the ongoing effects of confinement to a culture of poverty. Clearly child development services must be made available in preschool years to enable low-income families to place their children on a more competitive footing with the children of the more affluent. Clearly more effective forms of compensatory education must be found to help ghetto schools do a better job of preparing their students for successful lives. And programs of integration within centercity school systems and cooperation between urban and suburban school districts can make the educational

*Note, however, that metropolitan areas often contain less affluent suburbs whose school systems may be even more severely underfinanced than the central city's.

benefits of integrated education immediately available to many ghetto children.

But none of these approaches is a panacea. The roots of the extreme social and economic tensions which threaten to divide the Nation, and of much educational deprivation, lie in the extreme racial and economic segregation of our urban areas. Only by making real choice available—choice for low-income families to live near suburban employment and integrated suburban schools, choice for middle-income families to live near centercity jobs and send their children to integrated schools as good as those in the suburbs—can we begin to defeat the destructive economic and educational impact of the ghetto.

## B. Causes of Metropolitan Segregation

The rigid economic and racial stratification of our urban areas did not take place by chance.

In his testimony before the committee, HUD Secretary Romney explained that the answer lies in "our country's tormented history of race relations."

> Throughout most of that history the dominant majority supported or condoned social and institutional separation of the races. This attitude became fixed in public law and public policy at every level of government and every branch of government, and thus it was adopted as a matter of course by the Federal Government when it entered the housing field in the 1930s. It continued after World War II.

As Secretary Romney indicated, the Federal Government playea a major role in building ghettos and creating residential segregation:

- Massive public housing projects which deliberately reinforced segregated living patterns.
- Federal highway programs which destroyed viable urban communities and amputated innercity from suburb.
- Urban renewal programs which promised better neighborhoods but produced other, more crowded slums.
- Location of Federal offices in suburbs which barred low- and moderate-income housing.

Since World War II, the FHA and Veterans Administration financed more than $120 billion worth of new housing—less than 2 percent of which has been available to nonwhite families, and much of that on a strictly segregated basis.

The Federal Government's involvement in residential segregation was not a matter of inadvertance or neglect. It was conscious, stated policy.

For example, the official FHA *Underwriting Manual* for 1938 contained the following warning:

> If a neighborhood is to retain stability, it is necessary that properties shall continue to be occupied by the same social and racial group.

The manual recommended use of restrictive covenants to keep out "inharmonious racial groups." In fact, it provided a model restrictive covenant for those needing assistance in pursuing this policy.

Secretary Romney acknowledged that a variety of Federal programs are in part responsible for today's segregated living patterns:

> Urban renewal, the interstate highway network, and other Federal programs have contributed to the segregation and isolation of the poor and minority groups in our cities. These Federal programs have thus aggravated the magnitude of the problem by preventing families from living within a reasonable distance of their daily activities.

Secretary Romney also amplified the FHA's role in creating and maintaining segregated housing:

> Unfortunately, the sound policy objectives of FHA were accompanied by both official and informal Federal encouragement of racial segregation. FHA refused to provide insurance in integrated neighborhoods on the grounds that the financial risk to the Government was too great. As a matter of fact, Congress declared as a matter of policy that the FHA had to limit insurance to those instances where they could prove the economic feasibility of the insurance, and with the attitudes that existed, this tended to be a restrictive policy . . .
>
> In addition to preventing minorities from gaining access to new housing, FHA policies also generally withheld insurance from existing housing in central city areas. This practice, called "redlining," involved an unwritten but well-understood agreement between financial institutions and FHA that many central city neighborhoods occupied largely by minority groups had an unfavorable economic future.

In addition to the Federal Government, other levels of government have also pursued policies designed to perpetuate residential segregation.

Many communities have rezoned parcels of land to block federally subsidized low- and moderate-income housing.

Richard Bellman, a staff attorney for the National Committee Against Discrimination in Housing, described such local barriers for the committee:

> In my opinion, one of the most serious impediments to the creation of integrated communities is the imposition by local communities of restrictive and exclusionary building code and land use requirements which effectively foreclose construction of new housing for low- and moderate-income citizens. The techniques used to accomplish this result vary from community to community. Many suburban cities and towns have simply zoned all residential areas exclusively for single-family uses eliminating the possibility of construction of townhouses and apartment units for the poor. Some communities impose large lot or minimum floor space requirements which have the same result other communities raise arbitrary building code requirements, or encourage construction only of luxury-type apartments while refusing to approve multiple dwellings with units to accommodate larger families. A host of barriers are created to exclude housing

projects which would service low- and moderate-income citizens.*

A second major barrier to the creation of integrated housing opportunities is the practice of many city housing authorities of confining public housing developments to ghetto areas within the city, which reinforces and expands the ghetto—often hastening middle-income white flight from the city and making it more difficult to attract middle-income families back to the city.

The result of these governmental policies and actions, coupled with the massive population migration from farm to city, and from South to North, has been pervasive racial and economic segregation flowing from residence—and isolation in schools, jobs, public services, consumer markets, in nearly every area of human endeavor and opportunity.

*The 14th Amendment*—There can be no sweeping generalizations about the legal impact of the wide variety of local policies inhibiting the elimination of residential segregation. Individual actions by local authorities have been found violative of 14th Amendment protections against racial and ethnic discrimination. (See, e.g., *Hunter* v. *Erickson* 303 U.S. 385 (1969); *Gautreaux* v. *Romney* 71–1073 (7th Cir. 1971); *Shannon* v. *HUD* 436 F. 2d 809 (3d Cir. 1970); *SASSO* v. *Union City* 424 F. 2d 291 (9th Cir. 1970); *CORE* v. *Norwalk Redevelopment Agency* 395 F. 2d 920 (2d Cir. 1968).)

On the other hand, the Supreme Court recently implied that (where racial motivation cannot be proved) at least some limitations may be constitutionally imposed to exclude families on the basis of low income, which would be prohibited if the motivation were shown to be racial rather than economic. (*James* v. *Valtierra*, 402 U.S. 137 [1971]).

The law in this area is still in a state of flux, and it may be several years before a clear-cut legal pattern emerges.

The extent to which Federal courts may be prepared to require metropolitan cooperation for school desegregation, based on evidence of discriminatory actions by State and local authorities to encourage both residential and school segregation within metropolitan areas, is also unclear. There are two cases which currently raise this issue: *Bradley* v. *Richmond*, involving school districts in the Richmond, Va., metropolitan area, and *Bradley* v. *Milliken*, involving the Detroit, Mich., metropolitan area.

An order requiring consolidation of districts and multidistrict desegregation was entered by a Federal district court in the Richmond case. The order has been reversed by the Fourth Circuit Court of Appeals, and an appeal is pending to the Supreme Court.

In the Detroit case, an order requiring extensive multidistrict desegregation has been remanded by the Sixth Circuit Court of Appeals to the Federal Circuit Court of Appeals for further hearings.

It is interesting to note that in both cases the centercity school disrict requested the joinder of its suburban neighbors.

Both the Detroit and Richmond cases rest upon district court findings of *de jure* segregation—that is, official involvement in fostering

* Hearings of the U.S. Senate Select Committee on Equal Educational Opportunity, Part 5—*De Facto Segregation and Housing Discrimination*, Aug. 27, 1970.

segregation—at both the State and school district levels.* Both cases rest on the theory that once the State has been shown to have fostered school segregation directly, or indirectly through housing discrimination, the State can be required to take action, including consolidation of school districts created by State law, to make effective desegregation possible even if the school district lines themselves were not drawn for discriminatory purposes.

The future of these housing and school desegregation decisions and the legal theories on which they rest cannot be predicted with confidence. What can be predicted is that courts are not the branch of Government best equipped to deal with the extremely complex issues involved in breaking down racial and economic barriers within metropolitan areas in ways that do justice to the legitimate concerns of all involved. A court cannot offer subsidies to compensate suburban communities for increased costs, including educational costs, of serving low-income families or provide assistance to replace revenues lost through location of tax-free public housing units; a court is ill equipped to require that low-income housing be scatter-site, rather than in huge apartment projects or to implement the metropolitan planning needed to prevent some suburban communities from being swamped by low-income housing while others are untouched. But if public officials at the local, Federal and State levels refuse to act, the courts will be left to their own, and very limited, devices.

---

*In the Richmond case the court found State involvement in fostering school segregation including:

- The original establishment of segregation by State law;
- State law permitting transportation of pupils across school district lines for the purpose of maintaining segregation;
- State tuition grant and pupil scholarship programs permitting students to cross school district lines or attend private schools in order to avoid desegregation.

The court also found State, Federal and local involvement in encouraging residential segregation, including:

- State enforcement of racially restrictive covenants;
- Location of urban renewal sites to perpetuate segregation;
- Location of public housing projects to perpetuate segregation;
- Action by the FHA and local realtors to refuse to make housing available to blacks in white residential areas.

In the Detroit case the court's findings include:

- Until 1948, the State enforced racial restrictions on the ownership of property which confined blacks to particular areas in the city of Detroit;
- Lending institutions, real estate associations and brokerage firms, together with agencies responsible for land use management, and the FHA and VA cooperated to prevent blacks from obtaining housing in white residential areas;
- State funding policies contributed to rendering educational opportunities in the city of Detroit inferior to those in the surrounding districts;
- The State legislature intervened to prevent voluntary implementation of a partial desegregation plan by the Detroit school board;
- Within the city of Detroit: (1) attendance zones were designed to increase segregation; (2) black students were bused away from closer white schools to attend black schools.

## C. Encouraging Integration of Metropolitan Schools

In many metropolitan areas, where centercity school districts contain concentrations of minority group and educationally disadvantaged children, the most promising approach to successful school integration would appear to be through cooperative arrangements between city and suburban school systems.

The primary methods for implementing voluntary multidistrict cooperative arrangements—acceptance of innercity students by suburban schools "magnet schools" and education parks, are discussed in Chapter 17.

Successful interdistrict integration programs involving attendance of centercity children in suburban schools have been implemented through cooperation of 30 school systems in the Boston, Mass., area (METCO), 5 school systems in Rochester, N.Y., and 14 Connecticut school districts (Project Concern)—including all the major cities in the State. However, these programs are limited in scope—involving fewer than 4,000 minority-group children—due in large part to an absence of adequate financing.

Other interdistrict approaches have been based in the concept of the "magnet school"—a ghetto school designed to attract advantaged students through an innovative educational program. Although a number of efforts to establish "magnet schools" have failed, the Trotter School in Boston and the World of Inquiry School in Rochester both have waiting lists of children from throughout their metropolitan areas.

With recent adoption of the Emergency School Aid Act, which reserves 5 percent of appropriated funds ($50 million annually if the bill is fully funded) for voluntary metropolitan area programs, and makes substantial additional funding available for both multidistrict and within-district efforts, adequate financing will be available for the first time to support existing programs—including cost of services to improve educational quality for all children within integrated classrooms—and to encourage adoption of similar programs by other communities. The committee hopes that the availability of Federal financial assistance will encourage a marked expansion in interdistrict cooperative efforts.

A third approach to metropolitan integration is the education park, discussed at length in Chapter 17. There are no existing education parks, largely because large initial construction costs are an effective deterrent to experimentation; but the park concept appears to be a promising approach to providing integrated education together with improved educational services and facilities. Certainly some experimental parks should be established, with Federal assistance, to put the concept into practice.*

*Encouraging Metropolitan Planning*—Financial assistance under the Emergency School Aid Act will be available both to support physical

*Although funding for education parks is made available in the Emergency School Aid Act, the Act eliminates grades K–6 from its definition of park. Because we believe integration efforts which begin in early grades had the most promise of success, we would hope that grants will be made to communities which will themselves support the K–6 aspects of a comprehensive park and we suggest prompt revision of the law.

costs of multidistrict integration and to provide help in improving the educational program for all students.

In addition, however, we believe that appropriate committees of the Senate and the House should consider special incentives and priority in the allocation of Federal assistance for education to reward school districts in metropolitan areas which voluntarily achieve broad-based involvement in planning and implementation of cooperative school integration efforts. Such metropolitan plans might be based on a "fair share" approach under which suburban school districts could agree to encourage and accept up to a given number of educationally disadvantaged and minority-group children from the centercity, or from other suburbs.*

## D. Providing Choice in Housing

In many communities, rigid housing restrictions limiting minority-group and low-income families to centercities and poor suburbs provide a formidable barrier to school integration for most children. As Senator Ribicoff said in a statement included in the committee's hearings:

> For years we have assumed that integrated education would lead to an integrated society . . . Integrated education is important. It deserves our continued support and assistance. But unless we also open the suburbs to those trapped in the city, we will labor in vain.**

### 1. TOWARD MEETING LEGITIMATE SUBURBAN CONCERNS

There can be no doubt that, in most areas of the country, there is substantial local resistance to low- and moderate-income housing and to the elimination of residential segregation. In 1968, the National Advisory Commission on Civil Disorders found that:

> Housing programs serving low-income groups have been concentrated in the ghettos. Nonghetto areas, particularly suburbs, for the most part have steadfastly opposed low-income, rent supplement, or below-market interest rate housing, and have successfully restricted use of these programs outside the ghetto.

---

*In areas of high proportions of educationally disadvantaged children, the standard suggested by Senator Ribicoff's Urban Education Improvement Act might be adopted—that suburban school districts accept a proportion of disadvantaged students not in excess of half the metropolitan average.

The committee notes with approval that the recently adopted Emergency School Aid Act provides financial assistance for efforts to develop metropolitan plans where two-thirds of the districts serving two-thirds of the students in a metropolitan area join in the effort. However, this assistance is limited to plans under which each suburban school would achieve half the proportion of minority-group students found in the metropolitan area as a whole in each school within 10 years.

In some large metropolitan areas, it may be unreasonable to expect outlying school districts to meet the standard of the Act; in additon, the Act fails to include disadvantaged children who are not from minority groups in its approach.

**Hearings of the U.S. Senate Select Committee on Equal Educational Opportunity, Part 2—*Metropolitan Aspects of Educational Opportunity*, pp. 10910–32.

Today, 4 years later, the opposition is at least as great. There are often sound and legitimate reasons for suburban opposition to certain forms of low- and moderate-income housing.

*Preventing the Overburdening of Communities Which Accept Subsidized Housing*—Some communities which have responsibly opened their doors to federally subsidized housing have found that, precisely because there are so few communities willing to do so, they are soon overburdened. A tragic example is provided by the case of Beecher, Mich., a suburb of Flint, which adopted a policy permitting the development of federally subsidized housing. As Martin Sloan of the U.S. Commission on Civil Rights told the committee:

> . . . in the town of Beecher, Mich. a suburban area outside Flint, the construction of a substantial number of low-income units under the Section 235 program served to change the school system from a racially integrated one into a nearly all-black system. HUD officials disclaimed any responsibility for that, although the housing would never have been built in Beecher without express HUD approval. As one local HUD official was reported to say: "The impact on housing—any housing—on a community's schools is not my business, nor is racial balance."*

The construction of federally subsidized public housing takes land off the tax rolls, imposing a double burden on residential communities. Not only are children (with special educational needs) added to their school populations but the tax base which must support those needs is depleted at the same time.

And low- and moderate-income housing creates increased demands for public health, transportation, welfare, law enforcement and other municipal services in addition to education.

Federal housing programs must ensure that the experience of communities like Beecher—where local FHA officials ignored the impact of new subsidized housing on neighborhoods and schools—will not be repeated.

HUD has made an important step in the right direction through its new emphasis on scatter-site housing and small cluster developments in its regulations on "Project Selection Criteria," which became effective on February 7, 1972. The regulations establish a system of rating applications for Federal assistance for homeownership projects under Section 235 of the Housing and Urban Development Act for rental projects under Section 236 or rent supplement, and for public housing projects. Under the regulations, a project will be rated "superior," "adequate," or "poor," with respect to eight broad criteria. In order to qualify for assistance, a proposed project must obtain at least an

---

**Ibid.*

"adequate" rating on each of the eight criteria, a "poor" rating on any will disqualify the project.*

Under the new regulation, Federal support will be denied to proposals for subsidized housing which threaten to "tip" already integrated residential areas. In addition, subsidized housing located in existing areas of minority concentration will be supported only under a State or local development plan which provides comparable opportunities to minority families in integrated areas, or where housing needs cannot otherwise be met.

The new regulations are a vast improvement over prior HUD policy. For the first time, HUD and the Federal Government will use its site selection powers both to provide greater choice in housing opportunity. And, just as important, the new regulations embody a Federal commitment to preventing the kind of destructive influx of low-income housing which took place in Beecher, Mich.

However, the new regulations cannot be completely effective while their scope is limited to concern for the impact of Federal housing programs on segregation by race and national origin. The regulations should be broadened to reach the real problem, which is to provide wider choice in housing for all low-income families, while guaranteeing communities which accept federally assisted housing that they will not be overburdened.

Broadened as we have suggested, the new regulation can effectively guarantee that there will be no new Beechers.

*Reducing the Financial Burden*—The existing public housing program requires a waiver of local property taxes and merely permits a payment in lieu of taxes of 10 percent of shelter rent. This is totally inadequate. As one housing official observed:

> . . . very few suburban leaders are willing to make a political decision which calls for an influx of low-income families, a reduction in potential taxes from real estate, an increase

*(A) A superior rating shall be given if the proposed project will be located:

(1) So that, within the housing market area, it will provide opportunities for minorities for housing outside existing areas of minority concentration and outside areas which are already substantially racially mixed; or

(2) In an area of minority concentration, but the area is part of an official State or local agency development plan, and sufficient, comparable opportunities exist for housing for minority families, in the income range to be served by the proposed project, outside areas of minority concentration.

(B) An adequate rating shall be given if the proposed project will be located:

(1) Outside an area of minority concentration, but the area is racially mixed, and the proposed project will not cause a significant increase in the proportion of minority to nonminority residents in the area; or

(2) In an area of minority concentration and sufficient, comparable opportunities exist for housing for minority families, in the income range to be served by the proposed project, outside areas of minority concentration; or

(3) In an area of minority concentration, but is necessary to meet overriding housing needs which cannot otherwise feasibly be met in that housing market area. (An "overriding need" may not serve as the basis for an "adequate" rating if the only reason the need cannot otherwise feasibly be met is that discrimination on the basis of race, color or natural origin renders sites outside areas of minority concentration unavailable); or

(4) In a housing market area with few or no minority-group residents.

(C) A poor rating shall be given if the proposed project does not satisfy any of the above conditions, e.g., will cause a significant increase in the proportion of minority residents in an area which is not one of minority concentration, but which is racially mixed.

in the level of volume of public services, and therefore the possibility of a tax increase.

The Federal Government must reduce and seek to eliminate the financial burden on communities caused by low- and moderate-income housing.

Chapter 2, Section 6(d)(1) of the Housing and Urban Development Act of 1972, passed by the Senate on March 2, 1972, would eventually require all public housing projects to pay full real estate taxes. This provision will meet part of the local objections to public housing, by ending the depletion of available local tax revenues; and the committee urges its adoption by the Congress.

But we must also deal with the increased burdens placed on municipal services by both low- and moderate-income housing.

Education is by far the local service most directly affected by the addition of low- and moderate-income housing.

As a pertinent, short-term goal, committee witness Anthony Downs, of the Real Estate Research Corp. of Chicago, recommended the "creation of new educational subsidies, or new means of financing local educational costs, that take the financial penalty out of accepting low-income residents in a community, and convert it to an advantage." In fact, the Congress has already acted to provide such a program of educational subsidies. The Elementary and Secondary Education Amendments of 1969, signed into law in April 1970, added a new "Clause (c)" to the existing program of School Assistance in Federally Affected Areas (the so-called "Impact Aid" Program) authorizing a Federal payment to compensate local school districts for serving students from tax-free federally assisted public housing—in much the same way that school districts are compensated for serving children who live on military bases, Indian reservations, and other tax-exempt federally owned property. Unfortunately, this provision has not been funded. Full funding of the "Clause (c)" program is an absolutely essential first step toward a rational housing policy; past failures to make funds available are inexcusable. We must begin by fully funding this program, and then expand the concept to other types of federally subsidized housing, and other municipal services in addition to education.

President Nixon's Task Force on Urban Renewal approved this type of incentive to local communities, urging:

> . . . that additional legislation be requested to provide special Federal aid to help suburban communities meet the increased costs of education, public health, transportation, and other municipal services that result directly from expanding the supply of low- and moderate-income housing in the community.

*Avoiding Monolithic Housing Projects, Scatter-Site Housing and Cluster Developments*—Far more attention must be paid to the design of low- and moderate-income housing, to assure that it is consistent and compatible with surrounding residential areas and to avoid large low-income housing units which become "mini-ghettos".

As Anthony Downs observed, Federal policy should encourage the "location of many new low- and moderate-income housing units in suburban areas both in relatively small clusters and in individual scatteration in middle-income neighborhoods.

HUD's recently adopted "Project Selection Criteria" require all proposals of subsidized housing to meet the objective of providing "an attractive and well-planned physical environment." If properly implemented, these regulations could ensure that there will be no more large, institutionalized public housing projects which simply export a slice of urban poverty to the suburbs.

Present law permits Federal support for scatter-site housing and small multifamily units. But there is now only limited authority for a third approach: making individual housing allowances to enable recipients to obtain existing rental housing.

The Housing and Urban Development Act of 1970 authorized the Secretary of HUD to conduct research programs to demonstrate the feasibility of providing low-income families with housing allowances to assist them in obtaining existing standard rental housing of their choice.

This program should be continued—with the aim of adopting new legislation extending rent subsidies and public housing rent allowances to individual households.

The immediate costs for scatter-site housing, small multifamily units and housing allowances may be higher than for the construction of conventional public housing units. But the social benefits, in terms of school integration, reduced crime, increased access to jobs and more hopeful environment can more than compensate for these increased costs.

### 2. TOWARD A MORE EFFECTIVE POLICY UNDER EXISTING LEGISLATIVE AUTHORITY

*Encouraging Rational Site Selection*—The Civil Rights Commission points out that HUD can and should take a more active role in encouraging rational site selection for federally assisted housing.

> The project-by-project approach . . . reflects an unduly passive posture on the part of HUD, suggesting incorrectly that department officials have no alternative but to rely exclusively on the receipt of individual proposals drawn up in isolation from other such proposals. Under this approach, the department may often have to settle for less desirable projects, unrelated to rational metropolitan growth or to the problem of racial polarization.

The Commission suggests that the department—

> affirmatively seek out applications from builders and sponsors for housing located so as to contribute to the healthy growth of the entire metropolitan area [and] provide assistance to them to assure that they are able to build on desirable sites.

*Action Against Discriminatory Practices.*—Where zoning laws or other local ordinances discriminate against racial or national origin minorities, the committee believes that HUD is legally obligated to take enforcement action under Title VI of the Civil Rights Act of 1964 and the Fair Housing Act of 1968.*

---

*See analysis of HUD's power and duty to act against discriminatory zoning in the memorandum submitted by the National Committee Against Discrimination in Housing, pp. 2920–2926, Part 5, Hearings before Select Committee.

A recent statement on equal housing opportunity by the Leadership Conference on Civil Rights and nine other national public interest organizations aptly describes the need for adequate law enforcement in this field:

> The continuation of . . . Federal assistance unacompanied by civil rights standards subverts our major national housing goal—to provide a decent home in a suitable living environment for all American citizens.

*Location of Federal Facilities.*—The Federal Government is directly responsible for its own facilities location policies.

The Federal Government employs over 6 million men and women; and increasingly Federal facilities, like many businesses, are moving from the central cities. In the Washington, D.C. area alone, for example, many Government agencies—including the Geological Survey, the National Bureau of Standards, the U.S. Public Health Service, and the Atomic Energy Commission—have recently moved or plan to move to the suburbs.

To deal with this problem, the President issued Executive Order 11512 in February 1970, requiring that consideration should be given to the availability of adequate low- and moderate-income housing in the selection of sites for Federal facilities.

However, the Executive order has not solved the problem. The Civil Rights Commissioner finds that although it has great potential leverage on local communities because of the economic benefits flowing from location of Federal facilities, the Federal Government in relocating its facilities had made little or no effort to insure that its low- and moderate-income employees can find accessible housing nearby. In fact, Federal moves into the suburbs often result in the loss of jobs to low- and moderate-income employees who can no longer reach their place of employment.

As Senator Ribicoff observed:

> The absence of available housing near these locations has forced hundreds of dedicated low- and moderate-income black- and white workers to give up their jobs.

On June 14, 1971, the Department of Housing and Urban Development and the General Services Administration joined in a memorandum of understanding to help insure adequate housing near new Federal installations.* Under this agreement, HUD will advise GSA as to the availability of low- and moderate-income housing near a projected Government facility. If GSA decides to locate in an area where an adequate supply of such housing is not available, HUD, the involved Federal agency, and the community in which the installation is to be located will develop a written "affirmative action plan" to insure that an adequate supply of low- and moderate-income housing will be available within 6 months after the facility is to be occupied.

This new policy is an important step forward. The committee strongly hopes that these procedures will be implemented.

However, the committee believes that appropriate sanctions must be developed to insure compliance with the affirmative action plan called for under this agreement.

---

*Procedures for implementing this memorandum were issued on June 7, 1972.

In addition, the committee also believes that steps must be taken to insure that the facility location policies of Federal contractors and Federal grantees receiving substantial Federal funding comply with standards similar to those outlined in the memorandum.

If the Executive Branch fails to take such steps, the committee recommends serious consideration of legislation similar to that introduced by Senator Ribicoff on March 16, 1971. This legislation provides that before a Federal facility, or the facility of a Federal contractor or Federal grantee, may be located in any community, the agency or contractor involved must secure assurances judicially enforceable by the Federal Government that the community will provide at least one unit of adequate housing for each prospective low- or moderate-income employee.

As Senator Ribicoff observed:

> . . . this legislation will simply grant the economic benefits of site locations to those communities that are also willing to assume the responsibilities for the workers in those facilities.

### 3. TOWARD A MORE COMPREHENSIVE APPROACH

As suggested earlier, HUD regulation under existing authority can go far toward meeting the concerns of many communities that lowering barriers to low- and moderate-income housing may result in an avalanche. And HUD can do more under existing authority to advocate and encourage sensible site selection. But unless suburban communities agree to remove barriers to subsidized housing, the major burden will continue to fall on central cities, and racial and economic division will continue to grow.

A most promising approach has been adopted by the Miami Valley Regional Planning Association. The association, which represents the communities of the Dayton, Ohio, metropolitan area is implementing a unique plan designed to disperse the anticipated need for low- and moderate-income housing throughout the five-county Dayton metropolitan area.

The basic premise of this plan, adopted unanimously by the member governments of the Planning Association in September 1970, is that every community in a metropolitan area will accept its fair share of the low- and moderate-income housing required to meet the needs of the area's residents. As Mr. Dale Bertsch of the association testified:

> The housing plan essentially is based on computing low- and moderate-income housing needs by county and allocating shares of this housing to planning units throughout the region, each of which is based on groupings of municipalities and/or townships within a county. Locations of such housing is coordinated through voluntary agreements and working relationships with the MVRPC and through the A–95 review process. The plan is meant for immediate implementation, and it is already affecting the location of proposed housing in the region.*

---

*Hearings of the U.S. Senate Select Committee on Equal Educational Opportunity, Part 21—*Metropolitan Aspects of Educational Inequality*. Nov. 22, 1971.

Although the "fair share" is a goal, it is also a *ceiling*—no community will receive low- or moderate-income housing in excess of its "fair share." As Mr. Bertsch testified:

> One of the major complaints which is heard by elected officials across our region, when they begin to advocate low- and moderate-income housing within their communities, is that certain communities within the suburbs are going to become the pressure relief valve for the central city. Therefore, it is anticipated, and we have used—the Commission has used—the goal also as a shutoff valve for low- and moderate-income housing construction in the suburbs.

We do not pretend to have a detailed or final answer to the increasing educational, social and economic segregation of our metropolitan areas. But we do find that intense metropolitan segregation increasingly threatens the American commitment to equal opportunity based on individual merit. We believe that relevant committees of the House and Senate should consider legislation to encourage adoption of the "fair share" approach to allocation of federally subsidized housing in other metropolitan areas, and we believe that metropolitan plans should be encouraged to address the need to provide increased housing opportunities for middle-income families within central cities, as well as the need to provide housing opportunities for low-income families outside the central city.

As Father Theodore M. Hesburg, Chairman of the U.S. Civil Rights Commission, stated in testimony before the House Committee on Banking and Currency, such an approach:

> . . . has the greatest potential for meeting the housing problems of lower-income families in a way that would contribute to the social and economic health of the entire metropolitan area . . . for doing away with the irrationality of the existing system by which federally subsidized housing programs are operated, of making order out of what is now little short of chaos.

# Chapter 19—Recommendations

## A. Meeting Federal Responsibilities

### 1. FEDERAL LEADERSHIP

The committee's fundamental and most basic recommendation is that the Congress and the Executive Branch unite in a national policy which supports the Constitution, recognizes the potential benefits of quality integrated education, and is committed to helping local communities assure that desegregation—whether voluntary or under legal requirement—is responsive to the legitimate concerns of parents and students from all backgrounds.

The focus of national debate on the misleading issues of "massive busing" and "racial balance" has contributed to deteriorating public confidence in the justice of constitutional requirements and in the essential fairness of our judicial system. Our national commitment to equality of educational opportunity is in jeopardy.

At the same time, public discussion has largely ignored both the benefits of integrated education, and the legitimate concerns of parents—concern of minority group parents that their children not be subjected to unfair and discriminatory treatment within desegregated schools, concerns of all parents that desegregation improve and not impair their children's educational opportunities.

The immediate losers have been the Nation's children. And the greatest losers are the 11 million children already attending 1,500 desegregating school districts. Negative leadership discourages the local support necessary for successful school integration, and compounds the already difficult jobs of teachers and local school officials.

We must unite in an effort to make school desegregation work, or fail a fundamental test of our national character. As President Nixon said in his March 1970 message on school desegregation:

> Few issues facing us as a Nation are of such transcendent importance: important because of the vital role that our public schools play in the Nation's life and in its future; because the welfare of our children is at stake; and because it presents us a test of our capacity to live together in one Nation, in brotherhood and understanding.

### 2. REJECTION OF CONSTITUTIONAL AMENDMENTS

We recommend rejection of any proposal to amend the United States Constitution which would limit the existing authority of Federal courts to remedy racially discriminatory school segregation.

A number of proposed constitutional amendments were introduced in both Houses during the 92d Congress. Perhaps the most widely favored version, H.J. Res. 620, provides:

> Sec. 1. No public school student shall, because of his race, creed, or color, be assigned to or required to attend a particular school.
>
> Sec. 2. Congress shall have the power to enforce this article by appropriate legislation.

This language appears designed to reestablish "freedom of choice", proven ineffective as a means of disestablishing officially imposed school segregation over a 14-year trial period, as *per se* satisfying constitutional requirements even where no actual desegregation is produced.

This amendment would not only prevent the Federal courts from effectively remedying officially imposed segregation, it would also *prohibit* school authorities from adopting *wholly voluntary plans* (beyond "free choice") for the integration of schools as a matter of local decision.

Although this proposal, and others similar to it, are often described as "antibusing" amendments, their scope is far broader. They would establish constitutional prohibitions against using effective means to achieve school desegregation. In effect, they seek to establish national policy in support of apartheid in public education.

### 3. REJECTION OF "STUDENT TRANSPORTATION MORATORIUM ACT" AND "EQUAL EDUCATIONAL OPPORTUNITIES ACT"

We recommend against adoption of the "Student Transportation Moratorium Act", and the "Equal Educational Opportunities Act" proposed by the administration last Spring.

We find no justification for prohibiting all additional transportation on the elementary school level, as the "Equal Educational Opportunities Act" would do. The evidence indicates that school integration is most likely to produce increased academic achievement in educationally disadvantaged children if it begins in the elementary grades. Further, a policy of desegregation in secondary grades combined with extensive segregation in elementary grades increases the likelihood of continued racial tension in desegregated high schools and junior high schools.

We find no useful purpose in the Act's provisions making student transportation on the secondary level a "remedy of last resort" and requiring that transportation be undertaken only in conjunction with a long-term plan for adoption of an "alternative"—such as new school construction, establishment of magnet schools or educational parks. Under present law, school districts themselves have primary responsibility for drawing desegregation plans, and may adopt any method they wish, involving transportation or not, which meets constitutional standards. Most school districts presently choose transportation only as a "last resort". Further, several of the "alternatives" suggested in the bill, such as magnet schools and education parks, themselves commonly require student transportation, and therefore would not appear to be "alternatives" at all. In short, the Act's provisions "limiting" transportation at the secondary level are confusing and appear to be without point.

We do not agree with the Act's proposals to require court orders for desegregation to lapse after 10 years, and orders involving transportation after 5 years. While court orders remain flexible and subject to revision, and while courts may properly dismiss cases on an individual basis after discrimination has been ended, the "Equal Educational Opportunities Act" appears to invite a massive resegregation of schools at the end of 5 years. Nor do we agree with the Act's efforts to restrict the constitutional responsibility of State government for segregation which it has established, or to permit reopening of all existing court orders to litigate compliance with the Act—creating another round of divisive and embittering court suits, destructive of education even where existing court orders are eventually upheld.*

And we recommend rejection of companion legislation, the proposed Student Transportation Moratorium Act, which would prohibit implementation of desegregation plans requiring *any* change in existing transportation patterns during a period designed to permit Congressional action on the "Equal Educational Opportunities Act".** The moratorium would go so far as to prohibit adoption of plans transporting children shorter distances to achieve desegregation, and in many cases, would effectively require preservation of dual school systems intact during its life.

We find that guidelines for student transportation developed by the Supreme Court in *Swann* v. *Charlotte-Mecklenburg*, and applied to administrative proceedings under the Civil Rights Act by the Education Amendments of 1972, establish a sensible, enforceable and uniform standard for the use of transportation in eliminating the effects of racially discriminatory student assignment policies. Transportation will not be required over times and distances which risk children's health or impinge on their educations. If individual desegregation plans require unreasonable transportation, there are judicial remedies.

As discussed in Chapter 15, we find both of these legislative proposals to be of highly doubtful constitutionality. But beyond their questionable constitutionality, the "Equal Educational Opportunities Act" and the "Student Transportation Moratorium Act" would severely restrict remedies for unconstitutional school segregation while compounding the legitimate concerns which lie behind much opposition to school desegregation.

Without transportation, much unlawfully established segregation must be allowed to persist. The desegregation which does take place will often disproportionately involve nonminority-group students from less affluent, blue collar families whose homes are adjacent to minority group residential areas. Student bodies of desegregated schools will more often be predominantly minority-group and predominantly educationally disadvantaged—encouraging "white flight",

*The version of the Equal Educational Opportunities Act which passed the House of Representatives last September extended severe restrictions on the use of transportation to the high school as well as the elementary level. Although the bill would permit transportation of children to the "next nearest" as well as the nearest school, this alternation of the original formula would continue to assure that most desegregation outside of rural communities would be confined to the less affluent.

**The bill passed by the House Aug. 18, 1972 would have established a moratorium period ending July 1, 1973, or on adoption of the EEOA if sooner.

jeopardizing the academic benefits of integration, provoking legitimate concern of parents of more advantaged students assigned to these schools, and rendering the tasks of teachers and school officials far more difficult. Desegregation of elementary schools, where educational benefits are greatest, will be highly restricted, while desegregation of junior and senior high schools can be expected to be far less successful if based upon extensive segregation in elementary schools.

The Equal Educational Opportunities Act, and its companion legislation, the Student Transportation Moratorium Act, would amplify the inequities and injustices which can be caused by poorly designed desegregation plans, render stable integration far less likely, and impair the educational opportunities of all children, advantaged and disadvantaged, minority group and nonminority group, in desegregating school districts.

### 4. ENCOURAGING VOLUNTARY INTEGRATION

The committee strongly recommends Federal incentives to encourage voluntary school integration. We agree with the National Advisory Committee on the Education of Disadvantaged Children that "desegregation is the best form of compensatory education"; properly conducted, it can better prepare all children for life in a multiracial society.

Voluntary integration provides an opportunity for careful planning, to begin slowly and build public support, to take steps over a period of time. These are luxuries which, more than 18 years after *Brown*, are no longer available to districts desegregating under constitutional mandate.

The recently adopted $1 billion-a-year Emergency School Aid Act provides the necessary support for voluntary integration; it is essential that the bill be fully funded. In addition, those provisions of the proposed Equal Educational Opportunities Act which would divert Emergency School Aid funds for more general compensatory education should be rejected. Additional funds should be provided for general compensatory education, but funds devoted to encouraging and supporting voluntary integration should not be diverted for this purpose.

### 5. A UNIFORM NATIONAL POLICY OF LAW ENFORCEMENT

In exercising their responsibilities under the Civil Rights Act of 1964, the Departments of Justice and HEW must enforce constitutional 14th Amendment and Civil Rights Act guarantees against discrimination in public education on a uniform, national basis.

Unlawful public involvement in sponsoring school segregation is far more difficult to prove in those States where segregation was not caused by State law. But this does not explain why, although there are at least 22 active or complete school desegregation cases outside the Southern and Border States, the United States is or has been a party to only five.*

---

*This does not include recent efforts to intervene in the Detroit, Mich., and other cases to argue for postponement of desegregation plans.

We recommend a policy designed to enforce constitutional requirements on a national basis, which should include appropriate intervention under Title IX of the Civil Rights Act by the Justice Department as party plaintiff in existing lawsuits. Where needed, funds for additional personnel should be requested from the Congress.

We note that the recently adopted Education Amendments of 1972 authorize Federal district courts in their discretion to award the payment of reasonable attorneys' fees and costs to successful plaintiffs in suits to enforce the 14th Amendment and the Civil Rights Act in the area of public education. We strongly believe that continued private litigation is an essential component of a successful national strategy. And we recommend that Federal Assistance be made available, so that payment of attorneys' fees does not deplete education budgets.

### 6. FULL FUNDING OF EMERGENCY SCHOOL AID ACT

On June 23, 1972, the President signed into law the Emergency School Aid Act, as part of the comprehensive Education Amendments of 1972. The Act, which replaces the temporary $75 million Emergency School Assistance Program established by special appropriation in the Fall of 1970, authorizes an annual expenditure of $2 billion to support programs and projects related to the achievement of equal educational opportunities.

The Act is designed to provide assistance to school districts for programs to support voluntary integration or integration under legal requirement. It provides assistance for pilot programs to improve academic achievement in reading and math within racially and economically segregated urban schools. It provides a new and innovative program of bilingual education, and support for the innovative use of education television. And it provides for the funding of community organizations, groups of concerned parents and other nonprofit organizations, for development and implementation of programs to encourage and support the desegregation process.

Because this bipartisan legislation implements many of this committee's basic recommendations, we are most disappointed that funding was not requested in time for the beginning of the present school year. We are also gravely concerned by reports that, although $230 million were appropriated by the Congress in October for the remainder of this school year, administrative delays in preparing program regulations may prevent even continued funding under the new Act of programs which received assistance for the first semester under the earlier Emergency School Aid Program.

We recommend:

- Continued funding of programs and projects, for both school districts and nonprofit organizations, which received assistance for the first semester of this year under the Emergency School Assistance Program. If assistance cannot properly be made available under the Act, additional appropriations for the original ESAP program should be immediately requested.
- Full funding of the new Emergency School Aid Act for the 1973–74 school year. If the request is contained in the President's January budget message, school districts will have ample time

to prepare for the implementation of programs next Fall. We note that the $2 billion authorized by the Act for the 1973–74 school year is identical with the President's original request for the current 1972–73 school year.

### 7. FUNDING FOR TRANSPORTATION

We urge the Department of HEW to respect the clear mandate of the Congress, which defeated proposals to prohibit expenditure of Federal funds for desegregation-related transportation, by making funds available to support reasonable transportation upon request of appropriate local officials.

Great hardship has been caused by administration refusal to permit use of funds for transportation under the special desegregation appropriation for the 1971–72 and 1972–73 school years. If funds for additional transportation are not supplied by Federal sources, they must come either from an increase in funds from State or local sources or, far more likely, a cutback in existing services. And the lack of an adequate number of buses, caused by inadequate resources, has forced districts to adopt double and even overlapping triple sessions, so that buses can make an increase number of runs. These hardships can and should be ended with financial assistance under the Emergency School Aid Act.

### 8. ACTION AGAINST DISCRIMINATORY TREATMENT OF TEACHERS AND ADMINISTRATORS

We recommend prompt and decisive action against discriminatory treatment of minority-group teachers in recently desegregated school systems. HEW statistics reveal the demotion or dismissal of over 4,200 minority-group teachers in five States during the 1971–72 school year alone. The victims of such discrimination in employment are not only the thousands of minority-group teachers who have been fired or demoted but their families also. Every student in a newly desegregated school system is taught a profound lesson when desegregation of schools results in maltreatment of qualified minority-group men and women. This lesson once learned can leave a lifetime's legacy of bitterness.

### 9. ACTION AGAINST "SECOND GENERATION" DISCRIMINATION

Similarly prompt and effective action must be taken to remedy discrimination against minority-group children within "desegregated" schools.

We recommend prompt publication of a memorandum, promised to the committee in June of 1970, establishing Federal policy under Title VI of the Civil Rights Act of 1964 with respect to "second-generation" discrimination. And we recommend that the Departments of HEW and Justice enter into cooperative arrangements which will assure compliance of school districts desegregating under court order as well as under Title VI plan—a policy which was promised to the committee in the Spring of 1970 and never implemented.

### 10. DENIAL OF TAX-EXEMPT STATUS TO "SEGREGATED ACADEMIES"

We recommend that firm steps be taken to enforce the Internal Revenue Service Policy of July 10, 1970 that IRS:

> . . . can no longer legally justify allowing tax-exempt status to private schools which practice racial discrimination nor can it treat gifts to such schools as charitable deductions for income tax purposes.

Although there are no precise statistics, Reese Cleghorn of the Southern Education Foundation told the committee that in the Fall of 1970 over 400,000 students attended racially segregated private schools, many of these established for the purpose of avoiding public school desegration. In addition to the threat posed to support for public education in some school districts, many of these "segregation academies" provide grossly inadequate educational opportunities to their own students.

The Supreme Court's affirmance of *Green* v. *Kennedy* 404 U.S. 997 (1971) firmly establishes the legal standard and tax-favored status may not be given to:

> . . . private schools operating on a racially discriminatory basis as an alternative to white students seeking to avoid desegregated schools.

Joint arrangements should be entered into between IRS and HEW under which HEW civil rights personnel who would conduct onsite visits to determine compliance of private schools.

In addition, we note with approval that the recently adopted Emergency School Aid Act requires school districts receiving assistance to take reasonable precautions to avoid transfer of property or services to "segregated academies".

## B. Toward Stable, Quality Integrated Schools

### 1. ECONOMIC INTEGRATION

We recommend that wherever possible desegregation plans avoid the establishment of schools with majority-disadvantaged student bodies.

It appears from the available evidence that school integration is most likely to result in achievement gains for educationally disadvantaged children where integration is along economic as well as racial or ethnic lines.

In addition, parents of relatively advantaged students often fear that desegregation may result in placing their children in schools with students from the poorest and most deprived backgrounds.

The legitimate concerns of more advantaged families, and the educational interests of disadvantaged children from all racial and ethnic backgrounds, can best be served by assigning students to integrated schools in which a majority of students are educationally advantaged. This principle will not necessarily reduce transportation. But the result will be increased educational opportunities for all students.

Local school districts, not the Federal courts or Federal agencies, bear primary responsibility for the design of school desegregation plans. They, as well as the Office of Education in rendering technical assistance and in administering the Emergency School Aid Act, should bear in mind that neither minority-group or nonminority-group children can be expected to receive academic benefits from assignment to a school in which a majority of students are educationally disadvantaged.

## 2. PARENT, STUDENT, AND COMMUNITY INVOLVEMENT

We recommend that school officials make every effort to involve a broad cross-section of the community in planning for integration, including students, teachers, parents, representatives of business and labor groups, and other interested community members.

Representative committees should be established to work with school officials in planning both changes in school assignment policies and changes in the educational program to accompany desegregation. An excellent guideline is provided by the Emergency School Aid Act. Under the Act, at least half the membership of committees established to participate in planning and implementation of applications for assistance must be from minority groups, and at least half must be parents, to assure that the legitimate concerns of these crucial groups are fully raised. Where more than one minority group is substantially represented in a community, however, effective representation may require that more than half of committee members be from minority groups.

In addition to committees, the planning process should include a series of open hearings, to make absolutely certain that all segments of the community have been given an opportunity for a frank exchange of views with school officials. Final adoption of a plan should be accompanied by extensive public information efforts, including neighborhood meetings at which school officials or members of advisory committees can meet informally with interested parents, students, and other community members.

By assuring that all segments of the community are fully involved in the development of plans, resistance can be minimized, the public support which is essential to the success of any desegregation program can be substantially increased, and desegregation plans themselves can be made more responsive to community needs.

## 3. INTEGRATED CLASSROOMS

The committee recommends that school districts avoid classroom segregation along racial, ethnic, or socioeconomic lines within desegregated schools wherever possible. Federal enforcement officials should take prompt action against discriminatory practices designed to avoid the 14th Amendment mandate within "desegregated" schools. And in administering the Emergency School Aid Act, the Office of Education should encourage applications which maximize classroom integration.

## 4. MUTUAL UNDERSTANDING AND RESPECT

The most important aspect of a successfully integrated school is a warm and supportive environment for children from all racial and economic backgrounds, based upon mutual respect and acceptance among students and faculty.

To encourage the development of supportive classroom environment, we recommend that implementation of plans for school integration be accompanied by:

*First*, integration of faculty and staff.

*Second*, in-service faculty training on a continuing basis, to encourage sensitivity to the needs of children from varying backgrounds.

*Third*, reduction of student/adult ratios through employing additional professional and paraprofessional staff, and through use of volunteer aides, to permit more individual attention to each child.

*Fourth*, review of course content and materials to assure accuracy, sensitivity, and relevance for all students.

The committee notes that Federal financial assistance to support these activities will be available under the recently adopted Emergency School Aid Act.

### 5. FAIR TREATMENT FOR LANGUAGE MINORITY CHILDREN

Desegregation plans should include provisions for services to meet the needs of Mexican American, Puerto Rican, Oriental American, Portuguese, Indian and other children with special language-related educational needs.

While sensitive, integrated education is particularly beneficial to such children because it provides the best opportunity to exercise English language skills, it is essential that special bilingual services be provided to help them develop proficiency in both English and the other language spoken at home.

We note with approval that 4 percent of funds under the Emergency School Aid Act, $40 million annually if the Act is fully funded, will be available to support bilingual education, in addition to the $35 million budgeted for bilingual education under Title VII of the Elementary and Secondary Education Act.

Where possible, bilingual education and a bicultural curriculum should be made available to all students in areas with concentrations of language minority families, since language-minority children provide an irreplaceable educational resource. Where limited resources or a limited number of adequately trained personnel prohibit provision of bilingual education for all students, particular care should be taken not to scatter bilingual children so thin through the school population that they cannot be provided with the services they need. In addition, school authorities should encourage families to make use of cultural opportunities available outside of school itself—such for example as ethnic heritage studies centers established under the recently adopted Ethnic Heritage Studies Act—on a release-time basis, and should encourage the development of such opportunities.

### 6. EARLY INTEGRATION

We recommend that local school officials, and the Office of Education in providing technical assistance and administering the Emergency School Aid Act, bear in mind the crucial importance of integration during the elementary grades.

It appears from the available research, discussed in Chapter 16, that desegregation is most likely to produce gains in educational achievement when it takes place early in the academic experience. In addition, we believe the chances for successful integration of secondary grades are highest where students have attended integrated elementary schools.

## C. Metropolitan Approaches

### 1. MULTIDISTRICT SCHOOL INTEGRATION

We recommend Federal financial support for voluntary multidistrict cooperative integration efforts. Many centercity school districts can easily achieve substantial desegregation within their own boundaries. For others this is difficult or impossible, either because the numbers and proportions of minority group and educationally disadvantaged children are great, or because geographical considerations render integration across school district lines more feasible mechanically than within-district integration. And support is available under the newly adopted Emergency School Aid Act, which reserves 5 percent of funds ($100 million over 2 years if fully funded), for voluntary metropolitan approaches, and makes another $670 million annually available to support general integration programs, including multidistrict approaches.

We also recommend that appropriate committees of the Congress consider special incentives and priority allocation under general education programs to encourage voluntary metropolitan planning for school integration.

### 2. THE EDUCATION PARK

We recommend Federal support for the construction of some model education parks. A park would serve perhaps 12,000 to 20,000 students from kindergarten through high school, on a campus where space can be made available for location of junior college and postsecondary vocational facilities. To avoid the creation of an unwieldy and remote bureaucracy, we recommend that parks be divided into "mini-schools" of fewer than 600 students.

Although the Emergency School Aid Act does authorize Federal assistance for establishment of education parks, it excludes kindergarten through grade 7 from its definition of "educational park." Because of the crucial importance of integration in early years, we recommend that assistance under the Act be made available only to communities which themselves intend to supply the elementary component of a comprehensive educational park; and we recommend the prompt revision of the statutory provision to permit Federal assistance for the establishment of education parks serving grades kindergarten through 12.

The concept of the education park has received wide support. Only if two or three are tried in practice will it be possible to determine whether they deserve broader support from parents, educators, and the Federal Government; and because of the substantial initial cost, even though long-term savings may be realized, local communities will be unable to experiment with education parks without Federal support.

### 3. INTEGRATION OF NONPUBLIC SCHOOLS

We recommend that Federal assistance be made available for the purpose of encouraging and supporting school integration efforts by nonpublic schools.

Large numbers of middle-class children living in central cities attend private schools. These schools are a potentially important resource for providing integrated education to innercity children; and many are already excellent integrated schools. Funds under the Emergency School Aid Act are available to encourage and support integration programs in private schools; we urge the Department of Health, Education, and Welfare to make use of this authority.

### 4. HOUSING OPPORTUNITIES

In many communities, school segregation is closely linked with housing segregation. Our 80 percent of all black metropolitan residents live in center cities, while more than 60 percent of white residents live in suburbs; and this segregation is increasing. And housing segregation not only causes segregated schools; lack of suburban housing bars low income families from suburban jobs and forces them to raise their children in the social conditions of the ghetto.

*First*, the committee recommends an active role by the Department of Housing and Urban Development in encouraging rational site selection for federally assisted housing—both to encourage development of low- and moderate-income housing opportunities outside areas of present concentration, and to assure that communities which accept low- and moderate-income housing are not overburdened.

*Second*, we recommend that the Departments of Justice and Housing and Urban Development exercise their responsibilities under Title VI of the Civil Rights Act of 1964 and the Fair Housing Act of 1968 to take action against zoning laws, other local ordinances and practices which restrict housing opportunities on the basis of race or national origin.

*Third*, we recommend vigorous implementation by Executive order, of Federal policy under which Federal agencies will obtain assurance of adequate housing opportunities for low- and moderate-income employees as a prerequisite to location or relocation of facilities.

In the absence of adoption of such a policy, the committee recommends adoption of legislation similar to S. 1282, the Government Facilities Location Act introduced in the last Congress, to accomplish these purposes.

*Fourth*, we recommend that relevant committees of the Senate and House consider legislation to establish incentives for voluntary adoption of metropolitan plans based on the "fair share" approach to allocation of federally subsidized housing; such plans should be encouraged to address the needs for increased middle-income housing opportunities within central cities, as well as to provide housing opportunities for low-income families outside the central city.

The committee recognizes, however, that suburban communities and other middle-income areas often have legitimate reasons for opposition to federally assisted housing. Action to increase the opportunities of low-income families must be accompanied by action to protect the legitimate interests of suburban and other middle-income communities.

*Fifth*, we recommend vigorous application of the "Project Selection Criteria" which became effective February 1, 1972 to prevent funding of subsidized housing which threatens to "tip" already integrated residential areas. We recommend immediate expansion of the scope of these regulations beyond their present concern with preventing resegregation by race and national origin to a broader concern with preventing concentration of low- and moderate-income housing, regardless of the race or national origin of its occupants.

*Sixth*, we recommend immediate funding of "Clause (c)" of the "Impact Aid" program under P.L. 81–874—which has gone without funds since its enactment in 1970—to compensate public schools for the extra costs of serving children from public housing, and for the concurrent loss of public housing property from the tax rolls.

We recommend enactment of legislation to provide similar support for welfare, law enforcement, health and other additional costs, as recommended by the President's Task Force on Urban Renewal.

We recommend payment of real estate taxes by federally subsidized public housing projects, as provided in Chapter 2, Section 6(d)(1) of the proposed Housing and Urban Development Act of 1972, which passed the Senate and was pending in House Committee at the close of the 92d Congress.

And we recommend exploration of federally guaranteed insurance to protect home values in communities accepting federally subsidized low- and moderate-income housing.

*Seventh*, the committee recommends that HUD require adequate attention to the design of low- and moderate-income housing, to assure that housing is compatible with surrounding residential areas. To avoid large low-income housing units which become "mini-ghettos", we recommend location of federally subsidized housing in small clusters and on a scatter-site basis in middle-income neighborhoods, and we recommend continued experimentation with housing allowances, which enable recipients to obtain existing rental housing on the open market.

The immediate cost of scatter-site housing, small multifamily units and housing allowances may be higher than for the construction of conventional public housing units. But the committee is convinced that the social benefits, in terms of school integration, reduced crime, increased access to jobs and more hopeful environment, can more than compensate for these increased costs.

# Part V

# Education of Language Minorities

## Chapter 20—The Plight of the Language-Minority Child

The American child whose first language is other than English suffers a double disadvantage. Like black and poor white children he may be isolated in a rural slum or urban ghetto where he was born and lives and goes to school. If he is poor, he probably attends a school with other poor children of the same racial or ethnic background, usually an older school with less qualified teachers and fewer resources.

But when he arrives at school he faces a special disadvantage, for his language and culture are different, and often neither is valued or understood by those who teach him and run his school. His language is considered alien, his culture unimportant, and his manner unusual. He is probably told he must learn in English, a language which may be alien to him or at least is seldom spoken at home. He enters a new world where many of the values his parents taught him are now rejected, tacitly if not explicitly. He is asked to change into something different. Sometimes he is even forbidden to speak his native language.

What happens to this child was described by many of our witnesses. Mr. Frank Negron, a New York City dropout, in an exchange with the chairman stated as well as anyone the rejection and alienation felt by the Puerto Rican child.

> Senator Mondale. You said that you spoke Spanish at home. Your first days in school, I gather, you were taught by white teachers in English?
>
> Mr. Negron. That's right . . . I tell you what happens. You feel like you do not even belong there . . . You try to explain to your mother you do have a problem in communication, but you still have to go to school. It is frightening and, believe me, it is really boring.
>
> Senator Mondale. You did not receive any bilingual education or training at all in your earlier years at school; is that correct?
>
> Mr. Negron. One hour a day in elementary school.
>
> Senator Mondale. In your first year you did get some training in English; is that right?
>
> Mr. Negron. No. It started when I finally got to the second grade.

Senator Mondale. The first year you had no assistance whatsoever?

Mr. Negron. None.

Senator Mondale. Would you say that your language problem prevented you from learning much of anything?

Mr. Negron. I didn't learn my ABC's until I was in the third grade and I did not even know that too well.

Senator Mondale. Was this true of most of your classmates?

Mr. Negron. That's right.

Senator Mondale. What did you do then? You have someone speaking to you in a foreign tongue and you don't understand it. What do you do? Just sit there?

Mr. Negron. Try to develop an interest in something else. In my case I developed an interest in drawing and the teacher would always have me in the back of the room keeping me busy so I would not interfere with the process of education of the kids who could learn. . . .

* * * * * * *

. . . Otherwise I would be very uncooperative. I would interfere with any of the educational process in the class and I would stop the teacher from teaching. The teacher would either hit me on the head or send me to the principal's office. I would be sanctioned in some way.*

Unable to conform to his new world, the language-minority child is often labeled and stamped as inferior. His experiences fit a pattern which the committee heard repeated by witnesses relative to both their own lives and the experiences of others. The language-minority student is tested; the test he takes was designed for middle-class, English-speaking "Anglo" children; he fails or does poorly; he is then tracked into a class with slow learners; he sees himself as inferior; he becomes embarrassed about his culture and heritage, for there is little in his curriculum or his textbooks about his heroes or the history of his people, except perhaps descriptions that ridicule or otherwise distort his heritage; his world at home may be excluded from his world at school. These were the experiences of two of our witnesses, among others, who were assigned to classes for the mentally retarded in elementary school. They are among the few who made it. Uvaldo Palomares, whose testimony is quoted in Chapter 9, went to school from the prune fields of California. He is now a clinical psychologist with a doctorate in education from the University of California. Armando Martinez, Director of "Puente" in Boston, Mass., has a masters degree from Harvard and is studying for his doctorate. He is one of two Puerto Ricans out of 150,000 in Massachusetts who hold masters degrees. He was in a class for the mentally retarded until he was 13 years old.

These are two who made it. Hundreds of thousands of others don't—language minority children whose heritage is Spanish, Mexican, Puerto Rican, Portuguese, Oriental, American Indian or whose forbears may be from any of a large number of other foreign lands. The Depart-

---

*Hearings of the U.S. Senate Select Committee on Equal Educational Opportunity, Part 8—*Equal Educational Opportunity for Puerto Rican Children*, Nov. 24, 1970.

ment of Health, Education, and Welfare has estimated that there are 5 million school-age children in the United States who have at least some need for special language training programs. The 1970 HEW survey of public elementary and secondary schools provides some indication of the magnitude of the language minority education problem. Of 9.4 million minority-group public school children in the United States, 2.3 million are Spanish-surnamed, 209,000 are of Oriental heritage, and 197,000 are American Indian. Add to these many of the 416,000 children who are classified as "other minority" by the census, and approximately 3 million or 6 percent of our public schoolchildren are from language-minority groups. We have described the isolation of these children in Chapter 7—isolation which is no less detrimental, often no less the result of officially imposed discrimination than that of black children. In Chapter 9 we have related how language-minority as well as racial minority and poor children are the victims of discriminatory and mindless school practices including the misuse of tracking and testing and other forms of treatment that label them as failures. Chapter 11 describes the results of these inequalities: Low achievement and fewer years in school.

What these conditions add up to is a conscious or unconscious policy of linguistic and cultural exclusion and alienation.

The problem begins with the rejection of the child's language. It is reflected in the rejection of his culture and heritage of which his language is an extension. And it often results in his and his parents effective exclusion from the processes of education.

It is the conclusion of this committee that some of the most dramatic, wholesale failures of our public school systems occur among members of language minorities. Some examples of this failure were presented in testimony before the committee:

- In Boston, 62 percent of the Puerto Rican adults are illiterate in both English and Spanish.
- In 87 New York City schools with Puerto Rican majorities, 85 percent are below grade level in reading and a third are 2 years below grade level.
- In Chicago, Puerto Rican public school children are an average of 4 years behind in reading.
- Spanish-surnamed students in California leave the 12th grade 3½ years behind and in Illinois, 5 years behind.
- Texas describes 40 percent of its Spanish-speaking citizens as functional illiterates.

Perhaps even more devastating was the testimony we heard about the school dropout rates of language-minority children:

- In 1969 between 3,000 and 5,000 Spanish-speaking school-age children in Boston were not in school.
- Between 1965 and 1969, four out of Boston's estimated 7,000 Puerto Rican schoolchildren graduated from high school. In 1970, three graduated from Boston's public schools, four from parochial school.
- Philadelphia's Puerto Rican dropout rate is 70 percent.

- In Chicago, 60 percent of all Puerto Rican students drop out before they finish high school. 18,000 Puerto Ricans are enrolled in the public school system. Only 4,000 are in high schools.
- In Newark, N.J., out of 7,800 Puerto Rican students, 96 are in the 12th grade.
- In 1970 about 15 to 20 percent of all Mexican-American school-age children were not in any school at any time.
- The average Chicano child in the Southwest drops out of school by the 7th year.
- In Texas, the average Anglo over 25 years old has 12 years of schooling, the average black nearly 9 and the average Chicano 6.7.
- According to the U.S. Commission on Civil Rights, Survey on Mexican-American Education in 1969, 14 percent of Texas' Chicanos drop out of school before completing the 8th grade; 47 percent before high school graduation.

# Chapter 21—Bilingual and Bicultural Education

## A. The Problem and the Need

Unfortunately, all too often fluency in a foreign language is looked upon by public school systems as a handicap for the child who is deficient in his ability to communicate in English. While detailed surveys have not been undertaken for language minority groups, the U.S. Bureau of the Census estimates that of the 10 million Spanish language or Spanish-surnamed Americans in the United States, less than half usually speak English at home. In a survey conducted by the U.S. Commission on Civil Rights in 1969 it was estimated that nearly half the Mexican-American first graders in Arizona, California, Colorado, New Mexico, and Texas are deficient in English when they arrive at school. The survey also showed that the lower the socioeconomic status of the student and the higher the proportion of Mexican-American students in the school, the less likely it is that the Mexican-American child in the Southwest is proficient in English. Nor is the problem limited to Mexican-American children. In New York City, over 37,000 Puerto Rican students have been classified as having at least moderate language problems. Nevertheless, most of these children are given the standardized reading and achievement tests in English.

As the Commission stated in its May 1972 report on "The Excluded Student: Educational Practices Affecting Mexican Americans in the Southwest:"

> In poor and segregated barrio schools, only 30 percent of the Mexican-American children speak English as well as Anglos. In the contrast, in high socioeconomic schools where Mexican-American children are in the minority, more than 80 percent possess English in skills equal to that of Anglos.

Even greater proportions of American Indian children are deficient in English. In its report, "Indian Education: A National Tragedy—A National Challenge," the Senate Special Subcommittee on Indian Education reported that there are nearly 300 Indian languages in use today in the United States. The committee found that more than half our Indian youths between the ages of 6 and 18 use their native language at home and that two-thirds of Indian children entering Federal BIA schools have little or no skill in English.

Similarly, the Civil Rights Commission found in 1970 that almost three-fourths of the Puerto Rican population of New York City speaks Spanish at home, and more than one in every three Puerto Rican pupils (38.7 percent) had serious language problems.

The language minority child not only arrives at school with this handicap, he is immediately subjected to practices and policies and even legal prohibitions which attempt to keep him from communicating in his native language. In fact, until recently, many States had legal prohibitions forbidding teaching in public schools in any language other than English. California, for example, with nearly a million students whose first language is other than English, had such a law in effect until 1967. Texas and Arizona had similar laws in effect until 1969. As recently as October 1970, according to the Civil Rights Commission, a Mexican-American teacher in Texas was indicted under the Texas Penal Code for teaching a high school history class in Spanish.

Even in the absence of official State laws prohibiting foreign languages in schools many school districts prohibit or discourage the speaking of foreign languages. Of 5,800 schools in the Southwestern States surveyed by the Civil Rights Commission, a third admitted that use of the Spanish language was discouraged in their classrooms while 15 percent said they discouraged children from speaking Spanish anywhere on school premises. In Texas this "no Spanish" policy was in effect in classrooms in two-thirds and on school grounds in one-third of the schools surveyed.

It is particularly ironic that the Civil Rights Commission found that the more Mexican Americans there were in a school district the more likely it was that the district refused to recognize or prohibited Spanish from being spoken in the classroom.

These rules are enforced, often rigidly, through various forms of punishment: Detention after school hours, the payment of a few pennies in fines for each word of Spanish spoken, suspension from school, and even sometimes corporal punishment.

The discriminatory effects of rules and practices prohibiting the child's native language are compounded by his placement in classes for slow learners.

Mexican American and other language minority children are frequently placed in classes for the "educable mentally retarded" (EMR) in numbers that are far out of proportion to their representation in the school population as a whole.

In a recent California case contesting the disproportionate placement of Mexican-American children in EMR classes, *Diana* v. *State Board of Education*, plaintiffs charged that because of inadequate and discriminatory testing and evaluation, the percentage of Mexican-American children in EMR classes was twice their proportion in the school district. Studies by the California State Department of Education corroborated this inequity. In 1966–67, out of 85,000 children in EMR classes, children with Spanish surnames comprised 26 percent while they only accounted for 13 percent of the total school population. Other studies have estimated overrepresentation of Mexican-American children in special classes to be four to five times the expected number.

As a result of *Diana* and other litigation seeking to redress the discriminatory treatment of language minority children, the California legislature enacted legislation to assure the fair treatment of language minority children and provide funds for the development of culturally sensitive tests. The legislation requires testing in the home language of the child; the use of other measures than IQ tests, such as adaptive behavior tests; consideration of the home environment of the child; consultation with parents and a restriction of the number of language minority children placed in EMR classes to within 15 percent of the proportion of such children in the district as a whole.

Other States are also beginning to recognize the deficiencies in their bilingual education programs. For example, to help Puerto Rican and other language minority children, Massachusetts law now holds that transitional bilingual education must be offered in every school with 20 or more students with limited English.

The shortage of trained personnel such as bilingual psychologists who are sensitive to the individual needs of language minority children, the lack of tests which are relevant to the varied environments in which these children live, and the absence of bilingual programs as alternatives to special classes for mentally retarded children are further exacerbated by the existence of State laws and regulations which provide financial incentives to school districts that place children in EMR classes.

Edward Moreno, professor of Mexican-American Studies at San Fernando Valley State College in California, described to the committee how these incentives work:

> In California, there are extra funds above the normal amount of money allocated for children, for the EMR children, so you get your normal stipend, and you get X number of dollars more, so it is very convenient to corral blacks, whites and Mexicans and put them in EMR classes. You don't have to tell anybody what the kids are doing. You can jazz it up, and make it look like a pilot program.*

Twenty-six States allocate funds for special education on a classroom unit or per pupil basis. Ten of these States provide supplemental funds above the average per pupil expenditures for each pupil requiring special education. The financial incentives are particularly strong in those 16 States which allocate special education funds on a per unit basis. The majority of these States stipulate a minimum class size for eligibility for State funds with proportionately lower funding for classes below the minimum size. Some States, such as Kansas and Oklahoma, will not provide any supplemental help to school districts if special classes are less than the minimum size.

The per unit method of funding serves not only to place a premium on children who can be classified as mentally retarded in order to qualify for funds for special classes, but restricts alternatives to the self-contained classroom.

These problems can be avoided under State regulations such as those adopted in Minnesota, Tennessee, and Alabama which provide more flexible arrangements for funding so that supplemental assistance to mentally handicapped children is directed toward regular classroom situations. Regulations of this sort, along with guarantees of due process and appropriate testing and evaluation, can provide an opportunity for those who require special services to receive those services while at the same time preventing the improper and frequently harmful labeling of minority children.

Language is more than a means of communication. It is the embodiment of one's culture and heritage. It is through his language that a child communicates his values, his habits and the customs that he has learned from his family. The child who is told that he can no longer communicate in the only language he knows and that he must com-

---

*Hearings of the U.S. Senate Select Committee on Equal Educational Opportunity, Part 4, *Mexican-American Education*.

municate only in English at school often concludes that his culture is worthless as well. But the rejection of the minority child's language is also accompanied by the exclusion of his culture from the school curriculum. Most schools offer neither Spanish-surnamed, Indian, Oriental or other foreign language children an opportunity to learn about their heritage or folklore. Their textbooks either ignore the history of their people or present a distorted picture based on false stereotypes. As Marcos de Leon, past President of the Association of Mexican-American Educators, stated in 1968:

> Textbook after textbook supports the notion that the early settlers of the Southwest—Spanish and Indian and mixed-blood pioneers who came from Mexico, as well as Indians native to the region—wandered around in confusion until the Anglo-Saxon, with his superior wisdom and clearer vision vaulted the Rocky Mountains and brought order out of chaos.

At its hearings in San Francisco at which witnesses from the Chinese community testified, the committee heard the following description of the way school textbooks and other cultural materials depict the Chinese people:

> The Chinese have been given no fair treatment in school textbooks and in curriculum in general. Looking now at the school curriculum, it is ironic to note that it has so little to do with one of the most important races and cultures of the world . . . Our school curriculum continues to ignore the Chinese and their contribution to world civilization, denying, therefore, the American students the right to know more about China and her people and culture.
>
> In textbooks, almost without exception, the Chinese are depicted variously as vicious, cruel, stupid, sneaky, untrustworthy, inscrutable, filthy, etc. These depictions came directly from historical attitude and treatment of the Chinese in California. Unfortunately, little or nothing is being done to remove these obviously racist portrayals of the Chinese.

The witness, L. Ling Chi Wang, Director of the Youth Service Center in San Francisco's Chinatown, described the effects of these portrayals:

> The effects of these misconceptions of the Chinese are tremendous and quite detrimental to the welfare of the Chinese people in the United States. For example, many of our youngsters are brought up to be ashamed of their own people and to look down upon anything Chinese. They are taught exclusively white, Anglo-Saxon, middle-class values in schools . . . As a result, many have lost their self-respect and have developed a strong sense of inferiority complex.
>
> Others try to lose their Chinese identity and tongue by rebeling against their parents and refusing to have anything to do with their parents . . .
>
> Equally destructive are the effects of these racist depictions on fellow students and the general public. Oftentimes, Chinese become victims of public hostility and mistrust. We are denied equal employment and educational opportunity; we are prevented access to certain schools, recreational facilities and neighborhoods.

The Civil Rights Commission's survey of Mexican-American education found that only 4.3 percent of the elementary schools and 7.3 percent of the secondary schools in the Southwest offered Mexican-American history as part of their curriculum. And even these limited offerings were available to only 1.3 percent of the elementary school students and 0.6 percent of the secondary students in the States.

Witnesses before this and other committees also described history texts with degrading characterizations of Hispanic, Oriental, and American Indian peoples. Others described school censorship practices which deprive language minority children of the opportunity for exposure to the conditions of their people in America today.

Will Antell of the Minnesota Department of Education in testimony before the Indian Education Subcommittee described a standard textbook used until recently in public schools attended by American Indian children:

> One of the standard textbooks in Minnesota has been Marion Antoinette Ford's book *Star of the North* . . . We find it historically inaccurate and we find it very distasteful and offensive to the American Indian, Minnesota Indian, particularly. It cites them constantly as lazy, as doing a lot of drinking, of massacring white people, on the warpath, and in one particular section as I recall it, they referred to the American Indian male, saying the only work that he ever did was to stamp on wild rice during the wild rice season.

The Indian Education Subcommittee reported its findings on curriculum in public schools in November 1969:

> Public schools educating Indians rarely include coursework which recognizes Indian history, culture or language, and often use materials and approaches which are derogatory toward Indians.
>
> A. Public schools in many States use history and social studies textbooks which ignore the Indian's role in history or grossly distort that role.
>
> B. The primary result of the manner Indians are treated in the history textbooks in use today is propagation of inaccurate stereotypes.
>
> C. Most public schools do not take into consideration the language difficulties of many Indian students.
>
> D. There is a definite lack of bilingual and bicultural materials in schools educating Indians.

Teachers, principals and other school administrators sometimes deliberately discriminate against children who speak foreign languages, but usually these exclusionary practices are the result simply of insensitivity to the needs of children from different cultures. Educators often view it as the school's function, in the words of D. W. Brogan, "to teach Americanism, meaning not merely the political and patriotic dogma, but the habits necessary to American life—a common language, common tolerances, a common political and national faith."* Even those who recognize the importance of bilingualism justify it in terms such as those used by a school principal in answer to a questionnaire by the Civil Rights Commission:

---

*Brogan, D. W., *The American Character*. New York: Alfred A. Knopf, 1950, pp. 135–36.

Our school population is predominantly Latin American—97 percent. We try to discourage the use of Spanish on the playground, in the halls, and in the classrooms. We feel that the reason so many of our pupils are reading 2 to 3 years below grade level is because their English vocabulary is so limited . . . in our particular situation we must emphasize the correct usage of English. All of our textbooks are in English, all the testing is in English, and all job applications are also in English. We do a lot of counseling regarding the importance of learning correct English. We stress the fact that practice makes perfect—that English is a very difficult language to master. Our pupils speak Spanish at home, at dances, on the playground, at athletic events, and at other places they may congregate. We feel the least they can do is try to speak English at school as much as they possibly can. . . .

The basic problem with such justifications is that it assumes that it is the child who must change and conform, rather than the school that should adapt to the child and his cultural background and needs. As Dr. Tomas P. Carter of the University of Texas testified:

The school must adapt to the local cultural milieu; curriculums must reflect the real cultural content, not idealized middle-class culture. Children must learn to cope with the real society, not necessarily acquire idealized middle-class culture and norms—norms that the school imposes. The school must eliminate practices that are detrimental to individuals or groups of children. It must substitute positive, affirmative practices for present, negative ones.

In fact, sensitive bilingual, bicultural education should result in earlier comprehension of the English language and earlier learning of basic skills. A child who does not understand English adequately simply cannot learn when taught only in English.

It is clearly important that American children become proficient in the English language, but schools ought to take advantage of the minority child's language and culture rather than suppress it. To inject a new culture and language into the young child's environment at the age of 6 or 7 when he is learning to communicate and use language skills at an accelerated rate is to create a psychological conflict that may cause irreparable damage to the child. Dr. Manuel Ramirez, testifying before the United States Civil Rights Commission in 1968, told what happens to the child who is faced with conflicting cultures and asked to suppress his own:

My research has identified two different kinds of conflict. The first type arises as a result of the fact that the Mexican American is led to believe that he cannot be identified with two cultures at the same time. There is one message that is given by his parents, his relatives, and other Mexican-American students, who tell him that if he rejects Mexican-American culture and identifies with the Anglo culture, he may be considered a traitor to his ethnic group. . . .

The other message comes from teachers, employers, and Anglo friends, who tell him that if he doesn't reject the Mexican-American culture, he will be unable to reap the educational benefits that are in the Anglo culture.

> The second type is really a series of conflicts which come about because the Mexican-American student is bringing with him a series of behaviors, perceptions, methods of viewing the world, of doing things . . . and this conflicts with the value system of the Anglo middle class.

What is needed instead of these conflicting messages, is to develop the child's proficiency in communicative skills first through instruction in his own language.

Dr. Armando Martinez, Director of "Puente" in Boston, Mass., described to the committee the need for this approach.

> Children between five and seven use language at an accelerated rate for purpose of problem solving. To switch a child to a second language without first developing cognitive skills in the mother tongue can lead to what is called a non-lingual, a premature bilingual, whose function in both languages develops only in limited ways . . .
>
> To think that a non-English speaking child can learn to read and write in a language that he cannot speak is totally unrealistic and irrational. To continue forcing on our children the triple disadvantage of having to learn to speak English—a period of 2 to 3 years—before learning to read or write, forcing on them the frustrations of not understanding the language spoken around them, and leaving them only with nonverbal clues for communcation, is unjust. The result of this practice kills whatever motivation the child brings to the classroom, and breeds in him a strong feeling of inadequacy . . .*

### B. Present Programs

In recent years, many school systems have begun to recognize the tragic failure to provide a decent education for language minority children. Every witness before the committee who addressed the needs of these children stated that bilingual, bicultural education is absolutely essential to the successful school performance of chidren whose English speaking ability is limited. It is important as well to those children who may speak English adequately, but who come from families or live in communities where the dominant language is other than English.

Having limited resources of their own, States and school districts have relied principally upon two Federal programs to try to meet the needs of language-minority students: Title VII of the Elementary and Secondary Education Act, known as the Bilingual Education Act, and the "English as a Second Language" (ESL) program funded under Title I of ESEA.

Neither of these programs has been funded at a level which is adequate to even begin to meet the needs of language-minority children. While the Department of Health, Education, and Welfare is unable to supply the number of students participating in ESL programs, as of October 1972, only 109,000 children were being served by programs funded under the Bilingual Education Act. This compares with an

---

***Hearings of the U.S. Senate Select Committee on Equal Educational Opportunity, Part 8, *Equal Educational Opportunity for Puerto Rican Children*, Nov. 23, 1970.**

HEW estimate that over 5 million language-minority schoolchildren in the United States have at least some need for bilingual language training. The inadequacy of these programs was illustrated by figures supplied to the committee at its San Francisco hearing in March 1971. San Francisco has the largest concentration of Chinese-American students in the country. In 1969 the San Francisco school district conducted a survey which showed that 2,856, or 17 percent, of Chinese-American students needed special English language instruction; 1,539, or 54 percent, were at the elementary school level; 976 were at the junior high school level and 341 were in senior high. Forty-two percent of these elementary students received no special instruction in English and no bilingual education. That was true of 54 percent at the junior high and 22 percent at the senior high level. But even those who were receiving instruction in English received, at most, less than an hour's special training each school day. Similarly, a recent study of New York City reports that only 4,418 of that school system's 118,000 non-English speaking Spanish-surnamed students receive any kind of bilingual instruction. And in 1969, the Indian Education Subcommittee found that of the $7.5 million then appropriated for Title VII programs, only $306,000 was spent on bilingual programs benefiting 773 American Indian Children.

### 1. ENGLISH AS A SECOND LANGUAGE

ESL programs do not adequately serve the needs of language-minority children, for they cannot be described as either bilingual or bicultural education. The ESL program is designed only to teach English language skills on a part-time basis for a limited number of hours. Its specific objective is to turn language-minority students into confident speakers in the English language. The drawbacks of the ESL program were described at the committee's San Francisco hearings by L. Ling Chi Wang:

> . . . I strongly object to the use of ESL as an end in itself. I am referring specifically to the exclusive use of ESL in such a way that the native language, culture and knowledge of these children are systematically suppressed and down-graded. . . . Exclusive use of the ESL method entertains no consideration of the children's native intelligence, provides no respect for their native language and culture and ignores and negates everything they know in their native language. Inadvertently, students are humiliated and abused. I am fearful that we are doing injustice to our Chinese- and Spanish-speaking children and I regret that, by ignoring and suppressing the Chinese language and culture, we are depriving American students of one of the richest cultural heritages brought to this country by immigrant children.*

While no reliable national estimates are available indicating the number of children participating in the ESL programs, the Civil Rights Commission survey of the Southwestern States, Arizona, Cali-

***Ibid.*, Part 9A, *San Francisco and Berkeley, California*, Mar. 5, 1971.*

fornia, Colorado, New Mexico, and Texas, shows that an estimated 5.5 percent of the Mexican-American students in these States are receiving some ESL instruction with those in Texas having the highest enrollment in such programs.

While we believe it is important that language-minority children become proficient in English, we do not recommend the expansion of the ESL program as it is our judgment that ESL is an inadequate approach to dealing with the educational problems of language-minority children. We believe funds would be much better spent on bilingual, bicultural programs.

### 2. TITLE VII

While the Civil Rights Commission found in their 1969 survey that 5.5 percent of the Mexican Americans in the Southwest were enrolled in ESL programs, only 2.7 percent were enrolled in bilingual education programs under Title VII of ESEA. In terms of the needs of language-minority children. Title VII has been starved for funds. In the first year of the program's operation, fiscal year 1969, Congress appropriated only $7.5 million despite an authorization of $30 million. During the past year, 1972, $35 million was appropriated out of an authorized $100 million. For the present year, congressional efforts to increase Title VII funding to $60 million died with the veto of the Labor-HEW Appropriations Bill. Of the estimated 109,000 children presently served under Title VII, approximately 30 percent are not language-minority children. In terms of per pupil expenditures bilingual education assistance is a significant addition to the resources available for education. On the average, Title VII provided $321 per pupil served over and above State and local per pupil costs. But this average does not reflect the range of per pupil expenditures which, for fiscal year 1970, the Civil Rights Commission found to be as low as $271 in Texas and as high as $1,110 in Colorado.

Further illustrating the inadequacy, at least in quantitative terms, of Title VII programs is the fact that only 6.5 percent of the schools in the Southwestern States surveyed by the Civil Rights Commission had any sort of bilingual education program. In 1970 in these States there were well over a million Mexican-American students in school districts with 10 percent or more Mexican-American enrollment. Yet only 29,000 Mexican-American pupils and approximately 10,000 pupils from other ethnic groups participated in bilingual education classes.

What these statistics demonstrate is that the levels of participation and the resources available for Title VII are totally inadequate to meet the needs of this Nation's language-minority students.

Moreover, the funds that have been spent have not been distributed equitably. Illinois, which has 75,000 Spanish-speaking schoolchildren (3.6 percent of the country's total) received only $220,000 of Title VII funds during fiscal year 1971 (1 percent of the funds). This amounted to $2.90 for each Spanish-speaking student. New York, with 315,000 students, received $8,720,000 or $7.70 per Spanish-speaking student. The top 10 States, with nearly 700,000 Spanish-speaking students received between $10.17 and $41.55 per student.

### 3. LAW ENFORCEMENT

Section 601 of the Civil Rights Act of 1964 provides:

> No person in the United States shall, on the ground of race, color, or national origin, be excluded from participation in, be denied the benefits of, or be subjected to discrimination under any program or activity receiving Federal financial assistance.

Acting under his authority to interpret and enforce this section, J. Stanley Pottinger, Director of the Office for Civil Rights in HEW, issued a memorandum on May 25, 1970, to school districts enrolling more than 5 percent national origin minority-group children. The purpose of this memorandum was to define the obligations of school districts with relation to their treatment of language-minority children. In principle, the Pottinger memo said:

> (1) Where inability to speak and understand the English language excludes national origin-minority group children from effective participation in the educational program offered by a school district, the district must take affirmative steps to rectify the language deficiency in order to open its instructional program to these students.
>
> (2) School districts must not assign national origin-minority group students to classes for the mentally retarded on the basis of criteria which essentially measure or evaluate English language skills; nor may school districts deny national origin-minority group children access to college preparatory courses on a basis directly related to the failure of the school system to inculcate English language skills.
>
> (3) Any ability grouping or tracking system employed by the school system to deal with the special language skill needs of national origin-minority group children must be designed to meet such language skill needs as soon as possible and must not operate as an educational dead end or permanent track.
>
> (4) School districts have the responsibility to adequately notify national origin-minority group parents of school activities which are called to the attention of other parents. Such notice in order to be adequate may have to be provided in a language other than English.

The United States District Court for the Eastern District of Texas went a step further in August 1971, in the case of *U.S.* v. *Texas* (San Felipe—Del Rio ISD) ruling that the denial of bilingual services to Spanish-speaking children violates the equal protection clause of the 14th Amendment to the Constitution.

We believe the legal result arrived at by the court comports with sound educational policy. While enforcement of policy announced in the Pottinger memorandum has up to now been minimal, the committee is encouraged by the announcement from the Department of Health, Education, and Welfare that it has undertaken a major investigation of denials of equal educational opportunities to Spanish-speaking children in the New York City schools. We recommend increased funding for the Office of Civil Rights in HEW to permit more diligent efforts to conduct similar investigations in other districts throughout the country where language-minority children are suffering severe educational deprivation, as well as more diligent enforcement of its other responsibilities under Title VI of the Civil Rights Act of 1964.

## C. Recommendations

The U.S. Office of Education defines bilingual education in the following terms:

> Bilingual education is the use of two languages, one of which is English, as mediums of instruction for the same pupil population in a well-organized program which encompasses part or all of the curriculum and includes the study of the history and culture associated with the mother tongue. A complete program develops and maintains the children's self-esteem and a legitimate pride in both cultures.

Based on our studies and the testimony of witnesses before the committee we would add four qualifications to this definition:

*First*, children whose first language is other than English should begin to learn basic skills in their language while developing skills in English.

*Second*, language minorities themselves must be directly involved in both the development and implementation of bilingual education programs and teaching materials. More than that, they must become involved in the educational process. Without their direct and active participation we do not believe it likely that their language and culture will become an accepted, successful part of education.

*Third*, the education professions must recruit more members of language-minority groups and, through preservice and in-service training, assure an adequate supply of teachers and school administrators who are able to meet the needs of language-minority children. It is also believed that parents and students can be very successfully used as teachers' aides and tutors.

*Fourth*, culturally sensitive, bilingual instructional materials must be developed by specialists who are members of the language-minority groups being taught and used in the classroom.

### 1. Community Participation

In June 1972 the Congress passed the Emergency School Aid Act of 1972. Of the $2 billion authorized under that Act $80 million is set aside for programs "to meet the needs of minority-group children who are from an environment in which a dominant language is other than English and who, because of language barriers and cultural differences do not have equality of educational opportunity."

This program will supplement Title VII of ESEA, but it has several new features which we believe are essential to the development and implementation of effective bilingual and bicultural education.

*First*, to be eligible to receive a grant, a school district must establish a community committee which will fully participate in both the development and implementation of the program.

*Second*, private, nonprofit organizations may receive grants to originate bilingual and bicultural education curricula which will develop reading, writing and speaking skills in both English and the mother tongue of language-minority children. In addition, these curricula must be designed to develop an understanding of the history and cultural backgrounds of language-minority groups on the part of both language-minority and English-speaking children. To be eligible, the private nonprofit agency must establish a policy board which is representative of the minority and language groups involved.

Under these provisions both the policy board of the private curriculum development agency and school district community committee must be representative of parents, school officials, teachers, and other citizens. At least half the members must be parents and at least half members of language-minority groups.

We believe these provisions for private nonprofit organization curriculum development and for the establishment of community committees are among the most constructive and promising provisions that the Congress has adopted in Federal education legislation. We recommend that Title VII be amended to include the same requirements and that even in the absence of such amendments the Office of Education by regulation make these provisions applicable to Title VII programs.

The effective participation of language-minority groups, including parents, students, and other community representatives, is the cornerstone of any effective effort to deal with the problems of language-minority children. All too often educational decisions are made about language-minority and other disadvantaged children without the necessary consultation with parents and other community representatives. In some school districts, school officials are openly hostile to language-minority groups.

It is clear from all the testimony we have heard—from the educators, students, and other observers from both minority and nonminority groups—that unless ways can be found to involve minority groups in their own education and in their own schools, for them public education will remain a closed system and their lives will remain a series of lost opportunities.

But it is not enough that parents and students participate with teachers and school officials in their own schools. Community groups and private nonprofit organizations must all become involved in the development and implementation of new curricula and new programs and services to supplement formal public education for language-minority children. Many organizations in communities throughout the country are now providing counseling and tutoring services, English language instruction, courses in the history and the culture of language-minority groups, and other vitally needed educational services. These groups have often pointed the way for public school systems toward innovative policies and practices which will make public schools more responsive to the needs of language-minority children.

Several witnesses felt that only through the development of parallel schools outside the regular public education system would language-minority children receive a relevant education. While we do not reject such proposals, we believe the best path to educational reform is through change within the public schools themselves. Outside groups can play a vital role in this process. The Federal Government should encourage community groups to provide supplemental education programs and provide the funds to enable community groups to work with the school systems so that schools and the communities they serve can work together for educational reform.

### 2. THE NEED FOR BILINGUAL EDUCATIONAL PERSONNEL

The effectiveness of any bilingual education effort depends largely on the availability of teachers, principals, counselors, and other educational personnel who are capable of meeting the needs of language-minority children. Only if educators are sensitive to the needs of these children, understand and respect the language they speak and the culture and heritage of which they are proud, will education be a successful experience for minority-group children whose first language is not English.

There is presently a totally inadequate supply of trained teachers and other school personnel who are either themselves members of language-minority groups or are adequately trained to meet the need for bilingual education.

In New York, for example, there are 250,000 Puerto Rican children in the public schools—21 percent of the total school enrollment. At the same time, the school systems of New York employ only 495 professional educators of Puerto Rican background—a fraction of 1 percent of the school staff. In 1969, the San Francisco school system employed only 29 full-time and 15 part-time teachers to meet the special instructional needs of 2,856 non-English speaking Chinese students in that school system.

The Civil Rights Commission in its 1969 survey of Mexican-American education in the Southwest, found that less than 1 percent of the teachers in the Southwestern States participated in bilingual education programs. Moreover, most of those who did teach bilingual education had less than 6 semester hours of bilingual education training.

A 1970 HEW study of the first 76 bilingual education projects funded under Title VII showed that for those projects teachers received only a brief orientation session before the beginning of the school year. The study concluded that many teachers are just not adequately prepared to teach in bilingual education programs.

There are a number of reasons for this lack of adequate personnel for bilingual education.

*First*, the recruitment and training of bilingual teachers and administrative personnel has been largely neglected by our public school systems and by teacher education institutions.

*Second*, there has been neither an adequate commitment nor sufficient resources for the recruiting and training of bilingual teacher aides and paraprofessionals for minority groups.

*Third*, State legal requirements which are designed to set minimum standards of the employment of educational personnel often operate to discriminate against language-minority educators.

In Chapter 24, we have set forth our recommendations for more effective preservice and in-service training of teachers so that they may be adequately prepared to cope with needs of children from different backgrounds. These recommendations are particularly applicable to the recruitment and education of teachers who can meet the needs of language-minority children. Teacher training institutions in this country, particularly those in regions of the Nation containing substantial numbers of language-minority citizens, must include in their curricula, programs designed to acquaint prospective teachers with culture and heritage of language-minority children. Teachers should be encouraged to concentrate in this vital field. In addition a major effort should be undertaken by teacher training institutions to recruit members of language-minority groups.

There must also be intensive and well-planned in-service training programs for those now in the teaching profession who are employed by school systems with large numbers of language-minority children. These programs should be designed to make teachers aware of the cultural heritage and history of language-minority children. Teachers should be encouraged to attend in-service summer institutes such as those that were previously funded under the National Defense Education Act in 1964. These institutes can provide an effective and invaluable experience and improve teaching effectiveness for those teachers who have language-minority students in their classes.

The need for the training and recruitment of professional educators to meet the needs of language-minority students applies also to school administrators. In many school systems school principals, superintendents and other officials are unable to communicate effectively with language-minority students or their parents. Both preservice and in-service training for school administrators as well as teachers can be an important step in establishing a relationship of respect and confidence between the education profession and its clients.

Committee witnesses also emphasized the need for personnel in the counseling field—guidance counselors, school social workers and others who are familiar with the language and culture of the children and families of minority groups. Dr. David Sanchez, member of the San Francisco School Board, recommended that school counseling activities be more flexible and not restricted just to those times when school is open and in session. Counselors must develop an understanding of the family background and home environment in which the language-minority child comes. They must, in short, become family and community counselors as well as school counselors available on evenings and weekends.

In recent years, many school systems have come to realize that paraprofessionals are an invaluable aid to teachers, administrators, and counselors in working with all children. But this is particularly true with language minorities. The committee visited the Buena Vista School in San Francisco where parents and other local residents recruited from the local community are working as paraprofessionals in schools attended by language-minority children. Mr. Bob Jimenez, the principal of that school, testified:

> These parents, most of them from the community, some from very near the school, some with one or several children in the school . . . were like a replacement parent in the building. Their educational level was not important. What was important was how well they could talk to, understand, and help children.
>
> Our paraprofessionals pretty well duplicate the ethnic makeup of our student body. . . . We keep searching for persons, again, who will complement, balance out the teacher in the classroom.*

---

******Ibid.*, **Mar. 4, 1971.**

Mrs. Beatrice Meza, a teacher aide at Buena Vista, provided additional insight for the committee:

> To me, I think we are needed in the classroom. I mean the kids won't fall apart if we aren't there, but in our neighborhood, they are more secure. The parents bring children to my door, they tell me troubles they have at home, I listen to their troubles. They tell me when they have a new daddy, again, and they are going to get a new one in another 2 weeks; fine. You know what I am trying to say, I have to listen. Yet they won't tell the teacher these things because the teacher is, well, she has a little piece of paper and she is the teacher. I am still the mother image.

We believe that every school system should endeavor to make its clients a part of the educational process. The recruitment of community people as teacher aides can help meet the pressing needs for bilingual educational personnel.

There is another group of nonprofessionals who can make significant contributions to bilingual education. In Chapter 23, we have referred to the use of students as tutors. Children learn effectively from other children. In California, several school districts have undertaken programs in which volunteer high school and college students tutor and counsel young children on a one-to-one basis. Where these student-teachers are themselves bilingual they have served an especially crucial role supplementing the formal education of language-minority children. Some of these California proects have been funded by the Bilingual Education Act. Similar projects should be encouraged in other school districts.

Finally, ways must be found to ease the present restrictions in many States which operate to impede the recruitment of educators who are from language minority groups. Mrs. Sylvia Fox, Executive Director, of Aspira of Illinois, pointed out some of the ironies of certification standards to the committee:

> Certification and other requirements which systematically exclude persons whose native language is not English must be abolished from federally funded programs. Too many of the few Puerto Rican psychologists, teachers, and social workers do not get hired by the Board of Education because of failure to pass certification requirements which rely heavily on language, even when the crucial skill for the position is the ability to speak in Spanish. In the meantime, thousands of non-English speaking children are being tested, taught, diagnosed, and treated in a language which they do not fully understand. And while this is going on, armies of truant officers and community relations personnel, who cannot carry on a simply conversation with the parents, are being paid to retain the youth in school.*

Certification requirements have recently become the subject of successful court challenges. Objective standards for qualification are important to school systems in maintaining professional capability, but they can and have operated to exclude the very people that our public schools so vitally need. The committee endorses the principle of certifi-

---

**Ibid.*, Part 8, *Equal Educational Opportunities for Puerto Rican Children*, Nov. 23, 1970.

cation, but believes it must be implemented with much greater flexibility and sensitivity than has been heretofore practiced.

### 3. THE NEED FOR CULTURALLY SENSITIVE BILINGUAL EDUCATIONAL MATERIALS

As we have pointed out earlier in this chapter, few language-minority children have an opportunity to learn about the history of their people. All too often textbooks and other materials are entirely in English and present a distorted picture of language-minority cultures.

We believe a major effort should be undertaken, using Title VII and Emergency School Aid Act funds, to encourage the development of culturally sensitive bilingual educational textbooks and other materials. These materials should be developed by specialists who are themselves from the language-minority groups who will use the materials.

Experiences such as that at the Rough Rock School in Arizona, where the Navajo Indians have developed their own textbooks and teaching materials, have shown what can be done in this area.

We recommend that HEW fund bilingual educational development centers in every region of the Nation where there are substantial members of language-minority children and that these centers be staffed by specialists who are from the groups to be served.

### 4. FULL FUNDING OF BILINGUAL EDUCATION PROGRAMS

We believe it is essential that comprehensive bilingual, bicultural education be available for all language-minority children. Such programs should be a part of the curriculum in every school in which there are children from language-minority backgrounds. When bilingual programs are funded at a level sufficient to meet the needs of language-minority children, they should not only be available, but perhaps also required by the Office of Education as a condition to other Federal education assistance.

Together, Title VII of ESEA and the bilingual education programs of the Emergency School Aid Act are potentially the most promising programs designed to meet the needs of language-minority students. We recommend the full funding to the maximum authorized limit of both these programs. Title VII is presently funded at only 35 percent of the rate authorized by the Congress. While there has been a significant expansion of Title VII programs over the last 3 years, these programs do not begin to meet the need for bilingual education in any State, in any school district or in the Nation as a whole. The Emergency School Assistance Act bilingual education programs have not yet become operational. When they do, there should be close coordination between these programs and those under the Bilingual Education Act. As we have recommended above, Title VII programs should be operated in accordance with the provisions of the Emergency School Assistance bilingual program to assure the full participation of community members and nonprofit groups.

We recommend further that future funds for new bilingual education projects including those made available by the Emergency School Aid Act be allocated to help equalize the previous inequitable distribution of funds.

At the end of 2 years, when the Emergency School Assistance Program is scheduled to expire, these programs should be merged under Title VII. During that 2-year period we believe it is essential that HEW undertake a comprehensive evaluation of bilingual education programs. The Office of Education has recently funded an evaluation study designed to determine which present bilingual projects are most effective. We hope that as a result of this study the Office of Education will be able to provide a set of models which have proved successful and which can be replicated by school districts wishing to undertake bilingual education.

At the end of this 2-year period and with the help of a comprehensive evaluation, the Congress ought then be in a position to transform Title VII into a nationwide bilingual education program which can help financially hard-pressed school districts throughout the United States meet the needs of those children from families and communities where the dominant language is other than English.

But the Federal Government alone cannot make these programs successful. Ours is a culturally pluralistic society. State education agencies and local school districts must include in their curricula culturally pluralistic subject matter. No language-minority child should attend school, whatever his race or national origin, without learning about his own heritage in a way that will instill pride in his culture. No English language child should attend school without learning that his culture is neither exclusive nor dominant in our society. It is only through fulfillment of these goals that we will succeed in ending the prejudice and hostility born of ignorance which has so long characterized our society.

# Part VI

# Making Education More Responsive

## Chapter 22—The Need for Reform

Public education in this country has always had its critics. In recent years, however, our elementary and secondary school system has been the subject of a barrage of criticism and widespread debate both within and outside the ranks of professional educators and expert observers. It is a debate that goes beyond questions about educational equality and reflects widespread concern about educational goals, teaching methods and school organization.

Since the founding of our public school system, education has had among its principal goals the acquisition of the basic skills and knowledge and motivations necessary to enable a child to gain admission to college, find a job and advance his career. There is no doubt that from the standpoint of these traditional goals our public education system has been impressively successful. More children are better educated than they ever were; more are going on to junior colleges, colleges and vocational schools. More young adults are finding meaningful employment. More minority-group children are graduating from high school and continuing their education. The high levels of enrollment at every level of schooling in the United States are without parallel in any other society. Illiteracy in this country is almost nonexistant. Our school systems have responded magnificently to the need for scientists, engineers and other skilled technicians and workers in a technologically advanced complex society.

But most educators and observers of our school systems agree that schools should do more than teach children how to communicate and impart basic knowledge of a variety of subjects through a formal curriculum. Schools should also assist in the development of moral sensitivity and personal and social awareness; they should help children gain positive concepts about themselves and a concern and compassion for others.

Some critics of our public schools, however, do not view the present educational system as one which is either willing or able to act on these convictions. They say incentives for students flow in just the opposite direction. They are critical of those educational processes which treat the child as a passive observer, for whom conformity and passive acceptance of authority rather than individualism, independence, challenge and controversy are the permissible modes of behavior.

They ask that schools be more sensitive to feelings and emotions, that they reflect and encourage diversity, that they be client-oriented rather than professionally oriented, that they be child-centered rather than adult-centered.

To accomplish these ends, reformers believe there must be major changes in the ways schools are organized, controlled and evaluated. They seek changes in classroom teaching methods and the opening up of new learning experiences outside school as part of the formal education process. They demand that professional educators be made "accountable" and that parents and students have available to them a variety of educational choices.

These views are not limited to the experts. They are increasingly shared by students and their parents—the "clients" of public education—who want a greater role in the decisions that are made about their children's education and a greater choice among different kinds of school experiences.

As we have discussed earlier, many members of minority groups see the education system as unresponsive to their needs, unable to understand their cultures, unwilling to make room for diversity and insensitive to their heritage.

It is from this perspective that the committee has viewed the testimony of many witnesses who see the need for major reforms if our public school systems are to meet the needs of a diverse, sensitive, questioning and thoughtful generation of young Americans.

We do not presume to know how children learn or what they should be taught. We cannot write a prescription for educational reform or say that we know what will work. No one method of teaching or curriculum or school style or atmosphere is right for all children or every community. But our observations do provide an opportunity to suggest a number of things that ought to be tried, and if successful, replicated.

In short, there are many aspects of education that are beyond the scope of this committee's mandate or which, while they affect the education of minority-group and disadvantaged children, we have wanted but did not have the time to study.

Nevertheless, within these constraints, this committee's hearings, studies and the personal observations of its members and staff do point to the need for change in the ways many schools, particularly those that serve predominantly minority student populations, relate to the people they serve. We believe ways must be found to make teachers and administrators more sensitive to cultural diversity, better able to understand and meet the needs of disadvantaged students, and more responsive to their desires.

# Chapter 23—Schools and Their Communities

For more than half a century educators assumed that children learn most effectively through interactions in a box-shaped room with 20 or 30 of their peers and one adult. There is no doubt that this model has served many generations of American children admirably, and schooling conducted in this manner has provided most students with the knowledge, skills, and information about society sufficient to lead a productive past-school life. Yet there is good reason to believe that additional learning environments should be added to traditional classroom teaching in a world that has become infinitely more complex and where learning experiences outside school are becoming increasingly more important. A number of observers have concluded that the relative contribution of formal classroom instruction to the total knowledge the American child acquires is decreasing. As Dr. Mark Lohman testified:

> The percentage contribution of formal schooling toward implanting the total number of facts, opinions, values and beliefs held by a graduating high school senior has declined and will continue to decline as an independent source of knowledge. Some argue that less than half of the knowledge available to an individual person's active memory can be attributed to formal schooling alone.*

Yet education in most communities continues to function in a way that excludes outside learning experiences.

New learning environments both within the school and in the community should be considered legitimate and appropriate additions to the traditional school curriculum. Thus, a variety of learning experiences ought to be available within a school. At the same time schools should move toward becoming more integral parts of their communities. Learning should be a combined school-community effort. The community should be brought into the classroom, and pupils should be brought more often out of the classroom and into the community as part of their formal education.

There are many ways these things can be accomplished and a number of experiments have been tried. We only set forth several suggestions which, while certainly not appropriate for every community or every school, deserve further experimentation and use.

## A. Learning as a Community Experience

The allocation and distribution of resources to public schools has become a widespread concern in recent years. Cities are financially overburdened, rural areas are underfinanced and often ignored and

---

*Hearings of the U.S. Senate Select Committee on Equal Educational Opportunity, Part 20, *Unequal School Practices*, Nov. 8, 1971.

suburbs are pinched by soaring property taxes. Nationally, many school systems are operating on deficit budgets, and defeated educational bond referendums have become commonplace. Recent court decisions have provided the impetus for a more equitable distribution of resources. School systems of all types will need substantially greater financial support from the Federal Government if they are to survive in this decade, much less meet the needs of the next.

Dollars, however, are not the only resource necessary to make education in the 1970s or 1980s more effective. There are resources within businesses, universities, cultural institutions, service and other community organizations that are equally important, readily available and now largely unused in public education. Schools can and should make use of these resources. As stated previously, much if not most learning occurs outside the classroom. Schools should find ways to make the community part of the school learning experience.

Libraries, museums and zoos have long been used as resources outside the school. But they are almost always underused. Drs. Frederick David Erickson and Eliezer Krumbein have stated:

> Typical use of such facilities consists of a whirlwind tour. In Chicago, one sees these educational safaris at the Field Museum of Natural History. They arrived by bus, and led by the teacher and museum guide, proceed in lockstep from exhibit to exhibit on a half-day schedule through a million years of human evolution. Libraries have children's collections, story hours and a wide range of other materials, but they seldom are used effectively. History can come alive at the art museums, but it usually does not. Animals at the zoo are alive, but children rarely stay long enough to observe their life systematically.*

Perhaps the most successful and best publicized effort to integrate community resources into the formal learning process was the Parkway Program—the "School Without Walls"—developed several years ago in Philadelphia. This program made extensive use of the museums, theatres, libraries, businesses and government offices in downtown Philadelphia as learning, research and work experience sites for high school students. These locations were used not to supplement classroom activities; rather, history was taught at museums, mathematics at insurance companies, English at newspaper offices, and civics at government offices. The options were limited only by the imaginations of those in charge.**

In testimony before this committee, witnesses urged that schools be more open, less rigid and more in tune to the "real world" outside the classroom and that students be given an opportunity to understand how what they learn in school applies to their interests, concerns and needs.

Using community institutions would not only benefit students, it would involve the community in the education of its children. Businessmen, lawyers, accountants, public officials, health personnel, mem-

---

*"Systems Approach to the Reform of Schools," *New Models for American Education*, James W. Guthrie and Edward Wynne, Prentice-Hall, Inc. 1971.

**Hearings of the U.S. Senate Select Committee on Equal Educational Opportunity, Part 9A, *San Francisco and Berkeley, Calif.*, Mar. 6, 1971.

bers of industry and others could design educational programs to inform and educate young people about what they do and how they do it.

B. Students as Teachers

Beyond expanding the physical learning site there are other ways that the educational process can be restructured to take advantage of extra school resources. It has long been established, for example, that children learn effectively from other children. Where schools have had older children tutor younger children the experience has been found to benefit both. Dr. J. Russell Kent, School Superintendent in San Mateo County, Calif., for example, told the committee:

> We have found that in the Ravenswood School District, that using older youngsters, even who are poor achievers as tutors to younger youngsters, that this brings about spectacular results and improvement of each of these. It seems to have more effect on the performance of the kids than smaller classes under trained teachers or changing materials or methods of teaching, and this is a very difficult thing, you know, to isolate and say exactly what the cause and effect is. But it certainly has something to do with attitudes, self concept, belief in their self, this sort of thing. This probably is at the heart of it.*

In another California district, Santa Clara County, ESEA Title VII bilingual program funds are used in a preschool program in which bilingual Mexican-American housewives are teaching Spanish-speaking 3- and 4-year-olds in groups of five in their own homes. Dr. Glenn Hoffman, Santa Clara School Superintendent, said "We are having fantastic results." The district is expanding the program to include kindergarten children who are taught in both English and Spanish.

In another program in the same district, 2,500 volunteer college and high school students spend a semester tutoring underachieving younger children on a one-to-one basis. Dr. Hoffman said the program not only increased the reading and mathematical scores of the tutored children but had given the older children "something significant to do in their lives." In still another California district, Pasadena, the Superintendent said of a similar program:

> We are also finding that we are using some students who are not achieving too well themselves who are upper-grade students, junior and senior high school, with elementary school students who are not achieving too well, and we are finding in some cases this is the greatest motivation that has ever been discovered for these kids. In other words, the underachiever will start working. He has got to learn because he now has a real purpose, he really wants to help this little kid and he now has a chance to do so and so he learns himself so that he can do it and they both profit a great deal. We have 200 or 300 tutors in our district.*

What these and similar experiences demonstrate is that schools can develop new and imaginative and often unused ways to make use of community resources and people and make them a part of the

---

**Ibid.*

learning process. Such approaches will help make education a more practical and real experience and at the same time tap new, available and inexpensive resources that ought to be a part of formal education.

### C. Schools as Community Centers

A number of educators have proposed that schools be open longer hours and more days and that they provide both educational and noneducational services for adults as well as children.

A school might be open, for example, on a 12- to 14-hour basis 6 or 7 days a week. New school activities and educational programs might be planned, implemented and evaluated with the participation of parents, students and others in the community. Aside from the formal curriculum, late afternoon activities could be provided not just for children in the school, but for other children in the community as well. Education courses could be available for adults in the evening and the school would be open whenever possible for other kinds of community activities and meetings. The school could also be used to provide services such as health, legal aid and employment counseling. Paraprofessionals could be used both as teacher aides and in noneducational activities. The school itself would thus function as a community center for the educational and other community needs of all people in the neighborhood.

In this regard, we recommend prompt and serious consideration by the Congress of legislation such as the "Community School Center Development Act" introduced by Senators Church and Williams in the last session of Congress which was directed toward providing Federal support for programs and activities of the type outlined in this section.

# Chapter 24—Changing Roles for Educators and Their Clients

The growing demands for accountability in public education are in part a reflection of the fact that many schools are failing minority group and disadvantaged children and are often unable to recognize their needs. But they are also rooted in feeling among many parents and students from all backgrounds that public education is too often a closed society, overly defensive to criticism, and often resistant to change. In many communities citizens are unable to understand new curricula, standards for advancement, graduation or admission to college; arguments over the meanings and shortcomings of IQ and standardized tests and are confused about changing concepts of classroom instruction. Many school systems refuse to disclose information about student performance. Others are unable to explain to parents the reasons for poor performance or often wrongly blame the child. A few are openly hostile, secretive, and release only favorable information.

In short, for many communities the present educational structure does not provide its clients with adequate information about student and school performance or the data with which the public can judge the quality of education in its schools, compare them with those in other communities or compare individual schools with one another.

In poor and minority-group communities, particularly where poor educational services often combine with low-student performance, there is a rising mistrust of school officials and resentment of the tight control of educational policy by school boards and school professionals who determine, often without consulting those affected by their decisions, what should be taught and how, where and on what basis pupils are assigned, when students are "ready" for school, promotion, or special programs and even what kind of program (college preparatory, general or vocational, for example) is "best" for each student.

Often parents and students see themselves excluded from direct participation in educational matters. Increasingly, they are questioning the validity of the decisions professionals are making. They question the right of professionals to make such decisions *for* them and whether these decisions are made with their best interests in mind.

The result is that clients of education often feel they have few choices about the education of their children and little if any information with which to make such choices.

There are a number of actions which we believe should be taken to assure that parents, students and community residents have the information necessary to evaluate the performance of their schools, enable clients to participate in the decisions about education policy and programs, and afford choices among alternative methods of instruction, curricula and types of schools.

We have not been able to examine all the proposals, tried or untried, which are designed to make schools more accountable. However, we believe that any system designed to make schools more responsive must have five elements:

*First*, parents and students should become more directly involved in school affairs.

*Second*, the fullest possible, accurate information on school performance and other essential aspects of school life must be publicly available.

*Third*, school principals should be released from many of their present administrative burdens so they can be more active participants in the educational process and made more responsible for the outcomes of their schools.

*Fourth*, all teachers must be encouraged to become more sensitive to diversity and to the backgrounds of different children, and teachers must be freer to innovate, experiment and develop new instructional techniques.

*Fifth*, schools must be provided with the resources and sufficient incentives to innovate, experiment, and develop new instructional techniques.

## A. Community Participation in Education

In Part IV we have recommended that one of the keys to successful school integration is the more meaningful participation of students, parents, teachers and other community residents in the design of plans, educational programs and extra-curricular activities. Successful community participation in education is a two-way street. School administrators and professional educators must view community residents as an essential resource in educational decisionmaking. At the same time, parents and students must participate constructively and cooperatively. Joseph Featherstone in a series of articles on open schools in the *New Republic* in September 1971, has stated as well as anyone the need for restoring an appropriate balance between professionalism and community participation:

> In every case I know of where sound education is going on in America—including the best of the community-controlled schools—it is recognized that all parties to the educational process—children, parents, professionals and the general community—have rights and obligations. Where the pendulum has swung too far in one direction; where professionals are hiding behind administrative structures to keep parents out, as in so many of our big city systems, the balance has to be restored. Where parents seek to dictate teaching practices, even in the name of "open education," another balance has to be evened.
>
> As ideological battle lines sharpen we may forget the obvious point once made to me by a principal in a ghetto school: "If you aren't serving parents in a way that makes sense to them, you'd better close down."

We believe the establishment of community committees should be encouraged in all school districts whether or not they are developing plans for integrated education. Parent-citizen committees, adequately representative of minority groups, should be established for both individual schools and school districts with representatives of parents, students (at least at the high school level) and teachers. These committees, working with school superintendents, school principals, and other school officials should recommend specific objective goals for education, explore new educational programs and innovations, suggest changes in educational programs, and help develop appropriate ways to measure student performance and evaluate school performance. The committee might also explore new classroom techniques, find ways to involve the community in school activities, develop plans to make use of community resources, and help make the school become a more community-oriented institution, responsive to its clients.

These parent-citizen committees should receive financial support and have sufficient resources to tap the expertise of educational technicians and others who could be helpful in providing advice, counsel, and technical assistance and in developing ways to ask the right questions.

### B. Revitalizing the Role of the School Principal

In many ways the school principal is the most important and influential individual in any school. He is the person responsible for all the activities that occur in and around the school building. It is his leadership that sets the tone of the school, the climate for learning, the level of professionalism and morale of teachers and the degree of concern for what students may or may not become. He is the main link between the school and the community and the way he performs in that capacity largely determines the attitudes of students and parents about the school. If a school is a vibrant, innovative, child-centered place; if it has a reputation for excellence in teaching; if students are performing to the best of their ability one can almost always point to the principal's leadership as the key to success.

Joseph Featherstone has described in compelling terms what the best school principals in England see as their most important roles:

> They see themselves first and foremost as supporters and catalysts for the continued growth of their teaching staff. Many teach classes; those who can't, spend much of their day working in classrooms with teachers and children. They were chosen, among other things, for their ability to provide good examples of ways of working with children, for their talent in leading a teaching staff, not administering a plant.

Unfortunately, many of our school systems do little to encourage school principals to spend their time working closely with teachers and students. All too often, from the principal's perspective, schools are regarded as administrative units of a larger public system; the principal is too often a manager instead of an educational leader; and the priorities are on administration at the expense of teachers and students.

Our committee has not conducted an in-depth study of school administration. We have, however, seen enough schools in operation and heard sufficient testimony to draw some general conclusions about the needs to revitalize the leadership role of school principals, reduce their administrative burdens and permit them to exercise the kind of responsibility necessary to make education work. At the same time, we believe if schools are to be more accountable to their clients, as the person most responsible for education where it happens the principal should also be the person who is held accountable for the performance of the school, its teachers and students.

Accordingly, we urge that school districts take the following steps toward these goals:

*First*, the school principal should be unburdened from as many of his present administrative burdens as possible and given greater autonomy and responsibility for the improvement of instruction and other activities involving students within the school. He should be free to work with the teachers in experimenting and innovating and be responsible for the design and implementation of educational programs within the school. The principal and teachers should be free to experiment with new teaching methods and select appropriate instructional materials to meet the needs of students from diverse backgrounds. To the extent possible the States should relax their present restrictions on curriculum requirements and other matters to accomplish these aims.

*Second*, in exercising these responsibilities, principals should consult fully and directly with parent-citizen school committees described in the previous section. Changes in present educational practices, the development of new techniques and the design of new programs should be undertaken by principals and teachers in cooperation with parents and students involved in the school.

*Third*, in order to relieve the school principal from his present administrative burdens, he should have the resources to select a school administrator or manager to fill a position with the rank of assistant principal. The administrator should be responsible for noneducational, administrative, and managerial functions at the school. We believe that this would free the principal to be a full-time, active, responsible, and accountable educational leader.

*Fourth*, States and local communities should review the criteria under which principals are selected. More attention should also be paid to those essential traits which refine a prospective principal's capacity for educational leadership. Academic credentials, seniority, and administrative ability are important qualifications for any school principal, but the selection process should also be conducted in a manner to assure the appointment of qualified educators who are both leaders of teachers and responsive to the needs and desires of parents and students.

*Fifth*, consideration should also be given by States and school districts to the publication of an annual evaluation of school performance which would include the results of standardized achievement tests in schools and school districts. These results should be presented in such fashion that educators and their clients will be able to assess how well schools are doing.

We have attempted only to set forth some general guidelines which we believe ought to be further explored so that school principals can become more autonomous, free to experiment, relieved of many of their present administrative burdens and so that schools can become more accountable to their clients. We recognize that each State and school district will have to work out the details of such procedures in their own way. But we believe the key to success in every district will be the effective cooperation of the parents, citizens, and educators.

## C. Teachers and Their Education

Whatever else happens in schools and school systems, the interaction between teacher and child is a crucial component of the educational process. Effective teaching is the essential condition for education and insensitive or inadequate teaching will at least result in a lost opportunity, if not damage to the child.

We have reviewed in Chapter 11 how the attitudes and expectations of teachers and the treatment of minority-group and disadvantaged children can contribute to inequality in education. The elimination of such practices and the attainment of equal opportunity in the schools of this Nation will depend largely upon whether through their training and development, both before and during their service in the classroom, teachers can become more sensitive to cultural diversity and better able to cope with the needs of children from different backgrounds.

Indeed, no significant or lasting changes in education can take place in our schools without both the participation and leadership of teachers, their organizations and the people and institutions involved in teacher education and development.

### 1. PRESERVICE TEACHER EDUCATION

Like the classroom model of educating students, this Nation's model for educating and training teachers was developed in the last century and remains largely intact today. The preparation of potential teachers is fundamentally a process controlled by undergraduate teacher-training institutions. Only 5 percent of American public school teachers are not trained in undergraduate, 4-year programs on college and university campuses.

Typically, teacher training and certification involves the following five steps:

- General education courses usually required of all students regardless of their area of specialization.
- Subject area courses which provide in-depth knowledge at various age and grade levels.
- Courses on the history, philosophy and theory of education together with "methods" courses to bridge the gap between educational theory and practice.
- A brief on-the-job student teaching experience in a public school generally lasting 6 to 8 weeks, although sometimes a full semester.
- The award of a teaching certificate by a State and assignment to a teaching position in a school.

There are several features of this system which we believe need improvement if teachers are to be more adequately trained to meet the needs of public education today.

Certainly, every teacher must have a base of theoretical knowledge. Teachers must know how children function both independently and in groups. They should take courses in child psychology and behavior and understand how children develop mentally, physically and emotionally. But the prospective teacher must also know how to deal with and solve real problems that occur in the classroom. So far as possible this should be a part of any teacher's formal training. Teachers should be exposed to children's patterns of behavior and learn how children from different cultural backgrounds whom they will teach will react in school. They should be acquainted with the values children possess, how they are motivated, how they perceive themselves, their classmates and their teacher.

To accomplish these goals, we believe more teacher education should take place in public schools. Teachers should spend more time away from the physical setting and atmosphere of a college or university and work in classrooms with experienced teachers at various times throughout their period of training.

All too often today teacher education is largely removed from the practical day-to-day elementary and secondary school experience. In most schools of education, except for a short student-teaching experience, preparation is conducted within the college or university and the aspiring teacher must demonstrate his or her skills in the traditional way by taking tests and writing papers.

As Prof. Kevin Ryan, of the University of Chicago, stated in a paper prepared for the Select Committee:

> One of the most striking characteristics of the institutions in which teachers are prepared is that in them one rarely hears a child's voice.

One way of assuring that new teachers have the kind of practical training they need is to provide that a greater share of the responsibility for training teachers be undertaken by experienced classroom teachers not only with the student teacher in the public school classroom but also by bringing experienced teachers into teacher colleges and schools of education.

Unfortunately, most new teachers today are unprepared to meet or teach children who are poor or are from minority groups or who speak a different language or come from families with cultures and backgrounds different from their own. A number of schools of education are making serious efforts to emphasize the problems of disadvantaged and minority-group children. Yet, there is often little in the prospective teacher's training to provide the individual with sufficient understanding of the problems of disadvantaged and minority-group children. As a result many teachers find themselves frustrated in their attempts to work with children from backgrounds and cultures different from their own.

We urge that schools of education undertake greater efforts to assure that all teachers are adequately prepared to understand and meet the needs of children from minority groups.

## 2. TEACHER CENTERS

Teacher education does not stop with the issuance of a certificate or graduate degree. It is a continuous process of development. We believe teachers must have the time, freed from their classroom duties, to acquire new knowledge about subjects taught, about new classroom instructional methods and learn about new developments in education. They should have the opportunity to share experiences with each other so that new information will be disseminated into a variety of classrooms and schools.

One of the most hopeful, innovative models for the in-service development of teachers that the committee has found is in development of teacher centers, a concept that has become both popular and useful to teachers in England.

The teacher center concept is based upon the proposition, with which this committee is in complete accord, that fundamental educational change can best come through those charged with the responsibility for delivering educational services, that is, teachers. If education is to become more responsive, teachers must be able to define their own problems and work out ways to meet their needs in the classroom.

Initiated, organized and run by teachers, the primary function of the teacher center, as described by Professor Stephen K. Bailey of Syracuse University, is to "make possible a review of existing curricula and other educational practices by groups of teachers and to encourage teacher attempts to bring about changes." *

More than 500 such centers now exist in England.

While some centers meet after school, others meet in evenings, on weekends, holidays and more extensive sessions during the summer break. Professor Bailey provided the committee with a description of the kinds of activities that take place in a center.

> Typical after-school programs were: Lecture demonstration on understanding numbers, nine weekly meetings and discussions on how children learn, three lectures and workshops on visual aids, gymnastics and dance display, and devising a humanities course for leavers (those not planning further academic work beyond school-leaving age).
>
> The teachers' center also promotes and provides exhibits of new textbooks, programmed instruction, audio-visual aids, homecrafts and handicrafts and student art. Promotional and information activities (bulletins, newsletters, posters, etc.) are disseminated to keep all teachers and other interested people in the area informed about programs and exhibits. After-school experimental classes on family life, adolescent identity crises, and community problems are undertaken with selected students.**

He stated further that "the key to the success and enthusiasm associated with the teacher center notion is control by local teachers." Because of this, programs within the centers vary and options are readily available to teachers seeking all kinds of development and renewal. While some centers may be organized around subject areas such as mathematics, English, or reading, others may be organized by grade or region or focus on broader concepts such as child behavior or group dynamics. The alternatives are broad enough to include those seeking both general and specific knowledge.

This committee believes that the teacher center concept can have important implications for improved teacher and student perform-

---

*"Teachers' Centers: A British First," *Phi Delta Kappan*, November 1971.

**Hearings of the U.S. Senate Select Committee on Equal Educational Opportunity, Part 17—*Delivery Systems for Federal Aid to Disadvantaged Children*, Oct. 7, 1971.

ance in public schools in this country. With the cooperation of teacher organizations we believe teachers should endeavor to better mobilize their forces for educational progress than they have heretofore. Certainly, an American version of teacher centers could begin a process of relevant self-appraisal and development.

During this committee's visit to California, testimony was presented by teachers who participated in a voluntary and experimental effort of this kind. Other centers are in operation on a limited basis in other sections of the country. We believe that a more vigorous effort to engage teachers in educational and curricular renewal can be developed if other such experimental centers—sponsored by local teachers, unions, professional associations or other groups were established.

Although the establishment of teacher centers in this country will not alleviate all the problems inhibiting effective teacher-student interaction, it can begin to meet many teacher needs as well as initiate a process which will permit experienced and effective teachers to share their knowledge and skills with those new to the profession.

We believe a substantial effort should be undertaken with Federal funds to establish teacher centers in several communities throughout the United States. There is ample authority under existing programs for the funding of such centers and we recommend that Congress appropriate funds sufficient to establish teacher centers in a variety of school districts next year. After it has been determined that these centers are effective and useful such a program can be expanded in future years.

### D. Incentives for Education Quality

Many critics have suggested that the incentive structure of schools does not place enough emphasis on the provision of quality education to the schools' primary clients—its students.

The committee received testimony from representatives of the State of Michigan school system concerning an innovative program it has instituted to provide incentives for quality education. Michigan awards State aid to school districts partially on the basis of the educational progress of a school district's educationally disadvantaged students.

We believe schools should be provided encouragement for performing their basic functions well. We recommend that Title I of the Elementary and Secondary Education Act be amended to give States the option of participating in a new, federally funded, education achievement bonus program. Under this program, school districts would be provided a bonus for each Title I student who made adequate educational progress as measured by annual tests in reading and math. The bonus could be used by the school district as general assistance and would be in addition to regularly received Title I funds. The program would provide a strong incentive for school districts to find organizational structures and teaching techniques capable of teaching their Title I pupils effectively.

# Chapter 25—Compensatory Education and The Search for Solutions

## A. Compensatory Education

While our review of the results of school integration efforts have received much of the committee's time, we have also spent much time studying the problems of urban education, and of Federal aid programs which are designed to meet the needs of disadvantaged schoolchildren. The committee heard testimony concerning compensatory education programs from the school superintendents of Oakland, Calif.; Gary, Ind.; Kansas City, Mo.; Detroit, Mich.; and New York City.

In addition, the committee commissioned a study of the administration of Federal education programs by Prof. Michael W. Kirst of the Stanford University School of Education, entitled "Delivery Systems for Federal Aid to Disadvantaged Children: Problems and Prospects." That study has been published as part of our hearings, and we have also reviewed a number of recent reports evaluating compensatory education programs. Included is an important report by the Department of Health, Education, and Welfare, "The Effectiveness of Compensatory Education," analyzing the components of successful compensatory education programs conducted under Title I of the Elementary and Secondary Education Act of 1965.*

The results of these evaluations are often discouraging. The HEW report, for example, shows many instances in which compensatory education programs have either failed to show any significant achievement gain among participating students as compared with nonparticipating students, and instances where children receiving compensatory education services have fallen further behind. It shows further that in 1967 "a child who participated in a Title I project had only a 19 percent chance of a significant achievement gain, a 13 percent chance of a significant achievement loss, and a 68 percent chance of no change at all." Similar evidence is presented in other evaluation reports. But the HEW report also observes that Title I funds often have simply not been put to constructive use. The report notes:

> We know that the Federal compensatory education program has not been successful as a whole—that funds have not reached poor children in the correct proportion and that . . . significant amounts of funds [have been] spent in ways which

---

*Other reports include: A study by the Rand Corporation, *How Effective Is Schooling? A Critical Review and Synthesis of Research Findings* and a report by the American Institutes for Research evaluating ESEA Title I programs: *ESEA Title I: A Reanalysis and Synthesis of Evaluation Data From Fiscal Year 1965 Through 1970.*

have had only minor educational consequences for disadvantaged children.

A vivid description of Title I abuses is contained in "Title I of ESEA: Is It Helping Poor Children," a study of Title I conducted under the auspices of the Washington Research Project and the NAACP Legal Defense Fund.

In a real sense, compensatory education has never had a chance—services have often been diluted to the point of meaningless, and even extended to noneligible children. Funds have been expended on equipment which is never put to effective use. Most important, Title I-funded programs too often have lacked clear goals related to increasing academic achievement, as well as clearly defined strategies for reaching those goals.

But the reports also point to a number of programs which have been demonstrably successful. Identified by research groups referred to earlier, for example, are 41 projects which reported significant and successful achievement results. 14 were directed toward increasing IQ scores. 36 focused on the development of language arts and reading skills. One was aimed at the improvement of writing skills and 15 were directed to basic skills in mathematics.

These studies identify what we believe to be essential components of a successful compensatory education program—components usually not found in those projects which have failed to raise the achievement levels of disadvantaged students.

*First*, the program should have clearly stated objectives and be carefully planned.

*Second*, teachers should receive training in the specific methods of the project.

*Third*, compensatory education is more likely to be successful where instruction is either individualized or conducted in small groups.

*Fourth*, in successful programs there has often been active parent involvement in the projects.

*Fifth*, there has usually been a high intensity of treatment associated with the project.

The studies reveal that this last component, intensity of treatment, is among the most important. During fiscal years 1968 and 1969, the majority of elementary school children in Title I projects were found to have received less than an hour per day of compensatory education instruction. The most successful compensatory education programs that were studied ranged as high as 8 hours per day of instruction.

As former U.S. Commissioner of Education, Harold Howe, stated to the committee in August 1971:

> Probably nobody can give you clear proof that any particular amount of money ought to be spent per child. I believe, however, that the general concept of "a critical mass" makes good sense. Minor accretions of funds leading to minor changes in school services are in my judgment unlikely to provide sufficient difference in the education offered to have any potential for redressing severe environmental handicaps. The State of California has worked on this question and has come up with the idea that at least $300 per child is necessary in order to make the required differences. I believe that Connect-

> icut has reached about the same conclusion. To my knowledge, this is the best rule of thumb we have, and it would make sense to me to have the Federal programs operate in accordance with it. After all, $300 per pupil per year is only about $1.65 per child per day, surely not an extravagant amount for this important service.

Most recently, the critical mass concept has also been endorsed by the present administration. As President Nixon said on March 17, 1972:

> While there is a great deal yet to be learned about the designing of successful compensatory programs, the experience so far does point in one crucial direction: To the importance of providing sufficiently concentrated funding to establish the educational equivalent of a "critical mass," or threshold level. Where funds have been spread too thinly, they have been wasted or dissipated with little show for their expenditure. Where they have been concentrated, the results have been frequently encouraging and sometimes dramatic.

We note that, as former Commissioner Howe stated, it is probably not possible to fix an absolute amount that should be spent for each child. The amount of money it takes to compensate for the economic and educational disadvantages of minority-group and poor schoolchildren will certainly vary from State to State and among school districts within States. As we point out in Part VII of this Report, the costs of education and other municipal services can vary tremendously between different types of school districts even in the same metropolitan area. Nevertheless, $300 would seem in most cases to be an appropriate minimum guideline amount to begin to meet the needs of disadvantaged children.

The committee does not view compensatory education as in any way inconsistent with school integration. We believe that strong compensatory educational services are essential to increasing the educational opportunities of disadvantaged children in both integrated settings and in racially and economically isolated schools. We also find that compensatory education programs are most likely to succeed when they take place in an economically integrated setting.

## RECOMMENDATIONS

*First*, we recommend congressional adoption of a new program, modeled on the President's compensatory education proposals of March 17, 1972, and funded with a new and separate authorization of $1.5 billion annually.

These funds would be expanded in direct project grants from the Office of Education to school systems agreeing to use the new funds, together with funds under the preexisting Title I program, for highly concentrated, well-evaluated programs in reading and math.

The new programs, combined with a continuation of Title I, could provide compensatory services averaging $300 a year to 10 million of the estimated 17 million Title I-eligible students beginning in the Fall of 1973. Effective administration and full evaluation can build the record for increased funding to extend help to all disadvantaged children by the Fall of 1975.

*Second*, we recommend that the Office of Education make appropriate use of the "critical mass" concept in implementing other programs relating to the education of disadvantaged children, including school integration and compensatory education programs under the Emergency School Aid Act.

*Third*, we recommend that relevant committees of the House and Senate conduct in-depth hearings on the subject of compensatory education, involving a broad range of parents, teachers and administrators, as well as academic experts, in the next session of Congress.

*Fourth*, that the NIE undertake as one of its first priorities the monitoring and evaluation of federally funded compensatory education efforts.

## B. Indian Education

The education of American-Indian children must be a special concern of the Federal Government; for their present plight is only one more chapter in a long and bitter history of Federal Government injustice to Indian citizens.

The Indian Education Subcommittee, under the successive leadership of Senators Robert F. Kennedy, Wayne Morse and Edward M. Kennedy, thoroughly studied the problems of Indian education in this country. The subcommittee's report, "Indian Education: A National Tragedy—A National Challenge," issued in 1969, contains an eloquent summary of the state of Indian education, and concise recommendations for remedy.

The need for action is clear. The subcommittee found:

- Dropout rates are twice the national average in both public and private schools.
- Achievement levels of Indian children are 2 to 3 years below those of white students.
- One-fourth of elementary and secondary school teachers—by their own admission—would prefer not to teach Indian children.
- Indian children, more than any other minority group, believe themselves to be "below average" in intelligence, even though evidence is contrary to this belief.
- Only 18 percent of students in Federal Indian schools go to college; the national average is 50 percent.

### RECOMMENDATIONS

*First*, we recommend full funding and implementation of the Indian Education Act of 1972, which incorporates many of the Special Subcommittee's basic recommendations. The bill provides:

- Roughly $90 million in Federal assistance for use by local school systems in meeting the special educational needs of Indian children.
- For the pilot and demonstration programs employing innovative techniques for the education of Indian children, $35 million.
- For demonstrations and evaluation in the area of Indian adult education, $8 million.

- Requirement that Indian children participate equitably in the use of funds allocated to school systems under the Impact Aid Program because of the presence of Indian students, and extension of parent participation requirements to use of funds under the Indian Impact Aid Program.
- Establishment of an Office of Indian Education and a Deputy Commissioner of Indian Education in the Office of Education, and a National Advisory Council on Indian Education.

*Second*, we recommend immediate action by the Bureau of Indian Affairs to give control over Federal Indian schools to local Indian communities, in accordance with the President's message of July 1970.

*Third*, we recommend prompt action by the House and Senate Committees on Interior and Insular Affairs to reform the BIA education apparatus, and place control over federally run Indian schools in the hands of local Indian communities.

### C. Information, Research and Demonstration

Perhaps the greatest barrier to designing effective education programs, and effective compensatory programs in particular, is simply the absence of well-focused and evaluated research and demonstration programs, and failure to disseminate the results of those narrowly focused studies which have been conducted. As a result, the great national and academic debate over the potential effectiveness of education for disadvantaged children proceeds at a high level of abstraction.

Information, whether for meeting national educational needs, finding out the results of educational research, or striving for more efficient use of public resources, the participants in educational policymaking, be they public officials, educators, researchers or other citizens are presently severely handicapped by a lack of a systematic organized information system regarding schools and their effectiveness.

Formulating effective public policy for the support of elementary and secondary education requires a knowledge of:

(a) The demand for various kinds of educational services, both at present and in the foreseeable future.

(b) Estimates of their costs.

(c) A conception of equity in the distribution both of educational services and of the costs of those services.

(d) A continuous evaluation of the financial, and most important, educational impact of Federal programs in particular and of American education more generally.

Yet, we have found it difficult and often impossible to find information on these subjects.

This inadequacy may be traced to two causes:

*First*, and more important, data about education are not organized in a fashion that facilitates policy formulation.

*Second*, the data that are available are scattered among a variety of Federal agencies, and only the most time-consuming efforts can pull them together.

It is not so much the absolute absence of information as it is the failure to organize it for policymaking purposes which comprises the major shortcomings of current Federal data on education. Unfortunately, data about education is currently presented in unmanageable form and the significance of much statistical information can only be obtained, if at all, with painstaking effort.

In short, there is currently little attempt to present and interpret information in policy-oriented categories like those above. Much of the collection of statistical material on education is dominated by a laudable desire for accuracy and comprehensiveness. But the relation of data to issues of public policy is not being met. The haphazard quality of many of our Federal programs and the uncertainty and unpredictability of our thinking and planning on educational problems is traceable in large part to the inability of policymakers to draw upon relevant information as they pursue their deliberations.

The second major inadequacy is that information is scattered among a variety of Federal agencies. These include organizations such as the Office of Education and its subdivisions, the Office of Economic Opportunity, the Departments of Labor and Commerce, the Advisory Commission on Intergovernmental Relations, the Census Bureau, and the Office of Management and Budget. All these Federal agencies currently collect eduactional data or process it in some form.

State educational agencies and regional associations are additional sources of information, as are the many private organizations representing teachers, school administrators and school boards. The fact that multiple reporting and analytic sources exist is not itself the problem. The difficulty is that no single agency, including the U.S. Office of Education has undertaken the task of providing an overview of the entire educational information landscape.

The U.S. Office of Education has largely limited its efforts to the programs and data sources with which its programs are involved. Thus, for example, there is little data on early childhood education expenditures available at the National Center for Educational Statistics because its programs are administered by another Federal agency. Similarly, data collected on State and local finance of education by the Census of Governments and by the Advisory Commission on Intergovernmental Relations are seldom available from the NCES division of the Office of Education.

In short, the responsibility the Office of Education has carried since its founding in 1867, "to collect such statistics and facts as should show the condition and progress of education," has been subjected to a restrictive interpretation on the basis of jurisdictional lines that are unrelated to the substance of its mandate.

The National Center for Educational Statistics, created within USOE in 1965, has made major efforts to improve data collection procedures in recent years. However, the Center is severely limited in that almost 90 percent of elementary and secondary education information is collected at the Federal level by the program management bureaus of USOE, the Office of Civil Rights, the Bureau of the Census, and the Department of Agriculture. Though interagency cooperation is improving, the NCES is making a determined effort in this regard, much greater coordination is necessary.

NCES has by far the smallest budget of all major statistical agencies in the Federal Government. Given the pressing need for relevant and timely information and the multiplicity of problems associated with complete dependence upon State and local education agencies, the current budget of $5.7 million is grossly inadequate.

Not only are Federal policymakers lacking in useful data, but so also are State and local participants in education. State education agencies, teachers and school principals have no access to a nationwide information gathering system from which they can learn of new developments and the experiences of others. Further, if parents and local citizens are to be able to exercise choice and begin to shape schools more in keeping with their interests, then they need access to information at the level of the individual school, classroom, and child. While it may not always be practical to collect data using these latter two units, it is possible to use schools as the basic framework for collecting information. From that point, if carefully constructed, appropriate items of information can be aggregated at the school district, regional, State, and Federal levels. In such a system, decisionmakers at each level would be supplied with the data they need.

### RECOMMENDATION

We recommend immediate centralization of data collection and dissemination responsibility in the National Center for Education Statistics, and the preparation and implementation by NCES of a plan for a comprehensive data collection and dissemination system.

We further recommend that the next Federal budget request contain sufficient resources to permit an expanded and more effective role for NCES.

## D. Research and Demonstration

But information on current activities in education must be supplemented by new knowledge. We must not only collect, analyze and evaluate what schools are now doing at the State and local levels, we must also move ahead and establish new, innovative and hopeful efforts which show promise of progress toward quality education for all children.

As we have stated earlier in this Report, we have found a serious, indeed alarming, lack of knowledge about "what works" for different groups of children in our schools.

As President Nixon stated in his March 3, 1970, message on Education Reform:

> The *outcome* of schooling—what children learn—is profoundly different for different groups of children and different part of the country. Although we do not seem to understand just what it is in one school or school system that produces a different outcome from another, one conclusion is inescapable: *We do not yet have equal educational opportunity in America. . . .*
>
> The corresponding need in the school systems of the Nation is to begin the responsible, open measurement of how well the educational process is working. It matters very little how much a school building costs; it matters a great deal how much a child in that building learns.

Not only must we measure how well education is working, we must also have a major national effort to demonstrate new educational techniques, undertake basic research, and develop new educational models which seeks to achieve quality education for those not now receiving it.

The level of funding for educational research and demonstration is presently wholly inadequate.

As President Nixon noted in his Education Reform Message, we spend less than one-half of 1 percent of our educational budget on research. This compares with 5 percent of our health budget and 10 percent of our budget for national defense.

The Education Amendments of 1972 recently enacted by the Congress establish a National Institute of Education which has the potential of pointing the way toward more dependable knowledge about the process of learning. As the President stated in his message, the purpose of the National Institute is "to begin the serious, systematic search for new knowledge needed to make educational opportunity truly equal."

As stated in the enabling legislation, the purposes of the National Institute are to:

> Help to solve or to alleviate the problems of, and promote the reform and renewal of American education.
>
> Advance the practice of education, as an art, science, and profession.
>
> Strengthen the scientific and technological foundations of education.
>
> Build an effective educational research and development system.

### RECOMMENDATION

The National Institute of Education can perform an essential role in assuring an effective research base for American education. We recommend careful staffing of the Institute, and full and adequate funding.

## E. Council of Social Advisers

We must begin to recognize and analyze the whole spectrum of interrelated social needs in this country at the highest level. To undertake such efforts, the committee recommends the establishment of a Council of Social Advisers. Placed in the Executive Office of the President, the Council should be staffed with the most outstanding social scientists, just as the Council of Economic Advisers has been served by the Nation's leading economists.

A Council of Social Advisers could help to identify for the President and the Congress those problems that should be given the highest priorities. It would lead in the development of a comprehensive system of social indicators to show us how well—or how badly—we are doing. It would help us chart the course of social progress in dealing with our most pressing problems.

It is hard to believe how many times in recent years a great Nation like ours could have been shocked to discover the existence of monumental problems which sap our vitality and threaten us with disaster. A few years ago, for example, the U.S. Government first learned that malnutrition, and even hunger, were widespread in America. We had reams of data on soybeans, corn, meat and poultry—but we knew little about hunger.

We did not realize the scale on which hunger existed or where it was, what the reasons for it might be, what it would cost to feed the hungry or, perhaps more importantly, what it would cost not to feed the hungry in our midst. For it often happens that the cost of ignoring a problem is far greater than the cost of dealing with it promptly.

We have had similar situations in the fields of housing, and migratory labor, and health, and in other areas.

If we are to develop our capacity to recognize the existence of such problems, and improve our ability to deal with them, we will need new Government structures and processes. A Council of Social Advisers could help to focus decisionmaking in the Executive Branch on these strategic issues.

In turn, an annual social report to the Congress would eliminate some of the unstated choices which are implicit in the President's budget. A Joint Social Committee in the Congress, through hearings on such a report, would assist the Congress to reach the kind of independent decisions which are worthy of a coequal branch of Government.

The creation of a Council of Economic Advisors in 1946 vastly improved the sophistication of economic analysis in this Nation—permitting us to develop, refine, and use important economic indicators. The creation of a similiar council for social problems and the development of an annual social report, should help us to set our priorities more meaningfully and deal with our problems more effectively. This would enable us to plan where we should be going and how we should get there instead of doing what former Secretary of HEW John Gardner has termed "stumbling into the future".

We now have the capability for extremely complicated systems analysis. These skills must be brought to bear on the interrelated human resource problems which cut across the narrow boundaries of education, employment, health, housing and other areas of national concern. A comprehensive approach to social accounting and social reporting is essential if we are to do so.

# Part VII
# Education Finance

## Chapter 26—Toward an Equitable Educational Finance System

Our Nation's present arrangements for raising and distributing money for public education are both complex and fundamentally unfair. And while the details differ, the pattern is similar in nearly every State.*

The basic source of education finance is the local real estate property tax, which provides more than one-half of all school revenues. Heavy reliance on the local property tax enables rich school districts with large tax bases to spend large amounts for their children's education with low tax rates, while poor school districts which tax themselves more heavily still spend less.

The inequity of this tax system is not corrected by the bewildering variety of aid formulas through which the States finance most of the remaining costs of public education. In general, these formulas fail to equalize the revenue-raising abilities of rich and poor school districts; and, at worst, they aggravate the inequities resulting from reliance on the local property tax.

The California Supreme Court has found that our typical system of education finance conditions the fundamental right to education "on wealth, classifies its recipients on the basis of their collective affluence and makes the quality of a child's education depend upon the resources of his school district and ultimately upon the pocketbook of his parents." *Serrano* v. *Priest*, 487 P.2d 241 (1971).

In short, the way we finance our schools embodies the very definition of inequality in educational opportunity.

The existence of such inequitable State school finance systems alone would be enough to warrant fundamental reform. But these inequities are aggravated by the most serious fiscal crisis in education since the Depression. In nearly every area of the Nation, education costs have risen dramatically; and they continue to rise at a rate which threatens to outstrip the capacities of State and local governments to raise the revenues needed to meet present educational needs.

We face a financial crisis of emergency proportions which strikes not only large city school systems—with overwhelming educational problems, rising cost levels for education and other municipal services, and

*Hawaii which, at least for school finance purposes, has one statewide school district, and Minnesota which recently moved toward reform of its education finance system, are among the exceptions.

declining tax bases—but many rural and suburban school districts as well. As a result, teachers have been laid off, schools are closing early and basic educational programs are being curtailed.

Thus, we have an outmoded, unfair system of financing public education in this country and a state of near bankruptcy in many school systems.

Once again, in the face of decades of inaction by State and Federal authorities, the courts are taking the lead. On August 30, 1971, the California Supreme Court ruled in *Serrano* v. *Priest* that State-local systems of school finance—which link access to education funds with local wealth in real property valuation—violate the Equal Protection Clause of the 14th Amendment to the U.S. Constitution. Similar rulings have been handed down in cases affecting Texas and New Jersey. The *Serrano* principle is presently before the U.S. Supreme Court in *San Antonio* v. *Rodriguez*, 337 S. Supp. 280 (1971). If the holding of the three-judge United States District in *Rodriguez* is upheld, substantial changes will be required in the school finance systems of most, if not all, States.

But regardless of the Supreme Court's ultimate legal decision, the States and the Federal Government have both an opportunity and a responsibility to correct the inequities which the courts have brought to public attention. The challenge presented by *Serrano* and its progeny is to devise a system of education finance which allocates assistance fairly on the basis of need, rather than arbitrarily on the basis of local wealth.

While education is primarily a State function, the opportunity of every schoolchild for an equal education is a fundamental right in which the Nation as a whole and everyone of its citizens has a stake. The Federal Government can and should assist hard-pressed State and local governments in providing excellent educational opportunities for all children.

Our fairness in dealing with reform of education finance over the next decade will provide yet another test of our commitment to equal educational opportunity.

# Chapter 27—The Causes of Financial Inequality in Education

## A. How the System Works

### 1. A STATE RESPONSIBILITY

The major responsibility for education rests with State and local governments. Nearly every State constitution gives State government complete authority over arrangements for financing public schools. States typically specify the conditions under which localities may levy taxes for schools, appropriate State funds and determining how they shall be distributed among local districts, and set basic rules regarding school expenditures. However, although State governments have complete legal authority over arrangements for financing public schools, States have traditionally delegated much of their control over education to local school districts established under State law, 90 percent of which are independent of local government but dependent upon the State legislatures for their powers. This delegation has profound implications for school finance.

### 2. THE SOURCES OF EDUCATIONAL REVENUES

In 1970–71, States provided 41 percent of the funds used for public education, while local school district revenues—mainly from the property tax—provided 51 percent, and Federal revenues the same year accounted for only 7 percent. There have been only slight changes in the shares of these three levels of government in the past decade.* While the enactment of the Elementary and Secondary Education Act and other legislation more than doubled the Federal share from 4.4 percent to 8 percent in 1968, the Federal share has since declined to less than 7 percent in 1971. At the same time the State share increased from 39.1 percent in 1960 to 41.1 percent in 1971 while the local share declined from 56.5 percent to 52 percent during the same period. However, while the respective shares have remained relatively constant, there was a dramatic increase in the total revenues for education during the past decade. As Table 27–1 shows, revenues for public elementary and secondary schools rose from $14.7 billion in 1960 to $38.2 billion in 1970—an increase of $23.5 billion or nearly 160 percent. All but about $1.9 billion of this increase came from State and local sources.

*Note, however, that in any given State these proportions may vary substantially.

TABLE 27-1.—*Revenues for public elementary and secondary schools*

[In thousands]

| School year | Total | Federal | State | Local |
|---|---|---|---|---|
| 1959-60 | $14, 746, 618 | $651, 639 | $5, 768, 047 | $8, 326, 932 |
| 1961-62 | 17, 527, 707 | 760, 975 | 6, 789, 190 | 9, 977, 542 |
| 1963-64 | 20, 544, 182 | 896, 956 | 8, 078, 014 | 11, 569, 213 |
| 1965-66 | 25, 356, 858 | [1] 1, 996, 954 | 9, 920, 219 | 13, 439, 686 |
| 1966-67 [2] | 27, 256, 043 | 2, 162, 892 | 10, 661, 582 | 14, 431, 569 |
| 1967-68 [2] | 31, 092, 400 | 2, 472, 464 | 12, 231, 954 | 16, 387, 982 |
| 1968-69 [2] | 34, 756, 006 | 2, 570, 704 | 13, 866, 782 | 18, 318, 520 |
| 1969-70 [2] | 38, 246, 618 | 2, 549, 149 | 15, 634, 396 | 20, 063, 073 |
| Increase, 1959-60 to 1969-70: | | | | |
| Amount | 23, 500, 000 | 1, 897, 510 | 9, 866, 349 | 11, 736, 141 |
| Percent | 159. 4 | 191. 2 | 171. 1 | 140. 9 |
| Annual rate | 10. 0 | 11. 3 | 10. 5 | 9. 2 |

[1] Enactment of ESEA.
[2] NEA Research Division estimates. Estimates of Federal revenue may be lower than those which will be published later by the U.S. Office of Education because of partial omission of money value of food distribution for the school lunch program.
Source: U.S. Department of Health, Education, and Welfare, Office of Education "Statistics of State School Systems, 1965-66," Washington, D.C.: Government Printing Office, 1968, p. 11.
National Education Association Research Division, "Estimates of School Statistics, 1966-67, 1968-69, and 1969-70," Research Reports 1966-R20, 1968-R16 and 1969-R15. Washington, D.C.: the association, 1966, 1968 and 1969.
Financial Status of the Public Schools 1970, Committee on Educational Finance, National Education Association, Washington, D.C.

## B. THE CENTRAL SOURCE OF INEQUALITY

In the early 1930s there were approximately 130,000 local school districts in the country, including thousands of one-room, one-teacher districts. As a result of school district consolidation, the number of districts steadily declined during the 1940s, 1950s and 1960s until in 1969-70, there were only 18,904. It is the delegation of unequal taxing power by the States to such a vast and changing array of local jurisdictions that is the most pervasive single determinant of the quality and level of educational services in local schools. It has resulted in two central facts:

*First*, local school districts are grossly unequal in their local fiscal resources per pupil.

*Second*, the level of resources is often unrelated to the quantity or quality of educational services and programs needed by a district's pupils.

To compensate for these inequalities, most States have, in theory, designed their formulas for aiding local school districts to either equalize the tax burdens placed upon local jurisdictions or make provision for additional services in poorer districts. With few exceptions, however, most have succeeded in equalizing *neither* tax burdens *nor* educational services.

In addition to local disparities based on over-reliance on local property taxes, there are major differences in the ability of States to finance education. States such as Mississippi, with a per-pupil expenditure in 1970-71 which amounted to only two-thirds of the national average simply lack the tax base to match the expenditures of wealthier States.

## C. The Property Tax

### 1. HOW THE PROPERTY TAX SYSTEM WORKS

Fifty-one percent of all educational revenues are locally generated, almost all from property taxes.

The amount of revenue raised by property taxes depends upon two factors: the "assessed" value of the property to be taxed, and the amount of tax levied on that value. The assessed value is usually a percentage of the "market value" of the property—the price which it would bring if it were put up for sale. The amount of tax on the assessed value is determined by the "tax rate" which is usually expressed as the "millage rate." One mill is one-tenth of a cent or one-thousandth of a dollar. The millage rate applied to the assessed value determines the amount of tax to be paid.

Thus, for example, a house with a market value of $30,000 might be assessed at $10,000. If the tax were at the rate of 10 mills—$1 for each $100, or $10 for each $1,000 of assessed valuation—the tax would be $100.

It is evident that any one of three variables can affect the amount of tax money generated through this system:

*First*, the market value of the property.

*Second*, the percentage of market value assigned as assessed value.

*Third*, the tax rate.

Each of these variables may differ among school districts. The house, for example, with a market value of $30,000 in one community, or neighborhood, may be worth only $20,000 in another. In the latter, the taxing authority must either raise the assessed value to a higher percentage of market value or raise the tax rate or some combination of both to generate the same revenue.

In the aggregate, therefore, the money raised through property taxes in a given district depends first upon the total value of all the property or the district's "tax base." The standard method of measuring a district's tax base for school purposes is to divide the total assessed valuation by the number of pupils enrolled in the district's schools. It is this "assessed valuation per pupil" which defines the relative taxing "ability" of the school district. The tax rate or millage rate then measures the district's "effort" to support its schools. Note, however, that the best measure of taxing ability would be based on the market value rather than the assessed value of property located in the district.

### 2. THE UNEQUAL RESULTS OF PROPERTY TAXES

The amount of "effort" a district must make to raise money for its schools, therefore, depends upon the size of its tax base. Clearly, a wealthy district that has $100,000 of assessed valuation for each student would not have to tax itself as hard to raise the same revenue as a poor district that had only $10,000 of assessed value per student. In fact, the latter district would have to tax itself 10 times as hard as the former to generate the same dollar amount of money. This is not an unrealistic example. Table 27–2 displays recent property tax data for the State of Texas. One hundred and ten school districts are categorized and ranked in terms of their wealth per pupil. The mean tax rate for each $100 of assessed valuation was then calculated for each category. This tax was then applied against the wealth base to determine the dollar amount per pupil that could be raised by the average district in that category. As Table 27–2 shows, while the 10 districts with a market value of taxable property per pupil above $100,000 enjoyed a tax rate of 31 cents per $100, the poorest four districts, with less than $10,000 in market value per pupil had a tax rate of 70 cents. Nevertheless, the low rate of the rich districts yielded $585 per pupil, while the high tax effort of the poor districts yielded only $60 per pupil.

TABLE 27–2.—*The relationship of district wealth to tax effort and tax yield,*[1] *Texas school districts categorized by equalized property values, equalized tax rates, and yield of rates*

| Categories: Market value of taxable property per pupil | Equalized tax rates on $100 | Yield per pupi (equalized rate apl plied to district market value) |
|---|---|---|
| Above $100,000 (10 districts) | $0. 31 | $585 |
| $100,000 to $50,000 (26 districts) | . 38 | 262 |
| $50,000 to $30,000 (30 districts) | . 55 | 213 |
| $30,000 to $10,000 (40 districts) | . 72 | 162 |
| Below $10,000 (4 districts) | . 70 | 60 |

[1] Policy Institute, Syracuse University Research Corp., Syracuse, N.Y. From evidentiary affidavit of Joel S. Berke in *Rodriguez* v. *San Antonio.*

As the California Supreme Court concluded in *Serrano* v. *Priest:*

> . . . so long as the assessed valuation within a district's boundaries is a major determinant of how much it can spend for its schools, only a district with a large tax base will be truly able to decide how much it really cares about education. The poor district cannot freely choose to tax itself into an excellence which its tax rolls cannot provide. *Far from being necessary to promote local fiscal choice, the present financing system actually deprives the less wealthy districts of that option.* [Emphasis added.]

In California the assessed valuation per unit of average daily attendance of elementary schoolchildren in the school year 1969–70 ranged from a low of $103 to a high of $952,156, a ratio of nearly 1 to 10,000. It is not difficult to find similar disparities in many, if not most, other States.

### 3. THE REGRESSIVENESS OF PROPERTY TAXES

The property tax is an ancient tax first used when the value of real property owned by an individual served as the best measure of his ability to pay taxes. In today's society, however, personal income is perhaps the most accurate measure of ability to pay taxes. As the previous section demonstrates, property taxes are clearly regressive as they apply to rich and poor school districts. For the individual, housing represents a diminishing proportion of a person's income as he becomes wealthier. A family earning $10,000 a year may very well live in a house valued at twice that amount ($20,000), but another family with a $100,000 income is not as likely to live in a house valued at $200,000. To take a realistic example, suppose the $100,000 income-family lives in a home assessed at $80,000. A tax rate of $2.50 per $100 of assessed valuation (25 mills) will be a much larger burden for the lower income family. It will pay $500 in property taxes—5 percent of its income. Yet the $100,000 income family will pay $2,000 in taxes, four times as many dollars, but an amount equal to only 2 percent of their annual income.

Property taxes account for an average of 41.2 percent of all taxes raised by State and local governments in the United States. Among the 50 States the per-capita property tax as a percent of total per-capita State and local taxes range from 16.6 percent in Alabama to 61 percent in New Hampshire. The regressiveness of property taxes together with sales taxes account for the regressive nature of State and local taxes generally. Table 27–3 shows, for each State, the total tax burden as a percentage of family income. The variance is from 16.6 percent of the $3,000 income for a family in Maine to 3.1 percent for the family with a $50,000 income in Washington. Nationally the percentage of State and local taxes paid steadily decreases as income rises with the $3,000 family paying 12.8 percent, the $10,000 family 8.7 percent and the $50,000 family 5.4 percent.

TABLE 27-3.—*Differences in family tax burdens, distribution of State-local tax burdens relative to family income size, 50 States and all-State average, 1968**

[Tax burdens as percentages of income]

| State | Adjusted gross income, family of 4, 1968 | | | | | | | | | | | | | |
|---|---|---|---|---|---|---|---|---|---|---|---|---|---|---|
| | $3,000 | | $5,000 | | $7,500 | | $10,000 | | $17,500 | | $25,000 | | $50,000 | |
| | Percent | Rank | Percent | Rank | Percent | Rank | Percent | Rank | Percent | Rank | Percent | Rank | Percent | Rank |
| All States | 12. 8 | | 10. 9 | | 9. 4 | | 8. 7 | | 6. 5 | | 6. 5 | | 5. 4 | |
| Alabama | 10. 7 | 42 | 8. 8 | 44 | 7. 8 | 40 | 7. 5 | 39 | 5. 8 | 36 | 5. 7 | 36 | 4. 5 | 38 |
| Alaska | 12. 1 | 32 | 10. 5 | 30 | 9. 2 | 29 | 8. 5 | 29 | 6. 4 | 28 | 6. 5 | 27 | 6. 4 | 12 |
| Arizona | 14. 5 | 15 | 12. 6 | 10 | 10. 8 | 9 | 9. 8 | 10 | 7. 4 | 11 | 7. 7 | 8 | 7. 3 | 4 |
| Arkansas | 10. 4 | 44 | 8. 9 | 43 | 7. 7 | 42 | 7. 1 | 42 | 5. 6 | 40 | 5. 7 | 37 | 4. 8 | 35 |
| California | 12. 1 | 33 | 9. 8 | 34 | 8. 3 | 37 | 7. 9 | 35 | 6. 3 | 30 | 6. 9 | 22 | 6. 6 | 8 |
| Colorado | 12. 7 | 24 | 11. 1 | 21 | 9. 8 | 18 | 9. 3 | 18 | 7. 2 | 15 | 7. 7 | 9 | 6. 6 | 9 |
| Connecticut | 14. 6 | 12 | 11. 7 | 15 | 9. 5 | 21 | 8. 2 | 30 | 5. 9 | 35 | 5. 6 | 39 | 4. 4 | 40 |
| Delaware | 10. 9 | 37 | 9. 1 | 39 | 8. 2 | 38 | 8. 2 | 31 | 7. 1 | 18 | 7. 5 | 12 | 6. 2 | 13 |
| Florida | 15. 0 | 10 | 12. 2 | 13 | 10. 0 | 16 | 8. 7 | 26 | 6. 0 | 34 | 5. 8 | 35 | 4. 6 | 37 |
| Georgia | 13. 7 | 18 | 11. 2 | 20 | 9. 5 | 22 | 8. 8 | 23 | 7. 2 | 16 | 7. 6 | 11 | 5. 5 | 22 |
| Hawaii | 9. 7 | 48 | 9. 8 | 35 | 9. 6 | 20 | 9. 8 | 11 | 7. 5 | 8 | 7. 7 | 10 | 6. 8 | 6 |
| Idaho | 11. 9 | 34 | 10. 8 | 27 | 9. 1 | 31 | 8. 8 | 24 | 7. 0 | 21 | 7. 4 | 15 | 5. 9 | 15 |
| Illinois | 14. 6 | 13 | 11. 7 | 16 | 9. 5 | 23 | 8. 2 | 32 | 5. 6 | 41 | 5. 1 | 41 | 3. 9 | 43 |
| Indiana | 15. 4 | 6 | 13. 1 | 5 | 11. 2 | 4 | 10. 1 | 8 | 7. 5 | 9 | 7. 3 | 16 | 5. 7 | 18 |
| Iowa | 15. 0 | 11 | 13. 2 | 4 | 12. 0 | 3 | 11. 1 | 3 | 8. 0 | 6 | 8. 0 | 6 | 6. 0 | 14 |
| Kansas | 15. 5 | 5 | 12. 7 | 9 | 9. 3 | 26 | 9. 6 | 13 | 7. 3 | 14 | 7. 3 | 17 | 5. 7 | 19 |
| Kentucky | 12. 4 | 28 | 10. 9 | 26 | 10. 6 | 11 | 10. 4 | 5 | 7. 9 | 6 | 7. 8 | 7 | 5. 9 | 16 |
| Louisiana | 9. 7 | 49 | 8. 3 | 48 | 6. 7 | 49 | 6. 3 | 47 | 4. 5 | 46 | 4. 9 | 43 | 5. 2 | 26 |
| Maine | 16. 6 | 1 | 13. 7 | 2 | 11. 0 | 7 | 9. 6 | 14 | 6. 7 | 25 | 6. 3 | 30 | 4. 9 | 33 |
| Maryland | 14. 6 | 14 | 13. 0 | 7 | 12. 5 | 1 | 12. 6 | 1 | 9. 4 | 1 | 9. 7 | 2 | 7. 8 | 3 |
| Massachusetts [1] | 14. 3 | 16 | 12. 1 | 14 | 11. 2 | 5 | 10. 3 | 6 | 7. 6 | 7 | 7. 5 | 13 | 5. 5 | 23 |
| Michigan | 12. 9 | 22 | 11. 1 | 22 | 9. 5 | 24 | 8. 9 | 22 | 6. 9 | 24 | 6. 8 | 24 | 5. 2 | 27 |
| Minnesota | 12. 2 | 30 | 11. 3 | 18 | 10. 8 | 10 | 10. 7 | 4 | 8. 4 | 3 | 8. 7 | 4 | 6. 8 | 7 |
| Mississippi | 15. 2 | 8 | 12. 3 | 12 | 10. 4 | 15 | 9. 8 | 12 | 7. 4 | 12 | 7. 3 | 18 | 5. 7 | 20 |
| Missouri | 12. 8 | 23 | 11. 0 | 25 | 9. 4 | 25 | 8. 7 | 27 | 6. 4 | 29 | 6. 4 | 29 | 4. 9 | 34 |

| | | | | | | | | | | | | | |
|---|---|---|---|---|---|---|---|---|---|---|---|---|---|
| Montana | 10. 8 | 40 | 9. 1 | 40 | 8. 1 | 39 | 7. 7 | 37 | 6. 3 | 31 | 6. 3 | 31 | 4. 8 | 36 |
| Nebraska | 15. 1 | 9 | 12. 6 | 11 | 10. 5 | 12 | 9. 5 | 16 | 7. 5 | 10 | 6. 9 | 23 | 5. 8 | 17 |
| Nevada | 10. 7 | 43 | 8. 7 | 46 | 7. 0 | 47 | 6. 1 | 48 | 4. 3 | 49 | 4. 1 | 48 | 3. 3 | 48 |
| New Hampshire | 13. 5 | 19 | 10. 8 | 28 | 8. 7 | 34 | 7. 5 | 40 | 5. 3 | 42 | 5. 0 | 42 | 3. 7 | 46 |
| New Jersey [1] | 16. 3 | 3 | 13. 4 | 3 | 10. 9 | 8 | 9. 6 | 15 | 6. 7 | 26 | 6. 5 | 28 | 5. 2 | 28 |
| New Mexico | 12. 2 | 31 | 10. 4 | 31 | 9. 0 | 32 | 8. 1 | 33 | 5. 8 | 37 | 5. 7 | 38 | 5. 0 | 32 |
| New York | 13. 2 | 21 | 11. 5 | 17 | 10. 5 | 13 | 10. 2 | 7 | 8. 3 | 4 | 9. 7 | 3 | 9. 8 | 1 |
| North Carolina | 10. 4 | 45 | 9. 3 | 38 | 8. 8 | 33 | 8. 8 | 25 | 7. 0 | 22 | 7. 5 | 41 | 7. 3 | 5 |
| North Dakota | 13. 3 | 20 | 11. 1 | 23 | 9. 2 | 30 | 8. 5 | 29 | 7. 4 | 13 | 8. 1 | 5 | 6. 5 | 11 |
| Ohio | 10. 9 | 38 | 9. 1 | 41 | 7. 6 | 43 | 6. 8 | 44 | 4. 8 | 44 | 4. 7 | 45 | 3. 9 | 44 |
| Oklahoma | 12. 3 | 39 | 10. 2 | 33 | 8. 4 | 35 | 7. 7 | 38 | 5. 7 | 38 | 6. 0 | 33 | 5. 2 | 29 |
| Oregon | 10. 9 | 39 | 9. 7 | 36 | 9. 3 | 27 | 9. 2 | 20 | 7. 1 | 19 | 7. 3 | 19 | 5. 6 | 21 |
| Pennsylvania | 15. 4 | 7 | 13. 0 | 8 | 11. 1 | 6 | 9. 9 | 9 | 7. 0 | 23 | 6. 7 | 25 | 5. 2 | 30 |
| Rhode Island | 16. 4 | 2 | 13. 1 | 6 | 10. 5 | 14 | 9. 1 | 21 | 6. 5 | 27 | 6. 0 | 34 | 4. 5 | 39 |
| South Carolina | 9. 8 | 47 | 8. 3 | 49 | 7. 4 | 46 | 7. 1 | 42 | 6. 1 | 32 | 6. 6 | 26 | 5. 3 | 24 |
| South Dakota | 13. 9 | 17 | 11. 3 | 19 | 9. 3 | 28 | 8. 1 | 34 | 5. 7 | 39 | 5. 4 | 40 | 4. 3 | 41 |
| Tennessee | 12. 5 | 27 | 10. 3 | 32 | 8. 4 | 36 | 7. 4 | 41 | 5. 0 | 43 | 4. 9 | 44 | 4. 0 | 42 |
| Texas | 11. 3 | 36 | 9. 1 | 42 | 7. 5 | 44 | 6. 5 | 46 | 4. 6 | 45 | 4. 5 | 46 | 3. 7 | 47 |
| Utah | 12. 7 | 25 | 10. 8 | 29 | 9. 7 | 19 | 9. 3 | 19 | 7. 2 | 17 | 7. 0 | 21 | 5. 3 | 25 |
| Vermont | 12. 7 | 26 | 11. 1 | 24 | 9. 9 | 17 | 9. 4 | 17 | 7. 1 | 20 | 7. 3 | 20 | 6. 6 | 10 |
| Virginia | 10. 1 | 46 | 8. 8 | 45 | 7. 8 | 41 | 7. 8 | 36 | 6. 1 | 33 | 6. 2 | 32 | 5. 1 | 31 |
| Washington | 11. 7 | 35 | 9. 4 | 37 | 7. 5 | 45 | 6. 5 | 46 | 4. 4 | 47 | 4. 1 | 49 | 3. 1 | 50 |
| West Virginia | 9. 4 | 50 | 7. 8 | 50 | 6. 6 | 50 | 5. 9 | 50 | 4. 4 | 48 | 4. 3 | 47 | 3. 8 | 45 |
| Wisconsin | 15. 7 | 4 | 13. 8 | 1 | 12. 5 | 2 | 12. 2 | 2 | 9. 3 | 2 | 9. 9 | 1 | 8. 2 | 2 |
| Wyoming | 10. 8 | 41 | 8. 7 | 47 | 7. 0 | 48 | 7. 0 | 48 | 4. 3 | 50 | 4. 1 | 50 | 3. 3 | 49 |

[1] Massachusetts and New Jersey rely on property tax. No State income tax in New Jersey.

*Hearings of the U.S. Senate Select Committee on Equal Educational Opportunity, Part 16D–3, *Inequality in School Finance: General appendixes.*

It is clear that State and local taxes, generally, and residential property taxes, in particular, hit hardest on low-income families—especially retired households for whom payment of property taxes can consume as much as 50–60 percent of a family's limited income.

#### 4. THE ADMINISTRATION OF PROPERTY TAXES

Often the inequities inherent in the local property tax are compounded by administrative problems.

Too often assessors are inexpert in real estate appraisal techniques, especially when it comes to valuing complicated commercial and industrial properties. Too often the assessment process is subject to political pressures. As a consequence, assessment of equivalent properties may vary widely from community to community, and even within the same community. And in many school districts, where property values are constantly changing, assessors often are not given the resources to update assessments on a regular basis. Thus they do not reflect changes in property values due to inflation or the rising demand for housing. All of these imperfections may, alone or in concert, distort the evaluation process.

In addition, the historical tendency has been to allow the ratio of assessed value to full market value to decline—reducing the capacity of the school district to tap local funds. For example, the assessment ratio in the city of Detroit declined from 90 percent of market value in 1930 to about 50 percent in 1960. There was a similar decline in Baltimore from 90 percent in 1930 to 64 percent in 1960; from 80 percent to 45 percent in Cleveland; from 50 percent to 23 percent in Los Angeles; and, from 65 percent to 30 percent in St. Louis. These reductions are particularly restrictive in those States which limit local school taxing authority by imposing ceilings on tax rates, and even more restrictive on the many large cities for which taxing authority is limited even more stringently than for other school districts in the same State.

Finally, it has been pointed out that, nationally, it is the homeowner who bears the principal property tax burden—and that burden has become increasingly heavy over time. In 1957, residential property taxes accounted for 54.9 percent of all property taxes in the United States. By 1967 that share had increased to 60.8 percent.

Under legislative exemption and local assessment practice much commercial property is taxed at less than value, or not taxed at all. Ralph Nader told the committee:

> There are literally billions of dollars in potential property tax revenues that State and local governments have not begun to tax, and much of which they can tax simply by enforcing the laws as they are already written. It is our estimate that at least $7 billion in property tax revenues can be collected which are not collected each year.

### D. State Aid to Public Schools

About 41 percent of all revenues for education are supplied by the States for the operation of public elementary and secondary schools. If local property tax systems operate to classify school districts and determine the quality of education by wealth, the operation of State-aid formulas often aggravate and compound the inequity by purporting but failing to equalize the educational resources of local school districts.

Most State-aid formulas provide both a flat per-pupil grant to every school district regardless of its tax base or tax effort and an "equalization" grant which is distributed in an amount which bears an inverse relationship to the resources of the local school district. This, when added to the flat grant, is designed to guarantee a minimum per-pupil expenditure in every school district.

While State-aid formulas vary from State to State, California is fairly typical of the way these systems operate. It was described in the *Serrano* case:

> Most of the remaining school revenue comes from the State School Fund pursuant to the "foundation program," through which the State undertakes to supplement local taxes in order to provide a "minimum" amount of guaranteed support to all districts . . . With certain minor exceptions, the foundation program ensures that each school district will receive annually, from State or local funds, $355 for each elementary school pupil and $488 for each high school student.
>
> The State contribution is supplied in two principal forms. "Basic State aid" consists of a flat grant to each district of $125 per pupil per year, regardless of the relative wealth of the district. "Equalization aid" is distributed in inverse proportion to the wealth of the district.
>
> To compute the amount of equalization aid to which a district is entitled, the State Superintendent of Public Instruction first determines how much local property tax revenue would be generated if the district were to levy a hypothetical tax at a rate of $1 on each $100 assessed valuation in elementary school districts and $.80 per $100 in high school districts. To that figure, he adds the $125 per pupil basic aid grant. If the sum of those two amounts is less than the foundation program minimum for that district, the State contributes the difference. Thus, equalization funds guarantee to the poorer districts a basic minimum revenue, while wealthier districts are ineligible for such assistance.
>
> An additional State program of "supplemental aid" is available to subsidize particularly poor school districts which are willing to make an extra local tax effort. An elementary district with an assessed valuation of $12,500 or less per pupil may obtain up to $125 more for each child if it sets its local tax rate above a certain statutory level. A high school district whose assessed valuation does not exceed $24,500 per pupil is eligible for a supplement of up to $72 per child if its local tax is sufficiently high.

The Court went on to describe the inequities in this system:

> Although equalization aid and supplemental aid temper the disparities which result from the vast variations in real property assessed valuation, wide differentials remain in the revenue available to individual districts and, consequently, in the level of educational expenditures. For example, in Los Angeles County, where plaintiff children attend school, the

> Baldwin Park Unified School District expended only $577.49 to educate each of its pupils in 1968–69; during the same year the Pasadena Unified School District spent $840.19 on every student; and the Beverly Hills Unified School District paid out $1,231.72 per child . . .
>
> The source of these disparities is unmistakable: in Baldwin Park the assessed valuation per child totaled only $3,706; in Pasadena, assessed valuation was $13,706; while in Beverly Hills, the corresponding figure was $50,885—a ratio of 1 to 4 to 13. Thus, the State grants are inadequate to offset the inequalities inherent in a financing system based on widely varying local tax bases.
>
> Furthermore, basic aid, which constitutes about half of the State educational funds, actually widens the gap between rich and poor districts. Such aid is distributed on a uniform per pupil basis to all districts, irrespective of a district's wealth. Beverly Hills, as well as Baldwin Park, receives $125 from the State for each of its students.
>
> For Baldwin Park the basic grant is essentially meaningless. Under the foundation program the State must make up the difference between $355 per elementary child and $47.91, the amount of revenue per child which Baldwin Park could raise by levying a tax of $1 per $100 of assessed valuation. Although under present law, that difference is composed partly of basic aid and partly of equalization aid, if the basic aid grant did not exist, the district would still receive the same amount of State aid—all in equalizing funds.
>
> For Beverly Hills, however, the $125 flat grant has real financial significance. Since a tax rate of $1 per $100 there would produce $870 per elementary student, Beverly Hills is far too rich to qualify for equalizing aid. Nevertheless, it still receives $125 per child from the State, thus enlarging the economic chasm between it and Baldwin Park.*

As in California, most States prevent equalization grants from becoming totally operable by placing a ceiling on total State support. The further this ceiling is from the actual needs of poor-school districts the more the State-aid formula fails to equalize per-pupil expenditures within the State.

Thus, these aid formulas provide a minimum per-pupil expenditure for the poorest district which is well below that in wealthy districts which have high tax bases and can provide superior schools with relatively little tax effort. The result is shown in Table 27–4 which presents the wide variations in per-pupil expenditures among school districts within each State.

* *Serrano* v. *Priest*, 487 p. 2d 1241 (1971). Supreme Court of the State of California, Oct. 21, 1971.

TABLE 27-4.—*Intrastate disparities in per-pupil expenditures, 1969–70*

| | High | Low | High/low index |
|---|---|---|---|
| Alabama | $581 | $344 | 1. 7 |
| Alaska | 1, 810 | 480 | 3. 8 |
| Arizona | 2, 223 | 436 | 5. 1 |
| Arkansas | 664 | 343 | 2. 0 |
| California | 2, 414 | 569 | 4. 2 |
| Colorado | 2, 801 | 444 | 6. 3 |
| Connecticut | 1, 311 | 499 | 2. 6 |
| Delaware | 1, 081 | 633 | 1. 7 |
| District of Columbia | | | |
| Florida | 1, 036 | 593 | 1. 7 |
| Georgia | 736 | 365 | 2. 0 |
| Hawaii | | | |
| Idaho | 1, 763 | 474 | 3. 7 |
| Illinois | 2, 295 | 391 | 5. 9 |
| Indiana | 965 | 447 | 2. 2 |
| Iowa | 1, 167 | 592 | 2. 0 |
| Kansas | 1, 831 | 454 | 4. 0 |
| Kentucky | 885 | 358 | 2. 5 |
| Louisiana | 892 | 499 | 1. 8 |
| Maine | 1, 555 | 229 | 6. 8 |
| Maryland | 1, 037 | 635 | 1. 6 |
| Massachusetts | 1, 281 | 515 | 2. 5 |
| Michigan | 1, 364 | 491 | 2. 8 |
| Minnesota | 903 | 370 | 2. 4 |
| Mississippi | 825 | 283 | 3. 0 |
| Missouri | 1, 699 | 213 | 4. 0 |
| Montana average of groups | 1, 716 | 539 | 3. 2 |
| Nebraska average of groups | 1, 175 | 623 | 1. 9 |
| Nevada | 1, 679 | 746 | 2. 3 |
| New Hampshire | 1, 191 | 311 | 3. 8 |
| New Jersey 1968–69 | 1, 485 | 400 | 3. 7 |
| New Mexico | 1, 183 | 477 | 2. 5 |
| New York | 1, 889 | 669 | 2. 8 |
| North Carolina | 733 | 467 | 1. 4 |
| North Dakota county averages | 1, 623 | 686 | 2. 3 |
| Ohio | 1, 685 | 413 | 4. 0 |
| Oklahoma | 2, 566 | 342 | 7. 5 |
| Oregon | 1, 432 | 399 | 3. 5 |
| Pennslyvania | 1, 401 | 484 | 2. 9 |
| Rhode Island | 1, 206 | 531 | 2. 3 |
| South Carolina | 610 | 397 | 1. 5 |
| South Dakota | 1, 741 | 350 | 5. 0 |

Professor Michael Kirst of the Stanford University School of Education has summarized the effects of State educational finance formulas:

> At best, most State-aid equalization programs have helped to establish a minimum education program throughout the State—that is available to all students regardless of the fiscal ability of their local school district. At the same time these programs of "equalization" have provided opportunities for wealthy districts, whether the wealth is created by location of real property or high personal income, to supplement the minimum program to the extent they desire from their own local fiscal resources.

> The variation in equalized property per student is enormous within the States. This fact, coupled with the ceiling on State equalization grants, has caused differences of per-pupil expenditure among districts within a given State to vary by multiples of two or three in some instances. An additional comment on this situation is that, all too often, the district spending the lower amount for education is very often exceeding—in tax effort per $1,000 of personal income—the effort made by the district that is supporting education at the upper extremity of per-pupil expenditures.*

In short, not only do the children of the poor have less money spent for their schooling—and consequently unequal and less adequate school services—but also, relative to their income, their parents frequently pay more for those unequal services.

---

*Hearings of the U.S. Senate Select Committee on Equal Educational Opportunity, Part 17, *Delivery Systems for Federal Aid to Disadvantaged Children*, Oct. 7, 1971.

# Chapter 28—Equal Protection and Equitable Finance

Within the past year both Federal and State courts have begun to upset the inequitable patterns in the financing of elementary and secondary education. In a series of decisions which, may have the most profound significance for the future of education since the *Brown* decision in 1954, courts in California, Minnesota, Texas and New Jersey have held that the present educational finance systems in those States violate the Equal Protection Clause of the 14th Amendment to the U.S. Constitution.

Beginning with the California Supreme Court's pioneering decision in *Serrano* v. *Priest* (487 P. 2d 241) in August 1971, these courts have held that education is a "fundamental interest" entitled to constitutional protection; that public schoolchildren "enjoy a right under the equal protection guarantee of the 14th Amendment to have the level of spending for their education unaffected by variations in the taxable wealth in their school district or their parents"; and, that the States must change their finance systems to assure that the quality of education is no longer a function of wealth—other than the wealth of the State as a whole.

It is important to note what these decisions have *not* done. They have not imposed any particular finance formula upon the States. They have not said that per-pupil expenditures must be equal for every pupil, or in every school, or school district, or that educational dollars must be distributed in any particular manner. They have simply identified one criterion for distributing funds which should not be used—community wealth.

In the words of Judge Miles W. Lord of the Federal District Court in Minnesota:

> It is the singular virtue of the *Serrano* principle that the State remains free to pursue all imaginable interests except that of distributing education according to wealth. . . . The fiscal neutrality principle not only removes discrimination by wealth but also allows free play to local effort and choice and openly permits the State to adopt one of many optional school funding systems which do not violate the equal protection clause. This court in no way suggests to the Minnesota Legislature that it adopt any one particular financing system. Rather, this memorandum only recognizes a Constitutional standard through which the legislature may direct and measure its efforts.

It remains to be seen whether the U.S. Supreme Court will adopt the *Serrano* principles. The issue is now before the Court in the case of *San Antonio Independent School District* v. *Rodriquez* (S. Ct. No. 71–1332), challenging the school finance system of the State of

Texas. But in any event, the responsibility for designing equitable State finance systems rests squarely on the shoulders of State legislatures.

The decision to form elementary and secondary school finance confronts the States with a broad range of choices. The States clearly must assume an expanded role in financing education if they are to perform an equalizing function; however, full State financing is almost certainly not necessary. And the expanded State role can be financed in a variety of ways—conversion in whole or part from local to statewide property taxation, a progressive State income tax, or a regressive sales tax, and others.

The committee strongly suggests that a larger role in education finance be given to progressive income taxes. Unlike the property tax base, the income tax expands with the economy; and the income tax does not strike as unfairly at the elderly, and low- and moderate-income families.

An equally broad range of theoretical choices appears available for redesigning existing finance systems—ranging from efforts to achieve equal per-pupil expenditures in all school districts in the State* to the allocation of resources based on criteria of educational need.**

We do not believe that "dollar equity"—equal per-pupil spending in all school districts in a State—is an adequate response to the challenge of school finance reform. And we question whether such an approach would ultimately be upheld under the *Serrano* principle.

Mathematical statewide equality in expenditures will often result in continued educational inequality for cities and less-affluent suburban and rural areas, which suffer under existing finance systems. Equivalent educational resources may have costs which vary widely among different areas of a single State or even metropolitan area. And school districts serving above-average numbers of children with special needs will require additional resources.

Urban school systems clearly provide a case in point. City school districts with per-pupil expenditures which equal, or exceed those of many neighboring urban districts often find themselves unable to provide equivalent services—because of both higher urban costs and the greater proportion of children with educational difficulties contained in the urban population.

Moreover, in centercities education must compete for its share of the tax dollar with a broad range of other municipal services which also must be maintained from local taxes. Large city tax rates for education are often below the State average, while total city tax rates are often far above.

As a result, State imposition of a uniform education property tax rate could mean still higher taxes within central cities; while redistribution of existing education funds to achieve equal per-pupil expenditures would often mean reduced funds for central city school systems.

---

*Adjustment for differences in cost-of-education should be essential.

**A third approach suggested by Professor Jone E. Coons, is through so-called "power equalizing" State aid formulas. Under this proposal school districts would be permitted to tax themselves at different rates, but the State would assure that all districts taxing at any given rate are able to make equal per-pupil expenditures—by supplementing the tax revenues of poor districts and by requiring payment of a share of more affluent districts' tax revenues to the State treasury. There are an almost infinite variety of variations of this method.

Professor Joel S. Berke of Syracuse University and Professor John J. Callahan of the University of Virginia have analysed the effects of an educational finance system based on equal per-pupil school district expenditures in a study encompassing the central city school districts of the country's 37 largest metropolitan areas. The study* was published by the Select Committee in 1972. It demonstrates how most cities would pay more and receive less.

The authors hypothesized that the States in which these 37 cities are located assumed the full local share costs of education through a uniform statewide property tax and distributed State educational revenues on the basis of equal per-pupil expenditures in every district. The results are summarized below:

- In three-fourths of the cities, school taxes would rise.
- Out of 28 cities for which 1970 per-pupil expenditures were available, 18 would receive less money from the States than they presently receive under their existing revenue structures. Thus, not only would most large cities pay more in taxes for education, they would also receive less.
- If the cities were to apply new statewide tax rates to their own tax bases and keep the money for their own schools, 80 percent of the 37 cities would have had higher revenues than they would receive if the States were to distribute educational revenues equally in every school district. However, five out of 28 cities would still have less money than they did in 1970.

What the Berke-Callahan study demonstrates is that it is not enough simply to advocate State assumption of educational costs through uniform statewide tax rates, together with a reduction of educational expenditure disparities through the distribution of revenues on the basis of mathematical equality. States must devise educational finance plans that will match resources to the needs of school districts, and which will provide the special help needed for pupils with learning disadvantages.

We believe that reform of educational financing at the State level should be based on the following principles:

- If at all possible, school systems presently able to afford educational services of high quality from locally raised funds should not be required to sacrifice those services. This means that additional revenues must be made available to increase the resources available to school systems which are presently underfinanced.
- School finance reform should not be based on mathematical "dollar-equalization" but should take account of the special problems of urban and less-affluent rural and suburban areas, and the special costs of educating children who are educationally disadvantaged, bilingual, handicapped or have other special needs.
- The major role in financing education should be shifted away from the local property tax to State funding. In addition, education revenues should be borne in larger part by progressive State income taxes, rather than regressive sales or property taxes.

---

******The Financial Aspects of Equality of Educational Opportunity and Inequities in School Finance*, **committee print of the U.S. Senate Select Committee on Equal Educational Opportunity, January 1972.**

But we note that rapid elimination of property taxes might well result in unjustifiable windfall benefits to property owners in the form of increased land values.

- Property tax systems—whether conducted at the State or local level, or both—should be reformed through State requirements of fair, uniform and professional assessment practices.

It appears that there may be no legal obligation to equalize the ability to finance education among States. But we cannot defend a State of regional bias in the allocation of educational resources. We believe there is a special Federal responsibility to assist in equalizing the ability to finance public education at a State, as well as the local level. Our proposals contained in Chapter 30 for expanded aid for compensatory education and a broad new general aid initiative, would go far toward fulfilling that responsibility.

# Chapter 29—The Financial Crisis in Education

## A. The Gap Between Supply and Demand

As this Report goes to press, the Detroit School Board has voted to close the system's 300 schools for 8 weeks beginning December 21 because of inadequate funds.

Many school districts in this country are in a state of fiscal crisis. Since the end of World War II our public school system has experienced unparalleled growth. In the last 10 years alone, public elementary and secondary enrollment has increased more than 25 percent—from 36.6 million to 45.7 million students. While this growth rate has now begun to level off, by 1975 it is expected that at least another million students will be attending public school. At the same time, more children are completing a greater number of years of schooling and private school enrollment has declined significantly. This increased demand has been accompanied by improvements in educational services in our public schools. In the decade of the 1960s, for example, the number of pupils per instructional staff member was reduced—for the Nation as a whole—from 24.7 to 20.5. This change alone has been estimated to have added $2 billion a year to school costs or a total of $20 billion in the last decade.

This increase in demand for school services is reflected in a dramatic increase in total expenditures for elementary and secondary education. For the last decade alone, school costs have risen 153 percent—from $15.6 billion in 1960 to $39.5 billion in 1970. During this decade, school costs rose an average of 9.7 percent a year, substantially faster than the growth in the Nation's Gross National Product. Thus, during the same period when school costs increased more than 150 percent, the Gross National Product increased by 92.8 percent. Educational expenditures have therefore increased 43 percent faster than the increases in our economy, as a whole.

The burden of these higher educational costs has been borne principally by State and local government. Between 1960 and 1970, local taxpayers increased their share of educational costs by almost $12 billion, while State aid increased by nearly $10 billion. The Federal share increased by only $1.8 billion—from $651 million in 1960 to $2.6 billion in 1970.

But what is more significant than the rise in total educational costs is the fact that educational expenditures have made increasingly burdensome demands on State and local budgets for public services. Table 29–1 shows the percentage increases between 1953 and 1968 in State and local revenues for all purposes and those devoted to public elementary and secondary education. Using 1952 as the base year, State and local revenues from all sources increased 176 percent by 1968. At the same time, revenues for public education increased by 265 percent. A similar disparity exists when total revenues per pupil are compared with educational revenues per pupil. Total revenues increased by 101.1 percent from 1952 to 1968, while the amount per pupil increased by 168 percent.

**TABLE 29-1.**—*Percent increase over 1952 in per capita and per pupil in ADA amounts of State and local revenue, by purpose and level of Government, 1952–68**

| Fiscal year | Percent increase in amount per capita | | | | | | Percent increase in amount per pupil in ADA | | | | | |
|---|---|---|---|---|---|---|---|---|---|---|---|---|
| | State and local revenue for all purposes | | | State and local revenue for public elementary school education | | | State and local revenue for all purposes | | | State and local revenue for public elementary school education | | |
| | Total State and local | State | Local | Total State and local | State | Local | Total State and local | State | Local | Total State and local | State | Local |
| 1968 | 176. 0 | 187. 0 | 164. 8 | 265. 0 | 287. 5 | 250. 0 | 101. 1 | 108. 8 | 93. 2 | 168. 0 | 184. 0 | 157. 5 |
| 1967 | 153. 0 | 158. 7 | 147. 3 | | | | | | | | | |
| 1966 | 136. 6 | 140. 2 | 133. 0 | 200. 0 | 218. 8 | 187. 5 | 76. 3 | 78. 2 | 74. 1 | 124. 4 | 138. 7 | 115. 0 |
| 1965 | 117. 5 | 117. 4 | 117. 6 | | | | | | | | | |
| 1964 | 105. 5 | 104. 3 | 106. 6 | 157. 5 | 162. 5 | 154. 2 | 56. 2 | 54. 9 | 57. 5 | 97. 4 | 103. 8 | 93. 1 |
| 1963 | 91. 8 | 90. 2 | 93. 4 | | | | | | | | | |
| 1962 | 82. 5 | 77. 2 | 87. 9 | 127. 5 | 131. 2 | 125. 0 | 45. 3 | 40. 9 | 49. 8 | 81. 6 | 84. 9 | 79. 4 |
| 1961 | 72. 7 | 66. 3 | 79. 1 | | | | | | | | | |
| 1960 | 62. 8 | 58. 7 | 67. 0 | 97. 5 | 100. 0 | 95. 8 | 34. 2 | 30. 4 | 38. 1 | 63. 2 | 67. 9 | 60. 0 |
| 1959 | 48. 1 | 41. 3 | 54. 9 | | | | | | | | | |
| 1958 | 40. 4 | 34. 8 | 46. 2 | 70. 0 | 75. 0 | 66. 7 | 22. 2 | 17. 0 | 27. 3 | 47. 7 | 51. 9 | 45. 0 |
| 1957 | 35. 5 | 32. 6 | 38. 5 | | | | | | | | | |
| 1956 | 25. 7 | 22. 8 | 28. 6 | 37. 5 | 43. 8 | 33. 3 | 13. 1 | 10. 7 | 15. 5 | 25. 2 | 30. 2 | 28. 9 |
| 1955 | 15. 3 | 10. 9 | 19. 8 | | | | | | | | | |
| 1954 | 10. 4 | 7. 6 | 13. 2 | 17. 5 | 12. 5 | 20. 8 | 3. 4 | 1. 0 | 5. 8 | 10. 2 | 8. 5 | 11. 2 |
| 1953 | 5. 5 | 4. 3 | 6. 6 | | | | | | | | | |
| 1952 | | | | | | | | | | | | |

*U.S. Office of Education, National Center for Educational Statistics.

## B. The Taxpayer Revolt

Because the Federal contribution to education is relatively meager and because many States have been reluctant to increase their share of educational expenses, much of the growth in school spending has fallen upon local property taxpayers. The combined effect of growing tax rates and the inherent unfairness of the property tax has triggered a growing resistance among citizens to higher taxes for schools.

Many States place legal limits on the rates at which school districts can tax real property. Local voters must approve millage increases in tax override elections in order to raise any school revenue in excess of that generated by the State-mandated tax rate ceiling. Moreover, many States require a majority of two-thirds for such approval. In addition, aside from voter approval of tax increases, school districts must also seek approval of school bond issues.

The American voter at the local level is simply not tolerating many increases in additional money for schools. The most reliable indication of this resistance nationwide is indicated by the fact that between 1961 and 1969 the number of bond issues receiving voter approval dropped from 68.7 percent to 57.2 percent in school districts requiring a two-thirds majority, and from 81.1 percent to 65.1 percent where a simple majority was sufficient for passage. Similar evidence comes from an Investment Bankers' Association study which reveals that the percent of bond elections approved by voters declined from 89 percent in 1960 to 77 percent in 1965 and to 48 percent in 1970. Comparable findings are available for almost every State.

Thus, while school costs continue to rise, the principal source of school revenue is dwindling in its capacity to contribute.

## C. The Fiscal Crisis in the School District

The fiscal bind faced by public education today affects every type of school system—from rural communities with low tax bases, to suburban areas where property taxes have reached the saturation point, to cities where both the costs of municipal services and the numbers of disadvantaged schoolchildren have risen, often dramatically, over past decades. The committee has heard many examples.

Of more than 17,000 school districts in the Nation nearly 6,000, or a third, have less than 300 pupils. Some are simply too small to be economically self-sufficient. Many have inadequate facilities, limited curricula and low-paid teachers.

But the effects of size are not the only fiscal problem encountered by rural school districts. It is the lack of enough taxable real estate that especially puts many rural districts at a disadvantage.

Baldwin is a rural school district in southwest Michigan with 1,041 students. Twelve percent of its work force is unemployed, 25 percent of its population is elderly, and 40 percent of its families have incomes of less than $3,000. The school district covers 370 square miles. It ranks 494th out of 527 Michigan school districts in average annual teachers' salary. Even so, in the past 2 years, the Baldwin school district has run a deficit of between $80,000–$100,000. In testimony before the committee, Superintendent Edward C. McKinney described Baldwin's future:

> If the school system continues operating at the same level through June 30, 1972, the deficiency will be approximately $300,000, about 40 percent of our annual budget.
>
> At this time it appears that there is no reasonable way to cut an $750,000 annual budget enough to solve the problem in 1971–72 or even 1971–73, and still offer a program called "education." Few avenues are open with contracts signed, borrowing against anticipated taxes under questions because of the unresolved legal question of property taxes, and the concomitant requirement to reduce the budget and the improbability of doing so in midyear.
>
> If the problem is not resolved, by March or April the district will have exhausted all of its funds and be forced to close its doors. I have asked what happens if a school goes bankrupt? State authorities inform me that a school system cannot go bankrupt. The Baldwin Community Schools are far into the process of doing it. The Baldwin Schools are in trouble—deep, deep trouble.*

Covert, Mich. is more fortunate. It has about 1,000 students. It is a rural district, covering 35 square miles, not far from Baldwin. It has no industry and few large farms. A third of its students are from families on welfare. It now has only $5,000 in property valuation behind each of its pupils. But Covert is in the fortunate position of being about to acquire a windfall. Next year it will acquire its first industry, a nuclear power plant which is expected to raise its tax base from $5,000 to $45,000 per pupil.

Many suburban school districts are "bedroom" communities dependent upon residential real estate values and without an adequate commercial or industrial tax base to support their schools. Residents are understandably reluctant to see their property taxes go up year after year as school costs rise. Not untypical is the Ferguson-Florissant School District outside St. Louis, Mo. Dr. Warren M. Brown, school superintendent, described the fiscal plight of his district and others in suburban St. Louis:

> Last year our board of education conducted four elections in order to establish a property tax rate for school operations. The final vote was on the last day of the school year. This year it was necessary to hold six elections to establish a current operating rate which was finally passed on September 29, 1970. The opening of school had to be postponed from September 3 until September 14. Had the election failed on September 29, the district would soon have exhausted its operating fund balance and been forced to close.
>
> Five other school districts in St. Louis County were faced with a similar situation this year. Enrollments in these districts exceeded 75,000 pupils. At the present time there are two school districts in St. Louis County and one in out-State Missouri that have not yet established tax rates for the current

---

*Hearings of the U.S. Senate Select Committee on Equal Educational Opportunity, Part 19B, *Equal Educational Opportunity in Michigan*, Nov. 3. 1971.

fiscal year, which began July 1. One district, Hazelwood, expects to close on October 15. On September 1, 12 school districts in Missouri had not established tax rates. The total number of children affected by these crises (114,956) exceeded 10 percent of the total school population in the State. All of these districts were faced either with deferring the opening of school or operating schools for a limited time and closing for lack of local funds.

The Ferguson-Florissant Board of Education cut its budget five times since last February, in order to establish a tax rate which would receive voter approval and thus allow the school program to operate for a full year. The total reduction was in excess of $1,100,000. Since 85 percent of our operating budget is allocated to salaries and fringe benefits for personnel, the heaviest budget cuts were in terms of reduction in staff positions. These position cuts affected all areas: teachers, teacher aides, librarians, counselors, custodians, secretaries, maintenance, and transportation personnel. The board cut out at least 100 positions which it had originally budgeted, and thus reduced personnel services to children.

We also reduced the purchase of instructional materials by 40 percent in order to bring the budget down to a point where we could get voter approval, which we finally got on September 29, the fiscal year having begun on July 1. This obviously resulted in a qualitative decline in our school program which will take years to restore.*

In the central city school district the roots of the fiscal crisis in education are found in the redistribution of population from rural to urban areas and the movement of industry and commerce out of the city. For the past several decades, there has been a steady flow of more affluent people out of the central city and their replacement by expanding concentrations of poor, undereducated, elderly and minority-group citizens whose children require intensive and expensive educational services. This movement has been accompanied by the removal of industrial and retail business activity from the city to the suburbs, along with middle- and upper-income families. As a result, the tax bases of the city, along with the income levels of their residents, have been seriously eroded and the cities are often simply unable to meet the high costs of education and other public services. These other non-educational costs—such as the costs of law enforcement, welfare services, sanitation, etc.—often cause what is termed "municipal overburden." These costs compete with education for the scarce local tax dollar.

Further compounding the problem is the fact that educational programs and services in central cities often cost more than they do elsewhere. Teacher salaries have risen at a faster rate, maintenance costs are higher and the cost of land for school sites is practically prohibitive. In 1967, for example, Detroit paid an average price per acre for school sites in excess of $100,000, while surrounding suburban districts paid an average of $6,000. In the 25 largest cities, land costs per acre average $658,000, as contrasted with their contiguous suburbs where an acre can be purchased for an average of $3,500. There is no doubt

---

* *Ibid.*, Part 7, *Inequality of Economic Resources*, Oct. 6, 1970.

that the combination of a high-cost population, a stagnant and decreasing tax base, increasing demands and costs of noneducational services, higher costs of education, and the movement of industrial and commercial business to the suburbs all add up to a serious financial crisis in central city school districts.

### D. What Gets Cut

The consequences of this financial crisis are severe. While costs are rising, school districts all over the country have simply run out of money.

Last September, the National Education Association undertook a survey of those school systems enrolling 50,000 or more pupils. Of 63 systems responding to the survey, 41 reported at least some kind of rollbacks in educational services because of financial limitations; 13 systems reported "hold the line" budgets with no increases in services; and, only 9 reported they had sufficient funds both to support the prior year's educational program and to make some improvement. Of these 63 school systems, 23 had reduced their regular teaching positions by a total of 4,388. Many others were refusing to fill vacancies and had instituted job freezes.

The cutbacks caused by lack of funds are often concentrated in those school services which are among the most effective, particularly for disadvantaged children. Funds to pay teacher aides and substitute teachers have been eliminated or severely curtailed. Special teachers for art, music, drama, industrial arts, and physical education have been eliminated in many districts. But more important, where professional staff is reduced it is often in the area of special remedial programs for disadvantaged and handicapped children. Schools all over the Nation have reduced the number of course-hours for secondary students, have been forced into split sessions and shortened school years to cope with the educational financial crisis.

Perhaps the most compelling description of what happens in a bankrupt school system was given by Dr. Mark Shedd, former Philadelphia School Superintendent, in testimony before the committee.

> We have trimmed from the budget some 600 teachers and 800 support personnel in the past year alone. We have cut drastically on books, supplies and equipment. We have increased class size and have been forced by escalating debt service costs to halt our school building program, despite the fact that every day more than 30,000 youngsters attend school in Philadelphia in firetraps. We have cut the heart out of our night school program and closed our schools to community use. Only last week, we restored extracurricular activities to the budget based on the admittedly tenuous pledges from both candidates for Mayor and the present Mayor that they would get the money for us—somewhere.
>
> The interruption of our school construction program is especially crippling. In the past 6 years, we've been able to build three new high schools, four new middle schools, 25 new elementary schools, 77 major additions, and 13 supportive facilities, providing an additional 48,000 student spaces to handle an increased student population of some 17,000

and to ease overcrowding by 31,000 pupils. We've also been able to spend $53 million on alterations and improvements, including building libraries into 200 elementary schools where two existed in 1965.

But now we've got to stop, despite the fact that there are still some 30 nonfire-resistant buildings in use, class size is still far above accepted standards, and we have to rent an additional 400 rooms in churches and community buildings just to handle the overflow. Where we have an extreme need to invest another $480 million in our building program by 1980, we must now stop.

And the reason is simply that our operating budget no longer is able to handle the debt service, which has risen from some $10 million in 1965 to $56 million this year—which is equivalent to 16 percent of our total operating budget.

The story is the same in most big cities. Chicago is faced with the probability of having to shut down its schools for most of the month of December. New York had to borrow from this year's funds to finish last year, and now it faces a staggering deficit next Spring. Detroit cut 200 teaching positions last Spring, stopped repainting old schools, put its maintenance crews on a 4-day week, still finished the year with a $20 million deficit, and faces an additional deficit of some $50 million this year. Similar conditions exist in the cities from coast to coast.

The simple fact is that at a time when we should be bolstering urban education with new expertise, new programs and new enthusiasm to meet the critical problems that face us, we are constantly cutting back, spending most of our time trying to stem the flow of fiscal blood with bandaids and looking back over our shoulders at the specter of bankruptcy. Perhaps the worst part is the psychological impact on the school district staff as budget cut piles upon budget cut, and firings and demotions are the order of the day.*

The present fiscal crisis in education threatens not merely to stifle further progress, it is eroding the base of equality that now exists. As a Nation, we are being forced to offer fewer school services at a time in our history when many students need more.

---

**Ibid.*, Part 16A, *Inequality in School Finance*, Sept. 21, 1971.

# Chapter 30—The Federal Role in Financing Education

## A. The Inadequacy of Federal Funds

Present Federal aid for public elementary and secondary education is totally inadequate to deal with the growing fiscal crisis in education finance—it does not begin to provide the resources necessary to cope with the educational problems of disadvantaged children; and it has a negligible impact on the problem of financial inequity. In the last decade, Federal funds for public elementary and secondary schools have increased from $650 million to about $3.1 billion. Over the past 4 years the increase in Federal funds has been negligible; and, in fact, the Federal Government now provides less than 8 percent of the revenues for public education—and this share has steadily decreased since 1968.

In the face of a fiscal crisis in many school systems and totally inadequate funding of compensatory education programs, the Federal budget for fiscal year 1973 provides no increase in appropriations for compensatory education under Title I of the Elementary and Secondary Education Act—the largest single source of Federal funds for elementary and secondary schools. While Federal aid to education is leveling off and the Federal share declining, the costs of education are rising.

Compounding the inadequacy of Federal aid is the fact that no school district can count on the same amount, much less an increase, from one year to the next. New York City, for example, received from major Federal educational programs $31.48 for each pupil in 1966, $79.22 in 1967, and $39.89 in 1968.

Not only is Federal support for education declining and fluctuating, it fails to direct resources where the needs are greatest—toward offsetting the inequalities in State and local finance systems. In the aggregate, Federal aid does have a mildly equalizing affect because of the impact of compensatory education for educationally disadvantaged low-income children under Title I of the Elementary and Secondary Education Act, which provides nearly 40 percent of the Federal funds for elementary and secondary education. Within metropolitan areas, however, Federal funds are completely insufficient to overcome the advantages of those school districts with high tax bases.

A five-State study of Federal aid to education programs by the Syracuse University Research Corporation summarized the effects of Federal aid in compelling terms:

> The story in general is grossly disappointing . . . Many individual aid programs give more help to rich districts than they do to poorer ones. Fund flows over time are so uneven, both within school years and from year to year, that harried

school planners often end up shunting Federal aid funds to the least pressing, least important of their academic priorities. And problems of program administration further dilute the effect of Federal dollars. Most notable of all, the magnitudes of aid are so small—averaging from $22 to $50 per pupil in the five-State sample and from 3.3 percent to 10 percent of total revenues per pupil—that they must be found wanting when compared with the enormous tasks faced by, and the inadequate money available for, public education.

## B. Will More Money for Education Make a Difference?

There is no doubt that money alone will not produce quality educational opportunity. Educational effectiveness is determined by a great many other things: Most significantly by the child's family circumstances and home environment, and also by the interaction between teachers and their students, the quality of teaching, and, a host of other measurable and immeasurable factors. One can find superior education in underfinanced schools and inferior education in many rich schools with the best materials money can buy.

There are those who argue that the schools are powerless to improve the performance of disadvantaged children, that adequate academic performance is, to a large extent, unalterably forordained by the social and economic status of a student's parents.* It has even been suggested by a former White House adviser that the Federal Government would be better off giving funds presently devoted to compensatory education "to the kid or to his mother and let her take him to the beach."

We cannot agree. We do agree that, taken as a whole, our schools now are not effective in equalizing opportunity; but the schools are working under tremendous handicaps—little constructive research on which to rely, inadequate financial resources, inadequate opportunities for teachers who require special skills, and, a school organization under which teachers typically spend much of their time maintaining discipline and performing bureaucratic duties.

The question is not whether the schools are now enhancing the educational opportunities of disadvantaged children. The question is whether they can. We believe that the evidence produced in HEW Secretary Richardson's study (*The Effectiveness of Compensatory Education*, discussed in Chapter 25) of federally assisted compensatory education programs strongly indicates that carefully focused programs can be successful. And the evidence discussed in Chapter 16, suggests with equal strength that such compensatory efforts will be more successful if they are conducted within racially and economically integrated schools.

There is little that can be done to improve the quality of education in this country that does not cost money. While money by itself is not the answer to improving educational quality, adequate funding is an essential element. Money buys smaller classes, improved teacher materials, research, experimentation, new schools to achieve integration, counseling services, books, teachers, libraries, administrators and everything else that schools must do.

---

*See, e.g., Jencks, et al. *Inequality, A Reassessment of the Effect of Family and Schooling in America.*

Finally, this country simply cannot afford not to provide adequate funds for education, at a time when our public school systems are in a state of financial crisis. Education will continue to become more expensive. If help is not provided, more teachers will be fired. Future cutbacks in school programs will involve not just extracurricular activities or kindergarten classes or art or music, or school lunch or breakfast—the axe will fall on basic educational programs, libraries, and instructional materials. Also, there will be further reductions in class hours and pupil-teacher contact. If the Federal Government does not provide more funds many school systems will simply go bankrupt.

Neither a reversal of the present inequitable patterns of educational finance nor the development of new and more effective ways to help children learn can be accomplished without additional resources. The end result of a policy which fails to increase Federal aid to education is to throw roadblocks in the path of educational change and innovation—and to support the maintenance of a system of educational finance which often provides superb educational services to the most privileged, and yet provides the lowest quality services to educationally disadvantaged children who live in the poorest communities.

## C. A Renewed Federal Role

Our entire society benefits from the contributions of its educated citizens. This was the basic rationale for the establishment of a universal free public education system in the last century. It is also true that the entire Nation pays the costs of inadequate education—costs which are measurable in unemployment, lost income, welfare and crime costs, lack of participation in the political process and in many other ways.

In 1968 the Federal Government collected more than 71 percent of all the tax dollars in the United States, with State and local governments collecting 29 percent. The Federal Government collects 90 percent of all the Nation's personal income taxes and the Federal income tax is the Nation's most rapidly growing source of revenue.

Education must remain a local concern, subject to the local control which has always been basic to public education in this country. And the obligation for assuring an equitable distribution of resources for education rests primarily with State government. But we believe that the Federal Government* must assume the responsibility for providing a substantial increase in the support of public education—consistent with that local control—if this Nation seriously wishes to fulfill the goal of equal educational opportunity for all our citizens. The Federal Government must serve as a contributing, but junior partner, pressing for attention to the national concern for the poor and the powerless; for national objectives—such as a coordinated system of educational research—while leaving the operation of public education to the State and local communities, much as we leave key military decisions to commanders in the field.

We believe as well that there must be a major change in the Federal Government's role in financing public education. Present Federal

---

*If as is suggested in Chapter 13 there is a 7-for-4 return on tax revenues invested in education, more than 70 percent of that return accrues to the Federal Government while less than 30 percent accrues to State and local government.

policies and programs have not dealt adequately with the growing fiscal crisis, or provided the resources to those school districts and schoolchildren whose needs are greatest. Our Nation's schools must have additional Federal support simply to maintain present educational quality and to avoid further cutbacks in school services.

Additional Federal resources must be channeled so that those children who need extra help—the nearly 20 million who are from bilingual, minority-group and disadvantaged homes—receive educational services of such high quality that schools can begin to fulfill the goal of providing equal opportunity for all children regardless of their race or family backgrounds. An adequate program of compensatory education will go far toward relieving the financial crisis of our centercity and rural school districts.

And substantial additional funds must be provided to encourage and assist in the reform of State systems of school finance.

RECOMMENDATIONS

*First*, we recommend immediate expansion of Title I of the Elementary and Secondary Education Act through Congressional adoption of an additional new program, modeled on the President's compensatory education proposals of March 17, 1972, with an initial new and separate authorization of $1.5 billion annually. Adoption of this new initiative should not decrease funding for the Emergency School Aid Act, as would the original administration proposal.

These funds would be expended in direct project grants from the Office of Education to school systems agreeing to use the new funds, together with funds received under the preexisting Title I program, for highly concentrated, well-evaluated compensatory services in reading and math.

If vigorously administered by the Office of Education, such a new program can bring about the concentration of funds and focus on specific program goals which have been lacking in so many projects funded under Title I.* As the President said:

> While there is a great deal yet to be learned about the design of successful compensatory programs, the experience so far does point in one crucial direction: to the importance of providing sufficiently concentrated funding to establish the educational equivalent of a "critical mass," or threshold level. Where funds have been spread too thinly, they have been wasted or dissipated with little to show for their expenditure. Where they have been concentrated, the results have been frequently encouraging and sometimes dramatic.

The new program, combined with a continuation of Title I, could provide compensatory services averaging $300 a year to 10 million of the estimated 17 million Title I-eligible students beginning in the

*Two features combine to make enforcement of these requirements difficult under Title I. First, unlike the new proposal Title I is an "entitlement" program. While under the new proposal the applicant must prove the merits of its application, under Title I the burden is on HEW to show a violation of legal requirements in order to withhold funds allocated by statutory formula, until needed improvements are adopted. Second, under Title I administrative responsibility is vested in State government as well as the Office of Education, so that lines of authority are often unclear, in practice.

Fall of 1973. Effective administration on the local and Federal levels and full evaluation can build the record for increased funding to extend full compensatory help to all disadvantaged children by the Fall of 1975.

*Second*, we recommend that beginning next fiscal year and for at least the 3 succeeding fiscal years, $5 billion in additional Federal funds be authorized and appropriated to encourage and support reform of elementary and secondary education financing, along the following lines:

(a) Allocation of funds according to a formula which takes account of the varying ability, and effort, of States to adequately finance public education. Appropriate factors would be (1) need, as measured by the State's personal income per school-aged child, (2) effort, as measured by a State's total expenditures from State and local sources for elementary and secondary education, and (3) the number of school-aged children in the State. State allocations should be adjusted for regional variation in cost of education.

(b) Grant of financial assistance for implementation of State plans to provide fairer treatment for the many rural and suburban, as well as center-city, school districts which have inadequate revenue-raising ability under existing school finance systems. Plans should include (1) substantial reduction in per-pupil expenditure disparities based on local wealth; (2) adequate attention to the higher cost of educating disadvantaged, handicapped, and other children with special needs; (3) adequate attention to differences in the cost of education among regional areas in the State and within metropolitan areas, and to the problem of municipal tax overburden; and (4) reform of property tax collection and assessment procedures.

(c) Provision that local education agencies be required to adopt effective procedures, including objective measurements of educational achievement, for the annual evaluation of the effectiveness of education programs. In addition, States should be encouraged to undertake comprehensive statewide educational assessment programs through a setaside of funds for States with such programs.

We believe our recommendations for these substantial increases in Title I funds and new funds for elementary and secondary education will relieve the immediate financial crisis in public education, fulfill the promise and potential of compensatory education that was made when the Elementary and Secondary Education Act was passed in 1965, and encourage the States to shift from regressive inequitable education finance structures to progressive and equitable finance plans.

*Third*, we recommend more adequate funding for existing Federal elementary and secondary education programs, including support for vocational education and the education of handicapped children. And we note our recommendations contained elsewhere in this Report, for full funding of the Indian Education Act, the Bilingual Education Act (Title VII of the Elementary and Secondary Education Act of 1965), and the Emergency School Aid Act.

# Part VIII

# Rural Education

## Chapter 31—Inequality in Rural Education

More than 53 million Americans—about 26 percent of our population—live in the Nation's rural areas. And, as Dr. Lewis Tamblyn, executive secretary, Department of Rural Education, National Education Association, noted during hearings before this committee, this is equivalent to the world's ninth largest country:

> Although declining, its total population still exceeds the combined population of America's 100 largest cities. It is large enough so that rural America may be classified as the world's ninth largest country. (Only China, India, U.S.S.R., United States, Japan, Indonesia, Pakistan, and Brazil have total populations that exceed the rural population of the United States.) No country in Europe, and only one in Latin America (Brazil), has a total population that exceeds the size of America's rural population.*

As the following map shows, the percentage of population residing in nonmetropolitan areas ranges from 3 percent in Massachusetts to 100 percent in Alaska and Wyoming.

Among the Nation's nearly 70 million children under 18, 24.4 million live in communities of less than 10,000. Of these, 4.7 million live in towns with a population of between 2,500 and 10,000; 2.2 million are in communities with 1,000 to 2,500 residents; and 17.5 million live in what the Census classifies as "other rural areas," including 3.1 million who live on the Nation's farms. About 5 million of these rural children are from families with incomes below the poverty level and about 3 million are black. While precise census figures on other minorities are not available, substantially all of the Nation's Eskimos and large proportions of Spanish heritage and American Indian children are in rural areas.

Many rural children are in isolated school districts and schools which are simply too small to provide an adequate education. As

*Hearings of the U.S. Senate Select Committee on Equal Educational Opportunity, Part 15—*Education in Rural America*, Sept. 1, 1971.

Percentage of population, by States, residing in nonmetropolitan areas--1970

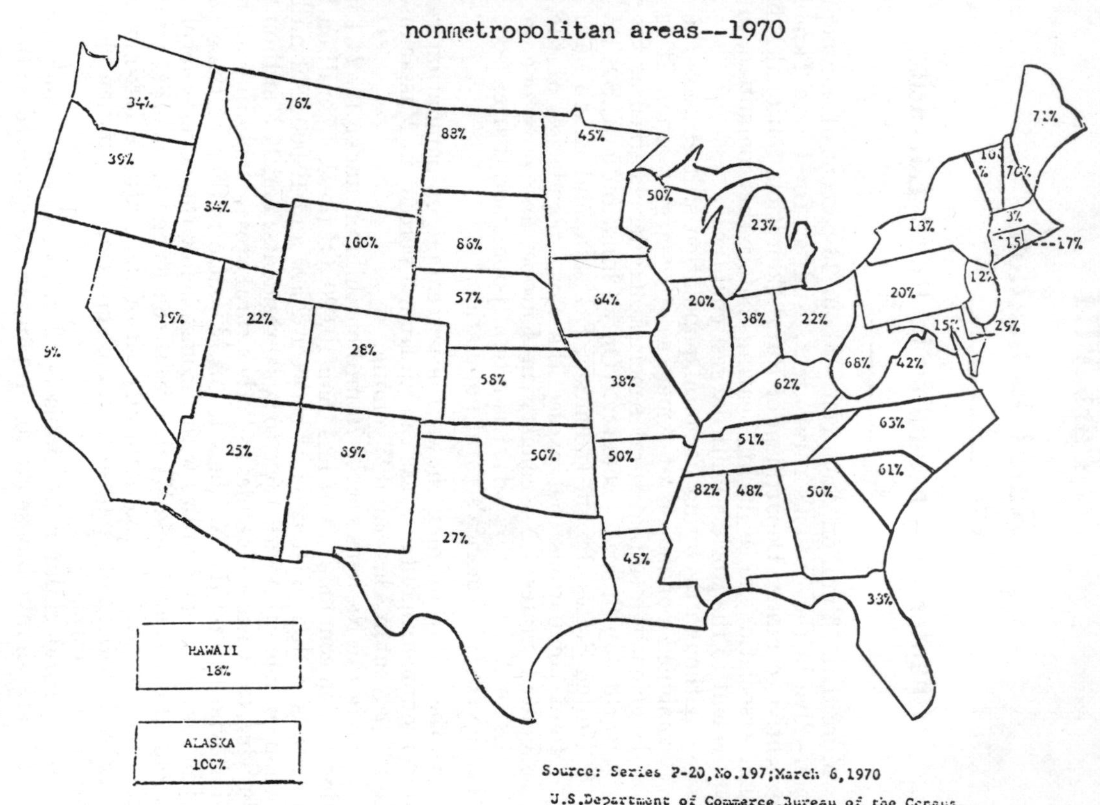


Source: Series P-20, No.197; March 6, 1970
U.S. Department of Commerce, Bureau of the Census.,

Table 31–1 shows, of more than 17,000 school districts in the United States, nearly 6,000, or about one-third, have less than 300 pupils. And about 3 million children are in school systems with less than 1,000 children.

TABLE 31–1.—*Distribution of operating local public school systems, by size of system: United States, Fall 1971* *

| Size of system | Public school systems | | Public school pupils | |
|---|---|---|---|---|
| | Number | Percent | Number [1] | Percent |
| Total operating systems | 16, 771 | 100. 0 | 45, 115, 164 | 100. 0 |
| Systems with 300 pupils or more | 11, 675 | 69. 6 | 44, 552, 210 | 98. 8 |
| 25,000 or more | 184 | 1. 1 | 13, 247, 458 | 29. 4 |
| 10,000 to 24,999 | 558 | 3. 3 | 8, 198, 133 | 18. 2 |
| 5,000 to 9,999 | 1, 110 | 6. 6 | 7, 725, 266 | 17. 1 |
| 2,500 to 4,999 | 2, 026 | 12. 1 | 7, 096, 504 | 15. 7 |
| 1,000 to 2,499 | 3, 506 | 20. 9 | 5, 741, 499 | 12. 7 |
| 600 to 999 | 1, 931 | 11. 5 | 1, 504, 080 | 3. 3 |
| 300 to 599 | 2, 360 | 14. 1 | 1, 039, 270 | 2. 3 |
| Systems with less than 300 pupils | 5, 096 | 30. 4 | 562, 954 | 1. 2 |

**Education Directory, 1971–72 Public School Systems*, National Center for Educational Statistics, U.S. Department of Health, Education, and Welfare.

[1] These figures represent the sums of the reported "enrollment" figures, which are not comparable from State to State (*see Introduction*). The official Office of Education Fall 1971 elementary-secondary enrollment figure will be reported in the forthcoming publication *Fall 1971 Statistics of Public School Systems*.

Education experts have suggested that it is difficult for the smaller school or school district to offer comprehensive educational programs. Dr. James B. Conant in *The American High School Today* concluded for example that a senior class of 100 pupils is the minimum necessary for an adequate high school educational program. This in turn would require a high school of about 500 students. Later research has tended to confirm, and even enlarge, on this figure. As W. D. McClurkin noted in a 1970 article which was included in the committee's hearing record:

> Research has clearly determined that the breadth and depth of educational opportunities are related to school size, and the scope of the all-important instructional programs and services increases in direct proportion to size up to about 600 in elementary schools and 1,200 to 1,500 students in high schools. Such enrollments are out of the question for remote schools in sparsely populated areas—whether the high school criterion is set as a desirable 1,200, a minimum of the valid 500, or the inadequate traditional 300. In 1966–67, 55 percent of all school districts had fewer than 600 total in all grades, 1 through 12. Again, extra support and supplements are essential in the small schools with limited programs and services.*

*"Rural Education in the United States," W. D. McClurkin, September 1970. New Mexico State University; see also Part 15, *Education in Rural America*.

Yet, smallness can also be an asset. The small school district seldom has overcrowded classrooms and teachers are more likely to be acquainted with their student's parents. The small town is more likely to be closely tied to the community. Often its school is the social center for the community. It is this sense of community, the feeling on the part of parents and students that they are participants in education, that is so seldom present in large school systems, especially in urban areas and particularly for minority groups.

But more often smallness means isolation. And it often means inadequate facilities, low per pupil expenditures, limited educational curricula and inadequately trained, low-paid teachers.

McDowell County, W. Va., is not atypical of many isolated school districts in Appalachia and other rural areas. There are 14,000 students in McDowell County attending 50 separate schools. While school consolidation has reduced the number of one-room schools substantially in recent years, two still remain in the hollows of Coon Branch Mountain. Both are elementary schools. One is attended by 28 students. It has no water, an outside privy, and it is heated in winter with a coal stove. In summer it is infested with wasps. Mrs. Birdie Powell who lives on Coon Branch Mountain described this one room school to the committee:

> I started to school at Grapevine—and I am 41 now. The school has always been in the same condition as it was when I started until it was burned down September 1. I never saw any improvement in it. There has never been a child from Coon Branch Mountain ever graduated. They are just operating to the sixth grade, then that's it. They just go home. There ain't nowhere else for them to go to school.*

There are relatively few one-room schools left in this country. Most have been consolidated into small town elementary, junior, and senior high schools. But these consolidated schools are often miles from the children's homes. Thus distance itself is often a severe handicap for the rural school child. The Coon Branch Mountain community is a 28-mile round trip bus ride to the nearest junior high and high schools. The road up the mountain is so steep it is often impossible in winter. Many Coon Branch children never attend junior or senior high school at all. The 54 who do often must walk down the mountain. As Mrs. Powell described it:

> They will try to walk for maybe a week or so. It is hard through the snow and ice. And when winter sets in they just have to quit. They have to leave about maybe 6 or 7 o'clock and get in way after dark. I have picked some of them up myself and brought them up after dark. Little bitty fellers had to walk right up Coon Branch.**

There are other handicaps faced by children in many rural schools. Witnesses before the committee, for example, presented the results of research studies showing that in rural areas fewer teachers have completed college or have advanced degrees than in urban areas. One witness from Tennessee said that as many as 30 percent of the teachers

---

*Hearings of the U.S. Senate Select Committee on Equal Educational Opportunity, Part 15, *Education in Rural America*, Sept. 2, 1971.

***Ibid.*

in a 13-county area with which she was familiar did not have bachelor's degrees.

Teachers' salaries are often as much as $2,000 or $3,000 less in rural than in other areas. This makes it extremely difficult for rural areas to attract well-trained teachers, especially those with advanced degrees.

Rural school districts also suffer from inadequate educational financing. Many rural school districts simply lack the tax base necessary to raise sufficient funds for public education. Thus, it is impossible to support modern facilities, pay teachers decent salaries, and purchase modern instructional equipment which can facilitate modern learning techniques. The small school district faces an additional financial disadvantage, for research studies show that the per pupil cost of educational services increases as the number of students in the school decreases. For this reason many rural schools are economically inefficient.

Compounding its fiscal problems, the rural school district is often unable to participate in those Federal aid programs which require local matching funds. Instead, the Federal funding assistance goes to the wealthier school district which may, with less tax effort, be able to provide the matching funds by law. The small school district suffers another disadvantage when it comes to acquiring Federal aid. Few such districts have the funds to hire an administrator for Federal aid programs. The superintendent or his assistant must not only run the school system, but prepare the complicated applications for Federal funds and pursue those applications through the Federal and State bureaucracies. They are usually in competition with wealthier school districts which may have their own public relations firms and often have an assistant superintendent in charge of Federal programs.

For the small rural school district fewer resources mean fewer educational services. Often rural education is described as overly textbook oriented. Few rural districts can afford to provide advanced courses in sciences or teach foreign languages. Many are even unable to provide the selection of courses necessary to meet college entrance requirements.

Equally if not more important is the lack of adequate vocational training often existing in rural school districts. Most rural youth today neither live on farms nor plan careers in agriculture upon graduation. Yet, much of the vocational training in rural school districts is agriculturally oriented. More than 300,000 American youth migrate from rural to urban areas each year. They move from the small towns, particularly in the rural South, to the major cities of the North and to other metropolitan areas in their own and nearby States. More often than not these youthful Americans are ill-prepared for urban living, untrained for available jobs and all too often are consigned to a life of poverty in the innercity more devastating than that from which they have escaped.

All these disadvantages of rural education result in lower achievement, low aspirations and motivations and low educational attainment among rural schoolchildren.

According to the 1970 Census our urban population 25 years of age and over had a median of 12.2 years of schooling. At the same time, nonfarm rural adults in this age group had completed 11.2 years and rural farm adults had completed 10.7 years of school. Similarly, 12.1 percent of our urban population has completed college as compared with 7.2 percent of our rural nonfarm and 4.6 percent of the farm population citizens. Studies published in 1967 revealed that 19 percent of rural youth were a year behind in school as compared with 12 percent of urban youth. The results of this and other research were summarized by Dr. Everett Edington of New Mexico State University in testimony before the committee:

> A review of the available research relevant to the characteristics of disadvantaged rural students shows them to be affected in seven general areas. The low socioeconomic status of large numbers of noncorporate-farm rural families is a characteristic of prime importance, particularly in view of the relationship between economic status and school achievement for rural as well as urban children. In addition, the educational and occupational aspirations of rural students appear to be negatively affected by their low economic status and possibly further depressed by factors related to geographic isolation. Many rural young people who will not be able to make a satisfactory living by farming do not aspire to any higher skilled urban occupations nor to the educational level which would prepare them for such work. Possibly related to socioeconomic status are other attitudes found among rural children which may further hinder their progress: low self-esteem, feelings of helplessness in the face of seemingly unconquerable environmental handicaps, and impoverished confidence in the value and importance of education as an answer to their problems. All of these attitudes understandably may contribute to the child's failure to benefit from his schooling.
>
> For the rural child, these three characteristics—socioeconomic status, low level of aspiration, and attitudes nonsupportive of educational progress—are linked with a fourth, educational achievement, to form part of a cycle of cause and effect the mechanisms of which available research does not yet permit us to specify. Disadvantaged rural students, like their urban and suburban counterparts, are characterized by achievement levels below national norms. Moreover, the mobility of rural and urban disadvantaged populations make it difficult to determine whether rural student achievement levels are more seriously retarded than urban disadvantaged student levels. Accompanying these characteristics is a pattern of slightly higher dropout rates, which indicates that educational retention is a more serious problem in rural than in urban areas.*

There is no doubt that many rural students in this country suffer severely in terms of educational performance as a result of all the factors which make rural education unequal.

---

**Ibid.*, Sept. 2, 1971.

## Chapter 32—Improving Rural Education

Educational inequality in rural America is but one of the disadvantages often suffered by our rural citizens. No program which is designed to improve rural education will alone create equal opportunity for rural children and adults, for life as a whole in rural America must also be improved. Robert McNair, former Governor of South Carolina, placed in perspective the inequality in rural education when he stated:

> As you examine the conditions which lead to educational inequality in rural America, you come to economic factors which undermine the essential quality of life, and I think this is something we have to emphasize, that with all the money that is needed, if it were immediately available and you built a quality educational program, unless you improve the economy, unless you improve living conditions, unless you improve the living environment, with job opportunities and the kinds of other things that go into good communities, you are simply going to be preparing people to move to another part of the country. . . .
>
> As long as we concentrate our industrial complexes in the major urban centers, or adjoining the major urban centers, and as long as our governments—and all levels of government fail to provide the type of basic services in rural areas which can open them up for economic growth, then no amount of educational excellence can stem the tide of migration from these rural areas.*

As we pointed out in the preceding Chapter, 300,000 rural youths migrate each year to the Nation's cities. It is perhaps ironic that this migration continues at a time when our cities are already overpopulated and overburdened with financial and other problems. It would certainly be advisable to at least diminish, if not reverse this trend. But there can be no serious effort to persuade American families to return to small towns in rural communities unless those communities are revitalized economically and educationally.

Witnesses before the committee presented a number of recommendations and described a number of promising efforts which could go a long way to improving rural public education.

South Carolina, for example, has reformed its vocational education programs by developing area vocational schools which serve several school districts and are attended on a part-time basis by both children and adults. Schoolchildren are bused to these schools for half a day after which they return to their regular schools for the remainder of the day. Adults are given basic literacy training as well as job-oriented vocational and technical training. South Carolina has also developed a system of job-oriented technical schools and occupational training centers in an effort to meet the needs of industry in that State.

---

*Hearings of the U.S. Senate Select Committee on Equal Educational Opportunity, Part 15, *Education in Rural America*, Sept. 3, 1971.

One of the most pressing problems in rural school districts is the lack of adequate transportation facilities. As witnesses from West Virginia, Michigan and a number of other States pointed out, bus transportation is often a major financial burden for rural school districts, since many rural children must often travel 20, 40 or 60 miles to and from school each day. It would be a major financial relief to these districts if the States were to assume full financial responsibility for school transportation costs.

One of the most hopeful efforts in providing equality of education in rural America has been undertaken by the Appalachian Regional Commission. The Commission has established Regional Education Service Agencies (RESA) to provide educational services to combinations of two or more school districts that wish to join together in efforts that the school districts could not afford to undertake alone.

One RESA has employed a guidance counsellor who has installed a computerized system to match job vacancies with available high school graduates in each of the high schools served. An RESA in New York State has employed a full-time school nurse and special teachers to work with classroom teachers on the educational problems of non-English speaking children and children who are mentally or physically handicapped. It has also employed music, art and physical education instructors. These regional personnel travel from school to school conducting classes and providing services which would otherwise be unavailable. Another RESA operates roving media centers—vans which deliver instructional films, closed circuit television equipment and consultant services to teachers. In another State, schools have delegated administrative functions, such as pupil accounting, scheduling, inventory control and other day-to-day management functions to the local RESA. RESA's have also been helpful in working with nearby universities in both preservice and in-service teacher training programs.

These Regional Education Service Agencies are now providing important educational and administrative services to many school teachers in Appalachian States. We believe the Federal Government should encourage these efforts in other areas of the country, for they not only provide much needed educational services, they make it possible for school districts to preserve the advantages of smallness and at the same time offer those services which large school districts can afford.

Rural education receives less priority than it deserves at the Federal level. We recommend the establishment of a rural school division in the United States Office of Education so that rural education will have a Federal spokesman whose sole task is to represent the interests of more than 20 million children in small towns and other rural areas in our Nation. This rural school division should act as the principal Federal agency for the development of rural education programs as well as be the advocate for rural school districts within the Federal bureaucracy so that these districts can compete for Federal funds on equal terms.

Finally, Federal aid to education programs must be both designed and administered with a recognition of the special needs of rural areas. Those rural school districts which are isolated and have low tax bases should receive increased financial assistance.

# Additional Views

---

## MR. JENNINGS RANDOLPH

### U.S. Senator From the State of West Virginia

The Select Committee on Equal Educational Opportunity was created on February 19, 1970, "to study the effectiveness of existing laws and policies in assuring equality of educational opportunity including policies of the United States with regard to segregation on the grounds of race, color, or national origin, whatever the form of such segregation, and to examine the extent to which policies are applied uniformly in all regions of the United States."

In more than 2 years of hearings, the views of many segments of our population—educators, public officials and private citizens—have been presented to this committee. The extensive hearing record, generally, reflects the genuine concern of citizens and their recognition of the importance of securing equal educational opportunity. The record of this committee's hearings represents a significant contribution toward the goal of improved educational programs for all citizens. It provides a wealth of testimony upon which educators, legislators, and policymakers can draw for future endeavors.

I support the broad program of educational advancements and initiatives outlined in the Report. Implementation of the committee's numerous suggestions and recommendations will, for the most part, benefit the educational process in our Nation's elementary and secondary schools.

Having stated my general agreement with the purposes of the Report, I respectfully submit a brief outline of my disagreement with the tone and content of certain parts of the chapters on "School Integration and Educational Opportunity."

I disagree with the Report's description of "racial balance" and "busing" as misleading issues. Clearly, "busing" and "racial balance" have been subjects of extremely emotional and often polarized debate. Many concerned educators, public officials, and private citizens hold very strong beliefs—for and against—the extensive use of busing to achieve a balance in the racial and socioeconomic mix in elementary and secondary schools. Yet, there are substantial numbers of persons who view these issues with mixed emotions. The Select Committee's Report, however, falls short of needed explanations and analysis to give deserved attention to the views of the majority of our citizens. By this, I do not mean that the Report should contain recommendations and findings to satisfy the beliefs of varying groups of people. What I do mean is that the Report, to gain optimum acceptance, should provide balanced discussion of the "busing" issue.

The Report focuses with great emphasis and eagerness on the need for busing to achieve school integration while minimizing the disruptions and hardships imposed upon students, families, communities and school systems. Nowhere can one find a clear, thorough and dispassionate analysis of the concerns—and, yes, fears—of those citizens residing in areas where busing has been instituted on a large scale. The Report does not clearly meet the issue which it raises in the following words: "Often parents are understandably concerned that desegregation may result in transfer of their children from schools with middle-class student bodies and highly motivated teachers to schools with educationally disadvantaged students bodies—where teacher motivation and academic opportunities may be decidedly inferior."

Likewise, the Report is lacking in any detailed discussion of the impact of court or Federal-ordered busing programs on school systems. The very limited references to testimony on the need for transportation funds, in my opinion, does not provide such a discussion. I recognize that the report has been approved by the majority of the committee members and, therefore, it is designed to reflect the views of the majority. However, the issues involved and concerns expressed, publicly and privately, by millions of citizens are of such import that they deserve a balanced presentation, notwithstanding the final recommendations and conclusions of the majority.

Failure to present this balanced discussion not only detracts from the findings and recommendations in the portions on "Integration and Education Opportunity," but it also calls into question the credibility of the entire Report—most of which, as I have stated, I support.

It is clear that a great many persons believe "racial balance" to be the ultimate objective of court desegregation orders and other Federal mandates. I, for one, hold this view. Despite the extensive public debate—including many hours in the Congress—and despite the fact that Congress has acted to prohibit busing to achieve racial balance, the Report quickly dismisses this as a "misleading issue." The basis cited for such dismissal is the Supreme Court decision that busing is not being imposed to achieve "racial balance." The repeated use of the Supreme Court decision does little, if anything, to help resolve this vital question. In no way, does it address the question of whether desegregation plans are in fact directed toward securing racial balance in our schools. On the contrary, the Report seemingly advocates utilization of busing at every level to obtain a student composition which is nothing more than "racial balance."

The issue of whether Federal court orders and Executive Branch directives have been reasonable is treated in the same manner, with the addition of overall national statistics to demonstrate that increases due to desegregation orders and plans have been minimal. Nevertheless, statistics on individual school systems show very substantial increases in transportation of students and increased cost. To minimize the problem of increased costs by stating that it is only a certain percent of the total operating budget of a school system, in my opinion, is faulty reasoning. While admitting that school systems operate on tight budgets, the Report through its one-sided approach to this problem, seemingly demonstrates a lack of understanding of the real impact of even limited cost increases in individual school districts and areas.

At this point, I should note that, in my judgment, recent court decisions—if followed through nationally and applied uniformly—could result in the busing of students to a degree which the people of this Nation—minorities and nonminorities—would never tolerate, and which school systems could never sustain. Yet, this seems to be exactly what the Select Committee's Report is strongly advocating.

I wish also, to address the issue of whether the Congress should legislate limitations or parameters under which the Federal courts can impose busing. The Report maintains that the Congress should not undertake such action. I disagree. It is my belief that this is a legitimate area of concern for the Congress and legislative proposals can and should be considered. There is no question in my mind that the Congress is in a better position to make the complex judgments involved in this issue; and, to legislate guidelines for desegregation plans encompassing busing and other remedial measures.

The committee's Report recognizes the limited capability of the courts to deal with these problem areas. It states:

> That courts are not the branch of government best equipped to deal with the extremely complex issues, involved in breaking down racial and economic barriers within metropolitan areas, in ways that do justice to the legitimate concerns of all involved. A court cannot offer subsidies to compensate suburban communities for increased costs—including educational costs—of serving low-income families or provide assistance to replace revenues lost through location of tax-free public housing units. A court is ill equipped to require that low-income housing be "scatter-site," rather than in huge apartment projects or to implement the metropolitan planning needed to prevent some suburban communities from being swamped by low-income housing while others are untouched.

The Report adds, however, that:

> . . . if public officials at the local, Federal and State levels refuse to act, the courts will be left to their own, and very limited, devices.

I strongly believe that the Federal courts, for the most part, are not in a position to fulfill the requirements of developing school integration as described in the Report: "along racial and socioeconomic lines, sensitively conducted," which "provides the best hope for improving the educational opportunities of educationally disadvantaged children."

The "very limited devices" at the disposal of the courts may well prove to be more damaging to the cause of integrated education over the long term.

For the Congress to leave to the courts and the Federal agencies the final resolution of how our Nation is to achieve quality integrated education constitutes an abdication of Congress' responsibility.

Finally, I make the following observations: The Report, at least in some degree, has allowed the advocacy of altering the composition of school systems to overshadow the questions of quality education and equal educational opportunity; it fails to recognize the realistic limitations of governmental ability to secure integrated schools; and that, in the final analysis, it must be our adherence to the moral and ethical concepts—rather than involuntary shifting of student populations—which will achieve quality education for all citizens in a barrier-free society.

JENNINGS RANDOLPH.

# Individual Views

## MR. JOHN L. McCLELLAN

### U.S. Senator From the State of Arkansas

### A. Introduction

Education is the keystone of the arch of freedom and progress. For the individual, the door of the schoolhouse leads to the richest treasures of our society. For the Nation, increasing the quality and availability of education is vital to both our national security and our domestic well-being. Yet we are faced with a serious problem: How can we provide the quality education that will endow each child with the knowledge and skills that will enable him to take his place in society? The Select Committee on Equal Educational Opportunity has explored at great length both the problems of equal educational opportunity and the means of providing that opportunity.

I will not comment in detail on either the report of the group led by the Chairman, the Honorable Walter Mondale, nor on that of the group led by the ranking minority member, the Honorable Roman Hruška. To the extent that my statement does not touch upon points made by either of these groups it is not to be assumed that I either agree or disagree with their views.

I wish to acknowledge the hard work, dedication and essential fairness of the Chairman of this Select Committee, the Honorable Walter Mondale of Minnesota. Without his willingness to spend many long hours in committee hearings and in preparation for them, far less information would have been developed by this committee. The Senator from Minnesota carefully explored the problems of inequalities in educational opportunity throughout our Nation; and, I am firmly convinced that information developed as a result of our hearings is in large part responsible for extending Federal antidiscrimination concern and activity into more of a nationwide effort. For this, I thank the Chairman. This extension has corrected the unfair concentration upon the Southern United States as a unique region in terms of unequal educational opportunity between races. The problem is nationwide, as is conclusively demonstrated in the hearing record, and is often more economic than racial. Discussing equality of educational opportunity in racial terms often obscures the real issues. I have therefore discussed racial matters only where necessary.

### B. Points of Agreement With the Committee Report

Equalization of educational financing should, in my opinion, have first priority for those interested in providing equal educational opportunity. Many educators believe that the single most important variable in a child's education is the quality of his teachers. In addition, outstanding educational programs across the country can usually be traced to a single administrative official of great ability—in the absence of whom the exceptional program rapidly deteriorates. Therefore, it would seem a prerequisite to equal educational opportunity that each school system throughout the country be on an equal basis in competing with other school systems with regard to the recruitment and retention of teaching and supervisory personnel. Equitable educational financing could be accomplished either by means of issuance of educational vouchers to individuals or by direct grants to public school systems.

I endorse the following recommendation of the Committee's Report which would equalize educational opportunity in terms of financing:

- Allocation of funds among the States on the basis of need as measured by the State's personal income per school-age child, on the basis of State effort as measured by a State's total State and local expenditures from its own sources for elementary and secondary education divided by the State's total personal income, and on the basis of the number of school-age children in the State. Need measure should be adjusted for regional differences in the cost of education.
- Grant of financial assistance conditioned on adoption and implementation of State plans for reform of education finance—including substantial reduction in per-pupil expenditure disparities based on local wealth; adequate attention to the higher cost of educating disadvantaged, handicapped, bilingual and other children with special needs; adequate attention to the higher cost of urban education and the greater overall demands on the urban tax dollar; and, reform of property tax assessment and collection procedures.
- Provision that local education agencies be required to adopt effective procedures, including objective measurements of educational achievement, for the annual evaluation of the effectiveness of education programs. In addition, States should be encouraged to undertake comprehensive statewide educational assessment programs through a setaside of funds for States with such programs.

I would, however, change the term "education" in the last line of the first endorsement, above, to "living."

## C. The Educational System

The Minority Views criticize the lack of emphasis in the Report on research and development, and suggests the need for development of new concepts of responsibility and accountability. I heartedly agree with these recommendations. But, I think both reports share a common failing in that they seem to assume that a deficiency in the education of a child, or a given group of children, is due primarily to the failure of the educational system without sufficient regard to the learning ability of a given child.

I would suggest that existing studies tend to demonstrate that there is a very limited variation in the achievement of a given individual student due solely to environmental manipulation. Hard scientific data should be developed so that we might make better judgments as to the amount of resources to be allocated for special programs for any particular group of students, given a limited possibility of success. The Report notes the lack of sufficient "longitudinal" studies to conclusively demonstrate the effect of existing programs upon the learning achievement levels of children exposed to different learning situations. However, as Professor David J. Armor, a noted Harvard sociologist, recently pointed out, the existing studies reject the tentative conclusions of the Select Committee's Report.

Every effort should be made within the school system to provide each child an equal opportunity to be educated in areas in which his aptitude is greatest—and at learning levels suited to his capabilities. Our children are no more homogeneous than our adults; but there is a disturbing trend toward treating children as a homogeneous mass. The tendency in many areas is to tell individuals and groups that lower achievement levels is due to discrimination rather than unequal ability. This is often misleading and obviously promotes racial disharmony.

### D. Busing

The most controversial and emotion-ridden issue in our school system is the degree—if any—to which our children should be bused out of their neighborhood for the purpose of achieving a "proper" socioeconomic—or racial—mix in the classrooms of our Nation. It is obvious that such busing lessens the extent of parental involvement in the school system to the extent that children are bused out of a neighborhood. The Committee's Report would agree that this loss of community control is an undesirable result.

Although the Coleman Report finds a great advantage to a socioeconomic mix in our school system and in the individual classroom, there is a great deal of evidence to the contrary. In the summer of 1972, Professor Armor published a research report in *Public Interest* entitled, "The Evidence of Busing." After analyzing busing projects in five Northern cities, he concluded that "busing is not an effective policy instrument for raising the achievement of black students or for increasing interracial harmony." Other scholars who have analyzed the Coleman Report and underlying data, have determined that Coleman's conclusion as to the beneficial effect of socioeconomic mix on education is incorrect.

Southerners have had no choice as to whether their children were bused. As a result of the hearings, however, many Northern cities have had their integration timetable stepped up. And, in the next few years, this lack of choice will be extended across our Nation. As the rest of our Nation joins the South in bearing the burdens of busing, there is no doubt in my mind that they too will conclude that the busing of children creates great problems that are not offset by any measurable educational or social gains. Our schools and our children have been asked to solve a problem which the rest of society has been unable to resolve over 100 years. That problem—achieving racial harmony and understanding—must be dealt with; but, the busing of children is not the appropriate means to a solution. As more and more educators and scholars conclude that no educational benefits accrue to either poor or rich, or black or white children as a result of busing, I hope that the advocates of busing as a means of improving educational levels will have the courage to admit that they are wrong. If so, they will join those who have opposed busing from the very beginning. We can expect such changes as the children of busing proponents join those presently being bused out of their neighborhoods. Many a miraculous overnight conversion to an antibusing position has already been observed in Michigan, Maryland, and Massachusetts during recent years. More will occur if busing is continued.

### E. Conclusion

Education is vital not only to the protection of our liberties and freedom, but is part of our obligation to posterity. Most of the children currently in our schools will live much of their lives in the 21st Century. We must provide a quality education for every child in the United States. The accident of place of a child's birth should not determine the quality of education he receives. Regardless of where in the United States a child is born, or the characteristics of its parent, it should, as the Committee's Report recommends: "have the same chance to participate and to succeed in life's activities." I believe the measures that I have advocated in these Individual Views would greatly help toward achievement of this goal—which all the members of the Select Committee share.

John L. McClellan.

## MR. WILLIAM B. SPONG, Jr.

### U.S. Senator From the State of Virginia

#### A. Introduction

Our Nation has reached a watershed period in public school desegregation, and the future currents are uncertain. In the nearly two decades since the decision in *Brown* v. *Board of Education* (347 U.S. 483 (1954)) much attention has focused on the successes and failures of attempts to desegregate public schools. In the South, we have seen State laws sanctioning segregation by race disappear and the utilization of various techniques such as pairing of schools, special assignments and busing to eliminate racially identifiable schools. Concurrently, we have seen a downward trend in public school enrollments compared to anticipated enrollments; an increase in private schools; charges of discrimination within schools; and, certain efforts to avoid racial mixing. In the North, we have seen a long period of quiet, followed finally by efforts to attack *de facto* segregation or to prove that *de facto* segregation is usually *de jure*.

The reaction, both South and North, has—in the face of direct confrontation with the problem of school desegregation—been the same. Some persons continue to claim that complete desegregation to the point of racial balancing is both morally necessary and educationally sound. Others claim that such a move is educationally counterproductive and unrealistic in terms of the burdens it imposes upon parents and children, both black and white. The two opposing schools of thought have, unfortunately, resulted in violence both in the North and the South. Pontiac, Mich., was not unlike Clinton, Tenn.; Sturgis, Ky.; or Mansfield, Tex., in the 1950s.

The great majority of Americans, the polls tell us, support educational opportunities for all children but oppose forced busing of public school children. In numerous recent elections, the voters have reinforced the poll findings.

In recent years, a massive body of literature has risen to substantiate practically all positions—positions ranging from the necessity of busing to the genetic inferiority of certain minority groups.

It is from this mass of literature, from conflicting opinions and beliefs, that American education must chart its future. That course cannot be easy. It involves honest differences among educated men. It involves the hopes and aspirations—and the fears—of millions of Americans throughout our land. It involves the principles upon which our Nation was founded and the rights of citizens both black and white. It involves the future of scholastic attainments in our educational system, and the future atmosphere in which men of various backgrounds and color will relate to each other in our society as a whole.

It involves a testing of our Nation to determine if reason and rationality—by blacks and whites, by liberals and conservatives—can prevail over emotionalism, demagoguery and fear.

### B. Committee Background

In February 1970, over 2 years ago, the U.S. Senate agreed to the establishment of a Select Committee on Equal Educational Opportunity. The committee was charged with the "study [of] the effectiveness of existing laws and policies in assuring equality of educational opportunity including policies of the United States with regard to segregation on the ground of race, color or national origin, whatever the form of such segregation and whatever the origin or cause of such segregation, and to examine the extent to which policies are applied uniformly in all regions of the United States."

Senate action to create the committee came in the wake of a number of actions. First, the Senate had debated and accepteed the so-called Stennis amendment, offered by Senator John Stennis (D-Miss.)—calling for the uniform application in all parts of the United States of laws and the civil rights guidelines established by various agencies of the Federal Government pursuant to those laws. The Stennis amendment had several bases:

*First*, statistics released at that time were beginning to show that there was more desegregation of public schools in the South than in many areas of the North and West and, there was substantial belief that, in view of the statistics, it was unfair to continue to impose requirements upon the South which were not imposed upon the North.

*Second*, it was obvious that our Nation was on a threshold as far as desegregation of public schools was concerned. In the large majority of cases, direct *de jure* segregation, that is, officially sanctioned segregation, had been abolished. The question which was to face the country—the question which, to a large extent, was brought to the fore by the case of *Swann* v. *Charlotte-Mecklenburg* (402 U.S. 1 (1971))— was whether or not school districts were to be required to engage in massive busing and to follow assignment plans which in effect—if not in explicitness—were plans of racial balance. If racial balance is the goal, then school districts throughout the land should be required to make reassignments.

*Third*, there was substantial confusion over exactly what the law required—and what reason dictated—in school desegregation.

Two years have passed, and our Nation is still floundering with the questions which began to surface years ago. The answers are no more evident now than they were then, although there is the possibility that the Denver case (*Keys* v. *School District No. 1*, Denver 303 F. Supp. 279 (1969)) which the Supreme Court currently has before it; or that several other cases—which will undoubtedly be appealed to the court, such as the Richmond, Va., consolidation case—will result in clarification of the *de facto/de jure* matter and of what is now required under law in terms of desegregation and integration of schools.

It is rather obvious, from the activities associated with the passage of S. 659, the Higher Education Act Amendments of 1972, and the failure of the Senate in 1972 to act on H.R. 13915, that the Congress is so divided that it is unlikely that effective legislation can be passed.

Thus, recommendations made by this committee threaten to represent little more than an exercise—an exercise in presenting divergent views that fails to deal practically with the educational, legal and political problems which face our Nation.

I must, consequently, disassociate myself from the committee Report and the committee recommendations. In large measure, I believe the hearing record is a good one. It covered many of the significant questions relating to the provision of equal educational opportunity. I do, however, regret that certain witnesses—such as Daniel Moynihan, Nathan Glazer and Roy Innis—were not asked to testify, as I and others indicated in an August 28, 1970, letter to the chairman.

I am also concerned by the underlying implication that the Federal Government can, by producing billions of dollars, reform U.S. education. While the report does contain qualifying language on this, the basic recommendations are to spend more money.

I have, therefore, determined to present my own views of the legal, educational and practical questions and my recommendations for dealing with them.

### C. The De Facto/De Jure Controversy

In 1954, the U.S. Supreme Court ruled that separate but equal school systems were inherently unequal and that a dual school system violated the rights of minorities under the 14th Amendment of the U.S. Constitution. Segregation which resulted from State law or official action, that is, *de jure* segregation, was outlawed. At the time of the decision, Southern States had laws requiring separate school systems for blacks and whites.

In the years which followed the 1954 decision, steps were taken to dismantle the dual school systems. It is true that action was not swift and that there are a number of episodes from these years of which the South cannot be proud. On the other hand, by 1970 statistics were beginning to show that racially identifiable schools were being erased from the South and that school desegregation had reached substantial proportions.

One of the oft-used means of determining segregation is to view the number of black children attending schools in which a majority of the school population is white. Following is a table documenting the progress in school desegregation which had been made in the South by Fall 1971.

TABLE 1.—*Fall 1971 estimated projections of public school Negro enrollment compared with final Fall 1968 and 1970 data* [1]

| Geographic area | Total pupils | Negro pupils | | Negro pupils attending schools which are— 0 to 49.9 percent minority | | 80 to 100 percent minority | | 100 percent minority | |
|---|---|---|---|---|---|---|---|---|---|
| | | Number | Percent | Number | Percent | Number | Percent | Number | Percent |
| Continental United States: | | | | | | | | | |
| 1968 | 43, 353, 568 | 6, 282, 173 | 14. 5 | 1, 467, 291 | 23. 4 | 4, 274, 461 | 68. 0 | 2, 493, 398 | 39. 7 |
| 1970 | 44, 877, 547 | 6, 707, 411 | 14. 9 | 2, 223, 506 | 33. 1 | 3, 311, 372 | 49. 4 | 941, 111 | 14. 0 |
| 1971 estimate | 44, 691, 675 | 6, 724, 956 | 15. 0 | 2, 393, 824 | 35. 6 | 3, 084, 785 | 45. 9 | 778, 832 | 11. 6 |
| Difference 1970–71 | −185, 782 | 17, 000 | . 1 | 170, 318 | 2. 5 | −226, 587 | −3. 5 | −162, 279 | −2. 4 |
| 32 North and West: [2] | | | | | | | | | |
| 1968 | 28, 579, 766 | 2, 703, 056 | 9. 5 | 746, 030 | 27. 6 | 1, 550, 440 | 57. 4 | 332, 408 | 12. 3 |
| 1970 | 29, 451, 976 | 2, 889, 858 | 9. 8 | 793, 979 | 27. 5 | 1, 665, 926 | 57. 6 | 343, 629 | 11. 9 |
| 1971 estimate | 29, 299, 586 | 2, 913, 047 | 9. 9 | 810, 985 | 27. 8 | 1, 664, 771 | 57. 1 | 325, 874 | 11. 2 |
| Difference 1970–71 | −152, 390 | 23, 189 | . 1 | 16, 916 | . 3 | −1, 155 | −. 5 | −17, 755 | . 7 |
| 11 South: [3] | | | | | | | | | |
| 1968 | 11, 043, 485 | 2, 942, 960 | 26. 6 | 540, 692 | 18. 4 | 2, 317, 850 | 78. 8 | 2, 000, 486 | 68. 0 |
| 1970 | 11, 570, 351 | 3, 150, 192 | 27. 2 | 1, 230, 868 | 39. 1 | 1, 241, 050 | 39. 4 | 443, 073 | 14. 1 |
| 1971 estimate | 11, 551, 697 | 3, 139, 436 | 27. 2 | 1, 377, 847 | 43. 9 | 1, 010, 558 | 32. 2 | 290, 390 | 9. 2 |
| Difference 1970–71 | −18, 654 | −10, 756 | 0 | 146, 979 | 4. 8 | −230, 492 | −7. 2 | −152, 683 | −4. 9 |
| 6 Border and District of Columbia: [4] | | | | | | | | | |
| 1968 | 3, 730, 317 | 636, 157 | 17. 1 | 180, 569 | 28. 4 | 406, 171 | 63. 8 | 160, 504 | 25. 2 |
| 1970 | 3, 855, 221 | 667, 362 | 17. 3 | 198, 659 | 29. 8 | 404, 396 | 60. 6 | 154, 409 | 23. 1 |
| 1971 estimate | 3, 840, 392 | 672, 473 | 17. 5 | 205, 082 | 30. 5 | 409, 456 | 60. 9 | 162, 568 | 24. 2 |
| Difference 1970–71 | −14, 829 | 5, 111 | . 2 | 6, 423 | . 7 | 5, 060 | . 3 | 8, 159 | 1. 1 |

[1] 1971 figures are estimations based on latest available data and are subject to change upon final compilation.

[2] Alaska, Arizona, California, Colorado, Connecticut, Idaho, Illinois, Indiana, Iowa, Kansas, Maine, Massachusetts, Michigan, Minnesota, Montana, Nebraska, Nevada, New Hampshire, New Jersey, New Mexico, New York, North Dakota, Ohio, Oregon, Pennsylvania, Rhode Island, South Dakota, Utah, Vermont, Washington, Wisconsin, Wyoming.

[3] Alabama, Arkansas, Florida, Georgia, Louisiana, Mississippi, North Carolina, South Carolina, Tennessee, Texas, Virginia.

[4] Delaware, District of Columbia, Kentucky, Maryland, Missouri, Oklahoma, West Virginia.

At the same time, however, statistics revealed that segregation and racial isolation in the North and West, particularly in the large metropolitan areas was increasing. In Boston, for example, the percentage of blacks in majority white schools had decreased from 18 percent to 14.9 percent in the 2-year period between 1970 and 1972. In Cincinnati, the drop was 16.9 percent to 13.7 percent from 1970 to 1971. The figures can be given for many large cities as shown on the following table: *

*From the Congressional Record, Jan. 20, 1972.

TABLE 1-C.—*Fall 1971 survey districts reporting by Nov. 19, 1971, compared with Fall 1970 data for these same districts (fall 1971 data is unedited) Negro pupils in 77 of the 100 largest (1970) school districts*

| District | Total pupils | Negro pupils | | Negro pupils attending schools which are— | | | | | |
|---|---|---|---|---|---|---|---|---|---|
| | | | | 0 to 49.9 percent minority | | 80 to 100 percent minority | | 100 percent minority | |
| | | Number | Percent | Number | Percent | Number | Percent | Number | Percent |
| Akron, Ohio: | | | | | | | | | |
| 1970 | 56, 426 | 15, 413 | 27. 3 | 5, 624 | 36. 5 | 7, 594 | 49. 3 | 0 | 0 |
| 1971 | 55, 570 | 15, 454 | 27. 8 | 5, 208 | 33. 7 | 6, 214 | 40. 2 | 454 | 2. 9 |
| Albuquerque, N. Mex.: | | | | | | | | | |
| 1970 | 83, 781 | 2, 048 | 2. 4 | 742 | 36. 2 | 779 | 38. 0 | 0 | 0 |
| 1971 | 85, 473 | 2, 180 | 2. 6 | 750 | 34. 4 | 1, 022 | 46. 9 | 0 | 0 |
| Anne Arundel County, Md. (Annapolis): | | | | | | | | | |
| 1970 | 74, 021 | 9, 587 | 13. 0 | 7 547 | 78. 7 | 335 | 3. 5 | 0 | 0 |
| 1971 | 75, 654 | 9, 783 | 12. 9 | 7, 716 | 78. 9 | 305 | 3. 1 | 0 | 0 |
| Atlanta, Ga.: | | | | | | | | | |
| 1970 | 105, 598 | 72, 523 | 68. 7 | 4, 777 | 6. 6 | 63, 111 | 87. 0 | 24, 332 | 33. 6 |
| 1971 | 100, 316 | 72, 321 | 72. 1 | 5, 768 | 8. 0 | 62, 131 | 85. 9 | 15, 625 | 21. 6 |
| Austin, Tex.: | | | | | | | | | |
| 1970 | 54, 974 | 8, 284 | 15. 1 | 1, 323 | 16. 0 | 6, 507 | 78. 5 | 1, 216 | 14. 7 |
| 1971 | 55, 565 | 8, 147 | 14. 7 | 2, 938 | 36. 1 | 4, 735 | 58. 1 | 697 | 8. 6 |
| Boston, Mass.: | | | | | | | | | |
| 1970 | 96, 696 | 28, 822 | 29. 8 | 5, 174 | 16. 0 | 18, 757 | 65. 1 | 3, 172 | 11. 0 |
| 1971 | 96, 583 | 30, 654 | 31. 7 | 4, 574 | 14. 9 | 19, 381 | 63. 2 | 398 | 1. 3 |
| Brevard County, Fla. (Titusville): | | | | | | | | | |
| 1970 | 61, 908 | 6, 618 | 10. 7 | 5, 876 | 88. 8 | 742 | 11. 2 | 0 | 0 |
| 1971 | 61, 979 | 6, 872 | 11. 1 | 6, 151 | 89. 5 | 721 | 10. 5 | 0 | 0 |
| Broward County, Fla. (Fort Lauderdale): | | | | | | | | | |
| 1970 | 117, 324 | 27, 230 | 23. 2 | 14, 189 | 52. 1 | 11, 201 | 41. 1 | 4, 303 | 15. 8 |
| 1971 | 122, 376 | 28, 554 | 23. 3 | 22, 467 | 78. 7 | 2, 291 | 8. 0 | 650 | 2. 3 |
| Caddo Parish, La. (Shreveport): | | | | | | | | | |
| 1970 | 53, 866 | 26, 401 | 49. 0 | 6, 777 | 25. 7 | 17, 959 | 68. 0 | 11, 740 | 44. 5 |
| 1971 | 53, 420 | 26, 489 | 49. 6 | 6, 748 | 25. 5 | 17, 653 | 66. 6 | 8, 023 | 30. 3 |

| | | | | | | | | | |
|---|---|---|---|---|---|---|---|---|---|
| Charleston County, S.C.: | | | | | | | | | |
| 1970 | 57, 410 | 27, 059 | 47. 1 | 8, 332 | 30. 8 | 16, 197 | 59. 9 | 3, 675 | 13. 6 |
| 1971 | 57, 128 | 27, 445 | 48. 0 | 7, 866 | 28. 7 | 17, 113 | 62. 4 | 6, 838 | 24. 9 |
| Charlotte-Mecklenburg County, N.C.: | | | | | | | | | |
| 1970 | 82, 507 | 25, 404 | 30. 8 | 23, 050 | 90. 7 | 1, 053 | 4. 1 | 0 | 0 |
| 1971 | 81, 042 | 25, 796 | 31. 8 | 25, 253 | 97. 9 | 399 | 1. 5 | 0 | 0 |
| Chatham County, Ga. (Savannah): | | | | | | | | | |
| 1970 | 40, 897 | 17, 963 | 43. 9 | 3, 499 | 19. 5 | 12, 058 | 67. 1 | 2, 804 | 15. 6 |
| 1971 | 37, 712 | 18, 195 | 48. 2 | 10, 809 | 59. 4 | 1, 385 | 7. 6 | 0 | 0 |
| Cincinnati, Ohio: | | | | | | | | | |
| 1970 | 84, 199 | 37, 853 | 45. 0 | 6, 399 | 16. 9 | 20, 661 | 54. 6 | 5, 924 | 15. 7 |
| 1971 | 81, 879 | 37, 731 | 46. 1 | 5, 159 | 13. 7 | 20, 696 | 54. 9 | 3, 986 | 10. 6 |
| Clark County, Nev. (Las Vegas): | | | | | | | | | |
| 1970 | 73, 822 | 9, 567 | 13. 0 | 5, 960 | 62. 3 | 2, 870 | 30. 0 | 515 | 5. 4 |
| 1971 | 73, 745 | 9, 499 | 12. 9 | 6, 420 | 67. 6 | 1, 774 | 18. 7 | 353 | 3. 7 |
| Cleveland, Ohio: | | | | | | | | | |
| 1970 | 153, 619 | 88, 558 | 57. 6 | 3, 725 | 4. 2 | 80, 505 | 90. 9 | 30, 852 | 34. 8 |
| 1971 | 148, 854 | 85, 291 | 57. 3 | 3, 931 | 4. 6 | 77, 841 | 91. 3 | 30, 232 | 35. 4 |
| Cobb County, Ga. (Marietta): | | | | | | | | | |
| 1970 | 44, 504 | 1, 397 | 3. 1 | 1, 397 | 100. 0 | 0 | 0 | 0 | 0 |
| 1971 | 45, 661 | 1, 336 | 2. 9 | 1, 336 | 100. 0 | 0 | 0 | 0 | 0 |
| Columbus, Ohio: | | | | | | | | | |
| 1970 | 109, 329 | 29, 440 | 26. 9 | 7, 614 | 25. 9 | 15, 604 | 53. 0 | 655 | 2. 2 |
| 1971 | 110, 735 | 31, 279 | 28. 2 | 8, 788 | 28. 1 | 16, 862 | 53. 9 | 205 | . 7 |
| Compton, Calif.: | | | | | | | | | |
| 1970 | 40, 364 | 33, 486 | 83. 0 | 0 | 0 | 31, 056 | 92. 7 | 5, 303 | 15. 8 |
| 1971 | 39, 356 | 33, 471 | 84. 0 | 0 | 0 | 32, 740 | 97. 8 | 2, 483 | 7. 4 |
| Corpus Christi, Tex.: | | | | | | | | | |
| 1970 | 46, 292 | 2, 590 | 5. 6 | 71 | 2. 7 | 2, 176 | 84. 0 | 12 | . 5 |
| 1971 | 45, 900 | 2, 601 | 5. 7 | 143 | 5. 5 | 2, 080 | 80. 0 | 15 | . 5 |
| Dade County, Fla. (Miami): | | | | | | | | | |
| 1970 | 240, 447 | 60, 957 | 25. 4 | 13, 254 | 21. 7 | 32, 352 | 53. 1 | 7, 498 | 12. 3 |
| 1971 | 244, 765 | 62, 974 | 25. 7 | 14, 507 | 23. 0 | 33, 485 | 53. 2 | 8, 129 | 12. 9 |
| Dallas, Tex.: | | | | | | | | | |
| 1970 | 164, 736 | 55, 648 | 33. 8 | 1, 528 | 2. 7 | 52, 380 | 94. 1 | 12, 899 | 23. 2 |
| 1971 | 157, 799 | 57, 338 | 36. 3 | 8, 617 | 15. 0 | 47, 843 | 83. 4 | 6, 028 | 10. 5 |

TABLE 1-C.—*Fall 1971 survey districts reporting by Nov. 19, 1971, compared with Fall 1970 data for these same districts (Fall 1971 data is unedited) Negro pupils in 77 of the 100 largest (1970) school districts*—Continued

| District | Total pupils | Negro pupils | | Negro pupils attending school which are— 0 to 49.9 percent minority | | 80 to 100 percent minority | | 100 percent minority | |
|---|---|---|---|---|---|---|---|---|---|
| | | Number | Percent | Number | Percent | Number | Percent | Number | Percent |
| Dayton, Ohio: | | | | | | | | | |
| 1970 | 56, 609 | 23, 013 | 40. 7 | 2, 990 | 13. 0 | 17, 900 | 77. 8 | 2, 183 | 9. 5 |
| 1971 | 55, 041 | 23, 489 | 42. 7 | 3, 670 | 15. 6 | 18, 343 | 78. 1 | 3, 431 | 14. 6 |
| DeKalb County, Ga. (Decatur): | | | | | | | | | |
| 1970 | 85, 859 | 5, 379 | 6. 3 | 3, 793 | 70. 5 | 793 | 14. 7 | 48 | . 9 |
| 1971 | 88, 012 | 6, 351 | 7. 2 | 4, 462 | 70. 3 | 1, 412 | 22. 2 | 0 | 0 |
| Denver, Colo.: | | | | | | | | | |
| 1970 | 97, 928 | 14, 434 | 14. 7 | 6, 431 | 44. 6 | 6, 426 | 44. 5 | 0 | 0 |
| 1971 | 94, 808 | 14, 901 | 15. 7 | 6, 755 | 45. 3 | 5, 443 | 36. 5 | 0 | 0 |
| Des Moines, Iowa: | | | | | | | | | |
| 1970 | 45, 375 | 3, 751 | 8. 3 | 2, 193 | 58. 5 | 24 | . 6 | 0 | 0 |
| 1971 | 44, 340 | 3, 738 | 8. 4 | 2, 137 | 57. 2 | 298 | 8. 0 | 0 | 0 |
| Detroit, Mich.: | | | | | | | | | |
| 1970 | 284, 396 | 181, 538 | 63. 8 | 10, 618 | 5. 8 | 143, 946 | 79. 3 | 24, 809 | 13. 7 |
| 1971 | 282, 076 | 183, 262 | 65. 0 | 11, 629 | 6. 3 | 143, 992 | 78. 6 | 22, 105 | 12. 1 |
| Duval County, Fla. (Jacksonville): | | | | | | | | | |
| 1970 | 122, 493 | 36, 054 | 29. 4 | 9, 237 | 25. 6 | 20, 747 | 57. 5 | 13, 345 | 37. 0 |
| 1971 | 117, 576 | 36, 769 | 31. 3 | 13, 229 | 36. 0 | 14, 042 | 38. 2 | 8, 549 | 23. 3 |
| East Baton Rouge Parish, La.: | | | | | | | | | |
| 1970 | 64, 198 | 24, 785 | 38. 6 | 5, 457 | 22. 0 | 17, 810 | 71. 9 | 7, 211 | 29. 1 |
| 1971 | 65, 906 | 25, 723 | 39. 0 | 5, 897 | 22. 9 | 18, 531 | 72. 0 | 5, 399 | 21. 0 |
| El Paso, Tex.: | | | | | | | | | |
| 1970 | 62, 545 | 1, 887 | 3. 0 | 1, 090 | 57. 8 | 383 | 20. 3 | 60 | 3. 2 |
| 1971 | 62, 960 | 1, 915 | 3. 0 | 1, 358 | 70. 9 | 355 | 18. 5 | 0 | 0 |
| Escambia County, Fla. (Pensacola): | | | | | | | | | |
| 1970 | 46, 987 | 13, 443 | 28. 6 | 5, 548 | 41. 3 | 2, 225 | 16. 6 | 0 | 0 |
| 1971 | 44, 723 | 12, 713 | 28. 4 | 5, 391 | 42. 4 | 1, 938 | 15. 2 | 1 | 0 |

| | | | | | | | | | |
|---|---|---|---|---|---|---|---|---|---|
| Flint, Mich.: | | | | | | | | | |
| 1970 | 45, 659 | 18, 475 | 40. 5 | 3, 512 | 19. 0 | 7, 051 | 38. 2 | 385 | 2. 1 |
| 1971 | 41, 899 | 17, 116 | 40. 9 | 3, 494 | 20. 4 | 7, 973 | 46. 6 | 319 | 1. 9 |
| Fort Wayne, Ind.: | | | | | | | | | |
| 1970 | 43, 400 | 6, 492 | 15. 0 | 1, 921 | 29. 6 | 3, 194 | 49. 2 | 0 | 0 |
| 1971 | 42, 963 | 6, 720 | 15. 6 | 3, 440 | 51. 2 | 2, 429 | 36. 1 | 0 | 0 |
| Fort Worth, Tex.: | | | | | | | | | |
| 1970 | 88, 095 | 23, 542 | 26. 7 | 2, 309 | 9. 8 | 18, 845 | 80. 0 | 11, 399 | 48. 4 |
| 1971 | 82, 418 | 23, 311 | 28. 3 | 4, 993 | 21. 4 | 15, 623 | 67. 0 | 4, 767 | 20. 4 |
| Fresno, Calif.: | | | | | | | | | |
| 1970 | 57, 508 | 5, 133 | 8. 9 | 1, 255 | 24. 4 | 3, 441 | 67. 0 | 16 | 3 |
| 1971 | 55, 783 | 5, 190 | 9. 3 | 1, 506 | 29. 0 | 3, 322 | 64. 0 | 13 | 3 |
| Garden Grove, Calif.: | | | | | | | | | |
| 1970 | 52, 684 | 110 | . 2 | 110 | 100. 0 | 0 | 0 | 0 | 0 |
| 1971 | 51, 983 | 170 | . 3 | 170 | 100. 0 | 0 | 0 | 0 | 0 |
| Gary, Ind.: | | | | | | | | | |
| 1970 | 46, 595 | 30, 169 | 64. 7 | 1, 060 | 3. 5 | 27, 673 | 91. 7 | 11, 781 | 39. 1 |
| 1971 | 45, 332 | 30, 593 | 67. 5 | 1, 177 | 3. 8 | 29, 272 | 95. 7 | 5, 336 | 17. 4 |
| Greenville County, S.C.: | | | | | | | | | |
| 1970 | 57, 222 | 12, 788 | 22. 3 | 12, 594 | 98. 5 | 72 | . 6 | 0 | 0 |
| 1971 | 57, 559 | 12, 770 | 22. 2 | 12, 654 | 99. 1 | 0 | 0 | 0 | 0 |
| Hillsborough County, Fla., (Tampa): | | | | | | | | | |
| 1970 | 105, 347 | 20, 417 | 19. 4 | 4, 771 | 23. 4 | 12, 832 | 62. 8 | 2, 303 | 11. 3 |
| 1971 | 101, 298 | 19, 769 | 19. 5 | 19, 335 | 97. 8 | 90 | . 5 | 0 | 0 |
| Houston, Tex.: | | | | | | | | | |
| 1970 | 241, 139 | 85, 965 | 35. 6 | 7, 202 | 8. 4 | 73, 373 | 85. 4 | 7, 604 | 8. 8 |
| 1971 | 225, 681 | 85, 276 | 37. 8 | 7, 398 | 8. 7 | 73, 351 | 86. 0 | 7, 391 | 8. 7 |
| Indianapolis, Ind.: | | | | | | | | | |
| 1970 | 106, 239 | 38, 044 | 35. 8 | 7, 785 | 20. 5 | 22, 925 | 60. 3 | 3, 318 | 8. 7 |
| 1971 | 102, 326 | 38, 542 | 37. 7 | 9, 060 | 23. 5 | 23, 180 | 60. 1 | 4, 889 | 12. 7 |
| Jefferson County, Ala. (Birmingham area): | | | | | | | | | |
| 1970 | 59, 717 | 16, 776 | 28. 1 | 3, 240 | 19. 3 | 13, 159 | 78. 4 | 8, 020 | 47. 8 |
| 1971 | 56, 573 | 15, 110 | 26. 7 | 5, 952 | 39. 4 | 8, 563 | 56. 7 | 4, 528 | 30. 0 |
| Jefferson County, Ky. (Louisville): | | | | | | | | | |
| 1970 | 93, 454 | 3, 382 | 3. 6 | 2, 738 | 81. 0 | 644 | 19. 0 | 0 | 0 |
| 1971 | 95, 660 | 3, 590 | 3. 8 | 3, 082 | 85. 8 | 508 | 14. 2 | 0 | 0 |

TABLE 1–C.—*Fall 1971 survey districts reporting by Nov. 19, 1971, compared with Fall 1970 data for these same districts (Fall 1971 data is unedited) Negro pupils in 77 of the 100 largest (1970) school districts*—Continued

| District | Total pupils | Negro pupils | | Negro pupils attending school which are— 0 to 49.9 percent minority | | 80 to 100 percent minority | | 100 percent minority | |
|---|---|---|---|---|---|---|---|---|---|
| | | Number | Percent | Number | Percent | Number | Percent | Number | Percent |
| Jefferson Parish, La. (Gretna): | | | | | | | | | |
| 1970 | 63, 572 | 13, 201 | 20. 8 | 6, 425 | 48. 7 | 4, 791 | 36. 3 | 2, 577 | 19. 5 |
| 1971 | 61, 763 | 12, 790 | 20. 7 | 12, 015 | 93. 9 | 80 | . 6 | 0 | 0 |
| Kanawha County, W. Va. (Charleston): | | | | | | | | | |
| 1970 | 52, 888 | 3, 404 | 6. 4 | 2, 934 | 86. 2 | 0 | 0 | 0 | 0 |
| 1971 | 52, 617 | 3, 450 | 6. 6 | 3, 017 | 87. 4 | 0 | 0 | 0 | 0 |
| Kansas City, Mo.: | | | | | | | | | |
| 1970 | 70, 503 | 35, 375 | 50. 2 | 3, 301 | 9. 3 | 29, 504 | 83. 4 | 5, 275 | 14. 9 |
| 1971 | 68, 335 | 35, 657 | 52. 2 | 3, 468 | 9. 7 | 30, 793 | 86. 4 | 8, 871 | 24. 9 |
| Long Beach, Calif.: | | | | | | | | | |
| 1970 | 69, 927 | 6, 349 | 9. 1 | 2, 219 | 35. 0 | 0 | 0 | 0 | 0 |
| 1971 | 69, 205 | 6, 972 | 10. 1 | 2, 405 | 34. 5 | 0 | 0 | 0 | 0 |
| Los Angeles, Calif.: | | | | | | | | | |
| 1970 | 642, 895 | 154, 926 | 24. 1 | 9, 121 | 5. 9 | 134, 889 | 87. 1 | 13, 551 | 8. 7 |
| 1971 | 633, 951 | 157, 589 | 24. 9 | 10, 712 | 6. 8 | 136, 459 | 86. 6 | 12, 046 | 7. 6 |
| Louisville, Ky.: | | | | | | | | | |
| 1970 | 53, 197 | 25, 674 | 48. 3 | 3, 013 | 11. 7 | 19, 884 | 77. 4 | 1, 094 | 4. 3 |
| 1971 | 50, 440 | 24, 591 | 48. 8 | 3, 120 | 12. 7 | 20, 246 | 82. 3 | 3, 830 | 15. 6 |
| Milwaukee, Wis.: | | | | | | | | | |
| 1970 | 132, 349 | 34, 355 | 26. 0 | 4, 197 | 12. 2 | 26, 193 | 76. 2 | 0 | 0 |
| 1971 | 131, 815 | 36, 930 | 28. 0 | 5, 467 | 14. 8 | 29, 111 | 78. 8 | 2, 059 | 5. 6 |
| Minneapolis, Minn.: | | | | | | | | | |
| 1970 | 66, 938 | 5, 935 | 8. 9 | 3, 416 | 57. 6 | 0 | 0 | 0 | 0 |
| 1971 | 65, 201 | 6, 351 | 9. 7 | 4, 118 | 64. 8 | 428 | 6. 7 | 0 | 0 |
| Muscogee County, Ga. (Columbus): | | | | | | | | | |
| 1970 | 42, 010 | 13, 074 | 31. 1 | 1, 564 | 12. 0 | 11, 214 | 85. 8 | 8, 093 | 61. 9 |
| 1971 | 40, 341 | 13, 126 | 32. 5 | 12, 602 | 96. 0 | 211 | 1. 6 | 211 | 1. 6 |

| | | | | | | | | | |
|---|---|---|---|---|---|---|---|---|---|
| Nashville-Davidson County, Tenn.: | | | | | | | | | |
| 1970 | 95, 313 | 23, 473 | 24. 6 | 5, 877 | 25. 0 | 15, 727 | 67. 0 | 4, 942 | 21. 1 |
| 1971 | 88, 190 | 23, 963 | 27. 2 | 19, 820 | 82. 7 | 0 | 0 | 0 | 0 |
| Newark, N.J.: | | | | | | | | | |
| 1970 | 78, 456 | 56, 651 | 72. 2 | 1, 620 | 2. 9 | 51, 685 | 91. 2 | 11, 217 | 19. 8 |
| 1971 | 79, 661 | 57, 358 | 72. 0 | 1, 463 | 2. 6 | 52, 359 | 91. 3 | 12, 888 | 22. 5 |
| Norfolk, Va.: | | | | | | | | | |
| 1970 | 55, 117 | 24, 757 | 44. 9 | 8, 139 | 32. 9 | 13, 827 | 55. 9 | 6, 457 | 26. 1 |
| 1971 | 50, 791 | 24, 341 | 47. 9 | 12, 280 | 50. 4 | 285 | 1. 2 | 0 | 0 |
| Oakland, Calif.: | | | | | | | | | |
| 1970 | 67, 830 | 38, 567 | 56. 9 | 2, 498 | 6. 5 | 28, 988 | 75. 2 | 991 | 2. 6 |
| 1971 | 67, 323 | 39, 102 | 58. 1 | 2, 480 | 6. 3 | 28, 582 | 73. 1 | 634 | 1. 6 |
| Oklahoma City, Okla.: | | | | | | | | | |
| 1970 | 70, 042 | 16, 109 | 23. 0 | 3, 442 | 21. 4 | 12, 095 | 75. 1 | 3, 672 | 22. 8 |
| 1971 | 69, 130 | 16, 309 | 23. 6 | 3, 576 | 21. 9 | 11, 135 | 68. 3 | 5, 235 | 32. 1 |
| Orange County, Fla. (Orlando): | | | | | | | | | |
| 1970 | 85, 270 | 15, 398 | 18. 1 | 6, 265 | 40. 7 | 8, 005 | 52. 0 | 2, 553 | 16. 6 |
| 1971 | 84, 928 | 15, 638 | 18. 4 | 8, 173 | 52. 3 | 4, 428 | 28. 3 | 772 | 4. 9 |
| Orleans Parish, La. (New Orleans): | | | | | | | | | |
| 1970 | 109, 856 | 76, 388 | 69. 5 | 5, 925 | 7. 8 | 62, 567 | 81. 9 | 37, 053 | 48. 5 |
| 1971 | 108, 969 | 77, 538 | 71. 2 | 5, 079 | 6. 6 | 62, 669 | 80. 8 | 36, 587 | 47. 2 |
| Pinellas County, Fla. (Clearwater): | | | | | | | | | |
| 1970 | 85, 117 | 13, 766 | 16. 2 | 6, 264 | 45. 5 | 2, 881 | 20. 9 | 667 | 4. 8 |
| 1971 | 86, 878 | 14, 137 | 16. 3 | 13, 408 | 94. 8 | 0 | 0 | 0 | 0 |
| Polk County, Fla. (Bartow): | | | | | | | | | |
| 1970 | 54, 380 | 11, 899 | 21. 9 | 8, 622 | 72. 5 | 1, 444 | 12. 1 | 0 | 0 |
| 1971 | 55, 343 | 12, 217 | 22. 1 | 9, 761 | 79. 9 | 1, 433 | 11. 7 | 0 | 0 |
| Portland, Oreg.: | | | | | | | | | |
| 1970 | 76, 206 | 7, 008 | 9. 2 | 4, 352 | 62. 1 | 1, 494 | 21. 3 | 0 | 0 |
| 1971 | 72, 694 | 7, 103 | 9. 8 | 3, 721 | 52. 4 | 1, 504 | 21. 2 | 0 | 0 |
| Prince Georges County, Md. (District of Columbia area): | | | | | | | | | |
| 1970 | 160, 897 | 31, 994 | 19. 9 | 13, 040 | 40. 8 | 11, 190 | 35. 0 | 724 | 2. 3 |
| 1971 | 162, 828 | 36, 450 | 22. 4 | 14, 093 | 38. 7 | 14, 510 | 39. 8 | 550 | 1. 5 |
| Richmond, Calif.: | | | | | | | | | |
| 1970 | 41, 492 | 11, 389 | 27. 4 | 5, 730 | 50. 3 | 3, 781 | 33. 2 | 343 | 3. 0 |
| 1971 | 41, 390 | 11, 699 | 28. 3 | 5, 704 | 48. 8 | 3, 598 | 30. 8 | 345 | 2. 9 |

TABLE 1-C.—*Fall 1971 survey districts reporting by Nov. 19, 1971, compared with Fall 1970 data for these same districts (Fall 1971 data is unedited) Negro pupils in 77 of the 100 largest (1970) school districts*—Continued

| District | Total pupils | Negro pupils | | Negro pupils attending school which are— | | | | | |
|---|---|---|---|---|---|---|---|---|---|
| | | | | 0 to 49.9 percent minority | | 80 to 100 percent minority | | 100 percent minority | |
| | | Number | Percent | Number | Percent | Number | Percent | Number | Percent |
| Richmond, Va.: | | | | | | | | | |
| 1970 | 47, 988 | 30, 785 | 64. 2 | 3, 609 | 11. 7 | 17, 485 | 56. 8 | 2, 954 | 9. 6 |
| 1971 | 44, 989 | 31, 101 | 69. 1 | 1, 901 | 6. 1 | 11, 363 | 36. 5 | 32 | . 1 |
| Rochester, N.Y.: | | | | | | | | | |
| 1970 | 45, 500 | 15, 082 | 33. 1 | 6, 161 | 40. 9 | 6, 661 | 44. 2 | 0 | 0 |
| 1971 | 44, 152 | 15, 747 | 35. 7 | 7, 709 | 49. 0 | 5, 303 | 33. 7 | 0 | 0 |
| Rockford, Ill.: | | | | | | | | | |
| 1970 | 43, 116 | 5, 300 | 12. 3 | 2, 965 | 55. 9 | 412 | 7. 8 | 0 | 0 |
| 1971 | 42, 131 | 5, 385 | 12. 8 | 2, 999 | 55. 7 | 449 | 8. 3 | 0 | 0 |
| Sacramento, Calif.: | | | | | | | | | |
| 1970 | 52, 218 | 8, 012 | 15. 3 | 5, 273 | 65. 8 | 302 | 3. 8 | 0 | 0 |
| 1971 | 49, 658 | 8, 070 | 16. 3 | 5, 166 | 64. 0 | 540 | 6. 7 | 0 | 0 |
| San Antonio, Tex.: | | | | | | | | | |
| 1970 | 77, 253 | 11, 853 | 15. 3 | 1, 099 | 9. 3 | 7, 950 | 67. 1 | 1, 310 | 11. 1 |
| 1971 | 74, 955 | 11, 600 | 15. 5 | 958 | 8. 3 | 8, 260 | 71. 2 | 1, 463 | 12. 6 |
| Shawnee Mission, Kan. (Kansas City area): | | | | | | | | | |
| 1970 | 45, 289 | 140 | . 3 | 140 | 100. 0 | 0 | 0 | 0 | 0 |
| 1971 | 41, 936 | 157 | . 4 | 144 | 91. 7 | 3 | 1. 9 | 3 | 1. 9 |
| St. Louis, Mo.: | | | | | | | | | |
| 1970 | 111, 233 | 72, 965 | 65. 6 | 1, 827 | 2. 5 | 64, 166 | 87. 9 | 36, 316 | 49. 8 |
| 1971 | 107, 986 | 73, 149 | 67. 7 | 1, 545 | 2. 1 | 65, 668 | 89. 8 | 34, 717 | 47. 5 |

| | | | | | | | | | |
|---|---|---|---|---|---|---|---|---|---|
| St. Paul, Minn.: | | | | | | | | | |
| 1970 | 49, 732 | 3, 163 | 6. 4 | 2, 043 | 64. 6 | 340 | 10. 7 | 0 | 0 |
| 1971 | 50, 589 | 3, 541 | 7. 0 | 2, 421 | 68. 4 | 339 | 9. 6 | 0 | 0 |
| Toledo, Ohio: | | | | | | | | | |
| 1970 | 61, 699 | 16, 407 | 26. 6 | 3, 954 | 24. 1 | 9, 725 | 59. 3 | 579 | 3. 5 |
| 1971 | 62, 597 | 17, 052 | 27. 2 | 3, 838 | 22. 5 | 10, 121 | 59. 4 | 448 | 2. 6 |
| Virginia Beach, Va.: | | | | | | | | | |
| 1970 | 45, 245 | 4, 793 | 10. 6 | 4, 187 | 87. 4 | 606 | 12. 6 | 0 | 0 |
| 1971 | 46, 802 | 4, 793 | 10. 2 | 4, 793 | 100. 0 | 0 | 0 | 0 | 0 |
| Washington, D.C.: | | | | | | | | | |
| 1970 | 145, 330 | 137, 502 | 94. 6 | 1, 674 | 1. 2 | 133, 421 | 97. 0 | 46, 117 | 33. 5 |
| 1971 | 141, 806 | 135, 068 | 95. 2 | 455 | . 3 | 131, 844 | 97. 6 | 47, 516 | 35. 2 |
| Wichita, Kans.: | | | | | | | | | |
| 1970 | 63, 811 | 9, 362 | 14. 7 | 6, 025 | 64. 4 | 2, 950 | 31. 5 | 371 | 4. 0 |
| 1971 | 59, 868 | 9, 274 | 15. 5 | 9, 247 | 99. 7 | 0 | 0 | 0 | 0 |
| Winston-Salem-Forsyth County, N.C.: | | | | | | | | | |
| 1970 | 49, 514 | 13, 727 | 27. 7 | 5, 077 | 37. 0 | 7, 884 | 57. 4 | 6, 015 | 43. 8 |
| 1971 | 47, 937 | 14, 097 | 29. 4 | 13, 494 | 95. 7 | 383 | 2. 7 | 0 | 0 |

86-389 O—72——26

In addition to the statistics which showed the South making more progress in desegregation than the North, several other aspects of the situation began to receive attention.

*First*, 1954 had become an arbitrary dividing line. Because a State had a law in that year providing for a dual school system, it was considered to have *de jure* segregation and it was required to take a number of steps which had included assignment of teachers on a ratio plan, pairings of schools, redrawing of school boundaries, and busing of schoolchildren. Furthermore, there was no means whereby a State once *de jure* could ever be considered to have overcome its *de jure* status.

In a number of the Northern and Western States, however, there had also been laws either requiring dual school systems or permitting other forms of discrimination against minorities. Judge Walter Hoffman, of the Eastern District of Virginia, compiled a listing of some of these laws which he included as an appendix to an opinion in a school desegregation case. Following is Judge Hoffman's appendix:

### Judge Hoffman's Appendix

A list of States with discriminatory laws or judicial decisions, excluding Virginia, North Carolina, South Carolina, Georgia, Florida, Alabama, Mississippi, and Louisiana, in which mandatory school segregation laws existed on May 17, 1954.

#### ALASKA

In *Davis* v. *Sitka School Board*, 3 Alas. 481 (1908), it was held that semicivilized Indians did not have to be admitted to public schools. It went on to find that the stepchildren of "an industrious, law-abiding, intelligent native" Indian, who operated a store "according to civilized methods," and had adopted the white man's style of dress; spoke, read and wrote the English language; and was a member of the Presbyterian Church; were not civilized enough to attend white schools because they still lived with other members of their tribe.

*Sing* v. *Sitka School Board*, 7 Alas. 616 (1927), upheld separate but equal schools for Indians.

#### ARIZONA

*Arizona Code Ann.* (1939), section 54–416, provided for mandatory segregation in *elementary* schools. Under section 54–918, there was permissive segregation in *high* schools, where there were more than 25 blacks in the high school district and if approved by a majority vote of the electorate. By an amendment in 1951, section 54–416 was made permissive and section 54–918 was repealed.

#### ARKANSAS

*Ark. Stat. Ann.* (1947), section 80–509(c) required the establishment of separate schools for white and colored.

#### CALIFORNIA

While laws enacted in 1869–70 and 1880–81 provided (1) mandatory separate schools for Negro and Indian children, and (2) permissive separate schools for children of Mongolian or Chinese descent, a statute enacted in 1943 but repealed in 1947 reenacted the permissive separate school provision and provided that, if separate schools were established for Indian children or children of Chinese, Japanese or Mongolian parentage, they could not be admitted to any other school. *Cal. Educational Code*, section 8003 (Deering's 1944.) *See* also: *Cal. Laws* 1869–70, p. 838; *Cal. Political Code*, section 1662 (Deering's 1885).

## COLORADO

Miscegenation statute, *Col. Stats. Ann.* c. 107, sections 2, 3 (1935). Jackson v. Denver, 109 Col. 196, 124 P. (2d) 240 (1909) holds that an otherwise valid common law marriage between a black and a white was declared to be "immoral" and justified a conviction under a vagrancy statute defining same to include leading an "immoral course of life."

## CONNECTICUT

*Conn. Const.*, Art. VI, section 2 (1818), limited the electorate to white male citizens owning property. In 1845 the property qualification was deleted. In 1876 the Constitution was amended by removing the requirement that electors be white.

## DELAWARE

*Del. Const.*, Art. X, section 2 (1915) provided for separate schools. By the Del. Rev. Code, Ch. 71, section 9 (1935), two kinds of separate schools were authorized; "those for white children and those for colored children."

## DISTRICT OF COLUMBIA

*D.C. Code,* title 7, sections 249, 252 (1939 Supp.), authorizes separate schools for white and colored in the District.

## IDAHO

*Idaho Const.*, Art. 6, section 3 (1890), prohibits Chinese or Mongolians, not born in the United States, from voting, serving as jurors, or holding civil offices.

Miscegenation statute: 1867, p. 71, section 3; R. S. section 2425, reenacted Rev. Code section 2616; amended 1921, Ch. 115, section 1, p. 291.

## ILLINOIS

*Ill. Const.*, Art. II, section 27 (1919), limited the electorate to white males.

Although no statute respecting school segregation has been located, history is replete with evidence of discriminatory practices in operating separate schools for many years. *See* Ming, *The Elimination of Segregation in the Public Schools of the North and West*, 21 J. Negro Ed. 265, 268 (1952); B. H. Valien, *Racial Desegregation of the Public Schools in Southern Illinois*, 23 J. Negro Ed. 303 (1954); Shagoloff, *A Study of Community Acceptance of Desegregation in Two Selected Areas*, 23 J. Negro Ed. 330 (1954). *See* also: *United States* v. *School District 151 of Cook County, Ill.*, 301 F. Supp. 201, 217 (1969).

Thus, Illinois without a specific statute, practiced segregation in public schools prior to 1954, almost as much as in the "Deep South."

## INDIANA

*Ind. Stat. Ann.*, section 28–5104 (Burns 1933), provided for the establishment of separate schools for Negroes if the school authorities believed it to be necessary or proper but, if no separate schools were established, Negroes could attend white schools. In 1949, the separate school law was repealed, *Laws*, 1949, Ch. 186, section 11.

## IOWA

*Iowa Laws*, Ch. 99, section 6 (1846), provided that schools were to be open to all white persons.

*Iowa Laws*, Ch. 52, section 30 (1858), called for the education of colored children in separate schools except where there was unanimous consent of all attending the school to allow Negroes to attend the white school. This act was declared unconstitutional in *District* v. *City of Dubuque*, 7 Iowa 262 (1858), on the ground that the Constitution gave the power to legislate with regard to education to the Board of Education and not to the General Assembly. Thereafter, the Board of Education provided education for all "youth" and in *Clark* v. *The Board of Directors*, 24 Iowa 266 (1868), this was construed as requiring admission of Negroes into white schools.

The *Iowa Const.*, Art. II, section 1 (1858), provided that only white males could be electors. Iowa Code, Ch. 130, section 2388 ff. (1859), stated that no colored person could be a witness.

### KANSAS

*Kan. Gen. Stat.*, section 72–1724 (1949), gave authority to establish and maintain separate primary schools for whites and Negroes throughout the State, and separate high schools in Kansas City. *See: Brown* v. *Board of Education*, 347 U.S. 483 (1954).

### KENTUCKY

*Ky. Const.*, section 187, *Ky. Rev. Stat.*, section 158.020 (1946), required separate schools for white and colored children.

### MARYLAND

*Md. Code Ann.*, Art. 77, sections 124, 207 (1951), required the county boards of education to establish one or more separate schools for Negroes, provided that the colored population of any such district warranted, in the board's judgment, an establishment of separate colored educational facilities.

### MASSACHUSETTS

In *Roberts* v. *City of Boston*, 59 Mass. 198 (1849), the court stated that separate schools had been maintained for colored children "for half a century."

The court upheld the school committee in denying admission to a white school by a Negro child. However, 6 years later Massachusetts by statute abolished the practice of excluding on account of race, color or religion.

### MICHIGAN

A dissenting opinion in *The People* v. *The Board of Education of Detroit*, 18 Mich. 400 (1869), states that in 1841 separate schools for colored were established in Detroit. The court was construing an amendment to the general school law which provided that all residents had an equal right to attend schools and the statute was held to apply to Detroit.

In *Day* v. *Owen*, 5 Mich. 520 (1858), the court upheld a regulation excluding a Negro from the cabin of a steamer solely for the reason of his race.

*People* v. *Dean*, 14 Mich. 406 (1866), held that only whites, or those at least three-fourths white, could vote.

Miscegenation statute, C. L. 1857, 3209, C. L. 1871, 4724, prohibited marriages between whites and Negroes until the statute was amended in 1883.

### MINNESOTA

*Minn. Rev. Stat.*, Ch. 5, section 1 (1851), and Minn. Const., Art. VII, section 1 (1858), excluded Negroes from voting until amendment of November 3, 1868.

### MISSOURI

*Mo. Const.*, Art. XI, sections 1, 3 (1875), and *Mo. Rev. Stat.*, section 163.130 (1949), required separate schools and "it shall be unlawful for any colored child to attend any white school or for any white child to attend a colored school." These provisions were repealed in 1957, three years *after Brown I.*

### MONTANA

Mont. Ter. Laws, 1872, p. 627, provided for separate schools of children of African descent when requested by at least ten such children. This statute was repealed in 1895.

Miscegenation statute, *Mont. Rev. Code*, section 5700, (1935).

### NEBRASKA

*Neb. Rev. Stat.*, Ch. 48, section 8 (1866), imposed upon the local school directors the duty of taking an annual census of unmarried *white* youth between the ages of five and twenty-one for the purpose of school assignments. *Neb. Rev. Stat.*, Ch. 48, section (1866), establishing the school system states that it is "for the purpose of affording the advantage of a free education to all *white* youth of this territory," and further provides that all colored persons shall be "exempted from taxation for school purposes." These laws were repealed in 1969.

Miscegenation statute. *Neb. Rev. Stat.*, section 42–103 (1943).

### NEW JERSEY

*N.J. Com. Stat.*, pp. 4791–92, Schools sections 201–204, pp. 4814–16, Schools sections 262–267 (1911), established as industrial school for blacks.

In M. T. Wright, *Racial Integration in the Public Schools in New Jersey*, 23 J. Negro Ed. 282 (1954), there is reference to an 1850 statute permitting a township in Morris County to establish separate schools for colored children.

In Williams and Ryan, *Schools in Transition*, p. 122 (1954), it is said: "A survey of 62 school districts, initiated in the spring of 1948, revealed that two-thirds had segregated schools sanctioned by local custom and practice."

*N.J. Const.*, Art. II, section 1 (1844), limited suffrage to white males.

### NEW MEXICO

*N.M. Stat.*, section 55–1201 (1941 Annot.) allowed school boards to place children of African descent in separate schools if the facilities were equal.

### NEW YORK

*N.Y. Consol, Laws*, c. 15, section 921 (Cahill 1930), provided that trustees of any union school district organized under a special act "may establish separate schools for colored children provided that the facilities are equal." On March 25, 1938, this law was repealed.

### NORTH DAKOTA

Miscegenation states, N.D. Rev. Code, section 14–0304 (1943).

### OHIO

Under *Ohio Stat.*, Ch. 101, section 31 (1854), separate schools for colored children were authorized and required when there were more than thirty school-aged colored children in a township. This statute was repealed in 1887. It was held in *Garnes* v. *McCann*, 21 Ohio St. Rep. 198 (1871) that the existing statute deprived the Negroes of the right to admission at white schools.

Separation of races on an educational level under the separate but equal theory was upheld in *State ex rel. Weaver* v. *Trustees*, 126 Ohio St. Rep. 290 (1933).

### OKLAHOMA

Mandatory separate but equal schools required for black and white children. *Okla. Const.*, Art. I, section 5, Art. XIII, Section 3; *Okla. Stat.*, Title 70, Section 5–1 (1949 Supp.).

### OREGON

Miscegenation statute. *Ore. Comp. Laws Ann.*, section 63–102 (1940). Statute repealed 1951.

### PENNSYLVANIA

In *Hobbs* v. *Fogg*, 6 Watts 553 (Pa. 1837), the Court held that a free male Negro was not a freeman entitled to vote under the Pennsylvania Constitution providing that all freemen could vote. In 1838, the *Pennsylvania Constitution,* Art. I, restricted voters to white freemen. In 1874 this restriction was removed.

While unable to locate the statute, H. M. Bond, *The Education of the Negro in the American Social Order*, p. 378 (1934), states that in 1854 Pennsylvania enacted an optional separate school law where there were more than twenty Negroes in a district. This law was reportedly repealed in 1881.

### RHODE ISLAND

*Ammons* v. *Charlestown School District*, 7 R.I. 596 (1964), held that Indian tribes were not entitled to send their children to local public schools since the state had provided schools for Indians through a special state appropriation.

### SOUTH DAKOTA

Indians were required to attend federal schools established for them whenever such schools were available. S.D. Laws Ch. 138, sections 290–293 (1931) : S.D. Code, Section 15.3501 (1939).

### TENNESSEE

Mandatory separate schools for colored children. *Tenn. Const.*, Art. XI Section 12; *Tenn. Code.* Section 2377, 2393–9 (1932).

### TEXAS

Mandatory separate schools for colored children. *Tex. Const.*, Art. VII, section 7; *Tex. Ann. Rev. Civ. Stat.*, Articles 2719, 2900 (1925).

### UTAH

*Utah Laws and Ordinances*, 1851. An Ordinance to Incorporate Great Salt Lake City, section 6, provided "all free white male inhabitants are entitled to vote . . ."

Miscegenation statute. *Utah Code Ann.*, Section 40–1–2 (1943).

### WEST VIRGINIA

Mandatory separate schools for colored children. *W. Va. Code,* ch. 18, Art. 5, Section 14 (1931).

### WISCONSIN

Indians required to attend separate schools where such schools were available. *Wisc. Stat.*, section 40.71, (1949), Repealed in 1951.

Under *Wisc. Stat.*, section 75, 14(4), restrictions surviving the issuance of tax deeds (after tax sales which were valid and enforceable included those regarding the "character, race, and nationality of the owners." Statute repealed in 1951.

### WYOMING

*Wyo. Comp. Stat. Ann.*, section 67–624 (1945, but originally enacted in 1876), provided that the school boards could establish separate but equal schools for Negroes.

### SUMMARY

Only as to the states of Maine, New Hampshire, Vermont, Washington, Nevada, and Hawaii does it appear from this nonexhaustive re-

**search that no discriminatory laws appeared on the books at one time or another. No consideration has been given to Puerto Rico, Virgin Islands, Canal Zone or Guam.**

As can be noted, only six States in our Nation, that is, only 12 percent of our States, have been without discriminatory laws at some time in their history. Furthermore, several States outside the South which have had such laws, had them until quite recently: Indiana had laws permitting a dual school system until 1949; Arizona and Wisconsin had similar laws for Indians until 1951.

In view of this, is the arbitrary 1954 date fair? Is it reasonable to call a State which had a discriminatory law in 1954 a State with *de jure* segregation and not call a State which had such a law 3 or 4 years earlier a State with *de jure segregation?* Furthermore, is it reasonable to expect the citizens of those States, which had such laws in 1954, to bear more burdens and take more actions than States which had terminated their laws only several years earlier? Finally, is it reasonable to expect the citizens of States which had segregation statutes—but which have been taking steps to desegregate for 18 years—to take additional steps to overcome racial imbalances if other States, which now have more racial isolation, do not have to take the same steps? Does that represent equal protection of the laws for the citizens of those States which have been taking actions?

*Second*, the hypocrisy attached to the concept of *de jure* versus *de facto* segregation was beginning to be recognized in so far as education itself was concerned. If a minority-group child was deprived because he was racially isolated, then he suffered from that isolation no matter what its source might be. That is, the child in a predominantly black Detroit or Boston school suffered just as much as the child in a predominantly black rural Southern school. As Prof. James Coleman of Johns Hopkins University noted in testimony before the committee:

> . . . school segregation had classically, in the South, been protected by law, and in the North been protected by residence. Now it is even somewhat in the South protected by residence. The effect of segregation on children is quite independent of its origin, that is, whether it arises from law or from residence.*

Thus, as far as education is concerned—and education is our major concern—racial isolation is as detrimental to the black child in a Northern city as it is to a black child in the rural or urban South.

Yet, the Northern and Western areas sat behind a shield of *de facto* segregation. The argument was made that segregation resulted from housing patterns and other informal factors and that there was, therefore, no legal remedy. As recently as 1970, then-Assistant Attorney General Jerris Leonard referred me to the case of *Deal* v. *Cincinnati* (369 Fed. 2d 55, 6th Circuit (1966)) in which the Sixth Circuit Court of Appeals, in Mr. Leonard's words: ". . . rejected the contention that racial isolation, standing alone, not brought by official action of the school board, was a violation of the 14th Amendment. . . ." As a result the Department of Justice intervened in only six cases to bring about

---

*Hearings of the U.S. Senate Select Committee on Equal Educational Opportunity, Part 1A—*Equality of Educational Opportunity: An Introduction*, p. 106.

desegregation outside the South prior to July 1970—and the Department of Health, Education, and Welfare took little action. A challenge to Chicago schools—where in 1970 only 2.8 percent of the black students attended predominantly white schools—was quietly buried after Chicago Mayor Richard Daley made a telephone call to Washington in 1965. Also, it took more than 2 years for fund termination procedures to be taken against Boston, despite widely recognized discrimination in that school system.

In recent months, a number of cases have arisen in the North and West. In most of those instances where the court has spent the time and effort to examine closely the situation, the finding has tended to be, not that *de facto* segregation has produced racial isolation in the schools, but that purposive and deliberate actions on the part of school and other local officials, such as school construction and assignment plans, contributed to the development of racially identifiable schools.

Thus, there is evidence that the North and West have *de jure* segregation, too. Unfortunately, however, the general legal approach throughout many years has tended to be: To treat the South, where *de jure* segregation is easier to prove, as the guilty section; and, to move with much less than deliberate speed in the other parts of the Nation to deal with either racial isolation or with segregation, whatever the latter's origin or cause may be.

In view of this, I believe that the *de facto/de jure* distinction is a tweedle-dee/tweedle-dum distinction. It is misleading and has, to date, permitted sections of our Nation to hide their problems behind a shield which has allowed them to excuse the discriminatory actions which exist in their areas and to avoid the corrective actions which the Southern part of the Nation has been required to take.

I view the distinction as hypocritical and inequitable. Under this distinction, parents and schoolchildren in the South have been required to bear burdens of inconvenience and of cost which other sections of the Nation have, to date, not been required to bear—even after it has become obvious that the South has less racial isolation than many of these.

### D. The Current Busing Situation

We are, I believe, at a crossroads, where we have been for something like the past 2 years. The real questions are busing and racial balance: Are they required; should they be required; will they be required?

Statistics are often misleading, especially in the aggregate. Some of the figures now being quoted on busing are undoubtedly being mishandled. It is said that busing is used by a large percentage of the student population and always has been and that busing to achieve any type of racial balance is at a minimum.

At the moment this is somewhat true. Several important qualifications must, however, be made. School transportation is a fact of life for many schoolchildren, especially for those in small towns and rural areas, and, to some extent, in the sizable urban areas where large, consolidated high schools exist. In many of these areas, the need for the school bus will continue. In other areas, including a number of rural Southern counties, the amount of busing has actually declined in recent years. Several explanations are given for this: A decline in the overall student population; consolidation of dual school systems;

and, development in certain areas which has led to schools closer to homes.

In many Southern cities, we are, however, on the verge of requiring massive new school busing. In the area of Richmond, Va.—where a Federal judge has ordered consolidation—for example, 78 percent of the schoolchildren would be bused. Under a plan in Norfolk, Va., it is estimated than 26,000 out of a 1972–73 total enrollment of 44,000 need transportation to their school assignments. In Nashville, Tenn., 45,000 of 85,000 pupils are being bused. By almost any measure, these figures do represent a significant increase in forced busing in the South—especially in the cities. They also raise new questions about:

- Financing the additional cost of transportation.
- Consolidation of public school systems.
- Whether or not busing should be required of all city or metropolitan areas.

Furthermore, the signs are already evident that in those Southern districts where massive busing is being required, the white enrollment is dropping. Richmond, Va., lost 7,500 in enrollment during a 2-year period. Norfolk's enrollment dropped from 54,821 to 48,573 between 1970 and 1972. In Nashville, the September 1970 enrollment was 95,164, and in 1972, 85,411. Thus, the trends which so many Northern cities have already witnessed are becoming evident in the South. Southern cities are experiencing what Boston has experienced—where 198,000 whites have left the city during the past 10 years. And, what Chicago has experienced, where—between 1960 and 1970—almost 500,000 whites moved out of the city into the suburbs. The children who, according to *Equality of Educational Opportunity*, help produce a viable school system educationally are being withdrawn from the system.

As complex as the situation relating to busing is, the situation related to racial balance is even more complicated. Since the statewide *Georgia* case (*U.S.* v. *State of Georgia* (CA 12,972 (N.D. Ga.) Dec. 17, 1969), it has become accepted that teachers are assigned according to a ratio.

In the case of students, the *Charlotte-Mecklenburg* case is often cited. In that case, Chief Justice Burger noted:

> In some circumstances certain schools may remain all or largely of one race until new schools can be provided or neighborhood patterns change. Schools all or predominantly of one race in a district of mixed population will require close scrutiny to determine that school assignments are not part of State-enforced segregation. In light of the above, it should be clear that the existence of some small number of one-race, or virtually one-race, schools within a district is not in and of itself, the mark of a system which still practices segregation by law. The district judge or school authorities should make every effort to achieve the greatest possible degree of actual desegregation and will thus necessarily be concerned with the elimination of one-race schools.

Shortly thereafter, in *Winston-Salem/Forsyth County Board of Education* v. *Scott* (No. 71274, Denial of Application for Stay, August 31, 1971) Chief Justice Burger commented further:

> Nothing could be plainer, or so I had thought, than *Swann's* disapproval of the 71 percent–29 percent racial composition found in the *Swann* case as the controlling factor in assignment of pupils, simply because that was the racial composition of the whole school system. Elsewhere in the *Swann* opinion we had noted the necessity for a district court to determine what in fact was the racial balance as an obvious and necessary starting point to decide whether in fact any violation existed; we concluded, however, that "the very limited use made of the mathematical ratios was within the equitable remedial discretion of the District Court."

Yet, there are several significant facts about these statements.

*First*, they do not, clearly and concisely, say what the law does require. They are confusing.

*Second*, they fail to deal with the *de facto/de jure* controversy.

Furthermore, certain actions of the Court speak louder than its words. In the *Mobile* case *Davis* v. *School Commissioners of Mobile County* (402 U.S. 33 (1971), for example, all of the elementary schools except nine were racially balanced. Those nine were considered by local school officials as a special case since they were located in an area somewhat separated from the other parts of the city by a superhighway. The same Supreme Court for whom Chief Justice Burger spoke above, ruled that those schools—nine out of 58—had to be included in the desegregation plan.

In Norfolk, Va., the school assignment plan for 1971–72 was based on a balancing of students. As it worked out, a number of white children failed to show up at their assigned schools, presumably having left the system for another system or for private education, with the result that the balancing did not occur as planned.

Thus, whether or not the words bespeak of racial balance is unimportant. The important fact is that court rulings are in effect seeking racial balancing.

This, then, is what has happened in our Nation. In general, on the basis of the *de facto/de jure* distinction, greater efforts to achieve desegregation have been required in the South than in the North. These additional steps have been required despite the fact that the South is today more desegregated than the North and despite the fact that there is growing evidence that Northern segregation and racial isolation has its roots in officially sanctioned actions, that is, in *de jure* segregation.

Under these circumstances, the entire Nation should be treated equally. The South should no longer be made the proving ground for the entire Nation. Laws and regulations should be applied equally and uniformly throughout our land.

### E. Wither Now?

Our question then becomes, what laws and regulations shall there be? What is required? What should we do—legally, educationally and socially—in order to see that each of our citizens enjoys the equal protection of the laws, that each child in our Nation receives an equal educational opportunity?

After years of confusion in our land over the constitutional requirements of desegregation, we continue without a final legal opinion. Proposals and counterproposals have been presented in Congress. Both legislation and constitutional amendments are pending. The U.S. Supreme Court had granted certiorari in the *Denver* case (*Keyes* v. *School District No. 1*, Denver 303 F. Supp. 279 (1969)), which could lead to resolution of the *de facto/de jure* distinction. It is probable that either the Richmond case or the Detroit case (*Bradley* v. *Milliken*, Civ. Action 35257 (E.D. Mich. 1971)) or a similar situation involving metropolitan consolidation will be accepted by the court. Unfortunately, a decision may not come soon. And, even when it comes, there is the possibility that the ruling will be on narrow grounds or on matters other than busing and racial balance. For the sake of our public schools, however, I hope that neither the gloomy prospect of judicial avoidance of the issue nor the likelihood of congressional inaction will prove true.

In the meantime, the legal questions remain: When is a dual school system dismantled? What constitutes a unitary school system? Does a school system which once had *de jure* segregation always have *de jure* segregation or are there other causes? Must every school in a school district reflect a racial balance in order for the school district to come from under the *de jure* categorization? Does every minority child have a right, under the U.S. Constitution and laws, to an education in a school in which his race is balanced with that of another race or races? Must schools constantly shift children—at the beginning of each year or during the year—in order to achieve some racial balance? What does equal protection of the laws mean—for black and for white schoolchildren?

The Constitution is and should be colorblind. I believe it is wrong to classify men by race. I believe that laws and policies which seek such a classification are illegal. That was the essence of the *Brown* decision.

As Nathan Glazer noted in a recent article:

> The promise of *Brown* is being realized. Black children may not be denied to any school on account of their race (except for the cases in which courts and Federal officials insist that they are to be denied admittance to schools with a black majority simply because they are black).*

I believe most school districts in the South have moved to eliminate the vestiges of the dual school system, that most of the racially-identifiable schools which remain are the results of housing and other patterns which make it difficult to deal with predominantly black or predominantly white schools.

Two principal means of dealing with racially identifiable schools are, however, being discussed at the moment: Busing and school district consolidation. The Supreme Court has said that busing may be used as a tool for dismantling dual school systems but it has not indicated when such a system shall be considered dismantled nor *what* shall be required in cases where dual school systems do not exist. Those are answers we need. And, we need *reasonable* answers, answers which provide opportunities but which do not impose unreasonable burdens or deny any citizens—black or white—the equal protection of the laws.

Educationally, the situation is almost as unclear as the legal aspects. There is a substantial body of material and analysis, much of it contradictory. As noted in the committee report, the most impressive and

---

******Commentary*, **March 1972, page 52.**

expansive study, the so-called Coleman Report named for Prof. James Coleman of Johns Hopkins University, *Equality of Educational Opportunity*, suggests that facilities and services have only a limited effect on the educational achievements and aspirations of schoolchildren. Far more important than facilities and services, the report concluded is the background of the children in a school. As the report states:

> Studies of school achievement have consistently shown that variations in family background account for far more variation in school achievement than do variations in school characteristics.*

Or, as another section of the report suggests:

> If a white pupil from a home that is strongly and effectively supportive of education is put in a school where most pupils do not come from such homes, his achievement will be little different than if he were in a school composed of others like himself. But if a minority pupil from a home without much educational strength is put with schoolmates with strong educational backgrounds, his achievement is likely to increase.**

Both Prof. Coleman and Dr. Thomas Pettigrew of Harvard agree, however, that there is a "tipping point" at which the number of advantaged children lose their beneficial effects on the disadvantaged group. For Dr. Pettigrew this point is about 35 percent, that is, when the number of disadvantaged reaches more than 35 percent then the beneficial aspects begin to diminish. For Coleman, the tipping point is slightly higher, running in the 40–50 percent range.

At any rate, the implication is that in order for the findings of the Coleman Report to be applied successfully to education, at least 50 percent, and preferably more, of the students in a class and school should be advantaged. Furthermore, sending a single or few advantaged children into a disadvantaged environment apparently does nothing for either the advantaged or disadvantaged child. Thus, where integration takes place, it would appear wise to keep in mind these basics of the Coleman data.

There are, furthermore, those who believe that facilities do make a difference—that numbers of library books, student services, teachers' aides—do matter.

I tend to believe that there are valid points to both views. Certain facilities and services are basic to education and to the provision of an equal educational opportunity for all our children. It does not take much—the tour of a selected number of schools within a school district—to determine that facilities and services are inequitably spread throughout most school systems. Efforts should be made to provide a minimum level of services and facilities to all children no matter what school they may attend. We must, however, remain aware of the literature which suggests that money and facilities alone do not guarantee a good education.

Furthermore, the study and analysis of the effects of integration are, at most, less than complete. Berkeley, Calif., which has experimented with a racial balance plan, has been proclaimed as both a suc-

---

* *Equality of Educational Opportunity*, p. 218.

** *Ibid.*, p. 22.

cess and a failure. Project Concern in Hartford, Conn., in which a number of innercity black students are bused into surrounding suburban areas on a voluntary basis, has been proclaimed a success, but it must be remembered that that project is largely a one-way program and limited in size. Finally, the recent study by David Armour should not be overlooked. All our learning, all our attempts to seek knowledge, are useless if we criticize findings without exploring them, if we are afraid to look at a situation as it is or might be. Our educational establishment might have saved time and money in the 1960s if it had not adopted so readily the unproven techniques which a December 1972 report by Paul Nachtigal of the Ford Foundation was to find unproductive. We should beware of making a mistake with busing and racial balance, especially in view of the cost and disruption involved.

To me, the evidence is far from clear that busing and racial balance bring the desired educational response, that they are a panacea for the educational ills of our Nation. We engage in what I have often referred to as the "politics of over-promise" if we present busing or racial balance as such to any group.

With the Coleman Report, the reanalysis of the Coleman Report, the other data which has been collected and the work of this committee ending in inconclusive findings about the value and results of various desegregation attempts and education programs, it would be an easy thing to call for an additional study. In a way, that seems to be what is required. Yet, that could lead to no more resolute conclusion and in the meanwhile the situation demands attention. A more positive approach, perhaps, is to admit that our knowledge is incomplete, the available research inconclusive, and to move within limited bounds.

Aside from the legal and constitutional questions which must be decided, there are substantive questions regarding education and our Nation's priorities which must also be considered. There is significant disaffection with U.S. education today. Questions range from the relevance of the curricula to the lifestyles of students to the failure of the system to meet the needs of many students.

If busing and racial balance are to be instituted—and we are facing that decision, for the South as well as for the North and East and West—then there must be an evaluation of the cost. In Norfolk, Va., for example, the courts ordered the city not only to implement a specific assignment plan but also to provide the free transportation to implement that plan. The estimates for the cost of the program were $2.3 million for capital costs (purchase of 200 buses and routine maintenance facility) if the city acquired a fleet of buses, plus an annual operating cost of about $780,000. As it turns out, the school system determined to contract, for the 1972–73 school year, with a local carrier at a cost of about $63 per student or $1.6 million per year.

The same questions face dozens of other school systems: How much will transportation plans cost? Who will pay? The figures are difficult to develop, but if we were to require busing in the 100 largest school districts or in the 212 standard metropolitan statistical areas, the cost would run into billions of dollars. In view of the limited findings of the educational research and information available, is this cost worth it? Is it worth it when thousands of schools and millions of schoolchildren need improved facilities and services, need special education help and attention, need assistance which requires dollars to provide?

The committee Report has discussed in some detail the inequities and burdens of the property tax. It is evident that the local property tax cannot sustain more major increases in local educational spending. Several alternatives were presented to the committee. At the moment, I am inclined toward the recommendations of the Advisory Commission on Intergovernmental Relations, which proposes that the Federal Government assume the major responsibility for welfare costs and that the States take over additional responsibilities for education. As Dr. John Shannon of the Advisory Commission on Intergovernmental Relations noted in testimony before the committee, "Our basic recommendation is that whereas the State should move in and pick up most of the tab for education, the National Government should facilitate this move by relieving the States of about $6 to $7 billion of public welfare responsibility that we believe much more logically rests with the National Government. If the National Government will assume full responsibility for funding of public welfare, and also generally strengthen the position of State and local governments through revenue-sharing, the States would be in a far better fiscal position to move ahead on the educational front." (Committee hearings, p. 3544.)

The advantages of such a system, as Dr. Shannon pointed out, are that:

*First*, the States could move toward the equalization of educational opportunity.

*Second*, political accountability for educational finance could be fixed at the doorstep of the Governor and State Legislature.

*Third*, greater impetus would be given to achievement testing and other means of accountability.

*Fourth*, State financing could lead to property tax relief.

*Fifth*, confining the local property tax to the financing of essentially municipal-type services such as police and fire protection would not only reduce interlocal fiscal disparities in education but it would also tend to mute those competitive forces that are balkanizing our metropolitan society.

Much of what is included here, I have said before. Some was expressed in two Senate floor speeches in 1970. Much was reiterated in a February 17, 1972 letter * to the President, which is included at the end of these views. The information developed by the committee has confirmed my belief that we should take certain steps to improve our Nation's schools: That we should seek to provide for an equalization of services and facilities and that we should make provision for majority-to-minority transfer to assure that a child can find an education in a school with more to offer than that closest to his home. I do not, however, believe that the evidence on the educational aspects of massive busing or racial balance is conclusive enough to demand the investment in time and money and the burdens it imposes upon our school districts. The time, the energy, the money, can be better used in other ways. Furthermore, I believe the imposition of such requirements will further erode the public support, both financial and philosophical, for our public school systems. Earlier in this Report, I cited statistics on white flight, the drop in the attendance of white children in our city schools while the attendance by black children increases. These coupled with election results of

---

*See p. 396.

recent years throughout the country indicate strongly that we cannot—and should not—force a massive social experiment upon our people. Compulsion on social issues seldom works, as the national experiment with Prohibition should have taught us.

There are, however, steps that we can and should take to improve the educational offerings for all our children.

*First*, we must have a single, uniform nationwide school desegregation policy, which obliterates once and for all the superficial distinction between *de facto* and *de jure* segregation. If it is educationally disadvantageous for a black child to attend an all-black school, then the child in the inner area of Boston or Detroit is as deprived as the black child in an all-black Southern school. Furthermore, there is currently more desegregation in the South than in many Northern and Western areas. It is understandable that Southerners should question why they should bear burdens of finance and inconvenience when other parts of the Nation—where the disadvantaged child is often receiving less opportunity—are not being asked to bear the same burdens.

Furthermore, is it equal protection of the laws to ask one section of the country to take actions not required of another when both have approximately the same degree of desegregation? And, does the U.S. Constitution require racial balance—in every case where there has been *de jure* segregation or where there are racially identifiable schools? I think not.

*Second*, we must reevaluate the neighborhood school concept as the basic unit for school assignment purposes. In view of the questions over the educational value of busing, the huge costs involved and the burdens it imposes upon parents and children, black and white, we must review the logical and most reasonable means of assigning children to schools.

At the same time, we must make new efforts to assist the deprived child. The long-term solution is, of course, a change in housing policies and patterns. But, that *is* long-term and in the interim there should be an extensive utilization of a majority-to-minority transfer provision, with the transfers financed by the local or State educational agency. In other words, any child in a school in which his race was in a majority could transfer to a school in which his race was in a minority, with his transportation costs paid by school authorities. The argument often made against this proposal is that the burden is placed upon the deprived child to rectify the inequities which exist. That is, to an extent, true. The child would, however, have the benefit of the transfer provision and an assured right to education in a desegregated environment. In recent years we have witnessed white flight to the suburbs and to private schools. Perhaps we ought now to ask ourselves how far we can follow white flight with the buses.

*Third*, in addition to reviewing our policy on the neighborhood school and majority-to-minority transfers, it is important to make every effort to remove the inequities which currently exist both within school districts and among them. There are, for example, currently, differences in facilities, services offered, libraries, the numbers of specially trained teachers, to name only a few. We must move once and for all to eliminate these disparities. And in doing so, we should remember that the disparities between urban and suburban school districts are generally exceeded by those between rural and urban/suburban districts. The latter problem was explored in some depth in hearings* which I conducted for this committee and is covered in the Report.

As I indicated earlier in these views, one means of overcoming existing disparities among school districts would be to adopt the financial arrangements proposed by the Advisory Commission on Intergovernmental Relations. Under these arrangements, States, which would be primarily responsible for funding of education programs, could make new efforts to remove inequities as well as to move toward greater accountability and to find substitutes for the property tax which may, for education purposes, soon be declared unconstitutional.

Finally, it is important to deal with another situation: The control of our school systems. The frustrations of our people who find themselves ordered by courts which are not responsible to them is understandable. The seemingly inability of elected representatives to act is another. We must take steps to see that local officials, officials responsible to an electorate, control, and administer our schools. We have heard this from both the black- and white-communities. The calls for decentralization and community control of schools have been widespread. Certainly, there are pitfalls in these procedures, pitfalls against which we must guard, but representative government, responsibility and accountability of public servants to those they serve, are a significant part of the American heritage.

Thus, local involvement and local control of public schools must be a significant feature of public school policy.

The suggestions presented above are not a cure-all for the Nation's educational ills. They are not a prescription with a guaranteed result. They will not satisfy the ideologue, the social planner, or the segregationist. They do, however, represent a means by which we may move forward in meeting a number of the problems in education in a practical, moderate and reasonable manner.

U.S. SENATE,
*Washington, D.C., February 17, 1972.*

HON. RICHARD M. NIXON,
*President of the United States,*
*The White House,*
*Washington, D.C.*

DEAR MR. PRESIDENT: I have concluded from actions taken prior to your departure today for the People's Republic of China that you and your advisors are involved in a reevaluation of the public school desegregation efforts throughout our country. As a representative of a State which has probably experienced as much litigation involving school desegregation as any other. I am compelled to share my own views with you.

The recent district court decision in the Richmond, Virginia, school case, the similar cases pending in other parts of our Nation, and the numerous pronouncements by our public officials have again brought confusion and misunderstanding to the issue of public school desegregation.

Our people are understandably perplexed and I have a deep sympathy for their feelings.

I appreciate, as I am certain you do, the fears of some of our citizens who have been subjected to discrimination in the past. I understand their apprehensions that the gains they have made through the *Brown* and certain subsequent decisions and the improved educational opportunity which has been made available to their children will be lost in a retreat.

---

*Hearings of the U.S. Senate Select Committee on Equal Educational Opportunity, Part 15—*Education in Rural America*, Sept. 1, 2, 3, 1971.

I appreciate, as I am certain you do, the fears of parents who are asked to put their children on buses for several hours a day, to send them miles from home, and often to send them to a school which is known to be no better than a school a few blocks from home in terms of facilities and services. It is quite understandable that these parents object to the sacrifices their children are being asked to make. I share their opposition to massive enforced busing to achieve racial balance, because I do not believe it will accomplish its purpose of providing equal educational opportunity.

Also, I appreciate the difficulties faced by local educational officials who find that they must make significant reassignments at the beginning of each school year, that they must constantly be reorganizing and that, in many cases, they must come up with additional sums of money for transportation costs, money which is in scarce supply at this time.

I am aware of the fact that in the past black children were bused past white schools to black ones and that white children were bused past black schools to white ones. That was wrong. But, I do not believe that we can rectify the mistakes of the past by experimenting with the schoolchildren of the present. I believe that we must seek to provide excellence in education for all our children. I believe that there are many situations which must be improved, where education needs vast renovations. But I do not feel that we accomplish much, either for our children or for our Nation's future, by pursuing a policy based solely on head counts and ratios.

We refuse to face reality when we refuse to acknowledge the fact that no parent wants a child to be bused far away from home to a school which is no better than a school close to home in terms of facilities, services, and educational offerings. We also refuse to face reality if we fail to acknowledge that parents, no matter what their color or economic condition, want the best education possible for their children.

The question then becomes quite simply, "How do we reconcile the desire of a parent for his child to be educated in the neighborhood school with the desire of a parent for his child to receive an education in a school superior to the one closest to his home, a parent who is often economically disadvantaged and of a minority?"

As we have all come to realize, there is no easy answer. Furthermore, the knowledge which we have about busing, racial balance and educational achievement, both cognitive and affective, is at best inconclusive. We have studies on compensatory education, which demonstrate that this approach tends not to succeed. We have the recent reports on the Berkeley experience, where racial balance was undertaken voluntarily, and again find failures.

Prof. James Coleman of Johns Hopkins University, in one of the most massive studies, has told us that parental background and the background of the peer group are generally the most influential factors on a child's development. Yet, this does not suggest that racial balancing is necessary. In fact, Dr. Coleman and Dr. Thomas Pettigrew of Harvard University suggested that there is a point at which balancing can produce a "tipping" effect which can be detrimental to educational offerings. Thus, it seems to me premature to determine the future of American education, especially when we are talking about busing, ratios and similar expensive and disruptive proceedures, on the little information which we have regarding their effects on educational opportunity.

Consequently, I believe we must look beyond court-imposed solutions. There is no perfect answer, but there are certain principles which should underlie our search for a reasonable and practical solution to the problem of public school desegregation.

*First*, we must have a single, uniform, nationwide policy on school desegregation, which obliterates the superficial distinction between *de facto* and *de jure* segregation. The statistics developed in the Department of Health, Education, and Welfare indicate that there is currently more desegregation in the South than in many parts of the North and West. Problems do remain, but they remain in every part of the Nation. If it is educationally disadvantageous for a black child to attend an all-black school, then the black child in a Detroit or

Boston innercity area is just as deprived educationally as a child in a black rural Southern school. And, it is meaningless to tell one child that his deprivation is wrong because it was *de jure* and the other that his is right because it is *de facto*. Educationally—and I hope education is our prime consideration—the result is the same. Thus, our goal should be the provision of a better education for every child, no matter what section of the country he lives in.

*Second*, we must reevaluate the neighborhood school concept as the basic unit for school assignment purposes, especially as far as elementary schoolchildren are concerned. It is logical in terms of cost, safety, and convenience for a parent to want a child in a school near his home. Many parents—black and white—feel that they have paid for that privilege in the purchase of their homes and the payment of taxes. There is every reason to believe that many parents in the future—again both black and white—will seek that same privilege. This, too, is a factor which cannot be ignored. We are told that we cannot change policy because of the desires of people. Frankly, I do not believe the desires of most of our people are based on race and segregation. I believe the large majority of Americans are fair-minded, that they do not want to deprive their fellow citizens of opportunity. But, understandably, parents' first concerns are for their own children—their education, safety and well-being.

We must see that these latter concerns are met or we shall certainly imperil public education. But, we shall also imperil public education if we fail to provide for our educationally deprived. I believe there could be merit in an extensive utilization of a majority-to-minority transfer provision, with the transfers financed by the local or State educational agency. In other words, any child in a school in which his race was in a majority could transfer to a school in which his race was in a minority, with his transportation costs paid by school authorities. The argument often made against this proposal is that the burden is placed upon the deprived child to rectify the inequities which exist. That is, to an extent, true. The child would, however, have the benefit of the transfer provision and an assured right to education in a desegregated environment. In recent years we have witnessed white flight to the suburbs and to private schools. Perhaps we ought now to ask ourselves how far we can follow white flight with the buses and to what extent we can discourage the enrollment in private schools. Is racial balancing and social engineering to the extent being contemplated in some areas, racial balancing and social engineering whose redeeming benefits are questionable, worth the possibility that our public school system may be deprived of even more advantaged students and of the degree of support needed to sustain public education? On the other hand, can we stop in midstream or stray backward? In both cases I would hope not.

*Third*, in addition to reviewing our policy on the neighborhood school and majority-to-minority transfers, it is important to make every effort to remove the inequities which currently exist both within school districts and among them. There are, for example, currently differences in facilities, services offered, libraries, the numbers of specially-trained teachers, to name only a few. We must move once and for all to eliminate these disparities. And in doing so, we should remember that the disparities between urban and suburban school districts are generally exceeded by those between rural and urban/suburban districts.

Finally, it is highly important for us to deal with a situation you discussed in the State of the Union Message: The control of our school systems. The frustrations of our people who find themselves ordered by courts which are not responsible to them is certainly understandable. The seeming inability of elected representatives to act is another. We must take steps and take them immediately to see that local officials, officials responsible to an electorate, control and administer our schools. We have heard this from both the black- and white-communities. The calls for decentralization and community control of schools have been widespread. Certainly, there are pitfalls in these procedures, pitfalls against which we must guard, but representative government and responsibility and accountability of public servants to those they serve are a significant part of the American heritage.

Thus, local involvement and local control of public schools must be a significant feature of public school policy.

The situation is, of course, complex. The proposals I have discussed are neither inclusive nor perfect. They have been attacked by those on the right and those on the left. This in itself, however, is probably evidence of their redeeming qualities.

In Senate floor speeches of July 20 and August 3, 1970, I tried to outline the conflicting court opinions and governmental actions which were resulting in confusion throughout our land. As a member of the U.S. Senate Select Committee on Equal Educational Opportunity, I have participated extensively in hearings on our school problems and have questioned several members of your Administration, including former Attorney General John Mitchell and former head of the Justice Department's Civil Rights Division, Jerris Leonard, regarding the issues which today confront us. Based on this, I introduced in the Senate on August 3, 1970, a bill which I felt sought a rational, moderate approach to our problems. This bill was drafted by Prof. Alexander Bickel of the Yale University Law School and Congressman Richardson Preyer of North Carolina. Hearings on this legislation were held before the Senate Education Subcommittee and the U.S. Senate Select Committee on Equal Educational Opportunity. The bill was attacked by the NAACP as well as by those in basic disagreement with the *Brown* decision. Despite the fact that the bill remained in Committee, there was excellent testimony by school officials from both Norfolk and Richmond, Va. I commend this testimony to you.

In my judgment, the decision in the *Charlotte-Mecklenburg* case, when coupled with that in the *Mobile* case, negated much of the thrust of the Bickel-Preyer proposals. Consequently, I joined in cosponsoring a constitutional amendment regarding this as the best available vehicle for provoking a public discussion of the need for a single, uniform, national school desegregation policy that all can understand—a policy that would end the present double standard of hypocrisy which prevails in our Nation today.

The unanimity of the *Charlotte-Mecklenburg* decision suggests that the opinion in that case represents consensus. The uncertainty of that consensus was, however, illustrated by statements made by Chief Justice Burger soon after the decision that appeared at odds with the findings of his own court. Despite the fact that nearly 20 years have passed since *Brown*, the Supreme Court continues to give maximum discretion to district judges and minimum guidance.

In addition to the principles I discussed earlier, which I believe should underlie our search for a solution, I would like to make several specific suggestions. On August 13, 1970, when the Attorney General appeared before the U.S. Senate Select Committee on Equal Educational Opportunity, he indicated a hope—a hope which I shared—that the *Charlotte-Mecklenburg* decision would answer many of the unanswered questions regarding public school desegregation. (Hearings before the U.S. Senate Select Committee on Equal Educational Opportunity, August 13, 1970, p. 1912.) Many of the questions were not answered and the Court has thus far avoided setting the *de facto/de jure* matter. Now, in the Richmond case, we have a new enforcement procedure, a procedure for which the Attorney General, also on August 13, 1970, in response to my questions, indicated there was no legal precedent. (Hearings referred to above, p. 1910.) Consequently, I would like to suggest and request that the Department of Justice enter, with amicus curiae briefs, those cases where it would be appropriate and where there is evidence that such action would contribute to the determination of a national school desegregation policy.

As you know, the Fourth Circuit Court of Appeals has granted a stay in the Richmond school case, pending appeal. In my judgment implementation of the order should be stayed until a *final* decision is rendered by the Supreme Court. It seems somewhat contradictory to find the Federal Government questioning the expansion of municipalities for racial reasons and at the same time ordering consolidation of political subdivisions for racial reasons.

The recommendations above are not intended to imply that Congress should be absolved of responsibility for this issue. In fact, I have stated on a number of occasions that Congress should act to clarify the existing situation, and I am pleased that both the Majority Leader and the Minority Leader of the Senate sought to contribute to the dialogue over possible courses of action during a Senate floor discussion on yesterday. Congress does have a responsibility to give consideration to all measures before it which are designed to bring clarification and rationality to efforts to resolve this pressing domestic problem. That responsibility should not be avoided because this is an election year.

Aside from the compulsory features of the recent decisions which threaten to undermine public education, there are equal rights involved which Americans will not long see abused. Parents black and white in Virginia's major cities might well ask why their private resources should go for bus fares and why their tax monies should go for the purchase of school buses when metropolitan areas throughout much of America are not burdened with this same cost and yet where black children are receiving less opportunity.

I have not always been proud of Virginia's past history with regard to education of minority pupils. I am, however, proud of the restraint most Virginians have displayed despite providing the proving ground for every new approach to a solution to the complex problem of meeting the constitutional rights of all children to an equal educational opportunity. The traditional respect of Virginians for the law and the common sense of our people has thus far always prevailed over the appeals of demagogues, the militant and the racist. However, it is difficult for people to comply with an interpretation of the law that they neither understand nor believe will achieve its stated purpose.

In view of the fact that several members of your cabinet and staff are involved with the matters discussed in this letter, I am taking the liberty of forwarding copies of this letter to them. I expect to reiterate and elaborate on a number of the principles I have discussed here in the report of the U.S. Senate Select Committee on Equal Educational Opportunity, on which I serve. Since you and your advisors are currenlty contemplating action in the field of school desegregation, I did, however, want to write to you at this time.

Sincerely,

William B. Spong, Jr.

## MR. SAM J. ERVIN, JR.

### U.S. SENATOR FROM THE STATE OF NORTH CAROLINA

---

### A. INTRODUCTION

I respectfully take exception to those chapters of the Report concerning "School Integration". This part of the Report accepts unquestioningly what are, in my opinion, some of the greatest dangers to constitutional government and individual freedom in America. I refer to the unconstitutional expansion of Federal judicial authority pursuant to a misguided interpretation of the Equal Protection Clause of the 14th Amendment to the U.S. Constitution, and to the unlawful interference by Federal agencies with respect to the public schools of this country.

By way of preface, I must state that I do not accept the label of "desegregation" which the committee's Report frequently uses to describe what is quite clearly nothing more nor less than "racial balance" in the public schools. Certainly the meaning of "desegregation" as set forth by the Supreme Court in its landmark 1954 decision of *Brown* v. *Board of Education of Topeka*, 347 U.S. 483 (1954), has nothing in common with the obvious, if not explicit, approach of many Federal courts and the Department of Health, Education, and Welfare to impose certain racial percentages in the public schools—an approach completely supported by this Report.

Furtherfore, I strongly disagree with the Report's characterization of "racial balance" and "busing" as "misleading issues." The Report relies upon the Supreme Court's own misleading words in *Swann* v. *Charlotte-Mecklenburg County Board of Education*, 402 U.S. 43 (1971), to reassure us that busing is not being imposed to achieve "racial balance," but merely to comply with the mandate of the Equal Protection Clause. Despite such comfortless words of assurance, it is as clear as a noonday sun in a cloudless sky that "racial balance" is precisely what the Federal courts imposed in the *Charlotte-Mecklenburg* school case and exactly what they have been requiring in numerous other school districts throughout the country.

The Supreme Court, in *Brown* v. *Board of Education of Topeka*, held racial segregation in the public schools to be in violation of the Equal Protection Clause of the 14th Amendment. I know of no State or local authority, today, which assigns children or teachers to schools on the basis of race. And yet, this Report asserts, "Racial discrimination, in the form of deliberate segregation of children by race or national origin, is widespread in public school systems throughout this country." Respectfully, this statement, insofar as I am aware, is absolutely unfounded in fact or in law. If those who drafted this Report sincerely believe that constitutionally-forbidden "deliberate segregation of children by race" is "widespread" in our public schools, the Report should strongly urge the Justice Department to initiate the appropriate legal action to correct what, in the Report's view, is a "widespread" violation of the Constitution. After reading the Report, I am compelled to conclude that what the Report calls for is not compliance with any reasonable interpretation of the 14th Amendment, but rather for "racial balance" in the public schools by any means whatsoever, including the massive use of busing.

The assumptions and analyses which underlie the Report's chapters on "School Integration" are assumptions and analyses with which I strongly disagree. Quite naturally, the directions toward which the Report points, based upon these faulty assumptions, are equally disagreeable. I might add that, in my opinion, most Americans disagree with the Report's understanding of, and approach to, what is generally referred to as the "desegregation of the public schools."

### B. The Equal Protection Clause of the 14th Amendment

It is strange indeed that the massive busing of helpless schoolchildren—and other means of forced integration—have been rationalized somehow under the Equal Protection Clause of the 14th Amendment. The Equal Protection Clause itself is a wise provision of law. It is a plain and unambiguous provision. It means that no State shall deny to any person within its boundaries the equal protection of the law. Properly interpreted, it prohibits a State from treating persons similarly situated in a different manner.

There is not one syllable in the Equal Protection Clause which authorizes the Supreme Court or the Department of Health, Education, and Welfare to place limitations upon the freedom of any individual. The Supreme Court's 1954 decision in *Brown* v. *Board of Education of Topeka* held that a State violates the clause if it denies any child admission to any of its public schools on account of the child's race. Over the last decade, both the Department of Health, Education, and Welfare and the Federal courts have turned their backs on the mandate of the 1954 Supreme Court decision—that race be eliminated as a determinant in assigning children to public schools. Paradoxically, the Supreme Court and the Department of Health, Education, and Welfare have now come to insist that race be used as a basis for pupil assignment. They have required the adoption of school assignment plans which are expressly designed to alter the racial composition of the schools in a manner sufficient to meet some mysterious mathematical level deemed by the court and the bureaucracy to be constitutionally acceptable. It is, indeed, a great and sad irony that the Federal courts and Federal bureaucracy would require the use of racial quotas and racial balancing to effectuate a constitutional principle which forbids Government to treat people differently on account of their race. In effect, the Federal courts have perverted and distorted the Equal Protection Clause.

As if signaling a warning for the future, Chief Judge John J. Parker, of the U.S. Court of Appeals for the Fourth Circuit, in an opinion correctly explaining the Supreme Court's decision in *Brown* v. *Board of Education of Topeka*, wrote:

> Having said this, it is important that we point out exactly what the Supreme Court has decided and what it is has not decided in this case. It has not decided to take over or regulate the public schools of the States. It has not decided that the States must mix persons of different races in the schools or must require them to attend schools or must deprive them of the right of choosing the schools they attend. What it has decided, and all that it has decided, is that a State may not deny to any person on account of race the right to attend any school that it maintains. This, under the decision of the Supreme Court, the State may not do directly or indirectly; but if the schools which it maintains are open to children of all races, no violation of the Constitution is involved even though the children of different races voluntarily attend different schools, as they attend different churches. Nothing in the Constitution or in the decision of the Supreme Court takes away from the people freedom to choose the schools they attend. The Constitution, in other words, does not require integration. It merely forbids discrimination. It does not forbid such segregation as occurs as the result of voluntary action. It merely forbids the use of governmental power to enforce segregation. The 14th Amendment is a limitation upon the exercise of power by the State or State agencies, not a limitation upon the freedom of individuals. [*Briggs* v. *Elliott*, 132 F. Supp. 776, 777]

Judge Parker's assertion—that when a State opens its schools to children of all races and grants to them freedom to choose the schools they attend, its action in so doing complies with the Equal Protection Clause—is absolutely sound. When the State takes such actions, it is treating all persons of all races exactly alike under like conditions and, thereby, fulfills the requirements of the 14th Amendment. No amount of judicial or bureaucratic jargon and sophistry, nor any congressional committee's repetition of such, can erase this obvious truth.

Not only have the Federal courts and Federal agencies perverted any reasonable meaning of the Equal Protection Clause, but they have also ignored congressional declarations as to this clause. In the Civil Rights Act of 1964, Congress incorporated the interpretation of the clause as set forth in *Brown* v. *Board of Education of Topeka.* Congress accepted the view that the Equal Protection Clause prohibits a State from taking into consideration the matter of race in assigning children to public schools. Section 401(b) of Title IV of this Act defines "desegregation" as "the assignment of students to public schools and within such schools without regard to their race, color, religion, or national origin." Other definitions and references in this Act amplify this definition. There is not a single syllable in Title IV of the Civil Rights Act of 1964 giving any support to a different interpretation.

The first clause of Section 401(b) of Title IV of the same law commands school boards to ignore race, color, religion, and national origin as factors in assigning students to public schools. Hence, it is self-evident that a school board complies with this statute if it opens the schools it operates to children of all races, colors, religions, and national origins, and allows them or their parents to choose the schools they attend.

The second clause of Section 401(b) denies to Federal courts jurisdiction to compel school boards to assign "students to public schools in order to overcome racial imbalance." Congress hereby clearly forbids Federal courts to issue decrees compelling school boards to take affirmative steps to integrate black- and white children in public schools in proportions which some social scientists and judicial activists may decide result in a unitary, nonracial system free of the vestiges of State-imposed segregation.

When officials of the Department of Health, Education, and Welfare ignored the clear intention of Congress, as set forth in the 1964 Act, Congress reacted by inserting in the 1965 Elementary and Secondary Education Act—the principal statute which empowers the Department of Health, Education, and Welfare to extend Federal financial assistance to public schools—the following provision:

> Nothing contained in this Act shall be construed to authorize any department, agency, officer, or employee of the United States to exercise any direction, supervision, or control over the personnel of any school system . . . or to require the assignment or transportation of students or teachers in order to overcome racial imbalance. [P.L. 89–10, Title VIII, Section 804; 20 U.S.C. Section 884]

Officials at the Department of Health, Education, and Welfare chose to ignore this congressional declaration also, whereupon Congress inserted an amendment in the 1968 Appropriations Act for the Department of Health, Education, and Welfare. Congress adopted the following prohibition:

> No part of the funds contained in this Act shall be used to force busing of students, the abolishment of any school or the attendance of students at a particular school in order to overcome racial imbalance as a condition precedent to obtaining Federal funds otherwise available to any State, school district or school. [P. L. 90–557, 82 Stat. 995]

During the second session of the 92d Congress, the Congress also made clear its opposition to forced busing. Section 309 of Public Law 92–48—the Education Appropriations Act of 1972—contains a prohibition against busing.

In addition, Public Law 92–318, enacted on June 23, 1972, incorporates several provisions concerning the busing of schoolchildren. Title VIII of this Act, entitled, "General Provisions Relating to the Assignment or Transportation of Students," includes sections designed to limit the authority of the Federal courts and Federal Executive Branch with respect to busing.

Section 805 of Title VIII, which I offered as an amendment to the original bill, is designed to eliminate the ruling in the case of *Swann v. Charlotte-Mecklenburg County Board of Education*, which had the effect of raising a presumption of continuing, unconstitutional discrimination with respect to Southern school systems which had been segregated by law prior to the 1954 *Brown* decision.

I also offered Section 806 which, I believe, prohibits all forced busing inasmuch as it makes the prohibition against busing in the 1964 Civil Rights Act applicable to all schools everywhere in the United States under all conditions and under all circumstances. Section 806 reads as follows:

APPLICATION OF PROVISO OF SECTION 407(a) OF THE CIVIL RIGHTS ACT OF 1964 TO THE ENTIRE UNITED STATES

> Sec. 806. The proviso of section 407(a) of the Civil Rights Act of 1964 providing in substance that no court or official of the United States shall be empowered to issue any order seeking to achieve a racial balance in any school by requiring the transportation of pupils or students from one school to another or one school district to another in order to achieve such racial balance, or otherwise enlarge the existing power of the court to insure compliance with constitutional standards shall apply to all public school pupils and to every public school system, public school and public school board, as defined by Title IV, under all circumstances and conditions and at all times in every State, district, territory, Commonwealth, or possession of the United States regardless of whether the residence of such public school pupils or the principal offices of such public school system, public school or public school board is situated in the northern, eastern, western, or southern part of the United States.

I offered this section to overcome the incredible ruling in the *Swann* v. *Charlotte-Mecklenburg County Board of Education* case which held that the Civil Rights Act of 1964 only applied to *de facto* segregation—a matter with respect to which, the Court said in this same decision, the Federal Government has no power. Certainly, the Supreme Court should presume that Congress is striving to legislate about matters over which it has jurisdiction rather than about matters over which it has no jurisdiction.

On numerous occasions, then, Congress has made it clear that its understanding of the Equal Protection Clause parallels that of the Supreme Court in the 1954 *Brown* v. *Board of Education of Topeka* decision. It has also made it clear that it opposes any view of that clause which would permit Federal courts or Federal bureaucrats to substitute federally-coerced school integration for outlawed, State-imposed school segregation.

In view of this history of congressional interpretation of the Equal Protection Clause, I must assert that this committee's Report, with respect to school integration, is contrary in every way to the expressed views of Congress.

### C. Jurisdiction of Federal Courts

In addition to embracing what I believe is a perverse interpretation of the Equal Protection Clause of the 14th Amendment, the Report also accepts and approves of what has been an unconstitutional and frightening expansion of Federal judicial interference with the local public schools of this country. In effect, the judicial activists have worked toward substituting Federal courts for local school boards. In many instances they have totally usurped the lawful authority of school boards and have exercised unlimited and arbitrary discretion in assigning pupils and teachers, drawing school attendance zones, and imposing massive busing of schoolchildren.

Defenders of such unprecedented Federal judicial intervention in the affairs of public schools often contend that these courts are merely enforcing plans for desegregation submitted to them by school boards. The truth is that, in almost every case, the desegregation plans are dictated by Federal judges. In the case of the Charlotte-Mecklenburg school desegregation plan, the Federal court actually employed an individual who was an expert witness for the plaintiffs in the case to draft a plan which the court subsequently imposed upon that community. I believe that this constituted an unprecedented violation of due process of law. In the case of *Hobson* v. *Hansen*, 269 F. Supp. 401, (1967), the Federal district court judge used 118 pages to instruct the District of Columbia Board of Education as to how it should perform its constitutional obligation to abolish *de facto* segregation produced in the public schools of the district by prevalent residential patterns. The judge in this case proceeded to dictate how the teachers of the district should teach their pupils.

The power to assign children to State-supported schools belongs to the public school board which operates them. The Equal Protection Clause does not undertake to transfer this power to the Federal courts. As long as the school board abides by the command of the Equal Protection Clause—that it must not exclude any child from any school on the basis of race—it has the lawful right to assign children to the schools it operates in any nondiscriminatory fashion satisfactory to itself. The Federal courts have no lawful authority to impose what they may view as a better assignment plan which will result in a different racial composition in the schools.

In addition to exceeding constitutional authority, Federal courts have exceeded their competence in drawing up school assignment plans which are imposed upon local school boards. Federal judges, as well as officials at the Department of Health, Education, and Welfare, simply lack the professional and practical ability to operate the schools. They have manifested this incompetence over recent years in their insistence upon integrating the bodies of schoolchildren—regardless of the impact upon the enlightenment of their minds.

Even this committee's Report concedes the incompetency of the courts as substitutes for school boards. It says:

> . . . courts are not the branch of government best equipped to deal with the extremely complex issues involved in breaking down racial and economic barriers within metropolitan areas in ways that do justice to the legitimate concerns of all involved.

Unfortunately, nevertheless, the Report goes on to insist that it may be necessary to rely on the courts and "their own, very limited, devices" when local and State authorities refuse to embrace the kind of forced integration advocated by the Report. Indeed, the Report at one point expressly embraces one of the most pernicious and arbitrary decisions ever promulgated by the Federal courts. The Report states:

> We find that the guidelines for student transportation by the Supreme Court in *Swann* v. *Charlotte-Mecklenburg* . . . establish a sensible, enforceable and uniform standard for

the use of transportation in eliminating the effects of racially discriminatory student assignment policies.

Federal courts have completely disregarded Congress' own declarations with respect to Federal jurisdiction as it affects public schools. Section 407(a)(2) of Title IV, of the 1964 Civil Rights Act reads:

> . . . nothing herein shall empower any official or court of the United States to issue any order seeking to achieve a racial balance in any school by requiring the transportation of pupils or students from one school to another or one school district to another in order to achieve such racial balance, or otherwise enlarge the existing power of the court to insure compliance with constitutional standards.

Herein Congress clearly deprived all Federal courts of the jurisdiction to order public school boards to bus children from one school to another, or from one school district to another, to remedy racial imbalances in public schools—regardless of whether such imbalances arise from innocent causes or discriminatory school board action.

Congress has unquestionable authority to restrict Federal courts in such a manner under Section 1, Article III of the Constitution. The pertinent part of that section reads:

> The judicial Power of the United States, shall be vested in one supreme Court, and in such inferior Courts as the Congress may from time to time ordain and establish.

Furthermore, Congress has undoubted power over the appellate jurisdiction of the Supreme Court pursuant to Section 2 of Article III, which reads:

> . . . the Supreme Court shall have appellate jurisdiction, both as to law and fact, with such exceptions, and under such regulations as the Congress shall make.

Despite the clear constitutional authority of Congress to define Federal judicial jurisdiction with respect to public schools; and, in face of congressional exercise of that authority, as set forth above, Federal courts have continually ignored these restrictions—thereby, both exceeded their constitutional authority and directly violated the law of the land.

When a school board violates the Equal Protection Clause, a Federal court has jurisdiction to order the school board to devise and implement a plan sufficient to remedy its discriminatory assignment of children to its schools; and, to punish the members of the school board for contempt of court if they fail to obey the order. Nevertheless, the power to devise and implement a plan to remedy the discriminatory assignment continues to reside in the school board, and the Federal court is without power to reject a nondiscriminatory plan submitted by the school board because such nondiscriminatory plans will not mix the races in the schools in numbers or proportions satisfactory to the Federal court.

Furthermore, the Federal court cannot usurp and exercise the power of the school board to devise a nondiscriminatory assignment plan merely because it wishes to mix the races in the schools in greater numbers or proportions than the nondiscriminatory plan of the school board envisages.

This Report's eagerness to permit continued Federal judicial and bureaucratic interference with the local public school systems of this country is underlined by its expressed opposition to recent legislative efforts to restrict such intervention. The Report specifically recommends against the adoption of the so-called "Student Transportation Moratorium Act" and the so-called "Equal Educational Opportunities Act." The Report states that these legislative proposals, if enacted, ". . . would severely restrict remedies for unconstitutional school segregation. . . . Without transportation, much unlawfully established segregation must be allowed to persist."

In other words, the Report advocates exactly what the Congress has opposed in the 1964 Civil Rights Act, namely, the busing of school children to achieve racial balance.

### D. Conclusion

Whatever one may think of the numerous assertions concerning the value of integrated education set forth in the majority report—assertions which are very much still a matter of dispute among professional educators—no American citizen who believes in constitutional government and in the sanctity of local control over education can be comforted by this committee's Report respecting school integration. At least in this part of its Report, the committee appears to be more committed to equal mixing of bodies in the schools than to the subject with which it was charged—equal educational opportunity. I am compelled to reach such a conclusion because the committee has clearly accepted, even advocated, the dangerous pattern of judicial and bureaucratic tyranny over local school boards which has emerged over the past few years.

I submit that the positions set forth in this part of the committee's Report not only directly conflict with Congress' expressed opposition to forced integration—especially when involving massive busing of schoolchildren—but also run counter to fundamental constitutional and legal principles long cherished in our Republic.

Sam J. Ervin, Jr.

## Minority Views

### MESSRS. HRUSKA (R-NEBR.), DOMINICK (R-COLO.) AND COOK (R-KY.)

#### A. INTRODUCTION

The Select Committee on Equal Educational Opportunity was authorized by the 91st Congress on February 18, 1970. Its reporting date was originally January 31, 1971, but three extensions of the Select Committee's life pushed the date forward to December 31, 1972.

Clearly the work of the committee spanned a period of considerable tumult in the elementary and secondary fields. Major new legislation was enacted in the form of Public Law 91–230 in the 91st Congress and the Education Amendments of 1972 (P.L. 92–318). Proposals dealing with child development and equal educational opportunity passed in one or both Houses, but were not enacted. Important judicial decisions, such as *Swann* and *Serrano*, were handed down. The report of the President's Commission on School Finance was released. And new initiatives for aid to education were presented to the President. The extensive hearing record compiled by the committee reflects the current attitudes and views of many segments of concerned educators and the public on problems of securing equal educational opportunity. The record is an impressive achievement of this Select Committee.

#### B. AGREEMENT WITH MAIN THRUST OF REPORT

The broad thrust of the Report is not disputed:

- Education is an important national concern, and the national interest requires the Federal Government to encourage both equal educational opportunity and equalization of educational attainment.
- Stable, quality integrated education is a desirable goal.
- In the short run, steps must be taken to restructure Federal aid to education; and, in the long run, it may be necessary to reduce the burden of property taxes used to finance education.

The hearings of the committee have documented the difficulty of achieving these goals, especially with respect to desegregation, in a pluralistic and increasingly suburbanized society. The roadblocks to integration by racial and ethnic groups, and also by social strata, have been mentioned by numerous participants in the hearings. Hence, it did seem worthwhile to widen the scope of the committee's inquiry so as to highlight the interdependence of schooling and other social programs or Federal initiatives, such as the concern for full employment, housing, and the elimination of poverty.

### C. Some Reservations and Criticisms of the Report

Despite the fact that the Report has summarized numerous suggestions of educators on how to improve school practices, and made a number of specific recommendations about steps to be taken by Congress and the Executive Branch to administer existing programs more uniformly; it is felt that in certain areas the Report falls short of being an adequate guide for Federal efforts to advance equality of educational opportunity. The following criticisms should be made:

- Despite its great length, the Report fails to deal with a number of widely discussed innovative or cost-cutting techniques, which bear on equal educational opportunity, such as educational vouchers, performance contracting, or year-round schools.
- The Report slights the complex relationships in school governance, and says little, if anything, about the roles of Chief State School Officers, school boards, central staffs and school superintendents. These relationships bear directly on efforts to assure quality education. Nor does the Report deal adequately with the role of professional associations or unions in the field of education.
- The Report is much stronger in documenting what is wrong with the schools than in mapping positive approaches. It does not suggest approaches which could be used to provide quality education for *all* children. Nor does it endorse fresh innovative strategies for Federal involvement in the education of children. It quite properly bemoans past failures, and then recommends that additional money be spent to fix wrongs which were not put right by largely unsuccessful programs in the past.
- The financial recommendations of the Report do not take into consideration the changing trends in national enrollment and, even more regrettably, fail to map out an adequate Federal policy for equalizing or providing adequate resources for quality education in the wake of *Serrano* and related decisions.

In the light of these shortcomings, we feel that dissenting views to the conclusions of the Report are in order.

### D. Special Education for the Disadvantaged

The Report cites disappointing results from current compensatory and remedial programs, and documents unsatisfactory arrangements for the planning and administration of these programs. However, it fails to draw the necessary conclusions from these findings, and largely recommends the infusion of additional funds into the school system on a basis which has not proved successful in the past.

We would like to go on record that considerable rethinking about the scope and methodology of present programs is required, especially in view of the expiration during the 93d Congress of the Elementary and Secondary Education Act and related authorities. To wit:

- Considerably more emphasis must be placed on diagnosing the reasons why students lag. A clear distinction must be made between failure due to motivation and failure due to slow learning rates, recognizing that each type of failure can spring from many causes.

- Programs must be designed to attack both of these causes of failure, and students and their parents must be assisted in finding appropriate programs.
- The current failure to tailor programs to students' individual needs has resulted in a dearth of acceptable mass approaches to remediation. The Report recognizes that: 1. Currently successful pilot programs cannot be replicated on a mass scale; and 2. A broader participation, especially by parents, is needed to achieve desirable results. But it stops there. The Report fails to point to ways in which the Federal Government could encourage research and development of viable programs. It fails, for example, to make the following important substantive points:

  (a) The necessity to develop reliable diagnostic tests to identify causes of student lag.

  (b) The need to develop consistent and theoretically sound programs either to produce interest in academic subjects or to accelerate the learning rate.

  (c) The need to train professionals *responsible* for achieving desirable results with lagging students. The Report addressed this question clearly only in connection with bilingual programs. If it is good for bilingual education, it should be good for other causes of educational disadvantage. In this regard the Congress can gain useful lessons from the history of Federal support for research, professional training, and program operations in special education for the physically and mentally handicapped.

  (d) The possibility and promise of encouraging the development of special organizational and administrative arrangements to deal with the problems of lagging students.

We believe that the principal objectives for Federal leverage in the education of young children should be:

*First*, the provision of adequate resources for the education of children from poor families and those with learning disabilities.

*Second*, the development of techniques, personnel, institutions, and administrative relationships to ensure that these resources are used effectively.

*Third*, the alleviation of the escalating cost of elementary and secondary education to taxpayers at the State and local levels, especially in light of *Serrano*-type expenditure equalization.

These considerations dictate the following priorities for Federal involvement in elementary and secondary education:

### 1. EMPHASIS ON RESEARCH AND DEVELOPMENT

A new emphasis on educational research and development is needed to encourage experimentation with more powerful methodologies to impart knowledge to educationally disadvantaged and handicapped students. Despite the considerably higher levels of educational research and development during the past 5 years, the Office of Education has failed to upgrade the status of educational research and development. The new National Institute of Education offers hopes of overcoming these failures. We would like to urge the Institute to launch a number of new initiatives. It is suggested that vaguely planned "social experiments" be de-emphasized, and rigorous, soundly based new techniques of teaching be researched.

### 2. DEVELOPMENT OF A NEW GROUP OF PROFESSIONALS

The realization that problems of school failure go beyond the schoolhouse dictates the creation of a new breed of professionals trained to interact with students, parents, administrators, and regular teachers. The Education Professions Development Act is an acceptable vehicle for this purpose.

### 3. DEVELOPMENT OF NEW CONCEPTS OF RESPONSIBILITY AND ACCOUNTABILITY

The difficult job of diagnosis, prevention, and remediation of school failure requires that clear-cut responsibilities be set up for the administration of special programs. While, on the one hand, some humility is in order about the role of the school in eliminating failure, the expectations of positive results can be enhanced if specific targets are the responsibility of a given group of program managers and operators.

### 4. DEVELOPMENT OF SPECIAL INSTITUTIONAL ARRANGEMENTS FOR REMEDIATION AND ENRICHMENT

Arrangements devoted to specific focused programs should be encouraged. Such arrangements may be either:

*First*, within regular school systems—preferably at special locations serving a number of schools, so as to assure a sufficient concentration and also avoid the disruption of diagnosis or therapy often caused by within-district pupil transfers. Such programs could be conducted on "released time" or after school.

*Second*, in competent nonprofit or profit-making institutions devoted to development, remediation, and enrichment of poor and minority students.

*Third*, in combinations of the above approaches.

While the reorganization of remedial and enrichment services is of high priority, we believe, also, in the great urgency of mounting programs which will obviate or reduce the need for remediation in the schools. Paramount among these are:

- The development of more effective tests, and the administration of existing tests, to diagnose certain types of learning disabilities at an early age. Much could be done, for instance, in diagnosing and remediating early hearing, speech and visual problems in very young children.
- Additional testing and introduction of early childhood education services. The development and popularization of successful methods for teaching parents to give very young children cognitive training in the home are recommended to reduce educational deficits.
- The development of effective early childhood education programs drawing on the expertise and close cooperation of both parents

and professionals. These programs should put the requisite emphasis on the cognitive and affective development of children. The Report is not specific enough on this point. Its reference to educating the whole child could be easily misunderstood as putting a stamp of approval on noncognitive approaches to early childhood education.

### E. Quality Education and Integration

The Constitutional requirement of the 1954 *Brown* decision to eliminate school segregation resulting from deliberate official action is no longer an issue in itself. Since that time, we have learned that desegregated schools are not by themselves a sufficient precondition for quality education. The courts and educators are now concerned with the processes of mixing majority and minority racial and ethnic groups. This carries with it acute questions concerning the future of neighborhood and community schools, and the involvement of courts and executive agencies in the responsibilities of State and local school officials.

It is becoming increasingly clear that integration of low achieving black or other minority children with low achieving whites does not necessarily result in quality education. Unfortunately, the Report has not addressed the conditions and the costs which will preserve academic standards in truly integrated schools. Nor has the Report suggested measures to reduce resegregation resulting from white flight, such as those referred to the 92d Congress in the proposed Equal Educational Opportunities Act. These questions heavily occupied the 92d Congress and may well occupy the 93d. They are matters of great national concern, and congressional positions are clear and on record. Pending Supreme Court decisions and the likelihood of new Executive Branch initiatives now present the Congress with major uncertainties.

It is generally accepted that incentives to truly integrated education of high quality must be provided by the Federal Government, and that standards for truly integrated schools must be applied impartially in all regions of the country. The Emergency School Aid Program under Title VII of the Education Amendments of 1972 (P.L. 92–318), helps to serve these purposes by authorizing aid to school districts desegregating under court order or compliance agreement, or undertaking voluntary measures to reduce racial isolation. Experience gained with Emergency School Aid can provide valuable guidance to the Nation in resolving some of the complex and divisive issues which obstruct bringing us together.

Furthermore, we believe that a strategy and legislation for stable, quality-integrated education must be more fully considered by the Congress in the light of recent court decisions. Major education decisions are expected to be handed down by the Supreme Court early in 1973, and these also will have to be weighed by the Congress. To these ends we favor acceptable legislation seeking the kinds of purposes advanced in the 92d Congress in the proposed Equal Educational Opportunities Act, should pending court decisions and Executive Branch initiatives indicate a continued need.

As indicated in Section F, below, it is our conviction that those in the Congress seeking to improve elementary and secondary education in the United States must find ways for the Federal Government to assist financially pressed school districts. Also, they must find ways to help assure that adequate educational resources are available and effectively used to meet the special educational needs of the poor, the disadvantaged and the handicapped. It is these approaches which will ultimately result in quality education for all children. Such measures as the involuntary transportation of children to schools many miles from their homes will hamper rather than help progress toward these goals.

### F. Future Direction of Federal Aid to Education

While we agree with the Report that access to quality education should not be affected by the resources of a given school district, we are concerned about the vagueness of the equalization recommendations in the Report. In the first place, the Report fails to focus adequately on the important differences between equalizing resources and equalizing expenditures. In the second place, it ignores the experience of such cities as Washington, D.C., where the reallocation of expenditures between schools pursuant to the decision in *Hobson* v. *Hansen* has, on occasion, penalized schools in poorer sections of the city, or failed to produce desirable educational outcomes even in those cases where small increments in resources were added to deserving schools.

After outlining some of the issues of equalization, the Report has tended to ignore them in its recommendations. Its main recommendations: (1) to provide $5 billion per year in immediate general aid for schools; and (2) to make project grants of $1.5 billion to supplement the operation of Title I of the Elementary and Secondary Education Act—familiarly known as ESEA—may, in some ways, be counter-productive.

The Report should take into account the projections of the President's Commission on School Finance, which showed that the rate of increase of educational expenditures is slowing down considerably. Some of the extreme financial difficulties of school districts were caused by temporary economic aberrations.

The slowing down of inflation, the moderation of the rate of increase in teachers' wages, and the rise in State and local revenues resulting from the upturn in economic activity are likely to take some of the edge off the school finance crisis. Hence, in the future it may be more desirable to allocate funds on a categorical basis, or according to clear special revenue-sharing priorities, for activities closer to the Federal interest in education, especially once one analyzes the uncertain effects of *Serrano*-type arrangements.

### G. Significance of Serrano-type Decisions

Since the California Supreme Court handed down its 1971 decision in *Serrano* v. *Priest*, a series of decisions in other States indicates a disposition among the courts to equalize local school expenditures. The significance of these *Serrano*-type decisions is that:

*First*, they will force States to assume a more important role in financing education.

*Second*, they deal with equalizing the financial resources of school districts at a given tax effort, but are not specific about the ground rules for the allocation of funds to equalize resources.

The rather general suggestion of the Report that these moves for equalization will contribute to reducing inequality in education—provided that there are adjustments for cost and resource differentials among school districts—raises a new set of issues.

It is not at all clear what kind of cost and resource differences should be taken into account. Should districts be encouraged or penalized for paying higher-than-average wages? Should the State shoulder the cost of programs, such as driver education or drama, outside the basic curriculum? Should it shoulder the cost of extracurricular programs? Smaller class sizes? And so forth . . . ?

The President's Commission on School Finance provides some general guidelines for Federal incentives to States to shoulder a greater part of education expenditures. We suggest that some part of the Federal aid funds be earmarked for those purposes.

We further suggest that the Federal policy take into consideration the impact of these equalization measures upon the finances of large cities and rural areas, where most of the disadvantaged students are concentrated, and assure that categorical programs or clear special revenue-sharing priorities provide for the special education needs of these groups.

## H. Immediate Financial Relief and General Aid to Education

The research commissioned by the President's Commission on School Finance indicates that elementary and secondary expenditures are likely to continue growing somewhat faster than the trend in the full-employment Gross National Product (GNP) until 1975. After that period, even if early childhood education services are expanded at an accelerated pace, it is not likely that this item of outlay will grow very much faster than the GNP.

The financial crisis experienced by education during the past few years was compounded by high rates of inflation; less-than-full employment economic conditions; and, limitations of State and local financial resources. With inflation moderating; an imminent return to full employment; and, progress realized in improving State and local revenues there are opportunities for more deliberate approaches to financial relief. Nevertheless, as long as the unemployment rate remains above desirable levels, we would be sympathetic to making available some $500 million for emergency relief to school districts—which despite State and local efforts are financially imperiled. The arrangements contrived, in 1969 and 1970, to fund the first Emergency School Aid Program suggest an approach which would recognize the urgency of the situations in certain school districts and give Congress and the Executive Branch opportunities to consider any needed long-range legislative authorities.

We view with misgivings the form of the Report's proposal for a general aid fund for education. Unless it takes into account the special needs of large cities, poor suburbs, and rural areas, the enactment of such general aid could well be counterproductive. It could be used by States to harden the present disparities in aid between school districts.

Forestalling this undesirable effect simply by imposing special allocation formulas does not appear to be feasible. The financial circumstances of school districts, State-by-State, school district-by-school district, should not—and, as a practical matter, probably could not—be determined by the Federal Government. Constitutionally, education has been defined as a State function, and it would not be desirable to encroach upon it.

Setting the level of general aid in accordance with certain eligibility criteria—for example, number of children in poor families, number of bilingual children, or children in preschool—does not appear to be desirable either. In the first place, these criteria are not all-encompassing; and in the second, just because these additional challenges to education do exist in a school district does not mean that they will be met. A general aid bill based on these or similar criteria will only contribute to reduce the drive for accountability of educational expenditures and be generally undesirable.

We would strongly suggest that greater attention be paid to general and special revenue sharing as ways of reducing pressure on State and local finances, especially if *Serrano*-type decisions make it imperative for States to shoulder a higher proportion of school outlays. The promise of general and special revenue sharing is far superior to rigidly earmarked funds for specific expenditures—the growth of which is likely to vary from time period to time period.

### I. Recommendations on Federal Aid to Education

The foregoing reservations expressed about the suggestions of the Report for increased aid to education were not meant to convey the impression that we are opposed to increasing the funding levels of Federal Government support for elementary and secondary education from current levels of 6–7 percent. On the contrary, we visualize that by the mid-1970s or early 1980s, it may be desirable for the Federal Government to shoulder 15–20 percent of total elementary and secondary school costs—perhaps as much as 30 percent as recently proposed by the U.S. Commissioner of Education.

This increased support to education, we propose, should be firmly based on:

- The provision of incentives to States and school districts to establish programs which will foster the Federal interest in education.
- Preserving the freedom of individual States and districts in shaping their educational delivery systems.

Perhaps a few words are in order to clarify what we believe to be the Federal interest in education. We share the view of the President's Commission on School Finance that the States must bear primary responsibility for designing, financing, and carrying out educational reforms. The Federal Government should provide sufficient incentives to enable the States and school districts to accomplish the great changes in the financing and distribution of educational resources necessary to deliver on the promises which the schools hold for our children. Furthermore, we believe that the Federal incentives must be presented in ways which serve the objectives of equalizing educational opportunity and attainment.

In the light of recent analyses of Coleman data (cf. Jencks, *et al.*), as well as the hearing record of the Select Committee, we are forced to conclude that the role of education in equalizing achievement or incomes is more limited than had been hoped. Nevertheless, education can and should have a role in providing the necessary skills to a far larger proportion of our population, to enable them to participate and compete in the U.S. economy. In other words, we believe that much still remains to be done to create environments where the vast majority of children attain the maximum possible levels of desirable skills, and where members of disadvantaged groups achieve to the maximum of their ability. What is more, we believe that programs can be mounted to reduce achievement disparities between social groups.

In order to mount such programs in a cost/effective manner—so as not to relive the disappointments which have beset us after expenditures of $3 billion for Head Start and $10 billion for ESEA Title I—we believe it is imperative to utilize the insights, theories, and techniques already at our disposal, and make a concerted effort to fill in the gaps in those areas where effective techniques do not exist.

In light of these comments, we commend to the attention of the Congress the need to deal more specifically with programs for early childhood education. As the President's Commission on School Finance has noted, there is a clear and discernible movement toward early childhood education, and that the provision of some form of regular education—beginning at age four—offers promise of improving the educational attainment of young children, and particularly those who are disadvantaged. We do not believe that the Report's advocacy of the comprehensive child development legislation considered by the 92d Congress adequately addresses the difficult issues involved.

A strong body of professional opinion holds that remediation costs are much lower, the earlier one begins to help the disadvantaged child. Unfortunately, current remedial and compensatory programs in the elementary grades have generally failed to sustain any cognitive gains realized in Head Start or ESEA Title I preschool programs. It is not clear how much of this failure should be attributed to shortcomings in preschool programs, nor how much to limitations in the regular grades.

In any case, if the hoped for cost savings of early childhood education are to be substantiated and then realized on a mass basis, there must be simultaneous and rigorous efforts to upgrade both preschool and regular grade programs with careful attention to the reciprocal influences between them.

It should now be clear to the Congress that the near simultaneous launchings of Head Start and ESEA Title I in the mid-1960s have resulted in costly, diverse and largely unevaluated experiments to help poor children overcome educational disadvantages. Educators and social service professionals have proceeded with little guidance about what could, much less what has, worked. Both Congress and the Executive Branch have advocated "concentration" of funds and project grants in the hope that these procedural measures would produce improvements in preschool and the regular grades. In the short run, there appear to be no other constructive alternatives. In the long run, more cost-effective alternatives must be devised. In the face of these circumstances, the Congress must now exercise initiative in a needed national reassessment of our early childhood education course.

We suggest that the Congress give careful attention to several steps which could successively test the merits of early childhood education, determine the prospects for sustaining early achievement gains in the regular grades, and then clarify the links which should exist between early learning programs and special education in the elementary schools.

In this vein, we suggest careful consideration of the following activities. For most, it would be appropriate for the Federal Government to consider shouldering a large share of developmental and initial program costs, and then a substantial share of total national operating costs of services targeted directly at the poor and disadvantaged.

- Establish diagnostic activities to identify speech, hearing, visual and other learning disabilities among very young children and treatment facilities for such disorders. National costs of incentives to hospitals and the medical professions to set up services could run $100 million per year for 5 years; and, to perform services about $300 million per year.
- Explore early learning programs with a primary reliance on a parent-training component. One or two successful models should be built, and simultaneously research and development moneys should be allocated for alternative approaches. This program could reasonably start with Federal support of $50 million for pilot operations, and some $10 million for research.
- Offer incentives to States and school districts to enroll children in quality, early childhood education programs. These should operate first on a pilot basis—to demonstrate successful early childhood education techniques—involving close cooperation between parents and professionals; then, as successful results become available, on a wider scale. A start of $150 million for demonstration, and $10–15 million for research, is probably as much as can be sensibly spent by the Federal Government before the merits could be determined.
- As first steps toward assessing the need for fuller responsibility for long-range programs for the disadvantaged, we urge the Congress to consider the needs for:

  (a) Serious research and development to develop effective remediation and enrichment techniques along the lines suggested above—in Section D—on the education of the disadvantaged.

  (b) Fundamental changes in the training and organization of professionals, as also suggested in Section D.

  An additional appropriation of $50 million for targeted research is recommended initially for programs aimed at the regular grades.

By the late 1970s or early 1980s it is possible that the Federal Government, the States and school districts would have to face up to shouldering and sharing a total national cost of dealing with disadvantaged students, from preschool through the regular grades, in the range of as much as $7-$10 billion per year.

We recommend that any Federal contribution for these purposes be channeled gradually as proven successes in remediation and enrichment are documented, and with ample consideration of the appropriate Federal role and financial share.

If these suggestions and estimates are taken seriously, it will be important for the Congress to face up to:

*First*, the potentially high national cost of special education for poor, disadvantaged, and handicapped children from preschool through high school.

*Second*, the Federal responsibility for such special education.

*Third*, the share of national costs appropriate to the Federal responsibility.

*Fourth*, the use of Federal support to influence reform of special education.

Should the costs of special education run relatively high and constitute a major share of total education costs, decisions to assume heavy Federal responsibility for these outlays may require difficult choices between channeling Federal support for general purposes or for categorical aid—including special revenue sharing priorities. Large appropriations for categorical aid to the disadvantaged could leave relatively limited amounts for general aid.

The Report does not address these questions directly or clearly. We have responded to them in ways sufficient to illustrate the kinds of policy choices facing the 93d and subsequent Congresses.

It would be unwise, we believe, to assume that a comprehensive child-development strategy, heavier ESEA Title I funding, and general aid—along the lines advocated in the Report—would purchase for the next generation of poor and disadvantaged children the level of achievement gains we have still failed to secure for the present generation.

## J. Other Specific Disagreements

### 1. CIVIL RIGHTS ENFORCEMENT

In its review of civil rights enforcement, the Report underemphasizes the burdens imposed upon the Departments of Health, Education, and Welfare and Justice by the May 27, 1968, Supreme Court decision in *Green* v. *County School Board of New Kent County, Virginia*, which, in effect, ended the era of "free choice" and "all deliberate speed." This decision, coupled with the October 29, 1969, decision in *Alexander* v. *Holmes County Board of Education* to terminate dual school systems at once, fundamentally altered the standards and timetables for school desegregation. The Report slights these altered circumstances in its criticisms of the July 3, 1969, joint statement issued by the Attorney General and the Secretary of Health, Education, and Welfare. This statement announced that ultimate enforcement responsibilities would shift from funding termination under Title VI of the Civil Rights Act of 1964 to court suits.

While the July 3, 1969, statement did contemplate a shift of ultimate enforcement to the courts on a selective basis where voluntary compliance could not be effected, this may have occurred in any event—with or without the statement. For the mandate of *Alexander* v. *Holmes*, which came 3 months later, was to bring all formerly *de jure* school districts under acceptable desegregation plans "at once." And it is questionable, in keeping with that decision, that prompt and total desegregation could have been brought to pass on a widespread basis without strong reliance upon the courts—in those cases where school districts refused to comply voluntarily with Department of Health, Education, and Welfare directives.

In more recent enforcement activities related to the Emergency School Aid Program (familiarly known as ESAP), we believe the Report's criticisms bear down more heavily than the facts warrant.

While there were weaknesses in pre-grant compliance under the first phase of the program, ESAP–I, the Department of Health, Education, and Welfare did field a compliance program designed to remedy abuses—such as those brought to public attention by the private survey, conducted by the six civil rights groups, cited in the Report. During the first year of funding (1970–71), about 300 school districts were visited by civil rights officials of the DHEW to determine adherence to the civil rights assurances submitted under ESAP. The majority of these districts were also reviewed, at the same time, for the purposes of determining Title VI compliance. Under both ESAP–I and ESAP–II (the second phase of the program) enforcement of the ESAP civil rights provisions was carried out on-site, and school districts in violation of these provisions were directed to correct any abuses. Where the evidence substantiated violations which the funded school districts refused to remedy, the districts were notified of an opportunity for a hearing with a view to termination of ESAP funds. In our view, the ESAP civil rights provisions served as a basis for bringing about positive change in many school districts.

It should be emphasized that the Emergency School Aid Act, which evolved from ESAP with the administration's initiative and support, was intended among other purposes to provide new tools—other than legal—to address problems of racial isolation in so-called non-*de jure* school districts. Given the evidentiary burdens in non-*de jure* cases, it has not been possible under Federal authority to accomplish, outside the South, anything approaching widespread desegregation. The President's proposal of the Emergency School Aid Act was an effort to encourage these school districts to cope with the problems of racial isolation on a voluntary basis. For that reason, the Act holds considerable promise for improving equal educational opportunity.

Any appraisal of the turbulent history of civil rights enforcement, since the 1954 *Brown* decision, will be affected by convictions concerning the proper and effective use of governmental enforcement to redress specific cases of legally defined discrimination—a use which we strongly uphold, and to moderate abhorrent prejudicial social values and attitudes.

In our judgment, the Nation now suffers in the area of school desegregation from tendencies to invoke governmental enforcement powers—well beyond the proper redressing of legally defined discrimination—for interventions in extremely complex conflicts of social values and attitudes. These conflicts, with deep roots in our national history, are reflected in our emerging pluralistic national culture, and, in the cultures carried to our shores by the many races and peoples who created this still-young Nation.

We believe that, in the troubled area of educational discrimination, clearer distinctions must be made between legal imperatives—subject to measured justice—and moral imperatives, implicit in concepts of equality. The latter must gain in force through an almost infinite number of individual and group actions—often over many generations—before they enjoy wide acceptance as legal imperatives.

The Congress and all of the people whom it represents need a new sense of realism about the proper balance at this stage in our Nation's history between governmental enforcement in redressing discrimination in the schools, and governmental actions in the field of education aimed at overcoming the disadvantages in skills and achievement which tend to reinforce and perpetuate popular prejudices against minority and social groups.

### 2. SCHOOL IMPACT AID

The Report recommends full funding of the P.L. 874 provisions which authorize impact-aid payments to school districts in relation to the number of children living in federally-assisted public housing. The cost would be about $300 million in fiscal year 1973.

The addition to total municipal overburden in large cities, as a result of heavy concentrations of poor and low-income families, deserves consideration on a more comprehensive basis than education. The Report recognizes this in its adoption of the recommendation of the President's Task Force on Urban Renewal—to provide support related to a variety of municipal services. Any urging of immediate full funding of school impact aid, related to public housing, would be a digression from the goal of more comprehensive urban support. It would also confuse current efforts to clarify P.L. 874 objectives with respect to school-district impact of military and civil service dependents.

### 3. BILINGUAL EDUCATION

Bilingual education programs deserve increased Federal support as they prove successful. However, the Report's recommendation to fund fully the existing programs would result in a several-fold increase. Experience over the past 10 years clearly indicates the danger of rapidly escalating education programs. As noted earlier, we recognize the soundness of most of the Report's recommendations in the bilingual field. At the same time, we favor a much more gradual rate of increase in Federal support—a rate which would assure careful building of quality programs.

### 4. COUNCIL OF SOCIAL ADVISORS

The Report's recommendation to establish a Council of Social Advisors aims at laudable objectives. We are, however, opposed to the creation of such a council, at this point in time, for the same reasons outlined in the Minority Views on S. 5, the Full Opportunities National Goals and Priority Act (Report 92–866). A new Council of Social Advisors would needlessly overlap with the Domestic Council established in the Executive Office of the President in 1970; and would be a counterproductive increase in the bureaucratic pollution which is already choking the Federal Government.

Increased attention, in recent years, to the quality of program analyses by the Office of Management and Budget and individual Federal agencies point in the right direction. The new National Institute of Education represents sound progress toward building a more systematic foundation for national education policy. It is unrealistic, in our judgment, to expect that a central council could compensate for current limitations of individual social science disciplines as evidenced, for example, in recent educational studies.

### 5. VOCATIONAL EDUCATION

The percentage of American students enrolled in vocational education has increased from 24 percent in fiscal year 1965 to 38 percent in fiscal year 1971. Federal expenditures for vocational education increased from $57 million in fiscal year 1963 to $507 million in fiscal year 1972, while State and local expenditures rose from $254 million in fiscal year 1963 to $1,951 million in fiscal year 1971.

We join in the Report's regret that greater attention was not devoted to this vital area of education. A recent General Accounting Office study (D-164031(1), Oct. 18, 1972) of four States revealed that between 44 percent and 75 percent of high school students needing vocational education were not receiving it—because of insufficient financial support at all levels of government; and, unfortunately, students held an unfavorable image of vocational education. We pledge ourselves to correcting this situation.

ROMAN L. HRUSKA,
PETER H. DOMINICK,
MARLOW W. COOK.

# SELECT COMMITTEE REFERENCES

## COMMITTEE HEARINGS



***Order by number only; no other title nor date needed.**
**†Not available from committee.**

COMMITTEE HEARINGS

| | Pages | Part No.* |
|---|---|---|
| Compensatory Education and Other Alternatives in Urban Schools. *July 14, 15; Aug. 3, 1971* | 5509–5841 | 12 |
| Quality and Control of Urban Schools. *July 27, 29; Aug. 5, 1971* | 5843–6177 | 13 |
| State Role in School Desegregation: Pennsylvania *Aug. 4, 1971* | 6179–6325 | 14 |
| Education in Rural America. *Sept. 1, 2, 3, 1971* | 6327–6599 | 15 |
| Inequality in School Finance. *Sept. 21, 22, 23, 1971* | 6601–6726 | 16A |
| ———. Continued. *Oct. 5; Sept. 29, 30, 28, 1971* | 6727–6892 | 16B |
| ———. Appendix I. Schools and Inequality | 6893–7449 | 16C |
| ———. General Appendixes | 7451–7788 | 16D–1 |
| ———. ———. Continued | 7789–8285 | 16D–2 |
| ———. ———. Continued | 8287–8614 | 16D–3 |
| Delivery Systems for Federal Aid to Disadvantaged Children *Oct. 7, 1971* | 8615–9006 | 17 |
| Pupil Transportation Costs. *Oct. 6, 1971* | 9007–9377 | 18 |
| Equal Educational Opportunity in Michigan. *Oct. 26; Nov. 1, 2, 1971* | 9379–9614 | 19A |
| ———. U.S. Senate Select Committee on Equal Educational Opportunity staff charts on Michigan's Educational Assessment Program | Chart | 19A–1 |
| ———. Continued. *Sept. 29; Oct. 1; Nov. 3, 4, 1971* | 9615–9901 | 19B |
| ———. Appendixes | 9903–10153 | 19C |
| Unequal School Practices. *Nov. 8, 1971* | 10155–10417 | 20 |
| Metropolitan Aspects of Educational Inequality *Nov. 22, 23, 30, 1971* | 10419–10948 | 21 |
| Education Information. *Dec. 1, 2, 3, 1971* | 10949–11155 | 22 |

*Order by number only; no other title nor date needed.

## COMMITTEE PRINTS

| | Print No.* |
|---|---|
| A Design for the Attainment of High Academic Achievement for the Students of the Public Elementary and Junior High Schools of Washington, D.C. *September 1970* | CP–1 |
| Interim Report *September 1970* | CP–2† |
| Emergency School Assistance Program—Background and Evaluations *April 1971* | CP–3 |
| Federal Aid to Public Education: Who Benefits? *April 1971* | CP–4 |
| The Financial Aspects of Equality of Educational Opportunity, *and* Inequities in School Finance. *January 1972* | CP–5 |
| The Costs to the Nation of Inadequate Education. *February 1972* | CP–6 |
| Court Decisions Relating to Equal Educational Opportunity. *March 1972* | CP–7 |
| Goals for Alternatives for the Education of Minority Group Students in Elementary and Secondary Schools. *June 1972* | CP–8 |
| Justice for Children *June 1972* | CP–9 |
| Environment, Intelligence, and Scholastic Achievement. *June 1972* | CP–10 |
| The Effects of Dropping Out *August 1972* | CP–11 |
| Issues in School Finance *September 1972* | CP–12 |
| Publications List and Researcher's Reference *December 1972* | CP–13 |
| The Report of the Select Committee on Equal Educational Opportunity *December 1972* | CP–14 |

*Order by number only; no other title nor date needed.
†Not available from committee.

# REMARKS AND STATEMENTS BY THE WITNESSES

| | *Hearing Dates* | *Part No.* |
|---|---|---|
| ABERNETHY, Donald D., superintendent, Hoke County Schools, Raeford, N.C. | June 17, 1970 | 3A |
| ACKER, Miss Chyrl, J. L. Mann High School, Greenville, S.C. | July 8, 1970 | 3B |
| ANDERSON, Jennifer, Lincoln School, Berkeley Unified School District, Calif. | Mar. 3, 1971 | 9 |
| ANDERSON, Mrs. Robert C., president PTA Council, Pontiac, Mich. | Nov. 4, 1971 | 19B |
| ANLIOT, Richard B., director, Division of Education, Pennsylvania Human Relations Commission, Harrisburg, Pa. | Aug. 4, 1971 | 14 |
| ANTHONY, John, principal, Morgan Community School, Washington, D.C. | July 29, 1971 | 13 |
| ANTONETTY, Mrs. Evelina, executive director, United Bronx Parents, New York City, N.Y. | Nov. 24, 1970 | 8 |
| AQUINO-BERMUNDEZ. Federico, City University, New York City, N.Y. | Nov. 24, 1970 | 8 |
| ARROYO, Mrs. Carmen, New York City, N.Y. | Nov. 24, 1970 | 8 |

—B—

| | | |
|---|---|---|
| BADENOCH, Mrs. Alice, teacher, James C. Mann High School, Greenville, S.C. | July 8, 1970 | 3B |
| BAILEY, Dr. Stephen K., chairman, Policy Institute, Syracuse University Research Corp.; and regent of the State of New York. | Oct. 7, 1971 | 17 |
| BAKAYLER, Elizabeth, student, Lincoln School, Berkeley Unified School District, Calif. | Mar. 3, 1971 | 9 |
| BANKS, J. F., associate director for secondary education, State Department of Education, Richmond, Va. | June 14, 1971 | 10 |
| BARRETT, Mrs. Catharine, president-elect, National Education Association. | Sept. 23, 1971 | 16A |
| BAXTER, Dr. Albert, professor, A.M. & N. College, Pine Bluff, Ark. | June 14, 1971 | 10 |
| BAXTER, Mrs. Louise, member, PAC, Morgan Community School, Washington, D.C. | July 29, 1971 | 13 |
| BEGAY, Mrs. Bessie, secretary-treasurer, Ramah Navaho School Board, Ramah, N. Mex. | June 8, 1970 | 2 |
| BELLMAN, Richard F., associate counsel, National Committee Against Discrimination in Housing, New York, N.Y. | Aug. 27, 1970 | 5 |
| BENSON, Charles S., professor, Department of Education, University of California (Berkeley). | Sept. 23, 1971 | 16A |

## REMARKS AND STATEMENTS BY THE WITNESSES

| | Hearing Dates | Part No. |
|---|---|---|
| BERKE, Joel S., director, Educational Finance and Governance Program, Policy Institute of the Syracuse University Research Corp. | Sept. 22, 1971<br>Dec. 1, 1971 | 16A<br>22 |
| BERRY, Dr. E. Ray, superintendent of schools, Riverside City Unified School District, Calif. | Mar. 6, 1971 | 9 |
| BERTSCH, Dale F., executive director, Miami Valley Regional Planning Commission, Dayton, Ohio. | Nov. 22, 1971 | 21 |
| BICKEL, Alexander M., professor of law, Yale University, New Haven, Conn. | Sept. 24, 1970<br>June 15, 1971 | 3E<br>11 |
| BLANCHARD, Dr. Robert W., superintendent of schools, Portland Public Schools, Portland, Oreg. | Sept. 21, 1971 | 16A |
| BOND, Hon. Julian, a member of the State assembly, Atlanta, Ga. | June 15, 1970 | 3A |
| BOYAN, Dr. Norman, dean, Graduate School of Education, University of California at Santa Barbara. | Dec. 3, 1971 | 22 |
| BRADDOCK, G. Holmes, chairman, Dade County School Board, Miami, Fla. | June 23, 1970 | 3B |
| BRADER, Jerry H., Director, Division of Equal Educational Opportunities, HEW. | Aug. 6, 1970 | 3C |
| BRADLEY, Mrs. Velma, president, Berkeley PTA, Calif. | Mar. 3, 5, 1971 | 9 |
| BREST, Paul, assistant professor, Stanford University of Law. | Oct. 8, 1970 | 3E |
| BRIGHT, William R., Jr., research associate, National Committee Against Discrimination in Housing, New York, N.Y. | Aug. 25, 1970 | 5 |
| BROOKS, Dr. Elbert D., director, Metropolitan Public Schools, Nashville, Tenn. | Oct. 6, 1971 | 18 |
| BROWN, Charles E., Ford Foundation, New York City, N.Y. | Apr. 27, 1970 | 1A |
| BROWN, Robert, chairman of the board, Morgan Community School, Washington, D.C. | July 29, 1971 | 13 |
| BROWN, Warren M., superintendent, Ferguson-Florissant School District, Ferguson, Mo. | Oct. 6, 1970 | 7 |

—C—

| | | |
|---|---|---|
| CALDWELL, Dr. George, superintendent of schools, San Bernardino City Unified School District, Calif. | Mar. 6, 1971 | |
| CALLAHAN, John, administrative assistant to the commissioner of education, State of Massachusetts. | May 21, 1970 | 2 |
| CARDENAS, Dr. Jose A., superintendent, Edgewood Independent School District, San Antonio, Tex. | Aug. 18, 1970 | 4 |
| CAREY, Mrs. Sarah C., assistant director, Lawyers Committee for Civil Rights Under Law. | Sept. 28, 1971 | 16B |
| CARLE, Dr. Wayne, superintendant of schools, Dayton, Ohio. | Oct. 6, 1971 | 18 |
| CARROLL, Donald, assistant commissioner, Basic Education for Professional Services, Harrisburg, Pa. | Aug. 4, 1971 | 14 |
| CARROLL, Ted, principal, Pelton Junior High School, Hunters Point, Calif. | Mar. 5, 1971 | 9 |

## REMARKS AND STATEMENTS BY THE WITNESSES

| | *Hearing Dates* | *Part No.* |
|---|---|---|
| CARTER, Robert L., president, National Committee Against Discrimination in Housing. | Aug. 25, 1970 | 5 |
| CARTER, Thomas P., professor of education, University of Texas at El Paso, Tex. | Aug. 21, 1970 | 4 |
| CASSO, Henry J., director, Development and Education Department, Mexican-American Legal Defense and Education Fund, Los Angeles Office. | Aug. 20, 1970 | 4 |
| CHAMBERS, Julius, NAACP Legal Defense Fund, Charlotte, N.C. | June 24, 1970 | 3B |
| | June 15, 1971 | 11 |
| CHRISTENBURY, Edward, Deputy Chief, Education Section, Office of the Attorney General. | July 13, 1970 | 3C |
| CLARK, Dr. Kenneth, professor of psychology, College of the City of New York. | Apr. 20, 1970 | 1A |
| CLARK, Hon. Ramsey, former Attorney General of the United States. | July 7, 1970 | 3C |
| CLEGHORN, Reese, director, leadership project, Southern Regional Council, Atlanta, Ga. | July 1, 1970 | 3D |
| CODY, Dr. Wilmer S., superintendent, Chapel Hill, N.C. | June 23, 1970 | 3B |
| COHEN, Arthur Mae, of Frogmore, S.C. | June 18, 1970 | 3B |
| COLEMAN, Herman, associate executive secretary for minority affairs, Michigan Education Association. | Nov. 2, 1971 | 19A |
| COLEMAN, Dr. James S., professor of social relations, Johns Hopkins University, Baltimore, Md. | Apr. 21, 1970 | 1A |
| CONKLIN, Miss Jan, teacher, Buena Vista School, Calif. | Mar. 4, 1971 | 9 |
| CONYERS, Hon. John, Jr., a U.S. Representative from the 1st District of the State of Michigan. | Nov. 4, 1971 | 19B |
| COONEY, Mrs. Joan Ganz, president, Children's Television Workshop, New York City. | July 30, 1970 | 2 |
| COONS, Dr. John, professor, School of Law, University of California. | Sept. 28, 1971 | 16B |

—D—

| | | |
|---|---|---|
| DANN, Michael, vice president, Children's Television Workshop, New York City. | July 30, 1970 | 2 |
| DAVIS, Caroline, chief, Education Division, U.S. Commission on Civil Rights. | Nov. 23, 1971 | 21 |
| DOWNS, Anthony, senior vice president, Real Estate Research Corp, Chicago, Ill. | Sept. 1, 1970 | 5 |
| DRACHLER, Dr. Norman, superintendent, Detroit Public Schools, Detroit, Mich. | May 12, 1970 | 1A |
| | Oct. 1, 1971 | 19B |
| DROSICK, Mr. John, superintendent of schools, McDowell County, W. Va. | Sept. 2, 1971 | 15 |
| DUNBAR, Mrs. Beatrice, chairman, education committee, Hunters Point, Calif. | Mar. 5, 1971 | 9 |
| DUNBAUGH, Frank, Deputy Assistant Attorney General. | July 13, 1970 | 3C |
| | Aug. 13, 1970 | 3C |

## REMARKS AND STATEMENTS BY THE WITNESSES

| | *Hearing Dates* | *Part No.* |
|---|---|---|
| DURAN, Leandre, student, King Junior High, Berkeley Unified School District, Calif. | Mar. 3, 1971 | 9 |
| —E— | | |
| EDINGTON, Dr. Everett D., head, Department of Educational Administration, New Mexico State University. | Sept. 2, 1971 | 15 |
| EDMONDS, Ronald, assistant superintendent, School and Community Affairs, Michigan Department of Education. | Oct. 26, 1971 | 19A |
| EDWARDS, Don, a U.S. Representative from the 9th District of the State of California. | Mar. 3, 4, 5, 1971 | 9 |
| ELIZONDA, Mrs. Gertrude, representative, Japanese-American Citizens League, San Francisco, Calif. | Mar. 5, 1971 | 9 |
| EPSTEIN, Dr. Benjamin, assistant superintendent in charge of secondary education, Newark, N.J. | June 14, 1971 | 10 |
| ETHRIDGE, assistant executive secretary for teacher's rights, National Edution Association. | June 16, 1970 | 3A |
| EVANS, Samuel A., deputy superintendent for business; Harrisburg Public School District, Harrisburg, Pa. | Aug. 4, 1971 | 14 |
| —F— | | |
| FAULK, Dr. Harry R., superintendent of schools, McKeesport Area School District, McKeesport, Pa. | Aug. 4, 1971 | 14 |
| FINNEY, Graham S., urban affairs consultant, Philadelphia, Pa. | June 8, 1970 | 2 |
| FISCHER, George, president, National Education Association. | June 16, 1970 | 3A |
| FISHER, Robert, supervisor for education, SEED project, Hunters Point, Calif. | Mar. 5, 1971 | 9 |
| FISS, Prof. Owen, University of Chicago Law School, Chicago, Ill. | June 15, 1971 | 11 |
| FLEISCHER, Hugh, Deputy Chief, Education Section, Office of the Attorney General. | July 13, 1970 | 3C |
| FLOYD, Miss Gertie, student, Lincoln High School, Greenville, S.C. | July 8, 1970 | 3B |
| FLOYD, Homer C., executive director, Pennsylvania Human Relations Commission, Harrisburg, Pa. | Aug. 4, 1971 | 14 |
| FORT, Dr. Edward B., superintendent, Inkster Public Schools, Inkster, Mich. | Sept. 29, 1971 | 19B |
| FOSTER, Dr. Marcus A., superintendent of schools, Oakland Public Schools, Oakland, Calif. | July 14, 1971 | 12 |
| FOSTER, Dr. Richard L., superintendent, Berkeley Unified School District, Calif. | Mar. 3, 1971 | 9 |
| FOX, Mrs. Sylvia, executive director, Aspira of Illinois, Inc. | Nov. 23, 1970 | 8 |
| FRANCO, Dr. John M., superintendent of schools, Rochester, N.Y. | Oct. 7, 1971 | 18 |
| FRANCO, Ralph A., bilingual intergroup specialist, Office of Intergroup Education, School District of Philadelphia, Pa. | Nov. 25, 1970 | 8 |

## REMARKS AND STATEMENTS BY THE WITNESSES

| | *Hearing Dates* | *Part No.* |
|---|---|---|
| FRYER, Mrs. Ed, member, Williamson County, Tenn. Quarterly County Court. | Sept. 1, 1971 | 15 |
| FUENTES, Luis, New York City, N.Y. | Nov. 24, 1970 | 8 |
| —G— | | |
| GARCIA, Dr. Hector, founder, American GI Forum; and former Ambassador to the U.N. | Aug. 20, 1970 | 4 |
| GEORGE, Thomas William, attorney, National Association of Secondary School Principals, Washington, D.C. | June 14, 1971 | 10 |
| GITTELL, Dr. Marilyn, professor of political science, Queens College, New York, N.Y. | July 14, 1971 | 12 |
| GOETTEL, Dr. Robert J., Syracuse University Research Corp., New York, N.Y. | Dec. 1, 1971 | 22 |
| GONZALES, Daniel, Filipino problems, San Francisco Unified School District, San Francisco, Calif. | Mar. 5, 1971 | 9 |
| GOVER, Bill, assistant director, Oklahomans for Indian Opportunity, Norman, Okla. | June 8, 1970 | 2 |
| GREEN, William, assistant principal, Bret Harte Elementary School, Hunters Point, Calif. | Mar. 5, 1971 | 9 |
| GREEN, Miss Winifred, on behalf of the American Friends Service Committee, Atlanta, Ga. | June 16, 1970 | 3A |
| GROSS, Michael, adviser and counsel to Ramah High School, Ramah, N. Mex. | June 8, 1970 | 2 |
| GULLEDGE, Eugene, Assistant Secretary for Housing Production and Mortgage Credit, HUD. | Aug. 26, 1970 | 5 |
| GUTHRIE, James W., assistant professor, School of Education, University of California at Berkeley, Calif. | Sept. 30, 1970 | 7 |
| —H— | | |
| HAFFNER, Dr. Hyman, deputy superintendent of program planning, Harrisburg Public School District, Harrisburg, Pa. | Aug. 4, 1971 | 14 |
| HALL, Dr. Donald, deputy superintendent of schools, Sacramento Unified School District, Calif. | Mar. 6, 1971 | 9 |
| HAMILTON, Dr. Charles, Department of Political Sciences, Columbia University, New York, N.Y. | June 15, 1971 | 11 |
| HARRIS, Inetta, student, West Campus, Berkeley Unified School District, Calif. | Mar. 3, 1971 | 9 |
| HART, Hon. Philip A., a U.S. Senator from the State of Michigan. | Oct. 26; Nov. 1, 2, 1971<br>Nov. 3, 4, 1971 | 19A<br>19B |
| HARVEY, James H., executive director, Housing Opportunities Council, Washington, D.C. | Sept. 1, 1970 | 5 |
| HASKINS, Kenneth W., former dean, Howard University School of Social Work, Washington, D.C. | July 27, 1971 | 13 |
| HATCHETT, Elbert, president, Pontiac Chapter NAACP, Pontiac, Mich. | Nov. 4, 1971 | 19B |
| HAWKINS, Alfred, principal, Covert Elementary School, Covert, Mich. | Nov. 3, 1971 | 19B |
| HAYMAN, Warren C., principal, Belle Haven School, East Palo Alto, Calif. | May 5, 1971 | 9 |

## REMARKS AND STATEMENTS BY THE WITNESSES

| | Hearing Dates | Part No. |
|---|---|---|
| HILL, James, law student, University of South Carolina, leading delegation from Greenville, S.C. | July 8, 1970 | 3B. |
| HILL, Marvin, teacher, Alston High School, Greenville, S.C. | July 8, 1970 | 3B |
| HILL, Miss Sandra, East Side High School, Greenville, S.C. | July 8, 1970 | 3B |
| HO, Miss Belinda, student, Vallejo High School, Calif. | Mar. 5, 1971 | 9 |
| HOBSON, Julius W., director, the Washington Institute for Quality Education, Washington, D.C. | Sept. 23, 1971 | 16A |
| HOFFMAN, Dr. Glenn, superintendent of schools, Santa Clara County School District, Calif. | Mar. 6, 1971 | 9 |
| HOLIDAY, Mrs. Jean, president, PTA, Morgan Community School, Washington, D.C. | July 29, 1971 | 18 |
| HOLLOWAY, Dr. Ruth Love, director, Right To Read Program, Office of Education, HEW. | July 15, 1971 | 12 |
| HOOVER, Robert S., director, Nairobi College Campus, East Palo Alto, Calif. | Mar. 5, 1971 | 9 |
| HORNBECK, Dr. Ralph, superintendent of schools, Pasadena Unified School District, Calif. | Mar. 6, 1971 | 9 |
| HOWE, Dr. Harold H., II, vice president for Education and Research, the Ford Foundation, New York City. | Aug. 3, 1971 | 12 |
| HOYT, Dr. Eugene C., director, education activities staff, Appalachian Regional Commission, Washington, D.C. | Sept. 3, 1971 | 15 |
| HUME, Robert, student, Wade Hampton High School, Greenville, S.C. | July 8, 1970 | 3B |
| HUNTER, Richard, principal, Longfellow School, Berkeley Unified School District, Calif. | Mar. 3, 5, 1971 | 9 |
| HUSSEY, Mrs. Judith, bus supervisor, Pontiac City School System, Pontiac, Mich. | Nov. 4, 1971 | 19B |

—I—

| | | |
|---|---|---|
| IRWIN, John K., president, Pontiac School Board, Pontiac, Mich. | Nov. 4, 1971 | 19B |
| ISENBERG, Robert M., associate executive, American Association of School Administrators. | Sept. 1, 1971 | 15 |

—J—

| | | |
|---|---|---|
| JACKSON, Gordon, director, Black House, Community High School, Berkeley Unified School District, Calif. | Mar. 3, 1971 | 9 |
| JENCKS, Dr. Christopher, Harvard Graduate School of Education. | Dec. 2, 1971 | 22 |
| JEROME, Lawrence B., chief, Exempt Organizations Examination Branch, Internal Revenue. | Aug. 12, 1970 | 3D |
| JIMINEZ, Robert, principal, Buena Vista School, Calif. | Mar. 4, 1971 | 9 |
| JOHNSON, Arthur, deputy superintendent, Community Relations, Detroit Public Schools, Detroit, Mich. | May 12, 1970 | 1A |

## REMARKS AND STATEMENTS BY THE WITNESSES

| | Hearing Dates | Part No. |
|---|---|---|
| JOHNSON, Mrs. Gertrude, special assistant, Connecticut Department of Community Affairs. | May 5, 1970 | 1A |
| JOHNSON, Mrs. Marie, chairman, Pontiac Neighborhood Education Center, Pontiac, Mich. | Nov. 4, 1971 | 19B |
| JOHNSON, Mrs. Patricia, teacher, Pontiac City School System, Pontiac, Mich. | Nov. 4, 1971 | 19B |
| JUSTICE, Mrs. Betty, McDowell County, W. Va. | Sept. 2, 1971 | 15 |

—K—

| | | |
|---|---|---|
| KEARNEY, Dr. Philip, associate superintendent, Research and School Administration, Michigan Department of Education. | Nov. 1, 1971 | 19A |
| KELLY, James A., program officer in public education, the Ford Foundation, New York, N.Y. | Sept. 22, 1971 | 16A |
| KENT, Dr. Russell, superintendent of schools, San Mateo County Unified School District, Calif. | Mar. 6, 1971 | 9 |
| KEPPEL, Dr. Francis, chairman of the board, General Learning Corp., New York, N.Y. | Dec. 1, 1971 | 22 |
| KIERNAN, Dr. Owen, executive secretary, National Association of Secondary School Principals, Washington, D.C. | June 14, 1971 | 10 |
| KING, E. V., human resources specialist, Mid-Cumberland Council of Governments. | Sept. 1, 1971 | 15 |
| KIRST, Dr. Michael W., School of Education and Business Administration, Stanford University. | Oct. 7, 1971 | 17 |
| KLEINDORFER, Dr. George, School of Education, University of California at Berkeley. | Dec. 3, 1971 | 22 |
| KLEINPETER, Anita, of Lake Providence, La. | June 18, 1970 | 3B |
| KRIEGER, William B., superintendent, Mackinac Island School District, Mackinac, Mich. | Nov. 3, 1971 | 19B |
| KRUEGER, Karen, chief, Housing Division, U.S. Commission on Civil Rights. | Nov. 23, 1971 | 21 |
| KRUGER, Dr. Daniel H., professor, School of Labor and Industrial Relations, Michigan State University, Lansing, Mich. | Oct. 26, 1971 | 19A |

—L—

| | | |
|---|---|---|
| LACY, William, school administration, Pontiac Public Schools, Pontiac, Mich. | Nov. 4, 1971 | 19B |
| LAFONTAINE, Hernan, founder, Puerto Rican Educators' Association; and principal, P.S. 25, New York City. | Nov. 25, 1970 | 8 |
| LANDSBERG, Brian, chief, Education Section, Office of the Attorney General. | July 13, 1970 | 3C |
| LANHAM, James H., community leader, Edgefield, S.C. | June 22, 1970 | 3B |
| LEE, Rev. Charles H., school-community coordinator, Hunters Point, Calif. | Mar. 5, 1971 | 9 |

## REMARKS AND STATEMENTS BY THE WITNESSES

| | *Hearing Dates* | *Part No.* |
|---|---|---|
| LEONARD, Jerris; Assistant Attorney General, Civil Rights Division. | July 13, 1970<br>Aug. 13, 1970 | 3C<br>3C |
| LEVENTHAL, Melvyn, NAACP Legal Defense Fund, Jackson, Miss. | June 24, 1970 | 3B |
| LEVIN, Henry M., associate professor of education and economics, Stanford University. | Oct. 1, 1970 | 7 |
| LEWIS, Lloyd, Jr., chairman, Dayton City Planning Board; and, member, Miami Valley Regional Planning Commission's Housing and Human Resources Advisory Committee, Dayton, Ohio. | Nov. 22, 1971 | 21 |
| LOHMAN, Dr. Mark R., assistant professor, School of Education, University of California at Riverside, Calif. | Nov. 8, 1971 | 20 |
| LOPEZ, Miss Aggie, New York City, N.Y. | Nov. 24, 1970 | 8 |
| LORENZO, Mrs. Bertha, vice president, Ramah Navaho School Board, Ramah, N. Mex. | June 8, 1970 | 2 |
| LOVETTE, Lowanda, of Rocky Mount, N.C. | June 18, 1970 | 3B |
| LOWENGARD, Benjamin, vice president, board of school directors, Harrisburg Public School District, Harrisburg, Pa. | Aug. 4, 1971 | 14 |
| LUKE, Dr. A. W., director, Division of Instructional Improvement, State Department of Education, Boise, Idaho. | Sept. 2, 1971 | 15 |

—Mc—

| | | |
|---|---|---|
| McANDREW, Dr. Gordon, superintendent of schools, Gary, Ind. | July 14, 1971 | 12 |
| McCABE, Mrs. Irene, chairman, National Action Group, Pontiac, Mich. | Nov. 4, 1971 | 19B |
| McCULLOUGH, Miss Elaine, Southside High School, Greenville, S.C. | July 8, 1970 | 3B |
| McFARLAND, Stanley J., assistant secretary, Office of Legislation and Federal Regulations, National Education Association. | June 16, 1970<br>Sept. 23, 1971 | 3A<br>16A |
| McGOVERN, Hon. George, a U.S. Senator from the State of South Dakota. | June 15, 1971 | 11 |
| McINTYRE, Lionel, of New Orleans, La. | June 18, 1970 | 3B |
| McKERR, Robert, associate superintendent, Business and Finance, Michigan Department of Education. | Oct. 26, 1971 | 19A |
| McKINNEY, Edward C., superintendent, Baldwin Public Schools, Baldwin, Mich. | Nov. 3, 1971 | 19B |
| McMAHAND, Miss Marilyn, student, Lincoln High School, Greenville, S.C. | July 8, 1970 | 3B |
| McNAIR, Hon. Robert, former Governor of the State of South Carolina. | Sept. 3, 1971 | 15 |

—M—

| | | |
|---|---|---|
| MANVEL, Allen D., consultant on Government Finance and Statistics, Washington, D.C. | Sept. 29, 1971 | 16B |

## REMARKS AND STATEMENTS BY THE WITNESSES

| | *Hearing Dates* | *Part No.* |
|---|---|---|
| MARISETT, Andrew, program associate, AFSC South Carolina community relations program, Frogmore, S.C. | June 22, 1970 | 3B |
| MARSH, Henry, NAACP Legal Defense Fund, Richmond, Va. | June 24, 1970 | 3B |
| MARSHALL, Dr. Thord M., superintendent of education, Savannah, Ga. | Oct. 6, 1971 | 18 |
| MARTIN, Mrs. Ruby, former director, Office of Civil Rights, HEW. | June 18, 1970<br>Aug. 4, 1970 | 3B<br>3C |
| MARTINEZ, Armando, director, Puente, Boston, Mass. | Nov. 23, 1970 | 8 |
| MEAD, William, advisory specialist, Human Relations, Title IV coordinator, Baldwin Public Schools, Baldwin, Mich. | Nov. 3, 1971 | 19B |
| MENDEZ, Manuel, president, Human Relations Council, Orange County, Calif. | Sept. 1, 1970 | 5 |
| MERCADO, Luis, New York City, N.Y. | Nov. 24, 1970 | 8 |
| MERCER, Dr. Jane, associate professor of sociology, University of California at Riverside, Calif. | Mar. 6, 1971 | 9 |
| MEYERS, Will, public finance staff, Advisory Commission on Intergovernmental Relations. | Oct. 6, 1970 | 7 |
| MEZA, Mrs. Beatrice, paraprofessional, Buena Vista School, Calif. | Mar. 4, 1971 | 9 |
| MILLER, Richard, president, Baldwin Education Association, Baldwin, Mich. | Nov. 3, 1971 | 19B |
| MITCHELL, Hon. John N., Attorney General of the United States. | Aug. 13, 1970 | 3C |
| MIZELL, M. Hayes, director, South Carolina community relations program, American Friends Service Committee, Columbia, S.C. | June 22, 1970 | 3B |
| MONACEL, Dr. Louis, deputy superintendent, Federal Projects, Detroit Public Schools, Detroit, Mich. | May 12, 1970<br>July 15, 1971 | 1A<br>12 |
| MOORHEAD, Mrs. Jean, teacher, Southside High School, Greenville, S.C. | July 8, 1970 | 3B |
| MORENO, Edward, professor of Mexican-American studies, San Fernando Valley State College, Northridge, Calif. | Aug. 18, 1970 | 4 |
| MUNEZ, Edward J., chief, Organizational Branch, Internal Revenue. | Aug. 12, 1970 | 3D |

—N—

| | | |
|---|---|---|
| NADER, Ralph, Public Interest Research Group, Washington, D.C. | Sept. 30, 1971 | 16B |
| NEGRON, Frank, assistant director, Center for Urban Education, New York City, N.Y. | Nov. 24, 25, 1970 | 8 |
| NORMAN, David L., Deputy Assistant Attorney General. | July 13, 1970 | 3C |
| NORTHRUP, Rhonda, Berkeley High School, Berkeley Unified School District, Calif. | Mar. 3, 1971 | 9 |
| NUNEZ, Angelo, New York City, N.Y. | Nov. 24, 1970 | 8 |
| NUNEZ, Louis, president, Aspira of America, New York City, N.Y. | Nov. 24, 1970 | 8 |

—O—

| | | |
|---|---|---|
| OBLEDO, Mario, director, Mexican-American Legal Defense and Education Fund, San Antonio, Tex. | Aug. 20, 1970 | 4 |

## REMARKS AND STATEMENTS BY THE WITNESSES

| | *Hearing Dates* | *Part No.* |
|---|---|---|
| OKAMURA, Raymond, representative, Japanese-American Citizens League, San Francisco, Calif. | Mar. 5, 1971 | 9 |
| OLDMAN, Dr. Oliver, professor of law and director of international tax programs, Harvard Law School, Cambridge, Mass. | Sept. 29, 1971 | 16B |
| ORFIELD, Gary, professor, Woodrow Wilson School of Public and International Affairs, Princeton University. | Oct. 8, 1970 | 3E |
| ORT, John, president, Michigan Education Association. | Nov. 2, 1971 | 19A |
| ORTIZ, Angel, Puerto Rican program director, New York City, N.Y. | Nov. 25, 1970 | 8 |
| ORTIZ, Ralph, New York City, N.Y. | Nov. 24, 1970 | 8 |
| —P— | | |
| PALOMARES, Dr. Uvaldo, director, Human Development Training Institute, San Diego, Calif. | Apr. 20, 1970 | 1A |
| PANETTA, Leon E., former director, Office for Civil Rights, HEW. | Aug. 4, 1970 | 3C |
| PANTOJA, Miss Antonio, founder, Aspira, Inc., Washington, D.C. | Nov. 23, 1970 | 8 |
| PERRONE, Dr. Vito, dean, New School of Behavioral Studies in Education, University of North Dakota. | Sept. 3, 1971 | 15 |
| PETTIGREW, Dr. Thomas, professor of social psychology, Department of Social Relations, Harvard University, Cambridge, Mass. | May 13, 1970 | 2 |
| PIERCE, Dr. Chester, professor of psychiatry, Harvard University, Cambridge, Mass. | July 30, 1970 | 2 |
| PLANTE, Dr. Alexander, chief, Bureau of Continuing Education, Connecticut State Department of Education, Hartford, Conn. | May 5, 1970 | 1A |
| POLLACK, Stephen J., former Assistant Attorney General, Civil Rights Division, Department of Justice. | Aug. 11, 1970 | 3C |
| POLLAK, Louis H., professor of law, Yale University. | Oct. 8, 1970 | 3E |
| PORTER, Dr. David H., superintendent, Harrisburg Public School District, Harrisburg, Pa. | Aug. 4, 1971 | 14 |
| POTTINGER, Stanley J., director, Office for Civil Rights, HEW. | Aug. 6, 1970 | 3C |
| POWELL, Mrs. Birdie, Coon Branch, W. Va. | Sept. 2, 1971 | 15 |
| PRESSLY, Dr. William L., president, Westminster Schools, Atlanta, Ga. | July 1, 1970 | 3D |
| PREYER, Hon. Richardson, a U.S. Representative from the 6th District of the State of North Carolina. | Sept. 24, 1970 | 3E |
| PRIDE, John, Housing Opportunities Council, Washington, D.C. | Sept. 1, 1970 | 5 |
| —Q— | | |
| QUAINTANCE, Charles, Jr., trial attorney, Minneapolis, Minn. | Sept. 22, 1970 | 6 |
| QUINONES, Nathan, vice president, Puerto Rican Educators' Association, New York City, N.Y. | Nov. 23, 1970 | 8 |

## REMARKS AND STATEMENTS BY THE WITNESSES

—R—



—S—

## REMARKS AND STATEMENTS BY THE WITNESSES

| | *Hearing Dates* | *Part No.* |
|---|---|---|
| SIMMONS, Samuel, Secretary of Equal Opportunity, HUD. | Aug. 26, 1970 | 5 |
| SIZEMORE, Dr. Barbara A., Center for Inner City Studies, Northeastern Illinois State College, Chicago, Ill. | July 27, 1971 | 13 |
| SMITH, Dr. Bettie M., principal, West Point Junior High School, West Point, Ga. | June 14, 1971 | 10 |
| SLOANE, Martin E., Acting Deputy Staff Director, U.S. Commission on Civil Rights. | Nov. 23, 1971 | 21 |
| SMITH, Dr. Charles H., associate director for social sciences, the Rockefeller Foundation, New York City. | Aug. 3, 1971 | 12 |
| SMITH, Dr. Donald H., director of educational development, Bernard Baruch College, New York, N.Y. | Aug. 5, 1971 | 13 |
| SMITH, William H., Deputy Commissioner of Internal Revenue. | Aug. 12, 1970 | 3D |
| SREBOTH, Raymond, superintendent, Benton Harbor Area Schools, Benton Harbor, Mich. | Nov. 3, 1971 | 19B |
| STEWART, Pelton, president, student association, Balboa High School, Calif. | Mar. 5, 1971 | 9 |
| STOLL, Mrs. Louise, president, Berkeley Story Committee, Berkeley, Calif. | Mar. 3, 1971 | 9 |
| STREET, Craig, student, Black House, Community High School, Berkeley Unified School District, Calif. | Mar. 3, 1971 | 9 |
| STRICKLER, George, Lawyers Constitutional Defense Committee, New Orleans, La. | June 24, 1970 | 3B |
| SULLIVAN, Dr. Neil V., commissioner of education, State of Massachusetts. | May 21, 1970 | 2 |
| SWEENEY, Mrs. Carole, of Pontiac, Mich. | Nov. 4, 1971 | 19B |

—T—

| | | |
|---|---|---|
| TAEUBER, Karl E., professor, University of Wisconsin. | Aug. 25, 1970 | 5 |
| TAMAYO, William, student, Lowell High School, Calif. | Mar. 5, 1971 | 9 |
| TAMBLYN, Lewis R., executive secretary, Department of Rural Education Asso., National Education Association. | Sept. 1, 1971 | 15 |
| TATE, Mrs. Jane, member at large, Michigan Association of Parents and Teachers. | Oct. 26, 1971 | 19A |
| TAYLOR, William L., director, Center for National Policy Review, Catholic University Law School. | Nov. 30, 1971 | 21 |
| THOMAS, Dr. Arthur E., director, Center for the Study of Student Citizenship, Rights, and Responsibilities, Dayton, Ohio. | Aug. 5, 1971 | 13 |
| THOMAS, Tyrone, of Mobile, Ala. | June 18, 1970 | 3B |
| THOMPSON, Sherwood, student, Greenville High School, Greenville, S.C. | July 8, 1970 | 3B |
| THROWER, Randolph W., Commissioner of Internal Revenue. | Aug. 12, 1970 | 3D |
| TOM, Benjamin, chairman, Chinese Advisory Counsel on Education, San Francisco, Calif. | Mar. 5, 1971 | 9 |

## REMARKS AND STATEMENTS BY THE WITNESSES

| | *Hearing Dates* | *Part No.* |
|---|---|---|
| TURNER, Benjamin, deputy superintendent for planning, Harrisburg Public School District, Harrisburg, Pa. | Aug. 4, 1971 | 14 |
| —U— | | |
| UKAI, Nancy, member, student council, Berkeley High School, Berkeley Unified School District, Calif. | Mar. 3, 1971 | 9 |
| UNO, Edison, assistant dean of students, San Francisco Medical Center, Calif. | Mar. 5, 1971 | 9 |
| URIEGAS, Jose V., member, Texas State Advisory Committee on Civil Rights. | Aug. 19, 1970 | 4 |
| —V— | | |
| VALDOQUIN, Mrs. Maria, New York City, N.Y. | Nov. 24, 1970 | 8 |
| VAN DUSEN, Richard C., Under Secretary of Housing and Urban Development. | Aug. 26, 1970 | 5 |
| VASQUEZ, Hector, Puerto Rican Forum, New York City, N.Y. | Nov. 23, 1970 | 8 |
| VAUGHN, Joseph, teacher, Hughes High School, Greenville, S.C. | July 8, 1970 | 3B |
| VELA, Carlos, attorney, former coordinator, Texas State Office of Civil Rights, HEW, Corpus Christi, Tex. | Aug. 20, 1970 | 4 |
| —W— | | |
| WALKER, Mrs. Jo Ann, reading teacher, Pontiac School System, Pontiac, Mich. | Nov. 4, 1971 | 19B |
| WANG, L. Ling-chi, director, Youth Service Center, Chinatown, San Francisco, Calif. | Mar. 5, 1971 | 9 |
| WATSON, Dr. Bernard C., professor of Urban Education, Temple University, Philadelphia, Pa. | Aug. 5, 1971 | 13 |
| WEBB, Mrs. Essie, member, Southeast Poverty Commission, Hunters Point, Calif. | Mar. 5, 1971 | 9 |
| WEBB, Miss Nelva, student, Parker High School, Greenville, S.C. | July 8, 1970 | 3B |
| WHEELER, Robert F., area superintendent, Division of Urban Education, School District of Kansas City, Mo. | July 15, 1971 | 12 |
| WEINER, Leon N., president, Leon N. Weiner & Asso., Inc., Wilmington, Del. | Sept. 1, 1970 | 5 |
| WELLS, Miss Janet, program associate, AFSC South Carolina community relations program, Aiken, S.C. | June 22, 1970 | 3B |
| WHITE, Franklin E., general counsel, New York City Commission on Human Rights, N.Y. | Aug. 27, 1970 | 5 |
| WHITMER, Dr. Dana, superintendent, Pontiac Public Schools, Pontiac, Mich. | Nov. 4, 1971 | 19B |
| WILEY, Eric, president, senior class, Berkeley High School, Berkeley Unified School District, Calif. | Mar. 3, 1971 | 9 |
| WILKS, Mrs. Gertrude, director, Nairobi Day School, East Palo Alto, Calif. | Mar. 5, 1971 | 9 |
| WILLIAMS, Mrs. Amada, representative, Community Forum, Berkeley, Calif. | Mar. 3, 1971 | 9 |

## REMARKS AND STATEMENTS BY THE WITNESSES

# BIBLIOGRAPHY

A convenient guide to the literature is Francesco Cordasco, *The Equality of Educational Opportunity: A Bibliography of Selected References* (Totowa, N.J.: Roman and Littlefield, 1973) which lists some 400 titles dealing with the American schools and the children of the poor: with the "minority child," (Blacks, Puerto Ricans, Mexican-Americans, Indians, the "Appalachian Poor," ethnics, migrants); the restiveness of community involvements; the desegregation of the schools; with educational experiments and innovative designs; and with the twin themes of alienation and disaffection. A main source of bibliographical information on the education of the disadvantaged child is the *IRCD* Bulletin (Informational Retrieval Center on the Disadvantaged, Teachers College, Columbia University) which is published five times a year under a contract with the U.S. Office of Education Educational Resources Information Center (*ERIC*). A vast resource of 1740 documents (Selected Documents on the Disadvantaged) dealing with the special educational needs of the disadvantaged is available from the U.S. Office of Education (Number and Author Index, OE 37001); (Subject Index, OE 37002). Additionally, see Meyer Weinberg, *The Education of the Minority Child* (Chicago: Integrated Education Associates, 1970) which is a listing of some 10,000 refences. Periodicals which contain bibliographical information include the *Journal of Negro Education; Urban Education; Urban Review*; and *Education and Urban Society*. The education of migrant children, Mexican-Americans, and Indians, has as a principal bibliographical resource the publications of the *ERIC* Clearinghouse on Rural Education and Small Schools (New Mexico State University), *e.g.*, *Migrant Education: A Selected Bibliography* (Las Cruces, New Mexico: New Mexico State University, 1969); and *Research Abstracts in Rural Education* (*Ibid.*, continuing). Bibliography for the Puerto Rican child is found in F. Cordasco and E. Bucchioni, *The Puerto Rican Community and Its Children on the Mainland: A Sourcebook for Teachers, Social Workers, and other Professionals* (Metuchen, N.J.: Scarecrow Press, 1972) which includes a comprehensive listing of some 500 entries. The most comprehensive guide to programs for the disadvantaged is Edmund W. Gordon and Doxey A. Wilkerson, *Compensatory Education for the Disadvantaged* (New York: College Entrance Examination Board, 1966), although this needs updating. Lastly, a serviceable general bibliographical guide to poverty is Freda L. Paltiel, *Poverty: An Annotated Bibliography* (Ottawa: Canadian Welfare Council, 1966); with continuing reference made to *Poverty and Human Resources Abstracts* (The Institute of Labor and Industrial Relations, University of Michigan) which is issued bimonthly and contains review articles, an annotated bibliography, and recent legislative developments related to all aspects of poverty and human resources.

*The Allen Commission Report: Desegregating the Public Schools of New York City*. New York: Institute of Urban Studies, Teachers College, Columbia University, 1964.

Alloway, David N. and Francesco Cordasco. *Minorities and the American City: A Sociological Primer for Educators*. New York: David McKay, 1970.

Armor, David J. "The Evidence on Busing," *The Public Interest* (Summer 1972), pp. 90-126.

Averch, Harvey A., *et. al. How Effective is Schooling? A Critical Review and Synthesis of Research Findings*. Santa Monica, Calif.: Rand Corporation, 1972.

Bagwell, William. *School Desegregation in the Carolinas: Two Case Studies*. Columbia: University of South Carolina Press, 1972.

Ballard, Allen B. *The Education of Black Folks*. New York: Harper & Row, 1973.

Benson, Charles S. "How to Beat Serrano: Rules for the Rich," *Saturday Review* (December 9, 1972), pp. 35-36.

Berg, Ivar. *Education and Jobs: The Great Training Robbery*. Boston: Beacon Press, 1971.

Berke, Joel S. "The Current Crisis in School Finance: Inadequacy and Inequity," *Phi Delta Kappan*, vol. 53 (September 1971), pp. 2-7.

Berke, Joel S., *et. al.* "Equality in Financing New York City's Schools: The Impact on Local, State, and Federal Policy," *Education and Urban Society*, vol. 4 (May 1972), pp. 261-291.

Berube, Maurice R. "Community Control: Key to Educational Achievement," *Social Policy* (July-August, 1970), p. 42-45.

[Boston] The Way We Go To School. *Task Force on Children Out of School*. Boston: Beacon Press, 1971.

Boudon, Raymond. *Education, Opportunity and Social Inequality: Changing Prospects in Western Society*. New York: John Wiley, 1974. (Originally, *L'Inégalité des Chances*, Paris: *Librairie Armand*, 1973).

Bradshaw, Thecla and Andre Renaud. *The Indian Child and Education*. Saskatoon: University of Saskatchewan, 1971.

Brecher, Charles. *The Impact of Federal Antipoverty Policies*. New York: Praeger, 1973. (Includes a foreword by Eli Ginzberg).

Brickman, William W. and Stanley Lehrer, eds. *Education and the Many Faces of the Disadvantaged: Cultural and Historical Perspectives*. New York: John Wiley, 1972.

Carter, Thomas P. *Mexican Americans in School: A History of Educational Neglect*. New York: College Entrance Examination Board, 1970. See review, F. Cordasco, *International Migration Review*, vol. 7 (Spring 1973), pp. 90-91. See also, Henry S. Johnson and William J. Hernandez, *Educating the Mexican-American*. Valley Forge, Pa.: Judson Press, 1970; and Herschel T. Manuel, *Spanish Speaking Children of the Southwest*. Austin: University of Texas Press, 1965.

Chachkin, Norman J. "Metropolitan School Desegregation: Evolving Law," *Integrated Education* (March-April 1972), pp. 13-25.

Chesler, M.A., *et. al.*, "When Northern Schools Desegregate," *American Education*, vol. 4 (1968), pp. 12-15.

*Chinese-Americans: School and Community Problems*. Chicago: Integrated Education Associates, 1972.

Cohen, David K. "School Resources and Racial Equality," *Education and Urban Society*, vol. 1 (February 1969), pp. 121-137.

Coleman, James S., *et al.*, *The Equality of Educational Opportunity*. Washington: Government Printing Office, 1966. The summary of the report is reprinted in F. Cordasco, *et al.*, *The School in the Social Order*. Scranton: Intext, 1970. See also, for a collection of reactions to the report, *Equal Educational Opportunity* (Harvard Educational Review). Harvard University, 1969. Also, Mosteller/Moynihan, and Jencks, *infra*.

Coleman, James S., *et al*, "Longitudinal Effects of Education on the Incomes and Occupational Prestige of Blacks and Whites," *Social Science Research* (September 1972).

[Community Education] "The Children Have Outgrown the Schools," *Phi Delta Kappan*, vol. 54 (November 1972), pp. 146-224.

Cordasco, Francesco. "The Catholic Urban School: Patterns of Survival," *Urban Education* (July/October, 1971), pp. 119-129.

Cordasco, Francesco, "Charles Loring Brace and the Dangerous Classes: Historical Analogues of the Urban Black Poor," *Journal of Human Relations*, vol. 20 (1972), pp. 379-386.

Cordasco, Francesco and Eugene Bucchioni. *The Puerto Rican Community and its Children on the Mainland: A Sourcebook for Teachers, Social Workers and other Professionals*. 2nd ed., Metuchen, N.J.: Scarecrow Press, 1972. See also F. Cordasco, "Puerto Ricans on the Mainland: The Educational Experience," *Journal of Human Relations*, vol. 20 (1972), pp. 343-378.

Cordasco, Francesco and David N. Alloway, eds. "Poverty in America: Economic Inequality, New Ideologies, and the Search for Educational Opportunity," *Journal of Human Relations*, vol. 20 (Third Quarter, 1972), pp. 234-396. (Articles on poverty contexts; minority responses to oppression; racial caste system; assimilation of Mexicans; educational neglect of Black, Puerto Rican, and Portuguese children).

Cordasco, Francesco. "America and the Quest for Educational Opportunity: A Prolegomenon and Overview," *British Journal of Educational Studies*, vol. 21 (February 1973), pp. 50-63.

Cordasco, Francesco. "Reforming Teacher Education in the 1970s," *Intellect/School & Society*, vol. 101 (March 1973), pp. 381-384.

Cordasco, Francesco. "The Children of Immigrants in Schools: Historical Analogues of Educational Deprivation," *Journal of Negro Education*, vol. 42 (Winter 1973), pp. 44-53.

Corwin, Ronald. *Reform and Organizational Survival: The Teacher Corps as an Instrument of Educational Change*. New York: John Wiley, 1973.

Crain, Robert L. *The Politics of School Desegregation*. Chicago: Aldine, 1968.

Crain, Robert L. "School Integration and Occupational Achievement of Negroes," *American Journal of Sociology*, vol.

75 (January 1970), pp. 593-606.
Culver, Carmen M. and Gary J. Hoban, eds. *The Power to Change: Issues for the Innovative Educator*. New York: McGraw-Hill, 1974.
Daly, C.A., ed. *The Quality of Inequality*. Chicago, University of Chicago Policy Center, 1968.
Dentler, Robert A. "Equality of Educational Opportunity: A Special Review," *The Urban Review* (December 1966), pp. 14-31.
Douglas, John R. "Free Schooling: Alternative Education and its Documentation, *Wilson Library Bulletin*, vol. 47 (September 1972), pp. 48-54.
Downs, Anthony. *Who are the Urban Poor?* New York: Committee for Economic Development, 1970. See also, Herman P. Miller, *Rich Man, Poor Man*. New York: Thomas Y. Crowell, 1971.
Dugan, Denis J. and William H. Leahy, *Perspectives on Poverty*. New York: Praeger, 1973.
Dyer, Henry S. "School Factors," *Harvard Educational Review*, vol. 38 (Winter 1969), pp. 38-56.
[Education Policies Commission] *American Education and the Search for Equal Opportunity*. Washington: National Education Association, 1965.
[Ethnic Education] "The Imperatives of Ethnic Education," *Phi Delta Kappan*, vol. 53 (January 1972), pp. 265-343. (On White ethnics; Chicano children; Blacks; Puerto Ricans; Multi-ethnic schools).
Fantini, Mario and Marilyn Gittell. *Decentralization: Achieving Reform*. New York: Praeger, 1973.
Farber, Jerry. *The Student as Nigger*. New York: Pocketbooks, 1970.
Fein, Leonard J. *The Ecology of the Public Schools: An Enquiry into Community Control*. New York: Pegasus, 1971.
Fisher, Robert J. *Learning How to Learn: The English Primary School and American Education*. New York: Harcourt Brace, Jovanovich, 1972.
Ford, Nick A. *Black Studies: Threat or Challenge?* Port Washington, N.Y.: Kennikat Press, 1973.
Gans, Herbert J. "The New Egalitarianism," *Saturday Review* (May 6, 1972), pp. 43-46.
Garcia, F. Chris. *Political Socialization of Chicano Children: A Comparative Study with Anglos in California Schools*. New York: Praeger, 1973.
Gartner, Alan, *et al.* eds. *The New Assault on Equality: IQ and Social Stratification*. New York: Harper & Row, 1973.
Gartner, Alan and Colin Greer, Frank Riessman, eds. *After Deschooling, What?* New York: Harper & Row, 1973.
*Ghetto Education: A Symposium*. Berkeley, Calif.: Center for Democratic Institutions, 1968.
Gintis, Herbert. "I.Q. in the U.S. Class Structure," *Social Policy* (January 1973).
Glazer, Nathan. "Is Busing Necessary?" *Commentary* (March 1972), pp. 39-52. See also responses, *Ibid.*, (July 1972), pp. 6-31.
Ginsburg, H. *The Myth of the Deprived Child*. Englewood Cliffs, N.J.: Prentice-Hall, 1972.

Gordon, Ira J. *Parent Involvement in Compensatory Education.* Urbana, Illinois: University of Illinois Press, 1971.

Grant, William. "Community Control Versus School Integration in Detroit," *Public Interest* (Summer, 1971), pp. 62-79.

Graubard, Allen. *Free the Children: Radical Reform and the Free School Movement.* New York: Pantheon, 1972.

Greeley, Andrew and Paul Sheatsley. "Attitudes Toward Racial Integration," *Scientific American*, vol. 225 (December 1971), pp. 13-19. See also, Jon P. Alston, "White Parental Acceptance of Varying Degrees of School Desegregation: 1965 and 1970," *Public Opinion Quarterly*, vol. 36 (Winter 1971-73), pp. 585-591; and Gwen Bellesfield, "White Attitudes Toward Racial Integration and the Urban Riots of the 1960s," *Public Opinion Quarterly*, vol. 36 (Winter 1972-73), 579-584.

Greenbaum, William N. "Serrano v. Priest: Implications for Educational Equality," *Harvard Educational Review* (November 1971); also in *Current* (March 1972), pp. 3-6.

Greer, Colin, ed. *The Solution as part of the Problem: Urban Education Reform in the 1960s.* New York: Harper & Row 1973.

Greer, Colin. "Immigrants, Negroes, and the Public Schools," *The Urban Review* (January 1969), pp. 9-12.

Greer, Colin. *Cobweb Attitudes: Essays on Educational and Cultural Mythology.* New York: Teachers College Press, Columbia University, 1970.

Greer, Colin. *The Great School Legend.* New York: Basic Books, 1972.

Greifer, Julian L. *Community Action for Social Change: A Casebook of Current Projects.* New York: Praeger, 1973.

Grier, George and Eunice Grier. *Equality and Beyond.* Chicago: Quadrangle Books, 1966.

Gross, Neal, *et al. Implementing Organizational Innovations: A Sociological Analysis of Planned Educational Change.* New York: Basic Books, 1971. (on change in an elementary school)

Guthrie, James W., *et al. Schools and Inequality.* Cambridge, Mass.: M.I.T. Press, 1969.

Guthrie, James W. *et al.*, "Dollars for Schools: The Reinforcement of Inequality," *Educational Administration Quarterly*, vol. 6 (Autumn 1970), pp. 32-45.

Harrison, Bennett. *Education, Training, and the Urban Ghetto.* Baltimore: Johns Hopkins Press, 1972.

Herndon, James. *How to Survive in Your Native Land.* New York: Simon and Schuster, 1971.

Hess, Robert D., *et al.*, "Some New Dimensions in Providing Equal Educational Opportunity," *Journal of Negro Education* (March 1968), pp. 220-230.

Hummel, Raymond C. and John M. Nagle. *Urban Education in America: Problems and Prospects.* New York: Oxford University Press, 1973. See F. Cordasco, "A Quartet of Volumes Preoccupied with Poverty," *Phi Delta Kappan*, vol. 54 (January 1973), pp. 354-355.

*Indian Education: Hearings Before the Special Subcommittee on Indian Education of the Committee on Labor and Public Welfare, U.S. Senate.* Washington: Government Printing Office,

1967-1968.

*Inequality in Education*. Cambridge, Mass.: Center for Law and Education, Harvard University. (A quarterly reporting on legal and paralegal questions about schools.)

*Integrated Education: Race and Schools*. Chicago: Integrated Education Associates. (Six issues annually, with articles speeches, reports mainly on race discrimination in schools.)

Jencks, Christopher. "Private Schools for Black Children," *The New York Times Magazine* (November 3, 1968), pp. 30-34.

Jencks, Christopher, *et al. Inequality: A Reassessment of the Effect of Family and Schooling in America*. New York: Basic Books, 1972. See also, Mary J. Bane and Christopher Jencks, "The Schools and Equal Opportunity," *Saturday Review*, vol. 55 (October 1972), pp. 37-42. For a critique of Jencks, see Thomas Pettigrew and James S. Coleman, *American Journal of Sociology*, vol. 781 (May 1973), pp. 1523-1527. See also, Godfrey Hodgson, "Do Schools Make a Difference," *Atlantic* (March 1973); and Donald M. Levine, "Educational Policy after Inequality," *Teachers College Record*, vol. 75 (December 1973), pp. 149-179; and "Perspectives on Inequality," *Harvard Educational Review*, vol. 43 (February 1973), a special issue of the Review.

Jensen, Arthur R. "How Much Can We Boost IQ and Scholastic Achievement?," *Harvard Educational Review*, vol. 39 (Winter 1969), pp. 78-88. Also, Arthur R. Jensen, "The Heritability of Intelligence," *Saturday Evening Post* (Summer 1972), 9, 12, 149-152. See also, Lillian Zach, "The IQ Debate," *Today's Education* (September 1972), pp. 40-43, 65-66, 68; David K. Cohen, "Does IQ Matter?," *Commentary* (April 1972), pp. 51-59; Walter F. Bodmer and Luigi Luca Cavilli-Sforza, "Intelligence and Race," *Scientific American* (October 1970), pp. 3-5, 10-13.

Johns, Roe L. and Kern Alexander. *Alternative Programs for Financing Education*. Gainsville, Fla.: National Educational Finance Project, 1971.

Keppel, Francis. *The Necessary Revolution in American Education*. New York: Harper & Row, 1966.

Kirp, David, "The Poor, The Schools, and Equal Protection," *Harvard Educational Review*, vol. 38 (Fall 1968), pp. 635-668.

Kirp, David. "Race, Class, and the Limits of Schooling," *The Urban Review*, May (1970), pp. 10-13.

Kohl, Herbert. *Thirty-Six Children*. New York: The New American Library, 1967.

Kohl, Herbert. *The Open Classroom*. New York: New York Review Press, 1970.

Kozol, Jonathan, *Death at an Early Age: The Destruction of the Hearts and Minds of Negro Children in the Boston Public Schools*. Boston: Houghton, Mifflin, 1967.

Kozol, Jonathan. *Free Schools*. Boston: Houghton, Mifflin, 1972.

Kraushaar, Otto F. *American Nonpublic Schools*. Baltimore: Johns Hopkins Press, 1972.

Kristol, Irving. "Decentralization for What?" *Public Interest* (Spring, 1968), pp. 17-25.

Lauter, Paul and Florence Howe. "How the School System is

Rigged for Failure," *New York Review of Books* (June 18, 1970), pp. 14-21.

Lekachman, Robert. "Schools, Money, and Politics: Financing Public Education," *The New Leader* (September 18, 1972), pp. 7-14.

Levin, Henry M. "What Difference Do Schools Make?," *Saturday Review*, vol. 51 (January 1968), p. 57, ff.

Levin, Henry M., "Why Ghetto Schools Fail," *Saturday Review* (March 21, 1970), pp. 68-69, 81-85.

Levin, Henry M., ed., *Community Control of Schools*. Washington: Brookings Institution, 1970.

Levin, Henry M., *et al.*, "School Achievement and Post-Secondary Success: A Review," *Review of Educational Research*, vol. 41 (February 1971), pp. 2-16.

Levin, Henry M. "Schooling and Inequality: The Social Science Objectivity Gap," *Saturday Review*, vol. 55 (December 1972), pp. 49-51.

Levine, Daniel U. "The Integration-Compensatory Education Controversy," *Educational Forum*, vol. 32 (March 1968), pp. 323-332.

Levine, Daniel U., 2nd ed., *Models for Integrated Education*. Belmont, Calif.: Wadsworth Publishing Co., 1971.

Levy, Frank. *Northern Schools and Civil Rights*. Cambridge, Mass.: M.I.T. Press, 1971.

May, Henry M., "Busing, Swann v. Charlotte-Mecklenburg, and the Fifth Circuit," *Texas Law Review*, vol. 39 (May 1971), pp. 884-911.

Micklenburger, James A. and Richard W. Hostrop, eds. *Educational Vouchers*. Homewood, Illinois: E.T.C. Publications, 1972.

[Migrant Children] *A Guide for Programs for the Education of Migrant Children*. Austin: Texas Education Agency, 1968.

Miller, La Mar P. and Edmund W. Gordon, eds. *Equality of Educational Opportunity: A Handbook for Research*. New York: AMS Press, 1974.

Milner, Murray, Jr. *The Illusion of Equality*. San Francisco: Jossey-Bass, 1972.

Milner, Murray, Jr. "On Getting Somewhere: Notes on Equal Opportunity and Other Convenient Delusions," *Columbia Forum*, Spring (1972), pp. 18-26.

Montague, Ashley, "Just What Is 'Equal Opportunity?,'' *Vista* (November 1970), pp. 23-25, 56.

Mosteller, Frederick and Daniel P. Moynihan, eds. *On Equality of Educational•Opportunity*. New York: Random House, 1972.

Moynihan, Daniel P. ed., *On Understanding Poverty*. New York: Basic Books, 1969.

Moynihan, Daniel P. *Maximum Feasible Misunderstanding: Community Action in the War on Poverty*. New York: Free Press, 1969.

Moynihan, Daniel P. "Equalizing Education: In Whose Benefit?" *The Public Interest* (Fall 1972), pp. 69-89.

Moynihan, Daniel P. *The Politics of a Guaranteed Income: The Nixon Administration and the Family Assistance Plan*. New York: Random House, 1973.

Nolte, M. Chester. "The Quest for Educational Equality," *The*

*American School Board Journal* (July 1972), pp. 25-26.

Overlan, S. Francis. "An Equal Chance to Learn," *The New Republic* (May 13, 1972), pp. 19-21.

Passow, A. Harry, ed. *Urban Education in the 1970s.* New York: Teachers College Press, Columbia University, 1971. See also, Maurie Hillson, Francesco Cordasco, Frances P. Purcell, *Education and the Urban Community: Schools and the Crises of the Cities.* New York: American Book Co., 1969.

Piven, Frances F. and Richard A. Cloward. *Regulating the Poor: The Functions of Public Welfare.* New York: Pantheon Books, 1971.

Ravitch, Diane. *The Great School Wars: New York City, 1805-1973: A History of the Public Schools as Battlefield of Social Change.* New York: Basic Books, 1974.

Ribich, Thomas. *Education and Poverty.* Washington: Brookings Institution, 1968.

[The] *Richmond School Decision.* Chicago: Integrated Associates, 1972. See also, "The Richmond Decision," *National Review* (February 4, 1972), pp. 82-33.

Riles, Wilson. "California and the *Serrano* Decision," *Planning and Changing: A Journal for School Administrators*, vol. 2 (January 1972), pp. 169-173.

Rist, Ray C. *The Urban School: A Factory for Failure.* Cambridge, Mass.: M.I.T. Press, 1974.

Robinson, Donald W. "An Interview with Christopher Jencks," *Phi Delta Kappan*, vol. 54 (December 1972), pp. 255-257.

Rubin, Lillian B. *Busing and Backlash.* Berkeley, Calif.: University of California Press, 1972. (Study of desegregation of Richmond, California schools).

Sacks, Seymour, *et al. City Schools/Suburban Schools: A History of Fiscal Conflict.* Syracuse: Syracuse University Press, 1972.

Shanks, Hershel, "Equal Education and the Law," *The American Scholar* (Spring 1970), pp. 255-269.

Shannon, Thomas A., "Rodriquez: A Dream Shattered or a call for Financial Reform?," *Phi Delta Kappa* (May 1973), pp. 587, 588, 640.

Silberman, Charles. *Crisis in the Classroom.* New York: Random House, 1970.

Silver, Catherine B. *Black Teachers in Urban Schools: The Case of Washington, D.C.* New York: Praeger, 1973. See also, A. Harry Passow, ed., *Toward Creating a Model Urban School System: A Study of the Washington, D.C. Public Schools.* New York: Teachers College Press, Columbia University, 1967.

Sowell, Thomas. *Black Education: Myths and Tragedies.* New York: David McKay, 1972.

St. John, Nancy H. "Desegregation and Minority Group Performance," *Review of Educational Research*, vol. 40 (February 1970), pp. 111-133.

Summerfield, Harry L. *The Neighborhood-Based Politics of Education.* Columbus: Charles Merrill, 1971. See also, Philip J. Meranto, *School Politics in the Metropolis.* Columbus: Charles Merrill, 1970.

Swanson, Bert. *The Struggle for Equality: The School Integration Controversy in New York.* New York: Hobbs, Dorman, 1966.

Tesconi, Charles A. and Emanuel Hurwitz, Jr., eds. *Education for Whom: The Question of Equal Educational Opportunity*. New York: Dodd, Mead, 1974.

Thurow, Lester C. "Education and Economic Equality," *The Public Interest* (Summer 1972), pp. 66-81.

[U.S. Civil Rights Commission] *Racial Isolation in the Public Schools*. 2 vols. Washington: Government Printing Office, 1967.

U.S. Commission on Civil Rights. *Mexican-American Study*. Washington: Government Printing Office, 1971.

[U.S. Department of Health, Education, and Welfare] *Do Teachers Make a Difference?* Washington: U.S. Government Printing Office, 1970.

[Urban Education] "The Reform of Urban Education," *Phi Delta Kappan*, vol. 52 (February 1971), pp. 327-390.

Walberg, Herbert J. and Andrew T. Koplan, eds. *Rethinking Urban Education*. San Francisco: Jossey-Bass, 1973.

Weinberg, Meyer, ed. *Integrated Education: A Reader*. Beverely Hills, Calif.: Glencoe Press, 1968.

Willie, Charles V. with Jerome Beker. *Race Mixing in the Public Schools*. New York: Praeger, 1973. See also, Thomas F. Pettigrew. *Racially Separate or Together?* New York: McGraw-Hill, 1971.

Wilson, Alan B. *Consequences of Segregation: Academic Achievement in a Northern Community*. Santa Barbara, Calif.: Glendassary Press, 1970. See also, J.S. Coleman and Edward McDill, "Educational Climates of High Schools: Their Effects and Sources," *American Journal of Sociology*, vol. 74 (May 1969), pp. 567-586; and Edward L. McDill and Leo C. Rigsby, *Structure and Process in Secondary Schools: The Academic Impact of Educational Climates*. Baltimore: Johns Hopkins Press, 1973.

Wise, Arthur E. *Rich Schools, Poor Schools: The Promise of Equal Educational Opportunity*. Chicago: University of Chicago Press, 1968.

Wise, Arthur E., "California Doctrine," *Saturday Review* (November 24, 1971), pp. 78-79.

Yudof, Mark G. *et al.*, "*Serrano* and Segregation," *Integrated Education*, vol. 50. (March-April 1972), pp. 71-74.

Ziegler H. and K. F. Johnson. *The Politics of Education in the States*. Indianapolis: Bobbs-Merrill, 1972.

Zimet, Melvin, *Decentralization and School Effectiveness: A Case Study of the 1969 Decentralization Law in New York City*. New York: Teachers College Press Columbia University, 1973. See also, McGeorge Bundy, Chairman, *Reconnection for Learning: A Community School System for New York City*. Mayor's Advisory Council on Decentralization of the New York City Schools. New York: Praeger, 1969.

# INDEX